THE TWILIGHT
OF THE GODDESSES

THE
TWILIGHT
OF THE
GODDESSES

Women and

Representation

in the French

Revolutionary

Era

MADELYN GUTWIRTH

RUTGERS UNIVERSITY PRESS

New Brunswick, New Jersey

Library of Congress Cataloging-in-Publication Data

Gutwirth, Madelyn.
    The twilight of the goddesses : women and representation in the French revolutionary
era / Madelyn Gutwirth.
        p.   cm.
    Includes bibliographical references and index.
    ISBN 0-8135-1787-7
    1. France—History—Revolution, 1789–1799—Women.   2. Women's rights—
France—History—18th century.   3. Sex discrimination—France—History—18th
century.   4. Women in popular culture—France—History—18th century.   5. Women
in art.   6. Women in literature.   I. Title.
DC158.8.G88   1992
944.04—dc20   91-30118
                                                                                    CIP

British Cataloging-in-Publication information available

In Memory of

Louis Alexander Katz

CONTENTS

IMAGES

PREFACE

COMMERCE between the women and men of French culture offers a salient example, in comparison with gender arrangements in some other nations, of a female omnipresence, not only at court, as queens, courtiers, and ostentatious mistresses to kings, but in literary arts, where from Marie de France to Marguerite Duras women have frequently enjoyed the rewards to which their gifts entitled them. What is more, the active, verbal, committed quality of the Frenchwoman has been manifest in all classes of society. Her sagacity and wit might well be roundly prized, and her communicative gifts might readily meet with the appreciation of both men and women. In fact, the relatively narrow social distance between the sexes is a distinguishing mark of French life.

This is why the situation of women in the years before, and then during, the French Revolution offers so fascinating an example of how the vicissitudes of gender interact with other impulses toward radical change. For while Frenchwomen have profited by their freedom of expression and action relative to the women of some other national cultures, they have not done so with impunity: French tradition has not failed to transmit a heritage of savagely misogynous denigration of women along with its greater toleration of their participation. Since the Revolution seems to have provided a republican point of no return for the relations of women and men in modern European democracies, we are moved to ask, which aspect of this dual heritage can have played the preponderant role in that turning? Can that massive trend, observed by so many historians, to an idealization of women's maternal role, gaining in force over the course of the eighteenth century and usually associated in France with the works of Jean-Jacques Rousseau, have borne any relationship to the Revolutionary temper? As we probe that question from the women's side, the story of the Revolution turns out to have had but little resemblance to that moment of soaring aspiration betrayed that was the men's Revolution.

The French Revolution, in its historiography, has undergone successive mutations. For most of the nineteenth century, it was a story of great men's actions and conflicts, to which a Michelet or another might add, as a sort of "women's auxiliary history," a brief, anecdotal, "human interest" account of distaff activities in that period. Marxist history of the Revolution, concentrating on economic forces, made little room for women as a factor important to its evolution. Historians of the Annales school with their longer-range optic and their bias toward social history have brought women's participation in the Revolution into distant focus in this way, allowing them, at least, back into the picture. This opening has allowed the present generation to enlarge that image and scrutinize events, ideology, and individual lives with an eye to reestablishing a degree of gender equilibrium in thinking about the world of 1789.

The origin of this particular exploration into the fate of women and their representation in the French Revolution lay in the conundrum raised for me, as a student of the works of the far from speechless Germaine de Staël, by her assertion in *On Literature* (1800) that "since the Revolution men had found it politically and morally useful to reduce women to the most absurd mediocrity." In the absence of an adequate context for thinking about women in the Revolutionary period, her words initially seemed to me merely paradoxical or excessive. Yet, with time, they became intriguingly gnomic for me.

To a literary scholar, concentrated almost exclusively upon the written word, further light upon this conundrum seemed at first available only from within the community of texts. It was in writing a long article on "Laclos and 'le Sexe': The Rack of Ambivalence" that I became more fully aware of a climate of debate in the 1780s surrounding upper-class women. Within that context, Laclos's novel *Les Liaisons dangereuses,* or *Dangerous Acquaintances,* itself began to take on a less extraordinary profile as a work: rather it could be seen as an expression of anxiety ambient in the author's own society, the precise content of which seemed forever elusive to us as later readers. Since, as Hans-Georg Gadamer has put it, the home of hermeneutics lies in the intermediate place between "the historically intended separate object and its belonging to a tradition," I sensed that a far more encompassing subject lay beyond my inquiry's probing into the relation of Laclos's novel to the gender outlook of his time.

A fortuitous challenge in the form of an invitation to contribute to a panel initiated by art historians at the 1983 meetings of the Consortium on Revolutionary Europe resulted in a paper, "The Goddess of Reason and the Queen of the Night," which drew me into a closer study of visual materials, as well as of the cultural climate around 1791, the year of the composition of Mozart's *Magic Flute.* I then formulated a plan of attack to explore Staël's enigmatic statement, now enlarged to ask what more generalizable validity her remark might contain, with the help of visual materials from the Revolutionary era, for which purpose I received a summer stipend from the National Endowment for the Humanities to do pictorial research in Paris in the summer of 1984 at the Musée Carnavalet and the Bibliothèque Nationale.

After scrutiny of the pictorial evidence, it became evident that the paradox Staël had posited about the Revolution's outcome for women demanded a far more comprehensive and interdisciplinary inquiry than my thus-far partial attempts had produced. If literary and visual works were a form of symbolic action, "a duplex compound made up of an inescapable past and an irreducible present," as Marshall Sahlins believes, a reading of the change intimated by Staël's remark would have to be set in a far fuller context, both symbolic and historical, to lend it something akin to breadth. I would have to become more alive than my literary training had made me to the ways in which "culture is . . . the organization of the present system in terms of a past."

Once immersed in the historical record, I saw clearly that exploration of the ground of what the Revolution had meant for women had been enjoying, and was enjoying still, almost a century of sustained interest. This exploration was no less intriguing for having been so consistently marginalized. Though seemingly all but invisible to me before, there was in fact no mystery attached to women's civil and political defeat by the Revolution itself, as Alphonse Aulard's 1898 "Le Féminisme pendant la Revolution" and Georges Ascoli's two articles on "Histoire des idées féministes en France" of 1906 attested. Their work was followed by Léon Abensour's *Histoire Générale du féminisme des origines à nos jours* (1921) and *La Femme et le féminisme avant la Revolution* (1923). Beginning in the 1950s a series of further studies like Elizabeth Racz's "The Women's Rights Movement in the French Revolution" (1952) and Scott Lytle's "The Second Sex—September 1793" (1955) began to make their appearance. During the sixties a more in-depth set of works began to emerge, beginning with Marie Cérati's book, *Le Club des citoyennes Révolutionnaires,* on the most militant of the political women of the Revolution, and then Paule-Marie Duhet's more general *Les Femmes et la Révolution 1789–1794* (1971). Studies essential to comprehending the Revolution's policies toward women followed by Margaret George, Olwen Hufton, Jane Abray, Mary Durham Johnson, Darline Gay Levy, and Harriet Bramson Applewhite, among others.

I want to acknowledge here my own greatest debts. The first is to Duhet's work, which because of the greater currency of Dominique Godineau's fine research is less evident in the citations in my own text, but whose temper and conclusions I responded to first, and most decisively. Olwen Hufton's article in *Past and Present* made a powerful impact upon my sense of the raw condition of the poorest classes of women that no serious account of women's alteration in status can fail to acknowledge. André Maindron's groundbreaking doctoral thesis on the evolution of the novel between 1789 and 1830 has provided me with much insight and data.

Despite the presence of increasingly full documentation of the conditions and participation of women in the Revolutionary years, many questions remained. If the outcome was inevitable, in what sense was this so? What did gender represent for the Revolutionary generation, and why and when did it come to represent what it did?

In the margin between art and history, Vera Lee published her charming and unclassifiable *The Reign of Women* (1975) and Françoise d'Eaubonne published a brief book called *Histoire de l'art et lutte des classes* (1977), a Jungian reading of neoclassicism in which she posited a link between it and the masculinist Revolutionary ideology. Hasty and polemical, her book is full of striking formulations. It came to me as confirmation of my own perception of the central issues but did not, I felt, document the case adequately. Carol Duncan's excellent articles on alterations in thematics of late eighteenth-century art proved powerfully suggestive for my own understanding of this evolution, as did Robert Rosenblum's *Transformations in Late Eighteenth-Century Art.* Finally, the probing Ph.D. dissertation of Diane Alstad acted as a spur to me to scrutinize the texts of the *philosophes,* which I had been teaching for decades, with respect to the issue of gender ideology. I have also enormously enjoyed my mute but lively dialogue with each of my other superb sources, which I have used not only for their authors' insights, but as repositories of voices of women and men of the era.

"Even where life changes violently, as in ages of revolution, far more of the old is preserved in the supposed transformation than anyone knows, and combines with the new to create a new value," writes Gadamer. I therefore chose to survey the ground of tradition as well as that of opinion. Even though I would try to give some place in this study to the demographic and medical ideologies of the eighteenth century, which seemed to me, as to other researchers in this field, to play a vital part in the redrawing of the gender map, as a literary rather than a historical scholar I have chosen to plant my own account of this reenactment of the "world historical defeat" of women firmly in literary and artistic rhetoric and in symbolics, which play out Gadamer's scenario of the old afloat in the new. In so doing, I believe I have established the framework of a far longer evolution for the essentially maternalist structuring of femininity that was then emerging than that of only the Revolution and its preceding decade; even though the place of Rousseau in this evolution has long been acknowledged, here I set his role in a wider movement, for which he becomes rather the spokesman than the initiator. The most novel aspect of this present work, then, lies not in the historical record of the women's fate in the Revolutionary period itself, which is well known and entirely reconstructed here from published sources, but in the four chapters of part 1 that build up the spectacle of gender tension that precedes Revolution, in the close examination of the rhetoric of the women's language in their *Cahiers* in chapter 5, and in chapters 6, 7, and 9, which concentrate on female imagery deployed in the symbolics of the Revolution that relates back to either the preoccupations of the earlier century, or to even older historical paradigms of female gendering by Western male culture.

This work is divided into two parts. Part 1 explores aesthetic, sexual, and social sites of gender tension in the era before the Revolution in three chapters, and the fourth attempts to describe their accumulated dimensions. This section is as long and sustained as it is so as to fully establish how the terms of gender definition came to be in question during a period, around midcentury, well anteceding the Revolution. The impact upon art, biological theory, Enlightenment thought, and polemics of the quarrel, which I try to demonstrate as one long festering, will be most fully appreciated by patient readers as they reach chapters 5 through 9.

Chapter 1 sets out some implications of the gender politics set in motion by the contestation of the rococo by its detractors, to situate the battle over taste in the context of its repercussions for notions of masculinity and femininity. Chapter 2 proceeds to advance evidence, both demographic and artistic, of the existence of a crisis mentality around issues of prostitution, sexuality, natality, infant mortality, nurturance, and parental roles. Chapter 3 explores the situation of women of privilege, from the court and from the salon, in terms of their actual powers and their limits, in the light of the quarrel over women's relationships to nature and to culture. It attempts to demonstrate trends of opinion concerning these women's prominence and to suggest the potential impact of strongly conflicting codes for women in the aristocracy and the Third Estate. Chapter 4 follows up exhaustively on social, literary, sexual, demographic, and artistic themes set out earlier as they impinge on the evolving gender redefinition of the decade immediately preceding the Revolution.

Part 2 considers women in the Revolution itself in five chapters. Chapter 5 deals with the already foreclosed general outlook of the women in the early Revolution, who use the language of the rigid terminology of their own limitations even as, in calling for relief from an array of grievances in their cahiers, they attempt to profit from this extraordinary moment of human liberation. Chapter 6 examines the complex role pictorial and verbal allegorization played in the rhetoric of Revolution for men and for women. Chapter 7 reviews the actions of the women of history in the era of the Terror and finds some element of affirmation in its politically disempowering aftermath. Chapter 8 surveys the myth of the Maenad-*tricoteuse* and its implications for the reconceptualization of women in a modern republican society. Chapter 9 investigates the thematics of the female breast as a code in Revolutionary art. Finally, the postlude attempts to characterize the nature of the gender ideology that emerged from the long evolution adumbrated, as well as the continuing resistance to it.

A word about my use of visual materials: I wished, insofar as I could unearth them, not only to provide pictorial instances of trends I discuss—that is, use them illustratively—but even more to find within the visual images intimations not spelled out at all in language, and so to mine them as the source of cultural change, that, among other things, they are. At times the visual material displaces my textual ruminations altogether; at times it will merely be cited to lend completeness to my documentation. But the visual material is never ancillary: it is as much the core of this demonstration as are the verbal texts.

Gadamer has also spoken of the need to express the tensions between the historical text and the present. As I wove my way through eighteenth-century quarrels over gender, the definitions of the family, of nurturance anxiety, of sexuality, of breast imagery, I was often aware of—but I rarely felt the need to underline—the tensions with present-day gender issues over child care, homophobia, abortion, divorce, and the definition of the family. Readers will, I do hope, make such associations for themselves. My own beliefs and situation have of course affected my shaping of the course I pursued in writing this work. The most material factors, no doubt, are a lifelong commitment to greater clarification of women's condition, and to its amelioration, and my experience as the mother of two women and a man. My critique of the French Revolution's construction of motherhood is meant to entail no particular scorn for any of its tenets (least of all breast-feeding, which I have actively advocated as a childbirth educator), but only a concern for the mode of their imposition upon women.

My thanks go to the following individuals and institutions for having, in one or another fashion, sustained the labors that produced this work. First, I salute the memory of Professor John J. Spagnoli, my mentor when I was an undergraduate at Brooklyn College, who shared his own canny devotion to French letters with me, inspiring my own; for professional support, Germaine Brée, Natalie Zemon Davis, Gita May, Frank Bowman, and Anne Firor Scott, without whose confidence in my efforts I could not have been enabled to proceed; to the National Endowment for the Humanities for its initial and essential grant of a summer stipend; to the American Council of Learned Societies and the National Humanities Center, whose fellowships in 1985–86 enabled me to research in superb circumstances for a year, and especially to the center's delightful and helpful staff for its assistance and friendliness; to the Bibliothèque Nationale and the Musée Carnavalet in Paris for the use of their resources; to the libraries of North Carolina State and Duke universities, and the University of North Carolina for the use of their facilities during my residence in that state; to the libraries and librarians of West Chester University and Haverford and Bryn Mawr colleges for their courtesy and assistance; to West Chester University for its resourcefulness in granting me a timely sabbatical leave, and for its financial and secretarial assistance; to the community of historians of women in the Revolution, including Vivian Cameron, Darline Levy, and Harriet Applewhite, who extended a cordial welcome to the literary interloper I must have seemed to them to be; to those who have lent materials or suggested leads—Simone Balayé, Frank Bowman, Géralde Nakam, Avriel Goldberger, Karyna Szmurlo and Judy Stein; to my Women's Studies reading group at West Chester University—Debbie Mahlstedt, Elizabeth Larson, Lynette McGrath, Gheeta Ramanathan, Carol Radich, Stacey Schlau, and Anne Dzamba—who read and commented on chapter 1, and to Anne, especially, for her steady encouragement; to Anne Rayburn for able assistance in preparing the first chapter of the text; to Marguerite Wagner for her generous expertise in completing it; to Sarah Gutwirth for her percipient advice about art and the warmth of her concern; to the love and commitment of my first mentor, my sister Jan; to my whole family, Eve, Jonathan, Nat, Terry, Isabel, and Mollye for challenging me to maintain my human commitments even in my scholarly endeavors; to dear friends, Gloria, Sylvia, Margaret, Avriel, Tracy, and Sibyl for sustaining affection; to Marcel, finally, for his devotedly lending his mind, his heart, and his feet to seeing this effort through.

I have dedicated this work, in a spirit of paradox, to the memory of my father, Louis A. Katz. It was his often verbalized disappointment in his failure to father a son that made me, the second of his three daughters, a feminist from childhood. But this same father who induced a permanent stubborn protest in me against my (own) female fate also lavished upon me, purely as his child, that intensity of affection that has allowed me to transcend impotent anger and go on asking, I hope ever more effectively, what lay behind this double message. I am, finally, grateful to him for both of these legacies.

All translations from the French are my own, unless otherwise indicated. I have taken some very slight liberties with punctuation in some of the texts cited, to promote ease of understanding.

In Jacques Godechot's review of Paule-Marie Duhet's *Les Femmes et la Revolution 1789–1794,* he tasks her, I believe unjustly, for not having shown "to what degree the mentality of contemporaries, even that of the most 'advanced' of the revolutionaries, was incapable of conceiving of a radical change in [women's] condition." This is precisely the lacuna I have moved toward filling in with this volume, though I hope also to have shown that a more radical mentality always coexisted with this dominant one.

Setting the account of the women's struggle in the time of the French Revolution within the more extended evolution of *mentalité* offered here, I believe, transforms its more familiar contour: it makes it part of a longer skein of evolution in men's and women's struggle to raise issues of gender to conscious awareness, rather than to reenact blindly the culturally imprinted scenarios that the pressures of unconscious tensions in sexuality have left as their legacy. It is to the battle for lucidity across the gender barrier, deeper than the battle for women's rights and governing its outcome, that I address myself here. This struggle is far from its end, and that is the import of an account like this one. For the structuring of the gestalt Woman has been molded by men in culture without the effective corrective collaboration of women's own reciprocal shaping of the notion Man, which women have not as yet gained sufficient power to impose. Here, in fact, we witness a skirmish in the life of culture where men, in the name of a movement for individual liberation, press back women's palpable advance, an advance that the men themselves had fostered and enjoyed, into a gender construct less challenging for themselves. It is as a contribution to the articulation by women of a critique of a momentous juncture in the life of modern culture that I offer this work.

This is the story as I have wished to tell it: filled to the brim with the voices of women and men of the era in question, and their commentators. It is time to let them be heard.

THE TWILIGHT
OF THE GODDESSES

ONE

Gender
and Culture
in the Late
Eighteenth
Century

Chapter

1

GENDERED ROCOCO AS POLITICAL PROVOCATION

Rococo woman is as a curve
that pursues its asymptote,
man, without ever reaching it.

ERNST TOTH

ONE of the first salvos in the battle over the rococo was fired by the Earl of Shaftesbury, who in 1713 denounced it as a revolting form exalting Sensation at the expense of Reason. He derided "that false Relish which is govern'd rather by what immediately strikes the sense, than by what consequently and by reflection pleases the Mind, and satisfies the thought and Reason." Our own contemporary, critic Michael Levey, rationalizes Shaftesbury's attack as understandable, arising from a critic of puritan temper in the Protestant nation most antagonistic to rococo art forms, England. But, as Levey points out, Shaftesbury "seems to anticipate the feminine bias of the rococo" in his caustic warning against its enticements: "Whilst we look on Paintings with the same eye, as we view commonly the rich Stuffs and colour'd Silks worn by our Ladys, and admir'd in Dress, Equipage, or Furniture, we must of necessity be effeminate in our Taste, and utterly set wrong as to all Judgment and Knowledge in the kind." Shaftesbury's implication, writes Levey, is that "the right type of painting was of an elevated masculine kind in subject as well as treatment," and that this virile art would necessarily be a "natural" and "moral" art, as opposed to that fey, artificial, and ostensibly feminine one. Levey concludes that "just while the rococo is getting under way, Shaftesbury seems to call for, in effect, neoclassical art. That is the dignified alternative to the rococo." [1]

A fuller measure of Shaftesbury's conception of the gender dichotomy as it relates to rococo art and to neoclassicism can be witnessed as we see him attempting to isolate the character of his goal of "manliness."

Childish, womanish, bestial, brutal. —Words! Words! Or are they anything more? But how then not a child? How least like a woman? How far from the beast? How removed and at a distance from anything of this kind? How properly a *man?* . . . ["Consider, then, by what you are distinguished on reason—from wild beasts—from cattle." Epict. Disc. Bk. II, C. x, #2]. A man, and not a woman; effeminate, soft, delicate, supine; impotent in pleasure, in anger, talk; pusillanimous, light, changeable, etc; but the contrary to this in each particular. —A man, and not a beast: . . . A man, and not a child: . . . the contraries: Manhood, manliness, humanity—manly, humane, masculine.[2]

Shaftesbury's fulmination draws gender parallels familiar to French as well as English culture. Women suggest the artifices and illusions fostered by high society—visual illusions of grace and languor that provided an ambiance conducive to verbal indirection in love and diplomacy. Its implicit opposite is a presumed masculine scorn of artifice, joined with a preference for simplicity and directness in self-presentation, in courtship and in moral matters.[3] Shaftesbury is careful to sustain his stance, significantly, by his reference to Epictetus. Recourse to ancient precedent is to become a potent arm in the round of gender struggle about to take place.

The delusion inherent in his terms, that this battle was one between masculine rectitude and female evasiveness, had had a long life. And in France, certainly, women had played a major role in devising that scheme of manners, Preciosity, that would eventuate a century later in rococo art. It was in Mlle de Scudéry's salon of the 1640s that the arts of indirection in courtship, linguistic and gestural, were developed and set in their arcadian mythological glade.[4] Seventeenth-century baroque painting had in its relative robustness rather overwhelmed the aimed-for piquancy of the literary genre of the pastoral. But by the eighteenth, Preciosity had so transformed upper-class social mores that, at least during the golden age of Watteau, its first and greatest moment of solemnity, a species of erotic democracy dominated the scene, as the refinement of men in love nearly coincides with and sometimes overcomes, as with the heroes of Prévost, the finesse of women. If those nineteenth-century *littérateurs* the Goncourts could confidently open their 1861 study of *Women in the Eighteenth Century* with the claim "It was the reign of women," in our own time critic Jean Starobinski revises their statement to read, "Woman reigns (she is led to believe she reigns)." Even as the fiction of woman's reign is, as Starobinski suggests while never exploring it, a male construct, that facile and widespread assignment of the rococo to women is of course equally misleading. Eighteenth-century France's rococo, though touched via Preciosity by a female sensibility in its beginnings, is a sensuous style by which the male imagination softened and divinized the mysteries of love and courtship and repressed the awareness of the crudities of coupling and the conflict inherent for both sexes in obtaining sexual access to the other. Rococo manners paint the scenarios of love with a lustrous, but thin, veneer. "Tender protestations are the

coded language of carnal impatience, the intelligent prelude to the defeats of reason. An entire refined system of attentions, of respect, of compliments, of notes
and portraits exchanged unfolds itself so as to achieve most assuredly the tumults
of animal satiety."[5] Starobinski structures his scenario as if there were no agent,
no subject, in action. But as we gather, this scenario must still have represented
the reign of men.

Analyst of the rococo Patrick Brady has fruitfully explored what he calls a "po-
etics of reduction" in such rococo lyrics as these (which are slightly racier in the
original):

> And why should I reproach Rosette
> If God's made her a bit coquette?
> What luck to find coquettes in love!
> Just one moment of coquetry
> Of folly and of wildest glee
> Is manna for the hungry heart!
> It's when one loves that raptures start!
> Coquette, it's then your arts are best;
> And deep inside you know you'd jest
> At constant lovers lacking art.

As Brady points out, this sort of trivialization of woman is not altogether an elimination of her. On the contrary, love and woman are yoked together in the rococo
lyric, but as the love we see here is pure ephemerality, a sheer moment of bliss,
woman is equally so.[6] The tremulous momentariness of perceiving her is echoed
in the terms of her representation: tumbled amongst clouds or passions, her features, moral and physical, are scrambled about so that all turn into sexual provo-
cations—breasts, goodness, buttocks, eyes, jests.

> Heaven gave you in full measure
> For your rank and for your treasure
> Just your youthful wayward sweetness
> Two breasts Cupid's own two hands
> Shaped to roundlets one fine day
> Simple goodness, spirit flighty
> Lilies, I still see them Philis,
> Of your dazzling cheeks of love,
> Buds of buttocks, Philis, gleaming,
> Dazzle even now my sight,
> Rivaling those of your fair eyes.[7]

Can the prime place given in art to empty, doll-faced, but seductive little goddesses of love set in splendidly stylized natural bowers be read as evidence of a
time of woman regnant? Brady thinks not: "It may be largely a myth. Those

women who exercised great influence at that time did so either at the price of
publicly occupying a position of great moral ambiguity (e.g. Pompadour) or at the
cost of great and continual effort on behalf of their followers (e.g. the famous
maîtresses de salon)." This "negative view of Woman as perched upon a very
precarious pedestal . . . is confirmed," Brady finds, by the poetry he examines.[8]

Brady attests to a loss in the poetry of this time of the metaphoric, and a
substitution for or reduction of it by the metonymic, which becomes manifest not
merely in the reduction of love, "but also in the synecdochic replacement of man
and woman by petit-maître and coquette, then by lap-dog and cat, by snuff-box
and fan, by china jar and bergère." In other words, by a systematically fetishized
sexuality.

Rococo, as even nowadays in its near-total fall from favor as a taste to be imitated, has from the start suggested a species of whorehouse elegance. Its heyday,
appropriately enough, was during the supremacy of the sexually adventurous regent, Philippe d'Orleans, who succeeded Louis XIV until the accession to the
throne of the Sun King's great-grandchild, Louis XV. It continued during the kingship of the Well-Beloved, a prince better equipped for life on the hunt and in the
boudoir than for councils of state. Rococo would come to be seen as the elite's art
of dissipation, of aristocratic slumming via the sensuality of art. Apart from the
unnumbered juveniles, like the *soeurs* Morphée and others of little or no birth
who peopled the king's Deerpark, where young women were frank sexual prey,
the king in his lifetime accorded to two mistresses, one bourgeois, the other of
common birth, such titles, wealth, and influence as to destabilize his own regal
position. Pompadour and Du Barry, great rococo ladies, would become potent
symbols of aristocratic arbitrariness in autocracy, of a squandering in sensual
showiness of a nation's vital substance.

One of the manifold paradoxes of rococo lies in its combination of rigidity and
fluidity, of relentlessly repetitive forms and contents portrayed via an infinite sinu-
osity of line and a gentle luminescence of frequently pastel color. "The rococo is
at once the most stylized and the least stylized of styles," in Brady's formulation;
he relates this problematic to the rococo's embodiment of what Lévi-Strauss would
term a "hot" society, characterized by huge gaps of fortune between classes. But
it connects, too, to a "breaking away from logic, rationalism, Cartesianism, towards a highly sophisticated skepticism" that "rejects vast rational hypotheses."[9]
Preceding, conditioning, and accompanying the Age of Reason, then, is an art of
near total Unreason, a celebration of tremulous, fleeting, passionate encounters.

The rococo's imperative to both sexes dictated that one remain on the surface,
the skin of experience, but there to find delight. Progressively, as we move from
the gentle momentousness and meditative sexuality of Watteau to the world of
Boucher and his company, canvases actually begin to lose all reference to any but
their own painted surfaces, to swirls and curves of flesh, leaf, cloud, or stuffs.
Turning away from the robust maturity and fleshliness of Rubens's rosy nudes,

Boucher and Fragonard generalize and incorporate women's divine attributes into standardized scenery and props.

Venus is the rococo's regnant deity, though all of her mythological and metonymic handmaidens are granted appearances as well. As historian James Leith has put it: "Through this pagan goddess an epicurean aristocracy expressed its preoccupation with the pleasures provided by women. Everywhere the nude female form was to be seen: in the murals, in state apartments, easel painting, book illustrations, upholstery fabrics, mantelpiece ornaments and jewelry." In these art forms elaborated by men "the 'feminine principle' was dominant and in fact glorified—an important facet of the male hedonism of the period." Candace Clements theorizes that the obsessive use of mythological scenes as the genre of choice for the rococo both high and low, both verbal and visual, arose "not only because of their origins in the classical past, but because of their utility as signposts in an increasingly social setting."[10] In this art of male desire, Venus's woman's body is the sign of a necessarily evanescent rapture. Erotic projections of Venus upon her couch seek to conjure up in us as observers, whether female or male, a mood of blissful seductiveness, a reassurance of the heavenliness of our sexual dreams, even as nature had begun its definitive retreat from us in the world.

The apology for love's inability to last is perfunctory: Both women and men, the poets repeat tirelessly, are *volage,* or flighty. "Women, they tell us, find it good that we, like them, change partners." And "Without liberty, desire soon becomes a mere trial." These stereotypical notions may well "represent the expression of the ephemeral character of love in Man, Woman being for man the natural symbol of this love and the nature of this love being expressed as a quality of this natural symbol." Thus do male artists indulge in psychological projection of their sex's characteristics upon the other. The many depictions of the swing in rococo art have been read as a shorthand reference to women's changeability in love, which to one critic "in part explains why one rarely sees any but women in swings in eighteenth-century art."[11]

The rococo's style of rendering visually the physical aura of sexual arousal incorporated as a vital constituent not merely the principals of the erotic narrative, but a sexualized secondary code of fetishized images. The broken pitcher or the dead bird signals abandoned virginity; the single tiny unshod foot or abandoned slipper of the woman represents her sexual availability.[12] The turtledoves of Venus that hover over the act of love; the fountains or waters flowing or the watering can representing the secretions of love; the phallic cane; the pet dog representing a sensual playfulness close to bestiality; the garden rakes standing for coition itself; the ambiguous use of putti as innocent fosterers of sexuality—these constitute an easily recognized and omnipresent code of intensifying teasers, augmenting the vocabulary of purely visual suggestion, a world, as art historian Mary Sheriff has said, of metaphors and props (fig. 1, Huet's *Lovers' Meeting*).[13] It is this secret, time-bound code that evokes a species of anxiety in modern viewers: we sense

1. J.-B. Huet, Lovers'
Meeting, *private collection*

this closed code; it is almost as if there appeared before us a sly yet heated flirtation between great-great-great-grandparents, whose sexuality, though manifest (in
ourselves) yet remains incomprehensible.

A further level of reading of such erotic works is possible. As Sheriff has emphasized, "an artist who knew how to manipulate the elements of this code could
continually manufacture new varieties of wit to amuse his audience, for sexual
allusions were activated in the beholder's imagination through association or recall. . . . Part of the pleasure taken in an erotic symbol was the pleasure of decep-
tion; the beholders who decoded these images were pleased and amused because
they could clearly perceive the sexual discourse hidden from innocent eyes. Such
pleasures belonged only to those privileged viewers well versed in the codes of
representation and permitted to enjoy forbidden subjects."[14]

This is of course the root of that prurience so endemic to this art: the knowing
wink of members of its audience at one another over the heads of ignorant sim-
pletons. In its convention of representing women as unknowing innocents, it
mocks their pretended ignorance; in this way it affirms itself as the men's code
and theirs alone (even if it has gaps). That the code was riddled with hypocrisy

becomes apparent in the reaction of the German observer Joachim C. Neimitz to the behavior of Parisian ladies at the bawdy spectacles presented at the *foires* (fairs) in which Harlequins, Columbines, and Scaramouches would go through their *commedia dell'arte* routines: "I have viewed with astonishment that even ladies of quality were able to bear and see the obscenities without blushing with shame; but what can I say, seeing that they feel contented and laugh from the heart? This is Parisian high society, the more drolerie is earthy and grotesque, the more one is entertained."[15] We divine from this comment that the women of the time, after all, did know, were not at all displeased to have their sexuality acknowledged.

The maximum degree of sexual suggestion, then, accompanied by the maximum pretense of a carefree innocence. This code presupposes "insiders" and "outsiders," but the secrecy of the code, as Sheriff insists, is a pure fiction that, though elitist and aristocratic, is shared basically by members of the male sex. It could be, and was, read by women and even children, but what it conveyed was necessarily a male construction of seduction and of pleasure. We may tend to agree with critic Roger Laufer's contention that the "great works of gallantry of the eighteenth century escape the platitudes of pornography to communicate the emotions felt by living flesh"; yet the play of insider versus outsider is one of seducer versus seduced, knower versus object. "Ah! Restif's fetishistic passion," exclaims the interpreter of fashion Perrot, as one of the novelist's heroines loses her slippers, revealing her lovely little feet. The libertine tactic of the slipper game consists of "getting it to fall off, thus granting the seducer a sight which is a stage in his progress." Men are the privileged viewers of this sensuous narrative, and the gender split extends as well to plastic representations. "Man is mover, actor and agent, and demands the use of techniques for representing recession, tension and action; woman is spectator and spectacle, and therefore tends to be shown as a stilled and extended display of forms."[16]

A major metaphor that Sheriff explores is that well-worn one so precious to the Age of Nature of woman as garden and man as gardener, seeder, waterer, plowman, a notion she applies to Fragonard's *Spring*, where she reads the man's scythe and gourd as signifiers of the male organs soon to fructify the woman-ground. Indeed, even as we consider the long lineage of works celebrating seasonal change and fertility, eighteenth-century painting seems far more preoccupied than the art of other periods of post-Renaissance art with the rose, that metaphor for the female genital (fig. 2, Greuze's *Young Girl with a Rose*). Garlands abound, flowers are strewn through the air, filling it with a sense of their transient beauty and joy in the polymorphously sexualized moment. And beneath it all, as the critic of the rococo Clements points out, is the woman as sublime spectacle.

Rococo is, then, a feminocentric art only in the sense that it adores woman in paint for her ability to inspire desire. Everything in it that enhances desire is present not for her sake but for her observer/lover's. Only in the sense that the

2. *J.-B. Greuze,* Young Girl with Rose, *Musée Cognac-Jay, Photo Giraudon/Art Resource, New York*

rococo commands heterosexuals to "make love, not war" can it be considered an art devised for women's sake. Rococo's is the quintessential representation of a sexuality that seeks to know no desire but the genital.

Frequently the viewer may sense something embarrassingly puerile in this style of eroticism, as compared, for example, with that of a Giorgione; a juvenilization, a miniaturization, a coy sweetness in the depicted object repels even as it attracts. Our malaise suggests we are in the presence of a mental construct lying along the margins between consciousness and fantasy, that region where we "may catch in the raw the process of transition from one system to the other, repression or the return of repressed material." What, we may ask ourselves, is repressed, what expressed in this vision of desire? "The origin of fantasy would lie in the hallucinatory satisfaction of desire; in the absence of a real object, the infant reproduces the experience of the original satisfaction in a hallucinated form. In this view the most fundamental fantasies would be those which tend to recover the hallucinated objects linked with the very earliest experiences of the rise and the resolution of desire." Laplanche and Pontalis add that the "Freudian model is incomprehensible unless one understands that it is not the real object but the lost object; not the

milk, but the breast as a signifier, which is the object of the primary halluci-
nation."[17]

Two psychological concepts relevant to the apprehension of the rococo impinge
with particular relevance here: that the origin of autoeroticism emerges at "the
moment when sexuality, disengaged from any natural object, moves into the field
of fantasy and by that very fact becomes sexuality"; and conversely, that "it is the
breaking in of fantasy which occasions the disjunction between sexuality and
need." Autoeroticism, once the intensity of drives has been removed from an
object to the self, fantasizes a sexuality; but this fantasy becomes a self-generating
system that systematically uncouples need from sexuality. The product of "the
anarchic activity of partial drives, autoeroticism is closely linked with the excitation of specific erogenous zones, an excitation which arises and is stilled on the
spot"; its fantasy discourse is "no longer addressed to anyone, all distinction between subject and object has been lost." This loss of the sense of the subject or
agency may be crucial to fantasy, inasmuch as it originates in a dream of incorporation with its object.[18]

Boucher's *Venus and Mars Surprised by Vulcan* (fig. 3) finds its amorous gods
interrupted in midecstasy. If it is true that the gaze has the power of appropriating
the object, Vulcan's gaze here, directed between the opened legs of Venus, certainly is meant to establish his claim to her, a claim disappointed in the event.[19]
In *The Odyssey*'s account it is Helios, the sun, who had uncovered the lovers
enlaced, thus fouling Hephaistos's marriage bed. Retaliating, Hephaistos fashions
on his anvil that magic snare to entrap them, "thin, like spider webs that not even
one of the blessed gods could see," a netting rendered here by the painter with the
lightest pressure of his brush. His brushwork's delicacy conveys Homer's final dis-
position of the lovers, who, after punishment, escape permanent entrapment, like
the unsnarable passion that had united them to begin with. As related visually, the
scene's conceit is one of unveiling: the clouds, opening out to cast Helios's light,
unveil the heavens; airborne putti raise the vaginally shaped, sheer, membrane-
like bridal veil; and we, ultimate voyeurs like the gods, look on at Venus's display
of the passive desire exposed. Birds, flowers, precious fabrics decorate the fleshly
scene as the putto at bottom exposes his rosy, dimpled rear. The desire depicted
concentrates on the figure of Venus its sheer projection of masculine longing. Her
whiteness, the languor of the postures of her head and prone leg, her reaching
beneath the arm of Mars as she raises her leg still enlaced with his, give to her
alone an aura of a longing unsuspecting of spectators' eyes. Though deliberately
unveiled, she yet retains remnants of the veil, even in her very abandonment to
love, in her closed eyes and insignificant, uncharacterized visage: she remains an
enigma still. The contrast between luminous white female and swarthy male flesh
heightens at once and paradoxically both her fleshliness and her vulnerable insubstantiality. The fantasy here is clearly "about woman," a male construct.[20] What

3. *François Boucher,* Venus
and Mars Surprised by Vulcan, *reproduced by permission
of the Trustees, The Wallace
Collection, London*

Mars is made to register is dismay at being uncovered in this less-than-material
posture: his gaze confronts Vulcan, the one with whom he fears he will have to
contend once this moment of dalliance has passed.

In this rendition of a dream of sexual fusion preempted by the male bond, the
arms that Mars has put off lie at the bottom of the image, reminders of man's other
prime function. And it is at the heart of this dichotomy that gender conflict lives.

Within the overdetermined sweetness and the heaping up of sub rosa erotic clues of the rococo mode lies a collective masculine fantasy of effortless infantile fusion in physical union. In its deliberate and virtually literal externalizations of sexual play, it presents an exhibitionist display of male longing. What is repressed, what deviates this longing from its objects, are of course the huge ambivalences surrounding sex acts: that sexuality arouses anxiety and hostility because, a union of separate beings, it can but rarely reproduce the wished-for fusion; or that this is a sexuality thrown up out of a Christian ethos of repressiveness. Even the interrupted ecstasies of Venus and Mars, as rendered by Boucher, retain their air of mildly comical bliss, essentially blessed by the gods. I will speak at greater length of those repressed dissonances later, but in the context of the rococo, it suffices to note that in its insistence on a fantasized reverie of fusion, this art denies or mutes a sense of agency in the realization of desire. In so doing, it reduces both sexes—but in a culture of male supremacy, more problematically the male—to a passive posture. This denial of agency enables it to convey a basic existential aspect of desire, that of its vast, invasive power, but in so doing it negates the effects of ego; and it is in this respect that rococo seems to us now to be the perfectly apposite art form for an absolute monarchy in decline.

The mockery of the cuckolded Vulcan in Boucher's painting provides an appropriate metaphor for the relation of this art form to the nonrococo classes. "Decorative mythological paintings designed to adorn aristocratic living spaces . . . constitute a system of meaning referring back to the room's inhabitants, announcing that fully displayed sexuality is the province of the privileged, just as it is the province of the gods and goddesses of legend."[21] To the smith Vulcan, coming in his sweat from the forge, the sight of the adulterous delights of this dallying class, of great-lady Venus and warrior Mars at his rest, is the sign of his disbarment from fantasy, hence ecstasy. If we compare the image of the relations between the sexes reserved for high art with those still regnant in eighteenth-century peasant culture, we gain some perspective not only on the potential for hostility toward rococo images on the part of the underclasses, but also a more rounded feeling for the consonances and dissonances they aroused even in aristocratic circles, despite their veneer of cultured overlay, ultimately bred upon the same rustic traditions. In the pervasive traditions of French society, absent wealth or nobility, and often even in their presence, women simply had no firm status outside marriage: it alone could confer a social identity upon them. Single or older women accepted roles as servants or adjuncts, or exiled themselves to the convent, or to an anonymous life—perhaps that of prostitution—in the cities. Even as the men determined woman's social and cultural existence, she remained for them a natural being who obtained her disturbing powers from the seasons and the lunar cycle. Among men, her pregnancies retained the aura of fearsome and mysterious irregularities, because foreign, not truly domesticated. Education was seen as a means of tempering women, of giving them a stake in good domestic order. But such cultural strategies were not widely trusted. Women kept about them their threat of sexual predation, sickness, and menace and were felt to be a continued source of potential social disorder. The function of community life was to limit their movement and their influence in the village.

The concepts of sexuality abroad in the peasant classes are by no means simple to ascertain. Certain recurrent proverbs illustrate some very ancient notions: the too amorous woman is dangerous, or as the saying from the Limousin has it, "When the hen seeks out the rooster, love isn't worth a nut." Yet, in support of at least one received notion concerning the French as a people, as we have seen the traveler Neimitz confirm, both *peuple* and high society in the Old Regime enjoyed an open reference to sexual and bodily realities, including female desire, that the nineteenth century would largely repress. Eighteenth-century France was still an agricultural world, where humans lived in the midst of animal couplings. This factor contributed on the one hand to a rural brutality about sex, and on the other to a relative indifference to it as compared, say, with worries about the harvest. In village life, women's sociability hovered about the fountain and the stream and was enjoyed exclusive of men, whereas segregated circles of men would congregate around fireside and drink.[22] I have more to say about this division in chapter 3.

Putting side by side, in even the most cursory way as here, the rococo aesthetic and the rustic outlook, we are overwhelmed by their contrasts. As against a stratified and hierarchized tradition featuring sexual segregation as a mode of male defense against a barely repressed anxiety concerning the menace of sexuality and women rampant, the rococo posits an entirely dissident scenario: its vision is an ostensibly timeless, high-cultural one, setting afloat the image of a sexuality coyly yet openly professed, even flaunted; a species of "democracy" of sensuality, where woman as metaphor for sex shares and frequently dominates visualization even as, in *Manon Lescaut,* she dominates the fiction. To the tradition's long-established order, rococo in its sheer repetitiveness of devices, in its use of the curve or the curlicue, the graphic figuration of femininity which characterized all of design in the first two-thirds of the century and could not be avoided, came to signify women's unprecedented and unauthorized presence—soon felt to be preeminence—in the social order. A gender provocation, then, via an aesthetic provocation and at the same time, a class provocation.

Among the nonrococo public, the assumption underlying this predominance of a feminized aesthetic might have been that "the men in charge had lost their heads," an intriguing preformulation of Revolutionary practice. The appearance of having forfeited a posture of male separateness and agency before women was infinitely heightened by the strong trend to an androgynous merging of male and female styles and manners. We listen to the Abbé Coyer in 1748 describing his interview with a twenty-five-year-old judge whom he wished to see in private. "He was being dressed. It was incumbent upon me to enjoy the whole of this

Spectacle which lasted longer than the time needed to explain my business; I thought I'd fallen in with an assault upon a duchess's curlings and perfumings. . . . Let our surprise henceforth cease in seeing male persons wearing earrings, doing embroidery, receiving company in their beds at noon, interrupting a serious conversation with a dog, speak to their own image in a mirror, caress their laces, grow enraged at the breaking of a trinket, fall into a faint over a sick parrot, steal, in sum, all its charms from the other sex."[23] A useful passage, giving its dual reading of the presumed-to-be foppish practices of some aristocratic dandies and its mirror portrait of what were deemed to be appropriately feminine absurdities. The abbé's gender outrage here reflects implicitly what Joan Landes has seen emerging with Rousseau: an opposition between "the iconic specularity of the Old Regime and the textual and legal order of the bourgeois public sphere."[24]

Impelled by courtly *préciosité* to effect ever more refined feats of artifice, the *petits-maîtres* of the midcentury created shock waves in the wider public. "Men didn't use to worry formerly about having a pretty face . . . but now they're just as concerned about it as women, and there is nothing they won't do so as to not look ugly."[25] High style decreed for the nobility a suppression of sexual dimorphism more extreme even than that of the seventeenth century. "Into the preciosity of their finery—which both hides unease and flaunts class superiority—they throw themselves body and soul." Wigs made of women's hair, cleanly shaven cheeks, perfumed and rouged visages, laces and satins, padded calves, the mouche near the lips to heighten their reddened color—all contribute to make these mincing courtiers to women masterpieces of imagination, or an affront to nature, according to one's outlook. In this world of rococo artfulness where, as Perrot reminds us, "not a vial, not a doorknob is not worked, incised, chiseled, stippled in the most delicate fashion so as to pleasure the eye and rejoice it in the comely climate of magic perfection," the arts of appearances have taken over an entire class. Since it is women who have traditionally been authorized to perfect the arts of appearances, it is upon them that this style leans. However, this exercise by women of the skills creating illusion, imitated by men so as to bring them closer to the presumed objects of their seduction, bears an ancient baggage of male scorn. Attacks upon women for vanity and perfidy are woven together in denunciations of them: a woman's "toilette is a resurrection that revives skeletons and embellishes cadavers and gives them a surprising attractiveness: teeth grow in them, dead eyes come back to life, breaths take on the odor of tuberoses and jasmin." These arts of women are close to charms or enchantments, the witch's forte, an extension into culture of the primitive and unruly powers women exercise upon men. Hostility to the reordering of female appearance to conform with the artifices of society reflects a deep and abiding source of male anxiety. Caraccioli, the critic of the mores of self-adornment, expostulates sarcastically: "They want plastered faces because they like duplicity; candor is no longer valued either in mores or in faces; it is a virtue good for villagers that really suits only peasant women and should be banned from our cities."[26] Such a concentration upon sensual experience and sexual adventures presented as major male enterprise was felt as a deep challenge to the West's traditions of manliness. The menacing possibilities inherent in male adoption of the manipulative strategies of the human object, woman, did not escape notice. Escape from this malaise could be imagined only in some primitive village, poor but honest. The now too evident self-reduction of a set of noblemen to the status of seeming objects seems to have struck a chord of fear in that set of men most anxious to maintain sexual dimorphism and hence stratification. What is perhaps not so surprising, in view of the protected status of the class in question, is that the most effective attack on such mores would come not as direct confrontation, but rather via a blast against rococo painting.

As noted at the start, the attack on the rococo arts that dominated court life goes back to Shaftesbury and the early years of the century at the least. In France, the offensive, probably long whispered before being shouted out in print, takes on public cogency with the aesthetic critic La Font de Saint-Yenne's *Reflections upon Some Causes for the Present State of Painting in France* in 1747, his commentaries on the Louvre exhibition of August of the preceding year. He would have agreed with Michael Florisoone's twentieth-century judgment: "instead of raising men to the gods—symbols of Antiquity—Boucher lowers Olympus to the lowliest places on earth, his nudes deprived of their ancient luminosity and of that holy desire that gave them a religious drapery, are no longer anything, once they've passed through Boucher's studio, than disrobed and primped-up models ready for the deer park." Florisoone adds that while the court had required of Boucher that he clean up nature, he had gone them one better, giving it an adorably fixed-up and antiqued look: "The milkmaid will become a beribboned shepherdess, the chimney-sweep a slippered shepherd, country life would be all pastorales, and the labor of the people transformed into games in which the false sensibility of a frivolous society will hide its sensual and egoistic instincts." Florisoone's attack is retrospective and seems to reflect the Revolution's passage.[27]

La Font himself does not blame a frivolous society for this failure; he blames its women. He begins his essay with the claim that "the painter of history is the only painter of the soul; the others paint for the eye alone."[28] It is for this dictum of La Font's that he is thought of as a father of neoclassicism. He advances the arresting argument that the extensive use of mirrors in decoration, which had come to the French court of Louis XIV from Italy, had reduced the function of painting to the status of a mere decorative adjunct, depicting allegories of the seasons, the arts, the senses, or the muses. And these mirrors had proven to have particularly devastating effects upon women: "Self-love, whose Rule is even more powerful than that of Fashion, had the art of presenting to the eyes, and above all to those of the Ladies, mirrors of themselves the more enchanting as they were less faithful" (23–24). Painters who pander to them have fallen into representing them in the fashionable mythological guises. His charge did not lack foundation:

after being taken to the palace at Sceaux in 1767, the scene of the long-deceased Duchesse du Maine's once lively salon, Horace Walpole noted, "the princess [who in reality was half hunchbacked] and her daughter were painted with the features of Venus and one of the graces. What insolent superiority could exert a more bald-faced tyranny, what feminine vanity demand a more humiliating homage?"[29] La Font finds in this practice (surely not new in his time, nor extinct in our own) the ultimate outrage. "What spectacle can be comparable, to a real or imaginary beauty, than to see herself eternally with the graces and the cup of Hebe, goddess of youth?" Or, he adds, as Flora, reflecting the image of a budding spring, or a goddess of the forest with a quiver on her back and hair blown gently by the wind? "How can she fail to believe herself the rival of the charming God who wounds all hearts? . . . She cannot doubt that Hebe's youth will avenge her for the insults of that least of galants, Time, that most impolite of all the Gods." La Font cites La Rochefoucauld's maxim that "the hell of pretty women is old age" and wonders, ironically, why painting should not put off from them their awareness of decline, or even "conceal entirely, if that were possible, the sight of their great-est torture" (25). La Font then "apologizes" for what he calls his "somewhat play-ful" (*égayées*) reflections, which he feels will not distress his public unduly (27). He does admit, though only in passing, that both of the sexes may fall subject to self-love.

What art history had agreed to constitute the central element of La Font's ar-gument is his call for the return to the noble style, to the models exemplified by Raphael, Rubens, Poussin, and Lebrun, and to the depiction of the moral gran-deurs of antiquity. He also called for the relatively greater simplicity and sobriety of style associated with these prerococo painters.[30] This "return," of course, would betoken a rejection of a gynocentric (though scarcely a feminist) art for an andro-centric one. La Font's argument, in its very terms, exhibits an all but overt aware-ness of this strategy.

First of all, he has derided women of style as both subjects and critics of art: it is their vanity that has pressed painting into the service of their fleeting charms, and their childish judgment that makes them incapable of a longer, deeper view. But even as he is attacking the frivolous egoism of women of the aristocracy, he falls into a wider statement about the nature of women in general: the tortures that aging presents to them make them resist it by resorting to strategies of dissem-bling; the ancient theme of the dishonesty of face-painting recurs in his charge. He thus ends by attacking women as a class—rather than a specific class of women—for minding that men love them best when young and, in a sense, for poisoning culture with their resentment by making art subservient to their trivial needs. He also establishes a dichotomy between the male of the species, whose representation evokes the stirrings of the soul, and the female, a shallow being who with her love of mirrors calls up nothing but the pleasures of the eye, mere appearances. Finally, he makes Time the ultimate arbiter in a war of the sexes:

Time, by virtue of the constant and renewable aggrandizement of Man through allusion to the consecrated History of the West, to which Woman is invisible or marginal, honors him as individual and as species. Painting must revivify and renew this endorsement. Time serves Man. But for Woman Time is nothing but a destroyer: she has no place in this history, and she is a ruin when her life is but half run. Unflattering as is La Font to works that attempt to enhance the sexual aura of women not young or lovely, he is deeply admiring in his description of a portrait by de Toque of a woman who simply looks her age. Although our own aesthetic, the historic inheritor of his, might well incline us to concur in his judgment, it is still evident that his position reflects a sexual anxiety as much as an aesthetic one. Ultimately a male reading of woman via the senses, calling upon long-established traditional tropes as well as the eighteenth century's own sensibility, La Font's dismissal of women does not fundamentally diverge very much from the rococo's own strategies of reduction of them. His mock-courtly "apology" bears this out. He has "decorated" his text by his discussion of them, and through a pretense of gallant courtesy he seeks to disarm their enmity and that of the men who might contest his terms. His pseudo-gracious mechanism of defusing not only women's antagonism, but all discourse on their behalf, will recur repeatedly in our study.

A concern for History and its preservation and enhancement by painting becomes in La Font's critique a defense against the intrusion of the sexual and existential anxieties produced by the preoccupation with the figures of women in the rococo. There is certainly a political as well as a psychological aspect to this discussion. By choosing to dislodge woman as focus for the masculine gaze, he seeks also to deprive her of a potent source of self-empowerment available to her in the current culture. If it is as goddesses that men have chosen to depict them (spurred to do so by the courtly and *précieux* precedents of the past), then goddesses women must seem, while all the while responding as earthlings to the blandishments of male sexuality. What is more, they embraced this goddess posture, deeply at odds as it was with the realities of their existences, as a font of fantasy for themselves, embellishing their own dreams of power, of freedom, or of fusion.

In mocking this feminized, debased form, La Font not only sets up an opposition between men and the women of the upper classes (though as we have seen, this attack could not be contained by class); he implicitly posits, as did Shaftesbury before him, a schism between those men who were prepared to sustain the gynocentric rococo and those who were not: La Font incites a scorn for the "feminized fops" as against the "real men."

These *Reflections* were followed up by other antirococo polemics.[31] Thomas Crow points to the potent quotient of incipient politics in this aesthetic struggle, which would long continue to dominate perceptions of rococo, even after the Revolution, when Delécluze, the rebellious pupil of David, was to launch his ridiculing cry "Van Loo, Pompadour, Rococo!"[32] His linkage of rococo with woman would not lack apropos: after all, was Pompadour not the lavish patron of "trivial" rococo art, who had installed her own relative Lenormant de Tournehem as the equivalent of minister of the arts? Crow certainly modifies such a view, claiming that actually her effect in hiring Tournehem was "to introduce a new seriousness and sobriety" into the domain of the arts.[33]

In fact, La Font's "moderate" polemic, although ultimately to be followed up by paintings embodying its thesis, met with much hostility initially. His book was greeted by an antagonistic response from the Abbé Leblanc, which featured as its frontispiece, originally by Boucher, the allegory of a despondent Art chased by a horde of asses, led by a Harpy. Until the 1770s and 1780s there was no war against the rococo, only sporadic skirmishes by a class of disaffected naysayers.[34]

Who were they? For the most part, it would seem that the established nobility, with some distinguished exceptions, had little interest in questions of taste. Effervescence around these issues arose among the rising classes, the recently ennobled and *parlementaires,* who sought in art "a common ground between old and aspiring elite groups." As Crow puts it, for the ambitious aspiring class it was because they were bourgeois parvenus that they "made it their policy to revive the standards and practices of Colbert's half-remembered golden age."[35]

In his review of the rhetoric of La Font's text, Crow brings out its fawning and suspect idealization of Roman virtue. Where else, it asks, but in Rome's republic could one find so insightful a conception of the state, or a people more modest and resistant to personal or to political ostentation, more hard-working and self-disciplined, more economical in its practices? Merciful conquerors devoid of cruelty, they felt themselves constrained by their fidelity to law. The crown of this image is love of country, a love "stronger than blood or nature." This was, Crow holds, "an untenable idealization, which took the legends of the early republic for general fact." Implicit in La Font's myth of the republic is his moral condemnation of the lavish lives of the aristocracy, of the unrelenting self-adoration of the monarchy and its slothful ways, which had seeped insidiously into the conduct of all of society's business.[36] The parlementaires, members of the judicial system under the *ancien régime,* were as a class more and more in conflict with monarchical power in the mideighteenth century. It was, Crow theorizes, in order to buttress the claims of this class, members of a *noblesse de robe* that had arisen during the last two centuries, that La Font made his case. The "new Romans," they alone were proper defenders of justice and law, possessed of an elevated sense of their heritage, capable of driving out the corruptions of courtiers and bankers. The rise of Pompadour and the Tournehem clan was presented by La Font and his party as "the culmination of an unholy alliance between Crown and finance."[37]

It was this parlementaire faction that consistently presented itself, in time-honored political fashion, as the "true" representative of public opinion, or of the Salon audience. Thomas Crow asks, "What, after all, would ambitious painting be like if it were not learned and difficult, artificial and self-referential in style, aspiring to the sophistication of literary classicism and the audience that all this implied? It would have been difficult to find some available point of reference by which a care-worn merchant or apprentice clerk could genuinely participate in that culture." It is certainly true that there was far more for a nonelite public, male and female, to respond to in the intimate erotic prints which approached the level of a folk art in their popularity, if not in the great oil canvases of Boucher or Fragonard or Van Loo. Yet it cannot be denied that the most aggressive case made later, around 1770, as Marigny and d'Angivilliers succeeded to the administration of the arts, was one that condemned Pompadour's agents, Tournehem, Marigny, and the class of the financiers that supported them. And this anticourt, antiwealth current possessed its powerful populist appeal. "The emphasis on history painting must be viewed within this context, not only as an aspect of a more general *retour à l'antique* initiated from within the art world, but also as a policy to separate the arts from the taste long associated with the kings, the financiers and with their women. History painting was a great and noble art, insofar as it was no longer linked to money or luxury."[38] Or to women, who were now becoming an especial target, along with rococo erotics and aesthetics, of the growing resentments of the French nation. These resentments found a useful target in the feminized court and society, which had given its women such freedoms and unprecedented notice, but on such an "illegitimate" eroticized basis.

In the midst of the rococo era, in the semigraciousness of a mock sexual egalitarianism, Diderot derides Boucher: "Wasn't there a time when he was seized with a fury to paint virgins? But what were his virgins? Sweet little *caillettes*. And his angels? Little libertine satyrs."[39] In an earlier version of this text *de gentilles petites caillettes* had been *de jolies petites catins,* or "pretty little tarts." The interchangeability of eager, effervescent young women and sexually venal ones is a convention necessary to the rococo.[40] Diderot is far from wrong: virginity is the last thing "on the mind" of a Boucher canvas, and the vaunted freshness and "innocence" of the caillette is meant rather to revive the aura of an everlasting dawn of desire for the use of the jaded. The visual rococo's female figures conjoin that lure of youthful sweetness bathed in sensuality with a "perverse" readiness to assent: the tension in the object is between a "seemly" indifference to love and postural, vestimentary, and/or semiotic clues that she is, on the contrary, more than ready to give her all.

The young girl in Fragonard's *Love Letters* (fig. 4) is not swinging, but immobile. Within a garden glade, flowers and foliage virtually caress the lovers upon whom the goddess Venus, poised above them, gazes. Their postures are characteristic of the placement of lovers in rococo: the woman's head rises over her lover's, his gaze lifts in dreamy contemplation of her as he risks a near embrace. The letter, bespeaking passion, is made the mental object of the beloved, but her doll-like mask gives no hint of affect. Her apparent placidity in the midst of the lover's gently caressing embrace nonetheless conveys an acceptance underscored by her gentle décolletage and the overskirt upswept over her relaxedly open knees

4. J.-H. Fragonard, Love
Letters, copyright the Frick
Collection, New York

and little crossed slippers. As they rehearse the pile of letters at left, it is understood that the lovers are using their words to fan their passion. Even as the man
concedes the center of the stage to his love in courtly fashion, what the work
revels in is his longing.

Love Letters positions the lovers within a frame of swirling feathery foliage, yet
rather concretely sitting and leaning (like the Venus herself) upon a marble pedestal: images of man-made matter, the letter papers themselves, temper the languorous fluidity of the scene. As Norman Bryson has observed, in both Boucher's
Venus and Vulcan and his Venus Surprised by Vulcan, "the females lower their lids
to conceal the eye, the males raise their pupils to reveal the eye. Semantically, the
lowering returns to the female the meaning of 'modesty' which her general appearance enormously contradicts, to a degree which threatens the gender-division
whereby sexuality is thought to be with the male. But from another aspect it
clearly announces the division of roles: Woman as Image, Man as Bearer of the
Look."[41] To women themselves, then, rococo conveys a paradox: it is in them that

lies the realization of men's desire, a desire they may not resist; but so as to present no threat to male desire, they must be seen neither to be aware of it, nor to feel their own. Bearing out Bryson's thesis, we observe how Fragonard's *Love Letters* exhibits an analogous structuring of the lover's gazing: his intensity of gaze compels her avoidance of it.

Gender ambiguities abound in rococo: they translate an enchantment with sexual passion itself, which exalted women's bodily magnetism within a space that is nowhere, where materiality is deliberately made moot. The smith Vulcan's very forge and tools virtually float off as he worships his unmajestic Venus, whose inert, emptily abstracted gaze seems to promise every fleshly delight except that of energetic return. Both lovers bathe in a languorous stasis, but onto the figure of the goddess a fantasy of desire is projected with such intensity that it immobilizes her in her inward fixity, on pedestal or cloud, even more than the lover who pursues her so gently.

Rococo art, which seems to extol woman's physicality in its fondness for the curve, loves only that in woman susceptible of releasing the dream of unfettered desire. As a social, courtly art, it celebrates and reinforces the pervasive notions of women as pleasers and teasers. Perhaps this art, in its palpable imprisonment of them within desire, gave some unconscious relief to unfree men, both in making and then gazing at images of women on display, sheer creatures of men's fettering fantasy. In terms of popular art, rococo of course can be, and has been, accused of abject frivolity for its concentration on pleasure. But that is also, certainly, where its power lies: as in a courtesan's bower, it tries to array acts of love in an aura of soft illusion, where all sense of effort in achieving satisfaction dissolves. It offers us images, far less dismissable than is sometimes thought, of a calm, acute longing, promising satiety.[42] These images disturb in their uneasy evocation of an infantile repletion rarely experienced in the land of adult sexuality. That such should have been the project of so triumphant a style of art and design cannot have been unrelated to pervasive underlying relational needs and pressures of that French society in which it flourished. Such, at any rate, is the hypothesis these pages will seek to verify.

Chapter

2

INFANT EROS
AND HUMAN INFANT

An unfortunate young woman, too
gentle, too easily moved, gave me my
life and died soon afterwards.

DIDEROT *LE FILS NATUREL*

WE already know the result: from a multitude of sources we have learned that at
the end of the eighteenth century in France the new family dispensation, that of
the closed nuclear family cell, as against the wider kinship clan, began its rise. But
this advent of the so-called modern family appeared there only after a significant
time lag as compared with England or Holland, where conceptions of privacy and
domesticity had taken root with the ascendancy of the bourgeoisie nearly a hundred years earlier.[1] In France, by contrast, not only had such an ideal failed to
emerge, but rather than a tightening of family ties, certain forms of child neglect
were actually increasing at exactly the same time as the nation was witness to "a
propagandist campaign for radical change" that would eventuate in bourgeois
preeminence.[2]

Such a national difference in the rate of change must not be considered simply
as a lag: it indicates that a more complex and compressed reaccommodation between women and men was coming into play, to be effected in France more
quickly and more explosively than elsewhere. This eruption, smacking of a campaign in a longer battle, must be counted among the factors leading to Revolution.
It would not, as elsewhere, come as an evolution, because the gender relationships
between French men and women were characterized by factors less pronounced
elsewhere.

There have been historians and commentators who have argued that the Revolution was overripe by '89, that it could have occurred in 1760, or in 1774.[3] "We
have long been aware that if a revolution born of misery and destitution was going
to take place, it would have occurred in 1774."[4] Michel Vovelle expresses willingness to absorb literary and artistic evidence, like that examined in the discussion

of the rococo, even though it may have originated in an elite layer of the culture, into the great stream of factors predetermining Revolution. "From Rousseauism to the Sadean theater of cruelty or to the Gothic novel, other trends appear which reveal deep changes in thought and feeling."[5]

Vovelle places the heart of alterations in collective outlooks and behavior not in the area of economic issues, nor of literacy, but within the family. And here he makes a striking claim: "If we approach the realm of attitudes to life at the most basic level—that of life given or received—we come across a cluster of surprisingly convergent data for several specific and important tests: contraception, illegitimacy, premarital conceptions and abandoned children." In pursuit of Vovelle's insight, I will seek in this chapter to explore some of the intersections between the factors he cites (adding to them prostitution and the welfare of indigent women) and structures of sexual accommodation, both traditional and libertine. As further evidence of the modifications in thought and feeling he alludes to, we find in the arts of the midcentury signs of new familial preoccupations and, consequently, new and influential avatars of gender definition. For as we move away from the rococo forms so closely identified as aristocratic and feminine toward the middle-class critique of their insubstantiality, we discern the ethical and political substratum of this struggle over style in works by Diderot, Rousseau, Hallé, Greuze, and Restif de la Bretonne. Moving from the historical to the conceptual, chapter 2 probes the ties between material conditions, insofar as these can be known, and the emergent conceptions of gender.[6]

In 1761 appeared the French edition of the work of the German Valens Acidalius, *Mulieres homines non esse* (*Women Are Not Men*), originally published in 1595. Its purport? Women were not human, but complex instruments of generation devoid of soul. The sins of women, like those of animals, were to be dismissed. The fact of female speech was not to be counted as a sign of humanity, since birds may speak, and Balaam's ass spoke, The eighteenth-century French translator of Acidalius professed to take no stock in these arguments, claiming to find much of the work reprehensible. But he nonetheless translated and published it in the belief that it would be read. One can only agree that its appearance is the sign of an "obsession with a struggle fed by the spectacular emergence of monsters buried, but most alive."[7] What was it about the midcentury of presumably rising Reason that should have made it so inviting an arena for rancor against women?

The first place to look has traditionally been the court. Although debauchery was certainly not new to the monarchy in the reign of Louis XIV, with the reigns first of the outrageously licentious regent, and then of Louis XV, the prestige of royalty waned. Already in the 1740s, the Well-Beloved's sexual flightiness had occasioned uneasiness, as he overstepped the conventions of a certain ceremoniousness in these matters, flagrantly taking and discarding in turn as mistress Mme de Mailly and her two sisters, Mmes de Vintimille and de la Tournelle.[8]

The role of king's mistress, which had acquired institutional status within the monarchy during the last two hundred years, was undermined by this treatment. Rumors about the monarch's Deerpark, his stable of amorous prey, reached well beyond the palace walls. Inside the court, as outside it, this era was the great age of the libertine. In 1741 so much licentious literature was in circulation that royal authorities felt they needed to take action against such works "contrary to good morals." They seized a quantity of them, but their action in no way stanched the flow.

Court society and high society in eighteenth-century France have, however, received such bad press regarding their morality in the wake of the Revolution that a slight caveat may be in order at the outset, especially as we move more intently into areas of disruption, which I intend to do here. The impartial Scots observer John Crawford made a point of emphasizing what he saw as the "decent freedom" of French eighteenth-century mores, a facet that never found the same sort of representation in the French novel as its parallel phenomenon in the English novel.[9] The sense fed to us by most of the texts, the record of the cultural imaginary, is of a jungle seething with heartless upper-class ambition and appetite, of an eruption of crass aristocratic bitterness made visible through the prejudicial screen of sentimental bourgeois moralism. Closer scrutiny suggests that this war of class pitting aristocratic against bourgeois culture was a subtle struggle, which, like that between the sexes, can find no easy definition in any purely Manichaean dualism of opposition.

The downward trajectory of the court, parallel to that of the declining rococo, can be seen in the degradation of the seventeenth century's idea, so strongly supported by women, of *galanterie,* which had proposed an ideal of social interaction and courtship between the sexes. The eighteenth century would now read the word narrowly, to denote an art of seduction. In illustration of this we see the very word *galanterie* falling so low as to become a mere euphemism for venereal disease.[10] The ideal of courtly worldliness is, by midcentury, a code of manners and of language, for the privileged classes that can indulge in it, fostering a ballet of sexual partnering, a ballet offering variety and adventure.[11] The women as well as the men of this set might engage in this game, but since infidelity remained the official privilege of the male, wives were charged with maintaining appearances, the *bienséances.* Although legally a man (though not his wife) had the right to prosecute his adulterous spouse, he who would do so risked appearing only an absurd cuckold to society. "In some ways, *galanterie* of the eighteenth century might be likened to a 'sexual revolution' which freed women in one area of their lives, but involved no structural changes."[12]

Between 1715 and 1792 there was in France no increase in births, but a decided increase in infant mortality. Population rose, but gradually, largely through the extension of the life span, giving rise to the belief that French couples were among the first to practice contraception deliberately.[13] No great famine occurred.

More grains were in fact grown. Agricultural techniques were improved, producing more and better food. Communications and commercial exchanges with other nations increased notably. On the other hand, the wars of Louis XV were systematically impoverishing the country's coffers. The rise of the commercial bourgeois class was taking place in an atmosphere of courtly abdication and loss of moral and economic power.

Passion's Threat to Patrimony

Many of the data Michel Vovelle refers to have of course arrested the attention of social historians. The unverifiable but challenging theses of Edward Shorter have shaped some of the debates and research on demographic issues. Shorter poses questions, perhaps problematic in themselves, such as: "Why did the family decide to cut the ties that held it within the surrounding social order? . . . Why did the family decide to cut the chain of generations, to no longer follow custom and tradition in arranging its life, to no longer bring up its offspring to perpetuate the patrimony? . . . Why did its various members decide that other values in life were more important than familial ones?"[14] In answering these questions, he has theorized poetically that romantic love displaced material considerations in bringing couples together. The romantic individualism that Shorter sees coming into play at the century's end did indeed dictate some rise, before the Revolution, in the idea of marriage by inclination.[15] However, this new assertion of the right to private passion as divorced from the perpetuation of patrimony was not all that new, nor did it prevail uncontested.[16] This attempt to break with tradition suggests to my mind, rather than the expression of an unfettered individualism, a drive to redirect and contain the loosed energy of desire. Sometimes this drive blends into the ideology of romantic love, which lends it form and credence.

Shorter also posits a change, this one more plausible, in the place the infant will henceforth occupy in the mother's "rational hierarchy of values. Whereas in traditional society the mother had been prepared to place many considerations—most of them related to the desperate struggle for existence—above the infant's welfare, in modern society the infant comes to be most important, maternal love would see to it that his well-being was second to nothing."[17] This affirmation, however, utterly begs the question of why maternal love should suddenly have emerged as so prominent a feature of social existence at this time. Nor does it tell us why the infants' cries, formerly so inaudible, should have so dramatically increased in decibel level.[18]

The scene into which Shorter introduces his maternal and romantic loves he depicts, probably rightly, as bleak and unloving indeed: in some places "the whole month of May was devoted to the sexual turning of the tables, in which women avenged themselves against wife-beaters and the like. But these were little flickers in an otherwise black night of female domestic passivity that was woman's place."[19] Shorter finds no parallel in female society for men's drunkenness and whoring with servants. Women's work in the agricultural setting, in addition to demanding of them backbreaking exertions, was to reproduce for and service men. Shorter contends that peasants and petty-bourgeois men saw their women as "baby-machines" and treated them "mechanically and without affection."[20]

Marriage, little though it may have been admired as a state, was still a goal for most maturing adults, a goal that had come to be increasingly out of the grasp of many. The general recoil of mortality meant that children would have to wait longer before inheritances would fall to them, and this made for a protracted period of dependency upon parents. The marriage of daughters was particularly burdensome to the family, since it forced it to expend its patrimony. In some regions, though not all, the economic hurdles to establishing a household sparked a rise in bachelorhood. For men in the Artois, for example, it went from 6.4 percent in 1710 to 18.2 percent in 1815, and for woman it rose from 5.2 percent to 16.2 percent.[21]

The country ideal of female beauty was "*grande et grosse,*" but not too much so, a far cry from the city's rococo tiny, slim model of pulchritude. Female chastity would be preserved in the upper classes by keeping the young woman cloistered, and in the peasantry by keeping her hard at work.

> Daughters and vineyards are hard to keep;
> Some passerby always wants a taste,

says the folklore. Or, "*Fille mariée, fille, sauvée*" (A daughter married is a daughter saved). Her "treasure" is in imminent danger, a danger against which, as for the hurricane, there is no human remedy. In Restif's *Paysan perverti (The Peasant Corrupted)*, the big boys who have already attained a master's status in their trade decide among themselves with their master's help which of them will get which neighborhood girl. As winter starts, they draw up their lists, either by lot or by consensus, and for an entire season each pressures the one who has fallen to him. "The girls don't even have the satisfaction of entertaining a boy who pleases them, and all winter long at evening *veillées* or social evenings around the fire, and on their doorstep whenever the moon is out, they have to suffer the company of a clumsy brute of a shepherd whom they detest."[22]

Though it is obviously the girl who is more at risk, the folklore insists that hers is the sex that imperils. An important litany of menace springs up around the dangers of city life. "An idle girl has evil thoughts." "A girl too much in the streets will soon be lost." In the eighteenth century girls go up from the country to the towns and cities to find work, while their brothers tend to remain in the villages and on the farms. A preponderance of boys results in the countryside, of unmarried girls in the towns. The number of the latter rose overall to a level of 13 percent of total city or town populations. This might mean that while these girls were becoming citified, acquiring city values, the boys remained ensconced in the traditional outlook of the peasantry. But what it meant to be citified for such young women was not exactly to be more refined than their male counterparts, just more wised-up. Pierre Bourdieu theorizes: "If women are more apt and precede men in adapting to urban cultural norms," it must be because "the city represents to them the hope of emancipation."[23]

Labors

As agricultural laborer, laundress, emptier of privies, vegetable carter, or domestic, a woman might perform the most abject services remaining to be accomplished in society. Sometimes a servant would fill in her "extra time" with lace-, glove-, or ribbon-making. The silk industry employed large numbers of such women, both single and married, in emptying cocoons and washing and unraveling the silk to ready it to be worked at the loom. In Lyon in 1716 a *tireuse* would earn six sous a day for eighteen hours of work. It was forbidden for women silk-reelers to rise to the rank of weaver.[24]

Usually a girl seeking a livelihood would go to a town not too far from her village of origin, less than thirty miles away. She might go where she had some ready relative to soften the blow of her exile. But some women lived in a state of permanent displacement, going wherever work might be found. The domestic *servante* was given a wage, which, she hoped, after five or ten years might constitute a reasonable dowry, though most had to work for fourteen to sixteen years before marriage. In addition, she received her room and board; on farms and in substantial households, she would also be clad and shod. As Olwen Hufton tells it, "the *servante,* starved of affection and unaccustomed to excitement, was ill-fitted to cope with the few hours of leisure she had on Sunday or feast day as the *déclarations de grossesse, surtout affaire de domestique* [pregnancy declarations] uniformly attest. She was the most usual target for the attentions of master, apprentice, and military alike, and the wonder is that illegitimacy rates were not even higher."[25]

Sara Maza perceptively exposes the explosive mix of sexual and class animosity serving women evoked. "Young unmarried men especially resented and attacked servants because these women were unmarried but unavailable, except by means of force or of patience." The hordes of young women working as domestics in eighteenth-century towns represented "a social and sexual capital hoarded by masters who had social power over their employees, and were already married, to boot. The rage and frustration these men felt at the sight of these women could just as easily be turned against their masters." Maza thus connects lower-class men's sexual resentment with their social, and ultimately their political, anger. She has estimated that between one-tenth and one-third of all recorded illegitimate pregnancies occurred as a consequence of the mating of masters and servants, though she considers the true percentage to have been higher, because of the ease with which masters could purchase the silence of the officials who recorded the *déclarations*.[26]

Hufton has graphically described the cramped living conditions of the married woman worker: her activities reflected none of what, through the nineteenth century's ideology, we have come to think of as homemaking. Living in close, rough, dirty, flea-ridden quarters with a few odds and ends of furniture and a pot or two for her rudimentary cookery, she would give her laundry out to a *blanchisseuse* for a few pennies and, with no minutes to spare, eat her own poor meal while seated at her loom or workbench. The advent of a child was the occasion of a struggle to find the time and strength adequate to tending and feeding it: and so it was that the women most likely to search out the wet nurse were the women in full-time employment, and particularly those townswomen working full-time in industry.

In the latter half of the century as much as 25 percent of the populace was admittedly *indigent,* that is, hungry, and this figure rose as high as 40 percent in those regions hit by a slump in the textile industry. This was a poverty that fell with inordinate pressure upon families with children. Mothers and children went about engaged in systematic beggary. In bad years, of textile slowdowns or poor harvests, fathers would go off as migrant workers and the abandoned mothers lived by their wits, begging, smuggling salt, or, when all else failed, prostituting themselves. Hufton pays tribute to "the sheer determination and ingenuity put into their efforts to make the family surmount disaster."[27]

The perpetually low wages earned by women workers and their state of servitude—they were often recruited like bond-slaves, as into soldiery, and could not break free from a life as harvesters or textile workers—in fact make elementally plain the appeal of prostitution. Père Houel was to claim there were no fewer than seventy thousand prostitutes in Paris before the Revolution.[28] Uncertainty concerning their numbers arose because the women who prostituted themselves were not always prostitutes, and passage to and from this life was common. It was in the cities, with the establishments of prostitution, that the greatest number of illegitimate births occurred. Contributing to this sum were the abundant fruit of the seduction of otherwise marriageable young women not in "the life." Numerous illegitimacies also resulted from "irregular" unions, in which the couple, ordinarily for financial reasons or because of disputes over inheritances, lived in a stable relationship without marriage. And finally, there were the children born inconveniently of adulterous liaisons.

Eros and the Evil Parent

"Things are changing between fathers and sons, between parents and children, probably also between men and women."[29] The tensions occasioned by change certainly would have played themselves out in the relations between the genders, and especially within the marriage bond. Dr. Brieude wrote from the Haute-Auvergne in 1782–83:

> Our young peasant lads, confident that their strength and industriousness will carry them through, take a spouse to satisfy their sexual needs. But the cold climate plus the precautions they fail to observe give them a numerous family. Becoming members of a community, they are burdened with taxes. As youths they were rich, as married men impoverished, because after taxes they have to feed and clothe a wife and children. The children languish and waste away for want of bread; the woman suffers in silence; the husband, unable to rise to so many demands, falls into melancholy and apathy. One must actually witness this cause of rural depopulation in order to comprehend it.[30]

The lack of affect in traditional French family life, sustained by hardship, will become the butt of social reformers, who will find the source of its defects and hence its alteration in the mothers: the greatest bogey will come to be that "she who gives birth will be no mother, she who marries will be no wife: arrayed against her own kind, she'll prostitute her sex in debauch and refuse it to the generation of the species."[31] The wording of this portentous apothegm compresses past and future: women have come to be neither mothers nor wives. They indulge their own appetites at the expense of the continuation of the species, to which they ought to be subordinate.

This moralism toward women as mother/wives will have healthy descendants. It seems to me to provide a text of concealment of a far more basic, though closely related problem: that of the abandonment of infants, first by their fathers, but then, in a species of default, by their mothers as well. A study of infants admitted to the Foundling Hospital of Paris (Enfants-trouvés) between 1670 and 1791 finds that there was a constant rise of such admissions between 1721 and 1772. Behind these statistics has been read the inability of parents to raise an illegitimate child in the countryside, and the fact that no hospices existed there to shelter such children.[32] Both the rise in illegitimacies, and the resultant increase of concern about the rogue desire's rupture of the social seams, were checked, though inadequately, by the still-powerful institutionalized tyranny of fathers, who would exercise sexual control over their sons (as well as daughters, of course) through their economic control. Paternal tyranny comes across as a potent and arbitrary repressor of the desire of sons.

Repression of any idea of affectional preference or of choice emerges in the story told by Restif de la Bretonne, born in 1734, of his father's finding a bride. Edmond, Restif's father, has been established as apprentice printer in Paris for two years when his boss proposes to him a match with his daughter. When Edmond writes his father about this development, the father replies by summoning him summarily, as if to his deathbed. Upon arriving, travel-worn, back in his native village, Edmond is told that his father is in blooming health and expecting him to show up over at the house of the wealthy M. Dondaine, the father of three girls. When he reaches M. Dondaine's, Edmond's father sermonizes his son thus: "Instead of a faithless, corrupt coquette from the city, I'm giving you a virtuous girl who'll cherish none but her husband. You might have more of a yen for a pretty miss wearing an elegant headdress; but I forbid you to think of it, and I won't have the slightest objection out of you, or my curse will come next. . . . To obey me must be your uppermost thought." Edmond's mother concurs absolutely in the father's view. Marie, the youngest of the three girls, suggests that Edmond ought at least be granted a right to refuse, since they have just met. "Dear father, I've nothing against this respectable young man, but we should see if we're suited to each other: in my case, obedience should foreclose any opinion from me, once my father has spoken; but I think that for a man it's not at all the same." Her father's response to even so feminine and self-denying an attempt to accommodate was the harsh reply, "Be silent." Edmond then accepts the bargain imposed on him and ritually recites the patriarchal litany: "I'd be most wretched and unworthy of becoming a father myself one day if I were to resist on such an occasion as this, which embodies the highest and most supreme exercise of the powers of a father; till death as in life, I will obey you, and my worthy mother."[33]

What Shorter sees coming out of this early eighteenth-century perception, whether embraced or decried, of an excess of fatherly control is a revolution of eroticism, especially among the lower classes, "in the direction of libertine sexual behavior." The economic divorce of home from workplace weakens patriarchy. "With fathers no longer emotionally nurturant, male children no longer had to obey them."[34] Is it Shorter's "freed eros" or Sarah Maza's "resentful eros" that better accounts for the rise of illegitimate births, accelerating around the time of Revolution and then increasing until the middle of the nineteenth century? In the light of later events, Maza's image of an eros of resentment seems the more compelling one. It plays itself out in an ethos of angry prescriptiveness toward deficient motherhood and in defiance, guilty or cheeky, of the consecrated sexual codes of the paternal order.

Prostitution: Sign of Disorder

A sense of antiaristocratic distress over sexual disorder permeates the discourse of commentators outside courtly circles and sounds a generalized alarm. Attacks against immorality are the cousins of misogyny, for they generally bear the imprint of the ancient gesture projecting guilt unwelcome to male consciousness upon women. Anger against prostitution and a feeling of disarray in attempting to deal with its growth are very much in evidence at the end of the century. The impressive figure, cited by a contemporary, of no fewer than thirty thousand women selling their favors at various rates to a Parisian male population of some two hundred thousand provides us with a gauge of the perception of the phenomenon.

The Church, sharing the widespread tendency to project guilt over sexuality onto women, did not depart from its traditional denunciations of the sins of the flesh and therefore was uninclined to lend its aid to ease the lives of harlots. The public, however, was less doctrinaire: it tended to show more indulgence to the common streetwalker than to the socially climbing one.

While virtually all the philosophes turned away from so distasteful a reality, lesser lights—reformers and the police—were not so delicate in their approach to the phenomenon. Written treatments of the question seem at times to be mere titillating burlesque, in the manner of Bernard Mandeville's English *Modest Defense of Public Stews* (1724): but even Mandeville's satire elaborates a plan for the sequestration of the prostitutes in brothels administered by the government. Moufle d'Angerville (1750) proposed that Paris prostitution should be organized under the care of a madam who would centralize trade and maximize profits.[35] In 1760 Turmeau de la Morandière advocated legislation to rid the streets of what he felt was intolerable vice. Turmeau was most exercised not at the attempts of any woman to earn her pennies, but by the depredations of courtesans, "*femmes-à-la-mode*." "If a public woman robs a Private Party of an *écu* by bestowing herself, there's no harm in that except to morals: but for a Young Lady with social graces to prostitute herself to a citizen and rob him of his fortune, the result is not only a moral evil, but a political one."[36] One senses some personal pique in his plaint. The offense here becomes truly grave when it undermines the family's patrimony: real money is involved.

The crotchety Restif de la Bretonne would provide in his 1769 *Pornographe* certainly one of the most detailed of these blueprints for a moralized, rationalized prostitution. The prostitutes would be sent to a set of *Parthénions* managed by the government. There they would be protected by bodyguards and allowed to enjoy medical and religious attentions. Customers would be masked (that is, remain nameless and faceless), but paradoxically, the women would retain a right of refusal to engage in sexual congress with a man who displeased them.

These conceptualizations of rationalized prostitution would be more modestly realized after the Revolution in the French *maisons de tolérance,* which were to dominate French treatment of prostitution until 1946. The essence of such proposals lies in their ostensible attempt to sequester and regularize wanton sexual impulse by penning in the women who would live by its exploitation: an underlying aim is to restrain women from flaunting and kindling desire on public streets and in menacing salons and boudoirs, where male control of self and property might go astray. The dimensions of the problem and the number and kind of responses to it reveal a pervasive anxiety. Cure is already envisaged here as separation, a sequestration of the unruly sector of female predators.

The attack in 1776 by the Baron d'Holbach, that friend of the philosophes, against the mores of high society features an interesting parallel to the stance of the sexual reformers, since he similarly finds that debauchery "is susceptible of producing destructive ravages upon society." But Holbach locates this evil not in the classes of courtesans and prostitutes alone; he essentializes it to all women. The problem lies in excessive commerce with them, in "the too frequent communications between the two sexes." As antidote, so as to dull the revulsion he feels about the "harpies" who suck men's blood, as well as against members of his own gender, those "vile seducers" abroad in society, Holbach posits a model of chaste marriage with women who, though not altogether sequestered, would learn to know and stay within their restricted place and space.

A sense of sexual crisis emerges from the confluence of these works dealing with prostitution. Its place in the "collective anxiety," religious, economic, political, has yet to be assessed. It is as if their authors were seeking relief from unmanageable sexual pressures: but what factors could have provided the occasion for this sense that matters were beyond control, that drastic measures would be called for to restrain and repossess all sexuality, projected as a "problem" of women's sexuality?[37]

In Carol Pateman's absorbing formulation, "the story of the sexual contract reveals that the patriarchal construction of the difference between masculinity and femininity is the political difference between freedom and subjection, and that sexual mastery is the major means through which men affirm their manhood."[38] Such a preoccupation with control over prostitution as we see here, then, displays distress with what is seen as the rampant power of women to profit from men's need to affirm their manhood via sexuality. The very definition of manhood seems to be at stake. Beneath the mania for control of prostitution, we find the search for a manhood that would not have to suffer the moral ravages of a "misplaced" sexuality.

The Illegitimate Son Seeks His Birthright

It is scarcely surprising that it should have been Denis Diderot, that restlessly candid and probing gadfly of the Enlightenment, who would come closest to exposing some of the hidden aspects of the rising bourgeoisie's gender paradoxes.[39] He did so most tellingly in his two plays, *Le Fils naturel* (*The Illegitimate Son*) (1757) and *Le Père de famille* (*The Father of a Family*) (1758), works usually regarded as examples of his pioneering attempt to wrest the theater away from its canonical underpinnings in classical history and mythology so as to lend it a counterrococo currency and social impact. For despite his novel aesthetic notions, a meliorist he was, and his strategy, in his need to move his audience, lay in an unblushing appeal to its sentimentality, that is, its awareness of the painful gap between the "is" and the "ought" of their moment in time.

Dorval, the hero of *The Illegitimate Son,* descends from Molière's misanthrope, Alceste, in his single-minded preoccupation with virtue, but unlike his blustering predecessor, Dorval is a melancholy puritan. Sad both in his conversation and his demeanor, he comes to life only when he speaks of virtue: "At such moments . . . his eyes took on brilliance and gentleness, his voice an inexpressible charm." Then he would display a combination of "austere ideas with touching images that could hold the attention in suspense and the soul in delight."[40] Yet after such sallies, his core of melancholy would repossess him as this magnificently live discourse died.

"Austere ideas and touching images," these masculinized and feminized poles of Diderot's thought, are combined in Dorval's single, androgynous person. But why such melancholy in so richly endowed a being? Diderot places its origin in Dorval's plight as natural son, unintegrated into the paternal order: for all his individual virtue, Dorval simply lacks the right accorded respectable birth. A bastard, no longer in this era a wild and blessed fruit of passion, he is deprived of all recognition of his basic expectation, as a man, for a father to acknowledge him as his seed. Dorval's is the pathetic marginality of the unwanted, though superior, man.

Diderot intensifies the pathos of his rootless status in Dorval's dialogue with Constance, his benefactor's daughter.

> DORVAL: Abandoned virtually at birth halfway between the wilderness and the world of society, when first I opened my eyes to grasp the ties that bound me to others, I could find nothing but fragments of ties. I'd been wandering through this debris for thirty years, Madame, isolated, unknown, and neglected, without ever meeting tender emotions from anyone who sought out my own, when one day I met your brother (88).

As our play opens, we find our representative of the eighteenth century's "new men," unpropertied but enriched by his own strenuous efforts, in the residence of his benefactor Clairville, a petty nobleman. Though comfortably ensconced there, Dorval is guiltily planning his getaway. Why? Because being as virtuous as we are tirelessly reminded he is, no longer can he share the dwelling of his friend, since he has—unwittingly—alienated the affections of Clairville's intended bride, the penniless Rosalie, also a natural child, whom the Clairvilles had generously sheltered. What is worse, Dorval had led Clairville's sister Constance to believe he would wed her. Uneasy over the duplicity of his unseemly passion, Dorval longs to leave this scene of confusion without a word to anyone: only that higher imperative, the male bond of friendship, impels him to remain.[41]

Contrasting markedly with the sexual confusion of the classless Dorval, Clairville's aristocratic rootedness authorizes him to feel and express passion: his at-oneness with his sentiments comes of a sense of entitlement that Dorval entirely lacks. Aflame with imperious male desire, even Clairville, all aquiver, feels he has to temper the volatility of his feeling: "What skill, what finesse I've had to employ to impose silence upon the forces of such a passion, to keep it mute!" (47). Clairville's hope of union with Rosalie has been impeded by two developments: her ailing mother had recently died in the Indies, and the father the girl had never seen was soon to appear in their midst. Most distressing of all, his beloved herself has turned "reserved, cold, indifferent" to him, seeming to love him no longer.

This play, closer in spirit to the comedies of Marivaux than *The Father of a Family* will be, still presents its *dramatis personae,* at the outset, in a near-rococo style; they believe themselves to be free amorous agents in a fictional Forest of Arden, tossed to and fro by the play of their emotions, divorced from considerations of power or consequence, though not of class. The conventions of this essentially verbal system of courtship are clothed in an artifice that acts like a social screen over "natural" sentiment, impeding the emergence of the "truth" of raw feeling, all the while toying with it. The resultant climate of suspicion around matters of love permits that rococo play of disclosure and badinage that gives such piquancy of social and erotic instability to Marivaux's work.[42] The pretense of a free and open society in which love is an unfettered force not subject to manipulation is belied in Diderot, as it is in Marivaux, by the gradual closing in of issues of power, class, and gender. In Diderot, these latter in fact become explicit.

Dorval attempts to dismiss Clairville's fears by ascribing Rosalie's chilliness to female humors, "these ups and downs to which even the best-born women are subject, and for which it is sometimes so sweet to have to forgive them" (48).[43] In fact, Dorval has fallen in love with the young and unformed Rosalie, and she with him: neither she nor he nor anyone else yet knows they are sister and brother, both products of a free union like the one they are now tempted to form. The mysterious bond between them is made to fuel the guilt of both: Rosalie, in an appropriately female display of self-abasement, even expresses self-hatred: "I cover myself with reproaches, I am wretched. I've lost all regard for myself" (54).

The least empowered of the four principal actors of the play, Rosalie is the one most fundamentally undone by her apparent lack of gratitude to her host family, the Clairvilles. In choosing Dorval to love, she fatally lacks appropriately submissive acquiescence to their will: it is only their kindness, after all, that has enabled her to survive. Rosalie's is therefore the ultimate underclass of the play. But Dorval appears to feel only a notch above her, for his own betrayal of the confidence of his friends Clairville and Constance fills him with dismay. Buffeted in his feelings, he asks himself despairingly, self-mockingly, "Where has candor fled? Has there been any in my conduct? . . . Oh you mortals, wretched toys of chance . . . go and take pride in your happiness and virtue." Coming into their house with a pure heart, he has brought nothing but trouble to all. "What greater harm could a scoundrel have done?" (60). With his morally ambiguous and yet pretentiously conscience-stricken protagonist, Diderot raises the issue of the vicissitudes of virtue, the difficulty of sustaining it unblemished in the face of the vagaries of an unbidden passion that can so easily drive it away from goodly intention.

The aristocratic Constance of the play, a wised-up young widow, is the female figure allowed by her social position and self-cultivation by both fiction and society to exercise some independence of judgment and conduct. She herself declares her own love for Dorval, and she tells him it is his virtue that draws her to him: he raises her up in her own eyes, providing her with a moral aspiration that without him she could never know (45). Despite the submissiveness of her wisdom, Dorval cannot feel love for this articulate and self-possessed woman. Yet she it is who has formed the charming Rosalie, having tailored her to suit her brother Clairville's needs: "He is headstrong, I made her prudent. He is violent, I cultivated her natural gentleness" (44). These accommodations to the stereotypes of gender and to male happiness Constance makes without pain, as a woman of the world.

The great void in this play, which despite many felicities lacks a core, comes of Dorval's silence, in which some would read absence. Faced by various trials—Constance reads his declaration of love for Rosalie and takes it to be for herself, he attempts to make a gift of his fortune to Rosalie—he is deprived by his guilt of adequate means of expression. This privation of language is attributable in the play's own terms to his lack of birthright: despite his vaunted virtue, he fails altogether to demonstrate the forthrightness of Clairville. Dorval's bourgeois moral aesthetic of loyalty tongue-ties him, as he discovers that sexual virtue is beyond his considerable powers.

Long-lost, the father, Lysimond, seized in the course of his journey to France, makes his initial appearance (in a description recounted to the two friends by the Clairvilles' servant, André) having suffered unjust imprisonment in an English cell. As André finds him "in the dark, lying naked on the humid earth," the old man whispers to him, "the wretched people here took advantage of my age and weakness by grabbing my bread from me and stealing the hay for my bed" (76). Together, the friends weep over the plight of one they believe to be the father only of Rosalie. This description conveys the pathos of a prodigal father's penance. Lysimond has returned from a long voyage to the tropics (a steamy allusion to his sexual wanderings) now to acknowledge his connection to his children. The unjust cruelty meted out to him in his dungeon makes of him a pathetic "innocent" victim since, as we are told, the old man's life has been "essentially" virtuous. This descent and return of the natural father are prophetic: they announce a non-Christian version of fatherhood, freed from sin and perdition by the grace of good intentions.

The game of incest played in *The Illegitimate Son* connects with the "stain" of namelessness that brother and sister share, a sensually liberating bond in its sexual origin. In a truly nameless world, would all chance sexual encounters be blameless? This uncontrollable incestuous impulse serves as Diderot's surrogate for the wild abandon of the life of the senses. Despite her enchantment with Dorval, Rosalie the powerless rebels slightly in act 4. He has finally confessed to her that he had been guilty of encouraging her to feel tenderness toward him (though he never does admit his love for her). In fact, all she does know is that she loves him, and that he does not seem to spurn her affection. In her outrage she expostulates to her maid Justine, "What do you think of Dorval now? . . . Look at this gentle

friend, this man so true, this virtuous mortal! Like all the others, he's nothing but
a scoundrel who mocks what is most sacred, love, friendship, virtue, truth itself!
How sorry I feel for Constance! He deceived me. He may well deceive her as well"
(83). Rosalie comes to equate Dorval with the rest of what she reads as his faithless, iniquitous sex. Her brother/lover stands as brother to all those men whose
volatile sexuality makes them unreliable lovers. "How wicked they are, these
men," she goes on, "and how simple-minded are we! . . . Look, Justine, at how
close truth lies to perjury in their hearts; how aspiration lies down with depravity
in them!" (71). The familial bond that might have authorized a gentle tenderness
has led here to its wild, unruly extreme: wayward, because unsocialized, sexual
impulse. And this, of course, is what a work about *The Illegitimate Son* must address: the taming of that refractory urge.

A salient and telling feature of the power relations of this shadow play of Diderot's with the question of illegitimacy is the Gothic third scene of act 5 where
Dorval, stirred by his primary objective of proving his fidelity to his beloved
friend Clairville, reduces Rosalie to the sorrowful acceptance of what she plainly
does not want: Clairville's hand.[44]

In a display of bourgeois eros of resentment, the "good" Dorval unveils Rosalie's
wayward desire, which he admits he himself had invited, in the presence of her
erstwhile suitor and benefactor. "We" must never "do evil," he tells her, sounding
like the smitten Reverend in Maugham's *Rain,* preaching chastity to the prostitute.
For her benefit, he delivers a sermon arraigning the mores of the time. "To be
wicked is to condemn yourself to living and finding pleasure among the wicked;
it is to wish to remain lost in a throng of unprincipled beings, without morality
or character" (104). Once you let go of the thread of the labyrinth, he threatens
her, "you are no longer master of your fate." In fact, at no moment of the play
is there any question for her of such mastery. Dorval, otherwise so speechless,
simply does not cease speaking until he has made Rosalie renounce her desire for
himself and return her troth to his friend Clairville. "What confidence can one
have in a woman when she has betrayed her lover? In a man when he has been
capable of betraying his friend? . . . You blush. You lower your eyes. . . . What is
it, then? Could it be that you are offended that I should find something in nature
more sacred than you are?" (105–106). I, Dorval, he proclaims, have returned to
virtue. Rosalie, he admonishes her, ought to have said to him all he has found it
necessary to say to her. If she had, "I would have looked upon her as a beneficent
goddess who held out her hand to me and steadied my faltering steps. At her
voice, virtue would have been rekindled in my heart" (106). She has failed to
represent his ideas, his ideal. Of course Rosalie succumbs to this torrent of bullying moral pressure, and virtually wordlessly. What could she have replied to his
denigration of her as less sacred to him than his friend, or to his disappointed
expectation that she behave as a chastening but benevolent goddess? Her discourse, her will, have been preempted by Dorval's. His manipulation of her sen-

timents is entire, his seduction of her will a success: this in a work whose surface claims to be a treatment of that end product of seduction, the illegitimate son.[45]

Dorval confesses to Constance his positive horror, as the scion of a nameless father, of fathering children, of marriage. "Could Dorval dare take on the burden of a woman's happiness! . . . When I think how, simply in being born, we've been thrust into the midst of prejudices, outrageousness, vice, and poverty, the very idea makes me quake with fear" (90). His comforter, Constance, reasons against such a negative construction, his shrinking so from life, his "phantoms." What she will offer Dorval as counterimage to his sullen, outcast state is the founding, with her, of his own patriarchal family. Guided by him, his children will think like him, have a conscience like his own. "Dorval, your daughters will be honest and decent, your sons noble and proud. All your children will be charming" (90). Her description of familial division of virtues by gender constitutes equally a program for the virtuous society: the women, who will be given charge over male sexuality, will be chaste and contained; the men's business will be the cultivation of proud accomplishment and a virtuous world. The charm with which Constance imbues this portrayal is not a mere embellishment: it is intended to lend an aesthetic prestige to the suggested dispensation that would make it not merely palatable, but the heart's desire. Diderot attempts to blend the sexual, the social, and the aesthetic in his stew of virtue. We hear Constance's preachment that "the effect of virtue on our souls is neither more nor less necessary, nor does it have a less powerful effect upon our senses, than that of beauty. For there is in the human heart a taste for order older than any conscious feeling. And this taste makes us feel shame, that shame that makes our fear of scorn greater even than that we feel before death" (91). Shame and virtue are concepts, needless to say, altogether alien to the rococo construction of love.

It is out of this familially based conception of virtue, so crucial to the Revolution's reading of Enlightenment, that Constance is moved to utter her celebrated and tragically misguided words; "The times of barbarousness are spent. Our age has become enlightened. Reason has become purified. Its precepts characterize the nation's labors" (92). You and your kind, she tells Dorval, must be honored and protected by the state as the rightful arbiters of its future, and that by virtue of your *sensibilité,* your empathy with suffering. Barbarians may yet remain, but their time is over.

Dorval will then finally confess to the articulate Constance his problematic origins. Her response might have been the early Revolution's motto: "Birth is given to us; but our virtues are ours alone" (94).

The gender politics of *The Illegitimate Son* are in no wise as simple as they present themselves as being: they convey no promise of an order devoid of inner stress between women and men. The force of character of the salon woman, Constance, who acts as the author's mouthpiece and proclaims her love and desire for Dorval, is decried in the *Premier entretien* or *First Discourse on The Illegitimate Son* as the author's *Moi* (Myself) criticizes her forwardness as being surprising in the theater. Dorval replies to him that her words would be thoroughly acceptable if spoken in a salon, her person having precedents in the life of that world.[46] Yet for all her eloquence, the Constance of the play is magniloquently submissive to her chosen "new man."

The play's bad faith in terms of gender is rounded out as Lysimond finally appears, revealing the relationship of sister to brother and announcing he will leave a great fortune to his children. This fantasy of reconciliation, in which "natural" mothers are suppressed, although it pretends to argue for and restore sexual "morality," simply makes women caretakers of sexual order, while integrating and celebrating the sexual foibles of the father. In fact, the dispossessed, penniless, sexually vulnerable *jeune fille* of the work is brought to such a state of abjection as virtually to invite abuse.

We find a state akin to Rosalie's of act 5 in Greuze's *Girl with a Dead Pigeon* (fig. 5), as the aftermath of desire creates a pathetic confusion destructive to the subject's self-possession. It draws its pathos from precisely this display of her vulnerability to her own senses. Although the stalwartly submissive Constance still figures importantly on Diderot's stage, under the forthcoming dispensation daugh-

5. *J.-B. Greuze,* Girl with a Dead Pigeon, *National Galleries of Scotland, Edinburgh*

ters will be asked to become silent Rosalies rather than eloquent Constances. The
new gender accommodation of that father's domain Diderot is attempting to create
here is erected on the rocky foundations of failed fatherhood, absent motherhood,
and ultimate complacency, even in its moralism, toward male sexual license.

In his *Troisième entretien sur le Fils natural,* Diderot invents a striking image
comparing the nefarious mixing of the genres to "a solemn senator at the feet of a
courtesan behaving in the most debauched of fashions, and members of political
factions plotting the downfall of a republic" (176). A telling analogy: abandoned
male sexuality (associated with the prostitute) is at the antipodes from the most
legitimate form of the state, in fact, endangers it. Despite his stated goal of introducing a sort of naturalness onto the stage, for Diderot the dissolute senator must
not be allowed to make his appearance in serious drama. If he were to do so, all
coherence would end. The subject of comedy only, the reduction of the official to
his unruly sexuality is to be left to the reconciling sublimations of laughter: it is
not to be subjected even to the mild probing of questions of class, birth, or gender
we find in *The Illegitimate Son.* Diderot has nevertheless insinuated in his play that
the sexual issues too were a major subtext, if not of overt discourse, certainly of
the mental life of his time.

Libertines

Not exactly hidden, but peeking tantalizingly through the interstices of our
documentary and artistic pictures, is the anarchic sexual code that undergirded
them and had transformed perceptions of the mores. Christian morality appeared
less and less operative as a moralizing check, and over and against it was posed
the code of the libertine. From its original sense—in Calvin, for example—as
referring to one who sought the right to freedom of spiritual judgment, the term
libertin, which in the seventeenth century still had philosophical relevance, had
come by the mid-eighteenth to apply merely to a sexual attitude, as the altered
meaning of the word *galanterie* attests. But even in this debased state a thread
connecting sexual, philosophic, and theological *libertinage* remained. Here is Grimod de la Reynière writing in his aristocratic rococo vein, "People nowadays con-
gratulate themselves as much on their *libertinage* as on their lack of faith: it would
seem that now we blush as much at appearing virtuous as formerly we blushed
for being devout."[47] Far too rarely have we understood the sexual arena as the
marketplace, the locus of exchange of human passions that it is, mediating between profane and sacred, ideal and real, inwardness and outwardness, personal
and social. In this respect our own late twentieth century bears a close resemblance to the end of the eighteenth, as sexual expression becomes, through displacement, the vehicle of a host of other repressed passions and potentialities,
personal, political, artistic. Viewed in this light, the libertin, stalking "freedom,"
becomes its *pantin,* a mere plaything of his own obsessive inability to envisage the

freedom of the whole man, rather than of his parts. His idea of sexual freedom is the form freedom itself assumes for the pre-Revolutionary eighteenth century, still enmired in the rigidities of its social and gender structures.

Women become the continents, rivers, mountains to "conquer," another or several each night. Bachaumont would write of his great passion for women, to whom he gives himself indiscriminately: since he seeks to make each one over so as to reflect the image of his own immediate need, for him it is best that they remain all the same, a malleable clay awaiting his imprint. If women themselves engage their appetites, sometimes heartily, in this round, it is never their game: on the contrary, it is precisely *not* their game. The sex for whom sexuality could (before effective contraception) never be altogether frivolous is objectified as so many game counters by the sex for whom it could be. "Everyone was talking about the insult to Mme de Gancé at a supper at Mme de Nesles'. The young men at the table with her fed her a variety of liqueurs which made her quite drunk. Afterwards, she danced, nearly naked, and then they gave her to some valets in an antechamber who had their will of her."[48]

This handing "down" of sexual prey from upper to lower class is a feature worthy of attention: it indicates the instant ability to strip women of class, mentally if not literally, and denotes women's essentially tenuous and less than necessary relationship to class hierarchy. According to Patrick Lasowski, the libertine imagination "takes fire at its belief that only the rough brutality of the common people could be adequate to unveiling the truth about this impossible sex. The libertine ritual of humiliation of the object is repeated in the story of the Countess of Bressac who, after becoming besotted, was undressed and had her sexual parts filled up with soft cheese mixed with salt and pepper."[49] This gesture, as Lasowski sees it, conveys a triumphantly scornful assessment by the dominant male mentality of women's "lack," their negativity and unreality as themselves sexual beings.

An anonymous popular print (fig. 6) entitled *She Fell, I Saw Her **** plays on the leering prurience toward women. A country girl carrying her product to market on the back of an ass is tumbled unceremoniously to earth by the beast. As a man beats the animal and a boy pulls at its tail, a dog yaps at the spectacle and two bourgeois passers-by whisper to each other that the woman's bottom is on show. In the loose abandonment of her fallen posture, her legs splayed apart, her arms flailing, she appears as luscious, vulnerable quarry of appetite, much like the cornucopia of cabbages, carrots, and turnips that seem to pour from between her open legs. Decidedly, women's sex is the dirtiest (that is, most unfathomable) of secrets.

Such male anxiety revolving around women's sexuality as is expressed in libertine hostility surely springs as much from terror of their fertility, which is felt as uniquely "theirs," as of their sensual appetites, which men share but are reluctant to acknowledge. The libertine strategy of handling these persistent, perhaps ineradicable, tensions apparently enjoyed, as Shorter has observed, wide, cross-class

6. She Fell, I Saw Her, *Bibliothèque Nationale, Paris*

consensus in the eighteenth century. As the Calvinist-born Rousseau recalls re-
provingly, around 1740 in the Parisian milieus he frequented, made up of officers
and musketeers, noblemen as well as businessmen, financiers, and food merchants, conversation would revolve about nothing except amorous adventures;
"chaste persons brought low, husbands deceived, women seduced, clandestine
childbirths, were the most usual of subjects, and he who had contributed most to
the foundling home [Enfants-trouvés] was always the most fervently applauded."
These unions, as well as their products, were objects of fraternal jocularity. Where
such sexual liaisons were not between persons of the same class, it was obviously
women of the lowest class who suffered their consequences most. "It is cruel,"
writes one commentator, "to see how carelessly . . . the common people are thus
eaten up by the rich. . . . Serving girls [are] handed over to bachelors in their age
of passion, finding themselves exposed to seductions hard to avoid: in the great
houses they are the toys of valets after having served as their master's plaything,
and they end up being dismissed by their mistresses. . . . Thus it is that we must
look among the lowest classes of the common people, for whom purity of morals
is not a paying proposition, to find the heart of corruption."[50]

A network of powerful resentments like those described by Maza must inevitably surround such a sexual system as this: the sexual resentment of the poor

men who cannot buy such pleasures against the rich; the grief and resentment of lower-class parents, brothers and sisters of women so used; and the repressed anger of the women themselves who have only such alternatives as these. If she should produce a child or children, the woman must suffer a traditional reproof, in all classes, unabated by the prevalence of sexual licence.

Flandrin makes the generalization from his far-reaching exploration of the documents over many centuries that "the more society became concerned with respecting sexual mores, the more harsh it showed itself to be toward unwed mothers and bastards, and the less chance it would give to the guilty mother of keeping her child, the visible sign of her fall."[51] To this I would add, the visible sign of *his* fall, as well. Does the vindictiveness exercised against the mothers spring from guilt repressed by the fathers?

Infant Humans—Abandoned

Of course attitudes to the child were not then entirely as they were later to become. Philippe Ariès has situated the evolution toward the modern private domestic conception of the family as occurring precisely in the latter half of the eighteenth century. This was an ideal at first for the privileged classes alone, which would trickle down only by minute stages over at least a century's time to the popular classes. Still, at midcentury and beyond, for the mass of French parents of even the children of marriage, there was "a subconscious awareness of emotional danger in becoming too fond of infants—best keep them at a distance in the care of wet nurses until the balance of probability tilted in favor of their survival." But if a child were to die, this death was to be regarded stoically: "God has afflicted us: we accept His will." John McManners reminds us how defensive a psychological armor this was for premodern parents. He sees it as protection from consciousness of that incessant slaughter of the innocents about them. Mortality must be read as a gift of the cards dealt to them. "To understand the mentality of the eighteenth century, the first step is to try to recapture the instinctive harshness, resignation, and fatalism of people who say their children were born to die rather than to live."[52] But more is in play here than simply child mortality.

After all, Jean-Louis Flandrin points out to us that in contrast to Africa, where the birth of a child has always been considered welcome, in the West, which was likewise subject to extensive infant mortality, it has never been regard as an unmixed blessing. While abortion and infanticide were virulently reproved by the Church, because these practices deprived potential beings of the cleansing powers of baptism, in practice, Flandrin argues, infanticide was actually fostered by Christianity, since the child made manifest to the eyes of all its parents' sexual sin, dishonoring them. It had ostensibly been to prevent such carnage of abortion and infanticide that, in the sixteenth century, Henri II's edict demanding that illicit pregnancies be declared became law. Since such intense sexual reproof still hung about these practices of desperation, what sprang up in their stead in the eighteenth century was a widespread abandonment of unwanted children, which was to prove itself a strategy slightly less lethal, and perhaps even more productive of guilt, than outright abortion or infanticide.

From 1670 to 1791 a curve representing the rate of admissions of foundlings to the Enfants-trouvés has been documented for Paris. It shows a constant progression until 1772, followed by a slight falling-off until 1791, the most persistent rise occurring between the years 1721 and 1772. This figure was stabilized at a figure of about 5,800 between 1780 and 1790, the most significant decade for the Revolution, after which it began to go down. The large number of these children brought to Paris from a wider circle of communities around Paris itself, Claude Delasselle tells us, merely shows us how frequent abandonment was in the provinces among those "desiring to see their embarrassing progeny swallowed up into an anonymous mass." Louis-Sébastien Mercier is one of the few to have left a description of the mode of portage of these infants to their destination. "It's a man who carries the new-born on his back in a box that could hold three of them. They stand in their diapers, breathing the air from above. The man stops only to take his meals and have them suck a bit of milk; when he opens his box, he will find one dead: he finishes his trip with the other two, inpatient to rid himself of his load. Once he's dropped them at the hospice, he immediately sets off again to do the job that earns him his bread."[53]

Nine-tenths of such infants, it is reported, would die before the age of three months. Among those born to mothers at the hospice of the Hôtel-Dieu in Paris, 87 percent were placed in the Foundling Home, leading Delasselle to conclude that the Hôtel-Dieu's lying-in facility was a sort of asylum for "sinful" girls coming up from the provinces solely in expectation of abandoning their children there. Mercier alludes to the lack of nourishment provided these babies, and Desbois de Rochefort confirms that they often went unfed, or were fed only wine. By a wide margin, it is the children from the Hôtel-Dieu who furnish the greatest tribute in deaths (83 percent die in the first month after their birth; scarcely 7 percent survive to the age of five, as against 17 percent of other classes of abandoned children). In any case, only a meager number of these children could have survived to adulthood.

The reason long adduced for this growth in abandonments (of which I have, of course, presented only a cursory and partial picture) is poverty. Mercier saw it arising out of "want, which in every era has been the cause of most of these disorders generally blamed on men's ignorance and barbarousness"; Desbois de Rochefort similarly saw it as a form of wretchedness especially visited upon the poorest of the people (*le petit peuple*). And indeed parallels have been found between rises in the price of grains and the number of infants abandoned in Paris. For not only illegitimate children but many legitimate children of indigents were given away in this fashion. Sometimes along with these infants would come ribbons or religious medals or figurines, indices of parents' hopes of recovering them. Only a few were in fact ever returned to their families: Delasselle mentions a figure of from 3 to 5 percent a year at the end of the old regime.[54]

Montlinot, a contemporary observer, however, offers a nuanced view of the contribution of poverty to this tableau. For him, as for Flandrin, poverty is not the sole cause of the abandonments of even legitimate children: "Misconduct, laziness, private misfortunes and even, it must be confessed, a lack of morality and probity on the part of fathers and mothers bring in their train the desertion of a progeny no longer safeguarded by paternal integrity."[55] A certain willful blindness on the part of parents has been noted concerning the real fate awaiting the abandoned young: the Foundling Hospital of Paris, after all, enjoyed an excellent reputation. Several commentators have not failed to observe that this very same refusal to know afflicted the Jean-Jacques Rousseau who, in giving his and Thérèse Levasseur's five infants out to the public charge held, in book 7 of his *Confessions,* that "he would have liked to have been raised and fed as they were." I intend to return to this stance of Rousseau's.

Montlinot thought that the secrecy—to which Rousseau's avowal is the great exception—surrounding desertion merely served to favor "the loosening of marriage bonds and made immorality secure." And Mercier likewise recognized that the very fact that the Foundling Home accepted all abandoned children without question put libertinage a bit more at its ease. As John McManners has so cruelly yet justly put it, "the fate of these unhappy infants throws a hard, cold light on the underside of the century of crystalline wit and rococo delicacy."[56]

A country lit by candlelight casts deep shadows into its corners. Shameful maternity was lived out in such shadowy places. In the eighteenth century the law fell with increased harshness upon the unmarried pregnant woman: her simple declaration identifying the father no longer sufficed. She now needed a virtually unattainable external witness to be believed. The whole dramatic ritual of confronting her lover babe-in-arms was suppressed. Few of these women, certainly, could afford to bring their sexual partners to trial.[57] Protective means had to be sought to guard pregnant girls from their fathers' wrath, a parental fury so potent that it impelled many of them to flee to the towns to give birth. Many pregnancies resulted from chance encounters between town- or countrywomen and transient male agricultural workers or soldiers. These men were from a cut of the population uprooted from their places of origin and not only without funds to establish themselves conjugally, but probably not inclined to do so and/or already married.

Two different sorts of images illustrate the theme of paternal abandonment. The first, *The Abandoned Mother* (fig. 7), is a sentimentalized prurient depiction of a nursing mother with her robust infant, hiding out in the protectively lush forest where she has gone to escape the hostile eyes of the community. Her naked breast is an offering as much to the viewer as to the child. The first stanza of the accompanying "Romance" reads:

7. The Abandoned Mother, *Biblio-thèque Nationale, Paris*
(Below) *8.* What Harsh Times These Are, *Musée Carnavalet, Photo Bulloz*

> Are there still some charms in life for me?
> No more of hope henceforth for my deep sorrow:
> Regret, remorse most cruel
> Fade the flower of my fair breasts.
> May the depths of this cavern
> Hide from nature my shame and my wretchedness.

This young mother, rendered with gracious artistry, is the reverse of the rococo coin. Her sexual use having resulted in pregnancy, now tarred with sexual guilt, she with her baby is (morally) expelled by a society that recognizes in her only the pathos of "her sin." This image exploits and has complicity with the system. The second (fig. 8), *What Harsh Times These Are,* shows us a patriarchal angel, Time, imperiously sending a mother with four small children away from a sheltering fortress into the cold, stony city streets. Time's autocratic gesture, the pleading stance of the children, the mother's openhanded wave of futility and pained look, all stress the harsh fate being dealt to unprotected women—whether widowed or unmarried—and their children. A protesting social conscience emerges in this print, which finds Time's stance abhorrent.

In attempting to illuminate this image of a loosened fabric of familial ties sustaining the life of the child, Vovelle alludes to the decline of the importance of religion, particularly in the lives of men, after 1750, which he speaks of as a "dismantling" of the age-old hold of the Church on the forms of life. This evolution affects men and women at different rates, with more men rejecting this regulation than women, to whom the Church, in the face of this weakening of the brake of religious controls, might still be seen as offering succor and comfort. Most significant to this present study is the gradual decline in the importance of the Virgin Mary, which Vovelle had observed in his perusal of Provençal wills. Her comfort and intercession, then, are less resorted to. If we can speak of the strong religious flavor permeating urban and petty-bourgeois life as being chiefly a female phenomenon, Leroi Ladurie has theorized that men's relative removal from Church influence may well have resulted from a struggle over their illicit contraceptive practices, basically coitus interruptus, newly emerging as a major factor in the population politics of the time. Vovelle's picture of the class structure of religious breakdown in Provence shows a distinct split, with aristocratic circles still remaining persistently observant, even as large numbers of persons from the commercial bourgeoisie and the liberal professions turned away from the Church.[58]

Nurture

To the gender conflict inherent in the problem of infantile abandonments must be added that surrounding wet-nursing, for these issues were closely related. The eighteenth century witnesses "the heyday of wet-nursing in France," where the system of giving the newborn to be nursed outside the cities was practiced not only among the more educated townspeople, but also, as we have seen, among the artisan and shopkeeping classes. Foundlings, too, were bundled off to wet nurses, so that this basic nurturant function developed into a flourishing venial industry. "The soaring numbers of children abandoned at foundling institutions and the widespread delinquency of parents in paying a nurse's wages, in particular, contributed to raising the price and lowering the quality of nursing services, especially in the last decades before the Revolution."[59]

By 1780, Charles-Pierre le Noir, the lieutenant-general of police of Paris, estimated that of the twenty thousand or more babies born in Paris yearly, only "one thirtieth sucks its mother's milk; an equal number is nursed in the mother's and father's home. Two or three thousand, belonging to the class of the well-to-do citizens, are dispersed around the suburbs and environs with wet nurses about whom the parents assure themselves and whom they pay all the more because they are closer and more to their liking." Le Noir adds that "the least wealthy and consequently the most numerous class was necessarily forced to take wet nurses at more considerable distances and in some ways at random." One study contends that the mothers of this less affluent group certainly did not hire wet nurses out of a desire to keep in with the fashions; rather they did so out of the press of their poverty. They felt they had to choose between the hazards for the nonbreast-fed infants in the insalubrious conditions of the cities, and the conflict posed for themselves between nursing and earning a living. For this stratum of society women's economic contribution could not be spared to accommodate a maternal breast-feeding function. At least that is how its priorities were organized.[60]

This wet-nursing industry arose, it must be remembered, long before artificial feeding had been made genuinely safe after Pasteur's discoveries a century later. Breast milk was still the only viable means of fostering infant survival. Cities like Paris and Lyons set up bureaus to oversee wet-nursing practices, but neither the supply of wet nurses nor surveillance of their conduct proved adequate to the need, occasioning at least in Lyons, as studied by Maurice Garden, a sort of *crise de conscience* against the tragic loss of nurslings.

Some idea of the dimensions of the problem can be gleaned from statistics gathered by Jacques Tenen of the Paris Bureau of wet nurses between 1770 and 1776. Through this agency 66,259 infants found wet nurses; 45,412 were to return to their parents, while 21,002 of them would die out in the countryside in the dwellings of their nurses. As George D. Sussman points out, this represents a mortality rate of 31–32 percent. The mean age of the dying babies was five or six months. But of course the fate of foundlings was far worse. Wet nurses were in too short supply to feed such destitute infants. This explains the catastrophic mortality of the figure cited for them. In 1781, 85.7 percent of newborns admitted to the foundling hospital of Paris in the last six months of the year died before their first birthday; 92.1 percent would die before their eighth birthday.[61] This latter figure certainly cannot be attributed to a lack of mother's milk, but to other deficiencies in child nurture.

Among a number of graphic works depicting departures, returns, or the stay of an infant with its wet nurse, we find Greuze's *Painful Privation* or *La privation sensible* (fig. 9). Here the tender scene of separation is softened by the juxtaposition of the baby's head against the full breasts of its wet nurse. The feminine cluster of figures on the stairs is contrasted with the darker grouping of the ass and its master with his strap poised to secure the purloined infant. The children terrorized by dogs intensify the sense of menace inherent in this consignment of the helpless newborn to an uncertain fate.

Shorter cites these illuminating remarks of a physician from the Orme: "The dwellings of many nurses are badly aired. Several have only a single room in which are crowded together a number of beds and chests. Some have but a single bed and three nurslings. Sometimes pigs, goats, sheep and poultry lived right with the family. Since the hearth gave as much cold air as heat, children's feet would freeze in their soaked clothing. The wet nurses are the poorest [women] in the

9. *J.-B. Greuze,* The Painful Privation, *Bibliothèque Nationale, Paris*

district, the most badly housed, and the most deprived of everything . . . for the nurse, staggering under the work of her own household and the burden of her own children, can pay but little attention to the cleanliness and physical exercise of which these children are in such need."[62] Elisabeth Badinter has ably summarized the picture of the treatment of the eighteenth-century French infant for us. Wet nurses would be selected with less care than that given to the choice of a groom for the horses. These indigent nurses were often ill and overworked. They might live in filth and dope their charges. The swaddling of infants was excessive and unsanitary. Many parents demonstrated a cool indifference to their newborns, and the aristocrat Talleyrand would claim that his mother had never made any inquiry concerning his well-being in all his four years with his wet nurse. In the upper classes, at the age of four or five children would be handed from the wet nurse to a governess, and at seven the boys would start their education with a preceptor. Badinter in fact, and I believe rightly, regards the use of wet-nursing as "a disguised form of infanticide," a mode of ridding people of their unsought-after progeny. She concludes that it would be deemed "necessary, at the end of the eighteenth century, to unleash many arguments to recall the mother to her 'instinctual' activities": "authorities" will call upon her to return to her sense of duty, "impel her to feel guilt and even threaten her so as to bring her back to her mothering and nurturing functions, defined as natural and spontaneous."[63]

This will certainly be one of the most salient outcomes of the eighteenth century's crisis of nurturance: the mothers, in line with their age-old functions as objects of male projection, will see assigned to them the guilt for their society's nurturant failures and will assume the consequences. As we recognize this, we are forced equally to acknowledge that it is essentially male guilt that is expressed in this campaign. Badinter comments that contemporaries, even as we ourselves tend to do, did not dare to engage in much moralizing against fathers concerning this holocaust of children. Indeed, she does not blame them, either, for "pressuring" women: rather she believes that a consensus of changed practices must have arisen out of some silent complicity between women and men. But in a world as patriarchal as that of eighteenth-century France, women could certainly have mounted no effective separate policy toward childhood: all the secular and religious institutions of life, the control over language, and the structuring of ideas were securely, though not unconflictedly, in men's charge. Can we say with Badinter that we are simply less shocked by the masculine attitude toward this vast loss of infantile life than the feminine, because "no one has ever, until the present day, proposed fatherly love as a universal law of nature?"

Certainly Badinter is right: motherhood was to be the parental role polemically arraigned before the tribunal of opinion in the late eighteenth century. And the mode of that arraignment will haul into court women's eroticism along with their maternity. But I want to reemphasize here that in this apparent campaign about motherhood, fatherhood is also being reconceptualized by French men. We witness this in the social and economic evolution as well as the cultural constructions

10. J.-B. Greuze, The Death of An Unnatural Father Abandoned by His Children, *Musée Municipal Greuze, Tournus*

of that era. Greuze's drawing *The Death of an Unnatural Father Abandoned by His Children* (fig. 10) captures, in the final contorted agonies of its emaciated progenitor, the hectic compound of grief and blame in play in this redefinition. The lifting of melancholy from Diderot's "Illegitimate Son" at the play's end by the embrace of his long-lost father is the portent that a new paradigm is rising.

Culture, Nurture, Eros, and Representation: the Philosophes

The rise to influence of women in court and salon society, which I treat more fully in chapter 3, was so established at the date of Montesquieu's *Persian Letters* of 1721 that the Persian visitor to Paris is made to write home his amazement that nothing could be done in the French capital without soliciting the aid of women. Even as it was enjoyed by the upper classes, this social arrangement could not but be greeted with hostility on the part of many, in a nation still living on the combined misogynistic traditions of Gaul and Christendom.[64]

A malaise, appearing most flagrantly in the domain of eros, arises about the precise location of the now disturbingly fluid gender borders we have glimpsed in the androgyny of rococo style. When Mme de Moysan undertook as administrator, in a meliorist female gesture that any nineteenth-century matron might have been lauded for, to humanize the atrocious conditions of the prison-hospital of the Salpêtrière, she was condemned by the Jansenist party not for her policy, but for her alleged turpitudes: "She is a procuress, a thief, she's had 2,558 lovers, she shows her breasts to the whole establishment, even though she's scarcely ever there." The terms of such sexually explicit denunciations—which are directed often, too, by men at men—betray in a public discourse a pervasive anxiety, an anxiety over the sexual tensions generated by women's public intercessions, seen as a species of unwelcome power play. Since men in culture have tended to define themselves as "not-woman," women—who, of course, bear their burden of human evil, but no more—have been assigned the function of representing sexual baseness and looseness, allowing man, qua male, to disengage himself from a full awareness of the vicissitudes of his own appetites. Woman played this role not only in the individual but in the social economy, which has seemed hectically to demand a redichotomization whenever the analogy between the sexes has become too close, too "threatening" to this convenient economy of blame.[65]

I have spoken of the androgyny of the rococo style, to which anticourt persons like La Font de Saint-Yenne reacted with outrage. Not quite outrage, but a nonetheless clear disquietude concerning androgyny emerges in Diderot's Salon critique of Noël Hallé's 1765 painting, *The Justice of Trajan* (fig. 11), in which the emperor's charity is implored by a matron he meets on the road with her two small children. Unimpressed as he is by the whole of the work, the critic seems exercised above all against the figure of the mother. For the woman, whose stricken facial expression ought, by rights he feels, to produce all the pathos of the scene, is presented from the back. "I said woman, but perhaps she's a young man. Nothing of her sex characterizes her. To believe she is one, I have to believe her hair or my program. And yet a woman is not more of a man from the rear than she is from the front; it's another fall of the hair, other haunches, other thighs, other legs, other feet" (6:50). Revolted by the unadorned and rooted sturdiness of this figure, Diderot finds it undeserving of a representation of pathos. The matron's figure, however, is not aberrant in terms of one's direct experience of women: such women existed then, and do still. The quarrel has to do with their representability. Diderot preaches to Hallé about what *he* would have wanted to see instead, and this turns out to be a perfect classical commonplace: the woman should be shown surrounded by women, and "For God's sake, don't show her to me from the rear. . . . Let her face reveal to me all her pain, let her be beautiful, let her display the nobility of her station, let her movements be strong and pathetic" (6:51). The novelty of the work lies in fact in its rejection of the drama of pathos for that of sheer encounter. Basically, Diderot is unhappy with this solitary, nonweeping mother since for him such a figure's right to pity must be tied closely to her sexual character. For him her beauty and her vulnerability must be one. Hallé's firm and protective maternal figure fails to speak to him. Diderot's discomfort with being confronted with our androgynous potential is patent.

11. Noël Hallé, The Justice of Trajan, *Musée des Beaux-Arts, Marseille, Photo Jean Belvisi*

In a species of organic recoil from the encroaching awareness of resemblances between the genders, such as those of intellect posited by the male feminist Poulain de la Barre in 1673, the eighteenth century's medical thinkers and some of the philosophes shared a move to an ideology of a more complete and biologically based dimorphism than had heretofore been propounded. This dimorphism, for the physician Roussel in 1775, was authorized by the differing ends of male and female physiology: the woman's organism being bent entirely toward its procreative tasks, her character is structured around feeling rather than ideas, of which she must necessarily know but little.

So to the tradition of sexual misogyny, we now add a new obsessive male emphasis on women's maternity: the two refuse to be dissociated, however. We distinguish this confusion in the kind of scorn directed at wet nurses, about whom such allegations might or might not be true, allowing for their general poverty and ignorance: "She who sells her milk has a mercenary heart," a lyric by Louis Racine teaches us. Such women suffer from a very bad press, becoming a butt, a scapegoat for nearly all the eighteenth century's authors. Peasant women of low station, they are usually held to have low impulses. All they want is money, or sex. Parents look upon them as mere machines. In such characterizations of these most vulnerable of all women the ancient war between sex and motherhood is fought most ruthlessly.[66]

Going back even to Galen, women had been instructed not to have sex during nursing because, it was believed, menstruation and a subsequent drying up of the milk would be provoked by coitus. In the eighteenth century it was thought that a woman discharged an emission like men's in intercourse, which could mix with her milk and spoil it. Ballexert held moralistically that passion was harmful to nursing: "An enamored woman is not a good wet nurse; for that you need a woman almost without passion." Boudier de Villemert, the self-styled "Friend of Women," held that a period of nursing would give women's temperament a rest and should not prove disagreeable to husbands. Milk production was to be held separate from heterosexual relations. Restif de la Bretonne, who advocated long-term maternal nursing in his utopian society, argued that during it husband and wife ought to live as sister and brother.[67] Whatever the physiological beliefs, the terms in which the desire to disassociate sex from maternity are expressed reflect concern about sexual passions and their link with motherhood. A developing male consensus that "good" maternal women cannot *at the same time* be sexual ones comes to the fore. From this it is but a quarter-turn to argue that mothers ought not be noticeably sexually active at all.

A related line of discourse develops concerning the wickedness of women who fail to nurse because they love their own freedom or pleasure to excess: two centuries earlier Michel de l'Hospital had written scornfully that "our beauties, raised amidst the sensuous delights of a city and given over solely to their own charms, are quite resentful at being subject to pregnancy; after bearing one child, they all refuse to feed their infants." And Henri Estienne a bit later would decry those "murderous" mothers who "used preservatives to keep them from pregnancy." This revulsion against the woman who prefers her pleasure to maternity returns with a sinister vengeance in the eighteenth century: Moheau writes in 1778, "Rich women whose greatest interest and sole preoccupation is sexual pleasure are not the only ones who regard the propagation of the species as a trickery of times past."[68] French society, faced with a breakdown of social restraints, appears bewildered over the havoc brought on by the growing failure of appeals to traditional Christian teachings to effect a measure of sexual continence. A nation that cannot look toward procreation with affirmation, but instead finds itself covered with confusion as it confronts it, is at risk. A mounting anxiety over the nature of sexuality is expressed in male reactions, whether they be a Rousseau's or a Sade's, and in each case these will turn on women's role in that sexuality.

There is being verbalized abroad, then, a quarrel not chiefly between men and women, whose views are in no way solicited; rather it is chiefly one between classes of men concerning what women should be held to represent. Libertine men are pleased to regard women as instrumental to their pleasure and, for the most part, accord them a lively sexual appetite, thereby somewhat justifying their own obsessions by assuming them to be wholly shared. These men and the women who are drawn to this code all see procreation as a boring and troublesome diversion. Another group of men, revolted perhaps by the "noise," the articulateness of the libertines whose speech about matters sexual seems almost to dominate eighteenth-century society, if not its actual sexual mores, is led, by its inability to identify with their sexual cynicism, to assume a dissenting posture. The form this dissent assumes reaffirms an economy tending toward an ideal of fidelity, sexual and emotional, for women; but it largely applies, at least on the affective plane, to men as well. Both of these groups agree on one issue: even the libertines regard female eroticism as more difficult to control than male. The moralists view it either as negligible, easily sacrificed to maternity, or monstrous. In the libertine code, which continues the *esprit gaulois* stress on appetite, maternity is in no way a consideration: eros is all. For the advocates of the rising family model, on the other hand, eros will either be familiarized or dismissed. But both factions express extreme discomfort with the alleged "unruliness" of female sexual appetite.

Missing Child—Guilty Mother

To Manon Lescaut, the heroine of Prevost's 1731 novel of a haunting obsessive love that persists through many vicissitudes, no child can be born. That is in part because the child has not yet emerged as a separate figure in either history or literature.

But it is also because questions of birth and nurturance have not yet surfaced as major conscious preoccupations of male society. As Philip Stewart has pointed out, childhood in the first half of the eighteenth century "is not only uninteresting but unimportant." The "hero's real 'birth' is a social one," occurring when she or he goes forth from home into the world as an adolescent like Marivaux's bouncy Jacob in *Le Paysan parvenu* or the resilient Marianne of his *Vie de Marianne*. Only sexual beings hold the prestige of real being, before Rousseau. But I would claim that even though the child indubitably gains ground as against its previous nonentity through Rousseau's intercession, children will long remain, though much spoken of, abstractions.[69]

Why? Perhaps the absence of the child is testimony to the cultural code's repression and denial of the arduous passage from sex to birth, from infancy to childhood: it lives in that unacculturated world of women, which impinges unavoidably but mystifyingly upon society. In the libertine code so prominent in the discourse of the first half of the century, this world was especially repressed.

Now, *theses* written by theologians and moralists on the duties owed by mothers to their infants were by no means lacking in eighteenth-century France. The familialist authors who now emerged had an object diametrically opposed to that of the libertines, that is, the protection of "the French family," and especially the nation's population. In reaffirmation of the ancient teaching inherited from Hippocrates that breasts were meant to give suck to infants, a new feature of their discourse will be their readiness not only to moralize, but also to offer practical advice, from their own concrete experience, to mothers.[70] Since the vast majority of such treatises, except for a few by midwives, were written by men, we are entitled to regard these works as male prescriptions, directed to both parents but geared particularly to the conduct of women.

The physician Jean-Charles Des Essartz addresses his remarks on the corporeal treatment of infants to fathers and mothers in the hope of instilling tender feelings in them for their progeny.[71] We distinguish Des Essartz's antilibertinism in his explanation for writing his book. "Every day we hear that Nature is degenerating and that soon, exhausted, she will begin her era of decline" (vi). Undismayed, Des Essartz finds such views exaggeratedly negative. As to the issue of depopulation, which marks his treatise as political and nationalistic, Essartz locates much of the problem as springing from "our fatal customs and ways, introduced by softness and luxury." A distinct antirococo scent emanates from this prose: attacks on nature are for him nothing but "miserable pretexts of our pride devised to disguise our vices of comportment and conduct, which are the true causes of the weakening of the human species" (x). While proclaiming his reluctance to compare humans to the animal kingdom in terms of their feeding of the young, he nonetheless goes on to do so in charmingly anthropomorphic terms. The mother hen gets his especial approval. *She* knows her brood needs her warmth to protect them from the cold. "There is no danger she will not confront so as to defend them and keep them safe; instead of fleeing, she attacks all those who threaten her young. This tenderness is the same in all animals; none abandon their little ones. Some lie down [or] kneel to bring their teats to the level of their young, others partly digest the food they gather before putting it into their mouths. . . . That is what Nature dictates to animals for the survival of their young" (xvii–xviii).

Des Essartz has an easy mark in contrasting this active animal maternal behavior with the picture of abandonments of infants to the wet nurse in the French family, a wet nurse being "the first one who offers herself" (xx). He claims his chief concern is only the health of the child, which needs fortifying by applications of good food, air, and exercise. Human beings must be to their progeny as a farmer is to his crop. "We," says Des Essartz, are not (xxv). This false universal "we" is a dodge, a use of the first person plural he does not long persist in, of whose inauthenticity he is vaguely aware. He goes on to attack "them." "We" are interested only in the happiness of society. "Let this motive serve as an excuse, as we investigate the way of life of most Demoiselles and ladies of high station. Certainly nothing so contributes to depopulation as the irregularity of life the fair sex has adopted, in devoting itself to its pleasures" (xxvi). These women cannot live as they do and give birth to healthy offspring.

Des Essartz berates those pregnant women whom one sees "walking out in the public gardens with their bosoms uncovered, exposed incautiously to the ravages and changes in climate, spending whole nights gaming and dining, singing, frolicking and even dancing with fervor" (22). Too free, too unharnessed, too wrapped up in their own lives, these mothers are too insubordinate to their biological maternity for Des Essartz to tolerate. Des Essartz and the other proponents of maternal nursing pose their arguments in a way that reveals a strategy of reducing the range of women's activities to the maternal sphere: reduction is the prime feature of their rhetoric.

Even so Des Essartz is significantly less restrictive toward women's physical capacities than end-of-century medical ideologues will become. The differences nature has established between women's constitution and men's does not need to lead them to be so delicate and weak that they cannot achieve "a health as firm and lasting as theirs through use of the same exercise." Women's present slackness was due only to their lack of activity, he claims, and he cites as his own counter-ideal the strong countrywoman. Yet Des Essartz is not above making the most abject threats against women who repress lactation. Their milk will only thicken within their bodies and become infected. And what then? "Deprived of the use of their legs, overcome with vapors and obstructions, weak, without appetite, covered with pimples as uncomfortable as they are disagreeable, they drag themselves through a painful and languishing life that finally ends in cancer, an ulcer of the uterus, or general consumption" (158). We may fairly judge from this degree of hostility that he treats a matter he deems to be of great consequence.

By the late 1770s there would be little interest in a relatively positive experiment with artificial or mixed feeding of infants. Emotional concern has been turned decisively toward mother's milk as a solution to degeneracy and depopulation. Yet the rumored depopulation was not held to be solely the result of the dearth of mother's milk, but also of allowing infants to be abandoned and maltreated in hospices. Such nurslings, like the children separated from their parents whom Anna Freud treated in an England bombarded by the Germans, appeared devoid of affect. The surgeon Léchevin wrote feelingly in 1775 that he wondered if it wasn't simply boredom that prevented these institutionalized children "from digesting and made them die slowly"; did they not need "to be played with, danced with, cheered," and were they really indifferent to the cries of pain of the infants around them?[72]

It was mothers who were held responsible for redeeming this appalling failure: more precisely, it was the milk of a race of subdued mothers that, according to the propagandists, held the promise of cure.

The Breast of Good, the Breast of Evil

Pierre Darmon calls the chapter of his *Mythology of Woman* relating to this era "The Battle of the Breast." He begins it by pointing out that in what he terms the "sacred pornography" of the eighteenth century, female nudity plays a central role in moralistic misogynistic outbursts; "but behind the misogynous façade of clumsy austerity hides a white-hot libido in which jubilation stews with despair."[73] The breast plays a focal role as sign in this discourse, as in fact it continues to do in the high style of female dress, as *robes à grant gore* come to flaunt the breast openly. Already in 1551 a friend of Jean Calvin's had attacked such exposure in "A Christian Instruction Touching on the Pretentious Dress of Dissolute Women." An eloquent text combining moral outrage with libidinal distress comes from a sermon by Canon Jean Polman in 1617:

> The worldly, the fleshly, the children of Babylon dart their lascivious looks upon this bare bosom; they throw their carnal thought between these two lumps of flesh, they lodge their wicked desires in the naked hollow between them; they attach their desires to these swelling mounds; they lay their desires down in this bed and lair of breasts, and there they commit their inward lecheries.[74]

Polman's emotional intensity concerning the breast as the focus of desire moves from the male desirer to the female breast, because the unveiling of the breast expresses a female desire unsettling to the male need to control sexual approach. Women prepared to admit their own lubricity all become Messalinas, violent and oversexed, in this system, metaphorically ready to leave the comfort of imperial beds (that is, the male ordering of sexuality with its attendant compensations to women who conform) for the sake of gratifying appetites of their own to which the code decrees they are not entitled. The system is so conceived as to present the menace of a limitless and open sexual provocation of men by women, which must be severely controlled.

Darmon hazards the view that the battle for the breast is "in fact inscribed in a far-reaching movement that aims at cutting women out of the concert of society." If, as I believe, this "movement" is not one fully under the conscious scrutiny of the culture and not an explicit program, its effects, the results of a massive psychological repressiveness embracing both sexes, have been nonetheless (and perhaps therefore) more politically successful than more overt political movements in history in slowing women's progress in emerging culture. When that 1761 French translation of Valens Acidalius's *Mulieres homines non esse* appeared, it reiterated the thesis that women were not human but rather complex instruments of generation devoid of a soul.[75] Now this translation of Acidalius's outrageous work seems to possess but little in common with works by Des Essartz and Rousseau on the face of it; and yet it was published in the same period as Des Essartz's treatise (1761) and Rousseau's *Emile* (1762). Can there be some underlying unity among these works—the one that assimilates women to bearing beasts, and those that call them back to an exclusive love for their young?

Rousseau and Maternal Nursing

Whatever words a host of other commentators had expended in fostering maternal nursing, Jean-Jacques Rousseau's prose would effectively wipe away.[76] He would use their evidence, their arguments; but it was his personalized voice, his supercharged eloquence uttering them that gave them their force and made them dominant over all other gender discourses.

And it is not without profound reasons that Rousseau would emerge as spokesman for the regeneration of infants: it is he above all who represents to all history the abdication of paternity, having given out all five of his and Thérèse Levasseur's infants to be raised at public expense as foundlings. As we have seen, his plight and his attitude to paternity were not exceptions at all, but common coin in his time. We cannot, however, ignore the fact that the thinker who most pressingly and persuasively constructed modern France's model of maternal devotion was a father who forced his troubled and unwilling mate to give up all her children. We must recall his essential words regarding the good conscience yielded by his self-examination with respect to these abandonments, for they lay out the tapestry of his rationalizations:

> Even if I was wrong in the result, nothing is more astonishing to me than the security of soul with which I took this action. Had I been one of those ill-born men, deaf to nature's gentle voice, in whom no feeling of justice or humanity ever took germ, this hardening would be quite simple. But this warmth of heart of mine, this lively sensibility, my ease in forming attachments, and the strength with which they subdue me, the cruel heartbreak for me of breaking them off, this innate benevolence toward others, this ardent love of the great, the true, the beautiful, the just, this horror of evil in all its guises, this inability to hate, to harm, and even to wish to do so, this pity, this lively yet gentle emotion I feel at the sight of all that is virtuous, generous, lovable: can all of this ever be harmonized in the same soul with a depravity that treads underfoot the gentlest of duties? No, I feel it, and I say to all, it is not possible. Never, for a single moment of his life, could Jean-Jacques have been a man without feeling, without compassion, an unnatural father. (*Confessions*, book 8).

Rousseau heaps on assertion after assertion of his goodness, his feeling for others, to demand the reader's assent to the appropriateness of his claim to peace of conscience. No plainer statement—this in despite of his professions of faith—of the absence of fear of God or men is possible than this. He dreads neither His wrath, nor that of his many equally delinquent but silent fellow fathers. Rousseau here pretends to assume that all share a discourse of male good conscience that need rest on nothing more than self-approval. Only a small "cranky" minority would contest such a claim to paternal complacency.[77] This is a text that roundly illustrates the guilt it denies, and so signals an emergence into print of the sense of a more generalized, more widely shared failure of fatherhood.

Since we know that Rousseau wrote the *Emile,* his great educational tract, and his *Social Contract* during the same period, we must regard with some seriousness his claim in the *Confessions* that in abandoning his children to public charity he acted as a citizen: "lacking the ability to raise them myself, in destining them for lives as workers or peasants rather than adventurers or tramps, I believed I acted as a citizen and a father, and I looked upon myself as a member of Plato's republic" (*Confessions,* book 8). Just as Des Essartz saw himself as a patriot in calling for women to dedicate themselves to motherhood, Rousseau regarded himself as a republican in making his children the wards of the state. The republic in these two views fosters guilty motherly devotion and complacent fatherly abdication.

Rousseau's last words on this issue are to the effect that he would have wished to have been raised and fed as his children had been fed. It is with the feeding of infants that the *Emile* begins, in paragraph two, right after his denunciation of Man and his exaltation of nature ("All is well as it leaves the hands of the Author of things, all degenerates in the hands of man").[78] And here he proclaims he is addressing himself above all to the "tender and foresighted mother" as reader. The issue of maternal nursing is supremely useful to Rousseau, for with it he can pose a whole series of dichotomies that obsess him: the tensions between nature and culture, country and city, the individual and society, authenticity and alienation, woman and man. Men mutilate and disfigure all: their institutions simply snuff out man's essential nature and put nothing in its place (5). It is the responsibility of the mothers to alter this nefarious course, for each of them can "preserve the newborn little being from collision with human opinion." While it is she who must set this barrier around the soul of the child, it will be for others to show it its way. Rousseau's barrier suggests a permanent womblike carapace intended to shield the individual. Emile's education in nature, the womb's successor, will complete that training in a plenitude that will allow him his fullest spiritual and mental development. This child, explicitly male, must not have his members confiningly swaddled, his infantile energies restricted. He is not destined for a passive destiny. "To live" is for him "not to breathe but to act" (13). But the selfsame nature that decrees that the male child be freed demands of his mother submission.

Rousseau indulges in the same moralizing criticism of women as his fellow propagandists: so many spoiled mothers reject their duty of nursing that a healthy wet nurse would be preferable to one of them. But he is equally acerbic about the wet nurse. "She who feeds another's child instead of her own is a bad mother; how could she be a good nurse?" (17). And yet, in his scorn for men and their culture, as he roots about for a source of regeneration for humankind, he finds he has no alternative but to turn to those very women who have been vitiated by their evilly socialized mothering practices. He turns to the sex that offers him semantic multiplicity, that can be metamorphosed in any way he chooses. Even so, we cannot help being thunderstruck by the enormity of his proposition:

> Do you want each and every one to return to his own duties? Begin with the mothers and you'll be amazed at the changes you will effect. Every privation comes sequentially out of this initial depravity [of wholesale wet-nursing]: the whole moral order is altered; the natural is extinguished in every heart; the interiors of homes take on a less vivid aspect; the touching scene of a family at

its birth no longer draws husbands, nor does it induce respect in strangers; we have less respect for mothers whose children we do not see; there is no abode for the family; habit no longer reinforces the ties of blood; there are neither fathers nor mothers, nor children, nor brothers nor sisters any more; all scarcely know each other; how could they love one another? Each one thinks only of himself. When the home is nothing but a sad solitude, one must go elsewhere for cheer. (18)

Privation and depravity in one, the denial of the breast is the seed of all personal and social evil, of all alienation, in its brutal break with nature at the very start of life. The result of this abrogation of connection is that we are then faced with the naked will of each and all. The husband (for it is from his, or from the cheated male child's, perspective that Rousseau speaks) is marooned, does not know how to find roots. We cannot respect a mother whose children are not around her, because she fails to affirm attachment by her person: she presumes instead to appear as an individual. In refusing her breast she does nothing less than annihilate all bonds, since without this first one, by Rousseau's definition, none other can be founded nor maintained.

This insistence on unity in the mother-infant dyad can be compared with Rousseau's vision of the solitary man of earlier human development in his *Discourse on the Origins of Inequality among Us:* he who would sit beneath an oak, drink at the nearest stream, and sleep at the foot of a tree and satisfy himself *sans effort.* This conjuring up of a passive primitive phase of human phylogeny free of obstacles to fulfillment is repeated in the dream of effortless satisfaction of the child at the maternal breast: both are fantasies of fusion with nature.[79] In the case of maternal nursing, the longed-for simplicity already escapes man because for Rousseau it is a miracle occurring within a house, a construct of culture. He compensates for this intrusion of culture by making the house itself sacred, a privileged place of communion. Located in the country, the house becomes a refuge, a womb/breast promising union, in which the act of nursing is placed like a jewel among the satins as the precious stone of rebirth.

We perceive how sensual this maternal image, like that of Greuze's portrait of a young mother overborne by her maternity (fig. 12, *The Well-Beloved Mother*), remains. And indeed a subtext of Rousseau's argument here lies in its potent expression of longing for release from repressive sexual mores that hamper the free play of the senses. In his imaginary state that will be repopulated because mothers will consent to nurse, the family will be "honorably" polymorphous, united in the flesh before they can be so by virtue of the social contract. Though the chief emotional burden of this regeneration falls upon mothers, fathers come in for their share of moralism as well. If Rousseau insists on the centrality of mothers—"the laws fail to give mothers adequate authority," (6) and their parental status is more certain, their duties more arduous, their care more important to the good ordering of a family—he certainly fulminates, if briefly, against the fathers of his time:

12. Print by Massard after J.-B. Greuze, The Well-Beloved Mother, *Musée Municipal Greuze, Tournus*

"Ambition, avarice, tyranny, their fake precautions, their negligence and harsh insensitivity are a hundred times more harmful to children than the blind tenderness of mothers" (6). In fact, to render his prescriptions more credible, Rousseau makes a hooded avowal of his own paternal dereliction in the *Emile*. While the mothers' powerlessness is passingly regretted, Rousseau intends to place chief responsibility in the fathers' hands. "He who cannot fulfill his duties as a father has no right to become one. There can be no poverty, no labor, no human respect which would dispense him from feeding and raising his own children. Readers, trust me, I believe that anyone with heart who neglects such holy duties will live to shed bitter tears over his failure, and will not be consoled" (23).

Despite this half-confession with its bitter undercurrent, mirroring a more generalized paternal bad conscience, Rousseau's indictment of the male sex for its sexual or social comportment as fathers remains transient and weak. It is perfectly evident that in leaving fatherhood so largely out of his emotional accounting Rousseau protects himself against heavier self-scrutiny. In his rush to escape, he instead turns back to women and, in a move fraught with ambivalence, ascribes to them in an unprecedented way, going far beyond the language of the apologists for maternal nursing, huge psychological powers with incalculable consequences for human life. If they would but give themselves once—body, mind, and soul—to this idyll of unity, they could create so profound an atmosphere of fusion between beings, such a solidarity of the flesh, that the plagues of alienation and immorality of the time would simply dissipate.

Romanticism will link such an ideal of fusion to the amorous couple rather than to the mother and child. Yet the family resemblance between these two models of demand for emotional intensity and their strongly sexual cast is striking. In Rousseau the image of nursing as the primordial human relationship confers on the later developing sexuality an atmosphere of spontaneity in necessity. Carnal needs must in no way be hindered but, as in the ideal—though certainly not necessarily the reality—of the infant at the breast, meet only with welcome and ease of contact.[80] Yet even for Rousseau himself, as for Romanticism, such unity is a threat to treasured individualism. A sense of this threat contributes to the thick atmosphere of ill-digested adoration of women and scorn for them that characterizes chapter 1 of *Emile*.

For the real mothers were far from the dream ones: like the men of the time, they were not particularly attuned to their primary being. Despite his kind words about motherly fondness being a hundredfold less destructive to children than fatherly failings, Rousseau issues a surly warning to mothers against the dangers attendant upon idolizing their child and not letting him live and suffer so as to become strong. "This is the law of nature," he scolds them. "Why do you work against it? Don't you see that in thinking to correct it, you destroy her work, you impede the effect of her care?" (20). Much as he tries to soften his attack by the use of *on* (one) and *nous* (23), we see that Rousseau lays primary blame on the frivolity of the class from whom he expects primary reform: the mothers.

> A child spends six or seven years in this fashion in the hands of women, victim of their caprices and his own; and after having loaded his memory with words he cannot comprehend, or things which are of no use to him; after stifling his nature by arousing passions in him, this artificial being is placed in the hands of his preceptor who completes the development of those seeds of artifice the preceptor finds already formed in him (21).

In this text we perceive that women's guilty artifice, the effect of culture, is the obverse of their capacity to fuse with the other. Rousseau's antagonism to and emotional distanciation from mothers as a class as contrasted with his fantasy of the solitary nursing mother's fusion with her infant finds expression in the *New Héloïse*'s insistence upon the separation of the sexes. In the idyllic setting of Clarens, Saint-Preux, the hero, writes, "each person belonging entirely to their sex, women live very separated from men" (433).[81] The scene of the gynaeceum in the novel best calls up his schema of sexual separation and its skein of the relations to the child and to sexuality.

In fact the women's retreat takes place in the children's room, a space into which Saint-Preux alone among men is allowed to penetrate. There they partake of an exquisitely simple repast of milk products, waffles and cakes, spice cakes, little tarts, and other dishes "to the taste of children and women." (No wine ever enters this sanctum: Dionysus is banished here.) Saint-Preux is transported with joy at this kind of meal and with the young mother who serves it. "Think," he exclaims, "what the products of a dairy run by Julie and eaten side by side with her might be like" (433–434).

> Julie laughed at my appetite. "I see," she said, giving me another plate of cream, "that your stomach does you honor and that you do no worse in consuming in women's company than you do among the people of the Valais."[82] "Not with more impunity," I replied; "one can become drunk sometimes in either company, and the reason can go astray just as easily in a chalet as in a wine cellar." She lowered her eyes without replying, blushed, and began to caress her children. That was enough to inspire my remorse. (434)

The link is luminous between this peaceful feminine space with its milk and sugary delicacies and the female breast. "Milk and sugar . . . are tastes natural to the fair sex and are akin to a symbol of innocence and gentleness that are its most affecting ornament" (435). Within the gynaeceum, a ravenous appetite is satisfied immediately, spontaneously, naturally: it suffers no intervention by any man or any social conception. Among these acultural women, desire is fulfilled beyond the conception of a barrier, just as the water in the rivulet flows toward the stream. But as Julie caresses her children—the gesture emblematic of the good mother who nurses—and as she veils her glance, she quite unveils the sexual current here which Saint-Preux has summoned by his words only to create the barrier— that of remorse for desire—once more. This very idyll is flawed by his verbal intervention.

A mood of menace may be called up by even so soft and nurturing a gesture as this on the part of a woman: the press of active desire or its expression shatters the reverie of oneness. Note the breathless anxiety in the grammatical clumsiness of this syntax: "With the ease women have in arousing men to sensual pleasure, often succeeding in reviving in the depths of their hearts the remains of a barely surviving amorousness, if there were some unhappy place on earth where philosophy had introduced such customs, especially in those hot climates where more women than men are born, tyrannized by them, men would be their victims and all would watch themselves dragged to death without ever being able to mount a defense" (*Emile*, 447). All active desire is alarming: but women's would be murderous. The terror occasioned by the possibility of sexual domination by women evoked by the Rousseau of the *Emile* impels him categorically to refuse the idea of attachment to this suspect sex unless it is shorn of menace and made comfortably passive. Since his rational side tells him "in all that does not pertain to sex, woman is man" (444), Rousseau elaborates in his texts a configuration of woman as *femme/sexe,* stripped of all human capacity outside the maternal and conjugal realms, to be realized in a single sexual/nurturant model of femininity.

In the *Confessions* Rousseau described this first erotic encounter, as Petit, with his protectress Mme de Warens, his Maman:

> I saw myself for the first time in a woman's arms, and those of a woman I adored. Was I happy? No, I experienced pleasure. I can't say what invincible sadness poisoned the charm of it. I felt as if I had committed incest. Two or three times, in enfolding her rapturously in my arms, I inundated her breast with my tears. As for her, she was neither sad nor lively; she was caressing and tranquil. Since she wasn't very sensual and had not sought delight, she never knew its ecstasy and never felt remorse because of it. (*Confessions,* book 1)

Female pleasure, elsewhere so terrifying, is here toothless. The incestuous anguish of Petit adds a sauce of transgression to his act, sublimated in the tears, his own utterable emission, which mix with the generous "milk" on the breast of the effaced Maman. The dream of fusion is destined to fail: where passion ends, conscience and memory intervene to impose their burden of guilt, their terror of loss. Union with woman is equally threatened by the selfhood she can never altogether repress. In Rousseau's texts, there is a will to silence her: Julie, who speaks only too much, dies; Sophie is raised to have nothing to say; and as for Emile's mother, did she ever speak?

It is especially noteworthy, as Mary Wollstonecraft recognized, that Rousseau refuses in his *Essay on the Origin of Languages* to see that the nursing that attaches mother or wet nurse to the child is not merely a solitary sensual act: it is at the same time the primordial social act.[83] For it is at the breast that the child first hears speech and begins to decipher vision and the nuances of the human voice and touch. Rousseau shows some awareness of this in his advice to women as first educatresses.[84] However, he cannot admit—in his fear of women's alterity and his emotional need to grant it space—that nursing is *for the mother* a profoundly social as well as personal act, in that it places the seal of bodily assent on her pact with the human community whose practices and mores she continues, in mimicking its conceptions and teaching its language. There is not the least reflection in the *Emile* on the mother's role beyond early childhood. The angelic Julie of the *New Hélöise,* after catching a fatal chill in saving her little boy from drowning, can accept death in her twenties because she has completed her role of raising her sons to the age when their serious education would begin. Male solitude and independence remain Rousseau's spiritual goals, even as he proposes the social contract. In spite of the individualism of his outlook, his influence upon the vogue of the family, including the seductive maternal role he ascribes to women, will be decisive.[85]

I have dwelt so much on Rousseau's maternal and erotic stances because their terms both recapitulate prominent formulations of their moment and in turn inform most forcefully the maternalist and family rhetoric of the Revolutionary era. Rousseau is not more condescending to women than other advocates of the new maternity: but his preoccupations are more philosophic, more psychological, and far more emotionally loaded than theirs, since he situates not merely the comfort and repopulation but also the happiness and regeneration of the French nation as lying within a woman's bosom. His failure—a word I do not flinch from using—arose from this more generalized incapacity to cope with intersubjectivity. An obsession with harmony made it impossible for him to think of relations between mother and child, between lovers, in terms of a mode of play, of reciprocity and intimate sociability that could withstand unforeseen surges of repressed desire.

For whether the eighteenth century's mores and attitudes were dipped in bemused irony about matters sexual like those voiced by the rococo Voltaire (whose heroes or heroines are never the worse for purely sexual encounters), or like Rousseau's by turns matter-of-fact in the gallic tradition, or mortified by sexual weaknesses, they were still engaged in a shadow war against repression.[86] A sense of the locus of that repression is not, however, a matter of consensus, but rather varies tremendously from text to text.

Nature's Body

The body, sometimes ignored, sometimes fetishized, sometimes divinized, can never find ease in this economy of sin and transgression, despite Reason's arguments. Its passion erupts either as joke or pathos, rapidly recontained to preserve the mercilessly mocked but relentless bienséances demanded by both social and religious hierarchies. French writing is most unbuttoned in posing the body's paradoxes in settings remotest from France, in imaginary confrontations with presumably more natural, distant lands than in the enervating zones of its own "civilized" society.

On the island called Lanciers a superstitious law controls population: "The child is crushed at its mother's breast, trodden to death beneath a priestess's feet," as men die, their throats cut by priests, or are castrated, while girls undergo infibulation—all "necessary and bizarre" cruelties unfathomable to modern minds. In Diderot's *Supplement to Bougainville's Voyage,* B exchanges ideas with A about such practices.[87] A sees in them the eternal moulting of supernatural and godly institutions, which become civil and national ones only to revert once more to the supernatural and divine. The violent death of infants at the feet of women, the murder of men by men, and the sexual mutilation and marking of girls lie at the core of this inquiry into sexuality, nature, and culture.

Voltaire's 1767 *Ingénu* had transported the Huron Indian hero to the coast of Brittany. Described as possessing the sexual prowess of a Hercules, whose name he then assumes, he has an idea of passion such that he can brook none of the niceties of sexual chastity and marriage placed in the way of his immediate union with Mlle de Saint-Yves. However, except for a brief comical episode of "barbaric" sexual directness, Voltaire's Hercules joins society and only reflects the perfection of a natural man in his "natural" ease in joining the "superior" civilization of eighteenth-century France.[88]

In a like demand for spontaneous combustion, the first act of Diderot's Tahitian Aoutourou, on his way back to France with Bougainville, is literally to throw himself upon the first European woman he sees, in his ardor to "show her the good manners" of his native land. Diderot, like Voltaire, needs to express the natural urgency of male desire, but neither of them is prepared to imply for more than the blink of an eye that Europeans could emulate their presumably "natural" sexual mores.

Bougainville himself had found in Tahiti the dreamed-of rococo paradise, "a new Cythera," where Tahitian men hospitably offer the traveler and his sailors young girls. "Venus here is the goddess of hospitality, her cult admits of no mystery."[89] But none of the Frenchman's rococo *douceurs d'amour* obtain here: only a utilitarian, procreative sexuality. Diderot imagines the meeting of this open code with the European, and he does so through the account of the grieving patriarch of the clan, who bewails the effects the coming of the Europeans has had upon Tahitian women and, in consequence, on the sexuality of the islanders.

What has happened? Formerly indifferent gestures of hospitality, their couplings have become intense, fraught, passionate. Whereas before the young Tahitian girl had given herself ecstatically to the embrace of the Tahitian boy, "waiting impatiently for her mother . . . to lift the veil that exposed her breasts, proud of exciting desire and the amorous looks of an unknown man, of her parents, her brother, even "the visual tribute of the throng," now, "a Tahitian girl is . . . twice possessed: she is the subject of the invader's physical embraces, but she must also bear the weight of his fantasies and participate in them" (207). Diderot views the pre-Europeanized Tahitian girl as less sexually coerced than the Frenchwoman, whom he recognizes as enslaved to a male construct of desire. Janet Whatley asks, since Diderot is claiming that the Europeans had brought a species of lust to Tahiti, "can it be that civilization preserves a kind of 'wildness' that Diderot's imagined Tahiti does not?" She observes perceptively that Diderot's ambivalence in this work about the *solitude à deux* of private coupling is posed against an exhibitionist, theatrical concept of sexual mating watched by the entire family and clan. Ideas of celibacy, but also of marital fidelity, are the target of Diderot's critical scrutiny, for their attempt to set into stone vows that beings of mere flesh, in a world so moving and crumbling that the very rocks wear themselves to powder, never can fulfill.[90]

Diderot's is a rumination on the ambient miseries of the sexual-social system he knew. Whatley alludes to his involvement in this work with "a peculiar sense of the domestic." She connects Diderot's voyeurism with that of Greuze's painting of the *Village Bride,* also a public spectacle of erotic confirmation, and with the "paternalism" he shows in his discussion of Greuze's *Girl with a Dead Bird* in his Salon piece on it. In these cases there is "a mingling of the domestic and erotic which leaves us uncomfortable because we feel that Diderot is not quite honest about the charge of these situations." This charge, I would claim, arises from the unstated juxtaposition of free-floating desire with sexual entrapment. As I suggested in speaking about *The Illegitimate Son,* an approach to incest, the sexuality of domestic enclosure, is present here: Diderot is "allowing himself an imaginative release in creating a little world in which the daughters do not have to choose irrevocably between fathers and husbands."[91]

But what repairs to the defective bourgeois French family can this Tahitian model offer? On the surface, Diderot proposes an end to the hypocrisies surrounding what he regards as Christian modes of chastity. And yet, as Whatley indicates, "the phony abolition of all tension, which we would expect to transform the family beyond recognition, produces an oddly bourgeois Utopia, where not only the family, but family status and even nagging mothers still exist."[92] This, then, is recapitulation in despite of critique. Diderot's entire demonstration of the superiority of the "natural" Tahitian family is supremely patriarchal: Aoutourou monitorily laments his own lost prerogatives to envious European father/husband readers, and intrusive reading women. As questioning of European sexual mores as Diderot is, his thought concerning their "rectification" still continues the tradition of reified, mythic, invincibly wild male desire. We witness its ungovernable strength in the "uncovering" of one of Bougainville's French servants on shipboard. Though untroubled by the European crew, whose sexual urges have been denatured by their culture, the servant is unceremoniously thrown to the ground and undressed by the Tahitian men to "present their compliments" to her: a girl, she had disguised herself so as to travel around the world. Neither the courage and good conduct B ascribes to her nor the strength of soul he accords to "those frail machines" are adequate to spare her assault by "real" non-European males. Natural male appetite is ineluctable, merciless.

The almoner's and Orou's tale in *Bougainville* is overtly patriarchal as well as sexually preemptive. Orou's wife and three daughters undress the visiting French almoner, wash his face, hands and feet, and serve him a meal. At bedtime, Orou brings in the four females, all naked, and presents them to his guest to make his choice: "A man needs a companion in bed by his side" (10:24). The almoner prissily refuses: his religion forbids him. But Thia insists: "Make me a mother. . . . If you accord me this favor, . . . I will bless you all my life; I will write your name on my arm and on your son's; we will say it always with joy; and when you leave this shore, my wishes will go with you over the seas until you reach your country" (21). Sex and reproductivity are made seamlessly indissociable here, in absolute variance with the reproductive picture of eighteenth-century France. Diderot here introduces a simple compensatory dream that will be one for the Revolution, too: that of a sexuality redeemed by a kindly maternity. The morally superior Tahitian Orou, mocking (libertine) ideas of seduction, of sexual dishonor, celebrates another code whereby couples mate only as long as they wish to. More arresting here, in light of the plight of French infants and orphans, are his society's ideas about the support of their children. Their arrival—in another searing contrast with much of French society—is greeted as an unmitigated good fortune by both domestic and public milieus, their death with tears. A woman who goes from her parents' to her husband's house takes her children with her as dowry; those born during cohabitation are shared. And in the passage introducing a contrast between the Flirtatious Venus and the Fertile Venus, we read, "The woman who attracts glances and whom desire pursues [notice the omnipresent subject disjoined from a person] is the one who holds the promise of many children . . . and active, intelligent, healthy robust ones at that." There is nothing in common between the Venus of the rococo, whose sexuality is divorced from motherhood, and this fecund one, whom Diderot replaces on his pedestal as a Venus of Maternity.

We perceive the compensatory emanations in Diderot's stance, as he proposes a Utopia where the children would never be made to suffer the ravages of their progenitors' sexual appetites, where sexual desire would be at once reassuringly banalized by availability and sanitized as an instrument of procreation. But this procreative paradise is achieved via some fatherly and husbandly tyranny that goes by uncommented on by either A or B. When Orou offers his women to the almoner, he proclaims, "They belong to me and I offer them to you: they belong to themselves and they offer themselves to you" (212). The first clause, however, is clearly prior to the second, which it contradicts. The father's desire to dispose of his daughter conditions, dictates, her desire. She cannot be said to belong to herself: this is precisely why Orou has to claim, in the teeth of his ownership, that her choice is a free one. So the women of this utopia are pawns to the men; their children bear the father's name—"fatherhood, like tribute, follows the child everywhere" (222)—and the memories of the departed fathers who have fleetingly inseminated them remain with them always. In these ways, Diderot's Tahiti is, as a utopia, a same-place rather than a no-place.

There is a marked resemblance between the social coding by veiling of the woman in this Tahiti and the codes of fundamentalist Moslem society and of Margaret Atwood's futuristic female nightmare, *The Handmaid's Tale,* where women are publicly designated to men as childbearers or not. Orou brags about the clarification that the system of white veils for the not yet available girls, the grey veil of the married, the black veils of the sterile, and the red veils of the menstruating brings to existence. Female sexuality here is not only reproductivity, but the only licit form their sexual life can take. All the same, women may still bear the burdens of a fierce moral reprobation in this class system: even in Tahiti, "dissolute old hags" who, doffing their black veils, go off with men are exiled to the north or enslaved; young girls who take off their white veil without parental consent (and in this case, the boys who share their transgression) are punished; women who feel their time of pregnancy is too long; or those unscrupulous about wearing the grey veil: all suffer social ostracism. Since men's fertility has longevity, there is never a thought about limiting their access to sex; no judgments are made about the appropriateness of their urges. This utopia of nature proposes a society in which they are the ones permitted to be "natural," while they subject women to their "culture," the code that fulfills the needs of their sexual nature.

It is significant that at the end of this work A should propose to B that they read Orou's interview with the almoner to some European women. B says he cannot imagine what they might say about it, but when A asks what they would *think,* B answers, "Perhaps the opposite of what they'd say" (249). His reply implies that women would like to approve Orou's world, with its enticements of a missing sexual plenitude and love of its fruit, but feel they may not. Both their thoughts and their words are complacently preempted. Women's own war of nature and culture is not spelled out: rather, it is left in limbo.

The great and more nuanced and complex existential image of man in society that B proposes in this work is this:

> Do you want to have a short account of almost all our wretchedness? Here it is. There was once a natural man. They put inside this natural man an artificial one; and there arose in this cavity a civil war that lasts all life long. Sometimes the natural man is the stronger; sometimes he's overwhelmed by the moral and artificial man; and in either case the sad monster is pulled about, torn, stretched on the wheel; ceaselessly groaning, ceaselessly wretched, either because a false enthusiasm for glory transports and inebriates him, or a false shame bends him over and beats him down. (245–246)

Diderot perfectly encapsulates the angst of natural man, especially sexual man, as entrapped in culture. The sense we find of the natural here as binding us into its unending series of mutations of form and impulse characterizes the late eighteenth century's metaphysics.[93] Diderot's *Bougainville* proposes a place of minimalist culture, friendly to human sexuality, where vice can simply be sidelined by language: if only, along with the words, the concepts of dishonor, adultery, infidelity might disappear. It is likewise magical thinking that makes his period—as well as Diderot himself—buy so heavily into a traditional idea of virtue stripped of its Christian trappings, yet strangely akin to it in its forms, dressed not in Tahitian garb but in the attire of the new bourgeois republicanism.

Bourgeois Pleasures

As Robert Mauzi has implied, bourgeois respectability comes to be dialectically tied to eroticism in a way paralleling the way devotion to work comes to be seen as the polar opposite of the pursuit of pleasure. For the bourgeoisie, "the debauchery of the worldly and the debauchery of the lower classes are equally shocking." Its emergent sexual code represents an attempt to squelch the ravages of debauch upon society. The cult of work is conjoined with the virtues of the new domesticity in this system, which will challenge the softness and sensuality of the dissolute lordly class. Turning away from the unpredictability of sexual impulse, "in his sentimental life the bourgeois pretends that passion and caprice, all irrational conduct, do not exist." Now Diderot's *Supplement to Bougainville's Voyage* also presents a model of a society devoid of debauchery, but via the rationalized expression of sexual impulse, rather than an outright repression of any overt appearance of it, as bourgeois culture would have it. Both Diderot's "counterculture" and the new bourgeois morality have this much in common: they both regard female sexuality and procreation as the domains to be recontained, to be tamed. And the personage who surfaces to perform this function will be the bourgeois father. "To the glory of the bourgeois businessman corresponds the seriousness and austerity of the bourgeois *père de famille*. The bourgeois' is a model of humanity that links the radiance of professional life to the rectitude and deep piety of private life."[94]

Even so, the concentration on fatherly power we find at the end of the century seethes with conflict. The relationship of king to subjects and of lords to vassals or underlings, now under severe strain, had always been conceived as one of a father to his children. The heightened ambivalence of the era concerning paternal authority surfaces most cogently in painting.

> The patriarchs in Salon paintings are often honored and obeyed; but their relationship to their sons are just as likely to be troubled or in crisis. Rebellious sons appear in these works with high frequency and in both ancient and modern dress. Authority, in the person of a pathetic or angry old man, is often challenged outright. . . . Even without rebellious sons, Salon patriarchs are prone to sorrow, suffer and die, or to be near death. . . . Pity, fear and guilt, alone or in combination, are the feelings these old men are most likely to inspire.

We have already seen the pathos of fatherhood expressed in the person of Lysimond in *The Illegitimate Son* and in Greuze's *Death of an Unnatural Father*. The eruption of an Oedipal theme in Diderot's works reflects that hatred of paternal powers in the old regime for its monopoly over private lives, decreeing in some cases that a man might remain a minor, unable to wed or enter into contracts, as long as his father was alive; or, as in the case of Mirabeau *père*, that a father might have his entire family put in prison. And yet, paradoxically, most of these willful fathers are represented in art as figures of pathos. As in Diderot's theater, Greuze's primary focus of attention settles on the father, whom he defends "with remarkable urgency." To judge by his paintings, "the answer to abuse of patriarchal authority is more and better patriarchy of the good, old-fashioned kind." Greuze's *Punished Son* of 1778 is a veritable fatherly wish-fulfillment tableau, displaying in its rhythmic melodramatics a scenario of family grief for the wayward son's failure to abide by paternal demands. Greuze's work points, in its deeply bourgeois aesthetic of struggle and reintegration, toward a return to a fatherhood not of repression, but of love and order.[95]

And so does Diderot's 1758 Greuzian *Père de famille* (*The Father of a Family*), a bourgeois drama that portrays a struggle between warring conceptions of fatherhood.[96] In it, as in the earlier play, mothers are again suppressed completely, while daughters are embattled. Diderot's *père de famille* is at once patriarch and mother surrogate.

Even in his dedication of the work to the Princess of Nassau-Saarbruch, Diderot cordially unveils his jealousy of her maternity, as he discloses that his central preoccupation will be with the character of parenthood. "Enlightened woman, tender mother, what sentiment might you not have expressed better than I? What ideas might you not have rendered more touching?" (3:259) Diderot does not bother concealing his seizure from her, from women, of the right of maternal discourse, any more than will Rousseau. "Whatever distance there may be between a poet's soul and that of a mother, I will dare descend into yours; and there read, if I can, and reveal some of the thoughts that preoccupy it. Let you but recognize and avow them as yours" (260). Thus he ventriloquizes for women. As does Rousseau, Diderot assumes the male right to repossession of the child less on biological grounds than on cultural ones. "My children are less mine perhaps because of the gift of life I gave them. It is in taking charge of their education that I reclaim them" (260).

Germeuil, the virtuous but unpropertied protégé of M. d'Orbesson, an impecunious widower of good social standing, is in love with his caustic, outspoken daughter, Cécile. They live in the house of Orbesson's crotchety brother-in-law, the Commander, who alone has the money that might enable Cécile and Orbesson's son Saint-Albin to find mates. Orbesson's daughter, whose marriage prospects are bleak, craves retreat to a convent as her sole dignified alternative, but her father harshly denounces this institution in emotional and naturalist terms: "Mademoiselle, never speak to me of a convent again. . . . I won't have given life to a child . . . only to let her bury herself alive in a tomb. . . . And who will repeople society with virtuous citizens, if the women most worthy of becoming mothers refuse to take on that state?" (294).

Saint-Albin, smitten with a poverty-stricken young girl who lives in a garret, at first finds himself unable even to tell his father about it. Germeuil, the "new man" without patrimony like Diderot's Dorval, acts as go-between, encouraging Saint-Albin's passion for Sophie. It is no accident that Saint-Albin has gone outside his class to love. "I need a chaste and feeling mate, who can help me bear the pains of life, and not a rich and titled woman who would increase them. Ah, wish me dead, and let heaven send her to me rather than a woman such as those I see" (307). Upper-class women are unworthy of forthright male passion. The imperious love this son feels for this poor, simple woman represents not-to-be-denied male sexual impulse become antisocial inasmuch as it threatens to destroy the father emotionally and economically. Fatherless, Sophie is seen as of lower station, is more "natural," than her lover: he will deliberately declass himself to pose as a poor man, Sergi, so as to disarm her defenses. That she is in danger from this lover is less important to the play than that she presents a danger to his family's order and economic security.[97]

Sophie's chaste virtuousness only just holds power adequate to moderate Saint-Albin's sexual ardor. Her powerlessness before male passion is underscored as Saint-Albin tells her he is resolved "to possess you, to be yours in spite of the whole world, in spite of you." Sophie replies aptly in the terms of gender power politics. "You show me the same scorn people use with poor wretches. They think everything is allowed with them" (371). Sophie is obliged to exhibit sagacity in controlling her lover.

At the play's core lies a dispute over the nature of fatherhood: the Commander-uncle's model of the "father" is arrogant, haughty, authoritarian, inflexible. He sets himself up in opposition to the young lovers, laying down the law to his nephew Saint-Albin: "All right, then, have your Sophie. Trample down your father's will, the law of decency, the expectations of your class. Ruin yourself. Debase yourself. Roll in the mud. I won't oppose you. You'll serve as example to all children who close their ears to the voice of reason" (320). A representative of the military caste, this unbending "father" is prepared to associate himself with the most tyrannical of all the powers of the political patriarchate in attempting to relegate Sophie to prison summarily by use of a *lettre de cachet.*

The "bad" father is outraged by the "good" father's slack inaction. To Orbesson's question as to whom he is expected to act against, the Commander replies, "Against whom? What a question! Against all." The disobedient son, the insolent daughter, and so on. "I would have exploded the whole lot long ago." Firmness is required, he thinks, and that is sadly lacking (353). A modern "liberal," Orbesson stoutly rejects his brother-in-law's rigorism along with his money and chooses instead fatherly affection, compromise, and forgiveness. "No . . . you won't make a cruel and unjust father of me nor an ungrateful and maleficent man. I will not commit violence because it is in my interest; and I will not make a desert of my house because things are happening here that displease me as much as they do you" (355).

In the play's climactic moment as the Commander takes his ultimate stand against his brother-in-law's laxness, we hear the echoing arraignment of French society. "While you sleep the sleep of an unprecedented security or give yourself up to a pointless melancholy, disorder has taken charge of your household. It has taken hold of everyone, the valets, the children, and their hangers-on. . . . There's never been any subordination in this place; consequently there's not a shred of decency or morals left here anymore" (386). And yet the Commander very nearly agrees to the marriage of Saint-Albin with Sophie (who in timely fashion is revealed to be the uncle's own niece, his impoverished sister's child). But the Commander remains the quintessential patriarchal tyrant, self-righteous and power-hungry within the family, a financial and emotional coward, refusing to part with any parcel of self for another. The rather odd factor that finally makes him reject all compromise, however, is his unreconstructed hatred for Cécile, who had insubordinately spoken words of condemnation to him unacceptable from a daughter, or, as here, a niece.

At the last, the furious Commander removed, Orbesson blesses the unions of his two children. The Good Father of the Family, absent any mother, has played the "mother's role" throughout: pained, pleading, imploring his son's acquiescence with emotional blackmail. "Go away"; "come back"; "I've never meant anything to you"; "you're poisoning my life"; "you want me dead" (315). Diderot incorporates into the figure of the compassionate father the affective volatility and emotional vulnerability of traditional maternity. This conception of the bourgeois father in effect leaves no space at all for a mother, even the sort of mother-surrogate-servant intercessors of Molière's plays. The new father figure proposed here, while embattled, triumphs through his invasive concern for the lives of his children and his benevolence (this being a paradox in Diderot) toward marriage and the family. As rejoinder to the crisis of sexuality and reproductivity, *The Father of a Family* projects a sense of towering need for kindly fatherly concern. The family we view under construction by bourgeois culture, then, at the century's end bears the deep scars of sexual and nurturance ambivalences, which lead it into profoundly misogynous formulations visible on the level of imagery.

Diderot was deeply moved by two paintings of tempest at sea by Joseph Vernet. Of one, the *Shipwreck by Moonlight* (fig. 13), he comments, "Reflect over these men busy attempting to restore this fainting woman by the fire they've lit beneath a rock, and admit you've seen one of the most interesting groupings imaginable." "Interesting"; that is, emotionally engaging. Nature is, for Diderot, dynamic and free-floating, forming and reforming itself infinitely, not good, not evil. But nature, reconceived in the traditional mode as feminine force—*La Nature*—recurs here as unfathomable destructiveness, akin to the power of passion in its unpredictability. Passion is indeed represented in the painting, both in the fierce tempest-tossed seas and skies and in the fainting but lissome surviving figure of the prostrate woman whose imminent loss lends the work its deep human pain. Nature's violence begins to recur in the art of this time as an awesome, incalculable Romantic power. This work, in its "tamed" wildness, the controlled horizontality of the depiction of the horizon, the stylized angling of ship and tree, conveys the struggle between nature and culture. Diderot asks us to note the "contrast between the weak and pale moonlight and the strong, red, sad, somber light of the lit fires."[98] The woman's moon pales before men's fires, the fires of culture, as they strive to revive the victim from her swoon. Nature, through struggle and despite

Dédié à Monsieur Godefroy.   Contrôleur Gnl. de la Marine.

13. C.-Joseph Vernet, Shipwreck by Moonlight, *Bibliothèque Nationale, Paris*

shipwreck, is here mastered by men. The pathetic woman, the driftwood of wild passion's excess, yet needed to preserve life, is sinking. Her feebleness seems terminal. Even the lights of civilization are lonely, "sad," "somber" ones. The men's link with women, already so tenuous, seems at a breaking point. Could it be restored sufficiently to serve as the bulwark against helplessness that humankind demands it to be?

Chapter

3

SOCIAL WOMAN: BETWEEN NATURE AND CULTURE

> Woman, among the savages, is a
> beast of burden, in the East, a piece
> of furniture, and among Europeans, a
> spoiled child.
>
> SÉNAC DE MEILHAN

ALCESTE, Molière's irredeemably plainspoken *Misanthrope,* addresses Célimène, his heart's desire, in a last desperate appeal to her probity, badly compromised for him by her dissimulating, contradictory letters to other suitors besides himself.

> *Alceste:* Woman, I'm willing to forget your shame,
> And clothe your treacheries in a sweeter name;
> I'll call them youthful errors instead of crimes,
> And lay the blame on these corrupting times.
> My one condition is that you agree
> To share my chosen fate, and fly with me
> To that wild, trackless, solitary place
> In which I shall forget the human race.
> Only by such a course can you atone
> For those atrocious letters; by that alone
> Can you remove my present horror of you,
> And make it possible for me to love you.
> *Célimène:* What! I renounce the world at my young age,
> And die of boredom in some hermitage?
> *Alceste:* Ah, if you really loved me as you ought,
> You wouldn't give the world a moment's thought;
> Must you have me and all the world beside?

> *Célimène:* Alas, at twenty one is terrified
> of solitude. I fear I lack the force
> And depth of soul to take so stern a course.[1]

Like the verbally forthright opponents of the rococo, Alceste demands of Célimène what she cannot give: a "manly" openness and candor. Her very ability to be present in society as a focus of male attention in her little circle cannot help but be hedged by evasions, circumlocutions, dodges. In fact these swerves and feints are what fill Célimène's company with delight at her acrobatic wit, while they distill in her a glee in which the verve of malice has its place. A euphoria of conversational interchange, the legacy to eighteenth-century society of its précieux predecessors, is the state that results from this higher form of play.[2] Alceste, the proto-bourgeois moralist, clearly enjoys his own verbal combat with Célimène, but he wants none of its ambiguities. He prefers to affirm that life, even love, are purely serious matters. But Célimène refuses to let them become so for her. Not yet, she pleads. To consent to a retired, private life's demands upon her would be to abandon society for the "rest of her life," that is, for domesticity, the dangers of reproduction, and a dwindling into slow sexual decline. But as Alceste sees it, her refusal is an index only of her shallowness, her frivolity, her lack of human gravity. Her love of autonomy simply cannot be combined with love for him.

This scene remarkably, almost prophetically, encapsulates—even to Alceste's Rousseauian readiness to forget the human race and Célimène's horror of his hermitage—the eighteenth-century's bemusement about its social women, their graces and talents, and their influence. The salon was, after all, this century's consummate social form, and it drew its centrifugal energies from women's interactions with men, verbal, visual, gestural, in the setting of a drawing room.

In this era the salon would altogether succeed the seventeenth century's court of the Sun King as France's cultural and social heart. It had been turned to originally precisely as a place spared the tensions of courtly intrigue. Nevertheless, the legacy of courtly life was carried forward in the manners of the salon. Castiglione's *Cortegiano* (1528) had set forth the Renaissance's conception of the qualities a lady ought to develop to sustain intelligent conversation: she would have to abandon the *taciturnitas* appropriate to the submissive domestic calling to which Christian teaching summoned her for a "public, promiscuous social role in which, by convention, she is the dominant partner; she is splendidly arrayed, in spite of moralists' warnings about the feminine weakness for vanity, ornament and luxury; she enjoys the delights of food, music and dancing despite her propensity to sensuality."[3] Salon women would occupy a niche unique to their own class, not to be generalized downward.

By the eighteenth century the inherent tension between the courtly woman and all others had not disappeared: instead, it had spread, even as it preserved the lineaments of a distinct social dichotomy. The flowering of the salon extended polite culture far beyond the confines of the court to nonnobles, among whom it yet remained the code of a (larger) elite class. The split remains, then, as a split between a mounting number of women of the rising bourgeoisie as well as those of the established aristocracy, and the rest: women who could never have dreamed of such ostentatious shows of self-display, which had to be buttressed by money and status. This chapter will concentrate on the former, because of their preeminent role in representation.

The realm of art is the central arena of women's long emergence into social prominence: women's self-presentation is bathed in its aura, which accounts for La Font's hostility to them. The rococo woman of society is expected, modestly but expertly, to practice the arts of drawing, music, and dance; she must present herself as an art object, harmoniously attuned in color and shading to wall panels of rococo cloud or bower, and she must speak with a tact, a grace, and a wit sufficient to bewitch her interlocutors; at no time may she be boring, a curse far more dreaded by this world than moral turpitude. Women are allied to art in their persons and attainments, therefore, and to artists whose efforts it is considered suitable for them to second. They are not seen as full-scale artists themselves, even when they are expert practitioners: their art is instead supposed to be embedded in their persons, in their capacity to please, not themselves, but others.[4]

An inevitable ambiguity crept into this socially sanctioned project. For some women, the medium would become the message: their narcissism would fire up as they perfected their abilities as artists-of-the-person. Such a concentration on mastery of the arts of the moment relates closely to what Simone de Beauvoir saw as the realm society has conceded as acceptable for women, that of immanence.[5] These women's pride in the perfection of their performance expanded with the enlargement of the stage on which they strutted. But the fact that women's chief energies were directed, by social imperatives that they joined rather than dictated, toward the goal of making of themselves their supreme creations could easily be interpreted as, and even become, a mere love of artifice. As we have seen, the problematics of artifice and ostentation will, in fact, come to be located by critics primarily in the persons of social women. And to this split between artifice and art, a series of other, more blatantly gendered dichotomies will be affixed: those of appearance and reality, of mind and body, of culture and nature, of outside and inside. None of these categories is susceptible of being gendered definitively; yet nearly all will be assigned and reassigned as feminine or masculine in the unsettled atmosphere that bathes gender relations toward the end of the Century of Light.

The central issue of eighteenth-century French culture, if we are obliged to choose one, revolves about the definitions of nature and of culture, their respective rights, and the determining of the most favorable valences between them. Social woman (in contradistinction to "natural" woman—of whom more will be said later), as the flagrant sign of the regnant culture, will be viewed by her most savage male critics as a triumph of cultural artifice, of appearance, as dazzling surface at best, as morally grotesque at worst. Note the report of Russian traveler Alexander Radischchev on French women in the cities: "On your cheeks there is rouge, on your heart rouge, on your conscience rouge, on your sincerity, soot."[6] Such a corrosive view reiterates consecrated male revulsion against female arts of self-adornment, so dreaded for their seductive power over men. Yet this is the very age celebrated as "the century of women" in which Frenchwomen were widely regarded as paragons of human cultivation—the female avant-garde of the world, for their freedoms and talents. Arthur Young observed that in France, women "though without virtue, are the masters and sovereigns [of their men]. . . . In all places and all times, the superiority of the females is readily acknowledged and submitted to by everyone, who has the least pretensions to education and politeness."[7] The rise of women in eighteenth-century society is confirmed by its century-long endurance and growth: yet in its very successes, it releases repressed anxieties and resentments over the freedoms and limits upon what was to be understood as masculine, what feminine, since it is the encounter between the sexes that sparks the incendiary vitality of this society.

La Pompadour

The person of the woman born with the decidedly plain-Jane name of Jeanne Poisson (or Fish), and who would become her own masterpiece, Louis XV's declared mistress par excellence Mme de Pompadour, provides a focus for some of the paradoxes of courtly femininity. To become mistress to the king was, in the eighteenth century, a summit of female ambition, consecrated in legend. The Pompadour herself reinforced the notion that this was her destiny by having Boucher depict, over and over, the scene of the fortune teller Mme Lebon's foreseeing in the hand of the nine-year-old Jeanne her fate as the king's companion. A final avatar of this scene (fig. 14), is the Beauvais tapestry of 1762, woven, after a cartoon by Boucher, by Cendre Charlemagne Charron. Mme Lebon's role in this myth was so vital that she was granted a pension through the offices of the grateful Pompadour.

Raised in the libertinage of the Regency, the king was reputedly interested solely in hunting and sex. But at least in his earlier years, the Well-Beloved could not truly have been said to have pronounced priapic tendencies. Only after the incompatibility of his union with the queen became evident, and after the birth of the required heir, did Louis turn decidedly to other women. Among them, an early favorite was the sort of lively tomboy, Mlle de Charolais, who did not become his mistress. Later he became enamored of the three de Nesle sisters. The first of these was Mme de Mailly, an individual of such a vivacious ugliness that she scandalized foreigners, who expected a king's mistress at least to have a pretty face, d'Argenson reported cattily. Her sister, the Duchess of Vintimille, was "a masculine type, large-limbed and ugly," while the third, Mme de la Tournelle, was

14. François Boucher and Cendre Charlemagne Charron, Tapestry, 1762, Mme Lebon Foretelling the Career of La Pompadour, *All rights reserved Metropolitan Museum of Art*

"tall and majestic, . . . with rather strong and regular features."[8] Not a rococo doll among them. In 1745, Mme de la Tournelle (Duchess of Chateauroux), the king's favorite immediately preceding the Pompadour, would become the target of public hatred when, in the midst of a sudden illness and fearing death, the king confessed his sins, begging forgiveness of the queen, Marie Leczinska, and of the ecclesiastical court for his disorderly life. While Louis, who persisted in living, was uneasily restored to sanctity, his "temptress" Mme de Chateauroux was showered with obloquy, avoided, called a slut. Falling ill that same year, she died at twenty-seven.

Her successor, Mlle Poisson, now become the young matron Mme d'Etioles, a bright and accomplished *bourgeoise,* through the prudent management and forethought of her family (she was planted to be seen by the king in her blue dress and pink carriage as he hunted close by her residence) easily found her mark. She arrived at the summit of power, becoming a marquise and the king's lover through that artful, civilized admixture of sexual and cultural lures that enabled women to express power drives "over" men. The rule massively was the obverse; but with the aid of culture, a Pompadour might sustain the illusion, through her activities and her graces, of woman regnant over a (weak) king.

Quentin de la Tour's portrait (fig. 15) presents us with that image she found most efficacious to her myth. In sensuous taffetas and laces, she is yet projected as a controlled and proper, rather than a seductive, figure, mistress over the many attributes she obviously wished to have associated with her personage: the violin and musical scores are piled in deliberate carelessness behind her, suggesting genuine use; the substantial leather-bound tomes beside her on the table, the title of one *Encyclopédie,* of another *The Spirit of Laws,* are again arranged slightly askew, to reinforce the conviction of her active literacy; the globe gives testimony to a wide curiosity; the musical score she fingers with her exquisitely graceful hand is another indicator of her musicality; the portfolio of prints on the floor beside her and the illustrative plate from the *Encyclopédie* hanging from the table merge with the general aura of textural luxuriance and mural decorativeness to bespeak Pompadour's love of visual art. The insistent seemliness of this figure, her willed neutrality of demeanor, her naturally alert readiness to smile and cajole, convey, however, a mild image of cultural advocacy, a sort of good-girl passivity and temperateness vis-à-vis these same implements of culture she ostensibly displays as her own. The only bit of turbulence in the image is nonetheless significant: it moves in the fold of her luminous skirt, outlining and testifying to the

15. Maurice Quentin de la Tour, Madame de Pompdour, *Musée du Louvre, Photo Musées Nationaux*

energy of her knees, and ending with the half-shod mule balanced on her toe:[9] the raised "stuck" portion of skirt, uncovering the petticoat, emphasizes this allusion to the sexual theater that the rest of the image downplays. This image thus tempers its identification of Pompadour with high culture by portraying her as its mutedly serene advocate, an amateur, not a creator, as it also slyly reminds us of the sexual route, the locus of her "real" power, that has led her to her high status.

As Pompadour, Jeanne Poisson conducted herself with an unbelievable tact and perspicacity, long providing the king with a trusted mate and counselor, mediating between him and artists and intellectuals, enhancing his reign with splendid architecture, paintings, sculptures, and porcelains, and acting as his accessory and agent in affairs both foreign and domestic. Her astounding public announcement in 1752 that she was no longer the king's mistress (her own sensuality is said to have found little satisfaction in the king's caresses) was a stroke of genius that fortified her political influence with Louis while freeing him to turn openly to his private Deerpark at Versailles, where he would keep young women sequestered for his use for a time before marrying them off with a pension.

Little given as he had been to libertinism as a young man, Louis was its enthusiastic practitioner as he grew older. Shades of the various published schemes for rationalized sex, there would be two to three occupants in his brothel at once, who were not allowed to communicate amongst themselves. Each occupant had her own chambermaid, lackey, and cook, while a manageress organized the household. The girls were allowed to go out to the Comédie, where they sat in a box with a grill. Although forbidden visitors, they were permitted to have whatever instructors they wished. The women thus used were selected carefully from the Paris brothels: the king tended over the years to younger and younger quarry, of fourteen or fifteen years of age, because it is said, he feared venereal infection. The monarch's visits were incognito; he posed as "a wealthy Polish nobleman": doubtless this was a mere pretense indulged by all involved.

The Deerpark features the tendency of the times to a carceral obsessiveness about sex in its prisonlike rigors of administration. Withal, in its encouragement of culture (play-going and lessons) on the part of the sequestered, it demonstrates the courtly identification of female sexuality with the veneer of cultivation. Even though they were no longer, as earlier, women of the court but lower-class persons, the king's sexual playmates had to be at least superficially acculturated to seem acceptable in bed. Like the fancified refinements of rococo art, cultivated forms and manners palliated the rawness of "natural" physical passion while adding a piquant suggestiveness in their contrast with it.

Still in the king's favor at the time of her death, Pompadour incurred the rage of many at court through her sometimes questionable influence upon him. Argenson would mutter in 1756, "More than ever was she the First Minister. She dominates the king as strong personalities dominate weak ones." At the same time, some of her most determined enemies admitted her abilities: the Duc de Croy saw her as having been born for the role she had been called upon to play in life.[10]

Amid a court rife with sexual and political intrigue, Pompadour, in suppressing curiosity over her own sexuality and in appearing to dominate herself, assumed a posture of eunuchoid impassivity and judiciousness.[11] "Everybody tells me they find Mme de Pompadour extremely polite. She is not nasty, she doesn't say unpleasant things about people, she doesn't even allow other people to do so. She is cheerful and likes to talk. Far from being proud, she continually refers to her family in the king's presence," wrote the Duke of Luynes.[12] That is to say that Pompadour brought the homelier values of her bourgeois background with her into the heart of court life: a courtly and cultivated "naturalness" expressed by a manner seemingly devoid of pretension, and a deeply politic ability to handle the most devious of courtiers, which she deployed in the service of a broad range of administrative functions. Pompadour was a beflowered and beflounced minister of the court, appreciated by many for her grasp of matters of state and of art. Voltaire was a particular admirer of her temperate and unmalicious conduct.

Yet among the philosophes Rousseau and Condillac could be unsparingly cruel in their remarks about this *parvenue* from their own class. And even Voltaire would vent his gallic misogyny in verse on the person of this woman, though on other levels of consciousness he was prepared to respect her as "that sincere and tender Pompadour."

> And thus we have this cheerful jade
> That nature joined with art hath made
> For bordello or opera
> But whom her crafty, sly mama
> Had raised for a tax-farmer's bed
> When Love himself with hand adroit
> Twixt monarch's sheets the jade he led.[13]

In seeming playfulness, Voltaire's doggerel brutally wipes away all of courtly society's protective sheen of aesthetic and cultural embellishment as it bares what it takes to be the sexual "reality" that undergirds Pompadour's status as favorite. Courtier that he is, he yet gives voice in this way to that nervous ambivalence concerning the source of social woman's power that afflicts in varying measure so large a proportion of the men of the time. What seems to eat at Voltaire is the usurpation inherent in the Pompadour's achievement of influence: she who lays claim to such refinement "really" operates as nothing but a common prostitute. Not a creature of culture at all, she has subdued the monarch through methods all too grossly natural. A potential Delilah, she manages a great man by stealth, by a calculated manipulation of his sexual vulnerability. Observe that, outside the princes of the Church, no one could with impunity blame the king for his sexuality: this being so, the full charge of a people's wrath against the tacit sanctioning of the privileges of the king and his class is reserved for the persons of royal mistresses, and failing that, of women of the upper classes, frequently presumed to be uniformly profligate.

Layered into this charge of resentment are deep contradictions about masculine and feminine roles in society and how these relate to sexuality. On the surface, Pompadour's sex seems not to preclude a social role because she adheres so exquisitely to every tenet of feminine practice prescribed by her society—except one: but that one undoes her entire structure. Her unauthorized exercise of political power and her seizure of the power of the purse was assimilated to her sexual power, somewhat erroneously, as it transpired, since the acme of her influence upon the king long outlasted their sexual union. The conflation in her person of sexuality with the assumption of otherwise unauthorized powers made her loom, in the spirits of some, and despite her apparently quintessential femininity, as a monstrous, masculinized figure. Reactions to Pompadour lay out to view the confusions surrounding gender: subjection to her charm and control emasculates the king, as their exercise masculinizes her. Too slavishly the creature of her culture, she yet manages to denature the male supremacist order of things by her own mastery over it. A hostile male response to her figure transcends her time; a twentieth-century observer can scarcely contain his outrage: "Womanish men bow their necks beneath the feet of mannish women on the model of Catherine, Maria Theresa, La Pompadour. Only sorrily do the downtrodden slaves revolt in sadistically wanton debauchery against their self-elected mistresses, and with a *raffiné* feminine sensual culture, woman erects the triumphant stele of her victory over man."[14] In such a perspective, all of the culture's moral depredations are attributed to these figures, its whole cultural system denounced for having allowed their emergence from anonymity.

In fact, the apoplectic, fascistic twentieth-century gallophobe Karl Toth would grasp, as a close reader rooting about for cultural scapegoats, some of the essential stakes in play in this figure: "For the Frenchwoman is the *man* of French civilization; masculine intelligence chills her passion, rouges her naturalness, forces its calculated way into social life and subtilized conduct, points her wit to a probing scalpel and bottles her vivacity."[15] Woman and culture constitute nothing but an oxymoron here. We divine that what makes it so is the connection with male desire. The problem seems to be that in the traditional male gender paradigm Frenchwomen's self-control, their critical subtlety, their intelligence even, exert a chill on male passion, despoiling it of free play. The Frenchwoman of eighteenth-century culture is understood by Toth to be ipso facto a sexual revolutionary. This enduring paradigm emerged in Pompadour's own era and served to uncouple women from the relatively intense participation in the life of the culture that they were indeed enjoying.

The Social Women and Their Powers

In Montesquieu's 1721 *Persian Letters* the Persian traveler Rica writes to Ibben back in Smyrna about life at the French court near the end of Louis XIV's reign.

"When I arrived in France, I found the late king absolutely governed by women, and yet at his age, I believe he was of all the monarchs on earth the one who needed them least." Rica listens to the conversations of women and observes with surprise that each has favorites suits she intends to press in aid of certain individuals, to obtain preference or a situation for them. At first Rica takes his example from the court, but he soon generalizes it to the nation at large:

> But the fact is that there is no one with any position at Court, in Paris or in the provinces, who doesn't have a woman through whose hands all the favors and sometimes the injustices that he may perform have to pass. These women all have relations amongst themselves and form a sort of republic whose ever-active members help and serve each other mutually; it's like a new State within a State; and whoever goes to Court, or to Paris or the provinces, and visits ministers, magistrates, and prelates in action, if he doesn't know the women who govern them, is like a man who sees a machine in movement, but has no idea of what makes it go. (107)[16]

Rica cautions Ibben not to be so gullible as to believe that a woman might become a man's mistress so as to have sex with him: no, she would only do so because she was determined to present him with five or six petitions every morning, and thus render "help" to others, who would then return the favor, enriching her. Rica ends on a note of smug Eastern male superiority. "People in Persia complain that the realm is governed by two or three women. It's far worse in France, where the women in general govern and not only take on the bulk of all authority, but even divide up its smallest parcels" (107).

These remarks, though carefully filtered by Montesquieu through Rica's patriarchal optic, convey in France to French men and women a sort of male bottom line of rejection of women's bossy interventions in men's affairs, which are displacing passion between the sexes, that is, women's dependent concentration on the love of men alone. A vast myth of female control, fueled by resentment, gains credence from Rica's repetition of this commonplace, never given the lie by another letter-writer here.

Usbek, another of our Persian correspondents, however, in a letter to Roxane, his sequestered favorite wife in Ispahan, fulminates quite differently against European women's painting themselves, their dress, "the care they take of their persons, which affronts virtue and insults their husbands" (26). *The Persian Letters* is primarily about the problematics of female constraint and freedom. Usbek admits to Roxane that in point of fact these women, painted and flirtatious as they are, are really less sexually abandoned than they seem. "They may pull loose from the external duties that modesty demands; but when it comes to taking the last step, their natures rebel." Surprisingly, even those provocative women have inner censors.[17] For Usbek, it is rather some incalculable quality of female desire that materializes into visibility in Frenchwomen's self-display.

Salon as Theater

The degree of the mixing of gender in French high society appears to be anomalous among European cultures.[18] Women in the salons, the scene of mixed gender, achieve a species of status in terms of social representation unparalleled before or since; but as we have already seen, this statement requires massive qualification. Certainly it was not as Rica claimed: women were not governing everything. Their legal position was poor, and their position in government non-existent. Although Elisabeth Badinter affirms, I believe justly, that women of the upper classes were respected and often had "a decisive and unprecedented influence on the course of things," Terry Eagleton, in speaking of England, cautions with equal justification that the meaning of women's prominence in this era must not be overestimated, but rather carefully assessed: "Male hegemony was merely to be sweetened in the eighteenth century by the participation of women in society, but by no means undermined." Roger Picard, earlier on, had also found the metaphor of the sweetener apposite: the French salon women were the sugar in the coffee of social life. To press this metaphor, the sweetener might materially alter the taste of the brew; it might even dominate its taste; but coffee it remained. The Duchess d'Abrantès, who was close enough to know, saw the ancien régime's social system as allowing women "a prestige and an influence that lent them the appearance of power, even if it was at bottom unreal."[19]

The fundamental fact remains that the eighteenth-century French salon was the stage of a social blend of female with male, a unique moment of human history during which a vital segment of public life combined the genders in such a way as to produce in both a heady charge of energy, a polymorphous delight. Salon life had of course inherited this on-paper parity from royalty's queens, princesses, and ladies-in-waiting; the female aristocracy had heritage, money, and influence to empower them in limited ways to strike bargains with its milieu. This bargaining power notwithstanding, it could not be said that there was any genuine male/female parity even in this institution. A salon hostess's male guests were her lions, outnumbering the women. She would have needed a capital of social standing, as well as a reasonable sum of money, to embark on the creation of her salon. In marked contrast with the sexual fate visited upon her, age, far from disabling her, lent her added authority. But this factor itself might generate male hostility. Although she certainly would have had to possess some variety of distinctiveness of mind or person to succeed, it was not required of her that she exhibit any deep cultivation. In the majority of cases, it was not expected that she dominate her company; rather, she was supposed to provide it with an alert medium and, with wit and tact, make herself the accomplice of men's self-regard by allowing each of them to say his piece effectively so that he would return home pleased with himself and prepared to return to her circle on another day. "Women both provided and structured the space—social and discursive—that was the salon, but men filled that space with their projects of enlightenment that would change the world through changing the common way of thinking," writes Dena Goodman. Of Mme Lambert's early eighteenth-century gatherings where aristocrats and writers would mix, d'Alembert would comment that "the latter would bring their knowledge and perceptiveness, the former that politeness and urbanity that even the meritorious must acquire. . . . The social set would come away more enlightened, the people of letters more amiable."[20] This was the effect their hostess sought. For some painfully gifted women like Mme du Deffand or Mme de Staël such an effaced role was not enough. Their seizure of a more aggressive role, whatever their personal gifts, might produce fierce criticism from others and inner torment in themselves.

Priestesses to the great, the salon women made of their living-rooms a species of leveling place, where scholars and youths, nobles and bourgeois, artists and foreigners, women and men, all might move beyond their narrower set and learn wider perspectives.[21]

In Charles-Antoine Coypel's portrait in pastel hues of the Marquise de Lamure (fig. 16) that lady is presented as in a loge, leaning gently against its balustrade. A muted but theatrical air lingers about her, emphasized by her emergence from the surrounding darkness and softened by the subtle palette chosen to depict her— the pink of iridescent silk next to luminous pale pink flesh so tender that it blends

16. *Charles-Antoine Coypel,* The Marquise de Lamure, *Worcester Art Museum, Worcester, Massachusetts*

into indistinctness from silk, velvet, pearl teardrops, languid buttons. Young as the sitter is, her colors endow her with an ageless cast. Powdered hair and lace mingle in airy but ordered confusion. The honeyed fur weaves in and out of the figure's major tonality as the burnished wood frame echoes and anchors its hue. The serenity of the hands expresses a poise that finds its echo in the directness of the sitter's glance, softened but not extinguished by her quarter-smile (a diminution of the Mona Lisa's). The glance is hooded, yet candid, conveying a subdued vivacity. The conceit of the portrait lies in its treatment of emergence from the loge/frame. The Marquise de Lamure's image offers itself even as, in its poise, it withholds, questions, perhaps mocks. Her personhood is tentative, yet distills some of the confidence of the woman sustained by birth and wealth. Mme de Lamure's is a fitting representation of social woman's paradox, that of a breaking through into subjectivity as an actor outside the frame, while remaining a sublimely desirable object.

Rococo Masquerades

Mythology informs the elite's rococo mode: Pompadour enacted Venus in plays of 1750; but her spectacular self-representations were only a few steps removed from the theatrics of the salon where, for the salon woman, an Olympian self-control was to prevail. Nothing, that is, was to be left to chance, yet all must seem perfectly spontaneous. Here, for example, is the Maréchale de Luxembourg, Rousseau's friend, described by Mme du Deffand: "Her gestures are so graceful, they are so natural and so attuned to what she says that it's hard not to be drawn into thinking and feeling as she does. She dominates wherever she goes and always makes precisely the impression she wishes to make." That double game of art calculatedly mimicking nature with wicked fidelity was, as in Diderot's *Paradox Concerning the Actor,* fully under Mme de Luxembourg's control.[22]

Theater invites spectators to watch actors: which are subjects; which are objects? In an obvious sense the actors are objects to the audience; but in its powerless, mute collectivity the audience acts only as a passive "subject," subjected, even subdued, by the actors' and the playwright's canny manipulations of its socially predetermined reactions. Yet off the stage, the actor is (socially) no one to reckon with, entirely outside the perimeters of power and influence: his or her fleeting power to subject is abrogated. As men performed in the salon, their representation within it perpetuated "naturally" their position of dominance in the society beyond: for them, there could be no "paradox of the actor." But women's self-representation in the salon posed precisely the actor's dilemma, with the exception that the salon leader would actually possess, not power to act alone, true subject status, but power to influence, to inflect, to alter and reshape the decisions of the holders of power. A further and highly potent factor here is that many men in this hierarchized elite world were little more powerful in any practical sense than the women, although the former's legal and consecrated status lent them the prestige of the upper class's masculinist tradition. Some of these men must inevitably have felt anger at the ability of the most adroit among the women of their class to effect, on occasion, what they could not. So the question of who is the subject, who object, is posed with an agonizing acuteness by the brilliance of salon women's representations.

This ambiguity of gender roles is reinforced by that retreat from clear sexual distinctiveness in dress previously alluded to. The history of gender is reflected in clothing, which alternates betweens waves of wide divergence in styles of sex marking to waves of close similarity. The French eighteenth century's stylish upper-class men ape the trappings of cultural femaleness: men wear only less exaggerated hip padding (*basques*) than women's generous wicker *paniers;* both go about clad in satins and laces and wear abundant artificial hair closer to the natural abundance of the female's than to the male's; and men entirely abandon facial hair, preferring to cultivate rosy, perfumed visages: indeed they did not stop at faces.[23] Like women, a number of men of the time might call aggressively upon pots of paint to stay or mitigate the ravages of time, like the Chevalier d'Arginy in his eighties, decked out in his beflowered breeches, his rouge, his pomaded wig, his eyebrows outlined in brown, his perfumes, his dentures.[24] Like his numerous female opposite numbers, the Chevalier represents the apogee of elite French culture's narcissistic fetishizing of the self.

Silvana Tomaselli attempts to encapsulate the situation of women vis-à-vis culture: "At the level of the real, women partake in and shape culture, but at the level of the symbolic or the imaginary, they are excluded from it and represented as belonging to the outside realm of the natural."[25] Tomaselli rightly affirms women's hold on the "real"—and this is the segment of their story that history in general has so painstakingly buried. But the ringing clarity of this formulation somewhat drowns out the dissonances and undertones of women's situation. Their problem arises precisely out of male culture's systemic antipathy to viewing their sex in any but the symbolic mode. Culture itself being largely imaginary, women enter the high culture that has been men's domain by correcting, editing, restating in ever more fundamental terms paradigms that have been basically conceived by men. When they move from segregation to integration into this world, women come bearing the ancient male-generated symbolic baggage defining them as temptresses, nurturers, or hags. These images they carry with them, even into their cultural work. Whether they saw themselves in this light or not—and not many did—the modes of cultural reception have generally painted them back into this framework. Culture then becomes the precondition of what may or may not occur in "reality."

Since nurturance per se is brutally rejected by rococo mores, women's representation in salon culture careens wildly to the side of the polymorphous tease whose whole person—her dress, her manners, her speech—bespeaks a generalized seductiveness; or, failing that, she may be assimilated to the category of the rejected or superannuated hag. Behavior patterns between the sexes—dress, gestures, language—take on forms intensely fetishized, attaching themselves to elaborate cultural signs. Manners so arch, so androgynous, then carry an electric, theatrical, seductive charge.

On this imaginary stage of gender parity—as in the theater itself, where women were allowed to enact something like the powerful, occasionally even preponderant, roles they but seldom played in the unequal world around them—the conceit is the old courtly one: culture is conducted under women's aegis, and taste is conducted to suit her presumed desire. The *petit-maître* or fop presumably imitates female graces so as to seduce: but as a member of a futile class, he finds himself idle and disempowered, akin to the other sex. In this rapprochement between the genders indulged in by the upper class, a strong vein of male narcissism, largely repressed in other cultural settings, emerges, expressing an envious seizure of the female's preeminent right to self-display in culture. Such a style of being as this authorizes male release into verbal expressiveness, as well as a flaunting of physical attractions. Society's theater comes to life in the forms of a heterosexual (and homosexual) play-acting, which paradoxically produces, from the female point of view, a new energy and drive. But what from the male side may have been intended only as a scene of enhanced sexual opportunity also enables women to assume at moments the stance of actual and vigorous predators. This was a right of which, despite their mimicry of indifference, the men were at bottom to prove jealous.

Desiring Women

There are roughly three stages in the life of the eighteenth-century salon, foreshadowed, though not slavishly, by its art. The first, that of the Regency, is usually thought of as combining sexual freedom with controlled, "classical" social forms of interaction. The second, the age of high rococo, freezes these modes into a sort of brittle lifelessness that begins the process of reaction. The first two stages are thoroughly theatrical; whereas the third stage, that of breakdown, will be riven, like Molière's Alceste's heart, by the issue of sincerity and the obsession with "naturalness."

The connection made between Montesquieu's seraglio and the salon invites me to speculate as to how the problematics of sexual energy in the salon might have operated upon the cultural relations between the genders.[26] In the salon itself, as I will explore it, an ideal of what some have seen as a species of eunuchoid mildness is imposed upon the comportment of men. As compared with the men of the surrounding culture, this represents a sublimation of desire into the chiefly verbal realms of flirtation and intellectuality. Hence the *Persian Letters'* obsession with continence and sexual expression. Of course culture itself, as Freud's illuminations have revealed, *means* sexual repression. Repression withdraws libido from circulation. But how can we speak of repression in this era and among this set where sexual venturesomeness appeared to be so free and so flagrant? Even the freest of cultures must be repressive, displacing raw sexual appetite to other levels of consciousness, or impressing it into alien-seeming forms. Freud's thesis, which applies so thoroughly to the eighteenth-century French case that he might have been addressing it, is specifically that "some obstacle is necessary to swell the tide of the libido at its height, and in all periods of history, whenever natural barriers in the way of satisfaction have not sufficed, mankind has erected conventional ones in order to enjoy love. This is true both of individuals and of nations. In times during which no obstacles to sexual satisfaction existed . . . love became worthless, life became empty, and strong reaction formations were necessary before the indispensable emotion value of love could be restored."[27] Salon society was certainly one such setting, where "natural barriers" to sexuality had lost much of their force.

Freud's discussion is limited by his refusal to distinguish between the differences in form and consequences between male and female desire. Libido may indeed be a free, cross-gendered energy, but the ability to claim it as one's own or give expression to it is massively skewed by gender politics, different everywhere for women and men in terms of their power differentials. While exploring how feelings of respect for women can inhibit male desire, Freud engages in no mediation on the implications of this psychological trend for women's cultural or sexual lives.[28] In the heterosexual world, such reflection would involve a rethinking of masculine sexuality as well. The "indispensable emotional value of love" must be hopelessly compromised by the excessive projection by the male gender upon women of attributes inimical to culture as a whole.

In a fiction within the fiction of *The Persian Letters,* Montesquieu, that familiar of Mme de Lambert's salon, processes in a folkloric vein the ancient male anxiety over female sexual insatiability. We may read this myth as intriguing its author in its retranslation of the conundrum of this age of the salon and the brothel, of women's near-reciprocal ability to command men's sexual favors in the one setting, and their status as sexual chattel in the other. A dream-story (letter 141) recorded by Rica is related by Zulema, a woman learned in the holy Koran. Its subject is whether Paradise is as favorable to men as this life is, and it begins with a violent revenge on the part of a man named Ibrahim against one of his wives for daring to complain of the tyranny under which she lives: in fury, he plunges a knife into her heart. With her dying breath, she calls for vengeance on behalf of her sisters of the seraglio. She is translated to Paradise, where all her senses are pampered with scents and music and two men are placed at her sexual disposal. So sated is she that she begs them to release her: "I'm dying from the violence of my pleasure." A prurient tour de force, this tale gives the masculine part of its audience the thrill and terror of glimpsing what a woman's natural, unfettered sex drive might be like. But then, as her senses are fulfilled, the wife turns meditative. Pondering her past wretchedness and that of her companions as contrasted with her present fulfillment, she resolves to act on their behalf. And so she sends one of her young lovers in the guise of her husband Ibrahim back to avenge her, a task which he accomplishes easily by virtue of his nonviolent, loverlike procedures. All Ibrahim's wives prefer the gentle false Ibrahim to the brutal real one, who stalks off in a rage, since sexual jealousy no longer has power over his household and his women are freed even from the veil.

This tale begins by playing with the idea of a freed female sexuality as heavenly reward for sexual injustice and disempowerment here below. The wife, freed by her power over her own sexuality, is fleetingly lent the ability to wreak vengeance on her murderous tyrant. But the tale ends with the benign, liberal tyranny of the false Ibrahim who institutes a new kind of harem, founded on his endowments as a good lover. Male sexuality is restored as the policing mechanism of social order. But the uneasy dialectic between the control of female passion by force or by self-control in the overall narrative is undercut and momentarily exploded by this dream of female passion freed, which dovetails with the subsequent "real" revolt of Roxane and the harem. After taking a lover of her own choice, Roxane imbibes poison and writes to her absent husband, "How could you have thought me so credulous as to believe that I was put in the world only to adore your caprices? That while you allow yourself everything, you could maintain the right to strike down my desires? No, I've been able to live in servitude, but I've always been free; I've reformulated your laws to meet Nature's, and my spirit has remained independent." Rather than love, Roxane has felt in Usbek's arms only a violent hatred, and she has found her sole violent joy in deceiving him (141). Nature, Roxane claims as would Freud, is parent to her passions as much as to Usbek's. She appeals to nature to redeem her rights.

In granting her the last word, Montesquieu seems to endorse her claim and the courage he has lent her in making it. Western culture, in a lesser degree to that of the East but still on a continuum of male supremacism with it, denied women's autonomy of desire. In so doing, it sapped the potential of sexuality to contribute to human happiness.

The Man of the Salon—Minimalism in the Pursuit of Happiness

The question now arises, how is happiness conceived of in the salon ethos? This is how one celebrated exploration characterizes it:

Happiness is only a timid efflorescence that has to be preserved in its fragility. It's merely a question of deciding on the minimal sense of the word and taking whatever reality it evokes at floor level, so to speak. Most often, such definitions are accompanied by a latent pessimism and a slightly forced smile: happiness is that frail margin won over a universal void and universal suffering.

Happiness, then, is but a small capital, permitting no lavish expenditures of passionate outburst or commitment; we might say, as would eventually be said by
critics of rococo mores, that this feeble notion entails no natural impulse. In fact,
this largely negative definition strongly suggests something like Usbek's passion-
less, eunuchlike state of repression and affectlessness, of *anomie*.[29]

In Mme du Deffand's description of her dear friend Jean-Baptiste Formont we
better grasp in all its contradictions the play of expression and repression in the
person she viewed as embodying the ideal of the civilized salon man.

> The facial expressions of M. Formont in no way announce what he is like; his
> face is cold, his demeanor indolent; yet he is easy and quick of wit, and has a
> gay and lively imagination.
>   This contrast of expression with wit is rarely met with, but nevertheless can
> easily be explained. Wit alone devoid of passion has not sufficient warmth to
> pierce, penetrate or make its imprint on our external organs. Neither M. de
> Fontenelle nor M. Formont are passionate beings, but M. Formont has a core of
> goodness that compensates his friends for all the sentiment he lacks. One does
> not feel needed by him, but once he believes he is needed, he fulfills all the
> duties of a friend, he actually takes the interest and has the feelings one needs
> him to have; the need once passed, he falls back into his indifference and he'll
> stay there for a long time unless someone thinks of drawing him out of it; but
> his goodness is ever at the ready and takes on all the forms one might want; I
> would dare say that it even takes on the aspect of love at times. If his senses are
> moved by some object or other, it is by a gentle, peaceful emotion; he desires,
> but without insistence or ardor, well removed from brazenness or jealousy; his
> own taste is subordinated to that of the other; if he sees he's no longer in favor,
> he ceases to make demands. Without vanity, without ambition, without love, I
> might almost say without friendship, he passes his days in a laziness and a sloth
> which render him quite independent of the opinions of men.

As to his behavior in the salon,

> Society is nothing but a spectacle for him in which he believes he takes no
> personal interest; that accounts for his timidity with very important persons and
> new acquaintances; he doesn't believe himself to be on stage, but rather in the
> audience or in the loges; it's not, however, that he's not participating in the play:
> he warms up and becomes animated when the conversation pleases him and he
> brings to it an appropriateness, gaiety and lightness of tone that make him one
> of the best companions. But once this moment passes, he becomes a spectator
> once more, stretches out in his armchair, resumes his dreamy and distracted
> look and takes no notice that with his inattentiveness he sometimes wounds
> those he's just pleased so much with the attractions of his wit.
>   No one is more virtuous than he or is of more relaxed mores; he excuses
> everything, forgives everything, his gentleness and tranquillity are inalterable.
> M. Formont is the model of the philosophic man and the image of the true
> friend.[30]

The hallmark of M. Formont's comportment seems to be, in this *portrait,* his basic, good-natured, controlled passivity. Though he can be stirred out of it, he lacks—or dams back—the active desire to make a gesture on his own initiative. Desiring sex itself only "without insistence or ardor," he quite lacks any sign either of "conviction" or of "passionate intensity," to cite Yeats.[31] This aura of coolness of his, which might seem at first to be at odds with the libertine climate in which he lives, is of course its precondition. Love is not a violent commotion, but a "gentle, peaceful emotion," which never must stir him overmuch but, like conversational wit, may have the ability to make him fleetingly "happy," that is, neither bored nor troubled, but amused, satiated.

Now, can this neutral state of living as if on ice, so at odds with ancient and consecrated conceptions of imperative masculinity, be attributed to the "reign of women," as the antirococo party tended to believe? Even Freud, taking an analogous tack, tries to "account for" male sexual bafflement before the women men respect: he does so by postulating that they may feel the need to degrade the feared mother so as to make her a fit "object for sensual desires." Is Formont, this "model of the philosophic man," so emotionally stalemated because the women he confronts as sexual partners from his own class fill him with apprehension? Certainly, a horde of unproblematic sexual partners was ready at hand to service his desire. But in a sense, in the ambiance if not the reality of Christian seemliness imposed upon public life, all sexuality was problematized, men's only less than women's, as the historian Flandrin argues.[32]

Men share with women, in salon society, the tortures of a fascinating limbo, of living in a eunuchoid, work-free aristocratic void, without ultimately making connections of any depth. Both sexes of the privileged classes share the sense of aimlessness of all courtiers not at war. Their ostensible aim—that of pleasing others—will be seen as demeaning and emasculating (by Rousseau among others) to men, but as women's full-time charge. Consequently, we find that both genders, in consenting to live so insistently in each other's company, undergo a degree of repression of their polymorphous libidinal vitality. Their crust of impassivity, their mores of fear, shield them from their own needs for engagement in experience, in work, society, family, their own sexuality.

Delon notes the philosophes' critique, shared by Voltaire and Montesquieu in the *Philosophical Dictionary* and *The Persian Letters,* of this notion: "Continence and avarice are equivalent. The eunuch is he who permits society to profit neither from his progeny nor by his investment." The philosophes' school sought a restoration of pleasure through profit, trusting that by putting into circulation more children and more money, history might progress rather than remain in its eunuchoid state.[33] Thus did the bourgeois intellectuals interpret the prevailing anomie, perceiving the sum of seminal fluid as a monetary fund. But their reading of the mores as a metaphor for the withholding of precious sexual and economic substance was far too schematic and mechanical. Of course, fear of dispersing precious inheritances conditions and impedes spontaneous circulation, both economic and sexual; but the affective repressiveness we witness here did not impede fluidity in sexual arrangements. On every side, what even the most privileged know best and fear most is abandonment, betrayal:[34] it is the withholding of commitment, its buying and selling, that makes all mistrustful of it. An emotional continence like Formont's cannot be precisely equated with avarice, although he spent emotion meagerly, as a precious quantity: for Formont, trust is so rare as to be perceived as a bankable asset, to be expended only with care and in reluctant melancholy.

Marquise

Such melancholy as Marie de Vichy-Champrond, the Marquise du Deffand, found so sympathetic in Formont was at least equally a quality of her own. Born into the old nobility, her family's origins were traceable back to the year 1000. But as was all too common, the financial fortunes of this illustrious clan had dimmed considerably over the centuries. Her own family's treatment of its children fell rigorously into the prescribed norms, and Marie was sent by her father to an elegant Paris convent that was decreed as the place of choice for girls of her class to be educated. Many years later she would inveigh against this mode of educating women: I quote her statement at length for the lucid precision of its cry of outrage against her own total unpreparedness for the experiences that would confront her. She is speaking of young girls like herself.

> Exiled . . . from the paternal home from birth, they are raised in religious houses where—and this is the least destructive thing that can be said of them—[the girls] receive no accurate idea of their state, nor of their duties, nor of honor, nor of decency, nor of society, nor of any of the situations they must meet with afterwards, and for which one must be prepared if one is to avoid their perils. Morality in women is based entirely upon arbitrary principle, their honor is not true honor; their decency is a false decency, and their whole merit, all the propriety of their state is constructed out of dissimulation and the misrepresentation of their natural feelings that a chimeric duty demands they subdue, but which, for all their efforts, they can never destroy. Imbued with such principles, on emerging from the convent they find themselves in the arms of an unknown man to whom they discover destiny has bound them with eternal and indissoluble ties. This is how, through the tyranny of our customs, marriage's gentle and sacred duties become outrages against a sense of decency; and the victim is immolated to the desires of a man who, armed with marriage rights, tears away the veil that propriety and the delicacy and finesse of tender and respectful love should have commanded him to put aside by slow stages and with timid diffidence. At that point the tumult of desire and the uncertainty about principles become equally great. Thrown into a world of whose dangers she knows noth-

ing, who will this girl, abandoned to herself, obey, given over as she is to a man who demands as her duty what her heart could grant only to a submissive lover capable of making it feel something? How can she find a way of distinguishing the essence of virtue from the precepts in those fairy tales of imaginary duties that cradled her in childhood? As she is made aware of their futility, will she not risk extending the scorn they deserve to even the most indispensable of virtues? By dint of having felt these virtues as shackles, she will then know no limits; and in equating real duties with arbitrary practices, . . . she'll find herself lost before she's even had her first sensible thought.[35]

The split between blind natural instincts and equally blind cultural imperatives baffles even the most "sophisticated" of the young women. The society's will to blind her, particularly, would have it so: a culture unable to cope with sexuality tells her, its mere object, nothing. It is then revolted by her resort to the use of the sexuality she has been brutally initiated into, by her use of her intelligence in subterfuges that express scorn of established morality. But it is noteworthy that, writing in 1756, the marquise already contrasts her past profligate morals with an idealized conception of domestic morality. She does so in the context of what she sees as the young married woman's own sexual right of consent and of "decent" sexual approach that would take into account her personal dignity. In making the generalization that this was in short supply, she understands the vitiation of women's devotion to the proclaimed moral code as arising from their hypocritical sexual treatment. Would she thus implicitly impose an "unnatural" demand upon male sexuality?

The other undercurrent of the marquise's remarks returns us to the issue of abandonment. This culture rips the child from her family, abandons her to the care of nuns ignorant of or concealing all she needs to learn, and delivers her without her consent literally into the hands of a stranger. At this point she realizes that she will be forever alone. If such is the perceived fate of one of the most privileged among Frenchwomen, what can we say of the rest?

Marie de Vichy-Champrond's life, even in its most skeletal outline, and despite the brilliance of her success in the salon, bears out this scenario of moral disaffection. Married in 1718 at eighteen to her distant cousin the Marquis de la Lande, she entered the most exalted circle in France, that of the regent, the Duke d'Orléans. The marriage that liberated her from convent and family was, in the event, to a man ill calculated to please her, a homebody whose young wife's appetite for stimulation and amusement met with no answering eagerness for social interchange in him. Her first lover was to be Regent Philippe d'Orléans himself, in a liaison that, according to her, lasted two entire weeks but in 1722 obtained for her an income of 6,000 pounds. Until his death in 1723, she remained part of his circle of intimates, the original *roués*.[36]

Some conception of the regent's pleasures comes from the Duke de Richelieu, his playmate. After a card game, the regent decided to get the ladies tipsy to see how they would act: himself becoming inebriated, he sang bawdy songs accompanied by lewd gestures at the women, all the men joining in. Then lights were lowered for a magic lantern show, as each man grabbed a woman. When Richelieu made his own play, he consistently found other hands in the way of his own.[37] What the marquise experienced in the regent's company was not verbal intercourse.

In the wake of the regent's demise, the marquise, legally separated from her husband without much financial security, threw herself into affair after affair and altogether compromised her reputation with a public opinion whose discourse on matters sexual rigorously parroted the Catholic bienséances in its pitilessness toward female adventurousness. In the end, she found a suitable *amant en titre,* Hénault, a rich, unattached widower and magistrate who bore the honorific of president. Gracious and successful among women, Hénault was the author of verse and of a mediocre history of France. The choice of Hénault enabled Mme du Deffand to continue her worldly life assisted by a man as avid for society and public approval as herself. Both were attached to the fabled court at Sceaux presided over by the Duchess du Maine, but this court would eventually give way as the center of aristocratic social life to the literary salon of Mme de Lambert. And it was there that literati and aristocrats would mix for the first time in a setting devoid of court etiquette.

Conversation

Duclos would remark that "in Paris, the mores accomplish what the spirit of government achieves in London: they blend together the ranks of society and equalize those classes that are separate and subordinated in the state."[38] The medium of this interchange is brilliant conversation: but irremediably lost to us as it is, few have been able to approach describing its magic adequately.

When Mme du Deffand started her own salon in 1747, her distinguished predecessor Mme de Lambert had been dead for fourteen years. She had been followed as a leader of society by Mme de Tencin, who, like Mme du Deffand, had begun her career with sexual adventures, forsaking the convent to which she had been consigned for the social vortex. The illegitimate infant Tencin had abandoned, having him placed on the steps of the church of Saint-John-the-Round, would become the celebrated mathematician and Encyclopedist Jean-le-Rond d'Alembert. Mme de Tencin's salon, at least as Marmontel would report it, was rather more like a men's billiard club than a gathering led by its mistress, even though all acknowledged her high intelligence and distinguished simplicity of manner. Mme de Tencin's successor and Mme du Deffand's great rival, who held court during the same era, was the bourgeoise Mme Geoffrin, host to the Encyclopedists' circle.

The salon can be viewed most fruitfully as a privileged space to which a hostess invites a company to game, eat, listen to music, and, primarily, converse. Though this space is her territory, in order to endow it with her own character, she has to provide a stable of men as its predicate, lending their authority to her gathering. Will the salon be brilliant and cynical (du Deffand), brilliant and philosophical (Geoffrin), passionate and philosophical (Lespinasse), morally earnest and philosophical (Necker), or passionate and political (Staël)? Those men become participants in each circle who enhance the salon woman's tastes and predispositions. The fact that the space is hers materially modifies the comportment of the assembled company: once the gentle Mme d'Holbach had taken refuge in a convent, her formerly seemly and civil salon became a blasphematory and salacious place.[39]

To Mme du Deffand's salon came some of the most distinguished women, as well as men, of the era. Among these was that extraordinary figure Madeleine-Angélique de Neufville-Villeroy, widow of the Duke de Boufflers, who would in 1750 wed her longtime lover, the Duke de Luxembourg. Following the pattern of Mmes de Tencin and du Deffand, this duchess not only had had an impressive libertine past but, like the others yet reputedly more so, cultivated not solely the graces, but the arts of nastiness. An example of this last was her treatment of her husband's gravely ill daughter, whom she accepted into her home under sufferance and mistreated, loudly announcing to all as she entered the sickroom of the dying, tubercular young woman that she couldn't stand the stench, that the reek of cadaverous flesh was suffocating her. A determined verbal acidulousness of course then characterized much of worldly discourse, but issuing from the lips of women, this mode becomes "bitchiness," a resolute turning away on the part of a woman from her pose of utter goodness, her maternal guise. In the apocryphal story of Mme du Luxembourg, the choice of an incident to relate from no doubt a larger number falls precisely in the domain of nursing the dying, so that the duchess's "unfeminine" aridity of heart (which in a man would not seem "unmasculine," but "inhuman,") should seem all the more scandalous. This arrogation by women of the privileges of public nastiness, begun in the seventeenth century, was well developed by eighteenth-century society. Yet like Mme du Deffand, Mme de Luxembourg was to become in her older age the most highly esteemed model of aristocratic comportment of her time (she lived until 1787). By her eighties, she was the absolute arbiter of taste, even among the skeptical young. Rousseau himself, suspicious of her reputation as the immoral Mme de Boufflers, let himself be utterly enchanted by her. "Scarcely had I seen her when I was subjugated. . . . I had expected to find her conversation mordant and full of epigrams. It wasn't like that at all, but much better. [It] doesn't bubble with wit. . . . It's of an exquisite delicacy that never seems odd and is always pleasing. Her flattery is all the more heady for its being so simple; it seems to escape from her without conscious thought, as though her heart were spilling over only because it was overfull."[40]

The earlier brashness had been a phase, productive of higher skills, of more encompassing perspectives, of richer talent, later in life. Mme du Deffand's own portrait of Mme de Luxembourg presents her as a far more imposing, less melting figure than Rousseau's: "She is so discerning as to make people tremble. She feels and passes judgment on the smallest bit of pretension, the slightest affectation, with the greatest possible severity; the fineness of her mind and the exquisiteness of her taste allow nothing to escape her." Withal, though feared for her formidable correctness, she had wit and gaiety of mien and constancy in friendship.[41]

The salon's aristocratic leaders before the 1760s, Tencin, Luxembourg, and Deffand, all survived rocky sexual experiences to arrive at maturity as respected, even revered women. Disabused early on, they became capable of a ruthless vindictiveness toward others. While they enjoyed their own sexual freedom, their reputations suffered, but, because of their high social station, not beyond recall. What is striking about this group of intellectually brilliant, sexually experienced women is their pronounced lack of sentimentality—not that they could not be sentimental, to a pet, for example, but that their code demanded that they know how to protect themselves first, since institutions and family structures could be counted on neither to respect nor to protect them. A deep acquaintance with the harshness of life seems to have stimulated their minds to develop that fruitful cynicism that made them natural allies of the social critics.

That the word *simplicity* endlessly recurs in the description of the refined manners of both sexes of this set, which we have come to think of as one of the most artificial societies in human history, forces us to wonder what can be meant by it. Here is some of Forcalquier's description of Mme du Deffand at forty: Mme Marquise "has liveliness and wit in her facial expressions, an agreeable laugh, charming eyes; all the fluctuations of her soul manage to be depicted on her visage; pleasure, boredom, wit, even to the smallest alteration in her feelings. Anyone could read her views before hearing them pronounced; and one never has to wait for her reaction, because of that total openness in her which makes for the charm and may perhaps be counted as the blemish in her character. It's impossible to have more wit than she has; it's so hard even to have as much as she, that I would place her above anyone I know, if only she might never see this portrait."[42]

Mme du Deffand positively shone with a personal brilliance far too great to allow her merely to second the self-expression of her guests, as did some of the other salon women. She was like quicksilver. M. du Chatel wrote to her in praise of her speech, "What variegation, what contrasts of feeling, of character and in modes of thinking you display! What simplicity, strength and aptness you have, even when you lose your train of thought! Nothing is lacking in it; it's enough to make one go mad with pleasure, impatience, and admiration. You are a priceless treasure to any *philosophic* [thoughtful] spectator."[43] Leading her own salon liberated Mme du Deffand to be as eloquent as she was capable of being: and to her self-display, so free and vivacious, her speech, so full of unexpected turns of mood and fresh ideas, her voice, so richly modulated in tone, people responded with an astonishment verging on adoration. She was an unparalleled intellectual performer: but her art was natural in the sense that it was unforced, a genuine improvisation coming from such pronounced verbal and intellectual gifts that it needed no props.

For contemporaries her chief flaw lay in her vehemence in expressing her opinions, that crack out of which her impotence to act seeped, causing anxiety in her hearers. In the "ideal speech situation," it has been suggested, "speech or discursive reflection is undominated, uncoerced, unmanipulated."[44] Descriptions of the marquise's conversation convey the impression of an astonishing approximation to this ideal, unprecedented in terms of female experience. It testifies to the unwonted flights of freedom of speech women achieved in these circles, which seems, paradoxically, to have been both authorized and yet limited by the speaker's ability to manipulate to her own ends the bienséances and the prevailing style of social rhetoric.

According to Craveri, du Deffand's cult of "naturalness" was the remnant of her classical background. "For her, as for her contemporaries, the natural is essentially a question of style, and artifice a failure of execution. But the style she chose is sober, concise, rapid, hard and cutting as crystal if compared with the fragile rococo porcelain." The marquise's unrelenting justness and effortlessness of tone would be parodied by others who could only imitate such style of polymorphous subtlety as hers, with premeditation. Thus Chamfort would report having seen in salons "the most elaborately thought-out calculations offered up with the apparent naiveté of a total, thoughtless unselfconsciousness."[45] Such trumped-up naturalness, akin to the fraudulent "lines" of sexual seduction that counterfeit love, disguising sexual impulse as a deeper form of longing, were anathema to du Deffand as to other persons of sensibility.

It is for good reason that the salon's conversation cannot be recaptured fully: it mimicked the free play of desire on the plane of the mind, with verbal balls flung wildly, only to be magically retrieved on the fingertips. Among these exchanges would come masterpieces of human contact, felicitous meetings of mind, explosions of the laughter of instantaneous mutual comprehension. Those devoid of the reflexes and skills of articulation needed to play this game (like Rousseau) could see it as being as unnatural an activity as a game of tennis would be to anyone without any spring in the knees. But though there is no way of dissembling in tennis, in social intercourse successful verbal forms have a tendency to become overimitated, and thus they die, are in fact long dead before their users become aware of their demise.

Mme du Deffand's reaction to the cheapening of rococo manners was to become brusque, outspoken, brutally truthful, so as to break up the mass of cobwebs gathering about social intercourse, making it airless and unfree. And this, says Craveri, is what made the determinedly candid d'Alembert so appealing to Mme du Deffand.

Bourgeois versus Rococo: the Lion, the Niece, and the Marquise

One of the two great dramas of the marquise's life, her relationship with d'Alembert and Julie de Lespinasse, would be characterized by the gap between the professed Christian sexual codes entrenched in the social forms, and the flagrant disregard displayed toward them in this segment of society.[46] D'Alembert, the natural son of Alexandrine de Tencin and a handsome artillery officer, Destouches, was a rising young man extraordinarily gifted in the sciences, living in relative poverty when the marquise first sought him out. Understandably scornful of aristocratic pretension, his posture toward the society where he would soon be enthroned as lion was adversarial. From du Deffand's portrait of him we perceive both the genesis of his own disregard for social hierarchy and the marquise's astonishing ability to identify with it: it exudes a species of pre-Revolutionary *ressentiment* in which the core issue of birthright emerges with a brilliant clarity:

> No one in his youth bothered to cultivate his mind or develop his character. The first thing he learned in beginning to think was that he owed nothing to anyone. He was at first consoled for this abandonment by the independence that resulted from it; but as he better understood it, he sought within himself some recourse against his misfortune. He told himself he was a child of nature, that he had to consult only her and obey only her . . . ; that his rank, his entitlement to the universe lay in his being a man; that nothing was above or below him; that only virtue and vice, talent and stupidity merit respect or scorn, that liberty was the real treasure of the sage; that one could always remain master over acquiring or enjoying it by avoiding the passions as well as all the occasions that might bring them to birth.[47]

In this all-but-closed social circle of birth privilege he had entered, nature alone could be appealed to as clement mother by this proud natural son, whose sense of injury takes refuge in the introversion of his passions. Like M. Formont, he puts them on ice, with the difference that d'Alembert, in the new bourgeois spirit, hopes thereby to cultivate a watchful virtue.

The marquise's abject admiration, her near-love for such a man lays open her dependence upon male genius to sustain, complement, and partner her own. Her espousal of the mode of being of this antiaristocrat was not an endorsement of his ideas, but rather of his rebellious psychological response to society: as du Deffand's comments on her convent education show, through her own disorienting experience of abandonment by a hypocritical system, she had herself acquired a revulsion against cant resembling d'Alembert's, and his greater aggressiveness (as a man and an illegitimate child) in expressing his scorn was tonic to her. Her enthusiasm for him remained permanently undimmed, and throughout their connection, she used all her considerable powers of persuasion in furthering his objectives, including his suit for a chair in the French Academy.

Growing blind from the age of fifty, the marquise found the need to resort to the expedient of a live-in companion to enable her to continue her Parisian existence. Her choice would fall upon Julie de Lespinasse, usually described simply as her niece. Such an allusion fails altogether to reflect the complexities of Julie's family background. Julie was the illegitimate daughter of Julie d'Albon, a married woman and member of a distinguished lineage. Long separated from her husband, Mme d'Albon had two extramarital children, a son, raised secretly in a convent, and then Julie. Unlike her less fortunate brother, Julie was recognized by her mother, allowed to grow up in her house, and given a family name. Her father was nowhere in sight; but seven years later he made a theatrical reappearance, not as Julie's parent, but as the new husband of Julie's half-sister, Mme d'Albon's own legitimate daughter. In terror that her beloved child might be disinherited, Mme d'Albon fawned over Julie and gave her a distinguished education. Julie's father, Mme du Deffand's older brother, Gaspard de Vichy, showed no loyalty to his bastard daughter, but only to his legitimate offspring. Yet he kept Julie in his household after her mother's death, at which time she learned the secret of her birth. As governess in the Vichy household, she lived as a Cinderella whose presence was a threat to the family. Sensitive, proud, and wretched, she prepared herself inwardly to escape by taking the veil. It was at this point that her aunt appeared, ready, not out of compassion exactly, but for her own reasons, to take this gifted girl with her to Paris.[48]

There Julie's youthful animation and sagacity would slowly transform her aging aunt's salon into one of her own. But as long as they were united, their combined milieu was the spirited apogee of the eighteenth century's salon life. The contrast, similar to the one between the disabused yet gracious wit of the aunt, obsessed with society yet scornful of it, and the passionate commitment, come what may, of her niece to life and to love, was noted by Sainte-Beuve when he spoke of the difference between the women who came before Rousseau and those who came after. A further salient difference between them was that unlike the marquise, the female performer, Julie's art lay in her intent listening, in putting others at ease. Even possessed as she was of great discernment, she would never put herself forward. D'Alembert praised above all her art of saying to others exactly what they were pleased to hear, of speaking little of herself, much of her interlocutors.[49] But for the salon woman self-effacement bore other perils than those incurred by self-display: her excessive adaptability to others might enslave her emotionally to her mania to please.

In historical retrospect, it is all too obvious why Julie and the bearish d'Alembert should have been so drawn to each other. As Marmontel would put it: "They were both what we call children of love." D'Alembert would have no emotional qualms about abandoning the blind and aging marquise for her meltingly impassioned niece. The older woman's love for him was stronger by far than his feeling for this caustic aristocrat. Craveri stresses Julie's overwhelming need for love, a need that the tired-hearted marquise was in no way able to offer her. Julie felt mistreated, enslaved—and probably cheated—by her aunt's relentless demands upon her. The triangular chase was intensified as d'Alembert accused du Deffand of siding with Palissot, the satirist of *The Philosophes,* and of mocking his own party. Writing to his ally (and du Deffand's friend) Voltaire, who had advised him to "get a good laugh" out of this skirmish, d'Alembert burst out, "I know that old whore du Deffand wrote to you and is perhaps still writing to you against me and my friends, but we should *get a good laugh* from it all and not give a damn [*se foutre de*] about old whores who are only good for that." One account of this worsening storm tells of du Deffand, in a scene worthy of Célimène, having read aloud to her in company one of her letters to her longtime correspondent Voltaire in which she played her mordant wit over d'Alembert's behavior. In the course of the reading, d'Alembert is said to have wandered into the salon. He is supposed to have made no comment on the spot, but that evening it was reported in Mme Geoffrin's rival salon that d'Alembert would surely get even with the marquise, and use Julie de Lespinasse as an instrument of his revenge.[50]

This is, in a sense, what would come to pass. Since the marquise received her guests in her apartments at the Convent of Saint Joseph only at six in the evening, Julie had taken to foregathering some of the most illustrious guests in her own quarters an hour beforehand, a group that became so congenial that it came to encroach on the hours of the marquise's invitation. The aunt's reaction was swift and violent: Julie, for whom she had done so much, was betraying her. She summarily ordered her out of her home.

Julie de Lespinasse then formed her own salon in which, instead of brilliant, saucy heterosexual conversation, a graver love of liberty and reform would prevail. Mlle de Lespinasse was herself the only woman Mme Geoffrin admitted to her philosophical salon. We take distinct note of the fact that the salons of these latter two more effaced women, rather than the salon of the fabled marquise, were the salons in which liberty and enlightenment were to become watchwords. As Goodman asserts, "Here it was not the philosophes who served the ends of the Salonnière, but the Salonnière who was selected to fulfill a necessary function for the philosophes."[51] Therefore, even within the salon, the revisionist canon came attached to a regression by salon women to a role as fosterers, not participants, in the verbal processing of ideas. The Marquise du Deffand's society would come to represent for the philosophes' party (though not for Voltaire) the acme of desiccated aristocratic charm. And yet we can find in her career elements of the same sense of revulsion against the mores, the debasement of the language, and the surrender of coherence accompanying it that motivated the society's critics as well.

This disaffected woman, writing to d'Alembert to plead for his friendship at the very moment when he is contemplating severing their connection forever, confesses her sorrowing conclusion that the most unhappy moment in life is the one when one is born. Her own birth and the births of d'Alembert and Julie de Lespinasse had been so freighted with ambiguity for their forbears, who had abandoned them in one fashion or another, that even these lives, some of the most auspicious ones in their time, were experienced as blighted. But to d'Alembert, poor and illegitimate as he was, diligent study and self-development could still bring a high calling in geometry, physics, and authorship. For his patroness and her niece, members of the frivolous sex of a frivolous caste—even though they may well have been the least frivolous among them—the extant code pitilessly decreed no spiritually engrossing alternatives to an obsession with sex or love in youth, and a sense of futility in age.[52] At any moment, moods might alter: the revered patroness might turn into a *putain,* as du Deffand did for d'Alembert once they were no longer of one mind: if the woman in culture cultivates herself to such an excess that she begins to believe she can make the rules, the remedy is to remind her and everyone else that she is nature, gross sexual nature, and nothing more.

The Dread Androgyny

I take Noël Hallé's painting (fig. 17) of Hippomenes and Atalanta, from the salon of 1765, as emblematic. It depicts the defeat of the fleet-of-foot Atalanta by her suitor's sowing along her path golden apples, which the avaricious young woman stoops to retrieve. A reflection of the long-lived paradigm of male-female competition inherited from antiquity, this work lent it a mid-eighteenth century French gloss. Diderot (who we recall was an eager critic of art in addition to his other manifold activities) is guardedly enthusiastic about Hallé's achievement: "I have regard for this work, and a great deal of it."[53] He praises the painting's composition and the lightness and grace of Hippomenes: "There in elegance in his figure, in his position, and in his whole person; the certainty of triumph and joy are in his eye." Diderot perceives Hippomenes' victory with satisfaction, reading a paternal benediction into it: from the joy he perceives on the face of the old man, he guesses he is Hippomenes's father. Yet Diderot would react with unease to something in this realization: "Perhaps this race is not natural enough; perhaps it's more of an opera ballet than a struggle"; perhaps, he wonders, when faced with losing the love of one's life a person might run in another fashion, his hair might fly back. Perhaps "he wouldn't rest on his toes, or . . . show off his fine legs and well-formed arms, or let an apple fall from the tips of his fingers as if he were rustling flowers." But then Diderot somewhat justifies these postures, since they comment on the race's outcome. Hippomenes has so clearly won that "he doesn't bother running; he shows off, he struts, he congratulates himself." Diderot understands and forgives the "natural ostentation" of Hallé's Hippomenes. He doubts, however, that "the chaste and savage Hippomenes" from the Grecian mountains would engage in the histrionics of Messieurs Vestris and Gardel, premier dancers at the opera.

Atalanta's depiction, on the contrary, evokes a spirited censure from him. Es-

17. *Noël Hallé,* Hippomenes and Atalanta, *Musée du Louvre, Photo Musées Nationaux*

pecially, he takes exception to her "long dry, nervous arm . . . for it is not in the nature of woman, but of a young man. I'm not sure whether this figure is stopping or running; she looks at the spectators dispersed along the barrier; she's leaning down; if she were trying to arrest their glances with her own so that she could surreptitiously pick up the apple . . . she would not have proceeded otherwise." Yet on the whole, he finds the work a poem whose blemishes are few.[54]

Whereas in his *Salons* Diderot usually achieves eloquence by his reaction to what he finds to be the emotional content of a scene, here the attempt at re-creation is relatively thin, for he identifies only with the father/son bond and with Hippomenes' victory. In this scene of mixed gender, some of the prominent female spectators seem to support Hippomenes' triumph, as does the benign cupid. The interest of this version of the race lies in the androgynous interchange between the effete grace and litheness of Hippomenes as contrasted with the determined and muscular but earthbound Atalanta. This rejection by Hallé of the visual conventions governing femininity and masculinity, also seen in his *Trajan* (fig. 11), especially the play of androgyny in Hallé's women, irritates Diderot. His objections spring to some extent from his antirococo convictions, for in likening the work's Hippomenes to posturing opera performers he regards him as a fugitive eighteenth-century dandy, resting only momentarily on one toe. But Diderot's perception of this work seems curiously off-base here: Hippomenes' hair does fly, he is running, albeit with a consummate balletic grace. It is Diderot far more than Hallé who imposes the notion of narcissistic self-congratulation on his performance. The work itself is more richly ambivalent.

What is more disingenuous is Diderot's total absence of rumination about the race itself or about Atalanta's defeat. He will not for an instant identify with her. The pathos of Atalanta's loss is expressed in the painting by the disarray of the figures at left center, the one who raises a hand in dismay (in parallel to Hippo- menes' expansive gesture of victory) and the one who looks down at Atalanta's reaching for the apple. Atalanta's muscularity, which Diderot finds so repellent, is the necessary sign of her mythic baffled strength. The puttoesque infant at the gate in the center reaching toward Atalanta translates the unconscious dimension of the story's equation of apples with babies. Those two noncourtly watchers fram- ing the foreground convey, in their mute and separated intentness, a sense of the seriousness (belied by Hippomenes' David-before-the-ark lightness) of Atalanta's defeat by stealth. Diderot seems in fact, in his commentary, to displace the idea of stealth from Hippomenes to Atalanta, as he reads Hallé's heroine as trying to dupe her audience by displacing their glances from her stooping to gather in the gold.

Hallé's *Hippomenes and Atalanta* provides us with a lushly realized metaphor for the conflict between the genders in this world: it puts "onstage," behind its fence, a mixed-gender society engrossed in the symbolic race between the two, the male suitor and his unconsenting female object, over whom he can prevail only by the institution of a "system," a stratagem. Cupid and the court bless this outcome, as only a few persons manifest disarray. The watchers—the man at left, the woman and child at right—who witness this struggle resemble the sex-segre- gated world outside salon and court, who regard the behaviors of both sexes within it as aberrant, unnatural, revolting.

Sociability in Popular Culture

To look outside the somewhat sexually unsegregated social life of the privileged classes is to see a scene starkly at odds with its mores, while not entirely divorced from them. What role did women play in the nature versus culture paradigms of popular culture?

As Robert Muchembled reminds us, in the traditional folk culture of France, mothers raised boys and girls until about the age of seven, when brothers would be taken under the father's aegis to learn his trade, while sisters remained under the mother's tutelage. The boys would become initiates into the men's world of farm and tavern life. Unmarried grown boys and men formed a sort of masculine *confrérie* until they married. At *veillées,* gatherings for courtship, it would most often be an old woman who would "make spines tingle as she related terrifying legends or stories revolving around werewolves, witches, monsters." A link be- tween this form of female eloquence, entirely licit in folk culture, and that of women of higher society is likely. Muchembled theorizes that this female lore of the veillée was a remnant of a maternal culture preserved by the women from mother to daughter, a culture viewed by authorities and by the Church as anathema in its continuing resort to the usages of a "multiform and magical world; a world that had resisted Christianization for more than a millennium," outwardly respecting its rituals while preserving the old lore with its numberless superstitions intact. French culture, among women as among men, was robustly *gauloise:* broad sexual jests and jokes about elimination—feces were *la matière joyeuse*— abounded in it, and vestiges of this candor remained in the mores, despite Christian censoriousness about the body. But in the wake of the Middle Ages, modes of sexual self-consciousness emerged, initially among those who could afford it, as first the lovers' bed and then their space were separated from those of the children. Nudity was banished in families, and reticence about the body became a valued mode. "Sexual brutality as Noël du Fail described it among the peasants and Brantôme describes it among the nobility gave way by the eighteenth century to a more restrained sexual behavior," as a severe set of controls involving "everything connected with excretion or with sexuality" infiltrated the sphere of human intimacy, at least as Muchembled interprets it.[55]

But these changes spread far more extensively among the upper class, and this schism in terms of customs and tastes made each class abhor the other with the near-visceral disgust that only people who cannot tolerate the same tastes and smells can have for each other. Muchembled theorizes that the church seems to have dominated sexual mores until around 1750 by dragging sexual offenders before the ecclesiastical courts. These, however, treated both clergy and laymen with lenience, while saving their greatest severity for women.[56]

"There should be no need to insist on the low status of the female condition in France before quite recent times."[57] Townswomen, especially, were the object of the wrath of preachers, for whom they represented the quintessence of sinfulness. But certainly village women were not spared, as the seventeenth century's witchcraft trials attest. Insofar as the sin of extramarital sexuality was imputed to the woman's sexual congress with the devil, her behavior was held to demand policing. Was this virulent anger against women aimed, as Muchembled suggests, against what he sees as their role in the folk culture, as keepers of an earlier pagan mode of mediation between the body and the world? Or did it spring from an even more fundamental and pervasive source? Surely both trends, the cultural and the naturally latent, were combined in the belief "among the people [that] all women were to some extent witches." And so, when women occasionally rose up in food riots, as in the *émotions* of the sixteenth century, a popular response, after sympathy, might well be terror of the "witches" acting *en masse*. French history, of at least some regions, records a relatively small but significant incidence of such outbursts of aggressiveness among women.[58]

The rise in literacy in the period preceding the eighteenth century only exacerbated the gap between women and men, since education was not generally available to women, even though some segregated schooling had been granted them since the seventeenth century in the north of France. This more pronounced distinction between the educations given each gender ensured to the males a monopoly over written culture, while the females, when literate at all, remained largely restricted to the literacy of the primer and to a largely oral culture. The resultant discrepancy became particularly salient in the more literate urban environments, where women were shown an increased level of scorn.[59]

Muchembled attempts to describe three sociocultural strata in eighteenth-century French society. The first was characterized by two dissident currents: the privileged aristocrats, sustained by the sense that their position came from God, were leavened by a minority of men of letters from the liberal aristocracy and the bourgeoisie. The middle level, that of the literate and acculturated, consisting of one Frenchperson out of three or four, contained only half as many women as men and far more northerners than southerners. Theirs was a mass culture, expressed in the *petites écoles* (elementary schools) popular imagery and the *Bibliothèque bleue,* the series of little blue books peddled by vendors from town to town. This second stratum of society lagged by as much as a century behind learned thought. It was in no sense a counterculture, but a past-oriented one, reflecting "a conquest by pictures and by books of an older oral civilization." Muchembled views the operation of these media on the popular imagination as involving a "fabrication of consent" forged in the seventeenth century, which survives in the audio-visual manipulations of our own day.[60]

Arlette Farge's analysis and reprint of the *Bibliothèque bleue* conveys a picture of so harsh a misogyny that she feels moved to caution modern readers against accepting it in a spirit devoid of nuance: "The amplitude of anger against women shocks our modern sensibilities: its virulence of terms, its passionate tone, its conviction of the unrelenting misery that woman represents, its beastly and degrading comparisons, its often ignoble and gross images" disconcert us by their rancor. This, then, an image of systematic negativity—of the female sex as death to man's life and hopes—is the received image of woman in the rising literate class. Farge quotes Achille de Barbantanne's summation in his 1754 *Discours sur les femmes:* "that's a woman for you, an error of nature, a body full of lies, a real monkey."[61]

This leaves the peasant culture as the numerically most significant stratum of society, from which the other two segments strove vigorously to separate themselves, as if from an ancient, superstitious, vile ancestor. And yet this powerfully rooted culture would resist the city's acculturations, maintaining itself in micro-cultures into the twentieth century. The major numerical split, then, would fall between the 20 to 30 percent of the French in or evolving toward cultural literacy, and the rest.

In the traditional culture, suspicion of women naturally made the social mixing of the sexes anathema. This of course would have been the case in educational settings: a belief that the development of intelligence involved the domination by mind over the body, the seat of evil, decreed separatist education. In the early eighteenth century, should a girl be accepted into a class of boys, this was enough to cause its schoolmaster to be dismissed. "The idea of mixing creates great fear."[62] And yet during this same period arguments were being made widely against the waste of the female mind, with the claim that if girls were not to be taught the things of the spirit (since these were believed beyond their ken), they ought at least to be trained to be intelligent mothers and mates.

Mixed Gender, Mixed Feelings

However inevitable the meeting of the sexes ultimately may be, the approach between them is traditionally fraught with tension. The non-Western society of the Ivory Coast provides us with an example distant from our scene in time and space. There, conjugal verbal intimacy is excluded as if the male/female boundary were an obstacle to the exchange of words. Luc Thoré consequently raises the hypothesis that alongside an incest taboo, there has been a tendency toward affective conversational restraint between women and men who are, or might in future be, tied by a consecrated sexual bond. He observes similarities between these African mores and those of the village in the modern Béarn studied in 1959–60 by Pierre Bourdieu. In the French setting boys and girls would be separated from childhood on, on school benches and at catechism. In churches, the men would gather about the pulpit or in the wings near the door as the women settled along the sides and in the nave. The men exclusively frequented the bars, and when the women needed to call their husbands, they did not go to fetch them themselves, but would send their sons. "The entirety of cultural apprenticeship and the sum of the system of values tend to develop in the members of each sex attitudes of reciprocal exclusion and to create a distance that cannot be crossed without embarrassment."[63]

Bourdieu offers some further insights in addition to those cited in chapter 2 concerning the men's diffidence about their own sex lives and, even more, their emotions. Bordieu points out that the girls of the village hold a monopoly over all questions of taste, which are seen prima facie as unmasculine. A man attentive to his dress would be absurd, *enmonsieuré,* pretending above his station to the manners of an emasculated class. "In a society dominated by masculine values, everything contributes to. . . encouraging a gruff and gross, rough and bellicose attitude."[64]

Martine Segalen offers a more highly inflected historical image of the undercurrents of peasant culture that obtained during the Century of Light. She notes the strong female/inside-male/outside dichotomy in most communities, with females caring for the young and domestic life and males hunting and fishing, and affirms that in the Aubrac the division of labor by roles, as distinct from tasks, would never be comparable or complementary. It would be the father who assumed all extrafamilial responsibilities. Consecrated physical spaces for each gender, as in

Bourdieu's study, were rigorously respected. Neither woman nor pig must ever leave the house, a Dauphiné proverb tells us.[65] While they might come into public to sell the barnyard fowl, to launder clothes communally, and to go to church, women would otherwise remain passive spectators of male activities in public, on those occasions where their presence was acceptable. The men engaged in commerce, gaming, and discussion in places like the public cafés or the village forge, or they would set up games like bowling, chess, dice, or cards.

Segalen, however, contradicts a too-easy assumption that this set of customs reflects only the historical domination of women by men. The traditional battle over the trousers and other images of women as boss, the terror of cuckoldry, the sheer volume of proverbs and sayings—"the hat must rule over the coif"—relative to the need to keep women in line, reveal permanent high tension in men around their "problem" of relating to women: "They reflect masculine fear before woman, a being with disquieting power, with sexual power, with powers of sorcery. Whence arises the desire to keep her out of all decisions."[66] Obviously, Segalen remarks, masculine power was far from absolute. It had to be ceaselessly undergirded by reinforcing the old social norms: those men who were henpecked or beaten by their wives could be charivaried mercilessly by the local youth. Their plight becomes dramatically visible in the popular prints on the theme of "the world turned upside down" (fig. 18), where women are depicted as usurping male prerogatives—smoking pipes, carrying muskets and canes—while making their spouses wield the distaff or cradle the baby on open and unwelcoming knees. Their exchange of headgear is the metaphor for it all: the female's activities must be crowned by a demure bonnet; the male's by a jaunty, military tricorn hat. Exchange of hats was disaster.

LA FEMME A LE MOUSQUET LA QUENOUILLE LÉPOUX
ET BERCE POUR SURCROIT LENFANT SUR SES GENOUX

18. La Folie des hommes ou le monde à l'envers, *Le Musée national des arts et traditions populaires, Photo Réunion des Musées Nationaux*

In the French peasant tradition, as in upper-class society, marriage alone admits women to society: without it, they have less than full social reality. Yet even within this sphere, the woman with her menstrual cycles and pregnancies still bathes in the aura of the natural world's mysteries for the men. Women pose a perpetual menace of death and social rupture by their being. French village culture strives to contain their potentially maleficent influence with a barrier of taboos. Within the house these render her manageable; but outside it she remains threatening, especially when she meets and communicates with other women. "Nothing is more feared, is perceived as more excluding, than a feminine group assembled around the wash-house or the oven." Farge corroborates this terror of assembled women: "Women among themselves: that's the worst. It's a certainty resounding in the whole of the literature." Their communal criticisms and denunciations—of men and of one another—are consecrated by proverbs: "At the fountain, the mill and the wash-house, women tell all" (Provence); "When the women come back from the stream, they could eat their husbands alive" (Gascony, Provence, Limousin).[67]

If men's discourse turns to public matters or techniques of making or doing things, women process the hidden and private parts of existence, the familial politics, intimate matters, sexuality. This division makes for a de facto complementarity of actual functions, within which women's and men's lives are deeply imbricated. Segalen insists that the women of this class would not necessarily feel dependency or inferiority, for they carry a huge share of social responsibility in terms both of arduous and needed physical labor, and in terms of their emotional burden as processors of family conflict and sustainers of the intimate rituals of life. The realities alone make for a certain congruence between women and men, a sense of parity between them in their daily existence.[68]

Nonetheless, *grosso modo,* their own culture, on the level of representation, maintains and continues an energetic traditionalist discourse affirming women's inferiority and subordination. So pervasive and so hostile are sayings, songs, and proverbs, which are summoned up at any moment in a variety of contexts, that they serve as a policing mechanism to restore women to silence whenever they break it, as they not infrequently do.

Important regional differences nonetheless obtain. Louis Marin, in *Regards sur la Lorraine* (1966) observed that in that area women advised their husbands with great discretion and were widely respected. Until the Revolution they sat in local councils after mass on Sundays and were integrated into public affairs. French peasant women in the south were severely enclosed spatially, and led more effaced lives, while those in the north—in Brittany or Lorraine, for example—enjoyed more freedom. The Basque country was widely held to be the land of the *femme forte.*[69]

There is nothing remotely surprising about this picture of peasant mores: we cannot believe these to have been materially less restrictive in the eighteenth century than in the twentieth.[70] If we juxtapose this set of factors with salon mores, we discern some huge and potentially anxiety-producing disparities. Instead of a peasant society segregated by gender and activity, the salon proposes a mixed company where women and men are potentially, at least, on a common footing. A more open world, the salon includes more members of the bourgeoisie in its composition, is devoid of a strictly prescribed social hierarchy. As against the system of verbal and emotional constraint between the sexes of traditional agricultural life, the salon offers a high degree of verbal freedom (albeit shaped by rhetorical formulas) to each sex in communicating with the other. Rather than the patriarchal immobilism of peasant life, the idea of the salon offers, especially to the sex most restricted by tradition, the promise of change, novelty, alterations in style, adventure, even escape. Contrasting with the willfully nonverbal and churlish attitudes of peasant men toward courtly manners and dress, we find the salon's men seeking their pleasures in just such masquerades and games.

But in fact there were no peasants of either gender worrying about whether or not to join salon society. These two realms were mutually exclusive social entities linked only by a deep mutual mistrust and contempt: the peasant class must needs despise the fecklessness or effeminacy of the salon's men, while the latter would find those rustics not far removed from their own barnyard beasts in comportment. The populace was comprised of 85 percent peasants and 8.5 percent bourgeois, with the most powerful classes making up the remainder. Fear and rage felt by the lower orders against the upper have to be counted in some significant degree as a sign of terror at a class of men who could not, or refused to, contain "its" own women who, from a peasant perspective, were "out of control." One can only imagine what popular opinion could make of an observation like J. J. Rutlidge's in 1770 that Frenchwomen's "influence is not confined within the circle of pleasure: they enter into areas of the greatest seriousness and the highest consequence."[71]

Women's Rights and Women's Role

Not surprisingly, it was the bourgeois class that bore the marks of conflict over the issue of the "proper" place of women in society, an issue the other classes were too profoundly polarized over even to address. But this conflict was not situated in the realities, always devilishly slippery to grapple with: rather it was displaced to the arena of representation. The mechanisms of traditional discourse policing women's behavior—mockery, the silencing of the other's voice, the equation of the woman with rococo profligacy and extravagance—were not proving adequately forceful, in this era of the weakening of Churchly belief, to the maintenance of a male supremacist overview like that of the revered churchman Jean Bodin, who in the sixteenth century classified wives as fifth in the household, after masters, parents, children and servants. Women had increasingly emerged into visibility as persons in the upper classes, as personages in society and authors of novels and tracts. The fiction governing the traditional gender complementarity was breaking down.[72] A revolution in representation would be needed to install a new one.

Boucher's appealing 1743 portrait of his wife (fig. 19), poised on her chaise longue, stands at the crossroads between rococo stylization and female individuation. An interior elaborately decorative in the current vogue, flowered and flounced, is yet rendered with bourgeois simplicity and limited to a few intimate details—the magot, the tea-set, the fallen thread. The erotic signs of the rococo code are present—Madame's tiny foot and its mule, the open drawer and the love letters. Her ruffled clothing, the soft bedclothes, and the nonchalantly draped curtain lend a sensuous softness to the setting, offset, however, by the more austere lines of the table's woodwork and, above all, by the subject's glance. If her coy hand has something of the reptilian look we later find in the hands of Ingres's women, the arm is firm, the glance firmer. The head appears indeed a bit outsized and ill positioned, so high is the forehead, so direct the gaze of this figure. Is she

19. *François Boucher*, Madame Boucher, *copyright the Frick Collection, New York*

amused by or judging the spectator? The ambiguous mouth and slightly hooded eyes present us with either possibility. The project of depicting this woman of the bourgeois class as a rococo erotic object is undermined and questioned by her own gaze.

We now better grasp some of Rica's ostensible comments to Ibben in *The Persian Letters,* as posing a question internal to French society's own schism regarding women, as much as it applies to any contrast between France and Persia.

> It is a great question, among men, as to whether it is more advantageous to take women's liberty from them or leave it to them; it seems to me there are many reasons for and against. If Europeans say there is no generosity in making people one loves unhappy, our Asiatics reply that there is a baseness about men giving up the power that Nature has given them over women." (38)

The terms of the argument are themselves intriguing: again, it is a struggle among the men; not, as yet, with women. Their struggle lies nakedly in deciding which is better for themselves, containing women's freedom or refraining from doing so. In the text's first sentence, women's freedom is conceived of as their natural right, stripped from them by men's superior force. Yet by the second sentence (and even allowing for the satiric thrust of the speaker's being representative of a harem-owning culture), that right has evaporated, to be replaced by a relationship, West as East, of sheerest dominion. Since it is within the European donor's gift to make women "happy" or "unhappy," why not grant them the "toy" of freedom? On the other hand, in the final clause, the Oriental appeals to nature to evoke male pride in a supremacy rooted in a physiology that it would be *lèse masculinité* not to uphold.

The Enlightenment's succeeding attitudes toward women are characterized by the same gymnastic contortions we find in Rica's remark. If he himself goes on to confess candidly that male power over women is sheer tyranny, he then somewhat excuses its absolutism as being only an answer to women's overpoweringly great seductive powers over men. Still, he does admit that men use every sort of stratagem to rob women of their courage: "Strengths would be equal if education too were equal." Rica moves in his letter from a consideration of male domination to a brief flirtation with the idea of equality. In his musing, he jettisons this notion for an expression of apprehension about the risk of female control, which illustrates that the salon aristocrat Montesquieu was not at all ignorant of the mentality of Segalen's peasants, with their bogey of "the world upside down." "It must be confessed, although it shocks our sense of rightness, that among the most polished peoples women have always had authority over their husbands" (38). Parisian society, that reputedly most polished of them all, cannot help terrorizing itself with such a specter of women in command.

The ambivalences revealed in this tiny sample proliferate on every side of educated discourse, revealing it to be in a state of disarray and recombination. The male discourse of the Encyclopedists, loosed from its theological moorings, in fact seemed rudderless in describing women's fate or in prescribing a better one. I cannot help speculating about the apparently mobilizing effects, not unlike those we see around us in our own time, of legislation inimical to women: such laws act to encourage those who would militate against them. On February 12, 1731, an *Ordonnance des donations* (ordering of gifts) was enacted by the Parlement of Paris, which in effect deprived women of equality before the law: it may be considered for the eighteenth century a "high water mark in the history of repressive legislation."[73] Was this development itself a response to women's aggressivity in upper-class circles? And was it the spur to a heating up of debate? Certainly, Boquel's 1744 *Superiority of Man over Woman* reaffirmed the view enacted in that law. But as Georges Ascoli has pointed out, after 1760 the great midcentury intensity of ferment of debate that had centered on the rights of women per se that we find in works by Mlle Archambault or Mme Galien, in Marivaux's *La Colonie* (1729), or in Dinouart's 1749 *Triumph of the Sex,* dedicated to Mme du Chatelet, is over. The powerful new bourgeois intelligentsia simply did not choose to make this issue, which had engaged the interest of Mme Lambert's salon entourage, its own.[74] Pothier would again essentially reiterate the Parlement's and Boquel's position in 1770: natural law had decreed a husband's hierarchical power over his wife, and this in turn authorized his demand that she acquiesce in an unqualified submission to his will in all things. Such views, however, were far from being universally acceptable. In 1753 the Jesuit Père Caffiaux published four volumes of *Defenses of the Fair Sex,* a reprise of Poullain de la Barre's 1673 *Equality of the Two Sexes,* and the quarrel wended its way on, in episodic bursts. Jean Bloch in fact discerns a renewal of interest in 1750 in the issues of women's role and their educability, which replaced the question of their rights as the locus of the quarrel.[75] By 1762, the date of Rousseau's *Emile,* such debates, with their new emphases, were still intense.

More Natural, More Terrible than Man

Once more we see how the new discourse about women circles obsessively round and round the issue of woman as nature. Generally speaking, women in traditional discourse had always been viewed as "more natural" than men, and the undergirding of such a structure was drawn from analogies with animal life. Agriculturally based arguments consistently drew upon the barnyard for images of gender relations: the cock (France's emblem) does this; the hen, that. Learned discourse often mimics this folklore in scientific terms. The defenders of women consistently reject reduction of women to this level, which projects human physicality upon women, positing instead a natural parity between the sexes. They tend to stress the idea that women's intellectual and moral qualities are akin to men's, arguing that men were simply guilty of rejecting evidence available to their senses in ignoring women's patent equality of natural endowment with them.[76] Even women's rights, then, could be seen as natural. In a sort of compensatory mechanism, egalitarians, feeling intensely the injustice in women's privation of rights, frequently resort to the strategy of making a case for women's superiority. These latter arguments then bog down in shows of questionable "gallantry" toward "the sex." In arguments for both sides, we see the scales flailing wildly up and down, rarely approaching anything like a balance of dispassionate evaluation. At the extremes of this discourse, women, permanent representatives of nature within culture, safeguard the warmth and coherence of men's private sexual and procreative existences and must be preserved from contamination by culture's artifices: they are now failing in their natural task, ruining culture itself, and must be restored to the purity of their conjugal and maternal functions. Conversely, it is to women that the highest of all cultural functions falls, that of purifying the mores: women in society are failing in their cultural task and must be pressed into performing it. The late eighteenth century's debate on women, whether it regards them as primarily natural or primarily cultural, sees their contribution to the commonweal increasingly as a private and moral one.

Silvana Tomaselli, we recall, had proposed as her formulation that "at the level of the real, women partake in and shape culture, but at the level of the symbolic or imaginary, they are excluded from it and represented as belonging to the outside realm of the natural." Insofar, J. P. Rutlidge implies, as the "real" French upper-class culture of this time approached matriliny in terms of descendance and gave foreigners the distinct impression that its women were, as civilized persons, superior to men, I would agree with Tomaselli. Women during that era acted as agents of culture to a significant degree. Therefore, in aristocratic circles, the Frenchmen of the time had to have known women as representatives of culture. But the discourse of Frenchmen would largely reject such anxiety-producing insights: it would resort instead to a remodeling of the traditional language, thereby containing the category "women" as a means of communication, essentially among themselves. As women would join in to defend themselves and their concerns, they could only do so, as Tomaselli points out, by "endorsing the position they [were] given in the symbolic and the imaginary, taking it literally, that is, considering themselves outside of culture, a position which they then [used] strategically to criticize the place they [were] given both within the real and the imaginary of the culture from which they [were] excluded and which they themselves reject[ed]."[77]

The severe dichotomies that come to overpower bourgeois gender discourse straitjacket both women's and men's expressivity: female/male; nature/culture; private/public; family/society; inside/outside; body/mind; passion/reason. But if these polarities recur with nauseating repetitiveness, it is certainly not as static categories, but along a continuum of possibilities. For example, "whereas female was often related to unmediated nature, as in the power to reproduce, male might also be so related as in the emphasis on brute sexual desire. In these ways a set of complex changing images was built up which both constrained and expressed tension and contradiction." As the pairs suggest, the symbolics of gender are a factor in intellectual history.[78] Identified more generally with the negative poles of cultural values, women's representation defines the character and limits not only of gender identity, but of all identity, and of culture itself.

Enlightened man often expresses consciousness of civilized man's tyranny over women, but he finds comfort in lamenting what he sees as its universality, excepting only, according to Diderot, in the Marianas Islands. Constant recapitulation of women's widespread subjection functions to reinforce the notion of its precultural, eternal naturalness. Diderot would note that while women were subjugated in civilized nations, they were utterly oppressed in primitive societies. "There is no kind of vexation that the savage does not exercise against his wife; the woman unhappy in cities is unhappier still in the deeps of the forest." Thomas would likewise observe that "women amongst the Indians are what Helots were among the Spartans, a vanquished people forced to work for its vanquishers."[79] As in Montesquieu's *Persian Letters,* the slave/master dichotomy marks this gender pairing, imprinting it with a newly minted expression of self-conscious male guilt.

The great Rohrschach blot that floods over this simple suspicion of gender injustice, obscuring its visibility, is the idea of beauty. "Man who has never missed an opportunity to abuse his power in rendering homage to beauty," (2) writes Thomas in his earnest attempt to undermine the emptiness of the courtly rococo flourish that poses so mountainous a barrier to taking women seriously. Diderot makes cruel mock of Thomas's timid attempt to dismantle the discourse of gallantry: "When you write of women, you must dip your pen in the rainbow and throw the dust of butterflies' wings over your lines; as with the pilgrim's little dog, each time you shake its paw, pearls should fall from it; and none fall from M. Thomas's" (10:48). With this precious, willful sally, Diderot displaces Thomas's attempt at rational speech about women, literally dissolving it in images of insubstantiality. Literary discourse is so enamored of beauty that it emerges in the most unsuspected contexts. Note how Diderot links it with other female attributes. "Beauty, talents, and wit, in every country of the world, savage or civilized, these will make a man fall prostrate before a woman; but these advantages peculiar to a few women will not establish anywhere a general tyranny of the weaker sex over the robust one. Man rules over nations even in nations where woman commands the nation" (46). Having evoked the notion of male sexual weakness before female beauty makes Diderot retaliate: he slots his argument back into the master/slave dichotomy, so as to insist that men *must never* be slaves to women, but that the reverse must remain true. Women's cultured powers are merely dangers that serve to conflate nature's own.

Even after that famous passage of Diderot's on society's victimization of women, "treated like imbecile children" by the laws and customs that have been superadded to nature's own cruelties (44), he still makes a scathing indictment of the women of his own culture: "Don't forget that inasmuch as they lack reflection and principle nothing can penetrate women's understanding to any depth of conviction; . . . and for all that they are more civilized than ourselves outwardly, they've remained real savages inside; all of them more or less Machiavellian, the symbol of women in general is the Apocalypse on whose forehead is inscribed, *Mystery.*" (48–49) For the atheistic Diderot, to whom virtually nothing else is unfathomable, women continue to be as much an unassimilable cognitive block as they were to the fathers of the Church. The graces of social woman, for the philosophic mentality, unfairly combine natural and cultivated charms with guile. The major charge leveled against her here is that of an alleged selfish, unloving, ungiving manipulativeness. This is a capital text by the most subtle of the philosophes. Although Diderot frequently expresses empathy and protectiveness toward women, here he reminds us that women's cultural participation—as in the formulation of central ideas like that of justice, for example—is deemed to be too shallow to be of value. Even after asserting women's victimization so powerfully, he fails utterly to imagine that women might feel some stake in justice.

Had he wished, Diderot might well have learned from some of the rhetoric of Mme du Châtelet's *Discourse on Happiness* (1761), in which she defends women's right to study as a compensation for their inequality. "Men have an infinity of resources to make them happy which are entirely lacking to women. They have many other means of achieving glory, and it's certain that to aspire to making your talents useful to your country and to serve your fellow citizens, either by abilities in the arts of war or by talents for government or in negotiation, is a [goal] superior to that of study; but women are excluded by their station from all species of glory, and when by chance one is born with a soul elevated enough [for such aspirations] she has only study left to her to console her for all the exclusions and all the dependencies she finds herself condemned to by her status."[80] Diderot was never able to concern himself in like concrete terms with the consequences of women's limitations.

Women, Calculation, and Spontaneity

A glance at the period's fiction allows us to judge the extent of the hardening into a *topos* of public conceptions of women as active participants in society. Novelistic representation makes the charge of artifice the locus of vituperation against women of society. In numerous works we find such women, "whose entire conduct is dictated by calculation; even in their moments of profligate abandon, they keep a cool head and carry out the plans their depraved reason has elaborated." Mme de Lurçay, the wickedly lucid society woman of Crébillon's *Bewilderments of Heart and Mind* (*Les Egarements du coeur et de l'esprit*), is a fine specimen of the type. Such unfeeling women as these "remain . . . seductresses, profiting by their arts of intrigue and their knowledge of men to lead a young man wherever it pleases them. They always take the initiative in words and acts, all the while preserving their respectability. For they are prudes." In fact, Laurent Versini claims that "the creation of the female demon is one of the most original features of the eighteenth century's novel."[81]

Versini interprets this development as reflecting disgust with a system of great sociability pretending to assure happiness in purity, which yet fails to warn young men against the traps they may find themselves caught in, set by jealous and rapacious women who willfully lay waste to happy relations between the sexes.

Although we certainly perceive the powerful resemblances between these female roués and their male counterparts, the emotional charge emitted by the former is of a far more repellent order. *Denatured* is the word they evoked and continue to evoke; and the word is intended to elicit panic. Men may act "unnaturally" to our horror, but this horror lies within the circle of our expectations of the range of men's acts. Women's abandonment of "their" nature is read as a wholesale abandonment of nature within the human psyche. If women are not to be sexual prey, but predators, then what can men be? What is under siege in these novels is nothing less than women's alleged uses of the arts of culture. In Dorat's *Sacrifices of Love* (1771) the wicked Mme d'Ercy is assimilated to a specific, suspect class. "It's in this century above all that a type of female intriguer has multiplied everywhere who has her own study as well as her boudoir; who reasons, decides, throws herself body and soul into politics, and basically, even while making macramé, dreams about administration."[82]

The effective charge against these women arraigns them for thinking, an activity seen as so unnatural to them that it can result only in the warping of social and sexual lives these novels elaborate. The reader is instructed thereby that women must not be allowed to pretend, as the upper-class ones seem to be doing, to full membership in culture. All of nature is made to cry out to them to abandon their evil ways and subdue their ambition to levels more comfortable to men. Women's initiative, beginning with the most primal one, but rising to the heights of government, is to be seen as nothing but deviance.

But this psychological and ideological equation is also coupled with a more direct and primitive fear. When women assume powers of initiative, their potential for a retaliation that male society feels to be not without its justifications is enormously augmented. Observe the vehemence in the wording of the Hostess's description, in Diderot's *Jacques le fataliste,* of Mme de la Pommeraye's state of mind when she realizes that her lover, for whom she had abandoned a blameless life, loved her no longer. "When the first fury abated, and she had enjoyed her indignation in tranquility, she thought of avenging herself, but in a cruel manner, in a way that would terrify all those who in the future would be tempted to seduce and deceive a chaste woman." (O.C, 12:146–147). In such cold fury, she sets about bringing into play her diabolical scheme of making her treacherous marquis fall desperately in love with a young and beautiful prostitute whom she finds a way of presenting to him as virginal. This plot involves the utmost conceivable self-control on la Pommeraye's part: she must in no way whatever divulge to the marquis what her real feelings for him are. In the end, the marquis does indeed love the prostitute: having been consistently subject to men's desire, she is acceptably vulnerable and responsive, the tool both of Mme de la Pommeraye and of men.

As Diderot's narrator defends Mme de la Pommeraye in the novel against a putative (male) objector, he seems here to be countering a current of opinion. "Her vengeance is atrocious, but it is not stained by any self-interest. . . . When she avenges a betrayal, you revolt against her instead of seeing that her resentment only makes you indignant because you are yourself incapable of feeling anything so deeply, or because you take almost no interest at all in the virtues of women" (12:187). The narration in this way flirts with regard for her depth of commitment. Setting before us in full the horror of this negative stereotype, the passage yet defends la Pommeraye's right to vengeance as a courageous assertion of her outraged integrity, and uses her to attack the failure of commitment by men.[83]

Can we really situate this void of trust within the women, or within the men who articulate this drama of vindictiveness? Whose manipulativeness and role in culture was most in question in such formulations? If women were under moral pressure to change, to move, where was it these men wanted them to go, and why?

Mothers

Evil, ignorant mothers, who ostensibly misuse nature's power by thwarting the desire of their daughters and enjoying desires of their own, are another frequent target of novelists. Accusations of failure at mothering so infiltrate all forms of discourse as to become inescapable, even to readers seeking "escape." In 1742 Godard d'Aucour depicts an unnatural mother, jealous of her daughter, who spies upon her, confiscates her letters, sequesters her, and tries to marry her off to a monstrous husband. She is described as a consummate actress, who "knows the art of feigning and of composing her facial expressions at will." So designing mothers may combine glacial self-composure with destructive will. Villaret's 1745 *La Belle Allemande, ou les galanteries de Thérèse* tells of a mean-spirited, profligate mother who deceives her baker-husband in a kneading trough and whose daughter defines herself as the "victim of her mother's ambition and avarice," not to say lubricity. A classically ambiguous role is played by Mme d'Aison in her prostitute daughter's life in Diderot's tale of Mme de la Pommeraye; she follows the pattern of many real mothers, driven to sell their daughters so that both might live. And in Laclos's novel of 1781, we will see how Sophie's mother's ignorance of how the world works wrecks her daughter's fate. Some of these novelistic mothers were from the lower classes, but not Laclos's model, so that mothers of any class might be incorporated into the "bad mother" trope. And so the Goncourt brothers will take the reputed unlovingness of Frenchwomen toward their offspring as a cornerstone of their description of *Women in Eighteenth-Century Society*.[84]

As I tried to demonstrate in chapter 2, an underlying distress, doubtless common to both sexes, over the loosening of the nexus of familial connections—the continuing formality that made children address parents as monsieur and madame, the infant mortalities, the dubious paternities—emerges in public discourse as a demand upon women to return to their "natural" role and reform themselves. Their reform becomes the cornerstone of moral regeneration. Only motherhood, it is promised (or threatened), will redeem women from "their" fallen actuality, and men from the vices of culture. England precedes France in espousing this ideal: John Locke's middle-class sanctification of marriage gave some intellectual impetus to this movement. In France, the sense of degeneration being deeper, the projection of resentment is more fierce, the tone of anger and reprimand more unmistakable. Threaded through calls to women to "return" to maternal sacrifice as their fundamental and natural contribution to the life of society are vehement denunciations, in dialectic with maternalist propaganda, of women's present vitiation of society as participants within it.

A Mother's Return to Mother-Love

In April 1756 Louise d'Esclavelles, the Marquise d'Epinay, a friend of the Encyclopedists, invited Jean-Jacques Rousseau to live in her country house, l'Ermitage. During the months of May and June Rousseau visited her at her chateau retreat at La Chevrette. But their acquaintance, of course, dated from earlier on. In January 1756, in an act signaling the decline of social women's preeminence, Mme d'Epinay had written the first of a series of so-called letters to her son (but really for herself and her friends). This revealed her to be already in the grip of the maternalist imperative, still admixed with reasoned argument.[85] Well before Rousseau's *Emile* (1762), but perhaps not before having conversed with Rousseau about education, Mme d'Epinay would assume personal charge of the affective and cognitive education of her nine-year-old Louis, thus consciously rejecting her class's mode of raising children for her own idea of an Enlightenment model. We see her self-denigration vis-à-vis Enlightenment itself in doing so.

> I haven't thought I should abandon you into the hands of strangers, or deprive myself of the pleasure of seeing your soul develop, formed by my care and in my sight; in so doing, I consulted my tender feelings less than your true interests, and right reason rather than the nearly universal example set by all heads of families. However limited I might be from the standpoint of insight, I thought that where the interest of what is dearest to me in the world is concerned, I ought not defer blindly to the views of another.[86]

But even as she thinks she acts only as an individual, d'Epinay is only in the avant-garde of a new mode.

D'Epinay stresses the absoluteness of her bond (Elisabeth Badinter calls it symbiotic) with her son. She makes plain her plan of total identification with him. "I'm happy in your satisfactions and in your pleasures, I suffer from your pain, I even suffer from the annoyances that it is my duty to cause you." She intends to make feeling for her son replace feeling for herself. Why? Because in doing so she gives herself a reason for being that others approve, and their approval is predicated on her show of a "natural" self-effacing connectedness to her child. No one may be interposed between mother and son, for the minute details of his personal care that "would tire a stranger . . . are just what makes for happiness of a mother; the more of them there are, the happier she is."[87] It seems plain that the marquise has calculated that her considerable intellectual and emotional capital must be invested this way. When her son, who has not been under her sole control from early childhood, proves intractable to her educational scheme, like the modern mother she is, she feels wounded in her own narcissism.

Accordingly, she turns to her younger and more pliant daughter, taking huge pride in her precocity and cleverness, in this way reaffirming her class pride in feminine achievements, even though these would now clash with her own nascent maternalist self-abnegation. Neither child, as is so often the case, will ultimately provide her with the narcissistic glow she had hoped for from such intense "natural" emotional investment. Hers might have proven a first emblematic exemplar of the paradox of maternalism: that a mother's individual devotion alone is by no means such a force as would be claimed, when pitted against virtually irresistible social structures and pressures. But neither she nor her society would read any caution into this fascination with the imperative to embrace mothering: it was, after all, becoming the new commonplace of displaced female ambition.[88]

Hell Hath No Fury like a Man Scorned

"Come, my Sophie, and let me afflict your unjust heart."
JEAN-JACQUES ROUSSEAU, letter addressed
but never sent to Sophie d'Houdetot

Through the generosity of Emilie d'Epinay, Rousseau was ensconced with his companion Thérèse Lavasseur and her mother at l'Ermitage in 1757, in his forty-fifth year. In his *Confessions* Rousseau tells us how he there received several visits from Mme d'Epinay's sister-in-law, Sophie d'Houdetot, just around the time he was conceiving his heroine, Julie, of the *Nouvelle Héloïse*. Nearing thirty, not a classical beauty, in fact somewhat marked by the pox, Sophie was nonetheless entrancing to him in her lively yet gentle expressiveness. On Sophie's first visit she had arrived wearing male riding garb. Although Rousseau claims he usually looked upon "such masquerades" with distaste, on this occasion, her boots and breeches bewitched him.[89]

She had the requisite talents for a lady of her class, some wit, a style of being *très naturel,* by which Rousseau meant that apparent lack of artifice that was the age's greatest of all artifices. In fact, she abounded in charming sallies that seemed to burst from her as if despite herself. She could dance and play the harpsichord and compose passable verse. "As to her character, it was angelic; gentleness of soul was its foundation; excepting only prudence and strength, it contained all the virtues" (189). Married young and unhappily, Sophie d'Houdetot was fully engaged in her liaison with the Marquis de Saint-Lambert. Her repeated visits with Jean-Jacques, while undoubtedly exciting to her as a flirtation with an acknowledged great man of the time, were by no means the center of her emotional life. Her cultivation of Rousseau's company proved, however, a prime provocation for the emotionally labile philosophe. "Shame, evil's companion" at first made him mute and trembling in her presence: "I didn't dare open my mouth or raise my eyes; I was in an indescribable confusion" (195). Falling in love with her, guiltily, yet filled with the suspicion that she and Saint-Lambert were making fun of his distress, Rousseau suffered, but not in silence. "We were both drunk with love, she for her lover, I for her: our sighs, our delicious tears blended together" (194). Her amorous privation—she had been six months away from Saint-Lambert— and his own heightened their mutuality of unassuaged desire. This love for Sophie, Rousseau tells us, was his sole great passion: "It was love this time, and love in all its energy and furor" (196). Neither hid their intimacy from their hostess, Mme d'Epinay, when they visited her at La Chevrette. "Women all have the art of hiding their rage," writes Rousseau, "especially when it is alive; Mme d'Epinay, violent but premeditating, preeminently possesses this art. She pretended not to see anything, to suspect anything."[90] Rousseau vents upon the person of his hostess his suspicions of her jealousy of this love, which in the event was to come to naught, leaving him dejected and heartsore.

Rousseau's subsequent refusal to accompany Louise d'Epinay to Geneva to see Dr. Tronchin, the most celebrated physician of the time, incensed their mutual friend Diderot, who wrote him an outraged letter, reproving him for his ingratitude to her.[91] After a long terminal interview with Sophie, who somehow conveyed to him her continuing fidelity to Saint-Lambert, Rousseau finally offered to leave l'Ermitage; but it was only after a stormy visit from Diderot and a virtual order to quit that residence that he actually departed, in December 1757.

It was at this precise moment, driven out of his refuge, having broken off with all his powerful and popular Parisian friends of the *Encyclopédie*—all of whom he knew to be gossiping behind his back about his presumed misdeeds—and having had to give up the only woman he claims to have loved, that Rousseau decided to write his *Letter to M. d'Alembert on Spectacle*.[92] He would write it from Montmorency while lodged in chilly, rickety quarters, ostensibly in response to d'Alembert's article "Geneva" in the *Encyclopédie*. And among the many scores Rousseau means to settle in this diatribe against Paris, its society and its pleasures, his vendetta against women is not the least of them.

Because d'Alembert had had the French cheek to suggest that the attractions of Geneva might be enhanced if its Calvinist city fathers relented in their opposition to the theater, Rousseau's Genevan chauvinism moves him to center his fire on that art. And so it is in the context of actresses "who force and drag" actors into immorality that he opens his discussion of the mixing of the sexes (188). He turns for his model of behavior between the sexes to England, where he claims the men are hard and fierce and the women gentle and timid. There the sexes live apart from each other; both are taciturn and slow to feel passion; and the women are as pleased to walk about solitary, in country parks, as to show themselves in town. Rousseau has chosen England as his model, he says, because there the two sexes have the most diametrically opposed mores. "If you want to know men, study women" (189). Women's morality, and hence men's, depends on their living a retired and domestic existence: "If I say," and he does so, consciously courting dissent, "that the peaceful care of a family and a household are their portion, that the dignity of their sex lies in its discretion, that shame and reticence are insepa-rable from decency in its modesty, that to seek out the glances of men is already to let oneself be corrupted, and that every woman who shows herself does herself dishonor, instantly that philosophy for a day that is born and dies in a corner of a great city will rise up against me and try to stifle that cry of nature, the unani-mous voice of humankind" (189).

God himself has decreed, writes Rousseau, that shame be natural to humanity. Should it be argued against this that desires are equal in both sexes, he asks, "What does that mean? Is there on both sides the same ability to satisfy them? What would happen to humankind if the order of attack and defense were altered?" (190). A painful question indeed, from one who has just suffered the most bruis-ing amorous setback of his life. Significantly, Rousseau here reduces all congress between the genders to the sexual and exposes a will to prohibit the expression of (misleading) female desire. Man alone must be actor/lover. Why? One only has to think of the differing consequences of sex for each gender, he argues: "Any woman without modesty is culpable and depraved, because she tramples under-foot a sentiment natural to her sex" (191). Their shyness, their vulnerability, ren-der women touching beings. "Why give her a more feeling heart, less speed in running, a less robust body, a shorter stature, more delicate muscles, if [nature] had not destined her to let herself be vanquished?" (192).

Despite the courtly distance of Rousseau's narrative voice in speaking of Sophie d'Houdetot in the *Confessions*, where he claims to have parted with her as a friend, keeping alive his regard for her, in the letter we find, on the contrary, the wrathful voice of a lover disappointed. The *Confessions* report that the Sophie who had sought him out had "granted me nothing that might render her unfaithful, and I had the humiliation of seeing that the heat that her slightest gestures toward me brought to my senses never caused the tiniest spark in her own" (*Conf.* 194). As he speaks of the imperative for women to stay out of sight, we sense his mortification at having been enchanted by the vision of Sophie. He turns this issue of female shamelessness obsessively about. In his own native mountain villages, women are modest and timid: a mere word is enough to make them blush. But in the wicked cities, modesty becomes "low and ignoble."

Surprisingly enough, in view of his rhetorical insistence upon the absolute naturalness of female modesty, Rousseau concedes on his very next page that even if one were to deny his assertion, and consider modesty a cultural rather than a natural factor, women should nonetheless live in domestic retirement, for timidity is a quality well worth cultivating in them. "Is there any more touching *spectacle* in the world than that of the mother of a family surrounded by her young, regulating the work of her servants, assuring her husband a happy life and wisely governing her home?" (193).[93] The obsessiveness of this section, which will find its outlet in the fictional domestic world of Julie, spins itself on. In antiquity, women lived shut away: "They rarely showed themselves in public, never with men; they never went walking with them, they did not have the best seats at entertainments nor did they put themselves on display; they were not even admitted everywhere, and we know that they courted the death penalty if they showed themselves at the Olympic games" (194). At home, they stayed in apartments men did not enter; they rarely ate with their husbands, or they would leave the table before the meal ended. There was no common assemblage of the two sexes: they never spent their days together. The answer to women's presumption is a restoration of ancient customs, still respected in Rousseau's day in village life only.

The punitive nastiness of Rousseau's advocacy of this model has to be measured against the mores of the women he had just been frequenting, Mesdames d'Houdetot and d'Epinay. He had just spent months in long daily rambles over the countryside with Sophie in "an intimacy almost unexampled between two friends of opposite sex" (*Conf.* 194), as well as numerous hours at La Chevrette in mixed company. These women now suddenly appall him utterly. While the break with Louise is clear, the underlying rage against Sophie is buried beneath this flood of summary judgment against women of this society, which he summons up all of received opinion to endorse. "People everywhere are convinced that in neglecting the manners of their sex, they neglect its duties; everywhere, then, we see that in turning their insolence against men's firm, male self-assurance, women vilify themselves by their odious imitation, thus simultaneously dishonoring both their own sex and ours" (193).

In his letter written as if for men, where women are alluded to repeatedly in the third person and never even implicitly included as readers or even overhearers of this discourse (but which he certainly intends them to hear) Rousseau purports to provide a warning to the male community about the sexual dangers inherent in allowing women such initiatives as he has suffered from. "A woman outside her home loses her greatest radiance, and shorn of her true adornments, shows herself indecently. If she has a husband, what is she out seeking among men?" (193). The adulteress Sophie, in her riding habit, had put herself in his path and torn his emotions to shreds by appealing so powerfully to his senses.[94] Something there was in Sophie's demeanor that made him feel unmanned, unable to affirm his own "firm, male self-assurance" when he was with her. Now, in the *Letter,* he denounces female self-assurance as if it were a plague of the entire female sex's invention to diminish men.

When Rousseau adverts to the separatist mores of the ancients as an antidote to the threat presented by women in the cities, he pointedly manipulates two prime ideological factors that will merge in the gender history of the Revolution: the first is class conflict, and the second is the issue of the remote past passing the baton of authenticity to the present. Appealing nakedly to an atavistic, precultural, male supremacist idyll of rural existence, to which men of all classes might resonate, he calls out of the shadows, into which cultivated life had partially repressed it, the energy of the ancient and infinitely renewable resentment against women. He summons up this sexually fueled passion to the threshold of consciousness with all the immense force of his rhetorical powers of suasion. A return is what he calls for, to the simple family hierarchy of a presumably less sublimated culture: but this culture, following the European historical imperative of the past four hundred years, had to find a base *within culture*—not in the purely agricultural societies—to be credible to his times; and this base, for Rousseau, as for La Font de Saint-Yenne, lay in classical antiquity.

Never mind that antiquity might need to be "rearranged" so as to prove the longevity and desirability of sexual segregation and female subordination.[95] The precedent of the misogyny of ancient democracies here becomes the guarantor of the moral purity of modern ones, as against the corrupt courtly tradition of the French aristocracy. The (ostensibly) sexually unstained, unwordly Swiss republicans are conflated with the morally unstained Greeks and Romans in Rousseau's text as natural protectors of the male supremacy expressed by democratic government. "It is certain," insists the Rousseau who certainly could affirm no such thing with such assurance, "that where women were segregated and maintained as submissive members of a household," domestic peace was generally on firmer ground, and greater union between the spouses obtained than that which we see about us today (194). Persians and Egyptians are also enlisted along with Greco-Roman civilization to ratify this dream scenario of gender relations in antiquity.

Gallantry, which is learned from the books popular in courts and cities, the (fallen) forms of courtship that have teased desire out of its cave of repression, is Rousseau's culprit. Wielded by women, it "makes one blush, and modesty, banished by woman from her discourse and her demeanor, takes refuge in men's hearts" (195). This, for Rousseau, is an unacceptable, even castrating, outcome for men who feel themselves impelled to adopt a value women ought to have upheld. There is a potentially important insight in germ here concerning the play of reciprocity in maintaining concepts of value between the sexes. But a grave absence of meditation on the nature of the interaction between the genders blocks his inquiry into the deeper sources of the conditions he so abhors. His reactive prejudice remains uppermost. In his assessment of the tenuous equilibrium between the sexes in the life of culture, Rousseau perceives chiefly men's loss, and he sees it as infinitely disastrous. When men are forced to face women as they have become, the women "lose only their morality, while we lose both morality and our fitness; for the weaker sex, physically unable to assume our way of life, which is too arduous for it, forces us to take on its own mode, too soft for us; and unwilling to suffer a separation between us, lacking the ability to make themselves into men, the women make women of us" (204). Incapable of conceiving of what women's needs might be or how the needs of both genders might be served, Rousseau is wholly attuned psychically to the menace of men's diminution. The status of men is most in peril in a free state like Geneva. "That a monarch may govern men or women must be a matter of indifference to him, as long as he is obeyed; but in a republic, we need men" (204).

"We need men"; what "we" of the republic do not need, therefore, is women. The concept "women" is ripped apart from the idea of the republic, not simply as not being germane to it, but as its very antithesis. A world of courtiers may be able to afford the detested commingling of the sexes. But if men are to be free, women must be *their* courtiers. The man who now spends his life amusing women in a salon "spends his life doing for them what they should do for us when, exhausted from doing work they are incapable of doing, our spirits need rest" (206). This allusion to women's weakness leads into a consideration of their weakness of intellect. By and large, he holds, they have no love for and very little knowledge of art, and they "have no genius." Capable they may be of creating small-scale works requiring lightness of touch, "but that celestial fire that warms and fires up the soul, that burning eloquence, those sublime transports that bring ecstasy into the depths of people's hearts will always be lacking in the works of women: [their works] are as cold and pretty as they themselves are: they may have as much wit as you please, but never any soul; they will be a hundred times more levelheaded than they ever will be passionate. They know neither how to feel nor to describe love itself" (206). He concludes that a society that allows itself to be dominated—for that is how he is describing French society—by the taste of such inferior beings cannot find help for its own poverty of spirit.

There is nonetheless a species of inner censor operating within Rousseau's discourse on women that acts to mitigate its excess. The whip hand flies out of control, and the gentle tamer reappears. An appearance of kindness of heart is so central to Rousseau's persona that he finds a means of tempering his androcentricity with a bow to women: this comes as so great a surprise that it provides a degree of relief out of consonance with its true weight. It is this relief that women readers sometimes interpreted as affection for them. After many pages of vituperation, he seems to turn to women's own interests. Present circumstances really serve them ill, we are astonished to learn—having been told the reverse, that everything was now being done for their sake. Here the personal and the larger social recrimination again converge. People "flatter women without loving them: they are surrounded by suitors, but they no longer have real lovers; and the worst is that the former, without the depth of feeling of the latter, nonetheless usurp their rights" (207). Rousseau's chagrin at having been spurned for the lightweight Saint-Lambert in Mme d'Houdetot's affections seems to find resonance here. Nevertheless it is for his defense of love as a deep and serious emotion rather than a frivolous and passing fancy that Rousseau's greater appeal to women would lie. "The way I conceive of this terrible passion, its disturbances, its wildness, its palpitations, its joys, its burning speech, its even more energetic silence, its inexpressible glances that its timidity makes courageous" (207). The promise tacit in his intensity of expression here, to find in love for a woman an overwhelming elixir, was what gave women an unreasoned devotion to the Rousseau who led them thereby to believe that their emotional lives might not be eternally trivialized, even if their role in society were to be severely circumscribed.[96]

But for Rousseau what he regards as the power of passionate love becomes increasingly tied, beyond the *Letter to d'Alembert,* to sexual segregation. We find this confirmed in both of his utopian visions, that of the *Emile* and in the account by Saint-Preux in the *Nouvelle Héloïse* of the ideal relationship between the genders obtaining at Warens. "Excessively intimate relations between the sexes never produce anything but evil." And if these are destructive socially, they are all the more to be feared sexually. Like Sophie and Emile, the women and men of the novel may see one another only "in glimpses and almost by stealth." Saint-Preux argues that this unfamiliarity itself safeguards the lability and plasticity of desire. In the same letter, a husband and wife are seen as rightly spending only their nights together: "Separation begins again at daylight, and the two sexes have no more in common than their meals, at most" (432). In bed at night, the man, I would hold, does not have to confront consciously the alterity of the object of his desire: she remains the pure complement of his sensuality, in a corporeal symbiosis akin to the maternal relationship of the nursling with its mother. Such "blind" moments are preserved for an entirely present-oriented sexuality, devoid of memories of the past or responsibilities for the future. Judith Shklar has characterized Rousseau's thinking about memory for us. "Memory makes us reflect. It cripples us, inhibits us, undoes us. It prevents us from consenting to the present by making us languish in the past."[97]

To live in the midst of a society is to live within a cultural memory: even Rousseau has to pick out a past to orient him in the present. But for Rousseauian man, to live in a society with women is debilitating, for it deprives him of what he most requires from them, the promise of an effortless ecstatic union between himself and his desire.

A good share of animus on Saint-Preux's part against the women of Paris—the quintessence of socialized womanhood—comes of what appears to have been a difficulty in approaching them. He tells Julie that these women have a "soldierly mien," a "grenadier's aspect," and when they speak, they do so in "harsh, bitter, imperious interrogative, mocking tones, louder than a man's" (*NH,* 246). The frankness of their glances above all else seems to upset him: "If anything remains in their tone that resembles female grace, their intrepid and inquiring way of staring at people succeeds in extinguishing it." These women blot out with their looking eyes all pretense that no subject person lies within: this evidence of a woman's own consciousness, of her aptitude for judgment above all else, is what makes her impossible to approach in desire, or to capture with a desire that seeks to remain preconscious, transparent. Yet we must not be misled into believing for a moment that these women—any more than Mme d'Houdetot for Rousseau him-self—held no appeal for Saint-Preux. In a move resembling the one previously described, of exchanging the whip hand for the caress, we find Saint-Preux re-porting how at a country party he had felt an initial antagonism for the Parisian ladies in the company parading their giddy, self-conscious *bons mots* before the men new to them in the group. But later he changes his mind and renders them this amazing tribute: by detaching women from "that eternal pretense that pleases them so, we soon see them as they are; and then all the aversion they at first inspired changes to friendship. . . . All foreigners agree unanimously that, setting aside questions of taste, there is no nation on earth where the women are more enlightened, in general speak more sensibly, more judiciously, or know how, if need be, to give better advice" (*NH,* 253).

This praise is significant. While it is true, as has been alleged by Sarah Kofman in Freudian terms with which I agree, that Rousseau rejects parity with women out of a fear of having to make himself respected by them, respect for him being a factor that would "throw desire into the dust by recalling man to the grandeur and even the sublimity of his nature," he cannot altogether reject the evidence of direct experience: that women too could demonstrate lucidity, frankness, and wisdom.[98] However, in the end he is prepared to sacrifice this French glory, the cultivated, socialized woman, to the imperatives of men's desire. For Saint-Preux's attitude to these women parallels that of the Rousseau of book 5 of the *Emile,* who mocks the qualities of the great courtesan and wit of the seventeenth-century Ninon de Lenclos. Ninon was widely reputed to have raised herself to the level of men. "But with all her high reputation, I would no more have wanted that man as my friend than as my mistress" (*Em.,* 488).

In his panic over the idea of sexual domination by a guileful Delilah—"her violence lies in her charms"—Rousseau, in consonance with his society on this score, reinvents a model for woman to whom a man need feel no fear in attaching himself. Since "in all that has nothing to do with sex, woman is man" (*Em.*, 444), just as he had done in the context of nurturant women he reaffirms "natural woman," *la femme/sexe,* stripped of all her human functions save the maternal and conjugal. And these duties women must perform at a comfortable remove from democratic male society.

For Frenchwomen are preventing Frenchmen from carrying on "their own" discourse on heavy matters of statecraft.[99] Among Genevans, some aspects of the ancient culture survive. "The men amongst themselves, not needing to lower their ideas to the level of women and to dress up their reason in gallantries, can engage in grave and serious speech without fear of ridicule. We dare speak of fatherland and of virtue without passing for a driveler; we dare to be ourselves without having to be enslaved by the maxims of a birdbrain. . . . There is no need to hold back from dispute; each person feeling himself attacked full force by his adversary is obliged to use all his own in defense. This is how the mind acquires justness and vigor." If a few salacious remarks are made, nobody gets offended, for "this boorishness of style is preferable to the more elaborate one in which the two sexes mutually seduce each other and gain a decent familiarity with vice" (*Lett.,* 207). Rousseau decisively shakes off the yoke of "feminine" society and its discourse of mutual flirtation as destructive to the discourse of free men.

Women of high society are rendered far more alien than they were before by this realignment, but they are not merely alien: they have been characterized as vicious enemies of liberated mankind. The young men who were then being trained up "for their amusement" are effeminate figures for Rousseau, who is terrified by them. Like women (and this Rousseau admits) they are kept out of the sun, the wind, the rain, the dust, and deprived of all exercise: "the only thing these women don't demand of these vile slaves is that they be consecrated to their service in the manner of Orientals" (*Lett.,* 213). A curious reentry of the eunuch recurs: Rousseau proposes a male ideal for modern democracy as a way of ridding the world of these effeminate puppets. In his own youth, he tells us, young males, though timid before their elders, had been adept at wrestling and fighting, could sustain wounds and even weep over them, only to then embrace their opponents and make up. This is the sort of youth that produces men "with the zeal to serve their country and blood to shed for her" (*Lett.,* 214).

A manhood developed apart from women is the only respectable male estate for Rousseau. And this is because women enslave men to a regime given over to love. "Love is the realm of women. In it women necessarily set the rules; because according to the order of nature, it is their role to resist, and men can defeat such resistance only at the price of their freedom" (*Lett.,* 159). A woman's freedom is "naturally" lost to her forever in Rousseau's *Letter* when a lover "takes" her. Yet in the Parisian society Rousseau had been a member of for some years, women were not sacrificing all other options in life to a first "defeat." Sexual mores were infinitely less overwrought than the one image of them in which he is so powerfully invested.

Since the theater for him is merely an extension of the realm of love and women, it becomes the wicked preceptor to young people, exerting a damaging power of enchantment over spectators like the nefarious power women wield over lovers. Even those most sublime theatrical expressions of masculinity, Racine's heroes, can find no favor in Rousseau's eyes. They may seem heroic, but "beneath their airs of courage and virtue, they exhibit the qualities of the young men I've spoken of, given over to gallantry, softness, and love, to all that can feminize man and cool his ardor for his true duties. The whole of the French theater breathes only the air of tenderness" (*Lett.,* 217).

It is not only the puny little mannered cocks-of-the-walk Rousseau is after here, but far more consequential game. He is after not only women, but the civil men who have created a higher discourse of the heart and mind that speaks to both genders, that sees the passions of love and politics as shared by women and men, as in the French classical theater. The battle Rousseau wishes to join opposes the most expressive tendencies of the French drama. He actively advocates a repression of male articulateness, is hostile to poetry, is against male conscience struggling with itself upon the stage, opposes the representation of maleness in conflict.[100] Rousseau does not merely espouse his more rustic model of masculinity, then: he pours opprobrium and scorn on the most accomplished works of French literary art as effeminate and degenerate productions.

In the emotional turmoil following his failed passion for Sophie d'Houdetot, Rousseau rejected more passionately than ever the claims of culture to any beneficent effect upon morality and proposed an ostensibly new but really quite ancient model of man.[101] This man is one totally available for service to his fellows, essentially to his nation. He will be hamstrung no longer by that fell passion, love. "Whoever feels tender love for his relations, his friends, his country, and humankind degrades himself in taking on a disordered attachment that soon harms all the others and yet is infinitely preferred to them all" (175). Love, a despised complicator, has been put back in its place. Rousseau self-disculpatingly confesses the self-serving nature of his arguments in the *Letter:* "Without noticing it, I described my present situation; I depicted Grimm, Mme d'Epinay, Mme d'Houdetot, Saint-Lambert, myself. While writing it what delicious tears I shed! Alas, one feels in it that too much of love, that fatal love I was trying to cure myself of, had not yet left my heart. What is more, a certain self-pity was admixed with it, for I felt as if I were dying and I wanted to say my final farewell to the public." Rousseau adds the significant note that this was "the first of my works during which I experienced delight in writing" (*Conf.,* 254–255).

This pleasure—of release, for it can have been no other—is that of vengeance against French society for the many slights he feels he has suffered via an exaltation of all that he considered to be antagonistic to it. And in this war, for it would be one, women of high society would be deliberately sacrificed. "Among us . . . the most esteemed woman is the one who makes the most noise, of whom the most is said, whom one sees most often out in society, at whose home people dine most frequently, who sets the tone most imperiously, who judges, lays down the law, decides, pronounces, awards positions for talent, merit, and virtue, and whose good opinions learned men curry slavishly" (*Lett.,* 161). An end to this outrageous "disorder," the disorder that put him in the posture of being evicted by Louise d'Epinay, is an imperative need, as he sees it. The remedy is not only a suppression of the theater, but of women's influence in the theater of wider life. The alternative "new" model of woman proposed will date from the time of Pericles' funeral oration. She will be out of sight and unheard from: "The most decent woman is the one of whom one speaks least" (*Lett.,* 160).

What Rousseau alludes to as the curious and singular tone of his *Letter* comes of its rhetoric being unambiguous, stripped of the feints and the careful masquerade of polite discourse. The gloves are off. The weakened victim of love turns to bullying both his competitors and his easier prey, the women. The entire machinery of culture is metaphorically brought down so as to punish the world for depriving Rousseau of his love, and mocking his vulnerability in loving.

But when Rousseau speaks, he speaks for a vast population of angry antiaristocratic male traditionalists and disaffected lovers of all classes in whom the idea of banishment of women from an active role in culture strikes a chord of deep, rancorous responsiveness. Hence the affection of Rousseau as well as his audience for Molière's Alceste, as he dismisses the worldly Célimène, who refuses to leave society and return "to nature" in his embrace:

> No, I detest you now. I could excuse
> Everything else, but since you refuse
> To love me wholly, as a wife should do
> And see the world in me, as I in you,
> Go! I reject your hand, and disenthrall
> My heart from your enchantments, once for all. (act 5, sc. 3)

Chapter

4

THE WAR OF THE SEXES: FROM THE FALL OF MERTEUIL TO THE RISE OF BRUTUS

All the nations have shown scorn for the
unchastity of women. . . . That's because their
virtue is one of the axes of public morality,
and its loss brings so many others along with
it that it is the forerunner of revolutions,
especially in states governed by popular
sovereignty.

JACQUES LESCURE DESMAISONS, 1783

AN imperious helmeted Minerva stands staunchly, grasping her great shield with
her left arm as she gestures daintily with her right hand toward her defeated
opponent in battle, Mars (fig. 20, *The Combat of Minerva and Mars*, attr. to David).
Lying among his strewn and futile implements of war—his abandoned helmet
and useless sword—the dark and muscular Mars looks up in confusion at this
victorious rival. His powerful, upthrust arm with its open, helpless hand is the
emblem of masculine power confounded. This work hovers between nascent male
neoclassicism and the feminized court tradition in its depicted confrontation between the idealized rigors of battlefield reality—the rearing horses and the slash-
ing soldiers at left rear, the foregrounded corpses, and the old-soldierly dismay of
the figures on the left—and the radiant Minerva. A revivified baroque emblem,
she dominates the composition, which is topped by the entirely rococo Venus
emerging from the clouds above: outstretched in a protective gesture toward her

20. *Attributed to David,* Combat of Minerva and Mars, *Musée du Louvre, Photo Musées Nationaux*

lover, her female hand provides a rhythmic counterpoint to his own. A "hectic, dashing piece, astonishing in its compositional sophistication and clear intimation of sexual warfare" is the way Anita Brookner characterized it.[1] What might some of the components of such sexual warfare be? In the period's context, Minerva may be read as the regal woman of the aristocracy or of the salon, employing a derived power merely lent her by her daughtership to Zeus, that is, by powerful protectors or by the Crown. Mars's dismay expresses anxiety in the face of the overthrow of male superordination: he lies there, cheated and bewildered by the thwarting of a victory to which his natural power would have entitled him. Seen in this light, the painting transmits at once a sense of the aspiration of women to engage in the world, albeit that of war, and that of the perplexity, close to anger, of men who long to engage with each other on the basis of their own masculine strength, removed from the tyranny of hierarchy and the intrusions of the other sex.

The gender split that becomes so patent in David's great neoclassical canvases of the eighties lies revealed here, its force scarcely muted at all by the weak Venus, who might have provided a visual focus attenuating the force of warfare. Her ineffectuality in the eye of the beholder conveys a sense of the growing fragility of the sexual tie: the putto, that infant emanation of love's liquefactions, seems, as does Venus herself, virtually to recede into the heavens as a factor in the gender battle that Minerva has (momentarily) won. Her victory would be one of the last great mythological evocations of the power of a goddess in the rococo vocabulary.

Thus far, I have attempted to delineate some of the gender dynamics inherent in the campaign against the rococo, which had as its major feature a denigration of the style as frivolous, morally tainted, erotic, and "feminine," in contrast with the heroic, virtuous, manly neoclassical. I went on to try to uncover some of the preconditions of this conflict in the erotic conceptions and the relational and familial substrata of mid-eighteenth century French life, and to look for the mode of their representation in the arts. I then turned to the high culture theater, to examine the conditions of upper-class women's prominence in the salon. There, I strove to emphasize both the potential it presented to women to exercise a degree of power and self-expression, as well as the marked masculine and lower-class resentment engendered by their omnipresence in upper-class society.

Now, having arrived at the immediate pre-Revolutionary period, while building upon the earlier examinations of emergent neoclassicism, altered conceptions of love and family, and the special animus growing in society against aristocratic women, I will emphasize alternatively some relevant historical developments and some major artistic formulations. This chapter moves in more or less chronological progression through the decade, which I regard as the era of a definitive ideological battle during which the new gender paradigm of separate spheres will, though not without struggle, have already congealed before the outbreak of the Revolution itself, as the arts, especially, of this era reveal.

More populist authors now give vent to a deepening and vociferously expressed misogyny, even as they expound the redemptive virtues of an eroticized maternalism. The relentlessness with which these trends are reiterated weakens women's already fragile capability for self-definition, either as individuals or as part of a group. As the chastity/corruption axis becomes more entwined in public discourse with the private/public polarity, a severe female/male dualism will achieve its greatest triumph in the creative arts, which, more than all other human productions, catch up and recreate the phantasms of collective life.

Even so, these rigid dichotomies, though they prove to be victorious in dominating public opinion, never prevail unchallenged by skeptical and dissenting voices. Such challenges as these produce the heightened dialogue engaged during the decade that ends with the Revolution, represented in the discussion that follows.

As Kings Wane, Do Queens Wax?

The defeat of Louis XV's armies in the Seven Years' War ratified his image as an inept, inert monarch. Much as he would be seen as failing the nation in strength through this military defeat, he was felt equally to be failing it in heart, through his wastefulness of life and money in the supremely self-engrossed luxury of his courtly and personal dissipations. A mood of apocalyptic hopelessness erupts into public discourse, which the crown attempts, harshly, to put down. The Parliament consigned to the flames Helvetius's *On Man* (1772), which had included the melancholy statement, "My country has accepted the yoke of despotism, whose nature it is to stifle thought in minds and virtue in souls. . . . This degraded nation is today the scorn of Europe. No salutary crisis will give it back its freedom." The people, associating their unenviable civic and economic difficulties, of summary judgment and abusive taxation, with their failing king, were observed to show little interest when he became mortally ill in 1774. You could not have arrested any more people for speaking ill of him than were arrested, or all of Paris would have ended up in jail, Félix Rocquain reports a contemporary to have concluded. On May 8 of that year, during the monarch's fatal sickness, the curate of Saint-Etienne du Mont felt impelled to administer a public scolding to his parishioners for their unfeelingness toward their king: "Are you Christians? Are you Frenchmen?" he cried, wonderingly.[2]

Louis's last four years, those of the lowly Du Barry's ascendancy at his side, eclipsed all that was left of regard for king and court. Despite the surge of hope accompanying his twenty-year-old grandson's accession to the throne and the people's initial enthusiasm for his fetching nineteen-year-old wife Marie-Antoinette, disaffection with monarchy now proved to be a chronic disease.[3]

Jacques Turgot, the Physiocrats' leader who assumed office as principal minister when Louis XVI came to the throne, attempted during his stewardship to impose on the monarchy a conception of the rule of equity, rather than the rule of power he identified with absolutism. But after only two brief years, the coalition of privilege reasserted itself. Turgot's desire to entrench a moral law applicable to all men without distinction of strength or interests clashed with the traditional monarchical understanding of untrammeled sovereignty.[4]

Such an insistence upon his regal prerogatives on the part of the young Louis invited further trouble. In this verbally licentious society, the king's claim to strength was undermined by his impotence. The clumsy prince's generative difficulties in his unfortunate match with a showily attractive princess (his marriage remained unconsummated for some years) gave rise to scurrilous lampoons concerning both. These in turn became so habitual, conditioning public perception of the monarchs, that their public sexual personae would remain virtually unaltered by events: the "insatiable" and ostensibly sexually unbridled queen retained her aura of debauchery, her husband his of sexual inadequacy, long after an operation had presumably corrected his impotence and a daughter, a son and heir in 1781, and a third child and second son were born to the couple. A good sample from out of the flood of *libelles* (scurrilous pamphlets) on such themes, *The Loves of Charlot and Toinette,* was published by the free presses of the Hague and of London to be smuggled into France. After its description of the queen masturbating, this rhymed ditty relates her alleged sexual revelries with the king's brother, the Count D'Artois. As to the king,

> It is well known that the poor Sire
> Three or four times condemned
> By the salubrious faculty [of medicine]
> For complete impotence,
> Cannot satisfy Antoinette.
> Quite convinced that this misfortune,
> Considering that his matchstick
> Is no bigger than a straw,
> Always limp and always curved,
> He has no p—except in his pocket;
> Instead of f—ing, he is f—ed
> Like the late prelate of Antioch.[5]

As Robert Darnton observes, though scurrilous satire has a respectably ancient pedigree in French politics, streams of such salacious lampoons simply overflowed during the reign of Louis XVI. Darnton argues that the power of such libelles as antiaristocratic propaganda has been underestimated, for it constituted the nation's "living folklore," with its colorful allegations (asserted as mock fact) of buggery, lesbianism, cuckoldry, venereal infection, illegitimacies, and impotence. "The ridiculing of Louis XVI must have done a great deal of damage when nobility was still identified with 'seminal fluid' and when the Salic Law still required that the royal 'race' be transmitted through a magical unbroken chain of males."[6] In consequence, after the history of the couple's initial sexual reproductive difficulties, and in the wake of the swarm of suggestive libelles about the queen's sexual habits, there would inevitably be a number who would never believe in the legitimacy of her offspring, hence in the continuation of the Capetian lineage. This sexual story, interweaving actuality with flights of accusatory fantasy, contributes enormously to the case against the Crown's becoming so largely a case against the queen. As Chantal Thomas has seen it, "in the reign of Louis XVI the arrogance of absolute power was entirely attributed to Marie-Antoinette, who thus managed to accumulate in her single person the vices traditional to the king and to his mistress."[7] Though the king continued high in the sentimental regard of his subjects, a sense of his own impotence would be merely reinforced, despite his consignment of several writers or publishers of libels against the queen to the Bastille, by his absolute inability to enforce respect for her.

Such a lack of congruence between the king's unaggressive sexual persona and the traditional ideal of male, not to say kingly, dominance acted as a stimulant to a set of men, of whom Restif de la Bretonne was the most vocal. In his *Gynographes* (1777), following Rousseau in spirit, he inveighs (via an imaginary female interlocutor) against the lack of women's subordination in society, most specifically against their claims to equality: he thus reveals that debate about this very question is alive. "The two sexes are not equal; to equalize them is to denature them" (41). One can virtually see not only the then-twenty-two-year-old Marie-Antoinette but all girls of upper-class pretensions indicated in Restif's furious outburst. "The girl raised as she is today has but one desire, and that is to command." She must instead be raised for submission to the will of father, brother, and (following the preachment of Rousseau, who taught that women must be acquiescent "even to men's injustice") "brutal, drunken husbands who would make them die of chagrin if they had the temerity to protest" (138). The Restif who proclaims that men owe no fealty, not even a core of basic respect, to women tacitly expresses exasperation with an "unmanly" king and a courtly code that, as far as he is concerned, has given women unnatural advantages, which must be wrested from them. Of course Restif is not everyman: but he makes his appeal to a spirit of domination over women he assumes (wrongly) that all men must share. He puts his diatribe against female equality, tellingly enough, into a plea ostensibly written by a woman. For in the sex-cum-class war this son of peasants is waging, he needs to co-opt the women's as well as the men's class resentments to his gender objective. Women are not his natural audience, however, as he is well aware: the mean coerciveness of his tone to them gives this away. His tactic with women— which, ironically in the case of the none-too-churchly Restif, continues the methods of the Church fathers—is simply to overwhelm them with affirmations of their self-evident folly and inadequacy. It is in effect but one more resort to deeply entrenched tradition by a thinker who thinks himself at odds with it.

A tale told at the start of *Gynographes* sets forth the gender/class structures his texts impose. In a certain family a gentle, pretty young girl too much spoiled by the reading of novels, falls in love with a young fop (we understand that he is either an aristocrat in fact or aspires to be one):[8] "opinionated, fatuous, quite impertinent, . . . drinking no wine because it spoils the breath, never uttering the least little swear-word, not even a 'damn it,' because it would give him a harsh, too-masculine tone, knowing all about Literature, and acting out plays in salons. . . . Wherever the ladies are, he's one of them and seems to have abjured his sex, so assiduously has he suppressed all his tastes; . . . he allows only a squeaky, whistling sound to escape from his throat; . . . his plumed hat . . . and his huge hairpiece resemble the coiffures of Prostitutes" (8). From his lips flows the language of "sentiment," "virtue," love's "flame." Naturally, the mindlessly impressionable girl falls for his game, rebuffing the "good" suitor, much admired and of admirable figure, a member of the magistrate class, who "occupies the top position in the judiciary of the town" (9). Restif is spurred by no such animus in elaborating a full description of this suitor as he had felt toward the petit-maître. The magistrate's class stature, entailing his rooted authority and his earnest dedication to precedent, is presumed to provide sufficient warrant of integrity and of a manliness totally at odds with the postures of that dandyish women-pleaser.

After the girl's parents have consigned her to a convent to cure her of her unseemly preference and failed, they "punish" her by allowing her to wed the man of her own choosing. Only two months later, she is disabused and wretched, justly punished for her claim to a penchant of her own for a different order of man than that of the new male ideal.

An unmanning obeisance to female desires and tastes, according to Restif's scenario, threatens to undermine rising bourgeois class consciousness; it would make women ungovernable and traitorous to their own class and to its men. Slavishness to women deprives manly men of the satisfaction both of gender pre-eminence, and of their prior right to the sexual enjoyment of "their" own women.

Feminist Consciousness Undermined: The Journal des dames

Our minds are flexible and thirsty.

MME DE MONTANCLOS

Restif taps into one important vein of gender conflict being mined in the pre-Revolutionary years. But there were strong countercurrents to his tendencies as well. The history of the *Journal des dames* provides a glimpse into some of these.[9] Isolated, antiphonal voices were raised quite regularly in defense of women, but the problems inherent in their discourse are immediately audible. "I am always astonished," wrote Marie-Anne Roumier-Robert in 1765–66, "that women have not yet banned together, formed a separate league, with an eye to avenging themselves against male injustices. May I live long enough to see them make such profitable use of their courage! But up until now, they have been too coquettish and dissipated to concern themselves seriously with the interests of their sex." As Nina Rattner Gelbart points out, women like Roumier-Robert were opposed to female frivolity and espoused puritanical Rousseauist family positions. Such moralism "went hand in hand with a growing political hostility to the regime."[10] Unfortunately, as I see it, this very moralism in argument merely reinforced, by its repetition, the association of women with frivolity it sought to combat.

Gelbart's account of the editorship of Mme Beaumer at the *Journal des dames* provides a striking instance of the vicissitudes of forthright advocacy of women, at a time when women editors were a rarity. Begun by and ending up in the hands of men, the *Journal* (1759–1778) was edited in its middle years by three women, of whom Mme Beaumer was the first. She served closest to midcentury, and her voice would prove to be the most militant among the three. A Huguenot, hence starting from a potentially oppositionist posture, she "crusaded for the poor and downtrodden, for social justice, religious toleration, Freemasonry, republican liberty, international peace, and equality before the law." But the most unacceptable item among her claims was that the subordination of women was related and even prior to the other injustices she deplored, and that its elimination would eventuate in harmonious equality between classes and nations. "How I would rejoice," she exclaimed, "to rid the whole earth of the injurious notion [that we are inferior], still held by some barbarians among our citizens, who have difficulty acknowledging that we can speak and write." Asking that relations between the sexes be based on equality and mutual trust, she told her presumably female audience, "if we educate ourselves, men will recognize that we are not only useful but indispensable." Obviously, she was not alluding solely to women's use as mothers and lovers: deploring the fact that war and peace are made "without us," she counseled women to abandon their mirrors for introspection.[11]

The response of male readers to this discourse was ridicule. Mme Beaumer's gravity itself was their butt as they strove reductively, as she put it, to metamorphose her "into an *Elégante*," or woman of fashion. "We women think under our coiffures as well as you do under your wigs. We are as capable of reasoning as you are. In fact, you lose your reason over us every day." With an unrelenting sting Beaumer denounces, though with a quite different emphasis, one of Restif's own targets, the "conceited dandies, bent on perpetuating flirtations, superficial relations between the sexes," for their behavior belittling women. Although her jaundiced view of the fops might seem to ally her passingly with Restif's rage against them, her own anger conveys no animus against any lack of manliness in them, as his most decidedly does. Beamer's meliorism departs materially from Restif's where women are concerned. Both despise the dominant social class and its manners, but whereas she envisages the rise of the bourgeoisie as fostering the establishment of sexual equality—with women as equal partners to men in their intimate relations as well as in the world of work, where they would practice all the sciences, metiers, and arts, Restif propounds an exactly opposite course.[12] Instead of sexual equality, Restif looks to change for its promise of male supremacy and toward deliverance of men from an effeminate culture. A touchstone of their conflicting views is Restif's deep Rousseauism as against Mme Beaumer's unalloyed rejection of Rousseau, whom she saw as negative, full of bewildering paradoxes, and tending to put humankind "back on all fours," thereby delaying both sexes in their need to progress.[13]

The fate of Mme Beaumer's editorship of the *Journal des dames* I take to be indicative of the fate of egalitarian feminism in the next half-century. In the wake of her call to her readership to make theirs "*le siècle des dames*—the century of the ladies," and her later wishful claim, in 1763, that the "women's revolution was gripping the entire world," the militant Beaumer, who called herself an *autrice* rather than a male *auteur* drops from sight. She was succeeded as editor by far more coy and conciliatory male and female voices, no doubt less disturbing to readers.[14] Women would increasingly find it uncomfortable to be thought of as given to "special pleading" in their own behalf.

The *Journal's* last female editor was the Baroness de Prinzen (later Mme de Montanclos). Under her stewardship and the protection of Marie-Antoinette, the magazine, like tastes in general in the seventies, turned maternalist, though still attempting to maintain some vestige of feminist flavor. The baroness herself became increasingly bourgeois and Rousseauist over time: "For over a decade," writes Gelbart, "Rousseau's ideas had been working a revolution in female psychology, and by the 1770's many women, especially mothers, had come to see him as their champion rather than their foe." Montanclos now preaches to her readers the joys of mothering, regarding its prerogatives as a right women had to reclaim, so as to demonstrate their value as tender nurturers to the state. Yet for her, mothers must at the same time be enlightened and even learned. "I do swear it my intention to force men to guarantee women the justice they have previously refused them on whim. . . . we can know everything, for our minds are flexible and thirsty, and we can do all the good of which humanity is capable."

References to children as "Cornelia's jewels" enable the *Journal des dames* to posit a Roman matron's status for women in the state, which would then owe to them some desperately needed allegiance and assistance in raising their offspring, in return for such maternal fealty. In an effort to shore up this bargain, Mme de Montanclos sought the support of the lawyer Delacroix in obtaining protective legislation for women. While she viewed him as her ally, his own allegiance to her cause by no means prevented him from referring to women as hummingbirds, to men as eagles.[15]

In Noël Hallé's painting (fig. 21) *Cornelia, Mother of the Gracchi,* neither woman suggests a hummingbird. This canvas from the 1779 Salon nakedly brings into confrontation the two contending styles of womanhood. Against the austerely neoclassical background the two women loom in the foreground, eyeing one another. The wealthy, bejeweled Roman matron, Cornelia's neighbor, elaborately coiffed, sits surrounded by her silks and satins, gems tumbling from her treasure box. Seated facing her is the simply clad mother of the Gracchi, unbejeweled except for the clasp of her cloak. Cornelia's posture is all appeal and the willed vulnerability of the strong woman. Stalwart, with sturdy knees and hand, she yet extends her neck and cocks her head to the side in a submissive plea that her child-jewels be recognized as superior to inert baubles.[16] The unprettified yet romanticized children's postures and the textures of their clothing blend into Cornelia's own to constitute a grouping that simply overwhelms the overdressed matron's figure.

21. *Noël Hallé,* Cornelia, Mother of the Gracchi, *Musée du Montpellier, Photo Claude O'Sughrue*

The latter's back is literally to the wall; her figure in its isolation appears bereft, as she seems to have to hold onto her perch to sustain the onslaughts of the love and pride of a mother of heroes. We may take this work as a sign of social women's retreat from preeminence in public esteem.

Shifts in Style, 1: The Tyranny of Opinion

The evolution of the *Journal des dames,* moving from the forthright gender egalitarianism of Mme Beaumer to the more politic familial feminism of Mme de Montanclos, retraces the trajectory of opinion concerning sex roles as the eighteenth century moves toward its end. Social attitudes that undergirded this change were being formed no longer at court (even Marie-Antoinette preferred Parisian social gatherings to the stuffiness of Versailles), but out in society, in cafés, salons, masonic lodges, and clubs. Yet despite our tendency to believe otherwise, François Furet argues that the aristocracy was in no wise in a phase of decadence. On the contrary, many members of the nobility actively espoused the progressive reformist views propagated in the later years of the century. In this respect, they too contributed to that deep alteration of sensibility that took place before Revolution was thought of. The "democratic sociability," that of the salon or the café that was displacing social hierarchy, at best provoked genuine social interpenetration and exchange, at worst might give birth to that monster "*On.*" "*On-dit*—they say . . .", this anxious rooting about for a confident new consensus might, on the one hand, dictate reforms to enlarge it like those granting the free trade of grain (1774), the suppression of the *corvée* (1776), freedom of conscience and the abolition of the *lettre de cachet* (1784), freedom of religion (1787), and the suppression of torture (1788). A less liberating effect of the pursuit of consensus lay in its giving way to storms of paranoid vindictiveness about individuals or groups. In terms of style, "usage, immovable scepter in hand, regulates all, commands all: there is no replying to these words: *they say, they do this, people think, they're wearing.*" As Sénac de Meilhan would affirm, the role of fashionability in the Revolution was to be its "super power," dictating both the acceptance of the guillotine as well as the flaunting courage of so many of its victims.[17]

According to Mercier, fealty to fashionability led petty-bourgeois women to seek to emulate the dress of marquises and duchesses, rudely taxing their spouses' pocketbooks. "Expenditures for fashion today exceed those for the table and for horses and carriage."[18] But even as bourgeois women attempted to emulate the surface embellishments of the aristocracy, the aristocracy's own value system was being infiltrated by bourgeois beliefs and ethics.

During the course of Louis XVI's reign, as Sénac tells us, a taste for private life became the rule, bringing with it a recoil from the free and piquant mores of the rule of Louis XV, and this rejection of the ways of the last generation affected even the manners and morals in court circles: "There was no longer as much grace in manners and speech as there had been, and yet there was no greater candor in people's souls; that gallantry that comes of a perpetual desire to please existed no more. Women had private arrangements which in terms of their duration and the serenity of possession were equivalent to marriages, but scandalous adventures were rare."[19] So much was this the case that the Juvenals of the time, claims Sénac, had little to chew on as compared with the previous reign.

Shifts in Style, 2: The Family-style Salon

No longer the exclusive apanage of aristocrats or even of philosophes, the salon continued to play a role important to the formation of opinion.

One of the most eminent salons before the Revolution was that of the irreproachably conjugal Genevans Suzanne Curchod Necker and her husband, the on-and-off minister of finance, Jacques Necker. The Neckers' Fridays drew inspiration and even support from the great Geoffrin and du Deffand salons of earlier decades, but apart from the whirlwind conversational pyrotechnics displayed on one of Diderot's occasional visits, their brilliance, as compared with those earlier salons, was muted. Mercier would state in 1781 that "the art of speaking is replacing eloquence, and that is quite another thing." What he meant by this was that a Diderot's or a du Deffand's solo improvisations were giving way to more egalitarian gatherings with fewer star turns, more exchanges of views, more reading of works—either fiction or projects for legislation. In the Neckers' case, the less playful tone was the inevitable consequence of the far more sedate, planned, and puritanical manners of the hosts, Protestant Genevans. The attractions of their mode of being lay in their (relative) candor, charitability, and earnestness, qualities not usually sought after by Parisian society. The none-too-sociable Necker would nod off, as his intelligent but self-conscious wife dutifully and skillfully prodded her guests. The addition of their astonishingly precocious little daughter Germaine, born in 1766, to the company of authors like Helvetius, Thomas, Morellet, Marmontel, and d'Alembert, sparked both company and child; it also expressed the new maternalistic solicitude of Suzanne Necker, who educated her daughter herself and had even tried to breast-feed her. Indeed the tiresome professions of familial devotion, often mocked in later times, of Mother and Father Necker as well as their daughter, were a near-slavish attempt on the part of the Swiss family to curry favor with a display of their allegiance to the nascent Rousseauist family mode in the 1770s and 1780s to a French public whose ideal it had become. Suzanne Necker's ostentatious public adulation of her husband, both verbally and in print, were, if anything, only surpassed by her daughter's filial piety. Much of Germaine de Staël's salon activity and of her writing would subsequently be devoted first to the success, and later to the rehabilitation, of her father's political career. Her own actions as a political woman, in fact, could be authorized even in her own eyes, in the decade of the eighties, only by the rationale of love for her father.[20]

Yet Suzanne Necker was only a selective Rousseauist, somewhat resembling in this respect Mme de Montanclos. She raised her daughter to be "like Emile" rather than his subordinate Sophie. And the career of Germaine de Staël, despite her panegyric of Rousseau written in this decade, the *Reflections of the Character and Writings of Jean-Jacques Rousseau,* would be imprinted by the struggle between the older code of salon women and the new familialism:[21] she would live her marital, amorous, and intellectual lives like a woman of the Old Regime's upper classes, but guilt, inspired by the new moralism, would afflict her ability to do so freely. Chiefly, more than any of the women who would pass from the old system to the new, her absolute inability to renounce public life was to mark her out as an anachronism among women.

Shifts in Style, 3: Digging Eros out from Underground

In 1776 "Paris was overtaking Venice as the vice capital of the world." Continuing the midcentury's interest in sexual control, numerous plans to regulate prostitution were advanced; the most sensational of these efforts to devise modes of organizing sexuality rationally was C.-N. Ledoux's plan for an *Ockéma,* a phallus-shaped structure without windows that was to serve as a sanitized municipal brothel. The terms of Ledoux's rationale do not lack interest: they prefigure the First Empire's for the rigid oversight of vice. "Here the good commands, it will neutralize the passions so as to prepare delicious access to hearts, and if it should appear to embrace apparent corruption, this is only to identify with the principle that maintains our great concern for the perpetuation of the generations."[22]

A sort of apprehension creeps into public discourse about the omnipresence of prostitutes, soliciting in every part of the city of Paris (not only in their usual haunts, the Palais Royal and its district), and about the general perception—whatever may actually have been the case—that France was following the path of Rome's fall in its too-visible sexual polymorphousness. In the 1780s "tribadism had become almost fashionable and sodomy seemed to many to be on the point of breaking through the old controls."[23] A terror of homosexuality fortifies the ambient gender anxiety of police and sexual reformers. So concerned will the latter be to reinforce sexual controls that pleas for the regulation of prostitution may even go so far as to ask men to abandon their encroachments on consecrated female professions, so as to ensure women "honest" work. Regulate women if you wish to reform men: this is a theme we will encounter again. Plans like Ledoux's uniformly regard women as instruments for the satisfaction of the individual male's sexuality, and of the regeneration and good ordering of the state.

Significant shifts in style in mores and attitudes redraw the moral map of the nation. On the one side we find the growing mood of moral earnestness, a concern with virtue and moral uplift that promises a harmonization between private mores and public policy (such as we find it expressed in the Necker family's public postures). The reverse or underside of these aspirations manifests itself in what we might call male blueprints of anxiety, those projects for a rationalized prostitution, expressed as a delirium of control of women's "uncontrollable" sexuality and venality, plans that situate in the persons of women, seen as irresistible foci of desire, the site of its enclosure and limitation.

Shifts in Style, 4: Fashion

A revolution before the Revolution: "The eighteenth century exhibits . . . a decisive mutation that Rousseau prefigured and exemplified and that the Revolution merely ratified by an acceleration of it." A different mode of seeing, of presenting and of representing the newly validated self comes to the fore. Spurred by a revulsion against the emotional aridity of the older modes, by Anglomania and the cult of antiquity, a mimesis of a fantasized natural austerity comes to be the imperative. The "privatization of morals and the rise of intimacy," Perrot believes, of discretion, and of isolation from society, "propagates a modesty that, by virtue of a well-known perverse effect, merely heightens desire." Instead of the now dreaded polymorphousness, fetishization will be directed elsewhere: to the woman-object-of-desire's diet, for example, which now consists of "vegetables and fresh fruit, milk and pure water," and not too much of them. "Parisiennes . . . are in despair when they begin to get fat, and drink vinegar to keep their figures," says the article on "Rouge" of the *Encyclopédie*.[24] The hygienic concern to restructure and constrict the female body and its appetites conflicts with the concurrent and frequently verbalized longing for freedom. This latter impulse ultimately finds its vestimentary concretion in the shift, which, as the whalebone corset is little by little put aside, will gradually come (by the time of the Directoire) to be the dominant female style of dress.

Even here the woman's body was the site of conflict among hygienicists, physicians, and traditionalists. The hygienicists advocated release from all stays, as the sole course consonant with nature's imperatives. "Nature is order," wrote Dr. Bressy in 1789; "every time we transgress it, disorder follows; where there is disorder in feeling beings, suffering ensues." But such evident advocacy of the freedom of the female body is almost always coupled with a prurient concern for ensuring its ability to entice the physicians' own sex. The unconstrained breasts of countrywomen, generous, rounded, with protuberant nipples, are viewed as a triumphant reproach to city women's flat and pendulous ones.[25] Exercise and an active life were what this group favored for women as well as infants. The more influential medical establishment did not agree with these prescriptions, however. To its eye, women appeared, as in Dr. Roussel's 1775 work, as irremediably bound by the telos of biology, their reproductive finality. "Nature" had created them as frail beings, uteri cloaked in an evanescent and fragile, inherently decaying medium of flesh. Both of these currents of masculinist opinion (like the projects for the regulation of prostitution) may be thought of as technocratic. What links them despite their huge differences—the first commending women to a life of hearty activity, the second to one of retirement and debility—is their common insistence on viewing women, and women only, solely as reproducers of their kind.

Fashion, recalcitrant to moralism or hygiene, moved in their direction in the late years of the era as the markedly less aristocratic *robe à l'anglaise* (fig. 22), often made of a simple cambric or muslin, became the mode of choice. It featured a fitted back and curved sides, following the natural line of a narrowly corseted waist and compressing the breasts upward, as in the past. "The princesses" in 1778, reports Elisabeth Vigée-Lebrun, "were not remarkable when seated on the benches, being dressed in cambric muslin gowns, with large straw hats and muslin veils," a costume universally adopted by females at that time.[26] The bustle put in a reappearance (it had been absent for most of the century). It was counterbalanced by a provocatively low, revealing neckline, coyly shrouded in a frothy fichu. Skirts were shorter, showing feet and ankles. The unbalancingly high heel of mid-century gave way to a dainty low slipper.[27] These elements of style present an unstable play of liberation, enticement, and control, which seem to have presented women with the illusion, at least of real choices.

22. Attributed to Elisabeth Vigée-Lebrun, Marie-Antoinette Wearing a "Gaulle," *National Gallery of Art, Timken Collection, Washington D.C.*

On the top of the fashionable woman's head there was also a war being waged, between the relatively short, soft, and simple coiffure, capped by a bourgeois *pouf,* or those huge constructions that amaze us still, built on an already high pyramid of hair or wig. At their apex these would feature displays of elaborate ribbons or flowers, whole tiny ships, or even farm buildings with cattle and minuscule people. Carmontelle's watercolor (fig. 23) of three such ladies at civilized tea in a garden glade shows us vividly the precarious quality of this construction of femininity. The figure at the left, with her simpler coif, still wears it atop a massive cone of hair. All three, amid the shower of their stylish stripes and ruffles, hold themselves with a precarious erectness that works against the lush, curving swirl of their leafy bower. Their gestures are calculated, their postures necessarily stiff: and yet Carmontelle lends them alert and attentive physiognomies. A sweet pathos issues from the visible strain they exhibit in upholding the weight of high cultural expectation. Mature civilized women, they suffer the pressures of their society with decorum.[28]

As to male costume, it too had become lighter, constructed out of less pretentious fabric. And men of lower class were increasingly conscious (such are the

23. *Louis de Carmontelle,*
Mesdames de Montesson,
du Crest, and de Damas
Taking Tea *(1771), Musée
Carnavalet, Paris*

vicissitudes of individuation) of their appearance. They took pains "not to look ugly," says Mercier, and dressed their hair more simply and, as he thought, "better."[29] For both women and men, then, the major alterations in costume can be read as diminishing the theater of rococo analogies of dress for simplifications that, revealing the body more nakedly, emphasize the basic dimorphism of the sexes.

The modes of the late century illustrate to what extent the drive to naturalness—for this will become progressively a period of consummately exquisite simplicity—is but partially realized. Clinging to the gracious forms that had given each sex access to the other, society reaches out yet tentatively toward the tabula rasa of purification. The loading of the woman's head with decorative messages, like the sweatshirt self-advertisements of our own day, seems, apart from its sheer narcissism, a coded means for her to manifest her personality, or even her ideas. The farm implies a Rousseauist soul, the galleon an adventurous one. But the sheer bulky insistence of this mode suggests a stressful overemphasis: why did these women need to make themselves appear so unnatural in this era of the cult of the natural? Were they forcing fashion to "speak" for them in despair at having their real voices heard? To me this mode suggests a last desperate stratagem on the part of upper-class women to make the dying rococo style, the style that had empowered them socially, imposing once more. On the other side, the cult of naturalness seems almost to call for no explanation, so overdetermined was it by Rousseauist, masonic, and politically reformist trends. And yet for women, acquiescence in this cult would have awesome consequences for their individual, family, and civic lives.

I have picked out several arenas of shift in style at the eighteenth century's end to stress here: the shift in manners, as an index of heightened democratization; the salon, for its more political, egalitarian, and familial tone; prostitution reform as a site of unrest and its imperative call for sexual reform; and fashion, as the visible summit of a submerged mountain of gender evolution. But the struggle around gender definition was not limited in the pre-Revolutionary era to such indirect modes of expression. For this was an age of polemics.

The Battle

Age-old quarreling over women's nature and role had by no means abated: but by the 1770s the debate seems to narrow in its scope and terminology. The Rousseauist camp now distinctly dominates discourse, as Carracioli (1767) and Fromageot (1772–24) defend women's right to education not as a right due them as persons, but for its promise of enabling mothers better to educate their children. Cerfvol (1772) argues that it is their motherhood that exalts women: women without children are respected "merely as human beings."[30]

The notion of the *citoyenne* is firmly tied in most representative thought with enlightened motherly attentiveness to the youth of the future *citoyen*. Women's present educational level is acknowledged to be wanting. This defect gave an opening to more feminist thinkers like the Abbé Le More (1774) and Riballier (1779), who propose that girls receive the same education as boys. "Look about us at the animal kingdom," the latter exclaims. "Where do male animals usurp authority over females, once the duty to reproduce is fulfilled? What difference is there between the two sexes as far as strength and courage, intelligence and industry are concerned? . . . Let's not flatter ourselves. Whichever way we may look, nature offers no example that authorizes our arrogant pretensions, our exclusive right to all the advantages that the education of the mind and the exercise of the body afford us."[31]

Even the considerable force of Riballier's plea is mitigated by two major rhetorical blocks. Such is the success of maternalist thinking that Riballier feels obliged to make the ritual concession that the award of equality is merited by women only once their reproductive duty has been met. He also deplores women's reluctance to nurse their infants and, blending sexual egalitarianism with the popular maternalist ideology, pleads, "Let us recognize women as beings like us, to whom we are superior only by virtue of the vain titles that tyrannical laws have afforded us. . . . Let's apply ourselves to making them strong, robust, courageous, educated and even learned as much as is possible and we will see, in the first generation to succeed us, humanity enter into all its vigor, all its splendor."[32] So powerful is the popular impulse to the regeneration of the nation that Riballier frames his argument for women's rights as a promise that they will bring it about.

The other feature that mitigates the force of Riballier's prose (a trait shared by most male commentators, mimicked even by some female ones in this time) is its insistent employment of the locutions of rococo male gallantry, with its accompanying condescension. The persistence of these formulas is an index of the tenacity with which the major construct shaping the courtship and sexuality of the literate class resisted all alteration. "Sex chosen by the Eternal to be the most brilliant proof of his supreme power, to make for the happiness and delight of the world, I want to break your chains," writes this advocate of equal rights.[33] Defenders of women claim to adore them: but their detractors use precisely the same terminology.

Riballier may well compose a stinging attack on Rousseau's sexism, but when he does so, he phrases it in nearly apologetic terms, after making due obeisance: "Oh you, most eloquent of our modern *Philosophers,* creator of the wondrous Julie," what were you doing when you gave us "so humiliating, so demeaning a portrait of the most beautiful, the most ravishing of nature's creations" as Sophie? Why do you want her to be weak, without powers of resistance, making her "ashamed even for being strong? Eh! Why?" he asks, deploring Rousseau's "Asiatic maxims."[34] But he is in the minority. "The feminist tendency did not prevail over masculine self-love, which Rousseau had endowed with new arguments."[35]

Jean Bloch has taken the important step in understanding their underlying *mentalité* of pointing to the relative timidity of women's own pleas for their sex in this period. "It might be argued that some of the pre-Revolutionary attitudes in fact encouraged defeatism or reinforced prejudice concerning women." I interpret this as further evidence, if any more were needed, that Rousseauist familialism had become in the decade preceding Revolution so prevalent, so insistent, that it can be seen as quasi-religious dogma, embracing all statements about women. Its imperatives are so absolute that they co-opt and deform all other frameworks for discussion. As Bloch points out, the Rousseauism regarding women that the public adopts lacks precise contour: it appears simply as a blanket endorsement of the popularization of general ideas of "humanity, motherhood, virtue, freedom, and reform," with the addition of some particulars, like the abolition of swaddling and the espousal of breast-feeding. So it is that the feminist Mme de Miremont writes, commenting on the prevailing mood in 1779, "Today we are obliged to fight off this new fervor that makes mothers nurse their infants." She rationalizes the appeal of this demand upon women. "It has become good form to be a nursing mother. Mothers have become more interesting."[36]

To dig into Mercier's 1781 *Tableau de la vie parisienne* is to find all this somewhat theoretical matter given some startling actuality. In Mercier's journalism sociological observation is braided together with moralistic prescription and sympathy regarding women. Its preoccupations are a precious index of what he deemed to be of deepest interest to his readership, as much as to himself. His remarks in these texts may, however, be classified into two categories, although they of course seep one into the other. The first is a more traditional and timeless one of complaint against women's insubordination, disorderliness, or moral defectiveness; the second, though also expressing age-old anxiety about sexual disorder, seems more directly rooted in actual problematic social practices. But there is always the mix of the two, the evil socialization, but of a readily spoilable female nature.

"As soon as a little girl knows how to stammer a few sounds, she receives her first lesson of smugness and coquettishness from us. There is nothing so ridiculous as our five-or-six-year-old dolls. They are children no longer." See how they make motions (with their hips) with those hoops (*paniers*), just like their mothers. "How dangerous must such absurdities appear to a thinking man?" Everyone says to these creatures, "'Stand up straight: *Here's your little husband.*'" The result? Simply that little girls "acquire the art of the mock grimace and all the artificial graces; for nothing corrupts natural grace as much as such imprudent and precocious impressions as these."[37] Although Mercier is implying, Rousseauistically, that the girls' natures would be quite graceful enough naturally, there is an animus in his depiction of the precocious expression of flirtatiousness that conveys his anger against female flirtation in general. This impression is borne out as he gives way, in some candor, to male anxiety: "If women attacked, what would become of us in the face of their charms, their audacious passion, and their amorous transports?[38] Nature has given them modesty in consequence of the strength it has wisely refused them. Today, certain women, out of idleness or curiosity or above all ambition are not at all abashed about taking the initiative [*l'attaque*]; but the system of nature is not broken because of this; men have the right to refuse . . . or to go no further than they care to." (4) Recapitulating Rousseau, almost verbatim, Mercier sets this consecrated male consternation about predatory women in the setting of the wicked city: what he has said will not even be understood in "fortunate lands where innocence still reigns," but, as he explains, it is of the turpitudes of Paris that he is speaking.

Concerns about women's sexual predatoriness is shadowed by continuing and open alarm—as earlier in the century—with women's ostensible control over opinion. Mercier is very coy in passages where this theme comes into play. He realizes he is courting trouble in denouncing women, but takes sly joy in doing so, for he knows deeper currents of prejudice are on his side. "The numerous crowd of Courtesans, who snare the most brilliant youths into their nets and steal them from other women, has brought to life a species of woman who, though not displaying the effrontery of vice, has none of the austere rigor of virtue, either." Such women declaim against the prostitutes, their rivals, and when they lose at gambling, they beg to borrow sums so as to avoid being scolded by their husbands "whom they know how to fear but not to respect." The current mores authorize these women to make public appearances at balls and spectacles: whenever they do, the circle of their female friends closes ranks and absolutely forbids anyone to make derogatory remarks about them; someone who did so would be shunned and called a "monster." This epithet, Mercier adds mischievously, "warns me to close my chapter quickly" (3–4). Disgust with the enduring rococo mores is palpable here; they license women to debauch the youth, rob men's pockets, and show disrespect for husbands, even as they foster a dangerous solidarity among women.

But Mercier is concerned too with what he views as structural problems he sees abroad in society. He worries, along with his cohort of populationist thinkers, about all the girls whom poverty or pride keep from marriage, for "are they not ceaselessly on the edge of the abyss, and will they not fall prey, sooner or later, to melancholy or to debauch?" Here he feels compelled to reflect about the men's role in creating this impasse: "There must be some radical vice in our legislation if men flee and fear to sign the sweetest of contracts." Mercier attributes their reluctance to the heavy financial weight that accompanies the title of "husband." "Either women have acted against themselves in giving themselves over to luxury, or we are not far from the last stages of corruption." Women without dowry cannot find spouses, and "men do not marry any longer, or marry only with regret." This is because vice rules the city and dissipated women scorn their duty, thus frightening the men. (1–2).

He is drawn back to this theme: people are not marrying, or are marrying late and having almost no children. He alights upon the unmarried woman: we see nothing about us but old maids who, having fled the duties of wives and mothers, trot from house to house. "Freed from the pleasures and pains of marriage, they must not usurp the consideration and respect due to the mother of a family surrounded by her offspring; we ought to look upon them as vines fruitless under the sun's rays, which rather than grapes produce only a few spare leaves." Inspired by his own imagery, he continues: "These girls past their prime are ordinarily more malicious, nastier, and more harshly avaricious than the ones who've had a husband and children" (165). Though Mercier deplores male celibacy too, these women untied to men strike him as an outright affront to nature's imperatives. So much is this so that he recommends that celibates, male and female, be made liable to the payment of fines. Arguing that it is often the law itself that forces people into sin, he advocates a revival of *mariages de la main gauche,* the keeping of official mistresses. "A concubine in the old days was not at all an immoral woman." It is from "*wanting to control men's liberty too much that* [women] *have been thrown into new delinquencies* [my emphasis]" (166).

Fearsome, nasty unmarried women, too-free married women taking advantage of men and controlling the public opinion that should be controlling them; marriage, left or right-handed, is the house Mercier wants them to reenter for the sake of society. Next to these unruly classes of women, the prostitutes appear positively virtuous: "They give themselves after all for what they are; they have one vice the less, hypocrisy: they cannot cause the ravages that a libertine and prudish woman often occasions under the false appearances of modesty and love." We see that Laclos's imminent creation, that queen of prude-hypocrites Mme de Merteuil, is no aberration as far as public perceptions are concerned. Common prostitutes, Mercier goes on, are "unfortunate victims of the poverty of or abandonment by their families, who only rarely have resolved to undertake this life because of any sensual temperament." Victims, not free agents, devoid of the power of enacting or feeling strong desire, "they take offense neither at injury nor at scorn; they are debased in their own eyes; and unable to dominate through grace and modesty, they deliver themselves to an opposite extreme and make a display of audacity and infamy." We witness the abrupt slide here in Mercier's prose from the prostitute as pathetic victim to the prostitute as victimizer. For him there are degrees even in such corruption as this: "Where the one gives herself wholly to pleasure and money: the other is a brutal being without sex who doesn't even feel the derision she inspires" (5).

It is the depth of Mercier's distaste (and that of Restif and other commentators) for the "shamelessness" of prostitutes that inspires us to visualize them along the streets, lifting their skirts, audaciously flaunting their hairy body parts or offering a naked breast (one had only to tear off the fichu) to tempt the potential buyer. These impudent women terrify men by word and deed in their unmediated summoning up of uncontrollable desire.

A continuing facet of pre-Revolutionary life in this decade was, still, the presence of large numbers of indigent women. The stability of poor families was fragile, with fathers abandoning wives and children, either for many months or altogether. Women and children would be reduced to begging or to eking out a living from the various expedients of abject need like smuggling salt or other contraband, or from prostitution. Hufton describes the desperation of the women of "the Auvergne who, during the hard winter of 1786, with their husbands absent, unable to borrow to finance themselves and their children, hammered, cold and hungry on the door of the *dépôt de mendicité* [poorhouse] and demanded to be arrested and imprisoned as beggars."[39] J.-J. Bachelier, in his *Mémoire* of 1789 to the legislators of the Estates-General on the education of women, bases his call for their enlightenment upon the "chain of disorders and crimes" he sees stemming from the comparison the poorest of women must inevitably make between their lot and that of flourishing courtesans: "They view with horror the rags that cover them, the coarse food they have to eat, and the sad hovel they live in. Should we be surprised to see them accept so often the help that the libertine life offers, when they have only to wish it to obtain all they could desire? Placed between bountiful crime and virtue in poverty, can we, without injustice, demand of them a sacrifice beyond our own strength, and cover them with opprobrium and scorn when a lack of education and talent is frequently the only cause of their unruliness?"[40] Is it only out of a care for tactics, in addressing a crowd of men, that Bachelier prefers here to attribute women's "immorality" to their lack of money or education rather than to indict men's needful complicity in such sexual disorder? Surely that is not the whole answer: the assignment to women of the lion's share of blame for a scourge of sexual corruption is so distinctly a well-nigh universal formula of the time that even an advocate for women like Bachelier has to restate it in making an appeal in their behalf.

Mercier, to return to him, finds the excessive number of prostitutes in Paris (in his own estimate, there were thirty thousand ordinary *vulgivagues,* or streetwalkers, and another ten thousand "less indecent" kept women) to be a factor in the "disorder of passion" and the loss of tone in speaking of love. Young men are assuming too free a manner in speaking even to "honest" women, so that "in so polite a century as this, we are coarse in love." For him, it is up to the women to change this: they must "establish reform by ceasing to allow those liberties they've been obliged to suffer under pain of passing for prudes" (6). Mercier's chief outrage is vented against neither the poverty of the women (which he had admitted) nor the part men play in this alarming commerce: it is reserved, visibly and flagrantly, for that "scorn for morals" he perceives in the persons of prostitutes. How can a father, he asks like Bachelier after him, expect to keep his daughter honest as she reaches the age of passion when she sees before their door a splendidly dressed prostitute, "attacking men, parading her vice, radiant in the midst of her debauchery, and, under the protection of the very laws, enjoying an unbridled license?" (7). A final street scene completes his portrait. After a nocturnal sweep, a bunch of prostitutes is made to kneel in the prison of the rue St. Martin to receive their sentences to be sent to the Salpêtrière. "They have no prosecutors, no advocates, no defenders. They are judged most arbitrarily." Next day the accused are put into a long, open cart where they "all stand pressed together. One weeps, another wails; this one covers her face; the most brazen ones look the public that is denouncing them in the eye; they reply indecently and confront the hoots that go up as they pass. This scandalous chariot goes through part of the city in broad daylight; and the outbursts its progress occasions are in themselves an affront to public morals" (8–9). Mercier cannot decide whether he is more outraged by or for these women.

Like Rousseau in the *Nouvelle Héloïse,* Mercier erects a counterideal to wicked
Paris in the Alpine countryside (he, too, was of Swiss origin) where a man may
live far from corruption, enjoying the chaste embraces of a tender wife and the
caresses of a beloved sister. "Ah! too happy republicans, keep . . . this purity of
morals" (9–10). Mercier counsels republicans to hold back the imprudent youth
who would give way to a licentious, luxury-filled existence.[41] It is striking that his
appeal is made to republicans as a collectivity to preserve the virtue of their suc-
cessors. In castigating women of "ill repute," he arraigns them as a class, but in
referring to their opposite number, the potential libertine, he uses the singular: he
is but a hapless youth. In this way he avoids an indictment of men's sexual practices while complacently indicting women's.

Jean-Jacques Rousseau's remark that the women of Paris had become so used
to appearing in all public places and mixing among the men that they had taken
on men's pride and audacity, their frank glances, and almost their walk is repeated
approvingly by Mercier. "Let us add that women, for several years now, have been
playing the role of business brokers. They write twenty letters a day . . . , lay siege
to ministers, exhaust clerks. They have their offices and their registries; and by
dint of whirling the wheel of fortune, they place their lovers, their favorites, their
husbands, and even those who pay them" (22). This remark is prefatory to laying
down the law to this gender whose manners and morals he depicts as so alien, as
if they were so divorced from those of his own. His solution will be the institution
of an order of sexual separation in which women will not presume to initiative.
The present weakness of their men, he tells us, has resulted in the women's heads
being "swelled by pride, rank, and wealth," making them become "dissipated,
spendthrift, licentious, and insolently haughty." Now, for Mercier, there is nothing
so shocking in woman as insolence or verbal abuse, for these make her lose her
"graces, her dignity, and her real power." Repeating Restif's anathema cited at the
beginning of this chapter that I suggested as possibly addressed to the queen,
Mercier explicitly applies his own to the idea of female royalty. "Nature has willed
that [woman] should never, by gesture or accent, raise herself above a man, under
threat of appearing odious and ridiculous. Nothing dispenses her from this eternal
subordination, even were she to be seated on the throne of the world" (23–24).

We must not, however, imagine that Mercier assumes these hostile postures
comfortably: he is in deep conflict over these issues. "Among republicans, women
are only housekeepers. But women are full of insight, of sense and experience"
(24). What to do? Are republicans to sacrifice this resource? He concludes, with
no attempt at logic, that they should be consulted only when the nation does not
yet exist or exists no longer. Probably he is prepared to accord them some such
role because he sees them in Paris "able to repair within their homes the evils that
legislation does outside." And he gives some praise to the upper-class women who
are "smiling, gentle, and amiable" as long as they play their subordinate parts in
public, even though they illegitimately subjugate their too-permissive husbands

at home. Essentially, though still attracted by rococo graces, Mercier intensely dislikes "our women" for having lost "the most touching characteristics of their sex, timidity, simplicity, naive modesty," and for having replaced this "immense loss" with "the attractions of wit, and grace of manners and language. They are more sought after, less respected: we love them without believing in their love; they have lovers and not friends." The old regime's pattern of woman, the emergent woman of society, is the object of Mercier's smoldering resentment. Their social initiatives merge with the sexual initiatives of the women who sell their sexual services to form a single bloc, in Mercier's outlook, calling for a renewal of male domination.

If Mercier's text sounds like a platform for gender reform, it is because it is one, and one accorded wide credence by the public. In opposition to these women of high society Mercier posits his ideal, the women of what he terms the second order of the bourgeoisie: "Attached to their husbands and children, prudent, economical, attentive to their homes, they offer a model of wisdom and of work. But these women have no vast fortunes, nor do they seek to amass them; they are not very brilliant and even less are they learned. We don't see them, and yet they are in Paris the honor of their sex" (24–25).

Les Liaisons dangereuses, *or the Assassination by Letter of the Rococo Spirit*

A portion of Mercier's animus against the excesses of prostitution is vented against attempts to limit men's freedom. With this as his context, he seems to reprove the increased moralism that makes men flee a too-puritanical conception of marriage, which would limit their sexual opportunities. Indeed the new stylish devotion to a rigidly sexually dimorphic gender order has as its not always spoken undercurrent the liberation of men, sexually and socially, from the perceived constraints of female opinion. Peter Nagy argues cogently that sentimentalism and libertinage often blend in this period because they express "the same muted struggle . . . for the liberation of the senses and the sentiments, for the maturation of a mentality and a psychology adapted to the total liberation to come; from midcentury on, everyone is more and more conscious of this."[42]

How does Laclos's *Liaisons dangereuses* (*Dangerous Acquaintances*), certainly one of the most fully realized novels of seduction of all time, relate to this human struggle, to this male struggle, and to the quarrel over women?[43]

Ludmilla Jordanova has observed that "when eighteenth-century commentators discussed such matters as pregnancy, childbirth, and adolescence, they did so with a lively realization of their dual physiological and social character." This is, I would claim, debatable. As she herself points out, in her skillful attempt to decipher the "language of nature" that was the battleground where the social and the biological fused, even the powerfully dichotomized terms that characterize this discourse would often overlap or merge. "In these ways a set of complex changing images was built up, which both constrained and expressed tension and contradiction."[44] These contradictions suggest confusion and uncertainty at the heart of sometimes ringing assertions about the social consequences of "necessity" as dictated by biology. Through their murky evasions of awareness, they are yet set forth rhetorically as if they had absolute truth value. In effect we see sweeping gender assertion here concealing as much as it reveals.

Although commentators on women's evolution in this period have chosen to dwell on the significance of Rousseau's *Nouvelle Héloïse* for the Revolutionary generation, the fact remains that it is the *Liaisons dangereuses* that best represents the preoccupations of this specific era.[45] Laclos had, I believe, no fully conscious objective in mind in creating his novel. Some indeed argue that its strength lies in its being a work concerning buried psychic forces.[46] Yet the ambient mood of resentment among ambitious younger antiaristocratic men with the code of the still regnant rococo elite seems to have combined in his spirit with personal frustration at his own mediocre career to produce the explosive charge of his novel. This is the charge that incinerates the viciously erotic duo of Valmont and Merteuil: and as between the two, the villainy of the latter is by far the more sensational. "Is it the misogyny of authors that so often assigns the chief role to a woman in comedies of wickedness? Or is it that the spirit of vengeance in the service of feminism is truer to feminine nature?" asks Laurent Versini. Versini, as we have seen, has elaborated from a set of literary precedents a villainous pre-Merteuil female fictional type: "The entire conduct of these literary characters is dictated by calculation; even in their debaucheries they keep a cool head and follow the plans their depraved reason has devised."[47] Merteuil, then, is *prima inter pares,* first among those of her type.

I would claim, in despite of the generations of literary critics who have chosen to read the *Liaisons* as devoid of preachment, that it is quite impossible for readers who peruse other texts of this time to miss how profoundly rooted Laclos's novel is in contemporary preoccupations and formulations about women and sexuality. In its sarcastically moralistic prologue, the novel mockingly addresses its female readers, officiously warning them that it is to them that the custodianship of chastity is entrusted, in their role as mothers who must diligently oversee their daughters' conduct, or as wives who may not stray. A comical abyss yawns between this prissy introduction and the elaborate, exquisitely nuanced account of the powers deployed in the will to seduce that follows. Yet, as Nancy Miller has said, the preface's admonitions establish for the novel "the grounding plausibility of its plots of seduction and betrayal, worldliness and innocence."[48]

The publisher's "warning" starts by casting doubt on the authenticity of the novel that follows on the ground that some of its characters have morals so evil that they cannot have lived in this century "of philosophy, when enlightenment, as all are aware, has made all the men so decent and all the women so chaste and reserved." These events can only have taken place elsewhere, at some other time. This awkward tongue-in-cheekiness reveals that the times are indeed in question. The author of the "preface" makes the case that it is but a "service to morals to unveil the means that those who have bad ones use to corrupt those with good ones" (7).[49] Crow observes the parallel insistence in the period's antirococo art criticism on "the action of unmasking"; the reader is urged over and over to attend to the outward signs by which the virtues or vices of an individual can be recognized. This unmasking, this laying bare of the true character, is most often reduced to questions of style—style in manner, in appearance, in written and spoken expression. "Villainous *gens en place* hide their true characters behind facades of rococo refinement, which invariably serve to disguise greed, depravity, and tyrannical design."[50] Laclos's preface suggests a similar project: but his novel, while carrying it out, ramifies it.

It subverts facile moralism by its delight in a depravity it makes the reader share: and such pleasure is part joy in sexual titillation, part pleasure in the skilled calculations of the manipulative characters themselves, part terror of the capacity of the sexual drive to alienate us from conscious intention. It is the odd teamwork of natural impulse with precise human engineering and careful forethought, expressed with grace and wit, that makes the Merteuil/Valmont correspondence so overwhelming. If Laclos had it somewhere in mind, as I believe, to express revulsion against the *moeurs* of the *noblesse d'épée,* in a sense he failed, for in this novel of the ravages of seduction he displays such feats of inventiveness of forms of evil for that class that we can only interpret his acts of imagination as a tribute. An ardent wonder seeps through his text at the sheer skill of his protagonists in organizing desire to suit highly civilized, if jaded, tastes. Laclos's ego as well as his id steam away in these letters.

What chiefly sustains the ardor of this exchange is the sex war, which is at once a sexual engagement between the vicomte who seeks to regain the marquise as his prize (while the marquise may still feel some affection for him), and an all-out contest between them as representatives of their sexes. In this latter respect, it is, quite simply, no war: the marquise knows her own sex to be beaten from the start. "So unequal is this match that our luck lies in not losing; your misfortune is not winning" (81)" Born, as she proclaims, "to avenge my sex and to master yours," she still operates from a defensive posture, and her claim is to a solely personal vengeance, since her concern is not for women but for herself alone. It is as entirely individual persons that Merteuil and Valmont are pitted against one another as gender champions. In this battle, the marquise with her subtler skills, sharpened by acute observation of human frailty and the ways of society and refined by literary elegance, is more than Valmont's equal. Her primacy is one she in no wise conceals: rather she gloats aggressively over him: "How your fears fill me with pity! What proof they are to me of my superiority over you! And you want to teach me, to lead me? Ah! my poor Valmont, what a distance there is between you and me! No, all the pride of your sex would not be enough to fill the gulf that separates us" (81).

The "pride of your sex": in the novel's implicit sex-cum-class war, male sexual pride will ultimately prevail. Merteuil's upper-class rococo aridity of heart, along with that of all women of her class who use their sexuality as a counter to gain power, is castigated. The "good" woman is the one like Tourvel, the simple and pious representative of the *parlementaire* class, who gives way to the longed-for and adored female vulnerability and allows herself to love her seducer/tormentor. Her example ultimately confirms the age-old masculinist creed that decrees that it is the women who shrink from probing the code of male hypocrisy and violence toward them who will inspire and find men's love, albeit, as here, a fatal one.

Where then can the "feminism" alleged by some to characterize this world lie?[51] We see it primarily in the laying bare of the gender system the letters display, especially in letter 81 where the marquise explicitly denounces the code of senti-mental libertinism—of public concealment and private profligacy—to which she has made herself impervious. We witness this in Merteuil's deliberate use of sen-timental pretense, in the Prévan episode, to being overcome with love so as to dupe her would-be seducer. And we see it in the fates especially of all the women except Merteuil, all used by the manipulators, each one unequal to coping with this arid, destructive code, which has authorized the upper class's right to pleasure in a play of puppetry with humans. But while Laclos's novel contains feminist insights in its critique of this code, it is not feminist. Rather it is hostile to its weak women, so much so that I have referred elsewhere to the work as exuding the atmosphere of a "concentration camp" for them.[52] All become will-less, witless, helpless toys in the course of it. This is not mere representation of the world's ways: it wallows in and reshapes them. Cécile, whose pregnancy is merely a lib-ertine joke for the novel (so much for reproductivity in this world) is pruriently absurd in her naïveté, and she ends in the hated convent where she began. Her criminally credulous mother has, by her misplaced confidence in Merteuil, done the very thing for her daughter she feared most to do.[53] Mme de Rosemonde is a doddering fool as conscience to Tourvel. And Tourvel, for the sake of the novel and in the interests of seduction, is made to give proof of lacking exactly the moral fiber that is her single claim to distinction.

All fall prey, but willing prey, to the emptied-out, vapid social codes of the bienséances, whose beflowered language is so admirably deployed that no ques-tions are asked of it. Through her studied practice of language alone, the self-professed prude Merteuil can convince all of her sanctity.[54] In the tougher case of Valmont, a known libertine can make Tourvel and Rosemonde swallow his self-definition as "good Samaritan." What makes all this hypocrisy palatable is a cer-tain jargon—"the sweet hopes"; "my charming friend"; "little Cécile"; "sovereign of my heart"; "I embrace your beloved daughter." This language is an amalgam of the old preciosity and the newer sensibilité, which mimics candor and devotion and is its reverse. Valmont, who speaks to Tourvel of his "tender eagerness" to please her but has only pleasing himself in mind, is, like Merteuil, master of this mode; but as ever, her version of gratuitous cruelty is one notch more lucidly assumed than his. We see this when she explains how she has learned to contain her emotions, to "repress the symptoms of unexpected happiness" beneath whatever mask she needs (81), or as she confesses to Valmont that the one reason she never remarried was to avoid having to deceive out of any necessity, but only "for my pleasure" (152).

The greater degree of Merteuil's monstrosity, then, derives from her autonomous willfulness, directed to deceitful control over the lives of others. Valmont professes the same creed as she, but he has no need to "explain" it, as she does in letter 81, because it is simply the male libertine's creed, which, though outraging the pieties, calls for no explanation or excuse. Merteuil buys wholesale into this creed, so much so—and this is how Merteuil becomes the work's allegorical effigy rather than a mere character in it—that she forces Valmont to live out to its bitter end the credo that the excellence of her analysis of the power relations in her world has forced her to adopt and master. Merteuil rather than Valmont becomes the Sign of this code. The marquise's human desiccation is given as more total than his, is by far the more terrifying in the sex that even she feels compelled to portray in her public persona as pure, gentle, and caressing in manner. In demanding that he treat Tourvel as an interchangeable part in the erotic scenario by sending her the all-purpose libertine letter, "It's not my fault," Merteuil attempts to stamp out the renascent lost connection between desire and affection that stirs in him for the *présidente*. "Adieu, my angel, I took you with pleasure, I leave you without regret: I may return to you. So the world goes. It's not my fault" (41) read the final words of this missive that she obliges Valmont, whose need to preserve his masculine freedom she has fired up by her taunts, to send to his toughest conquest. The mocking repetition of the disclaimer of responsibility, "It's not my fault," repeatedly enunciated in the work implies paradoxically that the libertine stance is one of a toy of desire, unfreely caught in its toils. Versini suggests that this refrain may express the new psychology that, in equating inner life with physical life, endows each occasion (carpe diem) in a series of erotic encounters with an "intensity and vivacity" that might rival the "depth and duration of the heroic passions whose secret has been lost, and for which one reserves only sarcasm."[55]

Erotic freedom, with its counterparts, freedom of movement and the ability to manipulate others, is the illegitimate power the woman Merteuil has usurped. Yet ultimately, eros as freedom appears to disappoint even the marquise as she is entrapped by her fugitive feeling for the vicomte, with whom she speaks nostalgically of renewing their lost happiness, not as he would have it, of merely spending a night as his trophy for conquering Tourvel. "But why be troubled by a happiness that cannot return? . . . First, I would ask sacrifices that you could not or would not wish to make for me, and that perhaps I don't deserve; and then, how to keep you?" (131). This is not the language of manipulation of the departed beloved, but a rueful awareness that her power over him has its limit. Merteuil evokes the image of the sacrifice of freedom—the demands—that the keeping of love imposes, as even she passingly feels the need of it. But Valmont so resists deeper self-knowledge that he has to be told by Merteuil that he loves Tourvel (145). In his arrogant wariness of being caught, entrapped, ensnared, he escapes to the end any awareness of the dialectic of love's perpetuation. Citing Paul Hoffmann's characterization of sexual possession as an act whereby "a man frees himself of woman's *power*: the power to bind and dominate that derived from *his* desire for her," Miller reads the masculine drive for possession as "a gesture performed in order to recover a lost *self*-possession; and we might also say that the seducers are as terrified of sex as their victims." Hence that anxious mania for a control of what escapes control, of which Merteuil and Valmont become the (eventually ill-fated) monster practitioners.[56]

Tourvel must die, her love and Valmont's murdered through the machinations of that willfully life-destroying antimother, Merteuil. Tourvel's death arrests our attention, for she is the sole character allowed openly to "cherish" her lover; once they have consummated their desire, she claims she loves him, in the traditional mode of feminine subservience, to the point of idolatry (132). Tourvel's ideal passion "begins in the heart, and ends in the senses" (133). In her (seduced) being, having fallen in love with her own passion for Valmont, the rupture between sentiment and sex seems momentarily repaired. But Tourvel's inability to survive transmits its statement about the precariousness of this precious new style of love. The novel's malevolent search by letter for a different social and sexual dispensation can come up only with the revalorization of the power of outraged innocence, sublimated in the person of Tourvel, made under duress to love "sincerely." What will come now to be seen as the new gender dispensation threatens to arrive at the expense of female intelligence, energy, will, affect, and sexual candor.

Les Liaisons dangereuses situates the sex war in the nexus of the entrapment of both sexes in the toils of that unruly sexuality they had shared with relative impunity in rococo culture. The novel grapples with the rococo idea of sexual freedom as operative chiefly for the sex that has ultimate control over what will be believed in and by society, as Prévan's victory over Merteuil, despoiling her reputation, confirms. Manipulative power demands an endless series of ever-renewable high-wire feats that engender a new sort of slavery to "freedom." Locked in their erotic tension and contention, both women and men seek, and seek freedom from, control. But despite its ultimate defeat of women, one of the singularities of this novel of sexual conflict, as is appropriate to the relatively greater balance between the sexes of rococo culture, is its near-admission of the deep resemblance of character and needs between the sexes. The androgyny of the Merteuil/Valmont paradigm is part of the scandal of the work and of its class/ gender structure. This is what made Aram Vartanian write that Merteuil's persona "is an embodiment of the thought, both perversely fascinating and obsessively disturbing, that the distinction between the sexes might not, after all, be real or necessary."[57] The perversity of this idea arises from our normative rejection of its implications, for these have insistently posited gender relations in terms of the dominance/submission syndrome. "You are neither the Lover nor the Friend of woman; but always her tyrant or her slave," (141) Merteuil proclaims as she denounces men in her final rage at Valmont's having sought to dominate her, of all women. It is partly just this parity in criminality between them that lends such wicked zest to the work. Laclos genuinely toys in his novel with that equality of endowments between the sexes that is being discussed and largely put down in the debates around him. But this novel's game of equality in evil has only the effect of branding sexual equality *as* evil.

Merteuil, with Valmont, but more than he, is the emblem of the rococo's cleverly ornate, hard-lacquered brilliance. Its purely decorative mores sacrifice sentiment for sensuality and intellectual primacy. Above all others, Merteuil exemplifies her caste in her aristocratic bearing, her refinement, her learning, and her autocratic style. In a woman, all of these qualities of her station turn to blemishes because of her concomitant usurpation of a pride and self-control associated with the new manhood. Not vulnerable, the very idea of her dismays, unmans. The bogey of Merteuil was a great construct called up in the novel to do the rococo spirit to death, and with it its women's hold over society.

Certainly the scope of the *liaisons* as art is not limited by its time-bound polemical factor: but that it has one is incontestable. Its mocking yet ultimately anguished excoriation of upper-class mores still shows evidence of love for what it purportedly hates. The spectacle of the cruel sexual freedoms of its protagonists, intended to be shown up as license, fascinates as much as it repels, since it purports to pull up society's skirts. And the hateful high priestess of this disorder is the unforgettable marquise, the woman as her culture had supposedly made her, devoid of all heart.

The Riccoboni Quarrel—Letters about Fiction?

Laclos's scandalous book came out early in the year 1782. In April, Mme Riccoboni, the former actress and an established and popular novelist since midcentury, wrote its author a brief and caustic note graciously praising its style, but expressing distress at the "revolting" idea it would give to foreigners of "the morals of the nation and the tastes of his compatriots." Most particularly, Riccoboni was exercised over the portrait of Merteuil, whose vices she believed Laclos had ornamented with unwonted charms.

Then followed an exchange of letters, four brief ones (including Riccoboni's original) from her pen, and four longer ones from Laclos. To Riccoboni's charge against the depiction of Merteuil, he responds that he could not in conscience remain silent about *what he has seen* (758). How else could one combat evil? As to the graces he has lent Merteuil, he compares them to the gentle draperies of a statue by Pigalle that cover a skeleton, a rapprochement that confirms that for him Merteuil is akin to an allegory of Death. Laclos's tone in this first missive is imperious and intimidating, as he announces to Mme Riccoboni that he has been unafraid of exposing unpleasant truths. He ends up with a recipe for severe artistic gender dimorphism, which he couches in the language of an incongruous gallantry. Citing Riccoboni's own novels, "*Ernestine, Fanny Catesby,* etc. etc. etc.," he opines that all readers may agree that "it is to women alone that belongs that precious sensibility, that easy and smiling imagination that embellishes all it touches, and creates objects as they ought to be; but that men, condemned to a more severe labor, have always performed well enough when they've rendered nature with exactitude and faithfulness" (759). Women's aesthetic, in his formulation, is made to appear to be rococo; men's, neoclassical. Riccoboni's responses tend to be short and self-deprecating; in her reply she claims she is not responding to his work qua author, but as a woman. "It is as a woman, Monsieur, as a Frenchwoman, as a patriot zealous for the honor of my nation that I've felt my heart wounded by the character of Mme de Merteuil" (759). Riccoboni, attempting to recapture patriotism for her sex, casts doubt on the possibility of there being a living model for such a woman as Merteuil, since she has never met one.

Perceiving Riccoboni's unwillingness to tangle with him despite her having dared write him, Laclos becomes passionately involved, and more and more verbose in his replies. He begins the next round by acknowledging that he may seem importunate: "I feel you have a right to remain silent," he admits, even that he should remain silent, but, he claims, "I've learned . . . to bear privation, but not to impose it on myself." He takes mock-gallant fire at her appeal to her womanhood and her Frenchness. "Eh bien! these two qualities hold no fears for me. I feel in my heart all that is needed not to dread this tribunal. . . . Perhaps these same *Liaisons dangereuses,* so reproved today by women, are a powerful proof that I've been most preoccupied by them; and how could one think about them and not love them?" (760).[58]

Some women, then, did indeed feel this novel as a threat. Laclos goes on to argue for his authorization to depict Merteuil by referring to the precedent of Molière's Tartuffe, whom he sees as an imaginary recombination of a horde of such hypocrites out in society. "I have therefore portrayed the base acts that depraved women have indulged themselves in, while covering their vices with the hypocrisy of the forms" (761). Laclos's moralism here, defensive or not, seems genuinely engaged.

In Riccoboni's turn, she then tells Laclos, "In spite of all your skill in justifying your intentions, you will always be reproached, Monsieur, for presenting your readers with a vile creature who has devoted herself from early youth to preparing herself for vice, to developing debauched principles, to shaping a mask for herself so as to hide from the gaze of all her designs of adopting the habits of one of those unfortunate women whom misery reduces to living from infamy. So much depravity irritates and does not instruct. We cry out on every page: this is not, it ought not be!" She then appeals to Laclos's claim to friendship for women: "You claim to love women? Silence them, then, appease their cries and calm their anger" (763). And she commends to him an interest in women's gentle friendship, which "becomes so agreeable to your sex, when its cooled passions allow it to look at [women] no longer as objects of its amusement," for they are capable of an infinity of delicate attentions, which men are not. "Change your system, Monsieur," she exhorts him, "or you will live burdened with the curse of half the world, excepting only my own." (764).

Only a light veil of politeness covers the animus in this exchange. It reveals a particular, if limited, shock wave among literate women over Laclos's Merteuil. Riccoboni's expression of outrage—in which she is conscious of speaking for her sex—spur Laclos's own, on both artistic and moral grounds. To Riccoboni's plea that he express his "love of her sex" by calming, rather than exciting, its fears, he behaves as if there were no such thing as misogyny, protesting that the actions of both sexes are condemned in his work, and seems, if anything, energized by his awareness of some women's hostility to his novel.[59] In their exchange, whereas Riccoboni speaks in the first person, Laclos, who knew her personally, responds in a haughty third-person style, as if holding at arm's length her distasteful communications, a posture he subsequently drops. His use of the formulas of gallantry is, in the end, an equivalent device for dealing with female discourse: the professions of admiration, the homages of respect and love, and even demands not to be deprived of precious commerce with the other sex intervene *mal à propos,* and certainly not only in Laclos's prose, to demean and trivialize the content of women's statements. Riccoboni in fact catches him out, but only in the most blatant of these Valmontish stratagems, as he chides her for not answering him, saying he feels "deprived" thereby. "One of your expressions seems to me quite singular. For a military man to set in the ranks of *privations* neglect by a woman whose name his grandmother might have mentioned! Doesn't that make you laugh, Monsieur?" (762).

But Riccoboni is not equal to Laclos's torrent of complacent language, filled with the self-righteousness of gender superiority, buttressed by chivalric condescension.

Laclos's division of the world of fictional art between a factitious female "ought" and a realistic male "is" effects the neat, but bogus, neoclassical gender split. For that split is far muddier than he admits: its complications emerge in his riposte to Riccoboni's objection to his portrayal of Merteuil's deliberate adoption, outside any financial need, of a life similar in its self-prostitutions to the lives of wretched common women of the streets. Repeating her own words, Laclos answers, "The mores I've depicted are not, Madame, those of *the unfortunates misery has reduced to living from infamy:* but they are those of that set of women even more vile, who know how to calculate what rank or fortune permit them to add to these infamous vices, and who multiply danger through their profanation of wit and grace" (767). What riles Laclos is not prostitution per se (that disturbs Riccoboni): it is the conflation of sex and upper-class standing with cultivated graces. The underlying reality of the sexual/class system was that the sizable and hated cadre of female predators it generated caused an intense male suspicion of women, which was warranted in the sense that calculation and the uses of seduction were important weapons for women in the struggle to survive. This suspicion, already overdetermined by cultural tradition, radiated its heat to the whole of *the sex.* Terror of the sexual freebooters cast a pall on women altogether. Laclos had exploited this rising tide of hatred and backlash in his novel.[60]

In the *Liaisons,* Mme de Rosemonde explains to Tourvel, in a reworking of a Rousseauian text, what pleasure is for men and for women. "The pleasure of the one is to satisfy his desire, that of the other is above all to bring desire about. To please for the man is a means of succeeding; whereas for her, it is success" (130). This dichotomy is pressed as the new idea of sexuality itself. The good woman must give up all claim to sexual desire, hence to initiative. Her role will be to create the ground of male desire. As Laclos tells Riccoboni, "whenever a woman is born with active senses and a heart incapable of love; some wit and vile soul; who is wicked, and whose wickedness has depth without efficacity, there will Mme de Merteuil be found, whatever costume she wears, with only local variants" (762).[61] Setting aside her stock villainy, it is the unloving heart and the active sexuality that precondition the awfulness of the rest of the picture. We divine now why even Tourvel's is an endangered species: her open readiness to love is coupled with open sexual responsiveness. That combination too, while piquant enough in a novel, holds terrors. What appears really to be wanted from women is deep love coupled with undemanding sexual compliance and a lack of desire of their own. Dominique Aury has observed that within the world of the *Liaisons* itself, "no one cries out: it's not cricket."[62] The more gratifying, therefore, it is that Riccoboni's lonely caveat has come down to us. She would finally terminate Laclos's flow of self-justification, still unreconstructed in her thinking. "To say what I do not believe seems to me a betrayal, and I would deceive you if I were to give in to your views" (768). For Riccoboni, Laclos's popular novel had an undeniably disquieting savage, political edge. In the heat generated by the evil splendor of the imaginary Merteuil, the seeds of the undoing of her class of women would germinate and flourish.

Misogyny and Its Discontents

Norbert Elias's thesis concerning marriage applies to our case here. He has posited the supposition that the power of husband over wife was broken in the seventeenth and eighteenth centuries for the first time: "The social power of the wife is almost equal to that of her husband. Social opinion is determined to a higher degree by women. And whereas society had hitherto acknowledged only the extramarital relations of men, regarding those of the 'weaker sex' as more or less reprehensible, the extramarital relationships of women now appear, in keeping with the transformation of the balance of social power between the sexes, as legitimate within certain limits."[63] This relative parity is what will now change, under the pressure of intensified dimorphic reconstructions of gender.

In the early years of the 1780s we find an erotico-moralizing visual rendition of seduction replacing the candidly salacious one, as Fragonard's *The Lock* inspires followers, a polymorphous eros giving way to a militant one.[64] Formerly latent elements in these scenes are now made overt. Locks and keys acquire a leaden significance. The physician Roussel would certify the male sexual need to break and aggress as he spoke of "the impetuous ardor pressing man to unite with woman" and noted this curious propensity: "After he has set all barriers aside, and marched from victory to victory," once he has found himself "master of all and has only to enjoy sex, he still likes to encounter an obstacle that suddenly stops him dead; he wants the passage he most wants to go through to be closed."[65] He wants, in effect, to defeat his partner by force. Hence the popularity of works depicting love as struggle—one to be "won" by the man, "lost" by the woman. Such a one is Louis Boilly's *Dispute over the Rose* (fig. 24), reviving yet once more

24. *Louis-Leopold Boilly,* The Dispute over the Rose, *Bibliothèque Nationale, Paris*

the conceit of defloration alive in French arts since the medieval *Roman de la rose*. Here, of course, many rococo elements recur: the dog for animality, the complicitous Cupid, the rose itself. The setting of seduction, however, is no longer the bower, the cloud, or the boudoir; it is a sofa in a stripped-down neoclassical interior, so that the struggle itself appears against no softening or embracing vision of natural forces or billowing bedclothes. A pure sex war, it powerfully resembles in its aesthetic the ethos of the *Liaisons dangereuses*. The doll-faced, half-smiling lover takes no notice of the dismay admixed with desire of his object: her struggle is foredoomed by her own sexuality, at war with her judgment. The impression of her fragility is heightened by the light shade of her garments and the listlessness of her pale arm, draped languidly over the dark arm of the lover who presses her breast. The mark of her complicity lies in the fabric of her dress, trailing over her suitor's leg, covering his arousal. She is in the very process of melting in his heat. Close to intercourse and/or tears, her image, not unlike the features of Greuze's abashed adolescents, liquidates that of the dry, pretty, cool self-composure of the rococo woman.

The woman should (this is the moral) have been able to resist. This scene plays on the guilty secret of women: they are not stalwart and chaste, as the Christian tradition has demanded them to be, but corrupt beings eaten up by sexual longing. Nagy cites Mirabeau's *Erotika Biblion*: "Pruritis begins only in the vulva, while the frantic mania for pleasure resides in the brain."[66] The age-old designation of the woman's body as the locus of human sexuality recurs here: as in Boilly's print, her waywardness is the image of his desire. Male evasion of the nature and consequences of man's own sexuality imprints itself in this representation.

By the 1780s the libertine spirit has been integrated into society, as the libertines, attracted by its liberal ethos, mouth the language of virtue of the philosophes. Self-proclaimed moralists of the bourgeoisie prefer a diction of sentiment, but sentimentalism and liberalism become intertwined because "both tendencies express the same mute struggle . . . for the liberation of the senses and the sentiments."[67] The two come together in a consensus promoting male domination that serves the needs of both groups, for whom ease of access to women is a primary, if unspoken, goal.

Restif's vision of the Gyneceum (1777) turns the screws of domination over women's sexuality a notch higher.[68] He makes a pair of women his spokespersons. Within the walls of this women's keep, those who were found to have allowed liberties like kisses were to receive on their knees a sentence either to go out only dressed as Old Women, or to stay indoors. A married woman convicted of "the whole sin," or even strongly suspected of it, would be "beaten with switches by two women charged with this task, condemned to an Old Woman's habit . . . , shaven, and if her husband wished, placed on bread and water." This project (1:94) of a resort to claustration as punishment for exhibiting any evidence of her own sexual nature expresses a desperate desire to banish women from society. "If the principle of J.-J. Rousseau is true, that ignorance contributes to happiness," writes Restif, "this only holds for Women; their absolute ignorance would be a real gain; they would be contented and peaceful, advantages surpassing all those they want to obtain in the sciences and the arts. Let the active being, Man, exert himself, feel, know, invent, throw himself beyond known boundaries . . . he is right. . . . Woman, on the contrary, cannot do these same things without a shade of ridicule; let us say more, without a species of indecency" (1:203).

For Restif in his *Pornographe* women must not be carriers or seekers of culture. At the same time, as merely sexual beings they are equally disquieting, and the lowliest ones predictably revolt him most. "Nothing proves better how passion makes us stray than the courage well-bred men frequently display in following a wretched woman of the people into a dusty hovel. . . . In order to satisfy their brutality, they are presented with an unclean and sickly object. All they see disgusts them, and if it were possible for a creature of this class to have any individual features, her bearing and manner would destroy any such illusion. Oh mortals! do you wish to see humanity fallen to the deepest degree of degradation? Follow one of these wretches to her filthy retreat; a thinking man will have nothing to fear for his passions there: he will feel only a sorrow and pity mixed with indignation." It was to regulate such abusive and unseductive conditions that Restif conceived his Gyneceum. Pity not only for the men but for the women breaks out momentarily in his account, for the "stew" that libertines make of such girls; but his dismay is overcome by disgust. He asks where, under such circumstances, a man can think his *triumph* lies [my emphasis]. "To triumph over a girl who languishes in want, or one who controls her tears as she speaks to you, or else over a wanton who is reduced to the acme of humiliation to get her bread, in all truth [a being] without either repugnance for crime or taste for pleasure; otherwise, coarse, unclean. Oh sad, detestable pleasure!"[69]

Anguish over the extremities into which sexual need leads men in this society colors much of the men's perception of the sex. In an ancient reenactment of sexual resentment, Restif reports in wrath that the prostitute's approach is often gentle, but once paid all she wants is to get rid of the man.[70] The meaninglessness of the act to her is unendurable to him. The alterations of women's status he prescribes follow from this: a sanitary, peaceful, undemanding setting for men's sexual relations with respectful, acquiescent women: such a vision would raise the lowest class of women while repressing the highest-placed of their gender.

Restif would describe, as had Mercier, how women's demanding behavior was making men flee marriage. But Mercier also complains bitterly that women, as well as men, were remaining unwed out of choice. "Sisters or friends arrange to live together and double their rent by placing their income in investments. This voluntary renunciation of a bond cherished with constancy by women, this anticonjugal system—now doesn't this show us something is remarkable about our mores?"[71]

The answer to this string of anxieties about women—that they were not conjugal enough, were too sexually liberal and unchaste, too culturally pretentious, too financially demanding, too emotionally uninvolved with men, too haughty or too lowly as sexual partners—was to lie in a restoration of hierarchy and discipline. The physician Roussel (1788) would be one of its high priests. "Man . . . having in himself the means of conserving his individuality throughout the time that nature has allotted him does not have all the means he needs to maintain his species." He needs to join with "a being who can help him reproduce, and that being is woman."[72] Roussel's formulation proclaims the kernel of the new ideology: it is just like the biblical one, but without God as creator. Given as a simple natural dispensation, without origin or evolution, it presents the human male, walking alone like Adam in Eden's garden, as the original being, the summum of creation. If he needs a mate, she is creation's afterthought, for purposes of procreation. It is their reproductive finality that makes Roussel conclude that "women are and *must naturally be* gentle and timid" (56).[73] Hierarchy and dimorphism are reinforced by the writer's coercive terminology of prescription, passed off as nature's. Since for Dr. Roussel woman's sole end is to attract through the seductions of her body the sexual union that will produce offspring, he rails, like Rousseau but still more pointedly and antiintellectually, at her pretensions to the use of her mind, for the activity of the female mind threatens that of her uterus. He maintains this opposition as he speaks of women's writings (and we may regard these as emblems of all of women's cultural work): they "always have an air of constraint about them that deprives them of naturalness and grace; and since they're so often not their own, we might compare them with spoils we go seeking in tombs; they're inanimate and cold like the ashes of the dead from whom they've been stolen; or else, if they are their own, insofar as they are the product of work, they have a rather strong resemblance to those aborted fruits lacking all savor that art wrests from nature so as to flatter the impatient rich" (149).[74] Hot-house fruits are aborted ones in this text, the result of illicit, unnatural arts. The opposition of head to uterus evokes images of abortion and death for Roussel, associated for him with the frivolous rich. Woman must allow her uterus to work its way within her, uncontested by mind. For him, there must not be any role in culture for women: in arguing that their efforts in this domain can never be anything but derivative, futile, and *destructive to the race,* he raises the stakes so high as to brook no reply. It would be hard to imagine a more decisive relegation of women to the domain of childbearing and immanence.[75]

Why should Roussel and his generation have so insisted on this schism? I have alluded often enough to bourgeois and lower-class rage (shared by many women as well as men) against the figure of the upper-class woman as emblem for the entire aristocracy. We must also take into account the explosive charge of growing resentment as gender mixing pervades segments of French society unaccustomed to it. These are overtly discernible phenomena. But as implied earlier, I believe there to be a more complex level to this attempt on the part of the new men to establish distance from women, along with their intense, angry relegation of them to baby-making and tending. Roussel's allusion to aborted fruit provides a confirming clue.

The dominant trend of opinion in this time exudes preoccupation about women's chastity and men's own paternity: women must act as mothers (and nothing else), and men's fatherly rights must be respected. These obsessions appear to arise from a heightened collective perception of Frenchmen's own failures as traditional fathers: the failures of Louis XV and Louis XVI to father their people; the illegitimate infants dying at birth or at the wet nurse's; the indigent abandoned women and children; the mobs of prostitutes, all daughters of someone; the search for individual sexual fulfillment at the expense (literally so, in the case of the most expensive courtesans) of children and patrimony. These currents surface to near-consciousness in tandem with the infinite increase in sentiment now attached to childhood. The crisis of parental conscience was not confined to women.[76] Both rich and poor increasingly found it difficult to see their children perish. As I see it, the transformation in mentalité then taking place enacts a drama of anguish for lost connections—the loosening of religious ties, of local loyalties and customs, but even more the weakening of the bonds of the flesh that had been anchored in their forms. For women, even those of the most favored classes, "privilege" had never been anything but random, conferring the chance for wealth and the appearance of social parity without securing them against poverty, emotional marginality, illness, and old age. So for the majority of women, the prospect of change would have seemed far from inimical, promising, as it did, the recognition of some of their deepest needs: a measure of longed-for respect for themselves and greater social concern for the survival of their young. For the men, however, the need for change held quite other valences. It sprang from an inchoate drive toward what they felt was rectification of an implicit, intolerable self-image: that of sexually incontinent wasters of infantile life. Hence, I contend, their fascination with prostitution and with parenthood, and the absoluteness of tone with which they demanded of women that abnegation to maternity that held the promise of relieving them of guilt.

The Embattled Paterfamilias Strikes Back

The relations between the sexes have been and will go on being human accommodations to species needs. I repeat Badinter's formulation: "No one until this day has ever erected paternal love into a universal law of nature." In pre-Revolutionary France, under modernizing industrial and ideological conditions, men had lost some of their traditional ground as enforcers of their own version of sexual accommodation. For the male mentality of France at this period, fatherhood is a cultural function, motherhood a natural one. Though men share with women the biological capacity for reproducing their kind, awareness of fatherhood has come late to human culture and, I would argue, remains relatively unintegrated into its structures, even in our own times.[77] On the other side of the equation, women have always shared in the making of culture, though their formulations have rarely proved decisive and their presence in its "higher realms" has been unwelcome. If we can still think of the Enlightenment as in any sense a phase in the widening of human consciousness, albeit partial and patchy, of a spreading notion of a core human identity for humankind, prior to languages, mores, nations, or governmental forms, its ideas of maternity and paternity or their absence would be crucial to shaping the new conceptions.[78]

The affect in Rousseau's own vision of fatherhood had downgraded it as a physical and moral bond. In comparing his own society unfavorably with that of Sparta, which toughened its children to enable them to survive and let the unfit perish, Rousseau seems to lament that the present state, "while making children onerous to fathers, kills them before they are born."[79] But then he himself goes on to reprove the ideas of family and of culture as intolerable impositions upon male freedom, with their burdens of memory and the barrier they pose to self-interest. As would Marx generations later, Rousseau comprehended the property aspect of family structure, but Rousseau did so solely from the male point of view, regretting that the idea of love led men into jealousy and contention, and that the bonds of responsibility imposed by society were only so many fetters to men's freedom. All this regret is expressed for natural man's privations. On the other hand, *The Social Contract* reiterates the consecrated notion of the family as the model for the state, with its chief the image of its father, the people, its children.[80] But this association is essential, for Rousseau, only so long as there is mutual need between child and father: yet he claims, sentimentally, that in the family the father's own love repays him for his care to his young, whereas in the state, the sheer love of command replaces affection. Of mothers there is no mention in these contexts.

The popular thinking of the eighties simultaneously conserves Rousseau's irritable suspicion of paternity and his nostalgic desire to see it enshrined in both familial and governmental institutions. The bourgeoisie, which until midcentury had been taking on aristocratic scorn for its own children, now turns about in resentment and aggressiveness to make decisive claims of its nurturant concern and fealty to family. Diderot's style of sentimental fatherliness enjoys a deepened popularity, as a painting like Aubry's 1775 *Paternal Love* attests (fig. 25). But at the same time, the bourgeoisie's family postures reinforce the subjugation of women and children. Roussel (1775) delivers the new law of nurturance in a tone of injured moral certainty: "All the animals made to nourish their young do not relegate such a sweet care to others; a species in which the father and mother would demonstrate ardor only to engender and would flee from the obligation to nourish their offspring would be a form dissonant in nature."[81] This movement of solicitude for the survival of the young, however, erupts in an actual family system where fathers frequently feel themselves poorly respected.

"Nothing," claims Mercier of Paris's manners, "more shocks a stranger than the

25. Etienne Aubry, Paternal Love, *Barber Institute of Fine Arts, University of Birmingham*

mocking and disrespectful way a son here speaks to his father. He makes fun of him, teases him, indulges in indecent language about the age of the author of his days; and the father is so feebly obliging that he laughs right along; the grand-mother applauds the so-called compliments of her grandson." In fact things are so bad you can scarcely locate a father in his own house. He's off in the corner somewhere chatting with humble folk. "How," asks Mercier, lamenting lost patri-mony, "have we come to annul to such a degree the powers of the head of the family? . . . Often the life of a bourgeois consists of being tyrannized over by his wife, disdained by his daughters, jeered at by his sons, disobeyed by his ser-vants: a nonentity in his house, he is a model either of stoical patience or of insensitivity."[82]

The balance of bourgeois family power, to judge from this text, is seen as slipping dangerously away from the father. The Mercier who is sometimes highly nuanced in his views of women readily admits male resentment of them. "Man always fears any superiority whatever in woman; he wants her to enjoy only half of her being. He cherishes modesty in woman; even more, her humility, as the finest of all her traits; and since woman has more natural wit than man, he doesn't at all care for her ease of perception, her penetration. He fears she may notice all his vices and especially his defects." Mercier yet reproves that mediocre male mob that "would like to demand a perpetual confession of inferiority from women."[83] We cannot help but be puzzled at how readily Mercier admits to and admires the intelligence and gifts of women as he thinks of them out in society or in the theater. And yet what is distilled in him as he considers their usurpation of power in the family and their withdrawal of automatic fealty in intimacy is wrath against the father's deprivation of his hallowed role of headship in his household.

The answer proposed to this sense of paternal loss, among these Grub Streeters who pretend to speak for and to the populace, is essentially a restoration of phallocracy. "Man has within him," writes Restif, "the divine and unbelievable faculty of giving life, through a member specific to him."[84] For Restif man is like God: "Every male has within him, like God whose most perfect image he is, . . . sperm."[85] Woman, certainly incorporating no such reflection of the godhead, is simply a lesser being. Restif's magnification of masculinity exemplifies that construct described by Andrea Dworkin wherein woman "is the thing in contradiction to which the male is human. Without her as fetish . . . the male, including the male homosexual, would be unable to experience his own selfhood, his own power, his own penile presence and sexual superiority."[86] A simple return by the culture to its rich vein of piety toward male sexual dominance promises potent reassurance to bruised bourgeois masculine self-esteem. The more extreme its banishment of women to some sphere alien to men, the better.

Whereas Mercier thought men wanted women to enjoy only half—the sexual and procreative half—of existence, Restif invades and occupies, on behalf of men, even that half, in that he believes in a male immortality secured via masculine generative power. Women, handed from male progenitor to their mate and then to male progeny, merely sustain that power by their nurture of the products of men's sperm.[87] The way chosen to restore the threatened supremacy of the phallus is to reinstate the fiction of an older, prearistocratic natural hierarchy of family order. Paternity is its touchstone, of course: as Ferrières put it, "however depraved a people may be, it will never reach that degree of corruption where it ought to be a matter of indifference to a husband whether he is or is not the father of the children his wife gives him." If he says this, it is because for many years it had indeed become "a matter of indifference."[88] It was to be so no longer, and the force of change was to be guaranteed by the rod, if necessary.

It is Mercier who calls for a return to beatings, if need be. "Now in the days in France when a lover beat his mistress, the father of the family beat his wife, his daughter, his woman servant, love still ruled: for to beat what one loves, to give it a few blows, that's the secret of an intensely loving heart and the proof of great love." Women nowadays do not recognize this, and at the least cuff they demand a separation: "It would be more advantageous to their attractiveness if we pulled out a few of their hairs instead of speaking too freely to them. They would be more celestial and more respected." "We" prefer woman as illusion, says Restif.

The threat of tacitly approved physically violent retaliation plays a policing role here. The remainder of the task of repression is accomplished through the ideology of an absolute dissymmetry between the sexes that, under the cover of the "natural," rejects all contradiction. Restif's extreme formulation of it is couched as total denial of any resemblance between women and men: "And so, I repeat to this century filled with error and folly, which seeks, despite nature, to confuse the two sexes in every way, man bears a greater resemblance to the male pig than to the woman who carries him in her womb, and in whose womb he places his son."[89] Women, with their uteri, are to be set outside the perimeter of the new, more democratic culture of men.

The archeological temper, in the wake of Winckelmann's exploration in 1764 of Herculaneum and the excavations of Pompei begun in 1748, provides a final time-tested consecration for gender dichotomy and male supremacy. In tune with sometimes trumped-up recapitulations of these past glories, Restif praises the "magnificent theogony" of the Chaldeans, who saw the Sun as the active (male) principle of intellectuality, angel of light, and the female as Earth, an "angel of darkness" and, presumably, of the principle of superstition. For his part, Mercier resorts to the precedent of classical antiquity as warrant for his belief in the value of beatings: "The Greeks and Romans, who were as good as we are, beat their wives and mistresses; for the great vice of love is languor or tepidness."[90]

Is it overdrawn to read disquiet and desperation in these overblown rejections of women as persons akin to themselves with whom society must be made? I think not. Simply, these men were hostile toward any mode of gender accommodation excepting one that would grant them, simply qua men, the promise of a limitless ego gratification, and that via the chimera of limitless female pliability and sexual accessibility, framed in terms of woman's maternal telos.[91]

The end result is the prescription to women in the terms provided by Dr. Roussel, who appears to be addressing the well-to-do, spoiled, young married belle: "It seems to me that a woman has a right to all the advantages a society may offer its members only when she has fulfilled all her duties; and she has performed only half the task when she does not nurse the infant she has borne. She is worthy of the rank she occupies only when, after having ornamented her society with her beauty, she has contributed to the increase of its strength in giving it vigorous, wholesome citizens who have received from her, with her milk, the example of an inviolable attachment to the sacred duties imposed on her."[92] Relegated by ideological totalitarianism to a being coterminous with the idea of her biological capacity for maternity, this woman's true excellence is located in the milk she feeds to future citizens of her nation. The stripped-down simplicity and isolation of her role make her a marginal being, confined during reproduction to house and bed, rewarded, in Roussel's prose, by some airings afterwards.

This is as Restif wished it to be, though his own concern is more directly sexual and more lyrically rococo. "Our Gynomanes want there to be only one sex; for it to be all men. But woman is the loveliest flower in nature." So lovely a flower could only be spoiled by the education we give a man. It would "deprive her of her lovable ignorance, her enchanting simplicity, her delicious timidity; it would prevent her from being the exact opposite of the courageous man. Let him be forever accursed who would ravish man of the inexpressible desire to be the protector, the defender, the *reassurer* of woman, against her childish fears that it is so delicious to calm! . . . We must therefore let women be women; just as we must not feminize men."[93] We note the slippage here in his argument: the champions of women—that is, the advocates of women's human rights (who evidently form a fair enough party to fire Restif's ire)—want to masculinize everyone. Restif pleads instead for gender polarization, but as a bulwark against . . . feminization! What he fears at both ends of the gender spectrum is unwelcome male identification with women, for this would hold men to a new and different level of consciousness that Restif and his generation were not prepared to contemplate. How, then, create man anew without severing all ties with women, while yet lending him a renewed masculine prestige? How does the invention of the popular "fixer," Figaro, fit into this project?

Figaro's Marriage (1784): New Man, Old Framework

Michel Delon is on the mark, I think, when he argues that the *folle journée*—that day of madness of Beaumarchais's play—could not have been placed in France and needed "indolent Spain" as the setting for its venturesomeness. "In the general framework of the old structures of life, changes of class, incest, and bisexuality seemed possible, people thought they could play with social and sexual categories."[94] Only removal from the contemporary crisis-ridden, transitional French world to that of an older, mythically settled Spanish society would allow the nervous miracle that is this work to succeed.

The Beaumarchais who could speak of his own style as "spermatic" shared with his rising contemporaries a search for an inspiriting profile for the new man. That play so rousingly scandalous to its time, so tame in ours, set in motion the simulacrum of a fresh and provocative class, that of Figaro and his "property," Suzanne, whose sheer energy and resourcefulness is more than adequate to the foiling of aristocratic pretension.[95] The pretension foiled is "spermatic": newly moralized as illicit, it is the Count Almaviva's claim of his proprietary right of desire to be exercised upon the person of Figaro's own bride. If there is any question of economics raised in this play, the coins in the count's "purse" are its means of exchange. Revolution's posterity has retrospectively read the work as a portrait of the fallen aristocracy challenged by an explosive social egalitarianism. Figaro's monologue in act 5, scene 3, with its account of his thwarted talents and his appeal for a free press lend some credence to this notion. As much as it is a social leveler, the play is on its surface a cheerful mechanism for debunking the now "tasteless" masculinity of the aristocratic libertine and his sex-cum-class arrogance in assuming his right to all the women.[96] Whereas the peccadilloes of the ordinary folk—the Marcelines and Bartholos, the Figaros and Suzannes, the Chérubins and Fanchettes—are for this work merely wholesome sexual appetites, the wicked, wayward id is definitively located in the personification of the lewd nobility, whose desire is grim acquisition, indifferent to response.

"Both the count and [later, in *La Mère Coupable* -(*The Guilty Mother*)] the count-ess' struggle with civilization and its discontents yield to natural lust, and long for its perpetuation as a source of regeneration, a reversal of time." Yet by the climatic garden scene, "desire . . . ricochets pleasingly if ludicrously, annihilating social distinctions or any distinctions at all." This whirlwind vision of a sublime comic democracy of sexual impulse can provide but momentary surcease either in class or in sex warfare. The fantasy of sexual freedom the darkness authorizes is quickly superseded by a ritual return to the old sex and class structures. Chérubin's grace-fully girlish adolescent being proves that "pleasure in its purest state is blind, careless of difference," indifferent even to any rigid sense of sexual identity.[97] That is what makes for the genius of his creation as comic amorous quicksilver. Yet even he ends up being paired with Fanchette in the end, as all are returned to pastoral coupledom, the dream resolution to every division.

The most palpably inauthentic aspect of this play is to have opposed to the count's "blameworthy morality" the countess's now fashionable "purity," a trait that makes her unwarrantedly too loving and long-suffering. Beaumarchais claimed he was roundly scolded for even the minitemptation she feels in her flirtatious pur-suit of Chérubin. The playwright felt impelled to "explain" his countess's com-portment by arguing that what pleases us in her is "to see her struggle frankly against the budding of a longing she reproves as well as against her legitimate resentments." The author sees the countess's conquest of herself and the return of the count as her triumph: "She is a model of virtue, the example of her sex and the love of our own."[98] We enjoy, that is, her struggle to contain herself, paralleled by the absence of such a struggle in her mate. In fact, in the play (act 5, sc. 19), at the moment when the count's imminent infidelity is exposed to all, he turns pleadingly to his countess: "Only a generous pardon," to which she immediately and smilingly replies, "You would say *no, no, no* in my place; and I, for the third time today, grant it unconditionally." The countess is herself, that is, made to restore the sexual double standard Beaumarchais had passingly striven to ques-tion. Without her beguilingly agreeable goodness, the play could not provide the epiphany it does, far more richly even in Da Ponte's line in Mozart's opera, *"Piu docile io sono, E dico de si,"* the line that allows for the heavenly strains of the ensemble, *"Ah! tutti contenti saremo cosi."* All torment is ended by the countess's capitulation. That this is a flimsy and bogus resolution, no one would want to know, so much are we in need of its deliverance.[99] The sublimity of genuine contrition and real forgiveness is stillborn here.

Suzanne and Marceline, however, present female counterpresences to the countess's. Though Figaro has the more bombastic role, Suzanne's energy and ingenuity make her the worthy descendant of Moliéresque and Marivaldian serving women with quick minds and sharp tongues. Whatever the play's structure is supposed to convey about her "place" as Figaro's property, she easily transcends such nonentity. After all, it is her desire for Figaro, as much as his for her, that all the action of the work projects. Her characterization overflows her role to represent something more than expected. We sense her exuding a force whose attractions could not be set aside by the author of a comic play about desire. Her scrappy vigor gives her a tonic parity with Figaro that enlivens our response to the work.

As for Marceline, her brief but celebrated "feminist" tirade in act 3, scene 19, when she has discovered she is Figaro's mother and can sue for his hand no longer, was cut out for a time by actors who felt it to be an embarrassment. As in a sense it was, for it is so blatantly *larmoyant,* displaced in tone, spoken by an absurd character high in comic relief. We can scarcely credit it as intended as straight statement, for it could easily be camped up to fine effect.[100] Yet its story is one palpably central to the mores of the time. "In the age of our illusions, of inexperience and need, while seducers lay siege to us, while poverty cuts us with its knife, what resistance can a girl-child offer to so many assembled enemies?" And as the men chorus "How right she is," Marceline excoriates those "worse than ungrateful men, who with your scorn soil the toys of your passions, your own victims!" We realize the tone has hardened into seriousness as the speech gets to economic issues. Not satisfied with sexual abuse, men even rob women of all honest work, by stealing from them the few trades that are theirs: "Tricked by outward signs of respect, in real servitude, treated as minors as far as our property goes, and as majors for our errors! Ah, in every way, your conduct with us inspires horror or pity." This eruption of a voice of outraged female complaint is difficult to integrate into a reading of the play. I will call it a corrective: a salute to a more liberal doctrine concerning women, and to an awareness of a hunger for its expression in his audience that Beaumarchais felt a need to address. It allows in a grain of suspicion concerning what the bogus pastoral ending would conceal.

Jack Undank claims that Beaumarchais's "genuine interest lies in the salvation of men haunted by the qualities women propose yet burdened by their own." He sees the polarity the playwright establishes, which we now recognize as culturally overdetermined, as one between women representatives of heart, sensibility, motherhood, home, hearth, and regeneration; while men are seen as disengaged, homeless, wily. This critic reads Beaumarchais's plays as a unit as "containing an aesthetics of resentment . . . masculine, artificial schemes for transforming rigid expressions into faces convulsed with tears." Undank asks, "How deeply lived or felt are his sentimental, female impersonations?" But then neither do the male impersonations project any affective core. Even Figaro, the effervescent fixer, is incapable of empathy, is self-interest incarnate. The busyness of the play hides its fear of futility. In addition to an impulse to "sink toward mother earth and a feminine ascesis," I see in the resolution of *The Marriage of Figaro* a related nostalgia for a sort of Rousseauian-cum-rococo order, headed by an Almaviva turned Wolmar, sweetened by an up-to-date construction of woman as gentle, acquiescent mediatrix.[101] Even though Beaumarchais's play itself offers elements that might dismantle this construction—the countess's fleetingly active desire, Suzanne's vigor, Marceline's protest—these other moments remain moments only. Yet he has not disdained to allow them into his play, for they offer instants of aesthetic release to his audience for its failures of feeling and awareness toward women.

The Milk of Human Kindness

It would not be men but women who were taxed with failures of feeling. Since their portion had been rearticulated afresh by Rousseau and everyone else as one of inspiring and sustaining sexual and familial love, all were pressed and cajoled to show themselves as paragons of the heart. Some resisted, but such is the force of fashion in France that most succumbed. After all, their own capacity to inspire love was involved in assuming this burden. The shorthand mode of transmitting this style of femininity was to pass what Shorter has sarcastically referred to as "the sacrifice test," whereby women were asked to subordinate their own desires and needs to those of their children, and most of all, their infants. In such appeals to women, the confrontationism of vulgar misogyny could be avoided entirely by the use of the language of devotion. It would be through an enticing propaganda of maternal intensity that women's adherence to a new femininity would be achieved. Dr. Roussel enthuses over the marvel of the traditional nursing position: "To hold the child beneath her eyes and in his mother's arms fosters an interesting exchange of tenderness, of care of innocent caresses between them, which better enable the one to express his needs, and the other to enjoy her own sacrifices in the continual contemplation of their object." Roussel's disclaimer of an element of sensual gratification in this description (maternal caresses are perforce innocent) reveals his concern with maternal privation of sexual responsiveness. His insistence on an absence of maternal gratification in nursing is at variance with French traditional belief, as reported by Dr. Théophile Bordeu (1722–1776), and represents a withdrawal of approval of the notion of such pleasure. Identification with the loved infant shapes Roussel's mode of describing nursing. The reciprocity he posits here has no parallel in the relations of adults. The mother's show of affect, which enables the infant to satisfy his will to power in compelling her to act as his surrogate, fills the doctor with a rewarding sense of his being a feeling man. For mothers, the appeal of this accrual of prestige to their concentration on their children was not easily denied. It had become indeed the sole means of engendering approval. Mme Le Rebours in her 1775 *Advice to Mothers Who Wish to Nurse Their Infants,* counsels, "In making yourselves more motherly, you make all hearts more human."[102]

l'Education de l'Homme commence à sa naissance,

26. Charles-Nicolas Cochin,
Frontispiece to the Emile,
Bibliothèque Nationale,
Photo Giraudon/Art
Resource, New York

Cochin's frontispiece to the 1782 edition of Emile (fig. 26) still distills a distinctly rococo feeling as it portrays the nursing role in society. Significantly enough, Rousseau had dispensed with a biological mother as nurse to Emile in favor of the far more easily controlled healthy wet nurse, whom we see depicted here with her multiple infant charges. Although she appears to be trying to read the Emile, open before her, her person with its wholesome solidity, bared breast, and solid unshod feet suggests peasant rusticity rather than theories of education. Seated on the earth at the foot of Rousseau's pedestal, she exudes natural simplicity. With her little girl apprentice—still a rococo female child with a suggestion of bosom—we see the wet nurse's preoccupation with the bas age (infancy) of humankind: the older children, all boys, have been entrusted to male masters, themselves sufficiently educated to "form men." The master gazes, with his somewhat equivocal expression, out into the future.

Marie-Antoinette, we remember, had acquired a nonmaternal stain from her initial inability to conceive a child, which the births of her three children never quite effaced. The death of the dauphin, her eldest son, in 1787—a period of governmental and economic stress—cannot have soothed the suspicions against her of a dominant opinion now so overwhelmingly turned toward maternalism. Marie-Antoinette herself, however, enthusiastically shared this conservative value with her detractors. Vigée-Lebrun painted her several times in affectionate if formal scenes with her children, as in the state portrait (fig. 27) of her comfortably seated in the nursery with her baby on her lap.

Of course the most suggestive of all links between Marie-Antoinette and the mothering movement lay in her construction of the *hameau* at Versailles, with its *laiterie de propreté* (creamery), a conception curiously analogous to the gynaeceum of the *Nouvelle Héloïse,* that women's retreat where, we recall, cheese, milk, and sweets were eaten, and meat and wine banned. Despite persistent myths, the queen neither seriously played at milking cows, nor did she invite her aristocratic guests to do so; she did keep cows in a building devised for the preparation of these wholesome foods, however. The laiterie, built in the eighties, was basically a "light and fresh summer dining-room where, on lovely marble tables . . . Marie-

27. *Elisabeth Vigée-Lebrun,* Marie Antoinette in the Nursery, *Musée de Versailles, Photo Musées Nationaux*

Antoinette took pleasure in setting forth for her guests a buffet of which fruit and milk products were the principal dishes."[103] Milk, butter, and cheese were foods for which the queen was known to have a decided predilection.

The royal drift toward a prejudice in favor of milk was of course preconditioned by the campaign for nursing that had been going on since midcentury. The implications of so pronounced a tendency as this are obviously important, if elusive. I have alluded to the apparent affective lack across French society we find in a broad spectrum of writing and in some of the demographic evidence, which can plausibly relate to this nursing propaganda as a form of psychic compensation. Many women accepted the implicit command that they at least try to nurse. Suzanne Necker attempted to nurse the infant Germaine de Staël and "failed"; Marie-Antoinette announced solemnly at the birth of her first child, "I want to live as a mother," promising that she would nurse the infant and devote herself to her education.[104] A huge weight of moral pressure was exerted upon women in this drive. They had little choice but to seem to accept it on some level as the ideal, even though many actually resisted the feeding of their own nurslings. Marie-Antoinette herself did not of course persist: she ultimately found a surrogate, "Mme Poitrine" ("Chest"). Still, we perceive in the impulse to build a laiterie a kind of embrace by women of a potentially more congenial separatism that might favor the celebration of women's maternal biological endowments as a refuge from the hostilities of sexual and moral tensions.

We recall the disastrous scale of the abandonment of foundlings. During the final two decades of the eighteenth century Parisian parents by themselves were abandoning something like 22 percent of those baptized. In the year 1788, six thousand abandoned infants were apportioned among sixteen hundred wet nurses; many of these died of infection, malnutrition, or starvation.[105]

There is a clear class dimension to this campaign for maternal nursing. Marie-France Morel points to the widespread belief that women transmitted their moral characteristics through their milk to their nurslings. Children placed with wet nurses "degenerated . . . because with their milk they take on their temperament, their character, and their habits." As Morel sees it, these women of the underclass are viewed as "guilty of making their nurslings suck in a milk infected with the vilest of passions, the most disordered desires, and the lowest of vices; it is to them, above all, that must be attributed the physical and moral degeneration of the great families that the moralists of the time so complain of."[106] The physicians regarded these women as impossible to influence, since they remained outside the written culture, Morel argues. The medical establishment chose to pose its "rationality," as a body of men of science, against the ignorance, poverty, and cruelty of "licentious" wet nurses who hampered enlightened medicine's desire to control the infants' milieu. But since experiment with animal feeding of human infants was still unsuccessful, a campaign to control women's nursing capacity seemed the only means available to the doctors. Yet the behavior of the wet nurses lay beyond the rim of their propaganda. Therefore the effect of the popular moralism so fulsomely expressed in the medical texts, while it reinforced technocratic male complacency, simultaneously had the effect of disculpating men of responsibility in the fate of their infants, and inducing guilt in upper-class (aristocratic and bourgeois) women, those most susceptible to written moral argument, around issues of mothering.

Liberal opinion joins the fashionable chorus of the socially concerned in demanding succor against the scourge of infant deaths. The queen would become patron in 1784 of the Society of Charity to Mothers (Société de charité maternelle) founded by Mme Fougeret d'Oultremont. In that same year—the year of *The Marriage of Figaro*'s great success—the playwright Beaumarchais spurred the creation in Lyon, by the archbishop, of an Institute of Assistance for Poor Nursing Mothers, to which Beaumarchais offered the proceeds from his play. We note the connection: if *The Marriage of Figaro* was thought of as a revolutionary play, maternal nursing was its surprising political action project. Observe the terms in which Beaumarchais couches his appeal for funds: "Out of a hundred infants born, wet-nursing carries off eighty, maternal nursing will preserve eighty. Each mother will have nursed her son; the father will no longer go to prison. . . . Women will be more modest, more attached to their homes. Little by little we will make it shameful to send one's children away; nature, customs, and the nation will all gain equally." Beaumarchais adds that with this new dispensation in force, more children would not be born, but more would be preserved so as to become "soldiers, workers, sailors." Nursing, whether private or commercial, is clearly public work, to be undertaken for the sake of the common weal.

In the print circulated to foster Beaumarchais's campaign, *Maternal Nursing Encouraged* (fig. 28), the legend tells us we are seeing a feeling philosopher indicating to Benevolence the objects to which she should present her gifts. Comedy, in the form of Figaro, holds great sacks and empties one at the feet of several mothers who give the breast to their children. Above is a statue of Humanity with a tablet inscribed "Help for Nursing Mothers." The class separation between courtly allegorical figures, raised on their pedestal, and the mass of nursing women (including a father freed to return to his family from the chains his wet-nursing debt had imposed on him) is plain. Civilized male largesse and female benevolence must save and restore the mother/infant bond, for which Figaro has become the advocate. There is a sentimental "naturalness" in this mass of women and infants seated on the ground at left, with the prison holding the delinquent fathers behind them. They act as a late-rococo reality principle, in their contrast with the courtly "elevation" of the allegorical group. A distinct charge of emotion attaches to the mothers, whom society is enjoined to help. Sheer bodily warmth provides a sort of stylistic reproach to the emotional aridity of aristocratic formalism. The question, then as now, was, was the nation so touched by such a spectacle that it would uncomplainingly put these women on the public rolls?

L'ALAITEMENT MATERNEL ENCOURAGE.

Un Philosophe Sensible indique à la bienfaisance les objets sur les quels elle doit verser ses dons.
La Comédie, sous la figure de Figaro, tient des gros Sacs. Elle en répand un aux pieds de plusieurs mères qui donnent le sein
à leurs enfans. Au dessus du Philosophe est la Statue de l'humanité, portant ces mots.   Secours pour les Mères nourrices.

A Paris, chez l'Auteur, rue de la Harpe, N.° 18. vis à vis la rue Serpente

28. Borel-Voysard, Maternal Nursing Encouraged, *Bibliothèque Nationale, Paris*

The other side of this tidal wave of insistence upon maternal nursing is that it never really worked, at least in Paris. Already in 1783 Mercier would write, "For awhile, women wanted to nurse themselves; but it was only a mode, it's over. The life of Paris will always be an obstacle to this sacred duty." Sacred duty though it continued verbally to be asserted to be this charge to women continued to be resisted by them. An upper-class woman like Mme de Genlis could scoff at this "*mode de la mamelle*" (fashion for the teat) and feel confident she was scorning it into disappearance. But for working women, nursing was simply a luxury they could not afford, as the police officer Prost de Royer clearly saw. "How can a woman, burdened with clothing, providing for and feeding an already numerous family, and working to sustain herself, have a nursling about?" Nonetheless, despite continuing resistance, the maternalist wave with its symbolic stress on mother's milk has to be counted a success in the shorter range. Although extant records are subject to serious doubt, the campaign did effect a decline in the number of infants sent to commercial nurses in the decade of Revolution and in the first decade of the nineteenth century. By the year 1801–02, 51 percent of newborns were held to have been nursed by their mothers as against 5 percent in 1780. The Parisian bourgeoisie gave up the discredited custom during the Revolution-

ary years. But rural wet-nursing, both officially sanctioned and black-market, remained a resource for working-class women throughout the nineteenth century.[107]
The practice of wet-nursing, as a response to material necessity, was not eradi-
cated by a war of ideas.

The Antimother

Curiously enough, it was in 1778, the year of her first pregnancy, that the
libelles against Marie-Antoinette assumed a destructive dimension. Charges of
bastardy against the royal infant (instigated by her hostile brother-in-law, the
Count de Provence) were so rampant that broadsheets appeared everywhere: the
queen uncovered one under her napkin; the king found one on his desk among
his papers; the queen was surprised by another in front of her armchair in her
own apartment. Such vicious charges were not abated by her further pregnancies.
Despite her motherly comportment with her children, her patronage of nursing
mothers, and her attraction to the Rousseauian matrix of her laiterie, this queen
came to be seen not as a bad mother, but as an antimother. As the nation's political
confusions rose she was no longer the object of sexual jealousy, but of fury.

Pornography and misogyny merge in the libelles as Marie-Antoinette's vagina
is no longer described as a precious sculpture but a "sponge" or a "dried-out
crust." No longer the goddess, a *Vénus divine,* she is all sexual appetite. And she
is most revolting of all when pregnant: "The queen's pregnancy advances; it is
monstrous, she has a huge breast that she affects to show off indecently."[108] We
witness how hatred for her person releases a return to more primitive forms of
misogyny. The queen becomes not only a devouring vagina: she is the blood-
sucker, who uses men sexually and destroys them.[109] In one version, she is made
to claim she uses men as oranges: "When I've sucked one, I throw the peel far
away from me."[110] In her erotic transports she dreams of drinking Frenchmen's
blood cupped in their craniums. Invited to imagine the queen in sexual congress
with one of her favorites, Mme de Polignac, along with the Count d'Artois, on the
sleeping body of Louis the king, we conflate her with all the Messalinas of history
and legend. Castrator of the nation, "she is a monster, product and instrument of
a plot that outstrips her and whose origin is essentially female." To eradicate her
would be equivalent to delivering the nation from the plague.[111] Her persona is
constructed to incarnate all of the nation's passionate reactions to its own perceived impurity.

Profound French xenophobia, as has often been noted, played a huge part in
the way this monstrous image evolved. Class animus was conjoined in it with
legitimate resentment against the queen's royal profligacies. And of course the
queen's enemies at court manipulated elements of this mythology in stirring up
anger against her. Yet the Marie-Antoinette mythology combines and recombines
xenophobia, misogynous rage, sexual jealousy, and reproductive and nurturance

anxiety. It is as if all the fury of sexual, social, and economic frustration were to be vented principally against this woman.

In the new maternalist morality, the tacit promise to women was that their maternity would redeem them from sexual accursedness. If Marie-Antoinette's case was to provide a vivid illustration that this system did not work, it was a warning that most Frenchwomen were in no way willing or able to act upon.

What kinds of response could women make to the encroaching sexual ideology? Even though answers to this question must be piecemeal and anecdotal, relevant examples can be brought to bear upon it.

Trapped in Ideology, 1: Sexual Politics in the Provinces

In a tranquil canton of Switzerland, the Vaud, lived what we now consider to be one of the foremost women of French letters of her time, the Dutch-born Belle van Zuylen, known to us by her husband's name, Charrière. Carrying with her from her native Utrecht an unsentimental ear for the tragic resonances of apparently placid intimate life, she recorded these in several novels: The *Lettres neuchâteloises,* an account of provincial life of 1784; the 1786 *Lettres écrites de Lausanne,* which relate the sentimental education of a young woman; *Mistriss Henley* of 1786, her attack on the marriage of a spirited woman with an unfeeling, distant spouse; and *Caliste* (1787), the original of the great-souled, inadequately loved courtesans of nineteenth-century literature.

The *Letters Written from Lausanne,* a sort of anti-*Liaisons dangereuses,* are communications from one mother to another conveying—in contrast to Mme de Volange's ignorant mothering—almost savage messages of sexual prudence to a young Cécile, Charrière's counter-Cécile to Laclos's entrapped adolescent. To this decade obsessed with mothering, Charrière presents some complications and some cautions regarding the limits of maternal influence.

Described intriguingly enough as a "handsome Savoyard dressed as a girl," Charrière's Cécile at marriageable age has not yet internalized all the female repressions.[112] This her mother strives to help her do, but not without a full awareness of the sacrifices of every sort involved for even women of such privilege as theirs. The mother writes, in her correspondence addressed to another mother, that her daughter's tutors wish her to acquire the talents that are pleasing to people, but without seeking actively to please. This repeats the paradox of Rousseau's Sophie, whose education retains traces of the rococo accomplishments—in music, for example—but miniaturized and kept within doll-house bounds. "Where the devil," asks Cécile's frustrated and downright mother, "can she find the patience and diligence for her harpsichord lessons if success is to be a matter of indifference to her? People want her to be at once frank and open, and reserved. What does that mean? They want her to fear censure without wanting praise. They applaud all my tender care of her; but they would like me to be less ceaselessly preoccupied with helping her avoid pain and find pleasure" (18). A mother of daughters asked to be the agent of repressiveness to a child she ardently desires to see bloom feels the perplexities of her conflicts and impotence. A far cry from those of male commentators, this mother's concern is with women's cultural, not biological, maternal task. To find her daughter a good husband, her avowed and realistic objective, she has to let her be seen, let her go to balls, where she must be allowed to dance, but not too much: "Yet she loves to dance with a passion; she is quite tall, well-formed, agile, has a perfect ear; to prevent her from dancing is to prevent a deer from running" (19). Charrière is perfectly lucid about what in female natural endowment is forced back upon itself, the energy and aspiration that, unwelcomed, go nowhere.

In the mother's conversation about Cécile's comportment with men, she gets at the sexual root of the question of dissipated energy. When Cécile in her youthful romanticism wishes to believe that a young man who has kissed her hand has some feeling for her, her mother warns her that this gesture does not mean the same thing to them both. "Yes, Cécile, you should be under no illusion: a man seeks to inspire, for himself alone, in each woman a feeling he has most often only for the species. Finding everywhere the means of satisfying his desire, what is often the great affair of our lives is nearly nothing for him" (48).

Cécile protests. Haven't men received the same laws as women? How can they disobey them and make women's observance of them so difficult? The mother's answer is ambiguous. Men too face difficulties: but she is inexorable. Women must exercise sexual self-control, because the very feeling men awaken in a woman terrifies them. Girls who are somewhat free please men more than those who are not, but these they do not marry. "A husband is so different from a lover that the one judges nothing the way the other used to do; they recall refusals with pleasure, and favors with distress. The confidence a too susceptible girl demonstrated no longer appears as anything but an imprudence she might allow herself toward all who might invite it. The too lively impression she has felt in her lover's show of love seems but a tendency to love all men" (51).

Men, Belle de Charrière thus claims, read into women's sexual surrender their own slavery to a generalized sensuality: this is what occasions their terror of any evidence of it in persons to whom they might attach themselves. She makes plain her awareness of women as sexual beings, but ones to whom prudence dictates a severe control of appetite. "I often find men odious," Cécile's mother confesses, "in what they demand and in the ways in which they make demands of women: but I don't find they are wrong in fearing what they fear." "Be prudent," she exhorts her child, "for if you are not, you will subject yourself to becoming too unhappy" (53).

To the image proposed of the stifling of talents and impulses in marriage and the injustices perpetrated by husbands, Cécile reasonably enough is moved to ask, would she lose much were she to refuse to marry? The sole reason adduced here in favor of marriage is the maternal imperative: "Yes, Cécile: you see how sweet it is to be a mother." But Belle de Charrière, like Emilie d'Epinay, attempts to fill this social command with a civilized human content worthy of a woman of mind. Significantly, she locates maternal dignity in the mother-daughter bond: it is in educating a daughter to cope with her bewilderingly rigged lot that a mother can demonstrate her effectiveness to society, while finding in the sweetness of that bond some reparation for the disillusionment of marriage, which offers her nothing of the kind.[113] Charrière's response to the imprisoning limits placed on upperclass women's potential is to describe them as such, stoically, despairing as she is of the male-female bond, and to set her gaze in the direction of a pared-down model of female aspiration, a subdued, but profound and kindly, maternal virtue.

Trapped in Ideology, 2: The Wild Bird of Female Ambition

Charrière's world is still an aristocratic and provincial one, where the woman's struggle is vain, her defeat foreordained. Charrière's tactic is to make it visible. For her, only a lucid, enlightened confrontation with women's limits can lessen their power. Germaine de Staël's purview widens as she sets the woman within Parisian society. With her birthright to a salon virtually guaranteed (as Suzanne Necker's daughter), a relative detachment from maternalism per se characterizes her works:[114] that drive becomes transmuted by her into something grander. Like Julie de Lespinasse's, her mentality is imprinted with an obsession with love, but she adds the new and revolutionary complication of love's absolute conflict with the expression of those female gifts Charrière so ruefully makes her Cécile abandon.[115]

Staël's early tale of the 1780's, *Adélaïde and Théodore,* quite transparently portrays the friction points between women of upper-class society and their altering status. Adélaïde, a highly conventional figure of the pretty orphan, is sent by her negligent uncle to be raised by an unsuitable female relation, Mme d'Orfeuil. This lady, a creature representing the new sensibility, thinks of nothing but of God and of love and raises her young charge in an atmosphere of religiosity and sentiment. The thoughtless uncle marries off his niece to a rich nobleman, and her hopes of romance are dashed.

When this undesired spouse conveniently expires after a few years, Adélaïde returns, still young and now wealthy, to Paris. "Pretty, amiable, people flattered her vanity and made her delight in her success" (161). Her vanity thus fed, she fears remarriage to a boring and/or demanding husband and throws herself enthusiastically into the delights of society. But then, in a foray into the country, she meets Théodore. Once a rake, now reformed, he is waiting for time to heal his bruised heart. Thus far, everything about his tale falls into stereotyped modes. Only with Théodore's characterization do we begin to find the heat of friction: a melancholic but expressive man, he owes much to Diderot's Dorval. But in him we see affective mobility pushed to its extremity, in an absolute inversion from

female to male of the imperatives to women. He has "the gift of love;" "he seemed
to live in what he loved, to serve his self-love by abandoning himself to the impulses of his heart, to act involuntarily the way reflection would have impelled
him to do; . . . in sum, he embellished the existence of the one he loved" (164).
How to resist so feeling a man? Adélaïde marries him, and of course they are
happy—but. While the husband has renounced society, recognizing its frivolity,
Adélaïde remains drawn to it by her own celebrity. When Théodore goes to the
baron uncle's to dine, he finds that at Adélaïde's entrance "the salon resounded
with the applause her beauty warranted." Much as she loves her Théodore, she
loves being lionized, too. "She dedicated her successes to him, but she wanted to
have them" (169). Théodore's reluctance to confess to her (selfishly, in his own
eyes) that he would wish her to sacrifice such pleasures for himself causes a cloud
of misunderstanding to separate them.

Staël's tale puts before us the spectacle of the woman of society of the eighties,
bathing still in the pleasure of her social preeminence, but now feeling the chill
menace of reproof from the man whose love and approval she seeks. Théodore,
the sober reformed libertine, is an Alceste-like, neoclassical "new man," almost
a Romantic hero, with the Staëlian gloss of living androgynously as a woman
"should," entirely in the heart.

The resolution of this story bears a curious connection to the theme of maternalism. Adélaïde makes a generous gesture for a friend that compromises her
reputation. Unaware of the facts and disappointed in her, Théodore goes off to
serve with his regiment. When Adélaïde finds herself pregnant, she asks Mme
d'Orfeuil to disculpate her by revealing the truth to Théodore about the compro-
mising incident, but not that she carries their child. "If he rejects the mother, both
mother and child must perish" (173). After a melodramatic scene, he forgives her,
but, sorely tried by her apparent betrayal of him, Théodore dies.[116] Adélaïde then
agrees to live only to fulfill her promise to him to allow the infant to be born, and
after delivering it, she puts it into the hands of the old women, takes opium, and
expires.

Motherhood here holds no promise worth living for, has no content at all, is
incomparably weaker than the sexual bond between the lovers, which in turn
exerts a power only equal to but, for this woman, not surpassing the heady applause of society. And yet it is motherhood that in effect snuffs out those other
attractions of Adélaïde's life and is given as the ultimate spoiler of it.

Written in 1786, Staël's story of *Mirza* is placed in one of those exotic settings
so congenial to the eighteenth-century imagination, this time in Haiti. An understated antislavery objective informs this tale, which begins with a denunciation
of the removal of Africans from Senegal to work on the sugar plantations of the
Caribbean. A tale within a tale, the inner narrative is related by Ximéo, whom the
traveler-narrator has met in his voyage. Already engaged to the lovely Ourika, to
whom he is still wed as he tells his story, Ximéo has one day been out hunting

when he hears a woman's voice resounding through the forest. Her song proclaims her love of freedom, her dread of slavery. Filled with curiosity, Ximéo draws near and learns that she has herself composed the words she sings. A daughter of the Jaloffes, the enemies of Ximéo's own tribe, Mirza had been taught to read by an old Frenchman. Ximéo is enchanted: "This was no longer a mere woman; it was a poet I thought I heard speaking; and never have the men among us who give themselves to the gods seemed to me so full of a noble enthusiasm." Believing he admires and does not love, convinced he is not betraying Ourika, Ximéo goes to stay repeatedly with the enchanting Mirza, who like Pygmalion refashions him into her Galatea, a being worthy of her sublimity. "In the end, inebriated by her grace, her wit, her glances, I felt I loved her," Ximéo recalls, "and I dared to tell her so: what did I not say to convey to her heart the exaltation I had found in her spirit! I was dying of passion and fear at her feet" (152). He swears falsely to Mirza that he has no ties to another; responding to his passion, she recalls to him in terms related to our thematic of abandonment and bonding that she has now sacrificed everything to him: her family, her home. "I must be as sacred as weakness, childhood, and misfortune in your eyes; I can have nothing to fear, no" (153). Using her visionary authority as poet, Mirza attempts to enforce the sanctity of the weak in binding Ximéo to herself.

Two months of bliss follow this avowal. Then, trembling inwardly at the thought that his father could never be reconciled to his marriage with a Jaloffe, though promising Mirza that he will return, Ximéo goes home to wed Ourika, the soft and pliant beauty his family had destined for him. Felled by his betrayal, Mirza rebuffs his offer of friendship. Rent by inner conflict, Ximéo goes into battle, hoping to die or to merit Mirza's esteem, and is taken prisoner. As the white men are in the act of choosing slaves from among their captives, Mirza appears and offers to take Ximéo place. We remembered, of course, that Mirza's song when first we met her in the forest was one in praise of freedom. Now she submits to slavery. "I will not find slavery demeaning, I will respect my master's power. . . . Ximéo must cherish life; he is loved!" Freedom without love has become worthless to her.

The "barbarous Europeans" are about to accept this bargain, but Ximéo pleads with them to respect Mirza's sex and reject her. Turning on him in fury, Mirza reviles him for defending her when he had abandoned her. "I prefer you guilty, since I know you to be unfeeling . . . : leave me the right of complaint" (157). She rejects a protection that would demand her silence as its price. As the governor comes forward to put an end to such a contest of self-sacrifice, Mirza pierces her heart with an arrow, saying to her lover, "Your very presence turns that blood that once boiled for love of you to ice; passionate souls know only extremes." But even this moment of vehement melodrama is not quite the end. Ximéo then buries Mirza and mourns for her every day of his life, admitting now his love of her as he had not while she lived. Prostrate on her tomb, he thinks he sees her, "but never does she appear to me as an 'angry mistress'; I hear her consoling and comforting me in my pain" (158).[117]

The sheer driven intensity of this tale makes for a hallucinating contrast with *Adélaïde and Théodore*. Mirza's unprecedented character as self-conscious poet and her demand to be free render her an anomalous creation among women. Her awareness of her own aberrant powers sends her into exile in the forest, where she lives as a solitary figure. Becoming her acolyte, Ximéo breaks into this virginal solitude, accepting in courtly platonistic fashion, her yoke, her learning, her ways, her law. But sexual love alters their platonized dream state. Accepting to share Ximéo's longing to complete their union, Mirza accedes to the dependency of the flesh. Her love then becomes unappeasable need, enlarging her love for Ximéo. Physical union has a reverse effect for him: it shrinks Mirza in his mind to the dimensions of an anywoman: why, then, not return to the Ourika to whom he is betrothed and who promises him reintegration into the paternal line? Mirza's grief and rage at her helplessness before Ximéo's abandonment flood the melodramatic ending in a vengefulness that the narration attempts ineffectually to deny.

The two tales from her youth place Staël's configurations at the confluence of the ideological struggle over women in the eighties. Adélaïde's model is the still rococo woman, and her inner conflict springs from her addiction to the social approval her salon talents and wealth entitle her to enjoy, and her husband's "mature" reproof of them. Her tale reflects the tension for women of society between their enjoyment of the exercise of their task of sociability and the increasing hostility to it in favor of the mothering function. As Adélaïde rejects motherhood, preferring death, she accuses the code that makes her choose between social and intimate life.

The narrative of *Mirza* is placed at its geographical remove so as to pose the woman's dilemma in the context of the debate over slavery and freedom. It demonstrates a pained awareness that the new code excludes women like the heroine. Depicted far more boldly than Adélaïde, Mirza is allowed to express openly the female will to power implicit in social woman's presence in society. A Romantic figure, her genius is an outcome of the Enlightenment's stress on the capacity for human growth and the cult of freedom, applied here to woman. But the same culture that had formed Mirza—a Frenchman, after all, has been her teacher—denies her integration. A foreigner and an outlaw in the eyes of her lover's tribe, she lives alone in the woods, enjoying the development of her capacities for her own sake alone. Ximéo offers Mirza a chance for connection through their love: but men persist in loving only those women who do not challenge their preeminence.

The story of *Mirza* features the great nineteenth-century split between the pliable domestic woman and the woman excessive in her talents and/or emotional demands, for this is the schism now abroad in society. The wrathful, jealous Mirza, who demands to be enslaved so that her lover can go free, is prepared to assume the yoke of slavery or even death, in a spirit not of abnegation, but of deep resentment and disappointment. The tale that sentences Ximéo to perpetual mourning for Mirza's shade sucks at the very marrow of his life. The insistence that she never reappears to him as angry, but as a consoling angel, reveals the struggle being waged, as in the *Liaisons dangereuses,* between the angel of vengeance and the angel of mercy.

Staël's story prophetically conveys the unresigned grief that those women, on the brink of breaking free to the release of their energies through a social revolution, now felt in the face of the imminent rejection by the Ximéos; for these very men, who owed them so much, were now prepared expressly to refuse them status as objects worthy both of love and of esteem.

Women Trapped in Ideology, 3: The Perils of Aspiration

The first of her line, M.-J. Phlipon (later to be known, after marriage, as Manon Roland) was to become as splendid embodiment of the contradictions of her career as a political woman. But it is her pre-Revolutionary sense of self that I want to explore here. Four evocations from Marie-Jeanne Phlipon's youth, as related in her *Memoirs,* rise to the notice of those intrigued by the development of this unique republican figure.[118]

The first is her report of having carried Mme Dacier's translation of Plutarch to church at Lent in the year 1763, when she was nine years old. "Plutarch seemed to be truly the pasture most congenial to me."[119] Plutarch's *Lives* exerted indeed a huge influence upon the schoolboys who became the revolutionaries. Volney, in fact, in his *Leçons d'histoire* (Lessons from History) (1795), would later trace the Revolution's impetus specifically to readings of Sallust, Livy, and Plutarch. Harold Parker discusses the passionate absorption of Desmoulins, Mercier, Brissot, and Mme Roland, all of whose ideas of republican Athens, Sparta, and Rome came from identification with the lives of heroes of antiquity. Exalted heroic sacrifices to virtue, the clashes of ambition and passion that made Plutarch's biographies a lay alternative to the lives of the Christian martyrs fed the sense of selfhood of the petty-bourgeois girl much as it did that of other youths. "Plutarch had disposed me to become a republican," she writes, without daring to reflect too closely upon the nature of liberty for republican womanhood. "He had awakened that strength and that pride that make for character; he had inspired in me real enthusiasm for public virtue and for liberty" (302).

A second reflection is one Manon makes concerning her mother's style of mothering, for it brings to light a brooding conflict between the two generations of women. "My mother, along with much goodness, had a certain coldness; she was more prudent than feeling, more measured than affectionate. . . . She wasn't in the least caressing, although her eyes shone with tenderness and were usually turned in my direction. . . . My mother had a dignity, of a touching sort to be sure, but it was dignity; the transports of my burning soul were repressed, and I understood the extent of my attachment to her only as I was thrown into despair and confusion at her loss" (263). This passionate child, fed on myths of aspiration to virtue, in the care of the fond yet prudent and emotionally wary eighteenth-century mother feels bottled up.[120] (Manon left all of her letters to her most intimate friend Sophie Cannet open, to be read by her mother.) The bourgeoise Mme Phlipon's style of restrained maternal comportment was evidently not limited to the upper classes. Manon herself would seek to express far more emotional expansiveness in her relations with her own daughter. The new generation, teased out of emotional remoteness by Rousseauism, seeks release. The path offered men is heroic virtue: what parallel path will there be for women?

A third probing reflection relates to the girl Manon's sense of the strangeness for her of the frontier between herself and society's perception of her. On the family's Sunday walks, as a young woman she would be—was it saluted, noticed, or teased provocatively?—by passers-by; it is difficult here to ascertain precisely the quality of the interaction. "I was not indifferent to the pleasures of going out on the public promenades; they offered a very brilliant spectacle, in which the young men played an agreeable role. The charms of a person were constantly given homages that modesty could not conceal from itself and for which a young girl's heart is always hungry. But they were not sufficient for mine; I felt after these excursions, during which my self-love was on the watch for all that could make me appear to my advantage . . . a dreadful void, a disquiet and disgust that extracted too high a price from me for the pleasures of vanity" (264). This open social approval of her sexual attractions, the candid sexual scrutiny of evaluating male eyes that was the mode of sexual measurement in her milieu, is for her both a temptation and an intolerable trial. We see in her response a disgust with the lot of the woman under the rococo ethos. "Is it then to sparkle to the sight, like the posies in a flower-bed, and receive a few vain tributes, that persons of my sex are trained up to virtue, and acquire talents?" (264). Manon deeply doubts the worth of such a fate, and she feels within herself the clash between wanting to be the creature reflected in the eyes of "admirers" and realizing her own dreams of sublimity of character.

The bourgeois tide demanding consciousness of individuality engulfed women as well as men; but women like the young Manon Phlipon encountered the entrenched sexual mores consigning women to sexuality, hence marginality, as a barrier impeding their development. In her assertion of a prudish middle-class refusal to be charmed, she felt anguish over the gaiety and excitement of the world of seductive play she was sacrificing; but as she felt it beneath the capacities she knew herself to possess—"Ah, no doubt I was meant for something better"— she remained unwilling to perpetuate a tradition so trivializing of her. Not that she thereby renounced seductiveness: *au contraire,* she often stresses her unfulfilled capacity for passion.[121]

The fourth reflection relates to her account of her attempted seduction in early adolescence by one of her engraver-father's pupils, a youth of fifteen or sixteen, who frequented her parents' home. Finding her alone in the studio, he first makes her touch and look at "something quite extraordinary," then cajoles and chides her for her ignorance, saying that what he's shown her "is in all the drawings," and warns her not to tell. She attempts to fathom the meaning of his actions and realizes that "his comparison with the drawings seemed faulty to me" (218). One day in the kitchen he scolds her for being angry with him, since "your mama plays the same way with your papa." The text then presents a scene in which Manon, having mounted a stool, is grabbed by the boy as she descends. He pulls her onto his erect penis. As she struggles free, pretending to smooth her clothes, he lays his hand on her crotch, "seeking to make it caressing." She looks at his face and is appalled by the lineaments of desire: "His eyes seemed to be coming out of his head, his nostrils flared; I was ready to faint" (219). This sexual approach utterly terrifies the girl. She tells her mother, whose reaction of alarm for her is such that "I felt myself so damned . . . the guiltiest person in the universe," and she cannot rest until she goes to confession, where ordinarily she went but rarely. "There I was, a penitent before I was a sinner."

Her inchoate despair about providing the occasion for sin makes her internalize it. She turns to religion, to prudery, to self-repression as a mode of avoiding trouble. "The devotions to which I gave myself changed me strangely; I acquired a profound humility, an inexpressible timidity; I looked at men with a sort of dread, which increased when some of them seemed likable to me" (220).

Whatever rearrangements the author has made to this narrative of *déniaisement* or initiation, as a tale of destructive female ignorance it demonstrates the classical features of seduction in postagricultural bourgeois society. These last incidents precede the recognition scene in which Manon feels repugnance against her own flirtatiousness and vanity, and the pull between sexuality and selfhood. But these are already implicit in the account of the attempted seduction, as we perceive her incomprehension of how this passion can be related to her, and why the youth's face is distended and unrecognizable. The attempted seduction as well as the remarks of the youths on the promenade are both felt as irrationally hostile and threatening, since she has no clue as to their origin, and they make absurd her visions of a life of personal virtue.

Little wonder, then, the sense of frustration she expresses to her friend Sophie at twenty-two: "In truth, I am quite bored with being a woman: I should have had another soul or another sex, or lived in another age. I ought to have been born a Spartan or Roman woman, or at least a French man. As such, I would have chosen as my nation the republic of letters, or one of those republics where one can be a man and obey only the laws. . . . I feel as if chained into a class and a way of being that isn't mine. . . . My spirit and my heart find barriers of opinion on all sides, the shackles of prejudice, and all my strength is exhausted in vainly rattling my chains." This young woman's discontent with the aridity of her society resembles that of her Revolutionary contemporaries, but it surpasses theirs in the realization that her enemy is not institutions so much as it is that chimera, opinion. "I lack everything; I'll never do anything worthwhile, and I'll forever be a little truncated being, displeasing to those of my sex because I don't resemble them, and not having learned enough to rise to the level of the other. I am as out of place as one can be."[122]

Manon gives vent here to the desperate absence of choice facing a highly intelligent, ambitious woman of her time and class, feeling the closedness of attitudes toward her, the absurdity of her sexual lot, the incongruity of the idea of woman she is supposed to emulate, yet withal fired with the idea of working toward freedom and living a life of distinction. It was an explosive compound.

The intellectually respectable and socially consecrated way out of this blind alley she improvised so as to be able to live her life would be to embrace Rousseau's conception of woman. Even before actually reading Rousseau, she had already imbibed the ambient cult of domesticity: in the same passage of the *Memoirs* where she speaks of the promenades, she refers to "the sublime and ravishing duties of wife and mother" that would some day be hers (264). But her memoirs affirm that it was her reading of *Julie ou la Nouvelle Héloïse* that provided Manon with her emotional fulcrum: she would identify with both Julie, an enlightened maternal bourgeoisie, and with Rousseau himself as an innocent and virtuous (passive) martyr to his sacred beliefs. The woman that she claims in her *Memoirs* to admire is not a pretty fool who cannot sustain her husband's interest, but a solid middle-class matron much like the mid-twentieth century's ideal. "I want a woman to keep or have others keep the linen and apparel in good condition, feed her children, order or even prepare her own meals without talking about it and with freedom of mind, and have enough time to leave her the ability to speak of other things, and to please with her good humor and the graces of her sex" (303).

I believe that Manon Phlipon espouses Rousseau's construct of Julie (it is not the *Emile* or the *Letter to d'Alembert* that she makes the object of her cult) because it lent women self-respect in housewifery and helpmeetery as well as domestic sexuality where nothing else was offered; therefore, by default. Her union with Roland de la Platière was, according to her report, entered into in a like spirit of stoical calculation: "If marriage was, as I thought, a severe bond, an association in which the woman ordinarily burdens herself with the happiness of both individuals, wasn't it better to exercise my faculties, my courage, in that honorable task than in the isolation I then lived in?" (332). The degree of her hard-nosed co-optation, considered her earlier expressed aspirations, is, however, astounding. "Never," this woman who had purported to long to join the republic of letters writes in her exceedingly well-wrought *Memoirs,* "did I feel the slightest temptation to become an author some day. I saw early on that a woman who earned this title lost much more than she'd acquired. Men don't like her and her own sex criticize her; if her works are bad, people make fun of her, rightly; if they're good, they take them away from her. If they're forced to recognize she's produced the better part of them, they so pick apart her character, her morals, her conduct, and her talent that you'd have to weigh her reputation for brains against the publicity given to her faults" (304).

Having perceived the depths of her contemporaries' misogyny toward women of aspiration, Manon Roland chooses as her coping strategy what Mary Trouille has called subversion. She splits her persona: as we guess, as we observe her lying to herself (and to us) about never having had the slightest desire to be an author, she represses the acute pain of this renunciation in espousing a displaced version of Julie, a further Plutarchian fantasy of the virtuous Roman or Spartan matron, always dutiful and generous, shunning the limelight. But the attempt to swallow up the conflict engendered by the social insult and rejection directed at her aspiring persona will prove only partially effective. As far as love is concerned, Manon Phlipon tells us, "I see pleasure, like happiness, only in unions that charm the heart as well as the senses and occasion no regrets" (253). Such emotional reciprocity as she believed she had bargained her higher ambitions away for was, however, not quite in the cards about to be dealt her. A concern for such reciprocity was distant indeed from two of the most celebrated literary works of the late eighties.

Justine *and* Virginie

No hazard lies in claiming that Bernardin de Saint-Pierre represented all that the Marquis de Sade stood against: and yet it has been rightly observed that the former's *Paul et Virginie* might just as well, like the latter's *Justine,* be subtitled, *The Misfortunes of Virtue.*[123] How, we must ask, can Bernardin's pious celebration of nature and Sade's assault upon every piety known to his culture be related to each other as stories of gender? Both of these works escape rational categorization, but by pursuing apparently radically divergent routes: both are far more deeply involved in substrata of representation than with its surface manifestations.

The sentimental tale that Bernardin read to the polite but perplexed sophisticates of Suzanne Necker's salon in 1786, and that was published in his *Etudes de la nature* (*Studies of Nature*) in 1788, was the antithesis of Sade's *Justine,* written in two weeks' time in 1787, though not published until the Revolution was under way, in 1791. The massive cultlike response to Bernardin's work—its author received four thousand letters—was not exactly emulated by the reception of Sade's novel, although it too would find its cultists. What interests us here is the phenomenon of two works authored by men that betray a crisis of transcendence, each placing a woman at its center.

What ties these disparate works together is that in the long-begun political struggle for greater individual autonomy, men were being driven toward all the forms of self-realization, including the sexual, yet all the while needing to contain, or recontain, these same drives among women.

Bernardin would make Virginie the soul of his work in emulation of Rousseau's Julie, the radiating sun of Clarens. As Marcel Hénaff has seen, since the novel's concern had been the evolution of the individual and of his/her desire, the ventriloquized female narrators of male writers, and even more so the female narrators of novels by women, constitute a provocation against "the masculine order, as the order of the state and its sublimating representatives, which strive only to reject the sexual connections far from the public space of the agora into the private and closed space of the house; by this same move woman is reduced to being the legitimitized prop of reproduction."[124]

Interest in the woman as the focus of the narration of erotic adventure is heightened in this period of transit to industrialization by the growing concentration on capitalist accumulation, since women have in numerous traditions functioned as a means of exchange among men. The circulating woman is a usable tool of fictional discovery because she does not know the male world and so, as a presumed *naive,* uncovers (pruriently) its sexual ways. But since the woman's only capital in this world of power and money is her body, her basic Sadean adventure is, as for most pornographic literature, that of prostitution. Yet for Sade, hers is not posed precisely as a prostitution born of poverty, but of "free libertine choice."[125] She is pressed to choose, that is, to become the body whose orifices serve the male member. Justine is to be forced to acknowledge her mute body as herself through the paradox of its speaking its pain. The conceit of female bodily innocence threatened is the target of both Sade and Bernardin, but for opposing reasons: for Sade, the defilement of the woman's body is triumphant proof that there is no soul; for Bernardin, Virginie's bodily sacrifice proves its existence.

Again we are thrown back upon the configurations of nature, the modes of conceiving of transcendence, espoused by these writers. As Max Horkheimer and Theodor Adorno see it: "In order to escape the superstitious fear of nature, [Enlightenment] wholly transformed objective entities and forms into mere veils of chaotic matter, and anathematized their influence on humanity as slavery, until the ideal form of the subject was no more than unique, unrestricted, though vacuous authority." We might well, then, speak of the late Enlightenment's dialectic of fear and attachment, felt as retrogressive, toward nature. Bernardin is straightforwardly, even comically, worshipful of natural Providence, as he alludes to the intrinsic sociability of the pumpkin, presegmented to be eaten comfortably by a family; or the blackness of lice, designed specifically to be caught on the white man's skin; or the philanthropic cow, whose abundant four teats enable her to feed not only her calf but all of humankind.[126] Needless to say, this abundant nature is a mother. Despite these pieties toward her, as Jacques van den Heuvel has noted, nature still retains for Bernardin some of that hectic, destructive profile observed by Horkheimer and Adorno. The wild, dry, rocky terrain of the island of Ile de France must be tamed by European skills and plants to produce paradise; and the hurricanes that visit that island are a constant reminder of nature's blind intemperateness.

For Sade, however, nature has replaced God—"No, Thérèse, no, there is no God, nature is sufficient to herself." For neither author, in these neoclassical years, is there a relevant past or a relevant cultural reality.[127] For Sade our present sexual nature, for Bernardin our present loss of our natural milieu, is all there is. Transcendence will have to show up in the here and now, or not at all. In Sade, as Hénaff sees it, the use of a woman as narrator helps authorize the force of the idea of libertinism as natural: "Nature herself is vice, cruelty, artifact; through woman libertinage achieves status as a truth of nature."[128]

Whatever nature may be for these novelists, motherhood as a state holds fantastically opposed meanings for each. For Sade it is, simply, the enemy of all sexual expression: the vagina, the passageway of birth, is the chief object of terror and revulsion. Examples of punishment and torture, verbal and physical, visited upon mothers abound. In *Justine,* a thirty-six-year-old six-months-pregnant woman is hoisted onto an eight-foot-high pedestal and made to stand on one leg while holding the other in the air. Around her are arrayed mattresses covered with thistles, a thick carpet of holly and pine. "When will she fall?" is the game that tickles the fancy of the Benedictine monks, as other women are employed in arousing them. "Pregnant as she is, the unfortunate woman stays in this position for nearly a quarter of an hour; finally her strength fails, she falls on the pine needles, and our scoundrels drunk with lust go and offer the abominable compliment of their ferocity to her body one last time" (152). Later we will have Mme Mistival, the mother of Aline in *Aline and Valcourt* (1795), who, having come to recover her daughter, is punished—for her effrontery in reclaiming her child from sexual abuse—and then scorned by her daughter, tortured, sodomized until she bleeds and avows her pleasure in sodomization, given the pox by forced intercourse with a valet, and finally has both the neck of her vagina and her anus sewn closed.

In the setting of the procreative and nurturant preoccupations of this time, Sade's violent rage against maternity seems far less extraordinary. "The state of pregnancy so revered in society," Omphale tells Justine, "is certain to be reproved here. . . . How often [the blows of the monks] cause to be aborted those fruits they decide to reject, and if they keep them, it is to take their sexual pleasure in them" (167). In lieu of the child, excrement is the adored product of the Sadean sodomite. Coprolagnia entails no future, impedes no impulse. Womb and vagina are the site, for Sade, of chastity and repression, but even more of a dreaded transcendence, furiously denied. Karen Horney has speculated that "at puberty a normal boy has already acquired a conscious knowledge of the vagina, but what he fears in women is something uncanny, unfamiliar, mysterious. If the grown man continues to regard women as the great mystery, . . . this feeling can relate ultimately to only one thing in her: the mystery of motherhood. Everything else is merely the residue of his dread of this."[129]

Horney suggests that the boy unable to surmount this fear withdraws into "a heightened phallic narcissism," an enactment in its rejection of woman of the wish to be a woman.[130] Sade's texts' expressed revulsion against motherhood certainly bear some such psychic scars, as we see in Bressac's jealously eloquent expostulation: "Ah, Thérèse . . . if only you knew the charms of this fantasy, if only you could comprehend what one feels in the sweet illusion of being only a woman! Unfathomable waywardness of the mind, we abhor this sex and wish to imitate it. Ah! how sweet it is . . . how delicious to be the whore of all those who want you. . . . To be, in turn, cherished, caressed, envied, threatened, beaten" (74). Oh to be "woman,' site of man's desire, but never mother, a personage of daunting biological potential, and in childhood cruel channeler of sexual impulses felt as not one's own, but transcending the self, blurring its outlines.

Of course anger against motherhood is not overt in *Paul et Virginie;* yet envy surfaces there in the sense that Bernardin's Caribbean utopia is a male fantasy of fatherless maternal love. Riven from all relations, Mme de la Tour and Marguerite, the first left a pregnant widow, the second abandoned when pregnant, triumphantly create a harmonious island world of female friendship, where motherhood becomes a diffuse power. We see how firmly Bernardin's fable follows the emotionally expansive maternalist vein of opinion.

The opening of the work is bathed in the warmth of a familial connectedness that no man emerges to disturb. Milk, breasts, affection, tears: we are back in Rousseau's gynaeceum. Having left wicked France where a sexual misstep—misplaced confidence in a gentleman who perfidiously promises marriage—has made Marguerite lose "the only dowry of a poor and honest girl, her reputation" (205), she finds refuge with her infant, Paul, among the protective rocks along the island's shore. Served by a resourceful and faithful couple, Dominque and Marie, the women create a blissful haven of reciprocity, a cooperative society (Bernardin finds nothing objectionable in the slaves' servitude, which is given as idyllically embraced). Their little community grants the Frenchwomen "cleanliness, liberty, property they owed entirely to their own labors, and servants full of zeal and affection. . . . All was shared between them" (211). Bernardin is careful to add that if any fires more ardent than those of friendship persisted in them, their religion's love of chastity drove their flames heavenward, purifying them. No compensations of fleshly communion may be granted even to these infinitely loving mothers' natures.

Far more than a paradise for mothers, their idyll is meant as a parable of enchanted infancy, devoid of the shadows perceived to be cast over mothering in French society, with its wet-nursing, its abandoned children, its aspiring, verbal, socially ambitious, sexually active, emotionally remote mothers. The mothers of Bernardin's novel submit to nature, seen here as largely benevolent. "The duties of nature added to the happiness of their circle. Their mutual friendship grew as they looked at their infants, the fruit of equally unfortunate loves. They took pleasure in putting them together in the same bath, to sleep in the same cradle. Often they exchanged them at the breast. 'My friend,' said Mme de la Tour, 'each of us will have two children and each of our children, two mothers' " (211–213). The displacement of erotic polymorphousness from the sexual to the maternal realm patent here is reinforced by the narrator's remark that the mothers were consoled by the thought that their children, whom they planned to unite in marriage, would "one day enjoy, far from the cruel prejudices of Europe, the pleasure of love and the happiness of equality."

Bernardin thus allows himself via this matriarchal reverie to attack European mores. There is a species of sentimental egalitarianism here, even a degree of sexual egalitarianism in forging utopia out of the sexually abused and neglected female remnant of French society. But utopia is attainable here only because the male sex is banned. The Old Man's response to Paul's question about the falseness of Europe's women is an anti-Sadean one: "Women are false in countries where men are tyrants. Everywhere it is violence that begets ruse" (327).

If motherhood is heaven for Bernardin and hell for Sade, they are less far apart concerning fatherhood: both bear witness to the crisis of fatherhood that is a theme of the present work. Both exhibit anxiety over the question of illegitimacy, Sade in his evocation of a rage to murder the products of conception, Bernardin in his rush to repair in fantasy the cruelty and lassitude of fathers in the actual French sexual order. Fathers, however, scarcely exist for either author on the level of consciousness of paternity, as they did, say, for Diderot. For Sade, fatherhood per se emerges as an issue of emotional fervor only in connection with a father's sexual rights over his child which are invoked precisely to deny the relevance of biological connection.[131] In *Paul et Virginie* the children's fathers are not even ghosts, and the Old Man, the surrogate patriarch, is a remote, if benign, presence in their lives. Indeed it is the work's absence of fathers that conveys its anguished statement of the incapacity of the two sexes to be conjoined, even in the interests of the children.

Manhood itself, for both authors, is embattled. In his stock manliness, the Paul of Bernardin's work—who has the form of a man and the simplicity of a child—betrays absolutely no signs of sexual interest: the erotic charge between himself and Virginie is projected entirely upon her person by the narrative. This vision of apparent male sexlessness perpetuates the culture's prime concealment: that male sexuality, as is evident to all, is a problematical force for the establishment of stable values. Sade's texts take the dialectically reverse route of erecting an order devised to serve male sexuality, making its satisfaction the sole value, and the power to fuck (with its concomitants of murder and plunder) the index of masculinity. To counter Paul's more socially acceptable posture, that of a feeble, repressed, sentimental species of lack of sexual will and energy, Sade proposes sexual predatoriness as the metaphor for the fierce exercise of will. A sultan, says Sarmiento in *Aline et Valcour,* commands his pleasures without respect to whether or not they are shared, an idea that would surely have made Paul burst into tears of outrage. Each man a potential sexual potentate, if he but have the determination: such is Sade's democratization of brotherhood, as far as his essentially hierarchial outlook will take him toward a proletarianization of sex. Carol Pateman locates Sade's moves through sexual permutations as deriving from the logic of contract theory, claiming that they provide "a vivid portrayal of the consequences of the absolute conquest of status as sexual difference by the individuals of the contractual imagination."[132] The "individual," a false universal, is a male master from whose psyche all sexual fantasies issue. The parallel sociosexual move toward presumed democratization by Bernardin is to make Paul, the peasant woman's son, an industrious laborer entirely without higher cultural pretensions. He is a pre-*sans-culotte* idol: the simple, earthy man, ignorant even of his own desire.

In response to Paul's and his milieu's (the society's) apparent demand that the rule of sentiment prevail, Sade's libertine hero cries out that all pity must be snuffed out. Woman as prime object of pity and prime pitier is the crux of the matter for both writers. If Paul can claim that he is nothing without Virginie, thereby constructing woman as All, Sade's spokesperson's persistent approving accounts of the destruction of women (and of youths and children) promise to make of woman, when representative of maternal creativity or of powerless spirituality, the great Nothing. Sade's negations feed, of course, on notions of sacred, spiritual femininity and maternity to achieve their prurient charge as blasphemy against ideas of the holiness of creation. Neither the portrait of Virginie nor that of Justine pretends to the least verisimilitude. The island maiden is the purest spun-sugar figurine, the sheer construct of a female goodness predestined for destruction by the world's cruel codes and disarmed before nature. And Justine, like Voltaire's Cunegonde, a rag doll, bloodied and battered, her orifices torn, her breasts bruised and bloodied, always gets up fresh and miraculously healed next morning to face fresh forms of battery and degradation. As Virginie is too weak and deficient as an ultimate standard of value, so is Justine inadequate as an image of nullification. Even these fictions could not generate constructions of women either as good or as destructible as their projects as texts would have dictated.

I view both *Justine* and *Paul et Virginie* as responding, if in diametrically opposed ways, to stubborn social realities, like the inability of many persons to marry, like the forcing upon women of the decision to wean and/or abandon their infants, or even more fundamental, to gestate infants to whom they would be forbidden by circumstances to relate. Sade's rejection of this nexus of "female troubles" is expressed in his worship of the penis as sterile organ of pleasure. In laughing all relationships to scorn, in his humorless way, he takes refuge instead in an onanistic frenzy of masculine solitude, celebrated in congress with other beings as instruments to spur the individual's pleasure. In so doing, he continues and exalts the libertine century's trend to male sexual autonomy, and furnishes its radical *reductio*. But he successfully explodes the machine of official secrecy around the actual sexual drive that gives this trend its mystery and power.

Bernardin instead apes Rousseau's handling of sexuality in his advocacy of the cover of an augmented, titillated sexual repression.[133] For Virginie's virginal adolescence, as she leaves Ile de France for her fatal trip to the French mainland, is filled with intimations of her unquenchable passionateness, that *mal inconnu* (unknown malady) that seizes her. "She was dressed in white muslin over pink taffeta. Her tall, lithe figure was perfectly visible beneath her stays, and her blond hair . . . admirably adorned her virginal head. . . . Her heart, agitated by contained passions, gave her complexion an animated flush and her voice an emotional pitch. The very contrast with her elegant adornments, which she seemed to be wearing in spite of herself, made her languor the more moving. No one could see or hear her and remain unmoved" (285–286).[134] Virginie's virginity and goodness offers us the paradigm of the young woman as consumable object, offering herself in her unconscious narcissism while yet holding appetite, her own or another's, at some remove; inviting desire, but only on pain, as we discover, of that death by drowning which finally allows the sensual languor of her body to flow, freed from chastity's imperative.[135] The dream of fusion that is *Paul et Virginie* terminates, no less than a Sadean orgy, in male solitude, for sexual fusion with the desired inevitably ends: better by far, says Sade, to enjoy oneself. Refusing through misplaced notions of sexual purity to be saved by disrobing and throwing herself into the raging seas from the vessel, approaching the shore, that was to return her to her family, Virginie by her death spares both Paul and herself what is seen as the inevitable wretchedness of mature sexuality; as the Old Man tells Paul, "How do you know that the object from whom you expected so pure a happiness might not have been the source of an infinity of suffering to you?" (359). The pathos of her loss is rendered starkly in J. Vernet's painting from the 1789 Salon (fig. 29). Ultimately, though of course far more regretfully, *Paul et Virginie* verifies the failure of human connection as surely as does Sade's *Justine*. In consigning woman—the one hatingly, the other lovingly—to nature, both works implicitly cast her outside the man's culture.

Although I am fully aware of how ludicrous such a rapprochement may seem, if we think of these two novels as connected in their tendency to relate human contentment to bodily states, we would have to assign *Justine* to the sphere of the penis, and *Paul et Virginie* to that of the breasts. As it flirts with utopia and release from constraint, the Revolution's imagery will recapitulate this split, as well as these anxious preoccupations with sexual and procreative themes. We will rediscover this split in propulsive outbursts of Sadean masculinist murderousness of mood in the streets and in the press, as well as in the persistent, prevalent, re-

29. *C.-Joseph Vernet,* The Death of Virginie, *Hermitage Museum, St. Petersburg*

pressive Bernardinian drive to foster a Rousseauist fusion through a rigged myth
of maternalist familialism: both trends were great perpetuators of gender schism.

The Antimyth: Condorcet, 1787

If we were to judge the prevailing French ideas concerning women on the eve
of Revolution solely on the basis of male texts like Restif's, Mercier's, Sade's, Bernardin's, or even, though to a lesser extent, Beaumarchais's, we should be impelled
to conclude that they were irremediably locked into the ancient dialectic between
chastity and corruption, angelism and diabolism. Enlightenment and nascent Romanticism had meanwhile evolved discourses of individual rights and the unique-
ness of personhood that, in a mode of silent denial, were simply presumed not to
apply to the female gender, although the *querelle* (debate) regarding women continued to engage a literate minority, both for and against women. How then can
we account for the decided oddity of the Marquis de Condorcet's publication, in
1787 and 1789, of his two texts advocating women's full civil rights, the *Letters of
a Resident from New-Haven to a Citizen of Virginia* and *On the Admission of Women
to the Rights of Citizens of a State?*[136]

Was the Marquis able to resist the traditional categories in thinking about
women because his overprotective mother had dressed him, well into childhood,

as a girl, to spare him the violence of boyish tussles?[137] Or was it because he had become the close friend of Julie de Lespinasse, that Muse of the *Encyclopédie* and of d'Alembert, whose circle was certainly the most liberally minded society of mixed gender of its time? Or was it because, as a mathematician—author of *On Integral Calculus* (1764)—and technocrat, he sought only rational and empirical answers to questions? Or was he incited by the ideal of human progress he shared with his mentor, the Physiocrat Jacques Turgot (who was finance minister to Louis XVI between 1773 and 1776) to apply the notion of progress to the condition of women? Or was it because he married, in 1786, a young woman of a distinctly feminist turn of mind, Sophie de Grouchy, who had such a passion for learning that she was dubbed *la Vénus lycéenne* (Academic Venus)? We cannot know the answers with any certainty. What the publication of these remarkable works for their date shows is that an interest in and a consequent elaboration of a discourse concerning women's rights were factors in the rising tide of hopes for governmental reform and national regeneration.

That it was a largely mute and easily repressed factor cannot be denied. But because of Condorcet's pamphlets the dearth of other overt statements cannot be evaluated as indicating indifference.[138] Even Condorcet, so courageous in these two early works, could not sustain his stance before the stubborn, intimidating silence that greeted his invitation to others to debate his proposals; he would back down from such demands for unequivocal democracy for women in his proposals to reform public education in 1790 and 1791. The climate of popular opinion was opposed to arguments for women's equality in the state and would only become more so. Is it that only someone as divinely tone-deaf to the meaning of the neoclassical and mass tempers as Condorcet could have missed their misogynist tonality? Or was it indeed that he had perceived it in the ferment of ideas around constitutional issues and was attempting to mount a counteroffensive of reason in opposition to the sullen inability of the men about him to affirm a concern for women's rights?

Certainly in his *Letters* to the American Mazzei he reveals his awareness of how outlandish his suggestion will appear. He opens the subject abruptly and unexpectedly: "Now I have an objection to raise to you."[139] He proceeds to argue that we call rights natural when they seem to arise from the original nature of man, and we believe that because men are sentient and sense-making beings, capable of reason and moral judgment, we accord them rights. Well then, he concludes, women having the same sensual and intellectual endowments, they must be entitled to exactly the same rights: and yet never, in any so-called free constitution, have they been granted the rights of citizens (280). Finding this distinction ungrounded in reason, he advocates that this right be women's.

Condorcet, even so, moves cautiously, exhibiting respect for the regnant familialist and separatist temper, as he advocates granting the franchise only to propertied widows and unmarried women, and he suggests that women may be more suited to some governmental functions than to others. But he achieves a height of visionary perception in recognizing that women too may have gifts of inventive genius as he expresses the wish that these gifts be repossessed for the use of society. What is more, in contradistinction to the tendencies of both Sade and Bernardin, Condorcet grants that women, like men, have will: since citizenship for him presupposes the ability to act out one's will, he sees that this power is for women the logical extension of their humanity (282). Laws should not limit women's role in any way, writes Condorcet, and when once they cease to do so, mores and education will so have evolved that present objections to their participation in government will seem entirely unreasonable.

Assuming a common human endowment across the sex barrier, Condorcet's statement now appears to be so prescient that it still bears a futurist tinge. His position here, as elaborated in *On the Admission of Women to Rights as Citizens of a State,* where he proposes how such rights could be implemented, can be seen as the summit of the Enlightenment's mostly emotionally driven consideration of women. As a late representative of the salon aristocracy, Condorcet knew and appreciated women unambiguously for their sagacity and energy. There is no suggestion whatever of a slyly demeaning or reductive esprit gaulois in the language of these texts. So totally does he avoid the related ploy of a posture of bogus rococo gallantry that he is driven to lament his lack of it: sighing philosophically, he observes that in robbing women of their myth by speaking of their "rights rather than their reign," he may fail to earn their approval, for he saw all about him the stampede among women to Rousseauist views. "Since Rousseau has earned women's approbation by saying they were made only to take care of us and good only to torment us, I have no hope they will end up approving of me (187). Yet he called firmly for reasonable responses to his proposals, responses that his public's doubts and fears and their greater sensitivity to the countertrends rendered impossible.

Doggedly linking up his advocacy of the freeing of the slaves and the emancipation of the Jews with this expanded view of women's potential, Condorcet rejected all suggestions that there were any basic distinctions among human beings sufficient to warrant the deprivation of natural rights. Even among the liberal Girondists, whose party he was to support until his death under the Terror in 1794, the article of women's rights would never prove popular. As Condorcet himself intuited, the sexual appeal of Rousseauist gender separatism crowded out his unrelentingly rational argument for a common human ground.

Jacques-Louis David's Brutus: 1788–89

The gender polarization evident in David's *Oath of the Horatii* (1784) has been commented on at length as prefiguring the Revolution's.[140] I hope the foregoing will have made it seem less unique in this respect, if not in the aesthetic completeness with which David's canvas expresses this schism. It is easy to see the *Oath*, with its swords uplifted and its tense array of arms and legs, as a phallic work, only intensified by the sorrowing inertia of its sarcophageal women. Considered already in its own day as a prescient political act, the *Oath* came to seem to contemporaries to have prefigured the Tennis Court Oath of 1789.[141] By the time David's *Brutus* came to be exhibited in the salon of the late summer of 1789, many of the crucial events of that year had already taken place, from the opening of the Estates-General in May to the storming of the Bastille in July. The *Brutus*, then, arrives as a sort of culmination.

In this work (fig. 30)—which we must not forget was commissioned by the king—David returns to the tradition of the *exemplum virtutis*, the modeling of individual virtue which was intended to inspire emulation. The figure of Brutus

30. Jacques-Louis David, The Lictors Bearing in His Sons to Brutus, *Musée du Louvre, Photo Musées Nationaux*

that David here exemplifies becomes progressively a personage of choice for republican sensibilities.[142] Whether or not David viewed this subject as possessing
political overtones, for there was as yet no republic in France, the work's reiteration of a starkly schematized gender split, coming in the wake of the *Horatii*'s,
represented a polarization impossible to ignore.

What David chose to portray is not represented by Livy or by Plutarch, nor
does it precisely reiterate the ending of Voltaire's tragedy of *Brutus* (1727), which
was to be performed with great resonance on Revolutionary stages after 1791.
Livy's background, which Thomas Crow rightly recalls to our attention, binds
Brutus to a severe moral code:[143] Brutus' opponent was Tarquin, who with his
wife, had murdered their previous spouses so as to wed; Tarquin had proceeded to
usurp the throne by murdering his wife's father. Brutus is the last remnant of a
family destroyed by this tyrant. His own sons had been seduced by their mother's
clan into a plan to collude with Tarquin and restore Rome to monarchy. Now
Brutus sacrifices them to preserve Rome as a republic.

But there simply is no reference in any of the historical texts to such a domestic
scene as David was to give us. The closest we come to it is the final scene of
Voltaire's play, where Brutus, seated alone, having condemned his son to death,
awaits confirmation of his demise. David had written of his own conception, "I
am working on a picture of my own invention, Brutus as man and as father.
Having robbed himself of his sons, he has returned to his house, where they are
brought back so that he may bury them. He is seated at the feet of the statue of
Roma, and his crying wife and daughters distract him from his sorrow."[144] Despite
his departure from textual authority in imagining his scene, David has taken the
utmost care to impart to his depiction the look of historical verisimilitude: he
derives his Brutus from a bust in the Capitoline Museum and his Roma from a
celebrated statue.[145] If he has chosen to set his scene at home rather than in the
forum, it is to emphasize the conflict between domestic sentiment and civic duty.
The silhouette of the statue of Roma set against the outdoor light, with the lictors
bearing in Brutus's sons behind her, form the civic masculine grouping. But the
gendered concept of the state here is complex. To be seated at the feet of the
goddess Roma is to acquiesce in fealty to her law, whatever the personal conflict.
But incised into the base of Roma's effigy is the Lupa, the she-wolf emblematic of
Rome, who suckled its founders Romulus and Remus as infants. Brutus therefore
sits before the sign of feral female nurturance as protectress of his statecraft. As
surely as the *Oresteia*'s version of the judgment of Athena—that the mother is no
parent to the child, but only the father—David's canvas portrays and reinforces
the same gender dispensation as inhered, for him, in the Roman republic. Rome
and the principle of female fecundity and nurture upon which her throne sits are
both firmly on the side of the legislator, Brutus.[146] The state, co-opting the powers of both the goddess and the Lupa, arrogates a parental power over the sons
superior to the mother's, which it swallows and incorporates.

31. J.-L. David, drawing,
The Lictors Bearing in His
Sons to Brutus, *Collection
of the J. Paul Getty Mu-
seum, Malibu, California*

David's preparatory drawing of the *Brutus* (fig. 31) has an entirely different
character from that of the ultimate painting. The chief distinction between the two
works lies in the painting's absoluteness of the division into gendered space. The
men of the drawing who had come to announce the tragedy and share the wom-
en's mourning will simply vanish from the canvas. Their postures expressive of
pity, and those of the drawing's male figures accompanying the bodies at right,
are gone: the women are now alone to face the violence of the state against what
is represented as their sole province, the closed-off interior of the family's emotional life. A choice has been made.

Jean Clay has stressed the separation here created between male and female
groupings by columns and drapes. The dominant column in fact acts almost as a
wall. As Crow writes, "One great gap occupies the center of the *Brutus*. Across it,
the opposition between male and female, between clenched angularity and sup-
ple, curvilinear form, between controlled and uncontrolled emotion verges on
dissociation."[147] Tensions here vacillate between stoicism and sentiment, virility
and grace, as much as between man and woman.[148] There is a sense of physical
closure about the women's quarter: nothing but grief reaches out from it toward
the dead youths. Pathos is lent the whole female grouping by the mother's open
hand, raised, as Crow puts it, toward a "neural void," by the rejection of the
abhorrent sight by the woman mourner at the right, and by the fainting, collapsing
postures of its girl-children, postures so much more extreme (as befits the scene,
to be sure) than those of the *Horatii*. The *Brutus* dramatizes the painful sexual
split, presented as inevitable, between public and private, a schism into which the
incapacity for innovation and the protective repetition anxiety resulting in the
reiteration of past classical structures had led Western culture.

David portrays the mother's simple, unhysterical, openhanded gesture here as a mute dumb-show of dismay: we might also call it capitulation. The daughter clutching at her breast, the daughter not daring to look, seem premonitory of women's helpless grief before warfare. The women alone, as Dorinda Outram has seen, react to male acts: therein lies their heroism. And women react in the interests of persons, rather than for any ideal. David's preoccupation with them, however, is primarily as foils for Brutus's anguished struggle between great *raisons d'état* and his personal conscience. The women "distract," they remind, they represent *his* sentiment, *his* paternity, *his* fleshly ties. It is *his* republic and its conflicts he ponders over as "he sits alone in his psychic autonomy."[149] Women will be welcome in it to sew and to weep. Yet David's tableau without them simply would not be what it is, as the artist was well aware. Even a schism is an accommodation between contending powers, acknowledging their existence as forces.

Yvon Belaval has delineated the victory of geometrization over late eighteenth-century thought. Carol Pateman sees as its resultant reconceptualization a male body "tightly enclosed within boundaries," whereas "women's bodies are permeable, their contours change shape and they are subject to cyclical processes."[150] This prestige of geometrization becomes concrete in neoclassicism. Alienation from both male and female bodies flows from its constrictions and prescriptions, which reject heterosexual juxtaposition and interconnection.

The growth in a drive to geometric control as between David's *Minerva and Mars* and his *Horatii* and *Brutus* has the force of evidence. To juxtapose the latter work with Vincent's more traditional *Zeuxis Choosing the Loveliest Maidens of Crotona* (fig. 32), also from 1789, is, I believe, to recover some of the dilemmas of the mental turn to a masculinity tied to measurability. Can works so utterly divergent thematically say anything to us about gender structures? Both canvases split male and female groupings, enclosing the women in a severely geometrized columned interior, heightening again the division between public man and private woman. In both a goddess (for Vincent, Athena) serves visually as spiritual protectress of the male group. In both the drama of dilemma lies with the male protagonist. In both the women are flesh, beauty, sexuality, mortality; the men statecraft or *techne*. The men exhibit noble restraint, the women vulnerability and pain. While the men act, yet appear stolid and static, the women merely in reacting express motion and emotion. The drawing of Aphrodite before which the painter Zeuxis sits is as rigorously measured and planned as David's and Vincent's paintings themselves. Objects stand forth visually along a single plane in that ontological relief so remarkable in the neoclassical formula of painting: vases, chair, sewing basket, hair, ribbons, all proclaim their creator's mathematical grasp of their volumes and shapes.

Thomas Crow casts intriguing light on the struggle of sensibility, and hence of ethical style, that contemporaries associated with artists like David, Vincent, and Drouais, the relentless classicizers. The younger painter Prud'hon would write from Rome to a friend in 1786–87 deploring their "violent desire to create an

32. *François-Andre Vincent,* Zeuxis Choosing the Loveliest Beauties of Crotona, *Musée du Louvre, Photo Musées Nationaux*

uproar" especially by offending those of "fine and delicate sensibility."[151] A conscious charge of terrorization of those still appreciative of tender sentiment was therefore associated with the *Horatii* and the *Brutus.* David's works steep us in the neoclassicists' style of a masculinity isolated from women, a distillate of that rage against his society's stifling of what he and the reformist men of his generation saw as manliness by hypocritical capitulation to the fancies and weaknesses of women. Here, at last, are men prepared to act as men, whatever the consequences to ties of sexuality or of blood.

The father prepared to murder his sons for the general good seems prescient to Ronald Paulson of Vergniaud's characterization of the Revolution as a Saturn, devouring its own children.[152] The barely contained intensity of the Revolution's cultural revival of classical history testifies to its character as a return of the repressed, of states where will escapes us, abandoning us to forces little understood and poorly controlled.

Beneath its show of gender separation, every lineament of David's *Brutus* bespeaks an anguish of male human will stranded on the shoals of love's consequences.[153] Brutus the father has broken the primary bond to wife and children through fealty to a cultural construct, the republic, that he sets above his love for the fruit of the passions of his loins. But he is shown in doubt. Will he turn his body toward the women, and weep also? Or is he locked into his solitary grief? In its apparent restatement of a classical masculinity severed from tenderness and the bond with women, David's painting taunts men to bond together in a pact that excludes women. But the canvas itself acknowledges the impossibility of exclusion; it raises the impinging question of the relationship between democracy and family; it makes a stubborn appeal to love between the sexes, even in the midst of its very attempt to subordinate it.

Yet ultimately, the move to a stark sexual division of men from women, emotional and physical, was espoused by many men of the rising bourgeoisie as a key to regeneration. David's *Brutus* gave stark expression, albeit in a tone permeated with grief, to this trend. For his was a work, reflecting the political tenor of his class, that recapitulated, reinstated, and reauthorized sexual separation, as Revolution was already under way.

The Abbé Raynal in 1780 had summarized what he deemed were the costs to Frenchmen of their present softness of fiber, their indulgence:

> A precocious libertinism that ruins the health of young men before they can become mature, and fades the beauty of women in the flower of their years; a race of men without education, strength, or courage, incapable of serving their country; magistrates devoid of dignity or principle; a preference for wit over common sense, for pleasure over virtue, courtesy over feelings of humanity, of the arts of pleasing to genuine talent and virtue; self-serving men rather than obliging ones; propositions without substance; unnumbered acquaintances and no friends; mistresses and never wives; lovers, but no longer any husbands; separations, divorces; children without upbringing; fortunes ruined; jealous mothers and women with vapors; nervous maladies; sorrowful old age and premature death.[154]

In the restructuring of society and its gender relations this passage passionately espouses, women's marginal grasp upon social life would be carved away, presumably so that men would be less corrupt, could aspire more greatly, might be empowered to clean out their Augean stable, so as to achieve a higher humanness. The world that Raynal had found so alienated from meaning and intention had already, in the course of this decade, completed its resolute turn away from what were held to be the superficial, hypocritical models of aristocratic life toward what it envisioned as simpler, purer forms. And it would now be given to women, as beings newly set apart, to represent national rebirth, as the other Revolution began.

T wo

1789
and
After

Chapter

5

WOMEN'S EARLY
REVOLUTION

Dependency decrees not merely economic
destiny; it decrees sexual and social destiny
as well.

JEAN STAROBINSKI

WOMEN were for the Revolution an object of masculine discourse, but, we have long been given to understand, one not of all that much moment; even when dramatized or romanticized, as by the orotund prose of a historian like Michelet, they come across as mere parentheses to a larger history.[1] This, at any rate, is how matters have been perceived by most historians until recent times, until the advent, that is, of doubters who have questioned and rejected this consecrated view. Now we are finally able to articulate the counterquestion: what were women as subjects of Revolution? How did they espouse it and act upon their beliefs?

Finding their moorings as actors or as reactors, women still breathed the air of men's language and institutions. "The subjective reality of women in the French Revolution is constructed by a contradictory movement, of acceptance and denial, of clarification and repression, of investment and displacement with regard to object/woman produced by masculine conduct in the Revolution."[2] There is no way of thinking about women in the Revolution without thinking of the complex of reactions of men to them: the material that follows should raise the question whether the reverse may not also be true.

What Elisabeth Guibert-Sledziewski describes in the quotation above is a hectic dynamic of constantly shifting accommodations between the sexes, here exacerbated by crisis, vacillating wildly between extremes of benevolence and hostility, and yet subject to the massive repression by society of a distinct consciousness of conflict. Awareness of such painful swings of mood is frequently displaced to some other, less emotionally threatening arena. "As of 1789, the father-son or father-child relationship is altering: doubtless the same is true of the man-woman tie," writes Michel Vovelle. Since, as we have seen, those alterations in family and love arrangements had long been under way, calling into question such practices as the older styles of courtship and the relaxed indifference to infidelity, to prostitution, to paternal abandonment, and to the influence wielded by women in society's affairs, Vovelle wonders aloud whether or not the Revolution can have done nothing more than shape up change "already in the air."[3] He decides this was not the case: instead, Revolution itself contributed enormously to the speed and nature of the changes already in process.

Turns of public events in these years would serve to heighten private tensions. In the wake of the king's betrayal of the Revolution at Varennes and his execution, the parricidal blocking out of the past—Barére would eventually claim that all libraries should be burned, for the Revolution wanted no memory save that of Revolution and its laws—would exert an emotional freeze upon revolutionary praxis: "It was necessary to repress affective attachments in order to act, and the greater the demands the more perfect the repression." As its connection with its despised origin, the Old Regime's paternalism, receded, suggests Lynn Hunt, "tradition lost its givenness, and the French people found themselves acting on Rousseau's conviction that the relationship between the social and the political (the social contract) could be rearranged." The Revolution was the cauldron into which differences of opinion as to what changes should or could be effected were cast. It is in the Revolution's "symbolic practices" that we search out the lineaments, the elaborations, of its evolving ideologies.[4]

Rousseau's own recasting of ideas of social relations had replaced king above and nation below with the society of "good men"; "the rich and powerful, the intellectuals, and women had all been stripped of their prestige in Rousseau's works, and on their vacated pedestals the 'man of virtue' and the 'virtuous state' had been enthroned."[5] Carol Blum speaks of the fanatical appropriation of Rousseau's expressed beliefs, most enthusiastically by some of the energetic younger men, and we know that his last station, at Ermenonville, had become virtually a shrine, revered even at the court of Marie-Antoinette. So we may finally refer, without exaggeration, to an atmosphere among the now-dominant bourgeois elite and its sympathizers, of a social stampede to the Rousseauist ethos, including as a central feature his version of the generally approved revision of gender politics.[6]

The trend to the expression of male civic dominance does not quicken neoclassical art alone: it infiltrates the manners of the times, coarsening the behavior of men. As the Count de Ségur would remember it, in Louis XVI's era,

> the failure to respect manners paralleled indecency in dress. . . . Already we greeted a woman carelessly; men said "tu" to each other in front of her; they would scarcely give her a chance to exit first. Under Louis XV we were corrupt, but at least we had some idea of granting deference to age and to sex. Under Louis XVI, we were just as full of vice, but we scarcely remembered what manners were. This state of affairs was one of the most detrimental imaginable to the existence of women. Some of them, in the city or at court, attempted by virtue

of age or the respect they enjoyed to offer a dignified opposition to this revolution in the mores. . . . They were permitted to speak. The younger ones, more
out of instinct than from any true comprehension, felt that their role in society
was becoming an unflattering one; but fashion drew them in, and sometimes
the decadence of customs is such that we prefer to be degraded to being made
to appear ridiculous.[7]

What Ségur records is the evident eruption of bourgeois male impatience and
intolerance of the code of gallantry and superficial obeisance to women's supposed
preferences, successfully undetermined by Rousseau and his acolytes. This code,
which had served to smooth over the roughness of sexual interaction in upper-
class life, had come to do so no longer. Set forever in Western culture either above
or below the male norm, women were tumbling from the higher to the lower
status just as men's collective consciousness of their own right to equality and
their drive to political representation came to be asserted in France. The most
telling part of Ségur's commentary lies in his assessment of the women's sense of
bafflement: unable to dissent effectively from a democratizing trend, for which
many of them must have felt considerable sympathy but which, as compared with
the previous courtly code, demeaned them in terms of their ordinary daily interactions, they seem to have acquiesced by default. If they gave in to those trends
of this reform in the mores, they did so in order not to seem "ridiculous," that is,
to appear to be entirely outside of the evolving separate spheres consensus, and
hence of absolutely no account in its reconstruction.[8]

The seemingly personal evasions and capitulations of a politically and socially
ambitious Germaine de Staël, for example, must be seen as part of this move by
women in general to the only ground—a Rousseauist one—offered by so-called
elite opinion.[9] We find this trend expressed with painful distinctness in that tellingly explicit and conflicted passage from Staël's letters on Rousseau already cited,
written in the 1780s: "Although Rousseau tried to prevent women from taking
part in public affairs, from playing a notable role, how he had the gift of pleasing
them in speaking to them! . . . If he wished to lessen their influence on men's
deliberations, how fully he consecrated their rule over men's happiness!"[10] This
prescient passage illustrates an awareness on the part of Staël, at least, that Rousseauism was enforcing upon women an embrace of the private realm that meant
the sacrifice of their aspirations to affect public life.

Jean Bethke Elshtain has enabled us to see how a woman like Staël, who espoused the liberal tradition of the philosophes, was forced by the terms in which
debate was posed to state her own claims in its language, a language that disbarred
her from giving voice to the private bases of female identity and disabled her from
allowing women's experience to "'speak to' the public realm." Repressing all evidence of her female identity, Staël would evoke in retrospect the nation's outlook
on the eve of the Estates-General held on May 5, 1789, that assemblage of the
nation's representatives last convened in 1614: it was a momentous event which

seemed to her to signify that philosophic enlightenment, "that is, the evaluation of things according to reason rather than according to habit," (*Considérations*, part 1, ch. 15) had made great inroads into society. Despite the obvious inner struggle she underwent over Rousseau's disbarring women from government, seen in her *Lettre*, her inner censor still forbids her from mentioning the issue of women's lack of participation as she reports her awe and sheer excitement at witnessing—as an observer in the crowd at Versailles—the amazing parade of the twelve hundred representatives of the French nation (*Consid.*, part 1, ch. 16).

As Elshtain points out, Rousseau had posited "an ambivalent relationship between the family and polity" in giving to a woman the charge of serving as nucleus to men's value system.[11] In the *Nouvelle Héloïse*, he seduces women away from public pretensions, while executing the rearguard action of excoriating and demeaning their historical effects upon men's (properly) public life. But although we must acknowledge that women had been essentially bought off by this emotional manipulation before active Revolution got under way, the vigorous restiveness and rebelliousness against such suppression of many among them, as among a number of men open to progressive ideas concerning male/female relations, would persist into and after 1789.

Whereas austere Rousseauist gender strictures already hemmed in women's reaction to their failure to achieve political representation from the left, the old rococo code still lay in wait to challenge them from the right. In an aristocrat's *Avis aux dames* (*Advice to the Ladies*) of 1788, the anonymous author threatens his ladies with loss of their feminine powers of attraction over his sex.[12] He had gone to a women's assemblage where "national liberty" was preached: "I've never seen anything as severe or pedantic as these pretty faces worked up to a pitch of *opposition*." While resistance to amorous pursuit makes you wonderfully attractive, he warns, "resistance to authority disfigures you, it pulls your features apart and fills your eyes, in which only the light of decency and gaiety should shine, with the somber and fateful fires of subversion." Disgusted by the "puritanical" aspect of these women whose minds are turned to economics rather than to flirtation, the writer digs deeper. He alludes to the pervasive political mood that he realizes may be turning women toward hopes of representation and redress. "It's true this century isn't very conjugal," he admits, and even guesses, rather percipiently, that "this secret spring might well precipitate the movement that is carrying us in its path; but is that any reason to upset the state, because you're mad at a husband who bothers or displeases you? That would be giving too much importance to household spats" (9).

Our author is upset by women's interest in matters of state. Why should all this—the calls for the Estates-General and the king's request for petitions of grievance—concern you in the least, he asks? "Nothing has changed for you; your Realm has the same brilliance; intrigues, honors, rewards, all the sources of glory and of recompense are still in your hands" (9). Cautioning women that it is not in their interest to support the men who urge change upon society, he makes this astounding prediction to them about the losses to be incurred by the sacrifice of women's aura of enchantment: "If we give Frenchmen other manners and tastes, only let this Anglican sap now fermenting in minds push us into the depths of politics and keep us there, and your scepter will be broken forever: the Graces once transformed into bourgeois Mothers of Families become pure population machines: take care, Republican Government is cold and severe; it scarcely lets itself be touched by gallantry"; whereas "Monarchy" engages us all in fantasy (11). A nasty threat, this, combining jocular flirtatiousness with hostility toward women for taking themselves seriously, but strangely lucid in its evaluation of the implications of women's alternatives.

Gender Accommodation: A Question of Distance

The *Advice* is an exemplar of the strategies resorted to before the Revolution to keep women's agenda (that is, their speech) from reaching the floor of opinion and, if it were to get there, to prevent it from appearing anything but marginal and laughable. Its author's argument is deployed precisely because he knows this agenda might prove to be so crucial and dangerous if heard. His jocose tone toward "the ladies" drips with the rococo's playful condescension and exhibits the aesthete's pose of intimacy, of a closing of the distance between the sexes as far as taste and comportment are concerned. The fact is that in a world without effective contraception and still rife with death in childbed, mortal abortions, infanticides, and the vicissitudes faced by abandoned children and women, some of which I have documented, this pretense of erotic parity was purest sham, robing love in uneasy charms.[13] Instead the new moralistic dispensation proposed an arrangement not unlike the harem's, that features the safety of gender distanciation.

A marked distance between the sexes may be felt by either or both as hostility, or as tranquilizing truce, as fundamentalist communities hold it to be. A drive to minimize difference between the sexes may be resorted to in a spirit of pacification—in the anxiety to move beyond conflict—or in a more combative vein, to fight for a conscious parity or equality. Frenchwomen on the brink of Revolution, whose cultural institutions had encouraged them to be verbal, but whose literacy level was half that of men, were sufficiently convinced of their stake in the equalizing potential implicit in constitutionalism to make a fair number among them ready to work toward narrowing gender distance in one domain or another.

The upper crust's women of the salons assumed that renewed institutions would offer them the same or increased opportunities for participation in public affairs as those they then had. Putting out of mind, as Ségur had foreseen, any sense of menace to their preeminence, they plunged into politics. While aristocratic lights gathered still at Mme de Beauvau's or Mme de Sabran's, Julie Talma entertained the artists, and Mesdames Helvétius's and Panckoucke's assemblies drew literary and philosophic figures. A new political salon like the Marquise de Chambonas's might attract acid wits like Rivarol or Champcenetz, the editors of the satiric *Actes des Apôtres* (*Acts of the Apostles*). The Orleanist faction gathered in the stately blue and gilt quarters of Félicité de Genlis, while the "patriots" of '89 would go to Mme Necker's, where Siéyès, Parny, Condorcet, Grimm, and Talleyrand jousted with her daughter, Germaine de Staël.

Underneath even the pretense of those liberals concerned with the improvement of women's lot—that things in general had only to get a bit better for women to be all right—lay the seething sexual and reproductive morass consecrated by the laws. Every woman still suffered from the delirium of the grotesque code: a man who had murdered his wife might die broken on the wheel after having been made to pay a fine, while a woman in Montbrison in 1786 convicted of poisoning her husband with arsenic had her hand hacked off and was immolated alive. The existence of a famous institution like the Salpêtrière, in which women—beggars, thieves, those who sold sexual favors, and women consigned there by a lettre de cachet—were imprisoned, conveyed its own mixed message to women about themselves.[14] In 1789 the Salpêtrière held 6,778 persons (abandoned boys until seven years of age, girls until twenty) herded by a staff of 1,200. There paralytics slept alone, the blind two to a bed, and the rest four to six in a bed. Madwomen were kept chained to benches in the open in every season of the year. This far from gallant prison reflected treatment before the law that had to give pause to any reflective woman.

Yet women were fettered in speaking their grievances by having to speak in language somehow alien to them, whether rococo or republican. Guibert-Sledziewski points to the felt problematic of daring to speak up for themselves in women's *Petition of the Women of the Third Estate to the King* of January 1789, where they dare raise their voices only as in a question.[15] In a time when some seek to return to servitude while others strive for release from the remnants of feudalism, "may not women, the constant objects of men's admiration and scorn, in this general agitation also make their voices heard?" In their defensively querelous query the women here virtually concede the whole battle, for as they perceive it, it is all but lost already. "Excluded from the National Assemblies by laws too well fixed to hope to alter them, they [we] do not ask, Sire, for permission to send deputies to the Estates-General."[16] "May not women ask?" "We do not seek . . ." *The Grievances and Complaints of Unhappily Married Women* also resorts to a rhetorically questioning voice, imploring release from the stance of defeat:[17] "Will this sex, all the more interesting for being the weaker one, forever be the slave of the stronger? Will its rights go on being discounted and scorned?"[18] Such is the tone of pained propitiation in which the women so generally feel forced to express their grievances that when we find affirmation we are struck dumb with admiration at this particular woman's Houdini-like escape from the chains of rhetorical servitude. Though it must be acknowledged that the numerous women's petitions are marred by failures to find an adequate form of speech, they nonetheless all break fruitfully with ancient, corporate, female silence.

In the heat of Revolutionary meliorism, the long-festering rights of "the persecuted class" of natural children were addressed as legislation suppressing bastardy was proposed, first in 1790.[19] A secondary concern of this proposed bill was to abolish all civil distinctions between natural and legitimate mothers, which would of course have tended to abrogate the division of mothers into good and bad ones and "cleanse" women and children of the "stain" of extramarital maternity or birth. Such generosity to both these mothers and their progeny would come a cropper in 1796, victim to a primary need of the Revolution's men, that of establishing a regime of father/brothers. Thus they would again shore up their "legitimate" families by protecting them against the traditional "search for the father" by women who had shared their vagrant sexuality. The complexity of this male dilemma meant that it could not really be resolved by legislation. Yet its presence as a factor undergirding the Revolution's failure of gender accommodation cannot be set aside.

Men as a caste, then, with some exceptions, have a conservative gender project as Revolution opens; whereas women, driven by expanding promises of constitutional guarantees, experience a broad and progressive drive to improve their lot, or against Old Regime male rule. If their impulse to participation has to be couched in familialist terms, they do not shrink from using this redundant vocabulary to their own ends. "Oh you! whose existence we must share and embellish, permit us to engage in the labors, the privations, the sacrifices that a new order of things today demands of your patriotism," writes a presumed citizeness, apostrophizing men, in a published letter to her friend. "Let's abjure forever our love of luxury and frivolity for the sacred tasks of mothers and citizenesses!" Women express their longing to contribute worthily to renewal, to renounce their "bad" educations, their "vices," for the sake of a restoration of virtue along with men in the bosom of mother France. Such a rebirth would present "the spectacle as touching as it is sublime of a France risen from its misfortunes through the union of men and women who first came to being in her loins."[20] The image of the nation as matriarchal symbol serves in this woman's prose to draw the two sexes, her children, together.

But the complaint of the mismatched, ill-married women mocks the simulacrum of unity and closeness they see about them. "What! marriage is a legitimate union, and in that union one is all, the other nothing!" Supposed to be one, one half commands, the other obeys. And this compact, for the oppressed partner, is unbreakable! Yet these harsh and ferocious husbands demand to be loved, for they claim love is a duty women owe them whatever they may be. The laws make women, like slaves, mere chattel of their husbands, the unhappily wed claim. Despite their show of anger in expressing their own truth, the women's actual demands are self-denyingly modest. To their own reflection that a valid objection might be raised that women ought to be subordinate to men in society, they write, "Agreed." Simply, they ask that they not be men's slaves.[21] They are seizing the opportunity provided by the possibility of constitutional redress by law to narrow, but not altogether to close, the gap in the humanity quotient Christian and Gallic codes had imposed upon the genders. Most speakers of the *cahiers* (petitions to redress grievances) are aware that the preponderance of men would not choose to hear them if they were to seek equality before the nation's laws openly. As the eventual popularity of women's demand for divorce was to prove, once the Revolution had enacted it, men were not wrong to be chary of greater equality in the home.[22]

Since Christianity had imperfectly protected women from the ravages of men's caprices, some women, and some men seeking fresh accommodation with the other sex, had turned to freemasonry. By 1783 there were seven hundred masonic lodges in France, though this figure had gone down by the end of the decade. Women had been originally excluded from masonic membership along with mercenaries, the salaried, Jews, actors, and artists. But a countermovement arose. Frère Procope (1684–1753), a Parisian mason, reflecting ruefully that Frenchmen "adored" the enchanting female sex without ever taking time to love it, was a supporter of mixed lodges. In them men received the names of prophets and women of sibyls. The vows women masons took, however, were marked by the same obsessions that characterized nonmasonic male thought: they pledged themselves to maintain modesty, candor, discretion, chastity, and fidelity.[23] Notwithstanding, freemasonry was so influential a counter-Christian force among prominent members of the Revolutionary generation that a camp within it that included women on a basis of parity, if not equality, could not but present a challenge to that uneasy hostile truce preserved by the gender accommodations of the folkways.

For readers of women's Cahiers, women claiming their rights has an unfamiliar sound. An odd problem of ventriloquism emerges: are the authors really female, or are they female impersonators? For numerous male lampoons of women's indictments of their treatment by men and society circulate, mockingly use language identical—defenses of the weakness of the sex, outbursts against the "immorality" of prostitution—to that employed by women. (The identity of the authors of many of these tracts is not always firmly established.) The presence of these lampoons exposes the play of hypocrisies of which the public is semiaware. All discourse on gender is so coded in euphemism as to seem suspect, hence easily turned to risibility. When the author of the *Remonstrances* chides the king for pretending that the Estates-General represents the whole of the nation when it includes only half of it, this complaint might just as easily be read as mockery of the very idea of representation as support of women's representation. A converse reading as masculine text is also possible: a travestying male sympathizer might also have been its originator. I choose to read this text as one of genuine female defiance. Whatever we may think is its origin, it describes a recognizable reaction to women's deprivation of the franchise. "Where does this humiliating scorn for our sex come from that forbids us all knowledge of and influence upon Government? How has it come about, Messieurs, that we should be pits of perdition, good, however, only to make men, those chosen vessels of honor?" Warning that "you do not know how far women's resentments may go," the text speaks to the historical juncture:

> What times have been chosen in which to do us this injustice? Times when our ostensibly more enlightened century wants to divest itself of the rust of barbarous ages and old prejudices? Isn't the dominance of men over women just such a one, overwhelming to our senses? Watch out, Messieurs, that we do not claim a superiority, which we might justly affirm; but at the least, let us have equality. When if ever, could we expect that such justice might be rendered, if not in these moments when frequent bursts of light hover about the throne?

Yet the writer suspects that a longing for men's bogus rhetoric of love and desire may prevail with women: "Do these proud men believe they can compensate us by the perfumes of their style of adoration and their tributes to our graces and charms by rushing forward to imitate one another in accepting and wearing our chains, even glorying in them?"[24] Such potent tributes to women's "powers" tend to maintain the sexes well apart in essence, the woman set "above," presumably so as to enhance the magnetism of sexual difference.

The terms of the unequal gender conflict have been set as the political battles that will produce the First French Republic begin. In the era of its greatest credibility, a public hearing for women's agenda was already hobbled by that uncontrollable "noise" of habit and preconceived notions Staël alludes to: it was this that prevented Reason from hearing much of either women's flights of eloquence or their sullen mutters.

Wanderers in the Forum, 1: The Time of Rising Hope, 1789–1792

Betty Rizzo has theorized with regard to the relationship of women to social class that classes are defined with reference to men's status, that of women being "entirely contingent" to it.[25] Women, she argues, might best be thought of as belonging to a "horizontal pool beneath the vertical line on which men are ranged, ready to be raised in status to the level of whichever man elects them." She concludes that "gender virtually equals class," in the eighteenth century certainly, and beyond. Although I find her argument persuasive, that is scarcely how either women or men conceived their gender situation to be in the Revolution. It is class conflict only that on the surface appears to inform the course of all activities and demands: as society becomes forcibly divided by class, this is the polarization that commands women's absolute fealty.

Even so, while during much of its earlier constitutionalist phase women of the upper bourgeoisie and even aristocratic women would write and act in support of their views, after 1792, when the battle was joined between middle-class and sans-culottes, it would be the turn of the women of the petty-bourgeoisie and the peuple to play preponderant roles.[26] At no time was gender not, somehow, an issue, albeit one carefully disguised in appeals to class interests.

A class division rose immediately in the wake of the king's regulation of January 24, 1789, allowing the same classes of women (those holding a fief) who had voted in municipal and provincial councils to be represented by proxy in electing representatives to the Estates-General. Propertied widows and unmarried women as well as female minors of the nobility thus held representation, in the ranks of the First Estate. So did women religious, who likewise sent deputies or proxies to their Second Estate. "So it happened that deputies from the nobility and the clergy in the Estates-General of 1789 owed their election to female voices."[27] In the subsequent eclipse of these classes this form of representation was not merely lost: women's influence in general became, in the radical mentality, associated with these hated categories to the point that the *Révolutions de Paris* of 1791 could claim that all women not of the peuple were aristocrats.

This barrier of class resentment is the backdrop against which the women's Cahiers, most of them the work of educated women, burst forth in their array of grievances never before given such play. While it may sometimes be useful to make a distinction between women's interests and the nation's, the women rarely make any clear-cut separation between patriotic and female concerns: their own demands *are* a national priority.[28] "Consider, . . . Messieurs, . . . the deplorable fate of a great number of mothers of families whose husbands have frittered away that ill-fated dowry and whom they've left nothing but debts and children; can you look upon these unfortunates as parasitic growths?" This class of women is very able, claims the motion's proponent, and would profit the nation if aid were given it to provide suitable work. Your happiness depends upon ours, she argues. But since the posture of most of the authors is that of petitioner to the real possessors of power, their tone readily turns to pathos. The woman's posture of victim is exacerbated by the need, even as she uses the terms of freedom, to plead: she ends her appeal by referring to the lot of the unwillingly cloistered women: "If all of us are born free and if you propose to break the bonds of servitude, you cannot abandon these dying captives, equally born to be free."[29]

Poor Javotte's 1790 *Motion*, whoever its originator, relates the tale of a provincial young woman whose family has known only hardship. She speaks to a group of women. Her brothers have gone forth seeking work, and found it; but she, her mother, and her sister are told there is none to be found for women. It turns out that the city is crammed full of poor women, begging at every corner. Javotte and her family do not want charity: she can sew and embroider, her mother is a dressmaker, her sister a lacemaker. An old lady tells her that practitioners of all these trades, whose customers were the upper classes, are now starving. "I want to be honest, and work," she objects. "You'll die of hunger," says the old lady. Javotte stalwartly insists her uncle has given her a good education: she can write and enter a business. "Only men are employed in business." To her objection that she can copy music, play the harp, draw, play the harpsichord, and give lessons, she gets always the same reply. The woman on her right tells her that "men are favored by Government from the beginning of their lives, and we are abandoned by it till the end of ours. There are several free schools for them, but almost none for us. People think of developing their talent: they want to teach us nothing but catechism."[30] Decent work is a basic and realistic requirement that Javotte, at least, reports is withheld from her by a government not hers. An adversarial note is struck against the unresponsive body with its pretensions to a sham universality and its perfidious claim to represent her interests.

Women's poverty, then, is vigorously denounced. So too, often enough, are marriage and love. One author excoriates insensitive men who barbarously treat women only as objects fit to satisfy a moment's passion: "The inexhaustible sources of [a woman's] feeling are untouched by such a man; she groans while feigning passion. And these men think they've felt pleasure!" The arraignment of marriage can be equally scathing. Here it is also deft and perceptive. "Marriage passes for being stupid, and so it is, through the vices of legislation. Women avenge themselves against the arbitrariness of husbands, and strangers give heirs to families. Either the father knows it and detests his wife's children; or he suspects it and then his uncertainty constrains him from natural feeling; or he doesn't know and he lavishes the caresses of a blind tenderness, care, and gifts upon ungrateful children whose natures remain unresponsive to his. Why so many fathers and sons who hate each other? Why so many brother-enemies?"[31]

Such forthright attacks are rare. Usually the women's appeals are mitigated, appallingly, by apologies for the deficiencies of their sex—their weaknesses of will or of education, or their immorality. The women thoroughly internalize the projection upon them of male sexual guilt.[32] The prime defensive strategy resorted to is one by no means unwarranted: it is that men's own happiness will be served by the amelioration of women's lot. But this is a position impossible to sustain in the face of the now-total exclusion from political representation (after the establishment of the Assemblée nationale and then the Assemblée constituante in 1789) which becomes for the women the sign that the new nation will be not "ours," but "theirs" alone. The *Remonstrances* (3) pick up precisely on the significance of this initial dispossession and angrily, yet saucily, give a riposte: what would you think, ask the authors, if "we opposed to yours a Body of Estates of our sex? Don't be surprised. Don't we have a real clergy, abbesses, prioresses, nuns without number, a nobility no lesser than yours, a respectable and numerous Third Estate . . . ?

What do you think, Messieurs? The idea may be new, but it nonetheless reflects reality." Since they have been so devastatingly excluded, some of the women themselves mockingly propose a separatist move of their own.

In her *Vues législatives,* Mlle Jodin offers an intriguing deconstructive perspective on the difficulties for women in relating to republican heroism. Recalling Rousseau's ill-tempered remark about the Parisian women's adoption, from living so much among men, of men's pride, their boldness of glance, even their walk, Jodin protests, why did he not say instead that the women had acquired men's virtues, their courage and their grandeur? She identifies these qualities of the ideal citizen as applicable to women, enhancing their capacity to fulfill nobler roles and not, as in Rousseau, defeminizing them. Her trend of thought leads her to consider how seldom women writers had belittled men in this fashion. The very idea makes her bellicose. It would not be hard at all, she thinks, to sully the laurels of your own celebrated male heroes. And so she attacks the sacred bulls of neoclassicism. Horace's reputed heroism, for example, so praised by history and art, "might be thought of merely as the action of a clever and fortunate soldier who owed his triumph to the overconfidence of his adversaries, to their negligence rather than to his courage. A Brutus or a Manlius, who kill their children against the advice of the senators and despite the prayers of the people, would appear instead as barbarians, not as ardent citizens." In place of the status of (Roman) male citizen, from which she is disbarred, she seems to proffer implicitly a heroism without military bombast, accessible to both sexes. It is in such ways that women's Cahiers attack not only the abuses to which women were subject, but the very principle of masculine privilege and its traditional source of renewal in the cult of antiquity.[33]

Men Who Heard

In light of the force of Rousseauist separatist notions of gender upon the Revolutionary generation, the small stubborn cadre of male thinkers who resist or qualify it is a powerful reminder of the endurance of a generous and rational countertrend among men resistant to their own privilege. But not unlike women, these men, though they speak in confident tones, experience difficulty in the choice of a register capable of swaying their fellows.

Condorcet, the Encyclopedists' heir who had broached the subject of women's vote in his *Lettres,* now persists. In July of 1790, he tosses into the ferment of constitutional debate an article published in the journal of the moderate Sociéte de 1789 entitled "On the Admission of Women to Civil Rights" ("Sur l'Admission des femmes aux droits de cité").[34] As before, Condorcet assumes that sharing a common sensorium and intelligence entitles women to full human status. "Either no individual in humankind has genuine rights, or all have the same ones." He points to the patent injustice in having proclaimed the Rights of Man (in 1789) and yet "tranquilly" depriving half of humankind of any role in the making of laws. In making his case for women's participation, Condorcet has to respond to the growing allegations of women's physiologically based unsuitability for public life: he does so by arguing that pregnancies are no more disabling than attacks of gout. But we also see how much Condorcet now feels forced to concede to the force of countervailing opinion. As to the man's superiority—in a sense the core of the question—he writes that "except for a small number of enlightened men, equality is complete between women and the rest of the men." Even though he goes on to express the faith that this male empyrean might yet be reached by better educated women, the concession is there, damagingly masculinist and elitist in its impact for both women and the "lesser men" among his readers. Then again, Condorcet accedes to popular tastes in expressing his accord with their view that women were superior to men in their "gentle domestic virtues," even though he corrects this stress in pointing to the heroism, "the virtues of a citizen," they have displayed in times of upheaval. Condorcet, who, as before in his *Lettre* to Mazzei, rarely falls into postures of coy gallantry, argues that women only seem "unreasonable" because their interests are not identical to men's; but he unwittingly trivializes them by saying that it is just as reasonable for a woman to fuss over her appearance as it was for Demosthenes to take pains with his voice and gestures. And indicating his essential accord with the emotional core of the separate spheres argument, Condorcet actually concedes the unsuitability of mothers for public service, as he gives assent to the view that women's primary obligations are the care of their homes and their children: yet he allows that while "this might provide justification for not giving them preference in elections, . . . it cannot be the source of legal exclusion."

Despite these concessions that weaken his case, Condorcet's stand toward women is positive and unflinchingly courageous. Not nature but nurture accounts for the gap between women and men in their sense of justice.[35] Women are kept from knowledge of business and the law, and so are said to have no sense of what they are. Opposing women's generalized dependency upon men, Condorcet thought equality of legal standing could correct this social inequality, and he tried to reassure his male audience that citizenship would no more make women desert the home than it made farmers desert the plow. The wording of his renewed call for debate reveals the ferment of mockery and support his view occasioned. "I now ask that respondents deign to refute these reasons by something other than jokes and speechmaking and above all that someone may make plain to me a natural difference between men and women that could furnish a legitimate foundation for the exclusion of rights."[36]

Probably no appeal for women's rights could have succeeded in the ambient climate of the time. But Condorcet's sweet reason was monomaniacally directed toward the rectification of legal disenfranchisement. It simply had nothing to say to the passions, though it aroused them, occasioning some elaborate counterdiscussions of his views. Many women of course enthusiastically supported his views, as the male respondent in the *Révolutions de Paris* of February 1791 admitted. But the separate spheres party projected a warm, sexually promising, utopian vision of marital concord, whereas Condorcet, despite his reassurances, proposed an idea of justice, of a female civil status, that seemed to promise only to isolate members of the family from one another, as all would become individual citizens with greater fealty to the state than to each other.

Other male advocates for women are far less independent of mind, far more straightjacketed by the current rhetorical imperatives. Bachelier's *Memoir* to the Estates-General in support of women's education is drenched in male perplexity regarding the purity/impurity syndrome. "Placed between good fortune in crime and indigence in virtue, can we without injustice demand of [women] sacrifices beyond our own strength and cover them with opprobrium and scorn when a lack of training is often the sole cause of their disorderliness? Alas! We might have preserved the purity of their morals and guaranteed their hearts against the approach of vice by giving them an education adequate to provide them with honest means of surviving in comfort."[37] Rather than question the interactions of male sexual mores along with the female, Bachelier prefers to turn to the education of women to cure the sexual mores. His attitude to women is kindly rather than reproving, but he still makes them the locus of present immorality.

If the deputy Pierre Guyomar's April 1793 preoccupations remain similar, his conclusions differ materially from Bachelier's. "I submit . . . that raised to the level of human dignity women will contribute powerfully to the maintenance of austere mores."[38] But for Guyomar the pattern for sexual equality is and has to be set in nature's plan. There are already intimations of the Fourierist and Saint-Simonian ideal of coupledom inherent in portions of his visionary ramblings. Corruption lies not in women, but in both sexes. He finds Frenchwomen worse off than the women of Hungary, England, or Russia, and feels appalled by this but inspired by the potentialities of the historic moment. "Will we admit or will we reject women in our social compact?" he asks, adding a reflection that casts a negative prophetic light, in retrospect. "Our own determination, without coercing other peoples, our brothers and allies, will have powerful influence upon their minds: it would be a fine thing if the Frenchman were to resolve the fate of women and give the universe an example of rigorous justice toward the companions of our travail. I go further: he must do so." Yet despite this ringing affirmation, what Guyomar supports is only a right for women to vote in local bodies, the *assemblées primaires.* He too verbalizes the consecrated split: "She takes care of matters within, while the man manages matters outside." Women, whether married or not, must lead sedentary lives; men active.

Berating men for their sexual pride and their ingratitude to their mothers, Guyomar—alas, far too confusedly and hastily—affirms that equality, including the right to divorce, will keep the conjugal peace, not destroy it, calling as witness to his claim the serenity of couples in which the man has simply granted equality to his wife. Guyomar's attempt at analysis is a stew of magnanimity and reserve toward change. He speaks in the universalist mode of "men of both sexes" and sees men paternalistically as the grantors of women's freedom—"let us free women from a slavery degrading to humanity"; but (and this is what lends his view superior insight) he hardheadedly finds both sexes to be equally responsible for vice, as for virtue. And Guyomar, like Condorcet—and this is the tie linking the genuine reformers—is altogether free from all nostalgia over antiquity that might intervene to prevent the utopian gesture of achieving sexual equality: "The rights and duties of nature are of an order superior to all institutions, whether ancient or modern."[39]

The Marquis de la Villette belonged to an additional set of men who in 1790 had called for the women's vote in primary assemblies.[40] All such men were potentially subject to the fierce ridicule of the masculinist majority (see fig. 90, *Grand Disbanding of the Constitutional Army,* a scabrous lampoon of the sexual and martial impotence of partisans of women). These men took their positions of advocacy with a great courage that deserves far more recognition than it has received.

Of course it is frequently claimed that this ferment was but a minority phenomenon, engaging only a small proportion even of the literate population. I rather doubt, though without the least documentation to prove it, that this was the case. A single writer may often speak the thoughts of a submerged group, and by verbalizing their dissidence concerning women's roles and nature, women authors of Cahiers and their male advocates surely spoke for a larger silenced, bullied segment of society.

Women's unfranchised struggle to participate in national renewal was played out against the backdrop of needing to present a seemly silhouette that only the most vociferous of sans-culotte or militant Jacobin women could resist. In imitation of that ceremony founded by wives of artists in Paris—Mesdames Moitte, Vernet, and David, who had made such a gift in the Assembly in 1789—the women of Orleans, dressed *à la romaine* in white and wearing the national cockade, followed a ritual of offering their jewels to the nation. They thus took on the semblance of ancient Roman matrons, making a highly acceptable gesture, whatever its novelty. The space occupied by women in such rituals gave them an apposite civic alternative to wandering about in public space. But by 1790, after a further ritual of the presentation of a flag to volunteers, a woman wrote a public letter in the *Orléanaise patriote* chiding the citoyennes for a lack of commitment to the carrying out of decrees. "Every day I hear of motions, but they're all made

by men, and not a single one from a woman. . . . This is dreadful. It would appear
in truth as if the fatherland is nothing to us, and we seem to be pouting because
our husbands spend nights on guard duty. Let us emerge, fellow citizenesses, from
our lethargy."[41] There is little doubt that the phrase "the fatherland is nothing to
us" might translate the sentiments of a number of women to whom its new language and policies already presented little promise. In that sense, the trumped-up
allegations of "aristocracy" leveled against bourgeois and aristocratic women were
in some sense a self-fulfilling prophecy: as Revolution progressed, although many
women remained fiercely loyal to it, a horde of others, seeing that they were not
its principal players but only walkers in the forum looking at events with a detachment born of ineffectuality, could well have removed themselves from intense
commitment to the Revolution. It would then prove to be the imperative to patriotism, as the women felt the need to be part of national consensus as France
went to war against Austria in the winter of 1791–92, that would impel women
to engage in active struggle.

Marie-Antoinette, Scourge of the French People

In the presence of the actual class warfare of the Revolution itself, the person
of the queen became more than ever the fulcrum of struggle, the terrain of passionate contention. Hatred of queenly usurpation of kingly prerogative is sump-
tuously endorsed in an eloquent image in circulation as Revolution begins. It bears
the legend "A people is without honor and merits its chains when it bends its
brow to the scepter of queens" (fig. 33). As the impotent old king drowses upon
his throne in heedless abandon, his scepter, with its scale of justice askew, is being
wrested from him by his half-bestial queen, who with her other hand raises her
goblet in triumph. Her sexual effrontery and wantonness are underscored by the
lissome grace of her face and bosom, as contrasted with the heavy, contorted
baroque curve of her dragon's tail. A lubricious goat climbs upon her apparently
complacent torso and belly. Rejected, an infant falls from the foot of the bed.
Naked truth on high with her torch exposes the usurper to full view, as the
sculpted satyr's head smiles his diabolical assent to this disorderly scene. Despised
by the xenophobic French for her Austrian origin—a factor that would lead her
from disfavor to disaster as Austria took on the role of the Revolution's principal
enemy—Marie-Antoinette was the palpable butt of such satire, mocked as sexually and financially profligate, but despised now above all as the usurper of
kingly powers.

"Certainly," writes L.-S. Mercier, "the queen did not enjoy the esteem or affection of the public."[42] This flagrant understatement is indicative of the embarrassment that characterizes outbreaks of wrath recollected in tranquility. As he speaks
of the fact that the public became accustomed to thinking of the little prince as

33. A People Is without Honor and Merits Its Chains, *Bibliothèque Nationale, Paris*

Un peuple est sans honneur, et mérite ses chaines
Quand il baisse le front sons le Sceptre des Reines.

"the fruit of her debauches," Mercier exhibits a nationalistic evasiveness not hard to comprehend: "People spoke only of her wantonness; it was such, true or merely suppositious, that only at that time was there open talk of a vice virtually unknown, which has no name in our language" (84). Lesbianism, as we have seen, was only one of the "crimes" attributed to Marie-Antoinette.

As Mme de Chastenay saw it, the queen was never at ease with the formality of court etiquette, especially when she arrived as a teenaged princess in France. She craved intimate friendships with women, which were scarcely viable under the pressures of court factionalism. Loving to flirt and gamble, she was drawn to marginal types, and she allowed herself the singular foolishness to express her scorn for the French aristocracy, allegedly claiming "there was no nobility in France."[43] The murmurs against her deeply unsettled her, but they were legion: court prudes loudly proclaimed their criticisms, echoed with sinister intent by the party of her political enemy, the king's brother, the Count de Provence, who, childless, could only gain by undermining the queen's reputation through gossip and libelles. The Count d'Artois, the king's libertine brother, was frequently linked in popular mythology with Antoinette as a figure given to sexual excess. In these ways, Marie-Antoinette assumed far too readily the part of scapegoat, locus of Evil, safety valve for French social and economic anxieties.

The vast scandal of the Diamond Necklace Affair, a true eighteenth-century-style tale of innocence, trickery, and bald-faced lies that broke upon public notice in 1785, cast the queen's reputation in its final rigid form. The Cardinal de Rohan, hungry for recognition by the court, allowed himself to be gulled by the parvenue Jeanne de La Motte into believing she could arrange a private meeting for him with the queen. La Motte provided the bower of Venus in which Rohan met with a blond milliner, heavily veiled, who acted the part of Antoinette convincingly enough to send Rohan off into an ecstasy of hope. Meanwhile, the necklace that would now come into question, originally created for Mme Du Barry, lay be-dimmed in the vaults of the jewelers Bohmer and Bassenge. Forging a letter osten-sibly from the queen authorizing Rohan to act as her agent in purchasing it, La Motte convinced them that Marie-Antoinette was prepared to buy it. La Motte's messenger, instead of delivering the necklace to the queen, parceled it out to be sold. Meanwhile, Rohan impatiently awaited some sign of gratitude from the queen, who, he thought, had received "his gift." It never came. The jewelers de-manded payment; La Motte herself told them they had been duped; and the whole scandal became known. Summoned by the king to explain himself, Rohan admit-ted having believed erroneously that he had had an interview with the queen. He was sent briefly to the Bastille, and his lawyer, Target, got him off on grounds of simple-mindedness. La Motte disappeared. Only the queen came out of it all more tarred than ever. "Mysteriously, it was the queen who emerged from this business portrayed as a vindictive slut who would stop at nothing to satisfy her appetites."[44]

As we have repeatedly seen, enormous power and influence along with mon-strous sexual appetite were imputed to this queen. As to the former, though she surely pressed the case for her favorite political operatives, as she did for Loménie de Brienne, she was too aware of the storm of disapproval of her "interference" to take a preemptive role in political affairs, which in any case she had inadequate influence, whether in France or in Austria, to sustain. Even her eventual self-serving collusion with the Austrians once war had begun was a backstairs, tragi-cally blind effort, and unavailing.

As to the queen's haughtiness, her critics claimed it showed in her collusion in the 1789 *Affaire des cocardes* (Cockade Affair). Allegedly, she had appeared uncere-moniously at a drunken party given by the Flanders Regiment of the Royal Guard at Versailles. If she encouraged the officers there to tear off their tricolored orna-ments in favor of her own and the king's black and white colors as was reputed, this would have been an ill-considered gesture of treachery against change. Stories about the event served to further embitter popular opinion among the Revolutionaries against her and helped precipitate the wrath of the October 5 march on Versailles. But a comment by the Englishman John Moore about her behavior in her appearance at the Assembly in 1792 provides us with an outsider's caution in evaluating the mob tendencies to observe in her only what would feed their vituperative unison against their chosen butt. "A person near me remarked that her face indicated rage and the most provoking arrogance. I perceived nothing of that nature; although the turn of the debate must have seemed highly insolent and provoking. On the whole, her behavior in this trying situation seemed full of propriety and dignified composure. I know not whether the height from which this unhappy princess has fallen, and her present deplorable situation, may not make me view her with additional interest and partiality; but I am surprised to find that the edge of rancor against her, seems to be in no way blunted by her misfortunes."[45]

Much of Edmund Burke's attack on the Revolution for its murder of chivalry he situates in the *lèse-majesté* of its treatment of the queen. And yet such were his own inner repressions that he would not tell a millionth of the story. Titles like "The Revelries of the Austrian Woman" or "The Uterine Transports of Marie-Antoinette" put on public display the body of the queen. The *Calendar of Court Pleasures* describes the hairy sexual parts of the queen and her friend the Duchess de Polignac: "The latter is shaded by a deep forest whose blackness contrasts admirably with her white skin. The Divine One's vessel, surrounded by a blond moss as gentle as silk contrasts with her alabaster body only at its coral edges." The offering made of the "wayward" queen's body to desiring citizens is only a first phase. "With the exacerbation of political tensions, rage wins out over reverie and her sex organs are no longer modeled in rococo style, but rather tossed off to the side of filth." She is made to speak her own nymphomaniacal lines. "My garden needs to be watered often. If it isn't, it becomes a dried-out crust. Hurry! I'm burning up!" The queen is nothing but raging female lust. As Chantal Thomas points out, there is no more rococo talk here of the Divine, nor are there allusions to goddesses like Venus. The virulence of these attacks catches up sexual energy for use by social and political animus. For the Revolution's pamphlets libertinism is a specifically aristocratic form of class arrogance, writes Thomas, and she quotes one pamphleteer's explanation: "All these plans of revenge and of blood were sealed with amorous favors. If Antoinette had not combined her lewd ardors with the most dreadful crimes, the story of her life would be only a dirty novel that would make indifference itself smile. But her crimes are so intimately linked to these amorous intrigues that we could not separate them."[46]

A searing social/sexual rage seethes in these passages: women like Antoinette or Polignac, imagined either as castrating vampires or supremely desirable *poules*

de luxe (high-priced prostitutes), are stripped of their class pretensions and reduced imaginatively to their status as enticing sexual prey, sometimes worthless
even as that. For resentful nonaristocratic men, the class privileges of such
women—especially the nonsexual powers of influence of the queen—are perceived as an affront to their masculine pride, which entitles them to judge women
of every class according to their sexual worth. The shape their fury assumes is
that the queen "is a monster, the product and instrument of a plot that goes
beyond her, but whose origin is essentially feminine." Like racism and anti-
Semitism, misogyny arises from the urge to cleanse the social body of the impurities, seen as despoiling the body politic, that stand in the way of homogeneity.
"At bottom, Marie-Antoinette creates unanimity."[47] As catch-all woman-at-the-
summit, this queen enticingly invites upon her person the potential venom of all
the dispossessed: the men leading the pack, but the women joining in with a
matching gloating rancor, which serves to bring them into a frenzy of harmony
with their men. Beugnot records in his *Memoirs* being in at least one bloodthirsty
crowd in the Place d'Armes, with people yelling for the queen, wanting to pull
her to pieces, one claiming a thigh, another her entrails. They danced heatedly
about, the women holding their aprons high in a provocative gesture of hatred,
self-loathing, and scorn, basking in the hatred they bore this presumptuous foreign female.[48]

Among numerous pictorial weapons, I choose here to scrutinize candid caricatures, rather than humorless licentious visualizations like the tribadic posture
of Antoinette with Polignac, or the heterosexual approach of Lafayette at her
knees, palpating her pubis, or of Artois's penis extended toward her vaginal ori-
fice. *The Austrian Hen* (fig. 34), La Poule (hen or prostitute) d'Autruche (a pun
combining *ostrich* with *Austrian*), of 1791 is a comic attack on Marie-Antoinette
as prime opponent to the Constitution, which the hen holds in her mouth. In the
legend she explains, "I digest gold and silver easily, but the constitution, that I
can't swallow." The stalwart posture of the legs and the arrogantly long, stiff neck
wittily render the artists' assessment of the queen's ignorant peacock pride, as seen
in the eye of her tail feathers. She is isolated in her solitude against the sky; the
sexual allusion is carried only by the title: here walks our Royal Prostitute, the
enemy of the people's Constitution. She is an insubstantial enemy here, whom it
might take but a small push to overthrow.

The Rare Beasts (fig. 35) comments on the removal of the royal family (here,
the menagerie) from the Tuileries to the Temple on August 20, 1792, herded by
their sans-culotte jailer, cracking his whip. The king, a small if central figure, is a
rather benign-looking turkey: his wife, his sister, and his children are wolves, but
the queen, whose face is rather prettified, is a she-wolf with human breasts seductively half-covered by human-looking hair. She bears a further unique feature: the
Gorgon snakes of disorder emerge menacingly from her head. In Neil Hertz's
Freudian formulation, this configuration, so entrenched in Western art, expresses

34. The Austrian Hen, *Musée Carnavalet, Photo Giraudon/Art Resource, New York*

(*Below*) 35. The Rare Beasts, *Bibliothèque Nationale, Paris*

LA POULLE D'AUTRŸCHE,

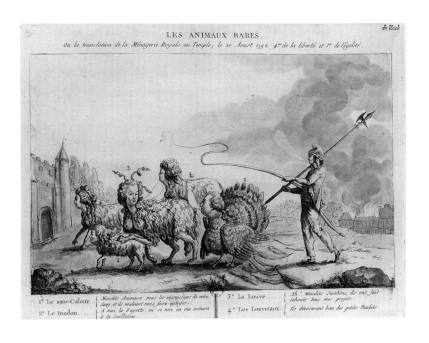

male dread of the vagina, which he finds used in times of political stress to evoke and tame ideas of chaos.[49] If this is so, the Revolution will find in this figure a consistently useful arm, as we shall see. The slightly sidelong glance of this seductively sphinxlike, yet threatening, apparition sustains Hertz's idea: this she-wolf is the chosen enemy of the sans-culottes, enticer and destroyer.

Such caricatures, whatever their sexual or political content, were shown in bookstalls and tolerated by those in authority, contributing mightily, in their "show and tell" art or artlessness, wit or witlessness, to the exchange of impressions of the populace. Of course there were countercurrents among royalists, and many like Burke who saw the queen as "a great lady" with the "dignity of a Roman matron." He recalled seeing her as dauphiness at Versailles, "glittering like the morning star, full of life and splendour, and joy. Oh! what a revolution! and what a heart must I have to contemplate without emotion that elevation and that fall!" This Burke exclaims in that core passage in which he declares the age of chivalry to have been killed by the Revolution, as he realizes that his belief that ten thousand swords would have "leaped from their scabbard to avenge even a look that threatened her with insult" no longer had any reality. Henceforth, Burke sees, there is to be no mitigation to the show of power. Along with the Revolution's exposure of aristocratic corruption and privilege, which Burke simply refuses to see, he *does* see that "all the decent drapery of life is to be rudely torn off." The euphemisms that cover our "naked, shivering nature" are to be exposed as useless. What is intriguing here is the aptness of Burke's characterization: the fundamental aridity of the gender implications of the stripping away of illusion. "On this scheme of things, a king is but a man, a queen is but a woman; a woman is but an animal, and an animal not of the highest order." Kings are to be reduced to being mere men, but women, even queens, become beasts of an inferior sort. Courtly traditions had concealed men's sexual fear and lack of regard for women; the rejection of these traditions has divested relations between the sexes of all the imperatives (such as they were) of magnanimity by the stronger regarding the weaker. Burke feels dismay. "All homage paid to the sex in general as such . . . is to be regarded as romance and folly."[50] He understands the queen's fall from favor as creating a new, unromantic gender order. What is meaningful to us is that though he idealizes the status quo unbelievably, he eloquently exposes the nudity and gender hatred implicit in the new order's incommensurable vituperation against Marie-Antoinette, and reveals its implications not only for her class, but for the whole of her sex.

Beugnot reports that wrath was particularly exercised against aristocratic women. "Yes, it is surely their mode of life, their elegant ways, the softness of their existence that was imputed to them as criminal. Talleyrand tells the women he knows to retire deep into some province where they run no risk of being recognized, and especially not to go to any chateaux."[51] But the lightning rod, in the early years of Revolution, continue to be the *Autrichienne*.

Antoinette-Médicis

In 1789 La Harpe is said to have circulated some doggerel with this content:

> Approach, oh woman detestable
> And look into the dread abyss
> Into which your crimes have plummeted us! . . .
> In vain my memory seeks
> Names of beings as abhorred as you.
> None can I find in history
> To be compared with you.
> Yes, I believe, unworthy queen,
> You're more licentious than that Egyptian
> Marc-Antony was so smitten with,
> Prouder than Agrippina,
> Lewder than Messalina,
> More cruel than the Medici.[52]

In the celebrated print (fig. 36) titled *The Austrian Pantheress* the silhouette of Marie-Antoinette's head is shown inside a lantern, for hanging. The frame of the

36. The Austrian Pantheress, *Musée Carnavalet, Photo Bulloz*

medallion holding her image identifies her as the Medici of the eighteenth century, and the extended racist legend, calling for that head to fall, tells us that "this frightful Messalina, born of the most licentious illicit union, is made up of heterogeneous materials fabricated from several races, part Lorraine, German, Austrian, Bohemian. . . . She shares the character of Judas; like him, she puts her hands into the plate to steal and squander France's treasures; her hard, treacherous, inflamed eyes light up only with the fires of destruction that will enact her unjust love of vengeance. Her nose is mottled and purpled by the corruption of her flesh . . . ; her fetid and diseased mouth holds a cruel tongue, held to be ever thirsty for French blood."

Prudhomme, editor of the *Révolutions de Paris,* habitually referred to the queen as Médicis-Antoinette. The factor that was to forever seal this association was Marie-Joseph Chénier's play, performed in October of 1789. This play had been scheduled to open in September of that year. However, the court, fearing that the audience would identify the defeat in the play of the honest Michel de L'Hospital, as minister to Charles IX, with the dismissal by Louis XVI of their contemporary, Jacques Necker, delayed granting permission for its performance.[53] But the events of October 5–6, in which women led the throng that brought Louis XVI and his family back to Paris from Versailles, had so heated up the political temperature that the noisiest element of the public became avid to see Chénier's political parable.[54] It had its preview, then, under the stress of opposition from those who saw the work as destructive of the *agape* that ought to obtain between a monarch and his subjects. But the threat to that bond, both in the play and, by extension, in the present monarchy, arose from a woman's overstepping her prescribed role.

Recreating the political struggle that preceded the Saint Bartholomew's Massacre of 1572, one of the bloodiest days in French historical memory for its mass murder of French Protestants at the hands of their Catholic brothers, the work presents the twenty-five-year-old, vacillating Charles IX as an easy enough prey to the wiles of the Catholic Guise party and the Cardinal of Lorraine; but it is his mother, Catherine, who exerts the most telling of emotional pressures upon him. In this neoclassical play centered upon statecraft, hers is the only female presence, and her spirit of calculation, of manipulation, is depicted as more extreme than that of any of its other actors. She pulls and tugs at her son, slyly warning him that the Protestant leader Coligny wants to become Charles's master and displace her as his chief adviser. A monster of political forethought, Catherine is also more overtly cruel than any of the men of the play. In act 4, it is she who advises the Council to proceed with the massacre. The Catholic party's rallying cry as it goes to the slaughter is "For God, Charles, and Medici."[55]

By far the most dramatic of the play's scenes is the one that pits Catherine against her son when, out of his great respect for Coligny and L'Hospital and his love for his people—"humanity is moving to me, he cries"—he has just revoked his own order for the slaughter. Catherine reveals to him that she has counter-manded his revocation, and in her rationale, she exposes both her scorn for his manhood and her hunger for authority. As he asks, somewhat ruefully, if it is she who reigns, she replies:

> No, but if I did no traitor would go free;
> My court and my council would be mastered by me;
> I would make all men fear, but myself ne'er feel terror;
> In my court all rebellion would be crushed as an error.
>
> (act 4, sc. 2)

And as Charles persists in his dread of the rage and sorrow of his people he is about to incur, Catherine intervenes: "Yes, I take all upon myself, all, even your remorse; Yes, I accept their hatred and leave to you the glory." In the wake of the awesome massacre of the Protestants, L'Hospital relates its horrors, including the presentation to Catherine of Coligny's head, borne by his murderer Bême, impaled upon his sword. The tender Charles has already turned against this awesome carnage that his bloodthirsty mother was ready to reassure him was necessary, when Henry of Navarre arrives to deliver his denunciation of her. It is her servile art of corruption and her alien Italian heritage that are destroying France. "You soil the name of Medici! You overturn the laws! You destroy your son!" (act 5, sc. 3) These charges are ultimate indictments of a woman for having presumed to exercise usurped, illegitimate powers: betrayal of her forefathers; betrayal of the forms of legal and social existence; betrayal of her motherhood. Like Lady Mac-beth and, Chénier suggests, Marie-Antoinette, this Catherine had sought out and found wayward spirits to unsex her and fill her "from the crown to the toe, top-full of direst cruelty."

The parterre at the revolutionary performances was filled with *tapes-dur* (hard-hitters), a band of sans-culottes dressed in rags, even bloodied rags, who subjected the actors to their caprices, singing, commenting, or mocking the action. Fleury wrote of them that they looked positively wild and did not lack a certain savage grandeur. To his mind, they suggested Shakespeare's Caliban. Mme de Chastenay was to recall the "almost incendiary" effect Chénier's *Charles IX* had upon its audience. What the review in the *Révolutions de Paris* saw in the play was its incitement of the audience to "detest ministerial despotism and the feminine in-trigues of court life." Chénier's exploitation of the Medici connection was a goad to the Calibans of the city to direct their corporate masculine hatred of monarchi-cal despotism to the person of the queen and, through her, women who stepped out of line. John Moore was to recollect the words of a petition addressed to the Assembly calling for all communication between king and queen to cease. "France will be saved only when this Medici no longer breathes her fury into the soul of the new Charles IX."[56] Implicitly, the women are being instructed that in the future only a very much more subdued and subordinate female comportment will be acceptable: but the women who had just broken into the public space thought this was a message addressed only to queens.

October Days: Women Seize the Forum

> Yourselves go to the front of each battalion;
> you must avenge the honor of your sex,
> compromised by one from amongst you.
>
> PRUDHOMME

> On the first of October, everything was
> spoiled by the women of Versailles. On the
> sixth, it was repaired by the women of Paris.
>
> MICHELET

Most women of the aristocracy, members of a privileged caste, of course identified with their caste status against the republican and constitutional leveling being proffered them. Women of the lower classes were by and large not bought out by prosperity and consequently freer to perceive and to identify with their needs as women. A great question raised concerning the women's active participation in the Revolution turns on the role played by food in impelling them to militancy. Olwen Hufton regards women's need to provide food for their families as an overwhelmingly validating, fully realistic motive for action and in no way flinches before the identification of women's militancy with periods of famine. Dominique Godineau tends to downplay this association, arguing that this "role as nourisher is anchored in people's minds, put forward in defense of women arrested for violence at bakers' or butchers' stalls empty of merchandise." Godineau warns that women's active engagement then seems justified only by such nurturant anxieties, the only ones smiled upon in women by the dominant ideology. And this is why women themselves tend to use nurturant language in providing the rationale for their interventions. Skepticism regarding the association "woman/food" may be intensified by a reading of Michelet, in whose view of the human economy women would never take Revolutionary action effectively unless impelled by a sense of pity.[57]

In point of fact, as Hufton argues accurately, women's role as food getters and preparers is a vital aspect of their lives, an interest of theirs, the prime item on their agenda, absolutely prior to any political role they might assume. To the charge that "theirs was only a politics of the stomach" or, variously, that "theirs was merely a politics of heart, to assuage hunger," we might reply that hunger is the true frontier of revolution, the locus where a people's survival instinct mobilizes to fight off lingering death. Pressed to the wall by the scarcity of food, unarmed women who have been schooled to accept their fates stoically find themselves tormented body and spirit: their own survival as well as the survival of those to whom they are tied in loyalty seems all at once to have fallen nakedly back into their own hands, out of the hands of the men, the ostensible organizers of supply, whose promise of material protection and agricultural abundance had been the society's given.

So pity is not the precise word to account for women's seizure of an active role, although we sense that Michelet, however reductively, touched a deeper note of women's entrapment. Rather it is a fierce protectiveness of the area of their human investment, closer in spirit to the mutterings of the Erinyes than to the sighs of the Virgin.

The huge existential gap between the ideology of gender and the in-the-home and on-the-street raw realities of women's actual behavior is nowhere more evident than in the story of the October Days. Just as we still jockey mentally in daily life with insistent ideas of female "goodness," "purity," and "beauty" in face of the full range of female "badness," "impurity," and lack of "beauty" we encounter, so did the eruption of a mob of women armed with pikes and muskets strain the ability of the Revolution's contemporaries to sort out the solecism of the Frenchwomen's playing so unforeseen a militant role as they did in their march on Versailles. In the wake of all the better-known great moments of 1789—May 5, the opening of the Estates-General; June 20, the Tennis Court Oath, in which delegates swore not to separate until a constitution for France had been established; July 14, the taking of the Bastille; August 4, the abandonment of privileges and partial aboli-tion of feudalism; August 26, the Declaration of the Rights of Man and Citizen—a sort of lull fell upon the political scene. Tales about Marie-Antoinette's riotous appearance at the Flanders Regiment banquet on October 1 took fire like tin-der in Paris, inflaming most of all the persons charged with finding bread, the women. Rumors of impending war with Austria menaced the country with further scarcities.

Flour for the making of bread was reduced to half of what was needed for full supply. Michelet tells us that there was in the female crowd gathering in the courtyard of the Hôtel de Ville (City Hall) on October 5 a core of women who had not eaten for thirty hours. But he also points out that many women in the crowd were not at all primarily motivated by hunger. He cites in example Made-leine Chabry, a seventeen-year-old wood sculptress whom the crowd took as its orator. Nor were the market women, well represented in the throng, motivated by literal hunger. Their own physical hunger might have been the gnawing center of the women's discontent, but it is a mere metaphor for the variety and ramifi-cations of their displeasure. The market-women, more specifically the fishwives (*poissardes*) of the market, had a ceremonial tie to the court, where they would be received by the queen once a year on the feast day of Saint-Louis. Many of them had been, and would soon enough again become, royalist sympathizers. Restif tells us that "by themselves, these ladies are never to be feared; they are good-

37. Formerly attributed to David, The Truck Gardener, *Musée des Beax-Arts, Ville de Lyon*

tempered and civic-minded." But he remarks that the crowd of these "good" women was infiltrated by men in skirts and by "vile creatures, the trash of civilization, who had been prostitutes in their youth and were now old dressmakers and procuresses."[58] For Restif, we might say that all the riffraff were "disguised as women": lowlifes posed as honest poissardes, and spies adopted female skirts. A crowd of women was so subversive that anything in it might not be what it seemed.

The painting (fig. 37), sometimes attributed to David, *The Truck Gardener* (*La Maraîchère*) pretends in somewhat idealized fashion to render a sense of these women as a type. Jane Kromm notes the "bland noncommital setting and the subtle counterbalancing shifts between torso, arms, and the somewhat furtive, or at least unusually subverted, gaze" of the figure.[59] Wrested out of all context, this personage, depicted in rich red tones, with strong, well-used arms aggressively folded, exudes a sense of challenge filled with misgiving. The frequent charge that the women of October were simply being used by men might certainly produce such wily, hooded glances as this *maraîchère's*. According to one such version,

Mirabeau had said insurrection could only succeed if it was hidden in women's skirts, and so Maillard, the march organizer, had lined them up.[60]

In any case, some women in the Palais-Royal on October 4, whether put up to it by others or on their own, floated the idea of going to Versailles to confront the king. Next morning, a grim, cold day, the market women and women of the Faubourg Saint-Antoine sounded the tocsin at the City Hall to demand not bread alone, but arms, and the return of the sovereigns to Paris. With Stanislas Maillard, the young hero of the seizure of the Bastille, as guide, between four and seven thousand women, impressing, often unceremoniously, women of other classes to join them, marched all day, gathering cannons from the Châtelet as they went. Loustalot describes their activities in the *Révolutions de Paris:* "They stop carriages, they charge their cannons that they drag along with cables; they carry gunpowder and cannon balls; some lead horses, others, seated on cannons, hold the fearsome fuses in their hands as well as other instruments of death."[61] The celebrated print *A Versailles* (fig. 38) is our best visual version of the scene. In it, the weight of cannons slows the women's forward progress, drawing against their long skirts. The rude, fierce camaraderie of this amazing scene of massed women emerges: this is an army in which the women look at each other, not, as would soldiers, ahead only. Those with pikes seem orderly, but several in the crowd brandish sabers joyously and aggressively: the woman at rear drags along the recalcitrant bourgeoise, the only figure here pulling back.

Arriving exhausted and hungry at Versailles at five in the afternoon, they were received unenthusiastically at the National Assembly by Mounier, who presided. Some of them drunk and verbally abusive, they sat down on benches alongside

38. A Versailles, à Versailles—October 5, 1789, *Bibliothèque Nationale, Paris*

the deputies (momentarily integrating the body by sex) and presented a petition for bread. Four to six among them were selected to be part of a deputation of the women to meet with the king. Marie-Rose Barre, a twenty-year-old milliner, complained to the king that only two barrels among the seventy destined for Paris had gotten to their destination. "The king promised them to have the flour escorted and said that if it depended on him, they would have bread then and there."[62] Pierrette Chabry, a delegation spokeswoman, having obtained the promise of flour, was accused of being bought out by the king's mild and politic response, and was kicked and pummeled for it.

But that was not the end of it. Alerted that the National Guard, led by Lafayette, was following the women to Versailles, Louis belatedly gave his assent to the Declaration of the Rights of Man, as well as to the decrees of August. The Assembly adjourned while the throng in the Place d'Armes, which had grown huge as Lafayette entered Versailles with twelve thousand troops, remained riveted to the spot, starved of both food and, despite the apparent concessions, of satisfaction. Mme de Chastenay, an aristocrat who may never have experienced real hunger, reports with revulsion the crowd's killing of a horse to eat: a *"repas de barbares!"*[63] The privileged tried to sleep, but in the early hours of the morning of the sixth, a violent contingent of militants entered the Cour de Marbre and ascended to the queen's chamber; we see them in a print (fig. 39) recreating the scenes of the women's mob palavering in the courtyard and attacking the queen. They assassinated her bodyguard, Miomandre de Sainte-Marie, as Antoinette fled for her life to the king's chambers. Lafayette's troops were summoned at this point to assist the king's guards, and a precarious order was restored. The king was then persuaded that he and his family had to leave the palace for Paris. When Lafayette asked the queen to show herself on the palace balcony, she did so holding her children by the hands: but the crowd protested, crying *"Pas d'enfants!"* She would have to appear alone. This reaction was tantamount to conveying to her that they refused to see her as a mother, the only category of women sacred to them. Lafayette turned the crowd around, however, by a gesture of courtly obeisance: when the queen reappeared without her children, the general bowed and kissed her hand. This scene of gallantry before the royal family's capitulation evoked a strange turnabout: now the cries were *"Vive la reine!"*

The labile quality of the women's response to the queen is so marked a feature as to deserve comment. The mob in the palace had made for the queen's bed, amid women's urgings to eviscerate her. "We must have the queen's heart!" With his characteristic simplicity, the king had asked the deputation, "Have you come to harm my wife?"[64] The rage of the women (by no means shared by them all) against the queen was certainly not unique to their sex, as the primarily male campaign of the libelles against her testifies. But it had the flavor of an extra animus felt by a disaffected caste against one of their number who had come to symbolize quintessentially the escape from all the female vises: ignorance, poverty,

39. The Terrible Night of the 5th to the 6th October, 1789, *Bibliothèque Nationale, Paris*

sexual bondage, slavery to their reproductive lives, unfreedom to act. This same syndrome of active female outrage against members of their sex emerges against other "exceptional" women. And what the men hated, the women had to hate with an inflated venomousness, as proof of their loyalty, especially in view of the blight Marie-Antoinette appeared to have cast on their sex. Even men's sexual scorn was echoed by women, to demonstrate their solidarity in matters sexual—not with women, but with men. To despise the "Austrian whore" became for women a sign not only of national loyalty, but of personal purity.

Mercier tells of the now huge mob's return with the monarchs to Paris, a most expansive scene (fig. 40): "Two hundred thousand men on the road, laughing, howling, dancing, yelling, saying: 'We've got him!' Each soldier holding a prostitute by the arm; the fishwives seated on the cannon, others wearing grenadiers' caps; wine barrels next to powder kegs; green branches attached to butts of rifles; joy, shouting, clamor, gaiety, . . . noise, the image of the ancient Saturnalia, noth-

Triomphe de l'Armée Parisienne réunis au Peuple à son retour de Versailles à Paris le 6.ᵉ Octobre 1789

40. Triumph of the French Army and the Peuple, Bringing the King Back from Versailles, October 6, 1789, *Bibliothèque Nationale, Paris*

ing could describe this convoy that brought the monarch back."⁶⁵ This boisterous account does not stress the two heads on pikes that led the procession.

The removal of the king to Paris brought government under the surveillance of the Parisians and consecrated the king's subordination to the people. But the impressive outbreak of female action that occasioned it aroused enormous anxiety. "The city fathers of all political persuasions viewed the women's part in the October Days as an aberration of nature that had exposed Paris to anarchy." What to some looked like near-anarchy was to others sheer triumph. The lyrics of a "Song of the Poissardes" composed to celebrate this exploit go: "To Versailles, like braggarts, we dragged our cannon. Although we were only women, we wanted to show a courage beyond reproach. We made men of spirit see that just like them we weren't afraid; guns and musketoons across our shoulders, we went off like Amadis of Gaul. . . . Everywhere, just like warriors, we carried off the laurels and the glory, and roused hopes for the glory of France." Whether written by a male or female hand, this song saucily celebrates the "women's hour" of courage and was evidently meant to be sung by women. The schism between the women's perception of their own acts as daring, courageous, and effective—a view shared by some men and not shared by some women—and the perception of it by the dominant trend of opinion as an aberration was extreme and consequential. As we listen to the proud and provocative assessment of the seizure of the royal family in a notice published in the women's magazine *Les Etrennes Nationales des*

Dames, the fears aroused by it fall into better focus. "Last October 5 the Parisiennes proved to men that they were at least as courageous as they, and just as enterprising. . . . We suffer more than men, who with their declarations of rights leave us in the state of inferiority and, let's be truthful, of slavery in which they've kept us so long. If there are husbands *aristocratic* enough in their households to oppose the sharing of patriotic honors, we'll use the arms we've just employed with such success against them." This writer bases her demands on the principle that women have proven their title to some share in civic honor by their action. This was a seditious sentiment, to which another reader of the *Etrennes* gave her support: "Having become free, [men] have not tired of treating us as their Third Estate." The women's formation of a crowd—a body—seemed to embolden them to articulate their own needs and desires. This could not be tolerated. The wind in women's sails had to be calmed. One of the ways of achieving this was, ironically enough, to set them up as *figures de proue,* goddesses on the prow of the ship Revolution, heading into the winds.[66]

Coping Strategies

Three of the Revolution's women express in their varying conduct the paradoxes of living in the midst of apparent political possibilities foreclosed against them by the Revolution's own ideology.

Manon Roland's solution, as we saw earlier, would be one of wholesale acquiescence on the surface. She would be almost accurate when she defended herself at her 1793 trial as never having presumed to have overstepped the limits prescribed for her sex: for she had consistently professed a primary allegiance well within these forms, to her husband and child. Silent in the salon company the Rolands gathered together in 1791—where Brissot, Pétion, Buzot, and Robespierre were major figures—Manon Phlipon would sit apart, knit, and listen. Only with the departure of the company would she engage in political strategizing with Roland, for whom she wrote speeches and correspondence. Her posture was to take at its word the ambient ideological imperative to marital fusion: her error lay in failing to efface herself within her marriage. Instead she exerted her impressive energies and gifts in the service of the objectives she held in common with her husband. These activities, taken under the cover of marriage, made her the most effective political woman of the Revolution. So whatever her professions of virtue, this activity made her suspect. Danton, in a public attack in the Assembly, hit an easy target in alleging that his enemy, Roland, was hag-ridden, for his collaboration with his "discreet" wife was no secret. "If you invite him, invite Mme Roland too; for everyone knows Roland does not run his department alone. I, on the other hand, am alone in mine."[67] Her strategy of glazing herself lightly in domesticity simply backfired: her blithe pose of being the subordinate domestic woman could not stand.

She would write in her plan for her defense, "I followed the progress of the

Revolution with interest, I kept abreast of public affairs with warmth, but I never went beyond the limits imposed upon my sex" (137). This seemingly conformist stance was coupled with a Rousseauist political apologia rooted in her master's ideology. "We want no empires but those of the heart, no thrones except in hearts." And yet both Mme Roland's political engagement and her love affair with Buzot scarred her as inadequate, not only in her Girondist politics but qua woman, as far as the Jacobin orthodoxy that would send her to the guillotine was concerned.

Germaine de Staël, unlike the lucid, deliberate Manon Roland, essentially had no strategy for remaining a woman of mind and energy as the Revolution bore down. Protected by wealth and station as Swedish ambassadress, she blindly expected a continuation of her life as an Enlightenment salon woman. Soon she was caught tragically unawares by the tide of disapproval of herself and her kind. Espousing constitutionalism with enthusiasm, she identified with Revolution, but her connection with her father, Necker, her class membership, and her irrepressible love of politics were to cast her into nearly permanent exile. The struggle she experienced with the new domestic code imprinted itself most powerfully in her fictions, and this record of inner strife, as we have seen, preceded the onset of Revolution, since the gender revolution had long since begun. At the Revolution's outset, her only published work has been her essay in (sometimes mitigated) praise of Rousseau. She had not yet committed herself fully to a life as a woman of letters. Until the summer of 1792, when she fled Paris, pregnant and in pursuit of her lover Narbonne, Staël, like Roland though far more uninhibitedly and essentially on her sole initiative, conducted a salon. This salon was patterned after the eighteenth-century model: it was not, like the Rolands', a purely partisan one. Although Staël had pronounced and public sympathies for constitutional monarchy at this period, she entertained company from divergent factions. Then as later, she engaged in discussions of political strategy and with her company would sit as a critic of speeches planned for the Assembly by some of her familiars who were its members. Her most intense energies were focused upon the furthering of the career of her lover, the Count of Narbonne-Lara, as minister of war. When Louis dismissed him in March of 1792, Staël's own position became untenable. Indeed, once her father had fled Paris, and at some considerable risk to herself, she had assisted friends to flee; her most pressing desire, once she had given birth to her child in Switzerland, was to pursue her lover to England. For the Jacobin Revolution, she was all that a woman should not have been.

Olympe de Gouges, a prolific playwright and a drifter, was a forty-one-year-old free agent when the Revolution began, with no establishment by birth or marriage to defend. A perfect representative of the problematics of lineage of the time, she was born to Anne-Olympe Mouisset and her husband, Pierre Gouze, a Montauban butcher, but she claimed to be the natural progeny of the Marquis LeFranc de Pompignan, Voltaire's favorite target as a pompous bigot.[68] Essentially a maverick, she was a far more representative figure, in terms of the problems facing the women of her nation, than the middle-class Roland or the upper-middle-class Staël. Born into a lower-class family, she was married at seventeen and widowed with a child a few months thereafter. Her life would take a number of picaresque turns. A rich bachelor transported the comely Olympe, with her child, to Paris and long provided for her. Spurning the patronymic of her dead husband, she invented a name for herself and acquired a reputation for the freedom of her sexual comportment. Though widely considered beautiful, she took to writing, in the teeth of the litany of the 1780s, that women's cultivation of literary talent only spoiled their "charms."[69] Olympe thus placed herself squarely against the rising tide of the reduction of women to the sexual/maternal dimensions and, despite the modesty of her social origins, laid claim to that lineage of French literary expression by women going back to the medieval Marie de France. She had never succeeded in getting her plays performed, but her luck seemed to have changed in 1789, when the Comédie-Française finally produced her *Zamore et Mirza (Black Slavery)*. It had been awaiting production for four years, while colonialists resisted its appearance. Met with derision on the part of one critic who claimed one needed to have a beard if one wanted to write good drama, the play's performance moved another to this reflection: "To maintain her right to French gallantry, a woman needs to appear in person. The spectator [of her play], become her judge, believes himself excused from being gallant, and no longer sees an amiable sex through the screen of pretentions that make all its graces disappear, without making us forget its weaknesses!"[70] The play disappeared from the boards.

In her 1791 play, *Mirabeau aux Champs-Elysées,* she put on the stage the seventeenth century's most famous femme fatale, Ninon de Lenclos, her spokesperson for women, to deplore the lot that men have accorded them. "I feel the injustice of it and cannot bear it," says Ninon. "I believe they have given to us all that is most frivolous and that men have kept all the real qualities for themselves. From this moment forth, I make of myself a man! I will blush no longer to use the precious gifts Nature has given me."[71] But there is also an exchange in the play in which Ninon remarks that women are usually content "to be women," are their own worst enemies, have little comprehension of their own best interests, and tend to unite in a surge of outrage at any one among them who stakes out a claim for them all. When France's great epistolary author Marie de Rabutin-Chantal, or "Sévigné" as she is called in the play, speaks the Revolution's oft-repeated yet little understood underground secret that "a government cannot stand if mores are not purified," "Ninon" replies that no Revolution can succeed if the souls of women are not raised up: as long as the nation fails to foster women's usefulness to society and their rationality, "as long as men are not great enough to be concerned with their true glory, the state cannot prosper: it is I who tell you so."[72]

The brute lot of most women, endured with so much less of the protective swaddling that enfolded the middle class, tormented the gifted intelligence of this energetic and striving woman. Her concerns were not confined only to women who, like herself, wanted to write; they extended to the most basic cruelties she saw about her: the one woman in four dying in childbed, the tyrannies perpetuated under the cover of marriage, the rights of unmarried mothers, illegitimate children, and workers' children, bereft. Her enlightened social sensibility impelled her, in a storm of writings, to propose refuges for the old, workshops for the unemployed. Some of her ideas were taken seriously by Mirabeau.

Meanwhile, Mary Wollstonecraft's 1791 *A Vindication of the Rights of Women,* inspired by the Revolution itself, had been translated into French and published that same year, as had Theodor Gottlieb von Hippel's analysis *On Improving the Status of Women.*[73] Following the ferment created by the October Days and Condorcet's repeated, though spurned, call for women's right to vote, these works and the discussion they occasioned created a fertile soil for de Gouges's 1791 reformulation in the feminine of the Rights of Man.

Manon Roland, like the Revolution's men, opted for a union of the sexes in difference within marriage that would close private distance between them; yet her conception departed from the male ideology in allowing the wife to express her capacities in actively fostering the objectives of her husband. Staël, although married in the fashion of the mid-eighteenth century's practice to a man she did not love, still energetically strove—at the outset—to conform to the new domestic code as she corresponded for her ambassador husband with the king of Sweden. The personal distance between them as a couple was considerable: the professional, less so. But their public pose was one of Old Regime social parity, a parity assumed by both into their separate sexual affairs. A longing for this species of interpersonal parity with men became increasingly unassuageable for Germaine de Staël, as the new gender accommodations placed it increasingly out of reach.

But even Olympe de Gouges, who, having less to lose, far more consciously demanded equality and the diminution of disparity between the sexes than the others, felt impelled to make concessions to the tyrannies of the Revolution's gender ideology. So much more is the wonder that this freebooting and marginal woman could have freed herself sufficiently to make so ringing and politically daring a call as her *Déclaration.*[74]

The *posttambule* that ends her tract is a sounding of the tocsin to alert women to come out and recognize their rights. We sense the desire to make so loud a noise that women would at last hear and be heard, for they are speaking out at last. And yet in her preamble she addresses men: "Man, are you capable of being just?" With a glance at the animal kingdom, she concludes that in nature the sexes cooperate harmoniously. Only man fails in this respect: "unpredictable, blind, puffed up with knowledge and degenerate in this century of enlightenment and wisdom," man wants "like a despot to govern a sex that has been gifted with all the intellectual faculties; to claim his own rights to equality, and say no more" (101). She speaks—utterly alone as she is—for all the "mothers, daughters, and sisters" of the nation and demands that women assemble to formulate viable and consistent moral principles applicable to both sexes. But listen to her rococo-cum-maternalist turn as she pulls out all the stops, to the left and the right as she speaks of "the sex superior in beauty as in courage in maternal suffering"; this is the sex that "recognizes and declares before the Supreme Being the following Rights of the Woman and Citizeness" (102).

Article One demands equality, but guardedly. "Woman is born free and remains equal to man in rights. Social distinctions may be founded only in a common utility." The latter clause may seem already to pander to the social distinctions insisted upon by the horde of separate spherist thinkers, who held that "social utility" demanded social separation between the sexes. But probably Olympe has made this proviso to ensure that society would cope with problems specific to women. After laying claim to rights of liberty, property, personal safety, and resistance to oppression, she demands for women in Article Six the right not only to vote, but to be admissible with men to all public dignities, positions, and employments, according to their capacities and without other restrictions than those of their virtues and talents (103). Equality before the law is called for in Articles Seven, Eight, and Nine. Article Ten contains her celebrated (and prophetic) formulation: woman has the right to mount to the scaffold, she must equally have the right to climb into the Tribune, providing that her manifestations do not trouble public order as established by law (104). (We note her defensiveness regarding allegations of female "disorderliness.") Women should have the right to affirm their children's paternity. Since their property rights are identical to men's, she affirms, women should share in the pains induced by taxation and civic duty, like the corvée, as well as the privileges of citizenship. And she asserts that women as a mass have the right to demand an accounting from governments for the administration of matters touching their interests.

Certainly an impressive document for an only approximately lettered, unpropertied figure without status or a distinct political profile: her Girondist sympathies sent her to the guillotine, and she dedicated her *Declaration* to Marie-Antoinette! The last section of this document contains a sorrowful appeal to women that rings with a special significance in its recognition that the Revolution is already failing women in the wake of October. "Man the slave, to multiply his strength, has needed to turn to your strength to break off his irons. Become free, he has turned unjust to his mate. Oh women! women, when will you cease to be blind? what advantages have you garnered in the Revolution? A more pronounced scorn, a more open disdain." Like Burke, she sees chivalry as dead, but she puts a moralistic gloss upon women's past collusion in its less alluring underside. "For corrupt centuries you've reigned only over the weakness of men. Your reign is ended; what remains to you now? A conviction of men's injustice" (106). She elaborates on the theme—which she palpably takes from men's discourse—of women's corruption. Their calculating wiles and nocturnal tricks gave them power: "They governed crime as they did virtue" (107). Women's ambition was thus vitiated, and this "formerly contemptible and respected sex" has now, since the Revolution, become "respectable and despised" (107). Rejecting marriage—"the grave of confidence and love"—she proposes contractual bonds allowing for extramarital unions by both sexes, whose children would then be embraced by the contractual couple. And the last section of this multifarious document, following its sinuous line of opposition to tyranny, is a ringing requisition to end the racism of the colonists, because for her it represents one more failure of human solidarity.

Olympe de Gouges's was a resounding declaration virtually unheard. "The men never took heed of it. The women preferred to keep a prudent silence."[75]

A woman of rococo tendencies to sexual freedom and an energetic ambition (after Olympe, few women would write thirty plays and agitate all over Paris to get them produced), the early Revolution represented to her the possibility of a true, not merely a decorative and demeaning, form of selfhood. It is this need for human expansiveness that her declaration proclaims, and nothing could have been more contrary to any of Rousseau's programs for women than this.[76] Yet it is true that in her rhetorical anxiety she will toss into her mix of argument anything lying about—a paean to women's beauty or courage or moral superiority, or accusations against their duplicity, or appeals to nature—that the popular demagoguery might find acceptable.[77] Her rhetorical task, in making this open claim for women's rights in the midst of the Revolution's climate, was severe: having adopted an entirely derivative framework from the men's rights document she careens in and out of resemblance with it and falls—though at moments only—into the tropes, allegorical and inflated, of Rousseauist sentimentality or even popular misogyny.

Despite these concessions to the old aesthetic or the new, *The Declaration of the Rights of Women* departs radically from any Rousseauist view in its plainspoken indictment of men for indulging in and maintaining, even into their Revolution waged in the name of political representation, the oppression of women. Liberated, like Mary Wollstonecraft, to speak in women's behalf precisely by her marginality, Olympe's voice still carries echoes of the bohemian and mixed-gender circles of those aspiring to make their impress on Parisian society. Styling herself "plus homme que femme," she was, in her challenging outspokenness, unafraid to address men. Listen to her cheeky tone in attacking Robespierre: "Tell me, Maximilien, of whom were you so afraid, in the convention, of the men of letters? Why did you thunder away in the electoral assembly against the philosophes to whom we owe the destruction of tyrants . . . ? Didn't you do so so as to end up dominating over the convention? You think yourself a Cato, but you're nothing but a caricature of him. . . . Maximilien! you proclaim peace to the whole world and make war on humankind!"[78]

While ready to speak the language of the men's politics, de Gouges forthrightly proposed a women's agenda to government to correct present injustices: the lack of inheritance and property rights; nonsupport of illegitimate children and their mothers; absence of freedom of expression both at home and in society, sexual rights, consistency and fairness in sexual matters, representation. These were chief factors that hamstrung women's advancement as men's equals, as genuine contributors to a common enterprise. Olympe de Gouges, unlike the more militant women in the Club of Revolutionary Republican Women two years later, was sufficiently identified with moderate positions to have been able to stand back and assess the fact: the Revolution was not improving women's lot, but worsening it.

And yet the early Revolution had not been so entirely closed against women as it would become. Even Robespierre, that great favorite of so many women, proposed in this period that women obtain representation. They did gain rights to inherit, to divorce, which implicitly granted them civic status, and to public education (a project soon aborted). The course of events—the internationalization of war against France and the menace of civil war—would entirely eclipse the consideration of other solutions to gender strife. Women's attempt to achieve recognition as individual citizens was already essentially over by the time the First Republic was founded on September 21, 1792. Even wresting the new republic's avenues of redress from the king proved to be a somewhat more feasible task for its men than any distinct improvement in women's condition. This simply did not lie in the cards dealt by the Revolution's gender ideology. Myth was to prove a potent tool in helping men arrest what they saw as an erosion of their own fragile, newly won rights.

Chapter

6

GODDESSES AND ALLEGORIES

Toi donc, Equité sainte, ô toi, vierge adorée . . .

ANDRÉ CHÉNIER

Once it was the wife of a conspirator carried in
triumph amongst the people . . . once an actress
who, the day before, had played the role of Venus or
of Juno . . . finally, a mythology more absurd than
that of the Ancients . . . , goddesses more vile than
those of Fable, were about to reign in France. The
Convention saw these conspirators. . . . They are no
more.

PAYAN

Is this liberty . . . a mere actress from the opera . . .
or that forty-six-foot-high statue David plans? If you
do not understand liberty, as I do, to refer to
principles, but only to a block of stone, there is no
more stupid and costly idolatry than ours.

CAMILLE DESMOULINS

THE symbolic vocabulary of the Revolution teems with metaphor: Truth is constantly being unveiled, Aristocracy impaled; Justice prevails, as Discord is routed
and Reason reigns. These verbal commonplaces of political speech and journalism
are matched by visual figures from the traditional iconographic stock, rendered
sometimes with radiant skill, but just as often with a naive but expressive lack of
it. The "goddesses" that now come into iconographic use are not total strangers
to the eye. Frequently they bear an arresting resemblance to the rococo's own
favorite goddesses: Venus primarily, of course, and sometimes Minerva or Juno.
Rococo representations of these goddesses had not been allegorical, however, but

anecdotal, conveying no ethical spillover. Rather than the visual analogue of a concept that we find in the Revolution, rococo depictions, as in Ovid's *Metamorphoses,* had seemed to convey the drama and motion of a goddess's story, her falling in love or out of it, her ascension to divine grace or her lapse from it. Language still faintly echoes this rococo tone: women are still "goddesses" but are now so referred to only in accents dripping with sarcasm, as on the police blotters that speak of the "*déesses dans la rue*" (goddesses of the streets).[1] Long since toppled from their courtly pedestals, women now fall prey to the passion for the restoration of virtue. The new order of representation, in its striving after "innocent" forms, resorts to a revival of moribund allegory, a form fallen into disuse in the bourgeois art of a Chardin or a Greuze. This was a revival, divorced from scenes of mythology, which would install the feminine noun and its female visualization in place of the rococo as the realm of (female) alterity. Whether "hot" and sexually suggestive, or "cool," remote, and monumental, allegory tends to remove the idea of woman from the play of passion and contention.

The intimation projected by the neoclassical avatar of the goddess-allegory of Roma we glimpsed in David's Brutus provides us with a clue to the nature of Revolutionary allegory: a dark, brooding shadow, she is a tutelary deity, not an active power. Although (especially in cartoons, above all in those from 1789–92) we may find our new goddesses in action, for the most part they will be passive, sculptural projections of what will be seen as the primary forces in play in the Revolutionary arena.

Why should the Revolution have turned so massively to allegory, a genre that was no longer alive and had literally to be disinterred, for its icons? And then, why to female figurations? Marie-Hélène Huet's formulation helpfully traces the end of the eighteenth century's evolution away from the iconic representation of royalty to a system of abstract symbols. The female figure had traditionally provided concretion for the latter. As Lynn Hunt has pointed out, Revolutionary rhetoric, of which allegory was a building block, was constructed only as the Revolution went along and acquired whatever unity it did from the sense that it was an event out of all historical context (except that of classical antiquity), for which a fresh "mythic present" had to be invented, to which the nation might give its consent.[2] Hunt in fact sees in this moment a "crisis of representation." As the monarchy's prestige withered, she points out, the use of woman as an alternative symbol of nation comes in to replace the monarch as effigy.

A cartoon (fig. 41) celebrating 1789 dramatically reflects this movement. The diminished little king, now called the Restorer of French Liberty, stands awkwardly on his pedestal, treading on the hydra of tyranny, with Clergy and Nobility below him, full-sized, acknowledging their day is over. On the ground sits the nursing mother with her four children, the boys playing at soldier, representing France and the French people. In her voluptuous corporeality, she has literally grown as her king shrinks. This awkwardly executed but eloquent image uncovers

LOUIS XVI.
*Restaurateur
de la Liberté
Française.*

A P.   1789

NOUVELLE PLACE DE LA BASTILLE
Ami le temps passé n'est plus rendons a César ce qui appartient a César et a la Nation ce qui est a la Nation

41. New Place de la Bastille, *Musée Carnavalet, Photo Giraudon/Art Resource, New York*

the sensual core at the heart of the political struggle: as counter to the lying artifices of rococo dress and the trappings of hierarchy of the monarchy, the half-naked nursing mother, the emblem of innocent fleshliness and healthy appetite, is here the image of choice. Seated as if rooted immutably to the ground, she calls forth a restoration to simplicity and "honest" sexuality, productive of children-soldiers, her prospective defenders. Images such as this one reflect the inconsistency and inner conflict of artists in addressing the "crisis of representation." Yes, they may have wished to build images of a world created as if de novo, stripped of the aestheticism of aristocratic society, but their very own sense of the visual world, not to mention their techniques of image-making, was unalterably shaped by the traditions they were now coming to despise. Neither in style nor in the modes selected to convey substance could they escape the vise of the past. In fact, in the artists' need for allegory, they would pillage the storehouses of art for precedents from antiquity and religious imagery. As with neoclassicism, a break with the immediate past would provide the appearance of novelty, even as it promised continuity with the authority of democracies of the remote past.

The allegorical figures thus pillaged, given ringing Revolutionary names like Liberty, Equality, or Justice, were deeply equivocal representations. Even outside the context of the Revolution, with its sea-change in tastes and values, allegories are never anything but ambiguous. As Angus Fletcher put it, they say one thing, meaning another. Even though this very ambiguity may be viewed as a rich skein of suggestiveness, on the whole its own commentators have not proven to be indulgent toward allegory. Coleridge viewed the links among the seen and the unseen aspects of allegory as shapeless and insubstantial, while Huizinga dismissed the genre as superficial. Paul de Man has spoken of the difficulty in interpreting these figures because of the surplus of meaning overflowing from them: "It is part of allegory that, despite its obliqueness and innate obscurity, the resistance to understanding emanates from difficulty or censorship in the statement and not from the devices of enunciation. . . . The difficulty of allegory is . . . that this emphatic clarity of representation does not stand in the service of something that can be represented." What intrigues us in our present context is the need to authenticate images through reference to past forms even when trying to convey an inchoate new code. Fletcher sees within the surface stasis of allegory a lively symbolic power struggle. It offers in a familiar, hence easily assimilable, form a compressed assessment, whether snide or laudatory, of some abstraction. In this way it creates a tension with the ideal, and so it is never as immobile as it may look. E. H. Gombrich has elaborated on the multiplicity of associations evoked by symbols: allegory invites par excellence an abandonment of sequential thinking for the associational. Because of its very platitudinous openness, Revolutionary allegory is often anchored by an "'elaborate explanation' (we find whole paragraphs, at times, of elucidation) together with specific emblems and attributes of these various personifications."[3]

Of course allegory in France is largely female because the abstract French nouns it represents are, on the first and overt level, feminine in gender. But the fact is that allegory thrives on the multiplicity of meanings men have attached to the female sex. Men's allegory (from the Greek *allos,* or other) needs woman to function. The philosopher of women's alterity Simone de Beauvoir explains: "Woman . . . seems to be the inessential who never goes back to being essential, to be the absolute Other, without reciprocity." The ontological void woman represents to the male culture apparently provides a perfect vehicle for the use of the female figure to represent virtually anything, even the ideal of car selling. But as a perusal of our Revolutionary allegories will show, woman is by no means so completely empty a category as allegory treats her as being: even though she herself may "incarnate no stable concept . . . through her is made unceasingly the passage from hope to frustration, from hate to love, from good to evil, from evil to good."[4] The allegorical Other is potentially all that the Self cannot control: she is pure projection of good or evil. In that sense, she becomes a distillate or essence, emptied of substance. But matters are not so simple. The overflow of ambiguity characteristic of allegory carries within it the contaminating impurities accruing to exemplary female figures in our misogynistic and idealizing cultural heritage.

Allegory is fundamentally conservative in its imagery, if not in its inner tensions: it is eternal recapitulation in that it offers us a culturally sanctioned, rigid assimilation of diverse and even warring phenomena to a predetermined sign.[5] In the Revolution's explosion of allegory reborn, we find, then, the repetition in ambiguity of old signs freshly charged with formerly repressed male passion, political, sexual, and religious. Fletcher remarks that "allegory is the most religious of the modes, obeying . . . the commands of the Superego, believing in Sin, portraying atonements through ritual." Further delineating what he sees as its neurotic religious character, he associates allegory with obsessive compulsion. Seeing how allegorical imagery tends to a deadness and coldness, Fletcher terms it "frozen agency." Using the work of psychologist Otto Fenichel, he equates the species of sexual isolation we may perceive in allegorical figures to an ancient taboo against touching.[6] His insight suggests to me that the allegorized female figure operates to reify female untouchability. Of course these effigies evoke such a nexus of feelings because they are depicted largely in isolation, observed by members of a culture in which women are usually perceived—and especially at this juncture—as performing the functions of connecting the people. This complexity of implication accounts for some of the chill called up by their mute remoteness.

Marina Warner has articulated the problematics for women implicit in allegory: "Onto the female body have been projected the fantasies and longings and terrors of men and through them of women, in order to conjure them into reality or exorcise them into oblivion." She tries to pin down the distinction that, despite universalizing claims made for allegory, must of necessity obtain between the female consumers' processing of such images and the male: "Often the recognition of a difference between the symbolic order, inhabited by ideal ideological figures, and the actual order, of judges, statesmen, soldiers, philosophers, inventors, depends on the unlikelihood of women practicing the concepts they represent." Lynn Hunt similarly applies such a logic to the Revolution. "The proliferation of the female allegory was made possible . . . by the exclusion of women from public affairs. Women could be representative of abstract qualities and collective dreams because women were not allowed to vote or govern."[7]

When women look at a female allegory, how do they react? Warner makes this crucial observation: "The representation of virtue in the female form interacts with ideas about femaleness and affects the way women act as well as appear, in that intermingling that Aristotle termed *mathexis*."[8] The power of allegory for women, an unempowered class, is palpable: for who could deny its charge of mimesis, of identification, of emulation? And yet even this charge inviting mimesis is steeped in ambiguity, in the ambivalences women must perforce experience about this reading-yet-not-reading of themselves by others, their masters. For women, the abstract representational force of female allegory must always be mitigated in some measure by its mimetic implications of prescription or proscription, the images' teaching regarding the containment of women's acts. Allegory thus represents a species of representational incarceration for women. The dynamic within women's response to it churns about on its own, in a fashion quite alien to the conceptions of its male makers.

On the most primitive level, it must have stimulated women's imaginations simply to have become, overnight as it were, so central and powerful a factor in the symbolic code of the new national identity. Whereas women were being alluded to by men dismissively as erotic rococo goddesses, now the idea of the various goddesses of freedom was swelled by an elevation and aspiration that cannot have left them unmoved. Of course I here recreate speculatively a state of mind that no one can affirm with certainty; but Michelet confirms something like it as he relates that an English legend was going the rounds about the famous historian of the Stuart dynasty "Mistriss Macaulay" (Catherine Sawbridge Macaulay-Graham). Her exploits, her genius, and her virtues had so inspired the aged minister Williams that he had had a statue of her in the form of the goddess of Liberty built to stand within a church. "Few were the women of letters then who did not dream of being France's Macaulay. The inspiriting goddess is found in every salon." And Dominique Godineau calls up the vision of the women of the people walking through the somber, narrow, muddy streets of the capital, brightened here and there by red bonnets or allegories of liberty painted by citizens on the walls of their houses. Along with the excited rhetoric of freedom and equality, the rash of allegory must have made it seem as though the figures of women were coming into a different focus.

An image that illustrates the sometimes absurd paradoxes of women's relationship to allegory is one (fig. 42) of a party of young women of the 1780s. In the original version of this print, the women were carrying flowers with their prayer to a statue of St. Nicolas de la Chesnée that he might find them husbands. With the outbreak of Revolution, the figure of the saint was rubbed out and replaced with an effigy of the Republic. This figure's height, muscularity, soldierly verticality, accoutrements, and allegorical emptiness of expression make her a ludicrously unsuitable goddess to be worshiped by a bevy of sweepingly ardent members of her own sex. The group's figures and this République's come out of conflicting codes. And yet the graphic substitution of the goddess for the saint makes an invitation to these maidens to adore the Republic, and that for which she stands, in his stead.

Before surveying the allegorical scene, it would be useful to review some of the iconographical commonplaces of Revolutionary times, as set forth in Gravelot and Cochin's 1791 edition of the *Iconography by Figures*. This work was the allegorists' bible, but like the Bible's own, its followers elaborated variations on its prescribed treatments.

Gravelot and Cochin present a set of split images—of an attribute with its presumed opposite—that is worth noticing. Affability (3), for example, represents two women, well dressed in eighteenth-century style, holding flowers and peacock feathers. It is yoked with Pride (Orgueil), a masculine noun nonetheless

42. Women at Prayer before a Statue of the Republic, *Bibliothèque Nationale, Photo Bulloz*

represented as a female with banded eyes, standing upon a ball and losing her equilibrium, thus exposing well-deserved rags beneath her finery. Affection (4) is a winged female, young and beautiful, shown with a lizard, while Animosity is an angry, menacing woman with a helmet, surrounded by flames. Happiness is a young nymph sowing roses, her head crowned with flowers. At her feet is Sadness (*Chagrin*), a masculine noun in French, here represented as an old man with a wound in his chest. While both positive and negative ideas may be represented by female figures, so that the presumably male viewer might identify with them, male figures would be selected to embody sadness or personal affliction.

Bravery, masculine in the iconology, is "a young vigorous man with bare arms and readying himself to stand up to the impetuosity of a furious bull." Its reverse, Cowardice, is an ill-dressed woman lying in a muddy place (19). Sorrow (Douleur), resisting the imperative of gender, is figured by a pale, sad old man dressed in black, while the presumably masculine Despair (Désespoir), takes shape as a pale, livid, bloodied woman, a knife in her breast, although a note here reads: "For greater exactitude, it would be better to represent Despair with the same attributes, but as a man, not a woman." There is little need to emphasize that the prescriptions for images of this iconology are perfectly congruent with idealizing or misogynous commonplaces concerning masculinity and femininity. But their unabashed rigging of gender stereotypes can nonetheless amaze a modern reader.

The description in Gravelot and Cochin's prose of pictured Liberty, the image most omnipresent in circulation, recommends that she be represented as a young woman dressed in white and holding a scepter in one hand and a bonnet in the other. "The scepter expresses the command that man, through her, has over himself" (31). We see the candor in envisaging Liberty as instrumental to men's freedom: yet the frail emblem (the scepter) supposed to convey this complex connection will probably fail to do so for most unenlightened viewers. The legend concerning a related figure, of Liberty acquired by Valor, is even more unsettlingly equivocal, since it is of a woman "holding a pike topped by a bonnet while she tramples a yoke underfoot" (33). This figure would not be the mere instrument of men's freedom; while she exhibits men's active temper, she is herself also acting to achieve it.

As we look at variations on this theme in the actual print literature, we find a broad range of interpretations, deeply incised with the imprint of warring conceptions of women in heroic posture. Two of these are gently alien rococo conceptions. *The Love of Liberty* (fig. 43) represents as if in a medallion a charmingly rounded angel with fasces capped by a Phrygian bonnet. Her single bared breast and obliquely posed head and gaze make her a fine transitional figure: as yet too effete and rococo to stand as Liberty herself, she sweetly and gravely portrays a distant feminine affection (in her abstracted gaze) for this great male passion. Though indeed offered as Liberty herself, *La Liberté* (fig. 44) is still distant from its most adequate allegorical form. A pretty-faced, half-dressed young woman stands here immobilized and insubstantial, her arms and figure devoid of muscularity or of tension. So relaxed are her posture and the drooping lines of her hands that she seems scarcely to grasp the tablets of the new Decalogue (the Rights of Man) or her staff. The cap atop the staff faces her as if it were not hers, but another's. Again, emanations of rococo gracility cling about this image, whose national rooster is its sole dynamic element. Only her breasts (a feature we will not fail to meet again), in their firm roundedness, face us with any sense of affirmation. This postrococo Liberty is representative of a class of such images, fit more for embraces than for battle: Liberty as heart's desire.

A host of other allegories of Liberty exhibit an opposite tendency. Though never unequivocally, these display Liberty as an active goddess. In the unsophisticated print of *Liberty Triumphant Destroying Abusive Powers* from the *Révolutions de France et de Brabant* (fig. 45), we find a goddess intriguingly ambiguous in her femininity. Her long, trailing, wavy locks, firmly rounded breasts, and vague glance stamp her as "feminine," but the artist's attempt to depict her in action alters this aspect of his project. The awkwardness of the legs and the feet shod in antique sandals springs from the conflict between presenting Liberty as passive—as her head and her still and centered torso suggest—and yet active, capturing bolts from the lightning in her left hand and raising the pike with her right arm. The result is that the figure, devoid of any appearance of weight or energy, stands uncertainly on her cloud: as with the rooster in the previous illustration,

L'AMOUR DE LA LIBERTE.

43. The Love of Liberty, *Musée Carnavalet, Photo Bulloz*

LA LIBERTÉ

44. *Boizot-Basset,* Liberty, *Musée Carnavalet, Photo Bulloz*

45. Liberty Triumphant Destroying Abusive Powers, *from* Révolutions de France
et de Brabant 6 (1790):628, *Courtesy of
University of North Carolina*

the "incidental" motifs, the billowing clouds and the *gloire* (sunburst) surrounding
Liberty, lend the image whatever dynamism it presents. Such images illustrate the
tensions associated with making heroic female imagery during the Revolution.

A number of more sophisticated artists resolve the problem more satisfactorily,
of course. A drawing by the able Boizot, engraved by the Citizeness Demouchy
(fig. 46), shows us a far more credibly powerful *Liberty* breaking the tyrants' yoke
over her poised leg, in a gesture prescribed by Gravelot and Cochin. The classical
draperies covering her nakedness downplay sexuality, as, isolated in her oval, she
looks out, helmeted and regal, directly at the observer. A neoclassical punctilious-
ness dominates this conception. Yet something doll-like in this Liberty's features
and a bias toward grace of line in the expression of her movement—the darker
curve of her back, the answering highlights of curved arms and leg—detract from
a sense of Liberty's force.

In an anonymous engraving based on the sculptor Moitte's bas-relief from the
1791 Salon (fig. 47), we find *Aristocracy and Her Agents Buried beneath the Ruins
of the Bastille*. Here Liberty, armed with her sword, tramples the Hydra underfoot,
as prisoners once victims of arbitrary power prostrate themselves before the altar
of the fatherland. The female figures, their draperies and wings unfurled through

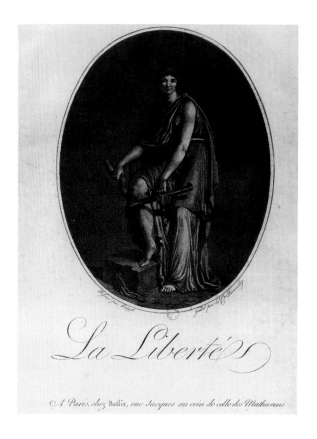

46. *Boizot/Demouchy, Liberty, Bibliothèque Nationale, Paris*

47. Aristocracy and Her Agents Buried beneath the Ruins of the Bastille, *Bibliothèque Nationale, Paris*

force of motion, strive determinedly and effectively against the enemy. Winged Liberty, though, is aerial and does not weigh upon the Hydra. Yet these are figures credibly both female and active at once, tutelary spirits with whose energy it would be possible to identify. The same, grosso modo, might be said of the less accomplished *Liberty Triumphant, or The Cowardly Run Aground* (fig. 48), where Liberty marches in the midst of clouds, the sun blazing about her, her skirts billowing, her pike thrust forward, her arms raised to cast thunderbolts against the Revolution's enemies, who lie about like so many broken rococo toys. The breadth of her stride is impressive. There is, as in *The Aristocracy and Her Agents Buried,* a minimum of tension in this print between the female figure and her function as dragon-slayer and defender of freedom.

In such images as these a threshold of credibility is reached for the allegory of Liberty via the consent to represent female strength and capability. For me, the most eloquent of the figures of Liberty is nonetheless a static one: the Copia engraving from a drawing by Prud'hon (fig. 49). Of course the sheer splendor of its design and execution raises it above less skillful works, to which it is unfair to compare it. But the conception embodied in it is of an astonishingly complex simplicity. Not in motion, Prud'hon's Liberty is at rest from her effective labors—the broken yoke of despotism falls from the chain in her hand over the gently undulant hair on the heads of slain despots, the Hydra of tyranny lies inert just behind her feet, and her raised leg rests on a severed crowned head. Through

48. Liberty Triumphant, or the Cowardly Run Aground, *Bibliothèque Nationale, Paris*

LA LIBERTÉ

Elle a renversé l'Hydre de la Tyrannie, et brisé
le joug du Despotisme.

49. Prud'hon/Copia, Liberty—She Has Overthrown the Hydra of Tyranny and Broken the Yoke of Despotism, *Musée Carnavalet, Photo Bulloz*

her efforts the reign of tyrants has been ended. The sheer force and relaxation of this gently muscled strong woman's body conveys a sense of easy athletic grace. Her powerful arm firmly grasping the axe, along with her direct glance at the observer, gives the work its essential note of tension. The head, with its laurel crown, is decorative but subdued. Gently moving ragged tatters neutralize any notion of prettification. Darkness hoods the glance of Liberty's strong features; the eyes, deep in shadow, are mysterious, as if unfathomed energies within her remain to be tapped. This allegory of Liberty looks equal to her task.

Prud'hon's allegory is sui generis, however. The 1796 cartoon *Liberty Hurling Thunderbolts against Royalism and Anarchy and Justice Pointing to the Monster of Speculation* (fig. 50) presents the two goddesses seated together on the throne. Here Liberty's figure, coiffed with graceful curls, suggests more the drawing room than the political arena. Justice in her traditional blindfold is a mere cipher, while the naked, cowering monster with her bulbous breasts below devours the public substance.

As is clear from my own reaction, a woman can easily identify kinesthetically with the most empowering of these allegorical figures, whereas the charge of identification with the more feeble figures is less compelling for her. The dilemma inherent in these powerful and effective figures lies in the differential between

50. *J. Chalette,* Liberty Hurling Thunderbolts against Royalism and Anarchy and Justice Pointing to the Monster of Speculation, *Musée Carnavalet, Photo Bulloz*

their psychic charge for the generality of women and of men. For many men, and many women as well, the too-self-sufficient goddess—acting without, and seeming to need no, male protectors—would have appeared not as liberating, but as threatening to the male supremacist gender accommodation.

Leaving Liberty for effigies of the Revolution's other themes, we discover similar ambivalences in the depiction of power and allure in women. *Equality* (fig. 51), embracing the fasces of unity, with the carpenter's level, her usual adjunct, held out on display, is a charming and purely decorative figure from whom no dynamism emanates. A revolutionary allegory of *Modesty* (La Pudeur) (fig. 52) is a simple translation of the Virgin Mary, complete with her lily, into the secular context. Unlike the others, it is a purely monitory image, obviously intended primarily to inspire emulation in women. We note that this is a figure stripped of both sexuality and vitality.

History (fig. 53) stands at her writing, surrounded by horn and books and the

51. Equality, *Musée Carnava-let, Photo Bulloz*

52. Modesty, *Musée Carnavalet, Photo Bulloz*

symbols of Revolution, the Phrygian cap and the masonic eye incised into her pedestal. Despite the allusion to inspiration in her distant glance, she lacks majesty and smacks too much of the comely live model to be effective as allegory. Somewhat more effective as allegory is *Law* (fig. 54), but this is because a wholly hieratic pose has been chosen for her. Except for the level and the cap by her side, and the rather bedraggled Hydra beneath her right foot, she might represent anything, anywhere. A *Truth* (fig. 55) from the same series, unveiling herself with her traditional mirror in hand, sits clumsily on her cloud, more an erotic than an allegorical statement.

Of course women's association with eros could not be entirely slighted by male allegorists nor, certainly, caricaturists. In *The Aristocracy's Nightmare* (fig. 56) we find a rather gothic, stripped-down neoclassical figure writhing upon her couch, at the foot of which the symbols of her past power are strewn. A figure of abject desperation, she is so not only, in her aristocracy—menaced by the carpenter's level and Phrygian bonnet that hang like a Damoclean sword over her breast—but in her sex. As allegory, she calls up an emotional response and gains dramatic impact from her sexual vulnerability; her breasts bared, her abandoned pose, the hand tearing at her hair as she twists helplessly. The mood of imminent rape is underscored by the figure of the satyr functioning as handle of the ewer on the left, whose lip points between her legs.

A far less fraught, comic image is the cartoon *Constitution of the Year III* (fig. 57), who sits incongruously in her slipped chiton—the gown consecrated in classical art covering one breast only—on a modern sofa. Without its legend, the image conveys nothing: "By raping me three times, they caused my death!!!" A riff on the ancient idea that rape never kills, this robust allegory comments ruefully on that constitution's failure through the repeated coups d'état of Fructidor, Floréal, and Prairial. Images of altogether entrenched and consecrated female sexual vulnerability undermine the ability to project female figures as allegories of strength and power. This problematic of Revolutionary allegorical representation, and the question of what women were and hence what they could symbolize, pervade these images.

Three representations of Aristocracy from political cartoons, for which no classical model could have proven suitable, also display the slipperiness of consensus, even among persons of similar political tendency. *Dying Aristocracy* (fig. 58) is portrayed in the depths of her death throes. A matron now stripped of all trappings of nobility, she still holds in her left hand the serpents of discord, as the legend warns: "Friends, mistrust her to the death. You know the blackness of her perfidy well enough to rightly fear that even at death's door, she may spring some fatal trick." So apparently mild, this contemporary figure conveys no sense of threat: her serpents and the legend alone give her away as vile. A far more fetching image of a meditative young woman is, we are instructed, equally to be feared (fig. 59): "*Aristocracy foiled,* reading so many decrees against her power, beneath

L'HISTOIRE

53. *Charpentier/Carré, History, Musée Carnavalet, Photo Bulloz*

LA LOI

54. Law, *Musée Carnavalet, Photo Bulloz*

55. Truth, *Musée Carnavalet,*
Photo Bulloz

(Below) 56. The Aristocracy's
Nightmare, *Musée Carnavalet,*
Photo Bulloz

En me violant trois fois ils m'ont causé la mort !!!

CONSTITUTION DE L'AN III.

57. Constitution of the Year III, *Musée Carnavalet, Photo Bulloz*

l'Aristocratie mourante,
Amis défiéz vous d'elle jusqu'à la mort;
Vous connoissé assez sa noire perfidie;
Pour avoir lieu de craindre encore qu'à l'agonie
Elle fasse jouer un funeste ressort,

58. Dying Aristocracy, *Bibliothèque Nationale, Paris*

l'Aristocratie interdite ,
Lisant contr-elle tant d'arrets ,
Dans son dépit cherche médite
Contre nous les plus noirs projets .

59. Aristocracy Foiled,
*Bibliothèque Nationale,
Paris*

this comely semblance seeks vengeance through the blackest of plots," we are told. In no way could we identify this figure as aristocratic—much less as an allegory of Aristocracy—so much is her style altered, without the legend, which seems essentially in this unallegorical representation to warn against trusting all benign-looking upperclass women. The same could never be said of the *Aristocratic Lady Cursing the Revolution* (fig. 60). A lusty caricature, her lavish old-fashioned dress and hectic decorativeness are also lampooned, marking as absurd the trappings of her class. This rococo harpy's grimacing frown, her tensed, muscular arms, her tiny, compressed waist, her feathers and furbelows, all are subordinated to those aging pendulous breasts, the iconographically consecrated emblem of the body of Discord. The fury compressed in her figure reflects a felt charge of fury toward her. She is all naked, impotent will.[9]

Dame Aristocrate maudissant la Révolution.

60. Aristocratic Lady
Cursing the Revolution,
*Musée Carnavalet, Photo
Bulloz*

Vive le Roi. Vive la Nation.

J'savois ben Qu'jaurions not'tour.

61. I Knew We'd Get Our Turn—The
Three Estates, *Musée Carnavalet, Photo
Bulloz*

A popular representation of the distaff half of the *Three Estates, I Knew We'd Get Our Turn,* (fig. 61; a masculine mate to this print exists as well) shows us the early Revolution's mode of allegorizing its victory. The hand-wringing nun in the lead is followed by Aristocratic Woman, loaded down already by her excess of hair and headdress (we note the allusion to this extravagant style), who now discovers what bearing weight is really like, as the Third Estate's young mother with babe at breast rides piggyback on her rump. The two elder matrons, the one asexual, the other past her prime, now give way to the vigorous young one at her sexual peak, as the legend reads, in peasant speech, "I always knew we'd get our turn."

The insistent recurrence of features from the traditional misogynous iconography reflects that facet of these allegories I have alluded to before: like Revolutionary discourse as a whole, it exudes a species of conservative lifelessness. Mona Ozouf builds on Jean Starobinski's observation concerning the lack of spontaneity of the great Revolutionary fêtes. She sees in them precisely an attempt to "wrest the Revolution from the improvisation of events."[10] Visual imagery, especially that of progressive tendency, shares this urge to stop the Revolution where it stands. And the imagery of political reaction, though like Jacobin images often enough furious in temper, naturally enough tends to distill nostalgia for a lost world. If the allegory of the print medium conveys images from hand to hand for individual or small-group delectation, the allegories raised in public places at the officially arranged governmental festivals were calculated to induce an ambience of unity, of aesthetically enforced consensus.

The center of these celebrations of common purpose was the figure of Liberty (which would become conflated with that of the Nation). Hunt believes this image of the proto-Marianne, which would become the emblem of the French Republic, was able to survive because, unlike the dramatic personalities of a Mirabeau or a Danton, it was an impersonal figure, free from historic taint.[11] In the print (fig. 62) of the *Federative Encampment at Lyons* of May 30, 1790, an early fête, Liberty with her pike and bonnet is jauntily enthroned atop a huge mound built around and towering over a temple pediment, thus combining natural and neoclassical cultural elements. A geometric formation of troops encloses her mountain in an encircling square, which produces a visual effect of holding it in check. The multitudes outside remain distant from this remote, grandiose altar.

Devotion to the Fatherland is the title of an image from 1792 (fig. 63) in which we again find Liberty enthroned. Here she is a far less remote figure as she sits hale, strong, and handsome, receiving the incense of citizens' devotion, the tribute of the heroes' departure for war, and the mother's dedication of her infant. The smaller statue of the winged male Genius of the Nation extends his blessing. A strong matriarchal feeling emanates from this scene, and it was doubtless the growth of this factor, along with the scandal of the live goddesses of Reason, that caused the reaction so ably reconstructed by Lynn Hunt.

Hunt has observed that before the Fête of August 1793, the deputies to the

62. Federative Camp at Lyon, *Musée Carnavalet, Photo Giraudon/Art Resource, New York*

63. Devotion to the Fatherland, *Bibliothèque Nationale, Paris*

Dévouement à la Patrie

Convention had voted to place the image of Hercules rather than that of Liberty on the national seal. Accordingly, with the Festival of Regeneration (also known as the Fête of the Unity and Indivisibility of the Republic) of August 10, at a time of swelling civil unrest and panic over the threat of foreign invasion, the Jacobin leadership sought to impress its own vision of natural hierarchy firmly upon the public mind. The Jacobin partisan Jacques-Louis David and his corps of artist-engineers erected five stations through which citizens should pass, in a sort of pseudo-masonic procession of initiation. David was careful to provide for recognition of women's contributions to Revolution, which his party could neither deny nor entirely dispense with. At the first station, on the site where the Bastille had stood, a throng of delegates to the Convention, departmental officials, and the throng of citizens stood before a huge statue of Nature (see fig. 115, *The Fountain of Regeneration*) from whose breasts flowed a milk (it was only water) of Regeneration. Having thus recapitulated its birth and infancy, the crowd moved toward a triumphal arch on the Boulevard Poissonnière, commemorating the women's march of October 1789. The third station was that of Liberty: in substitution for their now-dead monarch, a large, hieratic statue of Liberty was placed on the pedestal of the Place de la Révolution that had once held the likeness of the Well-Beloved, Louis XV. The equation "king or Liberty" was made explicit at the moment when both were superseded. The fourth station, at the Invalides, contained a huge statue that personified the French people, a twenty-four-foot-high Hercules complete with club, the bludgeoned Hydra of federalism at his feet. At the final station, in the Champ de Mars, was an image-free altar to the Fatherland, where the crowd swore fealty to the Constitution. As Hunt has pointed out, the placement of the Hercules was crucial. "By implication Liberty was important, but representative of one particular moment, a moment now passed." Politically, "in comparison to Liberty . . . Hercules represented a higher stage in the development of the Revolution—one characterized by the force and unity of the people, rather than by the sagacity of its representatives." By November, David was proposing that a colossus of a statue of Hercules (the work alluded to by Camille Desmoulins in the epigraph to this section, which Desmoulins still expected erroneously to be a female effigy of Liberty), designed to be forty-eight feet tall, should become the emblem of Republican France on all its official documents and coins. Only a few days before, in late October, the Convention had called a halt to women's concerted activity in the Revolution by placing its ban upon all women's associations.[12]

Hercules' symbolic enthronement signifies the ascension to power of the people as against the Convention. "The masculinity of Hercules reflected indirectly on the deputies themselves; through him," writes Hunt, "they reaffirmed the image of themselves as a band of brothers that had replaced the father-king." I would add that they saw themselves as a band of fatherers of families, as well. Hunt claims this was no happenstance: "In the eyes of the Jacobin leadership, women

were threatening to take Marianne [the female representation of France] as a metaphor for their own active participation. . . . Hercules put women back into perspective, in their place and relationship of dependency. The monumental male
was now the only active figure."[13] In the intricate web of connection between the
worlds of image and politics, this defeat of the active female allegory served to
reinforce the ideology that affirmed the marginality of configurations of, or participation by, women in the public space.

But there was a coda to this drama. As part of the Jacobin movement toward
dechristianization in the Year II, one of the very same spokesmen instrumental in
the banishment of women from the streets, Chaumette, as *procureur général* of the
Commune of Paris, proclaimed, in the face of the grinding on of the Terror, that
a celebration of the cult of Reason would take place on November 10, 1793, in
various churches of Paris and in some provincial cities. Living women were invited to play the role of Reason's goddess in these ceremonies. At Saint-Sulpice, a
magistrate's wife took the part; at Notre-Dame, now turned into a temple of Reason, Mlle Maillard, a celebrated actress, was divinized for a few hours. This attempt to incorporate real women as ideal figures into a substitute state religion
was not a success. A print (fig. 64) of such a goddess reveals the cheerful folly of
this positivist conception. A well-fleshed, known human quantity such as a Maillard could not convince as a goddess in postmonarchical France, where desacralization had just cast down both Venus and the Virgin Mary. Storms of resentful
gossip whirled up around these real women for presuming to represent Reason,
occasioning outbursts like that of Payan, Robespierre's acolyte, which is also an
epigraph to this section. Louis-Sébastien Mercier was revolted: "Drunk with wine
and blood, returning from the spectacle of the scaffold, the tottering priests and
priestesses of Reason followed in the wake of their impure divinity."[14] There was
obviously much more affect attached to this cult than to that of Liberty, especially
for women. One report held that just as churches before the Revolution attracted
many women and a paucity of men, "it's the same in the temples of Reason: few
men and many women." What was to put a decisive end to this form of devotion
was the execution in 1794 of Jacques René Hébert, who had ties with radical
women. "Many Parisians," writes Aulard, "saw only amusement in the cult of
Reason. Behind the goddesses' chariot, there was more than one skeptical rustic."
But in a less jocular vein, Annette Rosa reminds us that in the White Terror of
1795 some of the patriotic "goddesses" who had personified Reason or Liberty in
the Year II were to lose their lives, accused of "libertine masquerades."[15]

Reflecting this moment of Reason's passing from preeminence is an extraordinarily fine Prud'hon/Perée print (fig. 65), whose legend reads "The dawn of reason
begins to shine and the Genius of Liberty establishes the Realm of Wisdom on
earth." The large, helmeted, Minervan head of Sophia or Wisdom is purest allegory, divorced from female corporeality altogether. Male corporeality has replaced
it. The Genius figure is active, graceful, and seductive in his relaxed posture and
sidelong intentness of glance. Femaleness is frozen out and replaced in this co-
optive allegorical conception.

A LA PHILOSOPHIE

DÉESSE DE LA RAISON.

64. Goddess of Reason,
*Musée Carnavalet, Photo
Bulloz*

A cult akin to the Mosaic, of the Supreme Being, is what Payan then set forth in a speech to the Convention as a substitute for this debased female cult and, I would suggest, an escape from the peculiar gender struggle that had developed around allegorical representation. "We will have so sublime an idea of him that we will not degrade him by giving him a shape, a body like ours."[16] Instead of being consecrated to Reason, he pleads to the nation, let us give ourselves over to adoration of this (masculine) Being. The final fête of the Robespierre regime would be that of the Supreme Being, on June 8, 1794. Once more, this fête recapitulated hierarchy. It is generally conceded to have been a cheerful occasion. After Robespierre, holding aloft the torch of Reason, set fire to a statue of Atheism, a figure of Wisdom appeared to point toward the Champ de Mars, where a great mountain had been erected (fig. 66). This time, the hierarchy was compressed into the environs of the mountain: at the summit of it, eschewing anthropomorphic forms, the Jacobins now set a Tree of Liberty, topped with the pike and the Phrygian bonnet, formerly attributes of the goddess. On a high pedestal, standing alone against the sky but below the Tree, stood a Hercules, with minuscule, insubstan-

65. *Prud'hon/Pérée,* The Dawn of Reason, *Bibliothèque Nationale, Paris*

66. *Naudin,* Fête de l'Etre Suprême—June 1794, *Musée Carnavalet, Photo Bulloz*

tial figures of Liberty and Equality poised on a globe in his hand. The medallist Augustin Dupré's version (fig. 67) gives a better sense of the dimensions of the dwindling of the goddesses and the concurrent naked sans-culotte machismo, deliberately not filtered as in the Prud'hon by any mitigating grace. Hercules stands baldly and defiantly forth in his full frontal genitality as allegory of the people's—that is, its men's—unrefined physical power.

A closer look at the goddesses remaining on this scene is illuminating. The *View of the Chariot* (fig. 68; the chariot is visible in fig. 66 on the lower right) presents the image of France as a sort of Ceres, a goddess of abundance, a bulky deity with all the symbols of agriculture piled behind her. Her garish chariot suggests a carnivalesque mood, though the verse below the image urges the French people on to a life of industry and plenty. The plaster figure on the pedestal, with finger pointing heavenward, is a supremely vapid and passive effigy.

A celebrated print (fig. 69) created in honor of the Festival of the Supreme Being exhibits the final gender dispensation of the Jacobin Revolution at its most benign. Under the masonic eye of the Deity, a tender republican sans-culotte family adores the twin goddesses of nation and of plenty. The more Minervan figure, protectress of law and quality, stands stalwart, while her sister goddess, a surviving remnant of rococo elegance and stylization in her fetching headdress and abundantly fruited horn, sits passively, an offering to her people. This duo maintains the traditional male dualism between sexed and unsexed female figures. A sense of gentle resolution pervades the scene, which has drawn in these female emblems from antiquity to bless and restore the family system. Already, by June 1794, the goddesses have largely been reduced to subaltern figures, as in the image (fig. 70) in which they figure as caryatids to the Temple of the Supreme Being, within which men adore the tablets of the law as a very grandfatherlike God hovers overhead.

Liberty may still be summoned up (as in fig. 71, from November 1793) to become the foil for expressions of wrath against the Revolution. A sort of expressionless, lifeless antigoddess in this version, she turns a blind eye to the mob of aggrieved men, the soldiers and sufferers beneath her, who declaim against the horrors of "her" reign. Within a span of five years, the Revolution's goddesses have metamorphosed through phases as effete symbolic evocations mixing rococo style with neoclassical substance; as powerful, mythic actors; as immobilized endorsers of the status quo; as live embodiments of godlike Reason; and finally, with the souring experiences of shortage, war, and the guillotine, as goddess scapegoats. The final outrage of this evolution seems to have been the effrontery of trying to pass off real women, irretrievably scarred as they were by sexual taint, as pure, untouchable, remote representations of higher values in the fête dedicated to Reason.

The fundamental alterity of figurations of women had served Frenchmen in articulating their ideals and, as ever, had probably impeded perception of real women, in the forum or at home. For women, these allegories may have been

67. *Augustin Dupré*, Hercules, Hathor, Liberty, and
Equality, *Musée Carnava-
let, Photo SPADEM*

68. View of the Chariot, *Bibliothèque Nationale, Paris*

FÊTE CÉLÉBRÉE EN L'HONNEUR DE L'ÊTRE SUPRÊME.
Le 20 Prairiale l'an 2.e de la Rép.

Le véritable Prêtre de l'Être suprême, c'est la Nature, son temple l'Univers, son culte la Vérité, sa fête la joie d'un grand Peuple rassemblé pour resserer les doux noeuds de la Fraternité, et Jurer la mort des Tyrans.

69. Fête Celebrated in Honor of the Supreme Being, *Bibliothèque Nationale, Paris*

70. Homage to the Supreme Being, *Bibliothèque Nationale, Photo Giraudon/Art Resource, New York*

71. Liberty—November 10, 1793, *Bibliothèque Nationale, Photo Giraudon/ Art Resource, New York*

briefly inspiriting, but were more often irrelevant or distressing. They were not, after all, made for their use. For how could a woman, even of the right, identify with the anti-Revolutionary print of 1795 (fig. 72) depicting a huge proto-Marianne seated on a Trojan horse being dragged toward Paris by sans-culottes as bourgeois citizens, the pocket of one being picked by a woman of the people, stand helplessly by? The Latin inscription, from Vergil, reads "Yet we press on, heedless and blind with frenzy, and set the ill-omened monster on our hallowed citadel." This massive figure is not per se a figure of threat: rather she is bosomy and stalwart. Yet her size and the context of trickery evoke a feeling of dread of her monstrous and unwelcome entry into the city. In her hugeness and woman-liness she may well have called up the anxiety that object-relations psychology has suggested inheres in the maternal figure, the looming love-hate object of the child in infancy.[18] A species of counterrevolutionary revulsion against the Revolution's obsession with the goddesses emerges in this powerful print. The tranquil threat of its mute, gigantic female specter constitutes a warning to the populace against complacency toward apparent female harmlessness. This is an image whose allegorical overload sends women back into the deep recesses of the psychic closet.

72. Instamus tamen immemores coecique furore (*Trojan Horse*) (*Yet we press on . . .*), *Musée Carnavalet, Photo Bulloz*

François Furet speaks of the Revolution's attempt to restructure the French social system through the machinery of the imaginary. The allegorical impulse of the Revolution employed the female figure to that end, sometimes consciously, more often not. Mona Ozouf describes the government's solution, in the immediate post-Thermidorian era to the anguishing problem of how to "celebrate" the death of the king, and the train of executions it unleashed. "It was imperative to neutralize cruelty . . . and give preference to allegory over any symbol; the *peuple* must not see any scaffold." Instead, they set up a platform upon which "a colossal figure, heavily seated on a cube, tramples beneath her feet the 'signs of servitude': this is Liberty."[19] Thus the glorious female allegory is seen to have ended up in the role of priestess of the coverup, a meaningless catch-all whose ambiguity may comfortably conceal all turpitudes.

The very artifice—the return to conventions of antiquity—involved in the Revolution's resort to allegory ensured that even in its most splendid avatars, the new goddesses could not take on the life their creators hoped to imbue them with, and which they had nearly embodied in 1791, before the radical gulf was delineated between women's aspirations to Revolutionary participation and their enforced retirement from public life. On the other hand, allegory, simply as an idea, had to have suffered from its mustiness. For in the modern world, which now spoke the language of universal liberty and equality, women were already, for both the male and the female population, well past the era of radical alterity in which these conventions were invented.[20] Embattled though it was in this very respect, French society was fundamentally mixed by gender, and icons of other-ness ultimately could not prove meaningful beyond the short run of Revolutionary propaganda. Furthermore, the Revolution that desacralized Christianity could scarcely succeed in sacralizing man: so much the less could it have sacralized the other, the suspect sex. By Napoleon's time, allegories will have become mere pas-sive, decorative appendages, the embellishments to men's power we see still about us on our older government buildings, most especially our courts of law. Only intermittently would they return, revivified and so revivifying, as in Delacroix's *Liberty Leading the People,* to provide a momentary spur to men's flagging political hopes.

Chapter

7

THE LIMITS TO
WOMEN'S ACTION AS
EMPOWERMENT,
1792–1795

The greatest good for men is Liberty; but it is
not so for women.

RESTIF DE LA BRETONNE

Beneath Allegory—Women as Citizens

What meaning can this passage through the allegorical maze have possessed for the women who lived through this time? Since allegory removes the idea of woman to a plane of ideality, it tends to blur and skew perception of women on the ground. And on the ground, that struggle waged by women to make an impress on Revolution, to induce it to answer their needs and aspirations, went on. It was a struggle both to participate in the political life of Revolution with men and to ensure that their own needs were met. As has been seen, even when active women in no way militated for women's rights, their group struggles to affect policy expressed an inherently feminist project.[1] And so their eruptions upon the scene were frequently perceived, no matter their content, as disruptive outbursts. The sheer inability to cope with these manifestations by women, to integrate them conceptually or practically into ongoing policies, demonstrates the inability of political men, excepting those reflective few like Condorcet or Guyomar, to contemplate what the advent of a republic and its rhetoric of freedom might augur for women, or for men's relations with them.

What to do, for example, about an utterance like La Mère Duchesne's, that (supposedly) female counterpart of the foul-mouthed father-editor Le Père Duchesne: "Go puff yourself up, Mère Duchesne, you've got good reason, damn it. . . . Before, whenever we wanted to speak, they shut us up by saying to us ever so politely, 'You're reasoning like a woman'; that is, more or less like a fucking animal. Ah, bugger it all! Things sure are changed; we've really grown since the Revolution. . . . What wings liberty has given us! Now we fly like the eagle."[2]

Misogyny knows neither party nor class; it infects them all. But as we survey the Revolution, we cannot but ask which class or party among the chief contenders was most inimical, which least, to women's participation. Alas, none rises to the top of this list. In Condorcet's own largely upper-middle-class Girondist party, his lead in advocating women's active citizenship was by no means pursued, although many women collaborated with its associated clubs and supported constitutionalist objectives.[3] Among the sans-culottes, women's militancy was a more or less acceptable fact of life, their collaboration in the work of the world expected. Yet the most effective and articulate hostility toward women would arise from the ranks of lower-middle-class Jacobins: Among its voices none was more openly vituperative than that of the *Révolutions de Paris*. Its editor Prudhomme opens a series of articles on the theme of women published in three installments in 1791 by alluding to complaints coming to him from women readers who deplore the gender course of the Revolution.[4] "They report in many letters that for two years now it has seemed as if there is only one sex in France" (226). These women feel the men lack generosity and affirm that among the ancient Gauls women had a deliberative voice in assemblies and things went no worse. Visibly assuming he speaks for a respectable consensus, Prudhomme strikes back. For him, Versailles and all its works provide ample testimony against women's claims to influence: "The reign of courtesans brought on the ruin of the nation; the power of queens consummated it" (227). Rich bourgeois women merely imitated courtly corruption, frivolity, and calculation. "The compass of their domestic duties once crossed, women fear nothing, are free of doubt." Note this dismissive but telling image drawn from infancy: such women's heedlessness is comparable to playing "with a scepter as if it were a rattle," on the part of people who "think they can play with a nation as with their childhood doll" (228). We see the double-edged charge, leveled against frivolous rococo femininity exercised as power by queen and courtesan alike, that it is women's juggling with the scepter that has caused the nation's downfall. Forever children, they must be confined to the hearth.

Prudhomme cannot, however, escape acknowledging what women had done for the Revolution in the October Days. He accepts that the women of the peuple "showed themselves to be citizenesses," and courageous ones, at that. But he manages to use their courage as a device to slap down other "weak little women" (*femmelettes*) who did not meet October's challenge and thus displayed their (phallic) lack, as compared with men. These "others," he charges, "fled that male and imposing spectacle," fainted, had nervous fits, or aborted their young. "Few were able to make their organs rise to the pitch of revolution." As in the medical theories of the time, women's disability is uterine in origin for Prudhomme. Except to sport Revolutionary colors at parades, most of the women, he claims, had fled indoors to their salons and sofas. It is here that he comes to the conclusion that "all classes of women above that of the *peuple* are almost entirely aristocrats" (229). In this way, he reveals his vindictive anger against all women rising above poverty and necessary dependence.

Slightly aware of the sweeping injustice of his generalization, Prudhomme pretends to be "impartial." Women, he admits, whose former *adorers had changed their cult,* were in truth losing out by Revolution in many ways.[5] The sums previously expended for their embellishment were now going into male epaulettes (229). And here he mocks Condorcet: "Grave publicists" have claimed that women have the gift of language and ought to be allowed a role in legislative deliberations. While agreeing that women do indeed have powers of speech, Prudhomme immediately moves to his basic position, that nature herself has decreed separate functions for the sexes. Since they are simply devoid of all ardor for heroism, "civil and political liberty are, so to speak, useless to women, and consequently must be alien to them." From the moment of their birth to that of their death, women "are born for perpetual dependency and are gifted only with private virtues" (230–231).

Pleading with his women readers, whom he realizes full well he is offending with his strictures, he then begins to apostrophize them directly, as *vous* (you). In virtually supplicating tones, he begs them not to envy men the honors of politics, as he tries to enunciate what their own rightful place in Revolution ought to be. Even while staying home, they may be guardians of morality and education. And they may act not only as presenters of official rewards to men, but also *be* such rewards to them, providing men with occasions to share "chaste pleasures" (231). Thus he exhorts women to grant their sexual favors only to heroes. And yet he urges these domesticity-loving women to go out into the streets to embellish the fêtes with their daughters' sexual graces, and to offer them to such heroes, saying, "Good citizen, you will protect her with your sword." With this same sword, the citizen-hero will also enlighten his bride, as she will return that boon with her "esteem, attachment, and happiness" (232). An image of sheltered sexual abundance, under the sign of the phallic sword, is Prudhomme's Eden.

What Prudhomme in fact wants of women in public is that, like allegories, they represent and make manifest, the signs of Revolution: their sexual fealty of course comes first, as precondition to all the rest. But he also urges women as a mass to enact, to become the Revolution's outward manifestation of grief or of revolt. If a new Brutus should be cut down by a new Julius Caesar, "Citizenesses! All must mourn, and may your black scarves attest to the value you place on the loss of a martyr to liberty." Similarly, when the anniversary of the assassination of a counterrevolutionary general comes around, "gird yourselves with a red scarf" (232–233).

For Prudhomme, women at home may be allowed a certain individuality within the confines of "chaste" sensuality and private virtue: abroad, they must never appear but as a choral mass, the effluvium of the Republic's ideals and mental states. Much of the last part of his article, its ecstatic prescriptions to women, seems in the end to have been rationalization: "Woe unto you, woe unto us both, if through a rivalry fatal to both sexes, you were to become disgusted with your duties. . . . Do not be our rivals; let no misplaced jealousy alienate you from us . . . ; as long as you stay with us, we will not despair of our country's salvation" (235). The note of hopelessness and helpless pleading, added to his previous outbursts of menace and scorn, make Prudhomme's text a lesson in manipulative prose, constantly shifting its ground, first rebuffing, then fawning and appealing for sympathy. In this respect, his text is representative of the Jacobin discourse on women.

Women in Action: The Clash of Intention and Interpretation

Mercier was to claim that it was because its members had severed the head of their king from his body that the government was emboldened to take the heads of so many of its colleagues on the same spot. "It was a delirium of fury, vengeance, and rage, and I think there was in it much more of terror for themselves than for republicanism." The death of the king, "le bon papa," as many of his people still called him, on January 21, 1793, was a watershed. Insofar as monarchy could continue to feel like an everlasting, perdurant inevitability to the French nation after the monarchs' attempted flight by way of Varennes in June of 1791, the king's death was a traumatic closure. Was patriarchy itself passing with him? As with the death of God, did it mean that all was permitted? At the very least, as Mercier points out, the king's death carried an immediate menace to all who had sought to prevent it. A time of surly disorder followed. Between February and September of 1793 women in the marketplaces and public spaces of Paris would reach their greatest level of activity since the October Days. In part this effervescence may be attributed to the departure of so many men for service at the front, first against the enemy without, and then, in March in the Vendée, against the counterrevolution within, spurred by the regicide. On February 25–26 a crowd of women mobbed the storehouses and seized the sugar and coffee stored there. A couple of contingents of women went to the Convention to issue a threat to the legislators that they were prepared to stand in the way of recruitment, if the government should fail to impose price controls. The battle against the hoarders and speculators was brutal and inconclusive, since price controls were established (*le maximum*) by September 29, but these were never popular. Laundresses along the Seine pillaged barges in June for supplies they felt they desperately needed, and told officials they could not respect laws of property while their lives and the lives of their children were in danger. As Godineau points out, in such actions women often seized the initiative, later to be followed up by armed men.[6]

As women scholars have brought out, the very title they enjoyed of citizeness endowed women with a shadow right to a stake in the state, a fact long obscured.[7] Of course they would embrace the challenge of performing as citizens in diverse ways. Dominique Godineau charts about fifty women's or mixed popular societies and political clubs for the years 1789–93, virtually all over France. A number of these were charitable associations devoted to aiding poor women, and some had more extended and politically engaged projects. In March 1791 the handsome Dutch feminist Etta Palm d'Aelders founded the resoundingly named Patriotic and Charitable Society of the Women Friends of Truth, a cognate women's auxiliary to the Abbé Fouché's Friends of Truth party. An articulate moderate, by 1793 she and her nuanced but militantly feminist discourse had disappeared from public notice. The Girondist journalist Louise Kéralio had joined with her husband, François Robert, to form a mixed political club. Such activities gained in intensity day by day. In March 1792 Pauline Léon had gone to the Legislative Assembly with a petition bearing 319 names asking for women as citizens to be enabled to bear arms. Among its signers were some who would become members of the most celebrated of all the women's societies, the Revolutionary Republican Women, when it was established on May 10, 1793. As Godineau stresses, "the militant woman wills herself to be a citizen" by taking whatever action seems called for.[8]

On February 24, 1793, at the Convention, a petition supported by the Fraternal Society of the Two Sexes (the Kéralio-Robert group) would be presented under the name of the Assembly of Republican Women to protest the actions of monopolistic hoarders, squeezing the public out of soap. The rioting that broke out on February 25 was presented by newspaper reports as the work of a mob composed primarily of women, but in which men dressed in skirts had acted as provocateurs. Much noticed were the women's taunting, scabrous language and gestures, which, as Godineau writes, expressed more starkly than speeches that "the right to live is prior to the right to property."[9] This rebellious faction is thought to have been allied with the far-left wing of the Jacobins, Jacques Roux's Enragés, which took up the defense of the poorest class against the vicious hoarders whose speculations were depriving them of supplies basic to their sustenance and livelihoods. When the Convention, employing the ancient strategy of refusing to hear the women, adjourned their case until the following Tuesday, they went out muttering that when their children asked for milk, they couldn't tell them to come back the day after tomorrow.

The Club of Revolutionary Republican Women (henceforth referred to as CRRW or Républicaines) comprised about one hundred and seventy members, of whom about one hundred were active. This is the capital point: these women never dared, like the women who wrote the earlier Cahiers, to confront or refute openly the Revolution's compulsory language about woman as mother/wife. Nevertheless, their activity itself, a tacit refutation of that ideology, aroused such hostility as to herald their end from the outset. In perhaps the most radical of all women's requests, under the leadership of Pauline Léon they had reiterated Théroigne de Méricourt's demand for arms to defend the Revolution from inside the nation while the men were away at war. Under the cover of patriotism, they were challenging men's monopoly of their most closely protected realm, that which they felt most intimately defined them.[10] The CRRW women went parading through the Paris streets in formation, like a band of Amazons capped in red bonnets, to dramatize their claim. Allied with the Montagnards against the liberal Girondists, these women were a group rather mixed in age and in métier.[11] Their tactic was to use as their justification the invocation to them to be mothers above all. Their rationale? The Nation, their family, was summoning up their protective maternal ardor. They would station themselves aggressively in the Tuileries, through which people going to the National Assembly (later the Convention) would have to pass, and rabble-rouse there, or attend its debates in the galleries, often raucously insisting on the withdrawal of the Girondists, giving voice to waves of disapproval. Anxious to influence its deliberations in this way, they would heatedly contest when seats in the tribunal were awarded to anyone coming from the countryside or representing another political tendency. On May 15, 1793, the legendary Amazon of Liberty, who had drawn closer to the Girondists, Théroigne de Méricourt, holding her entry pass, was cruelly and violently whipped by such a band of Jacobin women.

Anne-Josèphe Théroigne was from Liège, the daughter of a well-to-do farmer, and had been reasonably well educated. She had led a peripatetic life with several lovers before ending up holding a salon in republican Paris. She was thirty-four in May of 1793. It was widely believed that she had been a major figure in the March on Versailles on October 5, dressed with her usual panache in her plumed hat and red Revolutionary sash, with a saber by her side. She proved to be agreeable to crowds, with her pleasing appearance, courage, and outspoken eloquence, as she took up her seat among Robespierre's partisans in the galleries at the Assembly. But she came to play a major role in a tragic episode, as she was implicated in the death of the counterrevolutionary journalist Suleau. Suleau, who had mercilessly made her the butt of his sneering commentary, was arrested on August 10, 1792, while walking on the terrace of the Feuillants. Théroigne did not deprive herself of the joy of publicly haranguing him on the spot for his views and behavior. Already infuriated against him, the crowd then tore Suleau apart, as his guard abdicated its duty to him. Some have found retributive justice in the fact that Théroigne was herself to suffer a similar, though not lethal, fate.

One odd print—probably not taken from life—depicting her (fig. 73) shows us a small, doll-like figure, holding an elaborate mirror, ostensibly primping before it. The dark, broad-brimmed hat that was her trademark is the only element that lends importance to her silhouette, coyly decorated by its flounces and feather. We perceive the unresolved paradox of depicting a charming young woman who has taken on an unforeseen political role: we could never divine anything significant about her career from this portrait. We could not dream that she had proposed legislation, warned the nation against division within when

73. Théroigne de Meri-
court, *Bibliothèque Nationale, Paris*

foreign agents roamed among them, plotting the Revolution's doom; or that she
was a visionary feminist, who urged that six women counselors be chosen each
month to deliberate with the citizens and moderate their incivility and lack of
respect for the freedom of opinion she held ought to prevail, even among women,
whose speech should be respected, not mocked.[12]

The market women (or were they, too, men in drag?) who whipped Théroigne
to the point of collapse, undressing her and withering her self-respect in May of
1793, were an angry mob indeed. Some of the wrath against her most probably
reflected class hatred: though already a sort of Revolutionary icon, she was not of
the peuple, either in her style or in her preoccupations. It was said that only Jean-
Paul Marat's intervention saved Théroigne from death on that occasion. It is abundantly clear that groups of women had become an important factor in popular
insurrection, often inciting it, and were consequently feared by authorities who
were uncertain as to what comportment to assume regarding them.

After the expulsion and arrest of the Girondists on June 2, the Constitution was
adopted by the Convention on June 24. Women, deprived of a vote there, nevertheless refused to be disbarred from voting in primary assemblies and took part
in votes by acclamation and in public oaths. Various individual women and clubs
went on record as regretting their lack of franchise. A police observer named

MARIE ANNE CHARLOTTE CORDAY

Née à St Saturnin les Vignaux

Agé de 25 ans moins trois mois,
a l'instant ou elle s'aperçoit qu'un des Auditeurs
est occupé a la Deßinée. Elle tourne la tête de
son côté.

74. Marie-Anne Charlotte Corday, *Bibliothèque Nationale, Paris*

75. Assassination of Jean-Paul Marat, *Bibliothèque Nationale, Photo Giraudon/Art Resource, New York*

ASSASSINAT DE J. P. MARAT

Perrière took note of the "gentle impression" that the word *equality* produces in women: "It would seem that, born slaves of men, they have a greater interest in its prevailing."[13] The mixed-gender popular society of the Arsenal section of Paris now declared that both sexes had a right to education, and a month later the Section of Free-Men of the Pont-Neuf would agree to accept women as full members.

But an event of considerable impact for the conception of women in the public imagination took place on July 13, 1793. Charlotte Corday d'Armans, a twenty-five-year-old Girondist sympathizer from Caen in Normandy, nurtured like Manon Roland on readings of Plutarch and Rousseau, gave herself a place in history by murdering the eloquent Jacobin journalist whose tongue was like a blade, Marat. An object of ardor for Jacobin women, he had been fiercely supported by them when he had been tried and acquitted by a tribunal in April of that year. Marat suffered from a painful skin disease that hampered his political activity. Having gained entry into his apartment by a stealthy appeal for help, Corday plunged a knife into his neck and wounded him to the death as he sat in his medicinal bath. As she was tried on the very next day, her demeanor in court was so serene and her defense so self-contained and rational—she claimed she was ridding France of a scourge that was ruining it, and took full and lucid responsibility for her act—that she caused consternation and rage in Marat's partisans and admiration in his enemies. This drama was much recorded. A portrait of Corday (fig. 74) seizes the moment at her trial when she noticed she was being drawn by an artist and turned toward him. This is an admirably unadorned and tranquil portrayal of a handsome head, a frank gaze, composed features. A rather even-handed interpretation of the assassination by Brion (fig. 75) presents its aftermath: Marat, already in the posture of a pietà, is borne away from the fatal bath by bearers; women at the center make a dramatic gesture of grief (shades of Prudhomme's prescribed ritual role for women) as the guilty Charlotte is taken prisoner. A discussion of the undercurrents from this woman's act will be deferred to a later point.

Mob Scenes

Despite such incidents of violence, on August 10, 1793, the most mellow and maternalist of all the festivals, that of Unity and Regeneration, took place, intended to weld the unwieldly French people into singleness of purpose.

Yet the Terror was about to be placed on the agenda to hunt down and destroy the Revolution's enemies, at the end of August. The Fête of Regeneration was a moment's surcease, of suspension of disbelief, for beginning in August and going on into September a disastrous dearth of bread paralyzed Paris. Lines formed at night to await delivery of supplies for the next day. Godineau describes the tenor of these mobs, which became a locus for both conviviality and for alarm. People would chatter, laugh, and hold each others' places if they had to go off to work or to nurse a baby. Neighbors in the area were enraged by the raucous noises continuing through the early morning hours. Journalists and the police observed that sexual unruliness seemed to flourish under the cover of darkness. "But the majority of women and men were scarcely interested in horsing around; tired, anxious, they are easily influenced, and these queues represent a potential site of ferment to riot."[14] Mercier tells of how the men, coming upon these assemblages, would survey the women on line: "Sixty-year-olds, valets, shopclerks pass by examining them row by row to pick out their 'lady loves.' Others, more shameless, rushed out upon the women, whom they embraced one after the next." This would be why a young woman linen worker would dress like a man "to get bread more easily, seeing as how in her neighborhood the men shove the women off and are alone to get bread at baker's doorways." When, as here, civilized restraints had broken down, argues Godineau, the women became disorderly, refused to stay in line, and, faced with their own and their children's hunger, preached insurrection.

Mercier saw it thus: "Morals evaporated, morals were perverted. Sentiments of brotherhood expired in every heart. Each person made it a maxim to prefer him or herself to anyone else. Soon women were struggling on a footing with men. Their characters became embittered."[15]

The women of the CRRW mourned Marat and called for an obelisk to be raised in his memory. They marched through the Paris streets behind the tub in which he had been murdered, four women bearing up the chair, the table, the writing desk, the pen and the paper he had used on that fatal day. They swore to give birth to a slew of little Marats to replace their sacrificed hero, using his shed blood as a metaphor for the seed they consented to gestate. Godineau is moved to wonder if there was not something alienating to the men about the intensity of these women's symbolic gestures at the ceremonies of July 16 and 28 commemorating Marat's death that might have turned the leadership of the Cordeliers and the Jacobins against them.[16] The delirium of intensity they demonstrated seemingly attached itself rather to Marat, the man of flesh, than to the Republic, and may well have unsettled a political regime striving to embed itself in patriotic abstractions.

Women and the Symbolic Order

This is a good moment to address ourselves to the most celebrated image of the militant Republican Woman (fig. 76). She stands stalwartly in her short skirt and boots, hand challengingly on hip, holding her pike with its legend "Liberty or Death." A strikingly timeless figure—after all, there was no ancient precedent for her—and simply garbed, with a touch of masculine style about her collar and tie, she is, even with her dashing, plumed hat (shades of Théroigne) a counterimage

FRANÇAISES DEVENUES LIBRES.

.... Et nous auſſi, nous ſavons combattre et vaincre.
Nous ſavons manier d'autres armes que l'aiguille et le fuſeau . O Bellone !
compagne de Mars, a ton exemple, toutes les femmes ne devroient-elles pas
marcher de front et d'un pas égal avec les hommes ? Deéſſe de la force et
du courage ! du moins tu n'auras point à rougir des *FRANÇAISES.*

Extrait d'une Prière des Amazones à Bellone

De la Collection Générale des Caricatures sur la Révolution Française de 1789.

Paris chez **Villeneuve** *Graveur,* rue Zacharie, *St Severin Maison du Passage* Nº 21.

76. Frenchwomen Become Free, *Musée Carnavalet, Photo Bulloz*

of femininity to those of allegory, of rococo, and of neoclassicism. We have only to compare this figure with that of Théroigne (fig. 73) to distinguish the refusal of prettiness or otherness here. A figure frankly female, with rounded arms, hips and breasts, she refuses the smile of submission. Standing solitary against the sky as a pre-Romantic figure should, her features are uncertain: they are overgeneralized—she does after all represent a type—and yet anxious. She looks straight at us, wondering what confronts her. Surrounded by broken chains, emblems of her past victories, she is given this speech by her creator: "And we too, we know how to fight and win. We are able to wield other arms than the needle and the distaff. Oh Bellona! companion to Mars, in emulation of you should not all women walk in ranks and in steps equal to men's? Goddess of strength and courage! at least you will not have to blush over FRENCHWOMEN." This caricature, *Frenchwomen Become Free,* is only very lightly satiric, and its elements of satire come primarily from the daintiness and insubstantiality of the hands and feet of the citizeness, and her pouty look, conventions of representation of women at this time.

The Républicaines as a club were, according to Godineau, moved more by political motives than by subsistance issues, though obviously the two could not be dissociated. The club agitated for the implementation of constitutional government and for their own political empowerment, while the demands uppermost in the popular mind were price controls and the availability of bread (the death penalty had been decreed for hoarders on July 26). This gap in perception separated the sans-culotte women from the women of the club in a way that government agitators may well have seized upon in initiating or exacerbating the women's so-called Cockade War.

As of April 1793, the Convention had required that citizens wear the tricolor cockade, but since women's status as citizens was still ambiguous, it appeared to them to be a voluntary matter. Women aspiring to citizenship, or even just wanting a sense of belonging, or to wear a fetching ornament, took it up. Since wearing the radicals' cockade could make one the butt of the jeers of the politically unsympathetic, or of the misogynists who reproved women's political commitment, the less enthusiastic women rejected it. The Républicaines passed a decree in their club that all its own members would sport it, and they invited the women of all the forty-eight sections of the Paris Commune to join them. In June members of the CRRW already complained of attacks on their members who wore it, and in August women members of the mixed popular society of Pont-Neuf also recorded their concern that they had been "insulted and mistreated by some women."[17] This situation worsened in September.

September was a time of severe crisis for the government of Robespierre: the federalist revolt had spread in July to over sixty departments, and French armies were retreating on all fronts. The nation was placed under conscription on August 23. On August 27 the royalists had turned Toulon over to the English. In the women's civil strife, the struggle over the symbol of Revolution continued heated. On the thirteenth, women of the Unity section threatened women not wearing the cockade and engaged in agitated confrontation with fishwives who would not hear of wearing it. From this moment on, this sort of brawl became common, the recalcitrant women rejecting the tyranny of the superpatriots, saying that only whores and Jacobin women would wear it, that women should busy themselves with their households and not with political matters, and that the cockade should be worn only by men. On the eighteenth an old woman was whipped and her clothes torn because she did not wear one, while in the Halles, the markets, a woman was chased because she was wearing it. The Convention then decreed that women should wear it, and that those who contested other women's right to do so would be punished by eight years of internment. Things quieted down. Godineau regards the militant women's victory as equally one for the popular movement.[18]

But this affair invites some speculation as to the relationship of the women of the various classes to patriotism, as reflected in the wearing of the cockade. As the legend beneath *Frenchwomen Become Free* suggests, the militant woman was seen as a Bellona, imitating Mars, trying to be a warrior like him. The women, like those of the market, rejected such masquerades, and indeed all politics, seen by them as men's game, lying outside their vital interests in survival issues. The rationale of their position was traditionalist and punitive toward the rebellious women who thought they had the luxury of contesting their assigned place. There is a sort of surly counterrevolutionary thrust in the sans-culotte women's scapegoating of the CRRW women, weak and vulnerable representatives of a government too powerful for them to oppose openly. These women's loyalty to the Revolution was steeped in skepticism. As to the upper-class women who rejected the cockade, some of them saw it as pulling them down from their rank, like the woman who felt she would look like a woman of the peuple wearing one.[19] Here it would seem that older class loyalties were prevailing among women, in preference to allegiance to the ever more masculine Revolution.

The Fall of the Club of Revolutionary Republican Women

In this same period, even the Républicaines, the women's group formerly in good odor at the Jacobins' club, would come under sudden and virulent attack, as François Chabot, himself under suspicion with Basire in the Convention, took its rostrum to deflect the wrath directed against himself by saying it was "time to tell the truth about these so-called revolutionary women." He then accused the CRRW's president, Claire Lacombe, and her associate, Jacques Leclerc, of participation in a counterrevolutionary plot. Chabot chose the easy path of attacking women as frivolous and unsuited to public authority. In taking on the Républicaines as target, the authorities were prepared to attribute to women the unrest then troubling Paris. Chabot even referred to Lacombe as "the new Corday," adding, "disappear, wretch, or we'll tear you to pieces."[20] Charging this club with formenting some of the previous riots over supplies, he created such an atmosphere of suspicion that Lacombe was arrested. She was freed the next day. But by then she and her club had become a convenient lightning rod for popular dissatisfaction. She was called a counterrevolutionary bacchante, fond of wine and men, a week later in the paper *La Feuille du salut public*. Soon the women of the club were denounced from all sides. Only the Enragé Jacques Roux would defend them. On October 10 the Society of Men (*sic!*) denounced the unpatriotic acts of these women and asked that they no longer be allowed to maintain a separate club. Lacombe ably defended the club's right of association and expression as universal ones. She also addressed herself to the obscurantist misogyny of the charges leveled against them: "Legislators, . . . plotters, and slanderers, unable to find us guilty of any crime, have dared to identify us with the Medici, with Elizabeth of England, with Antoinette, with Charlotte Corday. No doubt nature produced a monster who deprived us of [Marat], but are we responsible for her crime? Was Corday a member of our club?"[21]

Her lucidity concerning guilt by association was futile. The next step was an escalation in the war of symbols: it was now to be about the wearing of the Phrygian bonnet, and this was to prove the undoing of the CRRW.

Godineau makes the distinction: a woman wearing the cockade affirmed she was a citizen; but one who wore the red bonnet claimed the status of Revolutionary citizen. Godineau reads this further claim as a threat to men of a slippery slope of female demands: tomorrow the right to bear arms, after that heaven knew what. A foray into psychological reading may be equally plausible. Naomi Schor has drawn attention to the significance of the struggle around emblems. "For the archeology of detail, the sexism of rhetoric is of crucial significance. Neoclassical aesthetics is imbued with a sexist imaginary where the ornamental is inevitably bound up with the feminine." The battle over the cockade, though heated, could be conceded to women. Men's own use of it might well be understood as a seizure from women of a "feminine" detail, which had then been restituted to them. But the red bonnet is a cap: without abandoning ourselves to phallic analogies, we readily see that the French Revolution was about the beheading of one's enemies, the separation of their reason and their pretensions from their corporeal reality. Dominance over the head is extraordinarily significant for the post-Enlightenment the Jacobins' Revolution represents. The Phrygian bonnet, emblem of the freed slave, had been ludicrously imposed on the head of Louis XVI; now it had become a sign of shared sovereignty by the Revolutionaries, replacing the overthrown crown. To rejoin Godineau's view of it, the bonnet's adoption by women constituted a much graver contestation of shared male sovereignty than the affixing of the cockade had done.[22]

After the market women had protested that Républicaines had been forcibly attempting to impose the Liberty bonnets upon them, on October 28 a crowd of women in the gallery at a memorial to the Revolution's martyrs, Le Peletier de Saint-Fargeau and Marat, began to cry out "Down with the Jacobin women, the red bonnet, and the cockade!" A riot ensued in which the Républicaines were attacked and dragged along the ground. When they sought asylum in the local section, they were refused and rather than confront the huge crowd calling for their blood, were sent out through an alleyway. Next day, Robespierre's Committee of Public Safety saw fit to issue a poster attributing this incident to supporters of Brissot, hence to the discredited, arrested, and in-the-process-of-being-purged Girondists. This action strongly suggests that government provocateurs were actively engaged in these events. Now the market women who had originally taken umbrage, seeing their enemies discredited, requested of the Convention that the right to wear the red bonnet be denied to women. What is more, they called for them to abolish the Club of Revolutionary Republican Women altogether, arguing that "the misfortunes of France had only arisen through the agency of women, that is, Marie-Antoinette and Charlotte Corday."[23] Again, the ventriloquism question: are these the women's own voices? or women voicing what they think the men want them to say? or women whose words are dictated by men, hence men's words?

Corday, Antoinette, Medici . . .

The names of Antoinette and Corday could be summoned up out of the air because they were in the air. Charlotte Corday had been executed on July 19, and when an executioner held up her head he "had the infamy to slap her face two or three times." Even the radical *Révolutions de Paris* of July 19 was impelled to remark "there was but one cry of horror against the man who allowed himself such an atrocity." Corday's unwonted seizure of the right to political assassination was deeply disquieting, revolting to Maratists, male and female, and to those who dreaded women's active entry into affairs; on the other hand, to those women and men who shared her dread of her victim her act was seen as not unreasonable, even noble. Adam Lux, a German sympathizer with the Revolution, witnessing her courage in dying, became smitten with her and pronounced her "greater than Brutus." (He was to follow her to the guillotine in November.) Corday's heroic resolve was praised by Manon Roland, who saw her as having brought death "to the apostle of murder and brigandage." She looked upon her as "an astonishing woman," a heroine "worthy of a better age," deserving of the "admiration of the universe."[24] With her death, Corday became a symbol of women's activism, viewed alternatively as adorable or detestable.

In the turmoil of the fall of 1793 the trial of Marie-Antoinette was held. It was virtually guaranteed to be an occasion of republican solidarity, so substantial was the case the prosecutor Fouquier-Tinville set before the jury of her collusion with Austria. The superadding, to this charge of treachery against France, of an accusation, originating in an initiative of Jacques-René Hébert's, of incestuous acts practiced by the queen against her eight-year-old son, very nearly served to neutralize decades of hatred of her person. The interrogatory by the Revolutionary tribunal's president Hermann had sought to depict the queen as having usurped the king's powers and originated the monarchy's worst blunders, the fatal veto and the flight to Varennes. When Hébert produced a signed statement from the dauphin, who was then isolated in imprisonment with his keeper, Simon, that the queen and his aunt Mme Elisabeth had placed him between them in bed and induced him to masturbate, and that his mother had engaged in harmful acts of incest with him, the shocked reaction was palpable. Hébert even alleged that these excesses of the queen's were not called up by any true sensuality, but only by her desire to "secure domination over [her son's] mind."[25] Even an audience out for Antoinette's blood was taken aback by the enormity of Hébert's accusation. The simplicity of the queen's outraged appeal against it—"I call on all Mothers of

77. J.-L. *David*, Marie Antoinette on Her Way to the Guillotine, *Bibliothèque Nationale, Paris*

78. Execution of Marie-Antoinette, October 16, 1793, *Bibliothèque Nationale, Paris*

Journeé du 16 Octobre 1793

Paris chez l'Editeur Rue Honoré au dessus des cy devant Jacobins N. 1497

France here . . ."—nearly acted to generate a wave of sympathy for her. Fouquier-Tinville was therefore enraged by the near-boomerang caused by Hébert's overkill. The queen nonetheless went to her death on October 16. Unlike the king's death, which bore an air of ceremony—he rode in a closed carriage, in court dress, attended by his confessor—the queen rode to the guillotine in an open cart, her back to the driver, like a convict, "and no one," wrote an eyewitness, "dared to utter a prayer or breathe a sign on her behalf, but at the risk of his life." [26]

David's excessively well-known sketch of her (fig. 77) seems to reprove her proud, upright carriage as she sits bolt upright in the cart of her final journey. She looks like an aged hag (she was thirty-eight); her reduction could not have been represented as more abject. The very economy of line in David's quick drawing implies the contrast with the torrent of lines with which late rococo artists had depicted her, a contrast of profligate abundance with democratic austerity. The sketch declares that there were to be no more queens in France, and all should heed her fate. A sweeping vista frames an "arranged" scene of the queen's execution (fig. 78). The great stolid statue of Liberty sits in its relentless immobility above the scaffold, just as it did for all the guillotine's victims. An entirely bogus harmony, the sheer feathery grace of the trees behind the scene, quell a sense of its momentousness. The avid crowd, in which a large number of women may be seen, is kept at bay by a sea of soldiers and their muskets. In its serenity, the print seems to declare that justice has been done.

Germaine de Staël, from exile on Lake Geneva, had published her pamphlet *Reflections on the Trial of the Queen* the summer before, well before the trial had begun but as it was already under consideration. In this remarkable plea for Marie-Antoinette's life, Staël, who had never been close to her, assays the meaning of her loss. In a mood of clear moral disarray evoked by the storm of slander against the queen, Staël yet takes up a defensive posture, pandering to the popular pieties, and attempts to depict the queen as a simple, inoffensive wife and mother, a private woman life had forced into public notice. But realizing the inadequacy of these weak rationalizations, she searches for deeper reasons for the hatred against the queen. "What strength or what weakness gives these artificial passions such inexhaustible power?" She observes that the calumnies against her are sexual, of a sort used to soil all women's reputations. Staël also deplores the violent xenophobia of many of these accusations. But most pointedly, she appeals to women, at the outset and at the end of her plea: "I return to you, all women immolated by the crime committed against weakness by the destruction of pity: your reign is over if ferocity reigns, your destiny is over if your tears are shed in vain." [27] Whereas the courtly code had maintained a semblance of social integration for the women of the privileged class, the new republican code promises women honor as mothers. Staël clearly perceived that in killing the queen, a people "neither just nor generous" was expressing both the death of the old and the feebleness of the new dispensation.

Backlash

Sophie de Condorcet's reputed mot in reply to Bonaparte's expression of distaste for women concerned with politics—that in a country where women's heads could be cut off, it was natural for them to want to know why—went far deeper than a light sally, then. It expressed puzzlement at the simultaneous belittling women had undergone since the Revolution and the gravity and venom with which men were putting women to death, just as if they were free agents and political men. When Fabre d'Eglantine actually warned his fellows in the Convention that women would not stop with the red bonnet if allowed to don it, but go on to demand pistols, he formulated an anxiety endemic to the moment in the fall of 1793.

Since the question of the existence of the CRRW had been raised in the context of the public peace, Amar, speaking as head of the Committee of General Security on the ninth Brumaire (October 30) took action. From his description of the confrontation between a huge mob of women and a contingent of Revolutionary Women, it is clear that the latter were outnumbered, hence powerless. But since they were seen as having provided the occasion for the scuffle, they would have to be suppressed. It is at this point in the Revolution that the full armamentarium of the Rousseauist ideology about women, which had bathed in its atmosphere but had not given it its explicit official sanction, would be brought into play.[28] Asking rhetorically if women should exercise political rights, Amar now replies that they must not. They lack the "extensive knowledge, the application and the unlimited devotion, the severe impassiveness and the self-abnegation" to govern. His objections to the women's vote are themselves so sweeping that they allow him to extend his prohibition to all of women's rights of political association. Modesty should forbid women's participation in public rituals: "Do you wish women to be seen in the French Republic coming to the bar, to the tribune, to political assemblies like men, abandoning restraint, the source of all their sex's virtues, and the cares of their families?"[29]

The objections to Amar's reasoning raised by Deputy Charlier were—considering the kangaroo court atmosphere of this Convention session—most courageous. To murmurs of disapproval, he insisted that he saw no justification for depriving women of the right of assembly: unless one wanted to contest women's membership in mankind, Charlier asked, "can you take away this right common to all thinking beings?" While agreeing that a society that had disobeyed the laws should be punished, he found no justification for its suppression: "The fear of some abuses . . . ought not make you destroy the institution itself, for what institution is devoid of flaws?" But Basire quickly replied, in the paranoid temper that characterized this moment, that since women's societies had proved disruptive, "let no one speak to me of principles"; these associations must be forbidden, "at least during the Revolution."[30] Amar's motion then passed.

If such trouble was expressly taken to end women's right of association, this was because the reality of women's activities on every side, of every sort, was calling into question the dream of the republic of brothers. Women's multifarious presence was entirely unassimilated, psychologically and ideologically, hence productive of panic. It is not because women were ineffectual that the Revolution thus banned them: quite the contrary.[31]

We return to the guillotine. Olympe de Gouges went to her death, after vainly pleading pregnancy, on November 3, four days after the passage of Amar's motion, accused of having monarchical sympathies and fomenting civil war. No other woman had gone to the guillotine during the fortnight since Marie-Antoinette's execution. When her head fell, there was some applause, but many admired the firmness with which she had faced her death. In three days' time, Manon Roland was to be beheaded, after supposedly uttering her celebrated formula, "Liberty, what crimes are committed in thy name!"[32] That the cutting down of women's rights at the end of October should have come in the season when the heads of the most celebrated women of the Revolution were harvested seems less of an odd coincidence when seen as occurring at the confluence of national crisis and the chaos of unresolved gender issues.

The Revolution's New Women

Nevertheless, the Revolution had moved women and been moved by it. It had set off within them, as among men, an incalculable impetus toward individual and group realization, not wholly controllable by the ideology that had newly emerged to repress their liberationist impulses.

A last bloody scene remains to be evoked. After Thermidor, authority moved into the hands of men distinctly unsympathetic to the sans-culottes. They regarded the rabble, or *canaille,* "common coin in Thermidor for unruly women," as a disruptive, pillaging mob.[33] Young dandies with whips and canes were encouraged to harass "tricoteuses" and men and women of radical societies. 1795 brought a famine so grave that poor women were driven to commit suicide with their children.[34] The Thermidorians dreaded the resultant uprising among the people demanding not only bread, but a restoration of their rights. In the Prairial revolt of May 20, the tocsin was sounded in the fractious faubourgs Saint-Antoine and Saint-Marceau, and by ten o'clock a contingent of women moved into the Convention, led by the sound of their own drumbeat. That day the Convention was submerged by the throng calling for bread and a restoration of the Constitution of '93. The deputy Féraud was assassinated (two women were implicated in his murder) and his head set on a pike (fig. 79), which Boissy d'Anglas, who was presiding, contemplated impassively.

The size and openness of the women's invasion of this public forum is visible in the print. It illustrates what modern commentators have revealed: the women

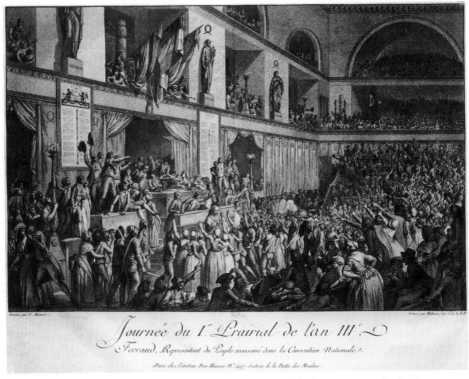

Journeé du I.ᵉʳ Prairial de l'an III.

Ferraud, Representant du Peuple assassiné dans la Convention Nationale.

Paris chez l'Auteur Rue Honoré N.º 1547. Section de la Butte des Moulins.

79. The Day of the First of Prairial, Year III, *Bibliothèque Nationale, Paris*

Madame sans Culotte

80. Madame Sans-Culotte, *Bibliothèque Nationale, Photo Giraudon/Art Resource, New York*

of the peuple did not simply go home when Amar told them to. The activists among them were too mobilized by the Revolution to yield so easily, and their needs were so acute that they were impelled to energetic protest. The National Convention had only a few months more to live, but in that time strict policing of all formerly militant women as well as suspect men would ensure that protest would henceforth be stifled.

A print claiming to portray Madame Sans-Culotte, dated 1792 (fig. 80), is a sentimental tribute. The air of a Chardinesque still life hangs about this image: Rather than evoking their undoubtedly turbulent and energetic sides, the work chooses to convey a tranquil vision of women of this class. Although she is an old woman, her trim, wiry figure conjures up memories of past activities. Seated among her solid but homely furnishings, at work knitting the cap of Liberty she pauses, raising one long, strong hand in admonition to offer some sagacious observation. Her cat, here her domestic totem, is an image of freedom kept within doors. A gentle harmoniousness rises from the neat stripes of her apron, the pleated flounces of her cap. She is given to us hopefully, as a spirit exuding order and wisdom.

A body of women, in despite of all the ruses of rhetoric that had first stirred them, then confined them in the vise of a restrictive ideology, had somehow managed to play a part in the first act of France's slow democratization. Their seizure of a participatory stance did not, however, prove to be the road to empowerment that those who took action hoped it might be. The degree of these women's enclosure in cultural concepts that impeded their ability to speak, to move, and to live in the polis was far greater than they supposed it to be. The climate in which their acts were received teemed with dissension, not the least of these centering on the appropriateness of women's acts. Only a small minority, among whom Etta Palm d'Aelders, Olympe de Gouges, Pauline Léon, Claire Lacombe, Théroigne de Mericourt, the authors of the Cahiers, and the women of the political clubs must be counted, grappled in any sort of awareness with the Revolution's paradoxical postures toward "the sex." As they were already powerless, even as the Revolution began, to affect its entrenched familialist rhetoric, they tried to make it work for them. This it could not be made to do, for it was a rhetoric specifically disempowering them. And yet the women could not help but be inspirited by the universality of the Revolution's pretensions. Like other oppressed nations and races, they would find their own fuel for revolt in its language, and even in its violence.

One of those splendid portraits by Jacques-Louis David (fig. 81), this one of Mme Trudaine, also known as Chalgrin, the wife of a deputy formerly of the upper classes, provides us with an appropriate representation of a woman living in Revolutionary times. Between this representation of her and our allegories, there is no common ground. Not a political figure, she is given to us as a distinctly private person, backgrounded against one of those antidécors David devised for his portraiture at this time. Its mottled texture allows him to dispense with super-

81. J.-L. David, Madame
Trudaine, also Known as
Chalgrin, Musée du Louvre,
Photo Musees Nationaux

fluous bric-a-brac and suggests movement and energy instead of stasis. Mme
Chalgrin's dress is aggressively simple, almost spartan, as devoid of coquetry as is
her posture. Composed, she looks into our faces, an almost modern woman, taking stock of what she sees. It is her grandly assertive head of red hair that lends
her a slightly dramatic and romantic aura: electric with vitality, it contrasts with
her placid air and suggests passion, a hint not erased by the subliminal smile that
plays about her lips. Her poise in the midst of turmoil is the aspect that David
had chosen to express. A single individual cannot stand for her sex. Mme Chalgrin
nevertheless reveals to us something of the new woman, stripped of her imprisoning rococo trappings, which, it had been found, were entirely superfluous to
her selfhood. Seated, her arms folded, in a posture that suggests self-constraint,
her questioning glance communicates her liberty of mind. In this she conveys the
paradox of the First Republic's women: her body still confined, her mind yet
roams, actively searching.

We turn now to the operations of those constructs of containment that would
continue to dog her, hampering her need to share in the responsibility for and the
direction of her world.

Chapter

8

THE MAENAD FACTOR;
OR SEX, POLITICS, AND
MURDEROUSNESS

> Dorval: When a peasant felt moved by remorse, he
> really believed there was a Fury inside him
> stirring him up; and what distress he must
> have felt at the sight of this phantom, rushing
> across the scene, her head bristling with
> serpents, and presenting to the guilty one's
> sight hands covered with blood. But as for
> ourselves, who know the vanity of all
> superstition! What of us?
> Myself: Well then, we have only to substitute our
> own devils for the Eumenides.
>
> DIDEROT

THAT the female form should have come to embody in legend the most sensational aspects of French Revolutionary murderousness is not an accident: it is instead a culturally overdetermined eventuality.

It is in *The Bacchae* of Euripides that we encounter that women's corps, dedicated to the worship of its god, Dionysus. His domain is that of humankind's deepest, most mystifying enchantment—that of sexuality, revelry, and drunkenness; those realms where self-possession escapes us, dubbed collectively by Sigmund Freud the libido. The women of this band, having "rebelled against shuttle and loom, answering the urge of Dionysus," rejoice in the ritual murder of its sacrifices. "How sweet, they sing the kill/ the fresh-smelling blood," and their hearts leap with joy when Bacchus (or Bromius or Dionysus; they are all one and the same god) summons them forth to the mountains.

> It is then that a girl like me
> Knows happiness. When she is free

> Like a filly playfully prancing round its mother
> In fields without fences.[1]

Euripides minces no words: the Bacchaes' once-a-year, world-upside-down revel frees them from a physical and moral imprisonment in home and family that squelches the expression of their sexuality, hence their will and energy.[2] The invocation of their wild romp with the god on Mount Cithaeron, their fierce rhythmic stomping to wild music, conveys an ancient male ambivalence over women's deprivation of freedom, an anxiety over the containment of their untamed, incompletely acculturated natures. For the culture knows, though it represses it, that women are made to conform to cultural norms they did not create and that were not devised for their needs. As a construct of the male-supremacist Greek culture, the Bacchaes' (or Maenads') legend and the women's involvement in the Dionysian cult "had a pronounced dual aspect: it provided rituals of mad hysteria in which sexual hostilities and pent-up frustration were released, and at the same time, it promoted a resolution of antagonism in harmonious family life."[3]

Like the rebellious Eumenides, or Furies, of Aeschylus' *Oresteia,* then, the Maenads are transformed into pillars of domesticity. Euripides' play, however, couples the maenadic explosion into revelry with raw dread: the release of the Bacchantes' ardor for physical freedom and sexual pleasure has dire consequences. For such an immoderate, unguarded turning against the rules of ordinary life as Dionysus plants in these women is seen as murderous to the fruit of their own sexuality, their children. Pentheus, the literal-minded, misogynistic moralist who rules over Thebes, is, significantly, tricked by Dionysus into donning women's clothes to spy upon the Maenads. Finding him huddled high in a pine tree, his own mother, Agave, taking him for a lion, slays him, and with her sisters tears him to pieces. These women, authorized by Dionysus to act as desiring subjects, to wield arms, the phallic surrogate, endanger their young. Maternal infanticide, their punishment for this usurpation, is the ultimate taboo of civilized life. The link Western culture has built between the idea of female empowerment and freedom, and child destruction, is thus a very old, very rooted one. It does not strain our credulity to relate this association to eighteenth-century French rhetoric already much cited, berating the privileged women of society for their supposed destructive unmotherliness to their young.

The Revolutionaries, as Carol Blum has so ably presented them, garbed in their tunics of moral virtue, bear a startling resemblance to the censorious Pentheus. Unable to bend to the pleas of wise old Teiresias to him, to relent and not use force with the Maenads, for moderation serves one best in ruling over men, Pentheus is all moral imperative, absolutely secure, like a Robespierre or a Saint-Just, in his strict construction of right, his expressed need to "put an end to this orgiastic filth."[4] What is more, the Revolutionaries mimic Pentheus in their horror of effeminacy, their striving to put as much distance as they can between men, and women and all their ways.[5]

Michel Vovelle cites Convention deputy Drulhe's statement to exemplify the Revolution's hostility concerning women's actions: "It must be said to my sex's honor that if one occasionally meets up with such ferocity of feeling it is scarcely ever found except in women" who give way to "the most dreadful abandon, either because vengeance, that passion so dear to weak souls, is dearer to their hearts, or because when they can do evil with impunity they joyfully seize the occasion to take revenge for their weakness, which makes them dependent upon fate." Drulhe takes care to point out that he is not speaking of subdued, educated women, but those "who have never known the virtues of their sex and who are scarcely found except in big cities where they are the sewer of all vices."[6]

Vovelle tells us that Drulhe's remarks have more to do with a certain male mentality than with women, and suggests that members of the radical club of the Cordeliers like Chabot and Basire shared with the partisan of the rival Hébertist faction Chaumette, who pronounced the anathema against women's mixing in politics, a misogyny that expressed a consensus among the sans-culotte population. Lynn Hunt, like François Furet, stresses the obsession with conspiracy that floods Revolutionary discourse with its venom and hyperbole.[7] Dearth, inflation, invasion, civil war, all were attributable to plots launched from various directions; speculators, aristocrats, Catholics, Austrians, or Englishmen might have been plotting against the people's government. In an atmosphere of near-universal paranoia, there were few who did not buy into some plot theory. Women in such an atmosphere inevitably came in for some share of the blame. As a society where the mixing of gender had made substantial inroads, the Revolution pressed toward purge (hence the popularity of the scatological enema in the cartoons of the time), toward the emptying out of foreign elements to whom it attributed its embattled state. The omnipresent and ever-problematic women were ready at hand as a target.

Mercier expresses his distress at how women became progressively hardened by experience: as the Revolution met with its setbacks, we recall, he claimed that "women's characters became embittered." Hufton points out that when the police official Pourvoyeur referred "in the year II to the bestialization of women and compared them to tigresses and vultures anxious for blood, the language seems rather strong, but the evidence to support it is not lacking."[8] In the male optic, women were losing, through the Revolution, that very softness and pliancy of female character whose reign the Revolution was expected to install.

Large numbers of the women of the people spoke a violent and unbridled language that was shocking to many: why this irritation should have proved so great in a nation where women's *bec* and *caquet* (their "lip") has always been mocked, but with pride in their irrepressibility, is somewhat difficult to comprehend.[9] Soboul quotes la Femme Baudry, lemonade seller of the Lepeletier Section, who said of "those who opposed the sans-culottes, she'd like to have their hearts to eat," and spoke even to her children of "nothing but cutting or tailoring heads and shedding ever more blood." It was a kingdom of language, writes Cobb, where words took on "a literal sense, a malevolent power" that was readily believed. At each village lynching, he tells us, one or two strident women, a Mère Fabre or Mère Barbasse, might boastfully dispute: "I was the one who slugged him . . . , I tore out his eyes, but I cut out *la b**** [*bite*, or penis], yes, . . . but I split his neck, but I split his skull with the axe . . . and my hands are covered with blood." The fact that women would use this murderous language with such gusto, unveiling as it did such usually repressed maenadic fury, alarmed many. Going far beyond the French tradition of female outspokenness, this bloodlust in women obviously transgressed the bounds of previously licit speech for them.

It must be added that Hébert's Père Duchesne and his "volcanic joy" provided the model for the breakdown of the linguistic frontier that stood before sexual and violent speech, with his eternal use of *buggering* and *fucking* as adjectives available to modify everything.[10] But Duchesne's speech, by analogy with male sexuality, could be licitly "volcanic," while women's similar excesses seemed unauthorized by the physiology that had come more and more to undergird gender beliefs. As an eruption of dire possibility, this style of women's speech revealed that the social order was not containing its women. Of course the men used identical language: "I'd like to eat your liver," or "I'd like to open your belly and eat your entrails," or "Let's eat a bourgeois's head." Though Hufton thinks that by 1793 women were "more frenzied, more intense, doubly credulous, doubly vindictive," but less publicly garrulous than their men, women's use of the current vile verbiage became targeted for what was interpreted as its deepseated impropriety.[11]

Women's watching eyes, too, were felt as a troubling element. Mercier, describing the terrorism of August 10, recreates how the king's Swiss guard was hunted down:

> In vain these wretches surrender their arms and beg on their knees for their lives; the drunken victor is deaf to their prayers: they are pitilessly struck down, massacred, run through with bayonets and knives. Their members, dispersed in different hands, seem reborn to fresh tortures. How can I say it? Can my trembling pen write this? Women, veritable furies, could see them roasted on braziers in the fire and, as their entrails went up in smoke, watch with dry eyes.[12]

The implication is plain: these women in their class solidarity were failing to exhibit the bourgeois conception of their assigned gender role, of empathizers with misfortune; for Mercier their dry eyes gave evidence of a failure of femininity unbearable to contemplate. This role of silent, pitiless watcher is the one history has associated with the tricoteuses. Pourvoyeur exhibited the consecrated male disquiet about these knitters, seated like the Fates, weaving before the spectacle of death. "It is astonishing how ferocious women have become. Every day they are present at executions."[13]

There are stories, undoubtedly many of them true, of women who passed from words and watching on to acts, like the one from Caen who is alleged to have eaten the heart or the genital of the Chevalier Belzunce, murdered in an atrocity by a mob in 1789. Restif would affirm it: "I close my eyes on the dreadful crime committed in Caen where there was seen . . . a hyena with a woman's face who made a trophy of the virility of young Belzunce." In the September attack on the La Force prison, Angélique Voyer was arrested along with her lover Nicolas and accused of "trampling on a cartful of cadavers, of kicking the not yet dead with her wooden clogs, and eating with bloodied hands." And Weber, Marie-Antoinette's *frère de lait,* who was imprisoned at La Force, where the Princess de Lamballe was also being held, reported hearing from the Revolutionary Collot d'Herbois that the princess's body was left to the fishwives: "These infamous creatures enjoyed making belts . . . out of her own entrails, and they dragged her nude cadaver through all the principal places of the city" before her head was displayed on its pike. Weber adds Collot's comment that if it had been up to him, he would have served up the princess's head on a covered platter to the queen. Annette Rosa asserts that there are firm grounds for concluding that Marseilles women helped eviscerate the commander of the citadel in 1790 and joined in dancing the far-andole while carrying his organs on their pikes and crying out "Who wants fresh meat?"[14] The exaltation of mob action unquestionably inspired women to words and acts of an unprecedented cruelty.

Then there was the army of hungry prostitutes and women criminals of the underworld who sponged on the Revolution and stripped the citizens of their assignats. Mercier describes the criminal element as sneaking in its underhanded way through the Palais-Royal. In the thick of the Terror, prostitutes thronged in the place de la Révolution (now Concorde), the site of executions, while pederasts gathered near the Seine's banks. Their predations became so aggressive that sentries stationed there had to be armed. In the Palais-Royal it was not unusual to be solicited by eight- to twelve-year-old girls or boys, "each sex about as bare as one's hand." The women among this population were even more devilishly clever, for Mercier, than the men: "The mouse who grabs a crumb of bread and rushes back into her hole in the wink of an eye, that is their image. One has no need to speak to them: they take one look at you and guess your vulnerabilities."[15] Such surreptitious thievery is a form of sorcery, the whisking away of one's substance by a minuscule beast of no importance who stores it in her burrow. His description has a resonance of Freudian fear and distaste for their secretive use of their sexuality.

More candidly sexual is Mercier's report of the obstreperousness of women condemned to the stocks who raised their skirts, insulting and terrifying passers-by with their obscene talk: "And as this departure from human reason was turning into a habit, the executioners were required to tie their skirts together and bind their hands."[16] This scene, added to that of the sexual predatoriness of prostitutes, suggest a mood of contempt for and confrontationism against men among a group of poorer women, played out mostly verbally, but also in acts, violent or symbolic, like exhibitionism.

Violence of language, style, or comportment among women is always observed with much anxiety and unease among men, as if it were an alien form of a familiar element. It was not lacking in the Revolution. Old ladies might call out "in Lady Macbeth-type language that children at the breast of a traitor should have their brains dashed out." Some women were attracted by a coiffure *à la sacrifiée,* in imitation of the chopped-off hair of women going to the guillotine, and some wore *bonnets à la lucarne,* to suggest the decapitating machine's contour. Cobb cites one femme Colon of Arles, a woman violent of tongue, seen at the head of "a horde of murderers, men, women and children armed with sabers and pistols, all shouting." Much of this women's violence, he says, was reserved for women. Of course in the general paranoia, "the woman concierge and the woman gatekeeper were queens."[17] Denunciations might make them so overnight, and such women were happy to betray their sisters as soon as or sooner than they would denounce the more powerful men.

Women's violence against other women meets with oceanic laughter by men: they have been checked by their own sex, momentarily releasing men from their own policing of their mores. The scene of the women of the markets setting upon members of the Révolutionnaires' club in their celebrated fracas, whether spontaneous or staged, is but one more instance of seething class-cum-sex resentment against women with pretensions, of any sort at all. Yet in acting against women who had presumed to make demands, the market women also enacted an intra-sexual quarrel, for they themselves were making demands. The Révolutionnaires were thus their competitors for those highly scarce commodities with groups of women, male attention and respect. The sheer bloodlust of Revolution was certainly often enough expressed by women. A throng of women gathered outside Robespierre's house on the day of his execution. It was said that a group of them did a dance to the clapping of hands of the multitude, as one of them cried out that his agony filled her with joy.

A prime example of nonlethal Revolutionary violence is the spanking. In the print from the *Révolutions de France et de Brabant* entitled *Discipline patriotique* (fig. 82) we see women administering a whipping to a nun in prayerful attitude before a small crowd of onlookers. "Upper-class women were whipped in the street: . . . women followers of Brissot and women of the Jacobin party challenged each other and meted out punishments."[18] Spankings represent for the victim a socially sanctioned reversion to the status of infant, unceremoniously undressed, tyrannized over and shamed by a hostile, looming set of parents. To be spanked by women, those parents society has rejected as figures of authority, is to add humiliation to infantilization.

These are some sketchy indications of ways in which women's violence and bloodlust contributed to the Revolutionary ambience. Women could denounce men or women; mobs of them could hunt down antagonists—as the Jacobin women did the unfortunate Suleau—and taunt them, spank them, or even do them grievous bodily harm; in a mob of men and women they might wield daggers along with the rest and help dismember or disembowel its victims. They

82. La Discipline Patriotique, *from* Révolutions de France et de Brabant *8, 74 (1791)*

might also act the role of inspiritors of destruction, through their yells and exhortations. Men might do all of these things as well, but they could additionally engage in a style of violence against women that had the sting of sexual sadism in its makeup.

Beatings by men of women might well incorporate the element of sexual degradation into an already humiliating scenario. In April of 1791, outmanned national guard troops looked on as a large band of men, some dressed as women, invaded Paris convents. A newspaper relates how "they saw sacred virgins of all ages, timid young ones, sickly aged ones . . . stripped naked, beaten with switches, pursued in that dreadful state of nudity in all the corners of their houses and gardens, hunted down, beaten black and blue, covered with curses more cruel than death. . . . They had in a word the grief of seeing poured out upon the persons of these innocent women all that an unbridled soldiery would allow itself in a vanquished city."[19] Such whipped-up crowd frenzies would lend themselves to a mood of gang rapism like that reported from Lyons on an Easter Sunday, as a Jacobin mob assaulted a congregation at prayer. As a witness recounts it, he saw "our women and girls dragged through the mud of our streets, publicly whipped and horribly violated. An image that can never fade from my mind! I saw one of them, bathed in tears, shorn of her clothing, her head thrown back in the muck, surrounded by bloodthirsty men. They felt her delicate members with their soiled hands, and took turns satisfying their need for debauchery and ferocity; they overwhelmed their victim with shame and sorrow." [20]

Cobb makes this gnomic remark about the society that spawned the Revolution: "There is nothing more revealing of the attitudes of a society, still in a state of savagery at the highest levels, than this apparently general acceptance of a state of affairs that left the women of the people largely unprotected against the casual or joyful violence of the male." [21] If so much could be claimed before 1789, it was not likely that the dislocations of Revolution would make it less true then.

After the September 2, 1792 siege of Verdun, the Commune rang the tocsin calling all citizens to arms, for the enemy was at their gate and treachery fermented all about them. The sense of menace from internal traitors turned the paranoid mobs toward the prisons, where the Republic's enemies still sat, largely unpunished, since the justice that was charged with trying them lacked direction and cohesion. "What then followed has no equal in atrocities committed by the French Revolution by any party." [22] In the subsequent killing of approximately fourteen hundred persons, Schama rightly reads a purge mentality directed at all the targets of the Revolution, aristocrats, priests, and whores. That the first two categories are political ones has never been in any doubt; that the third was political as well may now be clearer.

Moving from the Abbaye, where they hacked apart the bodies of nineteen out of twenty-four priests, the drunken crowd of murderers passed on to the Carmelites convent, where they killed 115 men. Meanwhile, the government sat still while "the people's justice" was done. Prisoners at Bicêtre, La Force and La Salpêtrière, were a motley population of criminals and vagrants, political prisoners, and people imprisoned by *lettre de cachet*. Among the 162 killed at Bicêtre, 43 were under eighteen. [23]

It was at La Force that the mob found its choice prize, the Princess de Lamballe, one of Marie-Antoinette's closest friends. Subjected at first to interrogation, the princess was pressed to swear oaths of loyalty to Liberty and Equality, and of eternal opposition to the king. To this she replied, with a fidelity surprising in a character so vilified by popular opinion, that she could take the first two oaths, but not the third. She was then put to death by hatchet and pike. Her head was severed from her body, and her clothing ripped off. The story that her body was sexually mutilated was widely retold. In Restif's story, the princess was made to climb upon a heap of cadavers, and the crowd demanded she repeat "Vive la nation!" When she refused, "a killer seized her, tore off her dress, and opened her belly. She fell and was finished off by others." (We may remember that Collot d'Herbois had said these others were "the fishwives.") Restif claims never to have seen a like horror, and so to have fainted. Thus no scene of sexual mutilation is reported by him. When he came to, he saw Lamballe's head on the pike. In the police report, the woman Millet claimed she had seen a member of the mob, Petit-Mamin, on the rue Saint-Antoine carrying and eating the heart of the princess.[24] Part of the mythology is the story told by Mercier that after the princess's bloody members had been divided up, someone from the mob cut out her vaginal parts and, as spectators watched, made a moustache out of them: another tale tells of a cannon charge made using one of her detached legs.[25]

A graphic Dutch print (fig. 83), which may well be apocryphal but bears some signs of fidelity to the scene, shows us two women, one with a sword at her waist, rejoicing as a man holds the princess's piked head on high. A sans-culotte slices a breast from her cadaver. In the middle and far distance we see other piked heads. Women are visible in the mob, but it is the men who have encircled and are about to kill another victim. The princess's head was paraded off to the Temple, where the queen was then lodged, as the crowd raucously called for her to come to the window to see it. A coiffeur had, reportedly, arranged the princess's hair for the occasion.

On September 4, at the Salpêtrière, that women's prison mentioned before that held madwomen, prostitutes, and women imprisoned for "misconduct" by their families, the crazed throng, intoxicated by its thirty-six-hour spree, forced its way in. Mortimer-Ternaux states that until then, except for the murders of the flower-seller at the Palais-Royal and of the Princess de Lamballe, women had been spared. Here, the men gave way to a small carnage, as thirty-five women, from teenagers

83. Het Vermoorden van de prinses van Lamballes (*The Death of the Princesse de Lamballes*), Musée Carnavalet, Photo Bulloz

to seventy-year-olds were sabred or hatcheted. From 52 to 213 were assaulted and/or raped by the assassins and then freed by them.[26] A substantial predisposition to know or not to know preconditions the willingness of commentators to evaluate these events. Pierre Caron, in his *Massacres de Septembre,* simply could find no substantiation in the documents of accounts of rape. The minutes of the Finistère Section, in whose jurisdiction the Salpêtrière fell, make no reference to such acts on September 4 and 5, and Caron believes they are merely suggested by Prudhomme's statement in his *Histoire générale et impartiale* that the mob spent the night there. Caron also doubts that the Princess de Lamballe's body was mutilated, though of course he acknowledges her decapitation.

The gap between popular beliefs and newspaper accounts and the testimony of official records is itself an index of the anxiety surrounding the violation of taboos that unleashes bloodletting and savagery. On the record, silence has traditionally shrouded unflattering outbursts of male sexual predations, so that silence in and of itself proves little.[27] Since the preoccupation of the present work is with what was thought about these events rather than with their exact historical nature, our pursuit of opinion leads us away from this quarrel and back to formulations of the meaning of the massacres for women. As soon as September 9, Mme Roland reported to her correspondent Bancal what she had heard. "If you knew the horrifying details of these expeditions! Women brutally raped before being torn apart by these tigers; entrails carved out, worn on ribbons, human flesh eaten raw." The Salpêtrière events were of course singular in that no then-apparent political motive seemed to have dictated them.[28]

A contemporary print entitled *Dreadful Massacre of Women Unprecedented in History* (fig. 84) claims to depict the scene of slaughter as the women, like the many men before them, were led out to summary destruction. On both sides of the print we see them herded, piteously pleading on the left, while on the right one woman throws up her arms among the forest of pikes in a gesture of despair. At center, their middle-class judge reads off their sentences, which are then executed by sans-culotte men with bludgeons, as we see the man with his raised weapon in the act of doing. At front the bodies of the slain and expiring lie on the cobbled street.

Restif spins his narrative of some of the drama taking place at La Force, where the gates of the women's prison, as he tells it, were pried open, filling its inmates with the expectation of deliverance. The women were called up in order of age, and Desrues's wife, the fourth or fifth to be summoned, "was the one who announced to the rest what their fate was to be by her horrendous shrieks, because the brigands amused themselves by subjecting her to indignities. Her body was not preserved from them after her death." Restif is moved by this incident to ask: "Why such violence?" Could it have been horror of her husband's crimes that inspired them? No, he answers, for horror of crime does not touch such people: rather, he thinks, "they had heard that she had been pretty." Her crime was that of having evoked desire. Forty women were killed in this way, he tells us. In other

84. Dreadful Massacre of Women Unprecedented in History, *Bibliothèque Nationale, Paris*

sections of La Force, another sort of scene is described: "It was not bloody, but never was there one so obscene. All the wretched women offered their liberators what they called their virginity. But let us turn our eyes away from this picture."[29]

In Restif's story, the pimps and the most vulgar of the men had gone only to that zone of La Force where the prostitutes were to be found, but others, libertines "more delicate in taste, though perhaps even more corrupt, had penetrated the asylum of the wretched girls who had been raised there under a regime of duress and celibacy." He reports it was into a room filled with "those depraved, ever vile beings spawned by chance in society that came the most villainous and immoral lot [of men] Europe had to offer. The libertines roam through the dormitories at the moment in the day when the girls were just awakening; they choose the ones who please them and, pressing them back on their berths and in front of the companions, take their pleasure from them. None of these girls was raped, for none resisted. As debased as Negresses, they obeyed at a sign to lie down or to turn over." The men took along as sexual booty the ones who most tickled their fancy. Restif believes himself to be "lightening" this somber scene as he tells us about a brewer from the faubourg Saint-Marcel who spotted a girl "giving some resistance" (so perhaps they were not all so acquiescent after all?) to a fat German who threatened to slap her. The Frenchman attacks the German with his stick and is set upon by his fellows for not minding his own "business." (The band of brothers, even with a foreigner, refuses to interfere in its members' sexual predations.) "Ah, my God," explains the Frenchman, "it's my sister. Do you want me to let her be fucked before my eyes?" The crowd then relents.

A similar drama supposedly told by Restif's informant is of a butcher-boy who, after running off after one of the prettiest girls, catches her and is about to put her to his use when she turns around. "Ah, my brother!" The brother reclothes himself and leads her away. But some are not so lucky and only recognize their attackers as blood relations afterwards. One "lucky one," Jacinte Gando, the "only perfectly pretty girl in the hospice," purposely making herself look ugly, takes it on herself to spy out the men and, choosing an attractive forty-year-old, throws herself on him, crying, "Papa, save me!" Noticing her good looks, he does; he takes her home and uses her sexually in full knowledge of his servants, but then the story ends "happily": they marry.[30]

These scenes as recounted by Restif are framed to the sexual tastes of the time to display the lurid melodrama of rape, while altogether shielding readers from its genital reality. Despite his appalling, racist claim that the women offered no resistance at all, we see in even his own account the resistance offered to the German's attack and Jacinte Gando's strategies to turn this holocaust to her own ends. But chiefly, while proclaiming its regret at the violence committed, Restif's account wallows in complicity with the mass rape as it describes the women as "pretty" or not, when in fact it is the male bond itself that initiates and perpetrates the group's sexual arousal and acts against the women, the rapable class. And the narrative's hypocritical tone of concern over the avoidance of incest covers intense pleasure with the idea of violating this taboo.

These sexual orgies, far from being peripheral, express a vital component in the character of the French Revolution. Cobb refers to the fact that as it went on, it became increasingly a movement of young and mature men, whipped into ever greater frenzy by a sense of danger.[31] And in Michel Delon's exploration of the idea of Energy in the Enlightenment, he speaks of the evolution toward the freeing up of vigor entrapped in frozen cultural forms. He concludes: "In the rigors of civic duty as in the emotions of the heart, in revolutionary planning as much as in sentimental individualism, energy impels men to an increase in being."[32] That this impulse has a core component in sexuality can no longer be ignored, so long after Freud's unveiling of the role of genitality in the human psyche. But we have only begun to comprehend how male hostility to women—what Restif character-ized as "the laughter of *atropolissonnerie*" or a reversion to the thuggery of primi-tive gestures of male dominance—connects with sexual impulse. Nor do we understand how sexual impulse in turn relates to spurts of violence, individual or collective, even though we all perceive the salience of this link. The mob's group fear of the prisoners as plotters is a near-conscious motive for the September massacres: but in that case, the attacks against women merely use them as a de-viated target of class wrath. These men vent their disappointed drives to domi-nance in sexual pleasure taken upon the persons of women in lieu of slaughter, in a satisfying spirit of hatred, and in brotherly impunity. The effect of these sexual crimes upon the community of women must be taken into account, just as would any pogrom on a community of Jews, or lynch mob action on a community of blacks. With this difference: that women must continue to live on in intimate connection with men, in the face of such outbreaks of ferocity, and pretend that such events are all aberrations.

In addition to the impunity of the actual rapists and murderers, most of whom were let off, Mortimer-Ternaux emphasizes the apologetics practiced by the Revolutionary press in recounting these events. He cites euphemisms like "an unforeseen event," "popular judgment," and "terrible but necessary justice" used in describing them.[33] In Prudhomme's account in the popular *Révolutions de Paris,* he wrote, "The peuple is human, but without weakness; wherever it smells out crime, it sets upon it, without concern for age, sex or the condition of the guilty." For him, the "sabers and pikes" wielded on that occasion were the "truncheon of the people—Hercules cleaning out the Augean stables." No wonder, then, that he fails to disapprove of sexual atrocities like those perpetrated on Mme de Lamballe. It is not incidental that in his justification that all was fair against the aristocrats (and not too many of the raped at La Force or La Salpêtrière were of that class), Prudhomme should have fired up fury against aristocratic women especially. He told the tale that aristocrats were serving up with their dessert as entertainment a miniguillotine made of mahogany with which dolls made in the image of prominent magistrates were executed, as little flagons allowed a liquid resembling blood to flow from their minuscule figures. "All those in attendance, the women especially, hastened to dip their handkerchiefs into this blood, which turns out to be a very tasty ambered water."[34] Mortimer-Ternaux claims no such little guillotines were ever found.

Caron claims, far from unwarrantedly, that in the massacres themselves, which exacted such a large toll of male life, women were largely spared, and that this moderation with regard to them was greater than the Old Regime's clemency toward them. But this is to evade the issue of what the Revolution's aspirations concerning women as a class really were. A new field of force, combining a new ethic of separatist protectiveness toward women with a release of hostile lubricity, surrounds the Revolution's treatment of them.

The breakdown of even the semblance of civil restraint toward women was coupled with a curious egalitarianism toward female crime, as we see from a discussion at the Convention on August 10, 1793. One Jeanne-Catherine Cler, fifty-five years old, a cook accused of making anti-Revolutionary statements in public, was condemned to death. The deputy Maguyer took her defense, claiming she was not herself when she made these statements, but drunk, and he asked for a stay of execution. Isnard supported his move, arguing that it was inappropriate to expect political responsibility from a woman: "It is not your intent that a woman who is unacquainted with politics . . ." A murmur of dissent from the floor was all that was needed to squelch this charitable move.[35] The Convention then passed on to its discussion . . . of freedom of speech. So women, though not to be thought of as full citizens, were nevertheless subject to equal punishment with men for infringements of patriotism. The contradictory muddle of male assertions of female accountability and, simultaneously, of female weakness and unaccountability is manifest in this example.

Another hostile male manifestation in the gender relations of the time was the tendency of thugs to seek out and affront the mostly more tender and traditionally susceptible sensibilities of women so as to elicit expressions of grief or outrage. We see one such lively portrayal of an attack (*Scene of Atrocity,* fig. 85) in which an assassin with an axe at right pursues a weeping woman (whose face is strategically unrepresented) with the bloodied head of her son or husband. So despite the presence of bloody-handed women, the consecrated sensibility gap between men and women was indeed present. Some other examples of such a phenomenon are found in reports given the police. Jean Debersche, a forty-five-year-old jeweler, was seen during the massacres with his sleeves rolled up, his arms dripping with blood. Turning on a citizeness witness of this scene who expressed her sorrow at the slaughter, he addressed "the most menacing remarks to her." Another, from a letter by Bazin, concerns Charles-Francois-Honoré Cortet, a carpenter, who claimed to have slain fourteen persons at the Conciergerie. His pregnant wife died

85. Massacre at Lyons, *Bibliothèque Nationale, Paris*

of a seizure after he returned home with blood on his face and arms. She "died of sorrow," and he was then imprisoned at the insistence of neighbors but was later released.[36]

Restif reports that horror-struck women in the crowd at Berthier's execution simply fell apart in fainting or sickness, and that the women in particular appeared stricken at the king's death.[37] Violence to women's perceived sensibilities was then and remains a tough's delight. Empathy, following Père Duchesne's lead, was simply counterrevolutionary.

Actual violence originating among men was of course more prevalent by far than that initiated by women. "The Revolution needs blood" was the maxim that fed the Terror. And rapine among the military is too entrenched a tradition to need documentation here. Klossowski, one of Sade's interpreters, tries to elucidate some of the forces at work. "The revolutionary community will be at its core secretly but intimately in collusion with the moral collapse of monarchical society, since it is thanks to that collapse that its members have acquired the strength and energy necessary to make bloody decisions." Delon focuses upon a tie between Sade's libertinism and Revolutionary violence: the libertine rationale is based upon the superior energy generated by sexual pleasure as compared with the feebler joys of the moral pleasure so vaunted by sentimentalists. Maximum intensity derives from the imposition of pain played out upon the body of another, so as not to cause the self "real" damage: "The displacement of violence onto the body of another permits the libertine to survive." So too with a member of a Revolutionary mob. The polymorphousness of desire erupts in a frenzied carnival of energies denied. Libertine and Revolutionary codes amalgamate in Terror. Cobb reminds us that some recent French historians have "suggested that the attachment felt by the sectionnaire to his pike could be explained in sexual terms; certainly, once deprived of it, he lost his sense of citizenship along with the visible emblem of militancy."[38] Violence intended to operate as the external sign of manhood incites mob action through an emulation that seals the male bond in cohesion. The Revolution's summons to atrocity broke out from the start as heads were cut off and lofted as quasi-religious effigies tying crowds together in a blood-bond.[39] Such apparently random atrocities as these and the September Massacres were followed up by the thousands of deliberate decapitations ordered by the Revolutionary tribunal's summary judgments. But even after the retreat from bloodshed following Thermidor, the spouting of blood could not be stanched. In the Year V, the disarmament decreed in the Year III had failed to quell its ravages in the southern countryside. "In the Rochegude area, barbarians butcher a father and stifle a baby in his cradle by compressing his skull. . . . At Velleron . . . the breast of a nursing mother is torn off by these cannibals. . . . Great God! where are we, where are we living, what has become of our country?" is the cry of an anguished citizen.[40]

Mercier captures beautifully the confusion and horror felt by the majority before the spectacle of its fractious, murdering members. Surveying the wreckage at the Tuileries on August 10, the members of a crowd of observers "were struck with a sorrowing stupor as they wandered slowly through the terrace littered with the debris of battle. They did not weep; they appeared to be petrified, annihilated. At each step, they recoiled in horror before the sight of those bleeding, humiliated, butchered, eviscerated cadavers, on whose faces wrath was still alive."[41]

A satiric allegory (fig. 86) of the Revolution by Taunay presents it as an all but entirely male hell. Except for the man coupling with the Phrygian bonneted woman (a militant?) at right front and one female figure with a child in the crowd, the personages and scenes evoked feature men, uniformly ripping, tearing, guillotining, skewering infants. Whether one believed in its worth or not, the Revolution was a men's affair, to which women offered their collaborative energies. Yet while it had been massively the work of men, its men were to call their tool of judicial murder, Dr. Guillotin's merciful invention, *La Veuve* (the Widow) or *La Sainte* (the Female Saint).

Demonic characterizations of women are slippery conceptions: they overlap curiously with heroic ones. Amazons and demons are often conflated in the Rev-

86. *Taunay,* Satiric Allegory of the Revolution, *Musée Carnavalet, Photo Bulloz*

olution's rhetoric. Even in presumably "heroic" representations, the Revolution's men may be staging projections of murderous impulses being played out by themselves upon figures of women. Barthélemy's painting in the Salon of 1791 displayed the scene of the Lacedemonian woman who, seeing her eldest son fall in defense of his city, calls out "Let his brother replace him!" And Naigeon's canvas in the 1793 Salon depicted Hasdrubal's wife as, after her husband's cowardly surrender, she murders her children.[42]

Welcome as the configuration of woman was as allegory to the Revolutionary sensibility, so unwelcome did real women become. That female activism that turned into such a core of gender anxiety for the Revolutionaries would be transmuted by its symbolism into Female Energy, since our vocabulary of signs allows us to codify forces seen as external to men only by tagging them as female.[43] Lairtullier, in his 1840 recreation, evokes a bunch of women rejoicing in their men's bloodshed at the guillotine, "doubling its atrocity by their devilish yelling; throwing off sinister sarcasms at the blood about to be shed, amid sardonic laughter at the lives about to end; crowding round the fatal plank so as to savor all the more the livid pallor, the mysterious trembling, and the death throes of the victim; rejoicing in the cowardly executioner, whose place they would take with delight; stamping their feet with joy at the moment of the bloody holocaust; panting with impatience after the dying one who, in their frightful lingo, jumps like a carp or sneezes in the sack; and then go off and dance hideous carmagnoles in celebration, at the very foot of the scaffold." These tricoteuses are not knitting, but neither are they the actors of the scene: they are its (aggressive) chorus, and like the undomesticated Eumenides, they are a chorus too vociferous, too public, voicing their own (vicarious) pleasure in the executions of the male republic they espouse too wholeheartedly. In Lairtullier's description, they are plainly assigned to serve as the site of all human bloodlust. "That corner of cruelty too often concealed in the human heart overflows in them and like the flood of a devouring poison invades the whole of their minds." Though fatiguing, it is worth pursuing Lairtullier's tirade to its end.

> These women were young, perhaps pretty, able to feel love; but all that was brutally repressed by their soiling contact with the world. Their hearts by stages hardened, dried out, were cast in bronze; they aspired to the drunkenness of bitter derision, savage irony, scorn for all things, and especially those that resemble human affections. That state of rage that gives rise to a feeling of censure replaced [the affections] and cried out for vengeance! A storm of threats, of curses and revolts, was piled up, always ready to burst out with shrieks and mud; women unsympathetic to the world, because it is lost to them, and by anticipation prepared for the ways of hell.[44]

The construct "tricoteuse" distills dread of a mass of women given over to irony and anger, venting it together in a public place, laying claim by their presence to participation in the ritual of slaughter and regeneration in which they have, by rights, no part. They are women who have failed to assimilate that the world is lost to them. Lairtullier's text shows a keen awareness of the powerlessness of these women, justified by a strenuous misogyny. For their (real or supposed) rejection of the ideology of gender, the knitting-women have been assigned the role of the Revolution's evil spirits.

A modern historian, Godineau stresses the patriotism of that group of sans-culotte women who expressed their status as part of the French people by their appearance at executions, and claims that attacks upon them conveyed the message that they must no longer presume to arrogate that role to themselves. She agrees with D. Arasse that the tricoteuses performed the function of "actress-spectators" at trials and executions that made them, as "others," unwelcome witnesses of the regime's acts.[45]

A fund of long-repressed rage motivated these women to indulge in their vile gestures and words. Their hatred of the status quo would have been, if anything, more intense than the men's. The ultimate acts had mostly to be foregone by them. The rage they elicited in the men was, as we have seen, constantly flung back upon them in representation, often as individual representatives of their militant type, but even more often as a group. A club of women, whether orderly or not, is for the author of a piece in *Les Révolutions de Paris* (185) an affront. Why a woman's club in Lyons, he asks? Why elect a president? Why have orderly meetings? Why keep minutes? Do we really need a ladies' club to teach Rousseau's *Social Contract* to young girls? "In the name of the fatherland they love with all their hearts, in the name of nature from whom we must never take leave, in the name of good domestic morals of which women's clubs are the plague because of the dissipation they bring with them, we implore the good citizenesses to stay home" (47).

A remarkable caricature by Chérieux of a women's club meeting in a church (fig. 87) expresses all this author's dismay and more. There they are, the women in the pulpit, on the dais beneath the Tricolor, arms flailing, breasts bobbing, accusing one another, making points of order, reading and writing minutes, some with babes in arms, some chatting, some vociferating. The artist endows them with a comically excessive energy for a sex with breasts. These semi-Bacchantes are no longer preoccupied by home and family. The men stand stolidly, over-dressed as compared with the females' display of flesh. The caricature in its deftness both mocks and does not mock: the women in their variety and intensity of posture are touching as much as absurd; their excess movingly spirited as much as ridiculous. But these are of course the same women—the Révolutionnaires—whom Chaumette called mannish. "Imprudent women, who want to be men, haven't you enough already?" The women who had gone into the streets urging other women to wear the red bonnet, he told them, merely soiled it. For him they were unnatural viragos whose sexual brazenness was simply too troublesome to the male citizenry.[46]

87. *Chérieux,* Women's Political Meeting in a Church, *Photo Bibliothèque Nationale, Paris*

Only a short step is needed, in this mentality, whether on the left or the right, to move from this image of the virago, denatured but still human, to a quintessential construct incorporating the tradition's loathing for all that cast-out content associated with the idea of woman. Not men, and refused recognition as women, the components of their female humanness rejected, the engaged women of the Revolution are transposed to a nonhuman plane. There they are refashioned into psychological scarecrows, for men to hate and for women to flee in fear of contamination. For dis-ease and monstrosity exude from these female monstrosities.

Restif's depiction of the Chimera is the image of the fetid rumors lofted into the air as the king's coming to Paris was debated. "The Chimera's head is that of a beautiful prostitute's whose eyes dart flames; her tongue is a serpent's from whose mouth venom sometimes spews, sometimes heroic words; whose hands are a harpy's; whose heart is empty or ferments only over lewd thoughts; whose middle, from her belt to her knees is a fountain of shameful evils; whose thigh is a goat's, her feet a pig's."[47] Like the virago, the chimera is a fiery, eloquent, lascivious creature, whose blatant and tempting sexual invitation is tied up with a heroic stance and an empty, because sexually aware, heart. Restif's portrait recaptures the spirit of a print of the lascivious harpy from the 1780's (see fig. 105), reputed to have been captured in Peru. This vile creature, an invention devised by the Count de Provence to undermine his sister-in-law Marie-Antoinette, was, because of the queen's sullied reputation, readily equated with her.

Sexual rage admixed with reluctant admiration for effrontery is the blend we find in men's representations of activist Revolutionary women. Thus we find Théroigne de Mericourt, "red goddess of death, surging up out of the waves, a new Venus, from the foam of the crowds." Théroigne acquired the moniker "Amazon of Liberty" for her arresting call to women to arm: "Let us arm; nature and even law give us the right to do so; let us show men that we are inferior to them neither in virtue nor in courage; let us show Europe that Frenchwomen know their rights and are up to the level of eighteenth-century enlightenment; [let us] scorn prejudices which, by dint simply of being prejudices, are absurd and often immoral, in that they make our virtues seem like crimes." Such patent ambition led to the stripping and thrashing administered to her a year later by "those indecent furies," the hating Montagnard women. Having gone mad, Théroigne spent the years from 1807 until her death in 1817 in the Salpêtrière. Louis Lacour tells us about the examination of this "aberrant" madwoman by the physician Esquiriol, who attributed her dementia to a misalignment of her colon. It was important, under Napoleon, to assign an innate cause to her dramatic departure from the prescribed norms. Her image as a Bacchante of the October Days, even though ultimately brought low by other Bacchantes, was only amplified by time. Baudelaire, in his tribute to Mme Sabatier's friend, Sisina, evokes her:

> Have you seen Théroigne, mistress of bloodshed,
> Exciting to arms a people ill-shod,
> Her cheeks and eyes aflame, playing her role,
> Mounting, saber in hand, the royal staircase?

Probably no more bloodthirsty than Danton or Brissot, Théroigne is yet cast as a livid, sexually enticing emblem of bloodshed.[48]

Twentieth-century history has not tired of "using" her in this fashion. Simon Schama found it apposite to end his huge survey of the Revolution with a tongue-smacking allusion to the mad Théroigne, naked in her cell, throwing off all her clothing, desperately attempting to cool down the heat of her diseased body. The metaphor of the Revolution as female sexual rage still has its uses. Théroigne, writes Schama, "oblivious of all visitors, concerned or callous, who saw her . . . now lived entirely inside the Revolution and the Revolution inside her. Sympathy seems out of place here, for in some sense the madness of Théroigne de Méricourt was a logical destination for the convulsions of revolutionary Idealism. Discovering, at last, a person of almost sublime transparency and presocial innocence, someone naked and purified with dousings of ice water, the Revolution could fill her up like a vessel."[49]

Only a metaphor from masculinity could adequately compass the reality of the French Revolution. But to find one, Schama would have had to sacrifice some of the luridness of his ending. Instead, he has recourse to this minor figure in the global Revolution's story. Sympathy is withheld from her as Schama paints Théroigne, with the stain of sexual stereotype, as a played-out Maenad: transparent (lacking substance), presocial (natural), and sexually fillable. Her fever becomes the metaphor for unquenchable sexual/political appetite. He chooses her as his scapegoat emblem for the blind heat of Revolutionary idealism he finds so tragically misplaced.[50] But in his own unreflecting sexual chauvinism, he has tragically misplaced her. Her own objectives as a woman and for women were not, ultimately, identical with the Revolution's, which outright rejected them. The charge of being presocial repeats the slander the Revolution itself directed against women like herself for being social, for assuming the right to speak and act in the state. This, after all, was her real dis-ease.

The chief allegations made against the queen, too, at her trial conflated unseemly sexual and political enterprise and took on the character of the Maenadic mythos. Her accuser, Hermann, pronounced her guilty of "intimate liaisons with infamous ministers, perfidious generals, unfaithful representatives of the people," as he described her as author of all the massacres of the Revolution, making all men wretched by tearing them away from the bosom of their families. We witness the furies of projection, the reinvention of phantasms of female evil far beyond the needs of even the Terror's justice, working within Hermann here: the massacres had arisen from the queen's person as evil enchantments exercised over men. The mode of exorcising her evil was to level Hébert's charge against her, that of the ultimate in unmotherliness: incest with her son. The monstrosity of this accusation placed the queen, as had the pamphlets and caricatures, squarely in the realm of bestiality, beyond the human pale. She was an "abominable fury," the devil incarnate, as Hébert asserted in urging throngs of people to attend her beheading. "Better kill the devil than the devil kill us." Elizabeth Colwill has best summarized the implications of her trial: "Thus stood Marie-Antoinette, accused and convicted of embodying woman as monstrosity. Beneath the formal charge of conspiracy lay covert accusations of adultery, homebreaking, and infanticide. The prosecution had mobilized the discourse on womanhood to stain the political prerogatives of queenship with the taint of dishonour. In making queenship itself a crime, the Revolutionary Tribunal had vanquished the aristocratic empire of woman." The queen was the ultimate Maenad. But the hated "aristocracy" in women was a slippery category, seeming to apply not only to a single class, but to women of any class who, like aristocratic women, presumed to think or to act, as the case of the petty aristocrat Charlotte Corday illustrates.[51]

Corday is another woman tagged by her enemies not only as the assassin she was, whatever her justification, but as a beast in female form. Chabot summed up her troubling effect: "She had the audacity of crime all over her face. She's capable

M.A. CHARLOTE CORDEY

88. *Haver,* Marie-Anne
Charlotte Corday, *Bibliothèque Nationale, Paris*

of the greatest misdeeds . . . one of those monsters that nature vomits up from
time to time to make humanity wretched. With wit, grace, and a superb face and
bearing, she seems to be possessed by a delirium and a courage fit to attempt
anything."[52] In juxtaposing Corday's murder of Marat and the onset of the Terror,
Jean Epois, Corday's biographer, seems to suggest a link: might her insubordinate
act not have been a "last straw" in the realm of disorder, as the myth or the reality
of the executioner's slapping of her face seems to imply? A painting by Haver
(fig. 88) shows us a dissolute Charlotte with a mad-dog look in her eye, wielding
her dagger, her breast uncovered, pointing to . . . herself.

The like the martyred Marat, Corday gradually acquired cult status. But in the
moment after the murder, she caused absolute consternation in the Jacobin party,
bordering on panic. Intense nervousness is evidenced by the preoccupation after
her execution with Corday's chastity, which was passionately denied by her detractors and affirmed by her Girondist supporters. So much was this the case that
her decapitated body was carried to the hospital of La Charité, where two physicians, accompanied by an illustrious Jacobin company including the painter David, scrutinized her genitalia to ascertain whether or not she had been a virgin.
They were much disappointed by her apparent intactness.[53] Yet other physicians
came forth to allege that her crime was the result of an unnatural chastity, unwonted in a twenty-five-year-old woman. In each case, her sexuality became the
core of argument for or against her.

The most arresting masculine attack upon her, obviously intended as a warning to women, was published just after her crime in the *Répertoire du tribunal révolutionnaire* in July 1793. It mixes fear with scorn and threat in its general anathema against female aspirations, conveniently annexed to class hatred.

> This woman, who they say was very pretty, was not pretty at all; she was a virago, fleshlier than fresh, graceless, unclean like almost all female wits and philosophers. . . . Charlotte Corday was twenty-five; that is, in our mores, almost an old maid, and especially with a mannish demeanor and a boyish stature. . . . This woman absolutely threw herself out of her sex; when nature recalled her to it, she felt only disgust and boredom; sentimental love and its gentle emotions cannot come near the heart of a woman with pretensions to knowledge, wit, strength of character, the politics of nations . . . or who burns to be noticed. Right-thinking, amiable men do not care for women of this type: so the latter make themselves scorn the sex that scorns them; these women take their disdain for character, their spite for strength. . . . Charlotte Corday, proud to excess . . . in her pride of birth and her conviction of the superiority of her mind and morals, failed to find about her food for her pride. Born into a proscribed caste, once proud and revered, today humbled, her spirit exalted by ill-digested readings, lacking admirers; her heart empty for lack of pleasure; unquiet and impatient in temper, this woman sought to end her life in the manner of Erostrates.[54]

Having, like Théroigne, assumed that arms provided the road to membership in her nation, Corday's ultimate vice was her claim to die a citizen's death.

Olympe de Gouges, too, would be assailed for presuming to depart from the bounds prescribed to her sex, thus becoming a nonwoman. The *Feuille du salut public* would comment, "Olympe de Gouges, born with an exalted imagination, took her delirium for natural inspiration. She wanted to be a statesman. She endorsed the stands of the traitors who wanted to divide France. It seems as though the law has punished this conspirator for having forgotten the virtues appropriate to her sex."[55]

It is always women's exaltation that is rebuked: it calls up an all too maenadic energy in women, and visibly most commentators experienced greater difficulty in discerning the difference between sexual and political fervor in women than in men. Women are virtually never anything but a homogeneous bloc in these polemics. This constricted mode of thought is what made Paule-Marie Duhet charge the Revolutionaries with racism with regard to women. When Claire Lacombe and her club fell into disfavor with the Jacobin leadership, we recall, she was accused of treachery as a "new Corday" by the women in the gallery as the members of the Jacobin club applauded. In her reply, she attempted to dissociate herself from the Medici, from Elizabeth of England, from Antoinette and Corday, crying out that Corday was indeed a monster, but "are we responsible for her crime? Was Corday a member of our club?" In fact, the women of the CRRW tried to throw the word back: they claimed that their sex had produced but one mon-

ster, whereas for four years the nation has been torn apart by the "monsters without number produced by the masculine sex."[56] No matter. When officialdom in
the person of Amar pronounces the doom of women's right of assemblage, it lumps
together all the women, now perceived to be on its right, together: the dead
queen, the dead Olympe, the dead Roland, all live in his text as usurpers of male
prerogative, hence on the right, for their various political positions are otherwise
too various to be associated together. "The Roland woman, a wit with great ambition, . . . was a monster in every way." Sacrificing nature and her own motherhood, "she wanted to rise above herself; her desire to be learned led her to forget
the virtues of her sex, and that forgetfulness, always dangerous, ended by making
her perish on the scaffold." Go home, then, you women in the clubs and streets,
he advises them in the spirit of Pentheus, and stay there.

In its article on the riot among women over the red bonnet, the *Révolutions de
Paris* (213) hands a final piece of advice to all women: "Keep yourselves in clothing appropriate to your habits and occupations, and always go on punishing as
bravely as you have just done any misdemeanor that would tend to disorganize
society, by the switching of the sexes or by indecently merging them, out of anti-
civic and perfidious intent."

Tradition

What resources did the iconic tradition offer to this struggle over the definition
of female identity? Like the nouns of order and goodness, virtually every word
designating disorder and enmity, as a noun expressing quality, is feminine in the
French tongue: all, then, are represented as female. Foremost among these, under
whose rubric I set all the others, is Discord, whom Gravelot and Cochin in their
visual recipe recommend be depicted as a "malevolent Divinity—with the air of a
Medusa, flying through the air, and in her passage pressing out the venom of her
fearful snakes" (70). But all her sisters run amok with her, and Licence, a naked
and disheveled young woman, breaks the bridle of Reason, tramples on the wheat
in a field, and vaults over a hedge surrounding her. Disobedience also bursts free
of her bridle; "daughter of pride and presumption, we would give her a peacock's
feathers and make arrogance and scorn manifest in her features and posture." In
contrast to the chaste charms of a modest young girl, Docility, Indocility is an
"ugly woman leaning on a pig and holding by its bridle an ass who refuses to obey
her." All of these images convey a sheer destructiveness inherent in female will.
Malignancy "is depicted as a thin, ugly woman with the equivocal smile of perfidy
on her face," while Wickedness is a hideous old hag with a wild look in her eye,
in menacing posture, with two knives in her hands. The great figures that match
the Revolution's obsessions are here too: Vengeance, a fury inflamed by wrath, a
militant helmet on her head, brandishing her knife; Calumny, "an atrocious vice
that could not be better represented than as a fury, with a wild glance, sparkling

eyes, and a head bristling with serpents, holding in her right hand a brazier, and in the left a votive cup that spreads her black poisons." Slander is not unlike her vicious sister; she stands there "old, thin, hideous . . . holding the torch of discord in one hand and a viper in the other." The most naked instance of projection in this series is exhibited by the contrast between the Angry One (Le Colérique) and Anger (La Colère). The former masculine noun is to be depicted as a male figure "thin, young, with yellowish cast, eyes sparkling, armed with a dagger and in a threatening pose": the latter is "a fury with the same emblems." The masculine figure menaces, but remains within human compass: the feminine transgresses human form to terrify.

Freud's interpretation of the snake hair of the Medusa, which appears on Athena's great breastplate in the *Iliad,* finds in it an allusion to unapproachable woman, repelling desire through her flaunted "terrifying" genitals, those of the taboo mother.[57] The representation of snakes as an attribute of a female figure render her a dread phallic woman, wielding dangerous powers. Athena's are contained by her daughtership and service to Zeus; but other such female allegories are unanchored, uncontained by allegiance to a father, and so hold incommensurable dangers.

The ancient male fear of women, most articulately analyzed in psychoanalytic terms by Karen Horney, has shaped male representation, and hence the historic configuration, of women. Horney quotes Wedekind's response to his "Earth Spirit," who destroys men because it is in her nature to do so. "It is not that I dread her; it is that she is herself malignant, capable of any crime, a beast of prey, a vampire, a witch, insatiable in her desires. She is the very personification of what is sinister." Horney posits that men feel fear in penetrating the vagina, even as they desire to do so. Their dread of being rejected and derided by women forces many men into evasion or overcompensation. As we recall, the masculine castration anxiety is, for Horney, an ego "response to the *wish to be a woman.*" As Freud and Klein affirm, maternal prohibitions and defections deflect infantile resentment onto the mother's person. For the man, "phallic impulses to penetrate merge with his anger at frustration, and the impulses take on a sadistic tinge."[58] If one means of reducing the pain involved in this masculine version of the "narcissistic scar" is to "adopt the attitudes described by Freud as the propensity to debase the love-object," the presence of a tradition instituting and representing such debasement reveals this strategy to be culturewide, by no means merely an individual mechanism of the psyche. The primitive magic women seem to distill in their sexuality, the pull it exerts on men's senses, the trouble and strife it creates in its resultant fertility, hover over the female persona, blocking out perception of women as persons.

The tradition, as we see it carried forward by this 1792 *Iconography,* unreflectingly continues to cast Evil (as well as Good) in female imagery. But in evil times, who ever thinks of Good?

89. The Patriotic Fairy, *Musée Carnavalet, Photo Bulloz*

90. Grand Disbanding of the Constitutional Army, *Bibliothèque Nationale, Paris*

Mona Ozouf takes note of the sort of magic thinking the Revolutionaries in-dulged in, so that at an angry glance of the people or of the Convention, the forces of evil were supposed to dissolve, even as they would in a comic strip, in a puff of smoke.[59] A print, actually a slight reworking of a 1626 engraving by Jan van de Velde, of *The Patriotic Fairy* (fig. 89) lavishly expresses this love of magic. This beneficent (from the Revolutionaries' point of view) Circe's wildly but neatly blown hair and magically globed breasts express female energy as she pours out her potions to slay the assorted beasts and dragons. The Bastille at left has been added to make the work timely. The fairy's necromantic fancies will avenge the nation.

In that sex is magic, a sexual metaphor powerfully augments propaganda or mockery of the other side. A skillfully executed rococo anti-Revolutionary print of the *Grand Disbanding of the Constitutional Army* (fig. 90) pretends to show "a detachment made up of the main chippies who've played a role in the Revolution presenting themselves to the Austrian Emperor's troops to make them disband [lose their erections], which succeeds completely, and we cease to be surprised at this Catastrophe, when we see Miss Théroigne showing her République." Among the women are "Mesdames Staël, Dondon, Sillery, Calo, Talmouse, Condor show-ing their Villette." Their corps is augmented by sans-culottes behind them who hang sausages and bottles from their pikes. The animus of the cartoonist puts the moderates like Mesdames Staël, Sillery, and Condorcet in the front rank: all are in the republican sack with that notorious woman of the political left, Théroigne, who at center presents herself frontally. The refusal to make distinctions among these members of "the sex" is plain. The Marquis de Villette, a constitutionalist traitor to his class, becomes a vagina in this reading for his advocacy of social assistance to women. The equation pitting female sexuality against male arms to the latter's detriment could not be more openly depicted.

From the left come two versions of the same work (figs. 91 and 92) represent-ing the woman of the people, demurely dressed and coiffed, a neat, lithe figure. In *The Democratic Woman Holding the Rights of Man,* she holds a folded paper inscribed Rights of Man; in the other, the close-up of *La Démocrate* fills her paper with a penis, upon which is inscribed "Right of Man," and underneath her effigy we read, "Ah, What a Good Decree." Perplexity overflows the association of women with rights that only a ribald invocation of male sexual authority seems able to contain.

A coming together of the sexual and the allegorical traditions is evident in the *Conduct of the Clergy 1790* (fig. 93), where the ecclesiastical image of Fanaticism with his crucifix leads Discord into France, while the genius of the realm uncovers their plots and threatens them with his sword. Discord here is as commanded by Gravelot and Cochin, a Medusa whose energetic step and bared breast suggest unleashed female passion. This image emanates from the left of the political spec-trum. But a post-Thermidorean image of *The Republic* (fig. 94) from the right uses

91. Democratic Woman Holding the Rights of Man, *Musée Carnavalet, Photo Bulloz*

92. Ah, What a Good Decree, *Musée Carnavalet, Photo Bulloz*

CONDUITE DU CLERGÉ EN 1790.

93. Conduct of the Clergy, 1790, *Musée Carnavalet, Photo Bulloz*

LA RÉPUBLIQUE.

94. The Republic, *Musée Carnavalet, Photo Bulloz*

95. The Abominable Ones, *Bibliothèque Nationale, Paris*

96. *Joseph Chinard,* Apollo Trampling Superstition Underfoot, *Musée Carnavalet, Photo Bulloz*

a similar model to convey the idea of the republic as discord. Here she is an old crone with pendulous, wasted breasts, her skirt covered with skulls and crossbones, brandishing her brand and dagger, embraced by the viciously poised phallic snake. About her we see the guillotine and its executioner parading a severed head, the emblems of overthrown authority at her feet, the city burning around her. All her creation. Still another (fig. 95), *The Abominable Ones,* depicts a like pairing of Discord with Jacobin violence.

The visual imagery of such popular allegory could only mitigate a sense of women as beings possessed of sobriety and mind akin to men's. Thus the iconic tradition aggressively wars against awareness of women as other than Other. In the wake of events involving real armed women, riotously aroused to action, verbally and physically abusive, armed with pikes and wearing the red bonnet, such images from the storehouse of icons could only reinforce misgynous fears embedded in the cultural design. A final example is one drawn from sculpture, Chinard's small but eloquent statue of *Apollo Trampling Superstition Underfoot* (fig. 96). This work represents the Revolution itself as a Golden Age Apollo arrayed, as his classical sunburst suggests, in all of French classicism's aesthetic aristocracy. His downtrodden victim, in her nun's habit, although she has borne a heavy cross now on the ground, recapitulates centuries of ecclesiastical sculptures of the defeated and despised Synagogue, beaten into submission by Christianity. Superstition is female in her deceit, her vulnerability, but even more, as the Synagogue had been formerly, in her sheer defeatedness.

Ambivalences of style and meaning shroud the rhetoric of Revolution and prevent such allegories from operating in the simple fashion they were intended to. Emblematized in these female figures we find the traces of the men's evasion of self-knowledge. Fortified by their tradition's ancient hatreds, these representations reinforce male sexual dominance in the very midst of the struggle against hierarchy.[60] The unavowed relationship of sexuality to issues of good and evil vitiates the Revolution and moves underground, next to the Eumenides, where it gives rise to the myth of the tricoteuses, those scapegoats of Revolution.

If, as Cobb claims, a tribal war between the sexes had before the Revolution impelled women of influence to "take revenge on the former seducers of their own kind," the dominant sex was now able to reassert itself, using all its weapons, political and cultural. Putting Sade into perspective, Cobb acknowledges that it was gender conflict that produced "the principal seam of violence in eighteenth-century France."[61]

It was, then, nothing new if on October 29, 1793, a group of men in a cabaret discussing the quarrel over the Républicaines' wearing of the red bonnet described them as armed with pikes and knives, a use of their own equipment they assessed as deliberately humiliating to their sex. Roused to wrath by this fearsome vision, they predicted that like Delilahs these women would murder their mates at their most vulnerable moment, and that if such behavior as theirs were not stamped out a Catherine de Medici would rise up from their midst and enslave men.[62]

It is this fear of women's domination, which had festered through the middle decades of the century, that surfaces here in so heated a form as to inspire the retaliation that came in November, with the women's exile from the public space. What can the allegation of women's greater propensity to violence conceal in its patent absurdity? Blood guilt has been similarly charged over the centuries to the Jews as a rationale for pogrom, and the collective memory of such allegations was the precondition of the holocaust. "The others" are seen, in these tribal scenarios, as lacking fundamental human qualities. Their "lack" makes it possible to reject and despise them. But between the sexes, a wholesale condemnation of women would threaten to end all possibility of union. The effect upon women of eruptions of women-hating has both a political and a psychological (a group and an individual) dimension. They force women as a group into so defensive a posture that they may not act together, and they make each woman afraid and hence submissive toward men so as not to be identified with "them," the out-of-bounds, abhorred Maenads. When women have submitted, it has been first of all so as to survive themselves, but also so as not to destroy society. The Maenad charge is the Revolution's substitute for the batterer's stick.

There is of course something more to this. Accusations of maenadism were leveled primarily at women who were thought to challenge men's monopoly over the armaments of death. Insofar as it is true that under the prevalent gender dispensation men identify with their weapons as if they were extensions of their physical strength and their genitalia, cutting, poking, exploding into the bodies of others, defiling and killing them, the seizure of such weapons by the other sex is viewed, as it was in this case, as castration. It is the culture's form of gender accommodation that dictates this interpretation. At its limit, the resultant division of labor has tended to make death men's work, life (birth and nurture) women's. In fact, this is what the Revolution prescribed to its women and its men. This eternal return of the binary gender opposition deprived the culture of the passionate capacity of its women so as to return to its men their prized conception of their sexuality as a tool of force analogous to the pikes and cannons they were using to wage war. Representation literally placed knives in the hands of women so as to prove the ever-ready charges of treachery against them, and thus provide the warrant for men's monopoly over the wielding of arms.

Women's activity blends into their active sexuality: both are indices of indocility, hence treachery. Words, women's only real arms, emerge from this battle as equal to men's in their cogency and sharpness, hence equally to be repressed. The Goncourts, building upon J.-N. Bouilly's memoir, *Mes Récapulations,* describe Germaine de Staël as a Maenad whose words, coming from such a hideous body, could scarcely be credited as human: "a woman with leonine face, purplish, pimpled, dry of lip, coming, going, sudden in her movements and ideas, making masculine gestures, tossing off in a boy's voice a robust or inflated sentence."[63]

Michelet sexualizes counterrevolution and allegorizes it as Woman. "The marquises and countesses, the royalist actresses boldly returning to France, emerging from their prisons and hiding-places worked unstintingly to royalize Terror; they clasped the Thermidoreans to their bodies and pressed their hands toward murder, sharpening their knives to bleed the Republic."[64] The Maenads are not dead in his prose. But Maenads know no national boundaries. The men of other nations find them equally useful and summon them up. It was Carlyle who first evoked Euripides' Maenads as he described the women of October as "a maenadic host." "Sight of sights," he exclaims, "Bacchantes, in these ultimate Formalized Ages!"[65] How, in modern times, could such an eruption of presumably civilized and repressed women be possible? Carlyle's English recreation of the massed Frenchwomen seems, however, utterly benign as compared with that of German littérateurs. As Suzanne Zantop has written, for them "it is as if by devouring their gluttonous, corpulent King, the French masses had themselves, turned into a cannibal queen." The Revolution metaphorized punitively as female trespass can never have been represented in a more roundly inflated fashion than in the prose of the German Girondist, Konrad Engelbert Oelsner, printed in his "Letter from Paris" in the *Hamburg Minerva* of August 14, 1792. If he has picked up on the Frenchmen's mood, he has decidedly improved on it. "The rejoicing of the women muffles the groans of terror. They slurp with brutal lust [*Wollust*] . . . the moans of the dying, and through their mouths, a devilish drunkenness mocks the last quivers of agony." He concludes with this overview of women's impact:

> And though it disgrace all womankind, I must say that it is the women who, in all the stormy scenes of the Revolution, have always been the first to invent and execute atrocities, or to incite men to commit new tortures and bloody deeds. During the night following that horrible day [August 10], they reportedly denuded themselves on the dead bodies, roasted the limbs of the killed men, and offered them as food. Even the morning after, I have seen women clawing among the dead, mutilating their limbs. This tendency toward excess was noticeable even among the educated class of women. I have always found that the weaker half of society has the greatest inclination to commit desperate and horrendous acts, and I could abhor women, were not that very same excitability, which in an eruption of hatred and revenge transforms them into repulsive monsters, almost the sole mainspring of their virtue.[66]

Repeating aloud to his distant readers the whispers he has heard, Oelsner moves effortlessly from the women's atrocities to an indictment of their entire sex as the bloodier of the two.

A sketchy allegorical drawing of the Terror (fig. 97), thought to be by Prud'hon, brings together various levels of the Maenad syndrome. The Revolution is seated on her pedestal in the Place de la Nation. A powerfully muscled female figure, her curls are modified versions of the serpents of Medusa. The flailing male figure upon her knees is the Nation, whose manhood Robespierre vainly protects with

*97. Attributed to P.-P.
Prud'hon,* Allegorical
Drawing of the Terror,
*Bibliothèque Nationale,
Photo Giraudon/Art
Resource, New York*

his outstretched arm as the beautiful, wrathful virago tears at his hair. Below lie
Revolution's victims, the martyred statesman, the decapitated trunk and random
heads, and the nubile, full-breasted women with their innocent children. Bonaparte prepares his entry at right. Revolution, her force unleashed, finds her ultimate representation as a murderous, wicked mother, tearing out the entrails of
her helpless son. Her empowerment means slaughter. The myth of the Maenads
was not gratuitous: it allowed men to emerge virtually unscathed in their own
eyes in the wake of massacre.

Chapter

9

CARITAS AND THE REPUBLIC: IMAGERIES OF THE BREAST

Is it to men that nature confided domestic care? Did she give us breasts to feed our children?

CHAUMETTE

THE skein of meaning surrounding the word *sein* in the French language lends substance to the value the Revolution (following the tendency of the eighteenth century, as the polemics over breast-feeding show) placed on the female breast. The Latin *sinus* is its sinuous origin, deriving from the S shape, concave/convex of the anterior body. Signifying at once the generalized human breast, site of the heart and lungs, and in the plural, the twin female organs of lactation, the sein is also the uterus, the place in the mother's body where the gestated infant grows. By extension it may also denote the core, or the center, or the heart even of abstraction, as in *au sein du bonheur,* at the heart of happiness. A *mamelle,* on the other hand, is nothing but a mammary gland, a female primary sex characteristic. An according uncertainty hangs over our readings of the representations of the breast that feature so impressively in French Revolutionary iconography and discourse. One thing we do know: this preoccupation was no innovation at the turn of the nineteenth century. On French soil the association of the female breast with magic is of very ancient lineage. At Le Combel, Pech Merle, just outside the original entry to the inner sanctum of a cave dating from approximately 15,000 B.C. is a stalactite in the exact form of the human female breast, which has been circled in red to mark it as a holy relic, and the inside of the cave holds an "amazing wreath of stone breasts." [1]

What is in question in a given representation in this era of the female breast? Is it given as a sexual appendage, there to titillate, or a maternal one? Is it neither maternal nor sexual precisely, but a generalized attribute of female ideality? Or if the maternal function is evoked, is it in virtually theological vein, to represent a primal natural harmony, a revolutionary synecdoche for the Virgin Mary? The breast is a floating signifier. Even marian iconography is marked by indeterminacy. Margaret Miles claims it "allowed a variety of interpretations, the most explicit of which focused on the Virgin's milk as a nourishing and cleansing substance through which nourishment passed not only to the infant Christ, but to all humankind. Mary was known as Mater omnium and nutrix omnium. Her milk was also the basis of her power to intercede for sinners."[2] In a period obsessed with food scarcity, the attempt to find a surrogate figuration for the Virgin's appeal is easily understood. For a Revolution that frequently speaks a rhetoric of national re-generation, to engender an image of purified maternity is to remain true to its own logic. But the breasts, being sexual organs as well as maternal ones, are, as Marina Warner has put it, "both sacred and polluting."[3]

So the Maenad factor is not so unrelated to the imagery of the breast as we might believe. A verse repeated by Père Duchesne catches up the mix of anacreontic bawdiness and gallic disgust with free-and-easy women.

> These women so scary
> Feed one and feed all
> From miraculous teats
> At a vast public feast
> And the liquid goes flowing
> The dread crowd a-growing
> It's not milk at all, but blood.[4]

Intarissables mamelles, magic teats that never go dry, may yet be wicked, profligate breasts, emitting blood. From the breasts of the tricoteuses, the people suck evil. Such flowing breasts are out of control, implying that their possessors were hideously oversexed, thus polluting their maternal function. A seemly yet coy contemporary sculpture by Clodion (fig. 98) extends the complications. It shows us two subdued Maenads with a greedy satyr who presses the breast of one of them as the other holds out a cup. Here the breast is erotic, and in that sense the work is purely rococo. The dionysiac implication is that the breast of the compliant Maenad will secrete wine. Sometimes emitting wine, sometimes blood, sometimes water, sometimes its own magic milk, the breast is the site of amazing secretion. Freud's principle of interchangeability of substances must be invoked here. Sexual secretions are caught up in the web of holiness and profanity. A site of conflict and at the same time of utopian dreams, the breast has long been the source of male fantasies of awe, and hence of incorporation.

98. Claude-Michel Clodion, Maenads with Satyr, *copyright the Frick Collection, New York*

99. Hapi, God of the Nile, *c. 1342* B.C., *Gift of Edward W. Forbes, Courtesy, Museum of Fine Arts, Boston*

Some ancient cosmologies feature the cow as Mother of All, creator of the universe. "With a flick of her udder, the horned moon cow creates the starry firmament; out of her flows the Milky Way in an abundant, never-ending stream. She gives birth daily to the life-giving sun."[5] The cult of the cow, usually occurring in ancient societies where cattle were raised, was tied to the worship of a Mother Goddess, like Egypt's Hathor. An image of a male god of the Nile (Hapi, ca. 1342 B.C.), incorporates females breasts as emblems of fruitfulness (fig. 99). Adjuncts of his power, these breasts are decoratively rather than naturalistically rendered, a point we will return to. Worship of the breast apparently antedates cultural awareness of the male contribution to reproduction. As sign of fertility in male-dominated cultures, the mysteriously potent organ of "the other," the breast has been considered more representable than the phallus, site of its own magic secretion.

Later art syncretizes the female deities and/or their attributes with the male. One of the ways Egyptian art integrates the image of Hathor is to present Ameno-pis simultaneously with her. She is depicted with cow ears: he stands under her head and drinks from her udder.[6] In this manner, her powers were subsumed by the Pharoahs. In like fashion, the Lupa (whom we have glimpsed on the base of Roma's statue in David's *Brutus,* fig. 30), that heroic she-wolf who fed Romulus and Remus, Rome's founders, in their infancy in the wilderness, achieves ancestral status in that city-state. Such maternal Ur-figures as these lend the imagery of statecraft an aura of precultural protectiveness, endowing it with a borrowed ambience of authorization by nature itself.

The Politics of the Breast

A major unspoken premise of breast imagery is its appeal not for men only, but for women, whose attachment to their own sexuality is invested in them. This ambiguity is cultivated in a series of eighteenth-century French prints in which women display/examine their own breasts or a friend's (fig. 100).[7] Like the women who were attracted by Rousseau's interest in their breasts via his advocacy of lactation, women would have been subtly flattered by the semisexual attention lavished on them by Revolutionary discourse. The female breast, so anchored in our experience of intimacy—maternal and sexual—is also the most public and ideological signifier available to channel private drives, via representation, into modes congenial to power.

We have seen how Rousseau had established maternal nursing as the precondition of national regeneration in his *Emile.* Raynal's highly successful *Histoire des deux Indes (History of the Two Indies)* (1770) pursued this line. For him, proof that his savages feel no less sympathy than Europeans lies in the treatment of their children. "A mother nurses her child until four or five, sometimes six or seven years of age." Children are never scolded or beaten. Raynal connects this pliant maternalism, which he sees as sacrificial on the mother's part, to the subsequent strength and independence of sons. So close is the bond with children among them that "if a young child dies, you see its parents going to weep over its tomb, and the mother letting the milk from her breast flow out over its grave."[8] Milk and tears are the substances of human charity for Raynal, the tragically missing factor in French society.

This profound movement toward making the breast the sign of a deepening of the mother-child (and hence the family's) bond becomes omnipresent in the *épouse et mère* (wife/mother) construct. Paradoxically, it will express itself in visual forms less direct than the topos of the nursling Christ-child with his mother. A Revolutionary print celebrating Rousseau's patronage of nursing mothers (fig. 101) illustrates its hierarchization. Beneath the medallion depicting the earnest Rousseau is a funeral relief on a tomb before which a couple of mothers, both with a baby at the breast, pay tribute to their spiritual patriarch, as the infants, like putti, play with a Phrygian bonnet. On the funeral relief we find effigies of Freedom, at left with pike and bonnet, and Equality, at right with her level; at center is the multibreasted goddess of Nature receiving her tribute of incense from the nation (the beehive). Hierarchy flows earthward: the paternal philosophe is at the summit; the nation and its emblems are his tributaries; and the women and children, expressing maternal joy and connection, seated on nature's ground, here provide a humanizing but more primitive focus to the grant man's higher abstractions. Women must be content to be the happy grounding of the nation's prosperity.

A print by Monnet-Vidal (fig. 102) provides inadvertent comic relief to this subject. It too is a tribute to Rousseau, for having "delivered childhood from the cruel shackles that exposed it to the most tragic accidents." A frowning Nature is depicted as a terrain of conflict at center, as her neglected infants, at her feet, implore her to act "as a tender, feeling mother"; meanwhile, blind Human Pride, "indignant at seeing his prejudices abolished, wants to oppose the benefits she is about to bestow on her young." Seizing mother Nature by her long locks, he tramples on the belly of an infant "to designate the part of his body that he plans especially to overwhelm with odious bondage" (a reference to the starvation of wet-nursed babies). But Virtue, with her scepter, chases Pride away, as naked Truth dissipates the clouds. In the distance at left is Rousseau's tomb. The value of this print lies in its portrayal of the mother's allegiance as the subject of a struggle whose outcome is at issue.

M.-J. Chénier and C. Dusausoir were the editors of the official handbook of Jacobin prayers and rituals for the temple services of the new republican faith. They cite as their precedent for ritual the Romans' worship of agriculture, in the person of the goddess Palès, by young farmers thronging to her sanctuary. "There, with satisfaction, they watched shepherdesses crowned with flowers, presenting the milk they had prepared for the goddess."[9] The conclusion Chénier and Dusausoir tirelessly press upon women is this: "Reflect, citizenesses, and tell me after

100. L.-L. Boilly, Ladies in a Park, Bibliothèque Nationale, Paris

101. Rousseau, Father of Maternal Nursing, Bibliothèque Nationale, Paris

102. Monnet-Vidal, To the Memory of J.-J. Rousseau, *Musée Carnavalet, Photo Bulloz*

this description . . . which of you can lack ambition to hold the sacred title of mother?" (13). They enumerate to them the consolations the devoted wife brings to her husband: "It is in the sweetness of your union that he comes to rest from his fatigue; it is in your bosom that . . . he comes to confide his pleasures and his pains; it is to your side that he runs to find that pure solace that makes him forget his labors and reanimates his ardor in the innocent caresses of his children." It is even to their tenderness that Chénier and Dusausoir attribute men's brilliant courage on the field of battle. "You are," they claim, in rococo but also magic language, "the greatest of all charms in life," from which "the gentling of character, purity of morals, and all the embellishments of society flow" (13–14). This line of propaganda to women blends rococo seductiveness with implications of women's present defectiveness and promises of power and honor in men's lives, confirmed in the milky ritual, should they conform.

An amazing speech by C. Du Laurent, entitled "The Good Mother," is also featured in this work aspiring to scriptural authority. It brings back into mind all the debates on the fallen birthrate and wet-nursing as it thunders prescriptively:

> Ah! why when maternity offers so many attractions can there be beings so denatured as to forget their primary duties and scorn its charms? How many mothers have we seen who commanded that infants they have just borne be taken out of their sight! Happily these monsters are rare on this earth, and the laws are there to avenge nature!
>
>   No, you will not be abandoned by all, you poor infants! The fatherland has heard your tender cries; for us it has become a second mother: the tree of liberty has spread its branches above you; it will cover your cradle with its hospitable shade. (60)

In this fatherland, wicked mothers will be punished by the privation of their babies' smiles. May you be struck down by sterility, is Du Laurent's curse, "may the precious germ of fecundity . . . dry up and perish! may you know of love, if ever love can enter your hearts, only its torments, its fury and its remorse" (61). A naked statement of sexual rage and jealousy is rare in a semiofficial document. Du Laurent positively proclaims popular wrath against "unmotherly" women and announces his emotional and sexual demands in men's name and the nation's upon its women. Since the laws would expressly forbid women all forms of public participation, they must place their pride and their (mitigated) pleasures in the satisfaction of their spouses and their young: for this is what the Nation-as-Mother orders them to do.

A last sampling of maternalist propaganda from this work is the poem of "The Wicked Mother" (La Marâtre). In its manipulations of women's consciences we see how the maternalist line operates less in the interests of children than in behalf of men themselves. Here the primary target is "selfish" women, given over to the frivolous pleasures of a corrupting luxury, who "forget . . . the sweet task of nurs-

ing" and "abandon to a mercenary bosom the fruit they had carried" (140). The
rage of the eighties against errant mothers continues unabated into the depths of
the age of Jacobin supremacy. The author of this piece plainly acts out a vendetta
against his own mother on the political plane that today might be resolved on the
analyst's couch. The sons of neglectful mothers like his own, when they return
home from strangers' hands at the age of puberty, are punished for the slightest
peccadillo in the paternal manse, even though the fault really lies with their mothers for providing so defective an education to their own sons (140–141). This is
but the prelude: the poem itself begins with a Hamlet-like lamentation addressed
to God.

> Could you have foreseen in mother's breast
> Her wild desire would come to rest?
> That out of this infernal fire
> A murderous poison would distill?
> A father sucks, his entrails fill . . . (142)

A monster vomited out of hell, this mother "degrades love, marriage, and nature
and profanes society." Of course I do not argue that no mother ever deserved such
rage. What fascinates here is the apparent authorization given to this seemingly
private wrath in so public and official a forum. A species of official sanction,
bespeaking wider consensus, bathes this orgy of vindictiveness against maternal
remissness, which is seen as sexual profligacy and felt as a deep betrayal of men's
affective needs and consequently a fundamental cause of their own evils.

> When your son is guilty, do you dare complain?
> Had your maternal care but formed his heart,
> Had he not learned from you the odious arts of deceit,
> Finally, if only your tenderness had banished his errors
> No doubt he would not now fear your presence. . . . (145)

Your children deny you the sainted name of mother, wish you dead, the poem
concludes.

So prevalent is the good-mother/bad-mother dichotomy that it is richly internalized by women: we find its pieties expressed by them ad nauseam. A letter of
a citoyenne to a friend speaks of the moment of becoming a mother and receiving
"this sacred title, the fairest title to a woman"; she will "press that cherished object
to her breast . . . and fill it lavishly with a nourishing and healthful milk." Echoing
Raynal, she writes that she will never hand it over to a stranger. "Such cruelties
will sully only the most barbarous of peoples; must it be, ah! can it be that in a
gracious, feeling, enlightened Nation we find so many . . . of them!" Echoing this
sense of national mission, the citizenesses of Avallon write, "As mothers we swear
to work unrelentingly to make our children cherish the constitution. . . . If until

now Frenchwomen have only created children, from this Revolution forth, they will create nothing but men." Marie Martin will proclaim, "Happy are women who give children to the fatherland, and pressing these tender fruits of conjugal love in their arms, make them suck in with their mother's milk the great principles of equality, a burning love for country and for liberty, and an inviolable devotion to the Constitution, with their mother's milk."[10] The women accept that the conditions laid before them for having sexual and maternal fulfillment involve these rituals of self-abnegation, including the fiction that their espousal of their role will bring into being a nation of courageous, democratic, liberty-loving men.

Some of the most militantly feminist of the women, as well as the men, too, resort to the rhetoric of maternalism, to shore up their own appearance of respectability.[11] Claire Lacombe warns family women not to follow her own lead in placing herself at the nation's disposal to defend it, addressing "you mothers of families whom I would find blameworthy if they left their children to follow my example," and adjures them to teach their children the love of liberty. Etta Palm cleverly recommends that women be entrusted with the organization of wet-nursing. "Ah! how essential it is that a maternal eye should oversee this administration whose guilty neglect makes nature tremble."[12] But on the whole, women's own discourse—it is, after all, the reflection of a literate class—uses maternalism to make more sweeping claims for women's abilities as guardians and educators. Women attempt to exploit the obsession with biological maternity as an opening wedge so as to break out of the narrower role prescribed to them, to find a broader, less constricted vision of their contribution to the state. At least equally poorly mothered (and fathered) as were the men, the women tend to fix their own critique of women only rarely on their maternal failings, and far more often on their frivolity, their immorality, or the poverty of their educations.[13]

This official maternalism looks within, to the family's bodily intimacies, to reinforce its internal exchanges of food and semen; it also looks without to the nation, and demands a parallel purification from egoism and a tightening of national bonds through women's approval, which, paradoxically, cannot be dispensed with even if it has to be coerced. Etta Palm repeats the double injunction. "It is right that women . . . should pay their tribute to France's regeneration; it is up to them to revive the morality of early childhood; it is up to them to see to it that this Revolution, to which their sex has contributed so much, is cherished and blessed by all." She recommends to women that they take on the care of their poor sisters and their lazy, frivolous ones: "To be mates of reborn Frenchmen, free men, we need patriotism, modesty, and virtue."[14]

Spurring himself on to an eloquent expansiveness, L. P. Dufourny, president of the Department of Paris, gave ample voice in a poster to what was probably a lavish personal expression of a popular view on June 30, 1793, in the midst of discussion over the role of the CRRW. We notice that he does not address himself to them, but to the whole of their sex.

Républicaines, in place of those vapid tributes made to degraded and servile beings, to slavish pleasures, to romantic phantoms, to languishing suitors and the sighs of the eternal seraglios of slave peoples among whom the sex vegetates, prefer the admiration of the only nation of free men; they restore their courage and bestow the crown of love only on those who've earned the civic crown. Republican wives and mothers, their hearth cannot contain the overflow of their affection. They sacrifice their pleasures to the nation.

Then he apostrophizes women directly, describing the national division of labor by sex.

Courage, Citizenesses, the Magistrates of the People recognize the Magistrates of nature; they confirm that power of persuasion she has given you; they place under the Law's protection that mission that comes to you both from your passions and your virtues. Sex insatiable in desire, sex impregnated with an immensity of love, no, your heart does not lie when it is never satisfied, and if when overcome with pleasure it sighs still for more, it is because it is telling you: Mothers of one generation, you are yet mothers of generations to come, their lives exist in you, and from the depths of your soul these generations already lay claim to your love; they make you feel you were born to prepare their happiness.[15]

The Revolution's gender perplexities transpire through Dufourny's incoherent prose. Scornful of rococo gallantries, as are the women he addresses, he yet can find no other register at the start than elaborate rococo compliments to women, who will "present the crown of love." In her role as arbiter of virtue, woman will throw off rococo servility and become worthy of the companionship of free men. As he moves into more properly republican rhetoric, in place of a tone of petition, he takes on an entirely hortatory tone, telling women what they are, what they must do. Here he lapses into an almost comical psycho-biologism, relating each woman's putative and dread sexual insatiability to a multiple maternal potential such that she disappears into a metaphoric sea of births. His text smacks of an extension into cosmic dimensions of pre-Oedipal object-relations needs, the infant demanding absolute maternal fealty, while suspecting the mother of unbridled sexual lusts that might tear her away from him. A spiritual bind is placed upon women, as keepers of the flame, to be the members of the French national family ultimately responsible for maintaining social coherence.

An embarrassed quasi-religiosity sometimes bathes attitudes to the breast. We glimpse it in Harmand's account of that moment in Charlotte Corday's trial after the witnesses had testified, but before the defendant had reread or signed her name to the record. As Harmand tells it, Chabot was interrogating her off the record, hoping for some revelation. He noticed a paper folded in her cleavage and made an abrupt gesture to get it; the movement she made to prevent Chabot's gesture made her pull her shoulders back so precipitately "that the pins and strings came out or broke completely, so that [her breast] was completely uncovered, and despite the immediacy with which she curved her chest and bent her head to her knees, she was nonetheless seen." Harmand was moved to comment, "What a situation! . . . I owe it to justice to state that, however susceptible some of those present might have been, none of them abused the situation; no untoward words were spoken, there were no sidelong glances, nor any gesture that decency might condemn."[16] No women being present, she turned to the wall and repaired the damage herself. But the observer Harmand entirely lost the thread of her testimony.

The virgin breast is of course the most promising, hence most protected, of them all. By contrast, the breast presumed to be the most sexualized is the most evil one. The rope-dancer Mme Saqui reports that as she was traveling down the rue St. Antoine her carriage was stopped by a crazed-looking mob of men emerging from the rue des Ballets. One of them carried on the tip of his pickaxe a bloody head upon which the hair hung down in sodden plaits; another, a coal man, displayed at the end of a stick a trophy with some shreds of a blouse. A few moments before, the Princess de Lamballe had been massacred.[17] Whether the trophy was Lamballe's breast or not matters little: the fact is that Saqui and others thought it was, and that the princess had been punished where she was presumed to have sinned.

The Breast in Visual Representation

We have witnessed the good breast in the print of Rousseau as Father of Maternal Nursing. Considering how ceaselessly women's duty to nurse is invoked, the yield of actual images of breast-feeding women is surprisingly spare. In fact, the solitary allegorical figure effectively sidelines the mother and child. That latter image would have been difficult to salvage as a non-Christian image at this moment of struggle against Catholicism, even for those of the Revolution's image-makers inclined to try. One of those we do find (fig. 103), a political allegory, features the good-breast/bad-breast struggle between the phallic anti-Mother, Envy, who tries to topple Necker, loosing the venom of the snakes circling her waist and arm against him, and Love, the nursing mother, protected by the angel of Glory. Necker's name will be inscribed in the temple of Memory by their efforts, despite Envy's vicious casting of her spell. Her pendulous breasts with phallic nipples and her Medusa-like hair, features we have seen previously in images of Discord, are death-dealing characteristics of goddess imagery far beyond the borders of France, as we see in a nineteenth-century copper sculpture (fig. 104) of Kali, the devouring Indian goddess of destruction. Of course the European print retains its suave fluency in the representation of Envy's body, but it incorporates all the elements of evil of the Indian avatar except the signs of sexual avidity: the

A L'IMMORTALITÉ

103. Necker, In Spite of Envy Your Name Will Rise to Glory, *Musée Carnavalet, Photo Bulloz*

104. Kali, nineteenth century, southern India, Victoria and Albert Museum

protuberant eyes and tongue, the stylized, snake-like hair, the extended arms, the energetically poised knees, readying to strike, the phallic snakes about the arm and waist. The very postures of the strong, active Envy and the languidly nursing prostrate Love, hiding her eyes, convey their prescriptions for good and bad female comportment.

Thoroughly grounded in medieval iconic tradition, the popular print *Harpy, Monstrous Living Amphibian* (fig. 105), circulated in the 1780s by Marie-Antoinette's enemies, was supposed to be a representation of her. The legend informs us that the twelve-foot-long beast, presumably discovered in Chile's Lake Fagua, has "a face like a man's, a very large mouth, . . . and two bull's horns, a donkey's ears, and a long mane like a lion's. It has two breasts like a woman's, bat's wings, and only two fat, short paws, each armed with five horned claws." Scaly below the waist, hairy above, this hugely carnivorous beast (consuming an ox and several pigs a day) is described as having been brought by slow stages to Europe to be

105. Harpy, Monstrous Living Amphibian, *Bibliothèque Nationale, Paris*

Harpie Monstre Amphibie Vivant

presented to the king. "The natives . . . say they have seen the female, and the viceroy has given orders to seize it so as to propagate the race in Europe." Presumably, then, this Harpy is not the female? Like traditional effigies of Satan, it has attributes of both sexes. But no, of course it comes across as female despite the text's pursuit of the masculine gender of the *Monstre*: everything about her is a distillate of the conventions of female monstrosity. Particularly the prominent, very humanoid, bearded breasts and belly of the Harpy, redolent of a fruitful, maternal fullness and roundness, provide a focus of shock in this monstrous context. If we read her head, with its fangs, as a hairy vagina dentata, and her grasping tail as another allusion to her snakelike nether parts, she emerges as one of the more astonishing pieces of misognynous imagery of the Age of Enlightenment. This representation totally outflanks its presumed target, the queen, to embrace Woman.

Two visions of the good breast attract our attention: the first is purely maternal, the second an abstraction. *Nature* (fig. 106) gives us a placid nursing mother feeding a black and a white infant, expressing the equality of the races as well as the rootedness in nature of this somewhat doll-like allegorical figure surrounded by fruit and sheaves of wheat. This image of her gift of her milky breasts to the egalitarian objectives of the state attempts to harmonize body and principle together in an apparent naturalness and fulfillment. Her face emptied of expression, her eyes focused within, Nature gives placid, mindless assent to her maternal function. She is a dream of acquiescent womanhood. An entirely symbolic avatar of the good breast, abstract and allusive, appears in a silhouetted allegory of Reason (fig. 107) with the Namibian lion as headpiece. Reason's breast is covered by a masonic eye of vigilance (a substitute for the nuturant nipple), surrounded by its radiance. This masonic symbolism makes the breast more than a vegetative bodily part suggesting bodily repletion: it becomes a site of widsom and intimates a relationship between these two notions.

By far the most difficult of all revolutionary breast iconography to account for are those "mysterious images of multibreasted nature" that so puzzled Ernst Gombrich.[18] Many-breasted mother figures are an ancient form, found as far distant as the Near East and in Mexico: the Mexican goddess Mayauel, for example, was dubbed "the woman with the four hundred breasts."[19] The Great Mother's reign is again reflected in such images.

However, the direct, classical origin of the multibreasted figures we find in the Revolution lies in the Diana of Ephesus, a Lady of the Beasts (fig. 108). Combining elements of the representation of Good and of Evil, this goddess, worshiped from India to the Mediterranean, began her symbolic odyssey as a beast, only later evolving into a goddess in human guise. At first she appears as an animal—cow, swamp-bird, ewe, lioness, or she-wolf—often, like Marie-Antoinette, as Harpy, bearing the fish-tail of the mermaid. Erich Neumann regards Artemis (Diana) as a "goddess of the 'outside,' of the free wild life in which as huntress she dominates the animal world." He sees her functioning as a projection of her role as "ruler

La Nature

106. Nature, *Musée Carnava-let, Photo Bulloz*

de Vinck

107. Reason, *Bibliothèque Nationale, Paris*

over the unconscious powers that still take on animal form in our dreams—the 'outside' of the world of culture and consciousness." But the second century's Diana is a benignly visaged static figure, trussed like a mummy in hieratic posture, swathed in rows of pendulous breasts that extend to her hips, and covered below and above with small beasts, presumably images of those sacrificed to her cult. She is at the antipodes from the strolling, cool, uncapturably free moon-goddess huntress of classical antiquity. Neumann raises the core issue presented by the recurrence of the multibreasted figures: "whether the duration of a culture or of one of its rituals corresponds to a living psychic reality, or is merely a consequence of the conservative tendency of mankind to cling to rituals that have long become atavistic." [20]

The Revolution's translations of Diana's multiple breasts spring from two sources. Piranesi's title page (fig. 109) of his *Diverse Means of Adorning Highways* (1769), mainly a pattern book for mantlepieces, with texts published in French, English, and Italian to appeal to an international market, had, in the climate of antiquarian mania, an immediate impact.[21] Its design features four decorative steles strongly reminiscent of the Ephesian Diana (having about the same ratio of breasts to beasts as decorative elements). Certainly Revolutionary artists who adapted her figure were acquainted with Piranesi's work. Ann Hope has explored a different source, to show that the figure of Nature in the 1778 edition of Cesare Ripa's *Iconology* illustrates changes wrought in that figure, precisely by the neo classicizing movement. Whereas Nature had been shown in editions of Ripa from various countries in 1643, 1669, 1709, and 1764 as a naturalistically posed, normally two-breasted female figure, she emerges in the 1778 London edition as a rigid, multibreasted stele (fig. 110) of the Diana of the Beasts. Gravelot and Cochin's *Iconography* of 1791 portrays as nursing mothers Charity, Education (whose flowing milk is "the emblem of spiritual food"), and Fecundity, who, like our Nature (fig. 106), nurses two babes at once. Nature, too, is a naked woman with only two breasts. But the text adds, "Mother of all beings, it is she who feeds them, which is the meaning of the milk we see flowing from her breast. It is according to this notion that antiquity showed her covered with breasts and surrounded by the different beasts that she produces." It is Earth, in Gravelot and Cochin, who is depicted as a species of Cybele with a horn of plenty and "a prodigious quantity of breasts, emblem of her fertility."[22]

How do these elements seep into Revolutionary iconography? *Mortals Are Equal—It Is Not Birth but Only Virtue That Makes for Difference* (fig. 111) proclaims a tribute to the decree of May 15 emancipating the slaves in the colonies. The inscription beneath tells us that Reason, holding the decree of the Declaration of the Rights of Man and crowned with the sacred flame of love, is placing her level over the heads of Black and White, as Nature, with fourteen breasts, sits on a leather gourd from which the demons of Aristocracy, Egoism, Injustice, and Disorder are violently expelled. Here we find that rather frequent division of func-

108. Diana of Ephesus, *Museo Nazionale, Naples*

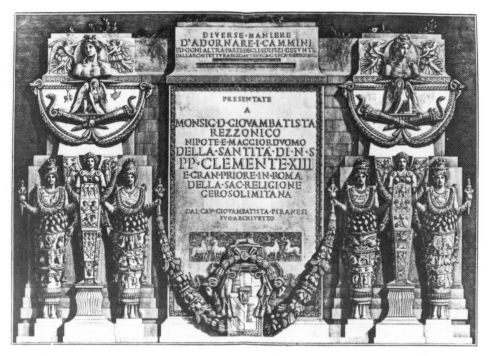

109. Giovanni-Battista Piranesi, Diverse Maniere d'adornare i cammini . . . , *frontispiece, 1767, Photo Library Company of Philadelphia*

tions between goddesses: Reason, serene and chastely covered, and Nature, disheveled and bestialized by her multibreastedness, combine forces to bring about a "natural" state, equality. The ancient association of multibreastedness with beasts is sustained by the hated monstrous symbols escaping from beneath her. Multibreasted Nature, and Reason, stand as forces outside of history, applying natural law to bring change to men.

A similar split between goddess figures, one stolid, the other active (fig. 112), recurs in *Philosophy Uncovering Truth.* Under the aegis of the bust of Rousseau, whose *Social Contract* and *Emile* are the Truth uncovered, we face the ambiguity of an energized female allegory holding aloft her torch, while in the corner the tiny, trapped, multibreasted effigy, a pallid emanation of a once-powerful ancient goddess, sits, checking the idea of female action with her reminder of women's underlying identity, as beings with breasts.

The multibreasted figures are perhaps a visual assurance that whatever our unconscious insatiability at our own mother's breast, whatever our jealousy at displacement from it, there is a realm of the imagination where a breast exists for all. Revolutionary representations of Equality call up this inviting association. In them the breasts are chaste, repeatable, decorative appendages, virtually stripped of reference to Diana's imperious biological mystery, or so it would seem. In the

110. Cesare Ripa, Iconology or Collection of Emblematical Figures . . . , *1778, plate 53, no. 202*

111. Mortals Are Equal—It Is Not Birth but Only Virtue That Makes for Difference, *Bibliothèque Nationale, Paris*

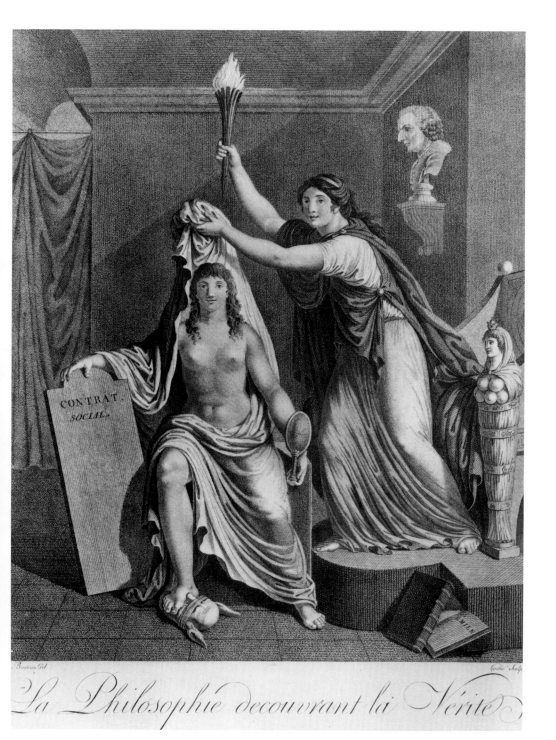

La Philosophie découvrant la Vérité

112. Philosophy Uncovering Truth, *Musée Carnavalet, Photo Bulloz*

Moitte-Janinet work (fig. 113) the monstrosity for moderns of the concept of the too-well-endowed Diana is countered by a hieratic figure whose own large, spherical breasts are, though carefully draped, still prominent. Again, the allegorical figure shares the scene with her attribute, a small multibreasted icon of fecundity with her fruited cornucopia. Another example of Equality (Rougemont-Allais, fig. 114) gives us a more chaste, classicized, and still vision of that goddess whose own breasts are draped in gentility. She leans serenely on the twin steles of fuller figures of Diana than the others, each dropping breasts like huge tears below their own two firm ones, from their strong bodies. From these pillar attributes, ostensibly fertile attributes of Equality's generosity, no breath of passion, neither love nor hate, emanates. They serve purely to reinforce an ancient warrant for seeing equality in terms of equal maternal nurturance.

We have long since come to believe that the creation of visual materials is impelled by laws internal to its own nature. The seizure of multibreastedness by Revolutionary artists from wider neoclassical trends certainly follows this tendency. But in the context of the breast fetish of the time, it necessarily takes on added significance. These multibreasted figures are overblown images, intrinsically alarming to women as well as men, in that they allude—even when stylized to exquisite dropletlike symmetry—to the repetitive nature of the mammaries of lower animals. Indeed Rousseau had discussed the number of mammaries in various species in evolutionary terms because of his desire to categorize humans as a vegetable- rather than a meat-eating species: "While mares, cows, goats, deer, and humans have two, cats, dogs, she-wolves, tigresses have six or eight." Darwin would later consider the "not very rare" phenomenon of supernumerary mammae in women and attribute it to reversion. Both sets of remarks reveal a male "scientific" concern with breasts as evidence of female linkage with the animal realm. Breasts are the salient evidence that women are cultural misfits, as compared with the norm, the flat-chested sex. This objectifying tradition would sustain its fascination beyond politics. Flaubert, for one, retains a remembrance of the Diana in cultural memory in his *Temptation of St. Anthony*. "Lions crouch upon her shoulders; fruits, flowers, and stars cross one another upon her chest; further down three rows of breasts are displayed, and from belly to feet a sheath enfolds her out of which bulls, stags, griffins, and bees sprout fourth."[23]

In propagandistic images like the ones just reviewed, multibreastedness neutralizes the power of primary female allegorical figures by their discreet decorative reference to female fecundity. Not intrepid goddesses representing untamed powers, but emblems of a wild maternity contained, the multibreasted figures confirm the subordination of women's fertility to a masculine, statist project. And yet such repeated deployment of these figures, as well as the harvest of good and bad breast imagery, points not only to repression by co-optation of women's biological power, but to its reverse, to its expression. It must be seen that the Revolution, even as it eventually suppresses this goddess cult, flirts with embracing it. Overthrow of the French monarch called up a more sentient icon as substitute for the

113. *Moitte-Janinet*, Equality, *Bibliothèque Nationale, Paris*

114. *Rougemont-Allais*, Equality, *Bibliothèque Nationale, Paris*

La Fontaine de la Régénération

Sur les Débris de la Bastille, le 10 août 1793.

115. The Fountain of Regeneraton, *Bibliothèque Nationale, Paris*

inadequate father: the body of a kindly mother, ultimately too disbelieved in to be viable, was nevertheless proposed, for a time, as a figure capable of conveying ideas of clemency and unity.

The work that expresses the essence of Revolutionary men's wish fulfillment fantasy of the feminine is the Fountain of Regeneration (fig. 115), already alluded to as one of the stations erected for the Fête of Unity and Indivisibility on August 10, 1793, staged by David and the composer Gossec. A huge statue of an Egyptian Hathor, seated between her two mastiffs, was erected, from whose breasts—chastely covered by her crossed arms—streamed the milk (we recall it was merely water) of rebirth. The propagandistic Monnet-Helmann print of the occasion shows us the immediate benefactors of her largesse, the distinguished legislators of the state, lined up before her, to make symbolic consumption of her bounty.

An aura of serene matriarchy hovers over this ritual, with its flaming torches, which flank the goddess. The French nation's seizure of nurturance is enacted by this scene. Yet for modern times, such an unwontedly huge effigy was, though not hideous, monstrous. Hathor, hieratically enthroned, is a dehumanized, remote figure whose nurturant gesture is carefully restricted to the Republic and its aims. Despite its ostensible obeisance to the goddess, the resort to Egyptian antiquity turns out to have been show business at its most high-toned. The hierarchy of access to the goddess's favors is plain: beyond the ranks of dignitaries stands a ring of soldiers with pikes; outside are the people, arrayed as nuclear families. A mother nursing her child sits on the stones fallen from the Bastille at center left; a mother with her young child points up at the marvel in the center foreground; two star-struck maidens kneel at far right. Such women as these presumably would have been well prepared for Hérault de Séchelles's official speech to them at the second station, a triumphal arch recalling the women's October march. "O women! liberty attacked by tyrants needs a people of heroes to defend it. It is for you to give them birth. Let every martial and generous virtue flow with your mother's milk into the hearts of the infants of France! The peoples' sovereign representatives offer you, instead of a flower to ornament your beauty, the laurel, emblem of courage and victory. You will transmit it to your children."[24] Even here, Hérault displaces his tribute to the woman from the despised rococo flower to a laurel meant not for her, but for her (male) children. In its drive to make a figure of nurturance into a symbol of the Nation Indivisible, Frenchmen had ignored the fact that nurture, like freedom itself, cannot be wrested from or imposed upon a people. The hierarchy enclosing Hathor ensured that her reign would be that of a day.

The sheer sterile aridity of this derivative, trumped-up breast imagery, divorced from its real subtexts both of transcendence—the ties linking sex, birth, death, and eternity—and of the warmth of fleshly human affinities, mark it as a fetishistic phenomenon. In the midst of the Jacobins' struggle to assert human equality, its men insisted to the last on the premise that signs of otherness can be exploited to express an ideal. A desperate insistence on the repetition of the forms of sexual dimorphism of other ages characterizes its major representations. The Revolution divorces the breast from its context; that is, from women's powers of intention, heart, and mind. The Revolutionaries' preoccupation with the breast is the indicator of a gender split in the new republican mentality so deep as to defy repair. Women's foreignness to republican culture was reified by its representation.[25] Increasingly locked into repetitive verbal and visual structures, by the era of Thermidor the new French political culture had definitively thrown away all grounds for anything akin to parity between women and men, even in difference.

Pursuant to this drama of suppression of the female principle by cooptation, breast imagery would revert to its male supremacist rococo norm, but with a Revolutionary flavor. The popular image of *Republican France Offering Her Breast to All Frenchmen* (fig. 116) is a democratic pinup. Despite her Phrygian bonnet and her level, with her glazed expression and eloquent breasts she proclaims nothing so much as Frenchmen's equality of sexual opportunity. Her wearing of the emblems of freedom and equality is a joke on her: she is reduced to her breasts. Of child nurturance there will henceforth be little more loud governmental talk. It recedes into conduct books for the consumption of a mainly female audience. The figuration of the breast has come home: a sign of universal charity no more, it has been restored as an adjunct to male eroticism.

LA FRANCE RÉPUBLICAINE.

Ouvrant son Sein à tous les Français.

Se vend à Paris chez les Citoyens Gamble & Corfel, Maison des Citoyens Arthur & Robert au le Boulevard, au coin de la rue des Piques.

116. *Boizot-Clement,* Republican France Offering Her Breast to All Frenchmen, *Bibliothèque Nationale, Paris*

Perhaps the earlier thundering movement to purification via the agape of maternal nursing was only a stratagem to bring about a less vexed tenor to men's sexual attitudes to women, in which children had never been anything but counters in the sex war. In the battle between nurture and eros, eros, now travestied as Domesticity, was victorious.

After Thermidor, despite the demise of the Jacobins, the regime of compulsory female conjugality was firmly in place, as it had been tending to become since well before the Revolution: the épouse et mère (wife-mother) was relentlessly installed as the sole acceptable ideal for women.[26] Of course many women, beginning with the Directorate, would subvert this edict in every way they could. But its grasp on the consensus remained strong, even as some of the imprisoning traditional imagery summoned up to buttress statism slowly receded.

A 1796 image attacking Babeuf's conspiracy of 1795 (Year V) (fig. 117) reiterates the age-old formula. France, as a "young, vigorous nursing mother, admires

117. Babeuf's Conspiracy, Year V (1795), Musée Carnavalet, Photo Bulloz

the Constitution," but "jealous, furious Anarchy, advised by an astute serpent," is about to plunge her poiniards "into the heart of the Nation." Fortunately, the Genius of the Republic is there to run Anarchy through. The young mother, standing outside the halls of state, conveys her enthusiastic assent to the new constitution. Only the wild and phallic jealous hag with pendulous breasts, in her natural alliance with the serpent of treachery, stands between the succulent mother and her mate, the constitutional hero. That hag, the postnurturant woman who would threaten absolute male supremacy, sexual and political, is no more. The compliant young woman with her nursling, then, is restored as the locus of that infantile Rosseauian dream of fusion, while her active older mother or sister, forever seen as a site of anarchy because she has outlasted her power to evoke desire, is impaled.

The good-breast/bad-breast imagery of the French Revolution uncovers a fundamental level of politics prior to the ordering of a state. As our survey of pre-

Revolutionary trends has shown, at the level of this substratum sits the individual's infantile, unassuageable demand for an order of nurture to be guaranteed: the early Revolution still thought this might be achieved by force of government. While major tendencies within Revolutionary rhetoric played with incorporating the symbolics of nurture, with making France into the image of the *Magna Mater,* the active fear and jealously of a majority of men would operate equally to reject, mock, and demean the breast.[27] Even this fetishized breast, whether good or bad, was ultimately felt by the Revolution's men to be incapable of integration as an emblem for the essentially male republic. The Magna Mater would instead return to her ancient status as a household deity. Her reduction, like the consignment of women to private life, signified that the vast human appetite for the body's most soulful needs, for food, love, warmth, and sexual expression, would stand entirely outside society's concerns and remain the domain of women, women who were unfortunately made to remain, spiritually and materially, utterly destitute of the means of fulfilling such desperate hopes and expectations.

POSTLUDE

DURING the long rococo dominance over the courtly style of eighteenth-century France, goddesses floated through the arts, in their seemingly eternal postures as erotic goal and prize. The sheer sensuality of this art of the elite class soothed its patrons, exuding a mood of ease of access to sexuality and of rapture in possessing gracious objects, human and material. Insofar as its forms and uses expressed the gentled, civil, masculine tastes of a society whose official fable was its obsession with pleasing its women, it came to be identified with them. In that it was an art conspicuously, ostentatiously consumed, women were seen as its profligate, self-absorbed consumers, adorning their settings and themselves in its lavish creations. In that it brought the sexes together in its forms of manner and dress, it aroused homophobic dread of the monster, androgyny. Inasmuch as it was an art form bathed in the aura of delight in women's sexual favors, their obverse, the sickly softness of erotic excess, eventually would hang over rococo women's persons, as the reaction against it crystallized. That reaction embraced a neoclassical aesthetic as the core of its alternative structuring of taste and of gender. It did so in the name of a putative republican model of manly probity and simplicity of mores, which, it claimed, was entirely at odds with courtly culture's tastes and manners. And this new manly style would necessarily force the too intrusive upper-class Frenchwomen, who held so prominent a place in midcentury life, into a far more constricted space. According to the lights of the rising male elite, the retreat of women from public notoriety had become an imperative to the renewal of French society.

Within this struggle over style, unverbalized as such, lay deeper levels of discontent. Pathologies of sexual relations and of family structure were exacerbating class conflict, as we have seen in the rise of illegitimate births begun at midcentury—a result of the slackening of the Church's influence upon men and the pervasive toleration of masculine sexual prerogatives. The very sweetness of rococo conceals a sea of misery: children surrendered by default to wet nurses; forsaken by fathers, and then by mothers; uncertainties of lineage and relationship; disinherited men, and abandoned and destitute women. Among the lower classes, satisfaction with the folkloric misogynous division by gender is unsettled by the upper class's toleration of the mixing of the sexes. Taxation, the expense of war, hunger, and privation fuel not only political but interclass angers.

Reaction to counter this deeper tide of trouble begins to be deployed primarily in two arenas, those of sexuality and of parenthood. In both the drive toward renewal found expression not in the reform of the mores of society at large, but in calls for alterations in the comportment of women of all classes: in the sexual realm via the reform of prostitution; and in the society at large through the idealizing assignment to women of an exclusively mothering role within the family.

In this way, male sexual resentment against women could be mobilized to feed the class rage of the Third Estate against the others, as the sexual and emotional interests of bourgeois and progressive aristocratic men flowed together into the mainstream of the tradition's peasant and sans-culotte suspicion of women as a sex. Rage against the presumptions of "the sex," forged by Rousseau, its most eloquent spokesman, into a potent rhetorical weapon, manifested itself progressively with greater force and more open hostility, buttressed by more restrictive medical theory, as the century neared its end. But never did it prevail free of the prodding and challenges of articulate opponents of this popular misogyny, who questioned its presuppositions from an Enlightenment standpoint. This debate was clouded, however, by the continuing use by "regenerators" of the cloak of the ideal in speaking of women, whose goddess aura hung on even as they were toppled from their structural postures as rococo deities. They would argue that the reimposition of a strict separation of the sexes throughout society would enchant sexuality itself, "restore" family harmony, and bring order to problems of lineage. All of this renewal was to be in the charge of women: the spiritual superiority (like Héloïse's) of the weaker sex would be the rectifying moral force to men's rough strength, their excessive intellectuality, their martial tendencies, and their sexual impulsiveness.

The stormy concealments inherent in this pre-Revolutionary reconstruction of gender illustrate the priority of fundamental human relations over politics. Repressed in this public representation of the new sexual order are awareness of men's own sexual guilt and the rawness of their anger at women, their troubled and vulnerable object. Repressed too is a lucidity in confronting the other sex that would have allowed a more adequate account of men's relationship to women, as full individuals of their own sex whose own interests would have to be accommodated, rather than as hostile rivals, whose rise must necessarily diminish men's own fragile hold upon citizenship and sexual and moral supremacy. This is the repressed that returns in the arts and in hectic, irrational polemics before Revolution. But the Revolution itself brings on a moment of truth: which facet of male culture's treatment of women shall prevail in dealing with sexual and familial conflicts—the new reign of Reason, with its emphasis on the prior worth of each person, or a continuing repression of women's complex reality from male consciousness, in favor of regarding them as contingent beings?

The symbolic practices of the Revolution display how the weapons of neoclassical representation and the tradition's arsenal of misogynous or idealizing allegory conjoined to ensure that there could be no question of the victory of Reason. With the public space dominated by beneficent or destructive female Others, the women of the Revolution could make but little impact on the imaginary life of the French people, whose violence itself would come to be labeled as a product of female rage.

Women's role in the French nation's mental life was thus made hostage in the crisis of the nation's evolution toward modernity. In fact, the enforcement of a regime of separate sexual spheres institutionalized under Jacobinism, with the women retired from all public participation, was to prove to be perhaps the single most unalterable measure effected by Revolution, surviving all the nineteenth century's changes of regime. What did this sexual paradigm effect; how did it alter the relations of women with men? I have implied that motives of sexual supremacy ultimately predominated over paternal drives in the Revolution's final gender dispensation. A glance at its laws to test this out seems mandatory.

In the *Archives parlementaires* of December 20, 1793, in the wake of the women's order into exile from public life, they were told,

> You of the lovable and generous sex whom feeling men count among the prime gifts of nature, and whom proud impostors had dared publicly to exclude from their presence so as to profane you in secret; you, over whom they dared affect a supremacy they never had, and that they dreamed up only to be able to hide their weakness and mask their criminal objectives, you too, listen to the voice of reason. It is you alone who can make it loved and temper its austerity. Let the delicacy of your organs and feeling serve no more as instruments of fanaticism and deception; reason tells you that nature has given you its precious gifts only to make men happy, and not to make them feel guilt.[1]

A complex text; it commends itself to women as a protection against those who would ban them from the public space only to use them more stealthily in private. But it continues the litany of blame, accusing all women of deceit and irrational behavior, even as it implores them to consent in the name of a reason informed by nature to ease men's consciences by renouncing all separate identity and consenting to lend themselves to the fostering of men's satisfactions.

Diane Alstad observed that although Napoleon's 1804 Civil Code was more conservative than Revolutionary family legislation, "there is great continuity between the two."[2] But what also seems clear is that the legal diminution of women followed the course of increasing ideological pressure to limit women's separate rights. We recall that at the end of the Old Regime women living in counties subject to written law enjoyed civil capacity to contract and even, as widows or property holders, to vote in regional assemblies. The early Revolutionaries, convinced that inequalities in legacies were contrary to natural law, decreed inheritance rights for women as well as younger sons, and passed laws giving women the right to bear witness in civil cases and to contract freely.[3] These laws were passed before the summer of 1793 and the hardening of Jacobin rule. The very first project proposed by Cambacérès for what would eventually become the Civil Code in fact contained no mention of marital power and granted to wife and husband equal rights in their common property. He was caught up short by the Convention, which rejected his proposal outright; reversing course to move with the political tide, he then submitted in his third proposal the revision that although the idea of equality ought to serve "as a regulator, it . . . is not infringed if we seek to maintain natural order and avoid debates that might spoil the charm of domestic life."[4] The Napoleonic minister and architect of the Code, Jean Portalis, seconded him: "Woman needs protection because she is weak; man is free because he is stronger."[5] Legislation thus instituted the lie that men (privately) could uniformly be counted on to sustain women's lives, and that women consequently had no need for freedom.

But the Revolution, in addition to rights of inheritance and witness, also gave liberally to women and to men the right to divorce, thus enacting the philosophes' notion that marriage ought to be merely a contract between individuals. As Roderick Phillips has shown in his study of statistics for Rouen between 1780 and 1800, divorce legislation had the effect, surprising to men, of being resorted to far more frequently by women than by themselves. In the wake of the 1792 divorce law, 1,046 divorces were decreed in Rouen during the eleven years preceding the suppression of divorce by Napoleon, about one divorce for every eight marriages. Women petitioned for no fewer than 71 percent of unilateral divorces. Marital violence was the chief ground alleged by women seeking to escape marriage, with drunkenness often its spur. Men's wrath would be exercised against pregnant wives because they doubted their paternity; or they would accuse wives of neglecting the care of the household, or of consorting with other men. "Clearly men's suspicion and fear of women's sexuality is an important factor to be considered in any study of relationships between women and men at this time," writes Phillips. Buttressed by religious and cultural tradition, a husband was able to beat a wife with impunity, to make her tolerate his adulteries, and to evict her with her children.[6]

The Napoleonic legislation of 1803 allowed divorce—after all, the soon-to-be emperor would himself have use for it—but under vastly more restricted conditions. It largely restored husbands' rights in its celebrated declaration that "the husband owes protection to his wife, the wife obedience to her husband" (Article 213).[7] Under the Restoration, in 1816, divorce was to be completely suppressed, until the advent of the Third Republic. The majority of men of all the intervening regimes continued to argue, in defiance of the palpable evidence of women's dissatisfactions with marriage revealed by their own use of divorce, that the marriage contract proffered them served the wife's and the family's interests primarily, not the husband's.

In a complex impulse compounded of the desire to suppress the paternity search required by the monarchy and to recognize the rights of their illegitimate children, the Revolution's men sought to abolish all distinctions between natural and legitimate motherhood, natural and legitimate children.[8] (This probably provided the root of the popularity of the image of the mother feeding "black" with "white" infants at the breast). It was the law of November 2, 1793, passed in the wake of the queen's execution, that granted them the most generous right: that of equal inheritance with legal offspring. This most radical moment of paternal conscience found legislators at their most demanding of men as progenitors, imposing on them the greatest responsibility for the fruit of their procreative activity. The Napoleonic conservative reaction then turned resolutely away from this crisis of male conscience to enact into lasting law the most lenient of standards toward male procreative laxness, with its corollary, the harshest of regimes toward women. The latter, deprived of separate legal or economic rights, would have no ability to make men acknowledge or protect the children conceived by them. Again, this change must not be seen to have occurred without serious, if ineffective, challenge within and among the legislators. Berlier, for example, would argue that he could not "divide paternity from its results . . . and that even as there were no half-truths, there could be no half-fathers." After Thermidor, the dominant trend already opposed such demanding voices, as male opinion turned decisively against the mother left outside marriage, and her children; this at a moment of the most meltingly mawkish sentimentality toward mothers and children within its presumed embrace. Society, Napoleon is reported as saying, had no interest in the recognition of bastards. In Articles 331 and 335, the Napoleonic Code expressly forbade the legitimation or recognition of children born of adulterous or incestuous intercourse, specifically disallowed them any right of inheritance, and forbade the paternity search. Brinton concludes, "It may well be argued that in its actual working out, the Code is rather harsher towards illegitimate children than was the jurisprudence of the Old Regime."[9]

No wonder, then, that scenes like that denounced by Fouché in 1806 had become common: "a crowd of individuals from twelve to fifteen years old who know no parents, . . . almost all pickpockets, crooks." This criminal element caused Fouché to wish piously that fewer children would be born outside wedlock: but as Lanzac de Laborie points out, in Paris and even more so in its environs, "the number of seduced girls went on growing as did that of natural children."[10]

Crane Brinton was to speak in 1936 of this legal management of sexual mores in a mode now so unfashionable as to seem quaint: he wondered how much of "all this post-revolutionary legislation was based on what the humanitarians would call 'masculine prejudices.'" Even though extramarital sexuality disgraced women and not men, maternity searches *were* authorized, because the state did not intend that children be altogether unparented. But in inflicting total parental responsibility upon these mothers, it was in no way prepared to grant them the civil and economic rights that might have enabled them to assume it effectively. On the contrary, it stripped them of the few they had previously possessed. It sometimes appeared that the misogynous substratum of masculine cultural contructs was rising perilously close to the surface, close enough to be remarked upon. Brinton quotes Perreau in the 1798 debates on the Civil Code: "'Do you not really think, if you would be honest, that for one false declaration [of paternity] there would be one hundred true ones?" He continued in a feminist vein rarely heard in France: "Let us be more just toward women, and let us not always make use against them of the fear of vices whose first cause can so frequently be imputed to us men. Let us not run the risk of the reproach that laws made by men seem to have been made but for them.'" [11] Perreau's cautionary and realistic stance found little response, as the other men closed brotherly ranks in protection of their sexual privilege.

Now, Carol Pateman has written illuminatingly that the institution of the husband's conjugal rights, in modern nations claiming their legitimacy in contract theory, illustrates how "political right as sex-right is translated through the marriage contract into the right of every member of the fraternity in daily life." The Civil Code, we then see, is at once a "denial of bodily integrity to wives" within marriage, but also to all other women but male-protected virgins outside it. Pateman believes that for the sexual contract the central question is, what does it mean to be a man? Of course the question of what it will mean to be a woman is also implicated in it. The contract decrees that "the satisfaction of men's natural sexual urges must be achieved through access to a woman, even if her body is not directly used sexually." Women's essential status in this regime is to be a class accessory to men's sexual use, whatever that may be. If we accord that "the exemplary display of masculinity is to engage in 'the sex act,'" we find Frenchmen's post-Revolutionary legislation closing ranks in protection of their own sexual privilege as they inscribe it afresh in civil privilege. As in the Revolution and its aftermath, "the brothers make the agreement to secure their natural liberty, part of which consists in the patriarchal right of men, the right of one sex. Only one sex has the right to enjoy civil freedom. Civil freedom includes right of sexual access to women and, more broadly, the enjoyment of mastery as a sex." [12]

In Brinton's résumé of the debates on illegitimacy, he observes that most speakers "frankly assumed the inevitability of a certain amount of masculine wild oats, and are not unduly disturbed by the plight of the women with whom the oats are sown. . . . The brief enthusiasm of the French Revolution merely seems to have given this attitude—sometimes known as the double standard—a firmer hold on French society." But laws alone could never have achieved the scale of repression of women effected by this era. Neither could the Republican and Napoleonic wars, powerful as their martial machinery and mythology proved to be. As John Stuart Mill would write one day, women's "masters require something more from them than actual service. Men do not want solely the obedience of women, they want their sentiments. All men, save the most brutish, desire to have not a forced slave but a willing one."[13] For this to obtain, the structures of gender themselves, and of mating, would have to be changed to fit the new pattern.

We have seen how this work had gone on in literature, art, medicine, and philosophy throughout half a century. Medicine now weighs in heavily, throwing its ideological prestige into the psychological battle. The woman's body (and the man's) had been remodeled by the physicians to meet the emergent individualist patriarchal family schema. "Every female individual is created solely for the sake of propagation; her sexual organs are the root and base of her entire system, *mulier propter uterum condita est;* all emanates from this source of organization, everything in her conspires with it." Woman's very force lies in her weakness, and she must resort to the restorative qualities of sperm as a strengthening agent. A mysterious, incomprehensible being, she is so even to herself, concealing within "impenetrable abysses . . . , inextricable labyrinths of caprice, of concealment, of inconstant will." Devoid of genius, her fate may still be "brilliant," since she may, indeed must, act as arbiter of taste and is the prime adornment of man's life. But the medical theorist Virey's physical description of her as the object of love is what most impresses us: it is as "a delicate, timid, powerless being, who is as if abandoned in nature," that she "naturally softens the human heart with pity." If man must be, according to Virey's version of nature's decrees, "magnanimous, open, generous, ardent, full of courage and daring, women will be timid, modest, chaste, frugal, reserved."[14] Hardening this pre-Revolutionary decree of sexual separation, the Consulate's doctor, the *Idéologue* Cabanis is even more specific: women's "fleshly fiber is weaker, and their cellular tissue more abundant than men's. . . . This muscular weakness creates an instinctive distaste for violent exercise; it leads rather to sedentary occupations . . . and amusements." They ought to "concentrate on small objects, on detail, for they will thus acquire greater finesse and penetration rather than [masculine] intellectual range and depth." Boys must contract habits and manners *absolutely opposed* to girls', for "man must be strong, brave, enterprising; woman, weak, timid, wily. Such is nature's law."[15]

"It is not liked that she be so strong," Cabanis decides. For this physician, woman's whole life is a succession of illnesses. To be sure, some of his apprehension was not unwarranted in a time before puerperal fever and a host of other gynecological problems were well understood: but there is clearly a more profound insistence on pathology here. The slippage from physical nature to mores, and thence to intellectual prohibitions, is too marked: "If they are not content to please through the graces of their natural wit and agreeable talents, and by those social arts that they no doubt possess to a higher degree than men, and go on to seek to astonish others by shows of virtuosity that combine the triumphs of knowledge with gentler and more certain victories, then all of their charms wither."[16]

Women must not hope to inspire sexual desire in men unless they make a prior display of capitulation in powerlessness, causing men to melt into pity. They are therefore called upon by all the means of emotional suasion wielded by authority and art to internalize this structure of female desirability. Carol Blum takes us back once more to Rousseau, whose problematics of sexuality were couched in "a vocabulary of transparency, of prolonged, painfully pleasurable tension of a cease-less pull toward dissolution into another who was an idealized representation of self, a compromise between struggling against and submitting to a hypnotic fe-male domination. It was a synthesis of sensuality and moral superiority in which the self longed for an eroticized fusion that made genitality almost irrelevant." Longing, then, replaces robust lust in Rousseau's affective economy, as wave re-places particle in physics: the site of desire is diffused, so that genitality appears "almost irrelevant." The "almost" is important: we are in the presence of a subli-mation of sexuality that will invest itself far beyond the libido. "Desire causes the current to flow, itself flows in turn, and breaks the flow." In the casting about for surrogate structures to invest with sexual intensity, the welling up of feeling be-comes the locus of fixation, the surge of pity displacing the object. Pity for the beloved, the lover's tears, become the synecdoche for "streams of desire" that "flow in real streams, real physical processes, in the stream of sperm, the stream of tears." [17]

As Pateman's "new private man of the sexual contract turns inward," his public attitudes feed his newly imperative demand for the good conscience that emo-tional lability provides. Blum speaks of Rousseauesque lust as "dissociated from responsibility": the structure of passion that now commends itself generally to men through representation derives from Rousseau's confessional practices to be-come a like "paean to intention with a corollary devaluation of the significance of action." [18] For pity need imply no action, is its own reward, as sobs cease and bodily equilibrium is restored. [19]

Under the monarchy the father-king could be the dispenser of charity, of par-don, of chance boons or favors. The conception of the First Republic, a society of propertied men (contested by sans-culotte rage), comprised no mechanism of charity except legislation, an entirely impersonal, administrative mode of dispens-ing generosity, expressing nothing, even in its ameliorations. Charity is intrinsi-cally impersonal: a virtue exercised "for love of God." Pity, on the other hand, is intensely personal, even as it expresses a finite, condescending surge of emotion from the safety of the shore for those lost in the flood. Compassion is the presum-ably horizontal and democratic ability to identify across hierarchical boundaries with the sufferings of others.

Bernardin's *Paul et Virginie* on the eve of Revolution had given huge impetus to the desire-as-pity movement. [20] The storm's flood tides had engulfed the beloved, chaste girl, the embodiment of female purity, weakness, and inadequacy as much as she was the externalization of a male sense of loss and longing for escape from dire consequences in death. The Revolution that followed, with its neoclassical aesthetic, provided a hiatus in the tide of popularity of this paradigm, as pity for women came to be expressed, in David's *Horatii* and *Brutus,* chiefly by the spectacle of its negation. In his history, Michelet insists with enormous intensity that women's initial support and subsequent opposition to the Revolution were both motivated by pity.[21] This merely confirms that for him, the woman as object of desire must be drenched in the pity of which he wants her to be the living emanation, an allegorical need. But what many women themselves probably thought they were filling was the void of compassion. The mission of loving-kindness had been definitively dealt them as their share of psychic work in the decade of the *Horatii*. But in the wake of the Terror, it would be the men in representation who would assume the Romantic postures of emotional lability, as their own political power was progressively stripped from them by Napoleonic politics. And in terms of the mythology of love, such lability could best be expressed by heroic, pitying grief for the lover's loss of his object.

André Chénier, the most accomplished French poet of the time, taking a leaf from Greek antiquity, devoted numerous lyrics to the drowned beloved. Whether he speaks of Néère, who, abandoning her mother, dies in the sea on her way to join Clinias her lover, or of the Young Tarentine, drowning amid the flood in his most famous poem, Chénier bemoans the loss in the swirling waters of the young girl about to come to the marriage bed or to her union with her lover. Pain, pity, and sexuality blend in this topos that dominates the representation of longing. I quote from Klaus Theweleit:

> A river without end, enormous and wide, flows through the world's literatures. Over and over again: the woman-in-the-water; woman as water, as a stormy, cavorting, cooling ocean, a raging stream, a waterfall . . . love as a process that washes people up as flotsam, soothing the sea again.[22]

Pity and sexuality flow together in this stream, evoking the object of love only to occasion the oceanic, orgasmic welling-up of pathetic feeling for the other's self as she disappears beneath the floods.

Prud'hon's *Phrosine et Mélidor* (fig. 118) is one of the many works that allow this sexual current to surface. His version of the legend of the girl who swims afar to join her lover, only to collapse, dying into his embrace as she reaches land, combines all the elements of gothic fantasy: the dark chateau on the cliffs above, the moon capping the waves with light, the lover in his dark cape clasping the naked and fainting swimmer as he kisses the wet tress on her shoulder. What preserves this depiction from absurdity, aside from the finesse of Prud'hon's technique, is in fact its candid sensuality in the handling of the solid Phrosine's body, the insistently large, impressive heads of both lovers, the fainting of both figures together in desire. But we sense that this engulfed beloved, like the others, is made

118. *P.-P. Prud'hon,* Phrosine et Mélidor, *Biblio-
thèque Nationale, Paris*

to lose consciousness, even life, so that she may not herself know a sexuality too threatening for her lover to confront. This young-woman-as-corpse is the representational emblem of post-Revolutionary womanhood.

David is sometimes thought to have contested the consignment of women to the combined role of object of pity and dispenser of compassion in his 1796–99 painting *The Intervention of the Sabine Women* (fig. 119). Here the Sabine mothers, raped after a previous encounter with the Romans three years earlier, come with the children born to them in captivity to separate the Roman and Sabine armies as the Sabines launch their counterassault. David's own critique of his earlier espousal of the aesthetic of the *Horatii* and the *Brutus* is often seen as emerging here. Norman Bryson has delivered a powerful reading of the vision of gender he finds in this work, which I believe achieves enhanced resonance here.

> Tatius' angular or submissive pose matches and complements the taut and dominating pose of Romulus; as if the male universe were self-enclosed and self-contained, and its inhabitants were distributing among themselves . . . male and female roles, disavowing the actual fact of sexual difference, and deflecting their

119. J.-L. David, The Intervention of the Sabine Women, *Musée du Louvre, Photo Musées Nationaux*

ideas of gender onto the fetishistic apparatus of sword, sheath, and shield. The women are attempting in unison, to break open the mirrored world of masculinities: they are not engaged in displaying the pathos of victims. . . . They are driving a wedge into the dyadic vision of men; they introduce true difference, differently gendered bodies, and their task is larger than the individual. . . . It requires a group momentum. The woman behind Hersilia, partly propelled by her companions' efforts . . . succeeds in breaking through that barrier, and in penetrating into the vision of the men, her arms dividing the dyad and interposing the collective force of the female body. Everything happens as if Hersilia were trying to reorient the masculine vision, align it around another term than a gaze of aggression located in mirrors; around a body which, by insisting on a different nature, breaks open the dangerous visual lock of Narcissus.[23]

A great statement on the Revolution and on Napoleonic warfare, steeped in the symbolics of Roman warfare, *The Sabines* attempts to cast women into the center of the conqueror/conquered dualism, unsettling it. David here admits what the Revolution had denied, that women and their sexuality affect and are affected by warfare: as spoils of war and, themselves or their infants, its victims.

The Sabines is a quintessentially post-Terror, Directoire work, expressive of that fleeting moment of doubt in the ultimate effectiveness of military might. The women, young and old, plunging into the midst of battle with their infants to defend the men against their own slaughter, in their postures as postulants or intercessors, all express maternal solicitude (or compassion) for the bare and vulnerable flesh of Roman and Sabine warriors, and for the children born of their sexuality. The figures of the kneeling woman with milk-filled breasts pleading for the lives of the infants and the old women desperately clutching her milkless ones provide a symbolic reproach, in their agonies, to the schematism of the soulless, statist nurturance emblematized by the suckling wolf of Rome on Romulus's shield. Hersilia's pacific gesture may be seen as a last, desperate expression of energy by the French Revolution's goddess of freedom: David calls her out of retirement one last time.[24] The piling-up of emotional energy at the center of the canvas produced by the small swarm of women overwhelms it as they attempt, as Bryson posits, to "reorient the masculine vision," to force themselves upon male consciousness and into visibility.

But the women are ineffectual on the canvas (though not with the viewer of it). Their eruption causes Romulus and Tatius only to pause: their eyes remain riveted upon each other. Within the work, the women remain unseen. This is perhaps appropriate in a work which, pretending to be a breakaway *for* pathos, yet plays the card *of* pathos. None of the female figures' pleading gestures hold any hope of providing more than momentary and symbolic resistance: indeed the posture of the Cassandra-like hooded woman at center conveys nothing but imminent doom.

The sexual undercurrent of this scene of war is palpable, as nude men and their horses stand forth in their muscular tension amidst a group of women carefully draped to expose or outline their breasts.[25] In Plutarch's account of the historical event, in the wake of Hersilia's move, "sentiments of love, conjugal, paternal, and fraternal, broke out in both armies."[26] *Conjugal, fraternal* and *paternal*—these are the bonds for which the Sabines plead, as unwitting tools of the system of warfare they believe themselves to be combating. The sexual code here is complex. The women's breasts, here the sign of their sexuality assimilated to reproductivity, remain a site of conflict among the men. As in the worst fears of Old Regime morality, the infants are mothers' children; their births, the work of rapine, can claim no firm fatherly allegiance. As in the campaign for maternal nursing and the debate over illegitimacy legislation, the Sabines' "solution" seals them into a powerlessly protesting symbiosis with their own deliciously vulnerable children. The delicately open-stretched hands of Hersilia, as devoid of the muscular tension of kinetic purposefulness as the Drs. Virey and Cabanis had decreed the ideal woman's to be, finally rob her figure of the fresh meaning it was meant to betoken. The

Sabine women remain valiant but helpless peacemakers, still entrapped in the Revolution's masculine dream of an eroticized maternal magic.

And yet, countertrends to this magic of sentimentality never ended. Louis Theremin published in the Year VII the most searching work by a man of this era about women, *The Condition of Women in Republics.*[27] Little disposed to the pieties of maternalist ideology, Theremin reasoned that women did not need to be constantly hectored to be domestic. Apparently he was then excoriated for taking women's "sacred duties" too lightly, and so he responded in a footnote that he simply found no need "to preach to them these duties everyone preaches to them." But basically, more plainly than anyone, especially at this date, Theremin affirmed that "in their quality as Citizenesses they must, as much as do men, draw the attention of the State, and they must not subsist solely by selling themselves or alienating themselves in any way whatever, for they are persons, not properties." He claimed that if women and men had similar physical training, they would come to have a greater bodily resemblance to each other. In fact, Theremin is for the most part boldly egalitarian, observantly taking his own sex to task: "By what right do you refuse women pleasures you liberally accord yourselves and force them to resist all their lives long that need to act which torments them even as it torments you, just as in former times you forced them into Convents. . . . Are you unaware that, forever victims of our despotism, they often know how to make us repent of it?"[28]

Theremin's stance is ultimately the one most delicately poised of them all between the Revolution's potential egalitariansim toward women, and its tendency to an idealizing allegorism regarding them. "Women," he reports, "have been entirely neglected in the Revolution of Liberty, as if they were unworthy of participating in it, or as if they had to have been basically indifferent to it." Having received no recognition by it, Theremin claims they had turned against it. Give women a stake in Revolution, he advises, and see how prodigiously they will sustain it. He nevertheless falls in with the dominant constructs of gender as he finds women both better than men, and yet more hideous when depraved than members of his own sex. In a passage that suggests interfertilization with David's *Sabines,* Theremin argues that women are the "Power that forgives in Republics . . . the pledges of universal peace and brotherhood. . . . It is through them that the conqueror becomes a friend, the protector, the father of the conquered. . . . They appease the wrath of cruel and bloodthirsty masters, like the Prayers, daughters of Jupiter whom Homer describes as modestly following the traces of insolent Fury who covers the earth with her light step, striking humankind to death; they come after her and cure all the evils she has committed; thus women soothe the evils of war."[29] Even Theremin has internalized the mythic tradition revived by iconography. Women are inspiritors of war, destroyers, then nurses to its consequences: allegorical sails to the wind.

But what of women's own responses to their fate of civil erasure and reduction to erotic ciphers of masculine romance? Paule-Marie Duhet finds among them a subdued picking up where Revolution had left off. Why not, since "no road seems to open, not even the consolation of telling one another that one day they will be able to try to change matters; all avenues have been closed off, even that of education. A generation was broken."[30]

As Theremin points out, many women, realizing how little a stake they had in Revolution, opposed it. Olwen Hufton has written movingly of the wrath of women starved by the famine of 1795 who would subsequently turn back to the Church. Deprived of the bread necessary to fulfilling the maternal function ceaselessly urged upon them, they sought a fount of pity the republic of men only was inadequate to supply. Rechristianization would then "pass through women," as the saying had it.[31] The result was one of the principal schisms of nineteenth-century life, of women's grosso modo turning toward a conservative religiosity, and men's toward politics.

Certain aspects of male representation of women during the Revolution and its aftermath—the fetishization of the female body, the mythology of the Maenad, the strict construction of women's sphere—powerfully suggest that all of these strategies at bottom may merely represent nothing more than more elaborate forms of the Australian aborigines' bullroarers, whose dreadful shrieks function to warn the women when it is time to "clear out." The women collude in the myth of their terror of what are represented to them as demonic voices by rushing away before them, pell-mell, even though they "know" exactly how these terrible noises are produced. "The women, by being frightened, help to persuade their teasers that there is something in it anyhow. The frightened women, acting as true believers, contribute immensely to the sense of reality that every ritual badly needs."[32] As J. S. Mill suggested, women's apparent assent is a feature essential to such a charade to lend it legitimacy. But in fact, the women do not stay banished: they are always back again when the bullroarer is sounded anew.

The forms and signs of Revolutionary masculinity, powerfully bolstered by its misogyny, bore a freight of martial nationalism and physical and sexual menace akin to the bullroarer's shriek. But the result of French gender scare tactics also much resembles the aborigines' style of gender accommodation. The women, though never relinquishing altogether the space they strove over and again to occupy, ostensibly collaborated in various ways in the new Republic and in all the subsequent regimes the men would found. Yet, as in the Australian case, all the women's gestures of cooperation did not take away "the antagonism that persists" which "finds the most diverse expressions."[33]

Driving the women away from the cultural turf left post-Terror France's social space an essentially masculine field.[34] The painter Elisabeth Vigée-Lebrun, returning to Paris from exile in 1801, was amazed to find a society segregated by sex. At Mme de Ségur's, "I was astonished on entering to see all the men on one side and all the women on the other; you might have supposed they were enemies in view of each other." In 1800, Germaine de Staël lamented that, as she saw it, "since the Revolution men had thought it politically and morally useful to reduce women to the most absurd mediocrity." And Mme de Rémusat would write in 1824, well after Bonaparte's fall, "There is no woman who, if she is sincere, does not agree that her posture in society is painful and constrained. . . . Rousseau said that when men were busier, women would have to renounce being mixed up in everything, and ready themselves for a life of withdrawal. The sentence may seem harsh, no doubt, but I fear there is no appeal from it."[35]

"In monarchies they have to fear ridicule, and in republics hatred." This is Staël's formula. She had witnessed the vicious campaigns of slander against the queen and the political women, including herself, in the Revolution. In her well-disguised discussion of women's lot, buried toward the end of *On Literature,* (1800), she buries even more deeply her most progressive remarks, knowing full well how contrary to the massively arrayed authority of opinion they might seem if fully exposed. "Enlighten, instruct, perfect women as you do men, nations as you do individuals, this is still the best secret for all reasonable goals and for all social and political relations to which you wish to provide a stable foundation." A still-unreconstructed believer in enlightenment and progress, Staël felt sure that women's advance was necessary. "If the situation of women is highly imperfect in the civil order, we should work toward the betterment of their fate, not the degradation of their minds." But she does not cling to this losing proposition. Using the Sabine arms that come to hand, she reasons that women should not be granted too frivolous or insipid a role in society, for then they would lose the power "to soften men's passions."[36] The argument for women's equality having failed utterly, only a separatist accommodation is now possible, and the politically astute Staël will strive to forge a positive role for women from the ingredients Theremin too had identified: a sense of women's potential must be contrived from whatever powers men have left on their plate.

Trapped in age-old misogynist rhetoric and categories, the radical Revolution ratified, rather than challenged, male sex-right. This is largely because the French Revolution itself arrived in the midst of a longer and broader struggle to resist women's advancement in society and to restore an unquestioned male supremacy. Had the many but powerless voices advancing women's cause prevailed, the men of the Revolution might have recognized women's basic equality as a first step in effecting their elusive universalist vision. They would have had to recognize women as possessing separate rights, congruent with their own, as beings like themselves. They would have had to acknowledge the deeper human consonances between the sexes, and not hate the feminine and fear the homosexual components of their own personalities. They would also have had to recognize women's surplus and separate needs as bearers of children, as Olympe de Gouges would have wished. But all of this was unthinkable in the languages, verbal and visual, of the time. The bourgeois gender outlook instituted by Revolution was one that

would instead borrow a certain softening of the manifest structures of gender
relations from aristocratic forms. But even as it did so, it reinforced Christian and
folkloric misogyny and hierarchy by sublimating its rougher manifestations into
codes of congenital female inferiority and a sexuality of "charity."

At the period of the founding of modern republics, then, men prescribed for
women, but not for themselves, a standard of chaste comportment and private
devotion to parenthood. In this same era women lost their erotic aura as goddesses
of the high culture and entered modernity stripped of energy and aspiration, as
man's mere, inferior, piously viewed, complement. Subsequent regimes, whether
monarchies or republics, did not choose to alter these decrees. To claim that something essential went awry when the sexes moved to a systemic accommodation
exiling women within private space and consigning them to civil and intellectual
inferiority is to accord far greater place in our cultural history than heretofore to

120. *J.-D. Ingres,* The Wounded Amazon, *Musée Bonnat, Bayonne, Photo SPADEM*

the import of sexual accommodation. The fact that all our claims to universal democracy have long rested on an evasion of the realities of gender interests is not foreign to the divorce we experience, even yet, between masculine public and feminine intimate realms. For the regime of separation splits our personalities, making us hope for far too much comfort from women, far too little from men and what remains essentially their world.

A superb early nineteenth-century drawing from the pen of Ingres, *The Wounded Amazon* (fig. 120), lends fitting closure to this long story of gender struggle. Superimposing her live, naked, pink-fleshed male slayer suggestively over the bloodless dying Amazon on her rearing horse, Ingres provides us with a final paradox of conflict between the sexes. Here is a male wish-fulfillment image of continued battle to the death with the untamable Amazonian will of the woman. A grand sexual symbiosis of man the warrior with woman the warrior is at once envisaged and denied. Defeated, as the temper of the time of her creation willed her to be, the Amazon's eloquently displayed strength implicitly denounces her destruction. Bleeding and pale as she appears on her steed, axe in hand, she bulks larger than her attacker, is more expressive than he in her luxuriant curls and flowing gown. Though bloodless and dying, the Amazon survives in Ingres's conception.

The women of history, too, survived the French Revolution, in and in spite of men's representations of them. For while their struggle to alter men's consciousness of their reality had met with pitiless civil and moral retribution, their resilience was imperishable.

NOTES

1. GENDERED ROCOCO

1. Cited by Michael Levey, *From Rococo to Revolution* (New York: Frederick W. Praeger, 1966), 121.
2. *The Life, Unpublished Letters, and Philosophical Regimen of Anthony, Earl of Shaftesbury,* ed. Benjamin Rand (London: Swan Sonenschein, 1900), 216–217.
3. This split between moral and aesthetic realms is evident in Molière's 1666 *Misanthrope,* as the excessively forthright and manly Alceste finally rejects what he sees as the subterfuges of lively young Célimène, a social butterfly. See chapter 3.
4. See Elizabeth Goldsmith, *Exclusive Conversations: The Art of Interaction in Seventeenth-Century France* (Philadelphia: University of Pennsylvania Press, 1988), 25–28 and passim.
5. Jean Starobinski, *L'Invention de la liberté* (Geneva: Skira, 1964), 55.
6. Patrick Brady, *Rococo Style versus Enlightenment Novel* (Geneva: Slatkine, 1984), 106, cites this verse, which I have translated, from Pezay. "Ephemerality," Brady, 150.
7. Brady, 108, discusses this ditty from Voltaire's *Epître des vous et des tu:*

> Le ciel ne te donnait alors,
> Pour tout rang et pour tous trésors,
> Que la douce erreur de ton âge,
> Deux tétons que le tendre Amour
> De ses mains arrondit un jour;
> Un coeur Simple, un esprit volage;
> Un cul (j'y pense encore, Philis)
> Sur qui j'ai vu briller des lis
> Jaloux de ceux de ton visage.

8. Edmond and Jules de Goncourt's advocacy of the "woman regnant" thesis, in their *La Femme au XVIIIe siecle* (Paris: 1877), has had an influence virtually unquestioned from the time of its publication. Jean Starobinski merely punctures it in his chapter "Règne fictif de la femme," in *L'Invention de la liberté.* "It may be largely a myth," Brady, 131.
9. "Synecdochic replacement," Brady, 132. "Cartesianism," Brady, 26.
10. James Leith, *The Idea of Art as Propaganda in France, 1789–1799* (Toronto: University of Toronto Press, 1965), 7. "Male hedonism," Brady, 51. Candace Clements, "The Academy and the Other: *Les Graces* and *Le Genre Galant,*" paper presented at conference, "Women and the Rococo," University of Missouri, Columbia, October 1987, 19–20.
11. Brady, 103, 102; Donald Posner, "The Swinging Women of Watteau and Fragonard," *Art Bulletin* 69 (March 1982): 76.
12. Posner (86–87) cites Brantôme's *Vie des dames galantes* (1665–66) as source for the folk wisdom "petit pied, grand con" (little foot, big cunt).
13. See Philip Stewart, "Representations of Love: The French Eighteenth Century," *Studies in Iconography* 4 (1978): 135.
14. Mary Sheriff, "The Erotics of Decoration," paper presented at conference, "Women and the Rococo," University of Missouri, Columbia, 1987, 5. I recommend Sheriff's attentive readings of Boucher and Fragonard canvases.

15. As quoted by Thomas Crow, in *Painters and Public Life in Eighteenth-Century Paris* (New Haven: Yale University Press, 1985), 52, from Neimitz's *Séjour à Paris* (1727).
16. Roger Laufer, *Style rococo, style des "lumières"* (Paris: Corti, 1963), 28. Philippe Perrot, *Le Travail des apparences ou les transformations du corps féminin, XVIIIe-XIXe siècle* (Paris: Seuil, 1984), 72. "Man is the mover," Clements, 19.
17. Jean Laplanche and J. B. Pontalis, "Fantasy and the Origin of Sexuality," part 1, *Journal of Psychoanalysis* 49 (1968): 12, 15, and note 36. Their formulation derives from Melanie Klein's object relations theory, as expressed, for example, in her "Envy and Gratitude."
18. Quoted material in this paragraph is from Laplanche and Pontalis, 15–16.
19. So many commentaries have taken up the question of the male gaze that a complete listing is inappropriate in this context. John Berger's was among the first. "I am in front of a typical female nude. She is painted with extreme sensuous emphasis. Yet her sexuality is only superficially manifest in her actions or her own expression; in a comparable figure within other art traditions this would not be so. Why? Because for Europe ownership is primary. The painting's sexuality is manifest not in what it shows but in the owner-spectator's (mine in this case) right to see her naked. Her nakedness is not a function of her sexuality but of the sexuality of those who have access to the picture. In the majority of European nudes there is a close parallel with the passivity which is endemic to prostitution." "The Past Seen from a Possible Future," in *Selected Essays and Articles* (London: Penguin, 1972), 215.
20. In Boucher's art, according to Norman Bryson, "the gaze of the male is phallic, and in this the male within the painting acts as surrogate for the male viewer, to whose sexuality the image is exclusively addressed." *Word and Image: French Painting of the Ancien Régime* (Cambridge: Cambridge University Press, 1980), 98.
21. Jeri Mitchell, "'Le Commerce des femmes:' Sexuality and Sociability in Eighteenth-Century French Representation," paper presented at conference, "Women and the Rococo," University of Missouri, Columbia, 1987, 10.
22. For material on mores, Martine Segalen, *Mari et femme dans la France rurale traditionnelle* (Paris: Flammarion, 1980) 138–139, 153.
23. Abbé Coyer, *L'Année Merveilleuse ou les Hommes-femmes* (1748), 1–2, as quoted by Perrot, 59.
24. Joan Landes, *Women and the Public Sphere in the French Revolution* (Ithaca: Cornell University Press, 1988), 67.
25. L.-C. Caraccioli, *Dictionnaire critique, pittoresque et sentencieux, propre à faire connaître les usages du siècle, ainsi que ses bizarreries* (Lyon: 1768), 1:353, quoted by Perrot, 56.
26. Perrot, 56, 41. Caraccioli, *La Critique des dames et des messieurs à leur toilette* (Paris: 1770), 5–6, 9, in Perrot, 46.
27. As noted in this chapter, "the deer park" was Louis XV's "stable" of sexual playmates. Michel Florisoone, *La Peinture française: le dix-huitième siècle* (Parie: Pierre Tisné, 1948), 45–46.
28. La Font de Saint-Yenne, *Réflexions sur quelques causes de l'état présent de la Peinture en France* (The Hague: 1747), 8. Further page references are given in the text.
29. Horace Walpole, *Horace Walpole's Correspondence with Mme du Deffand and Wiart*, ed. W. S. Lewis and Warren Huntington Smith (New Haven: Yale University Press, 1937–1974), 6:57, as quoted by Benedetta Craveri, *Madame du Deffand et son monde* (Paris: Seuil, 1982), 303.
30. Crow, *PPL,* 7.
31. J. Locquin, *La Peinture d'histoire en France de 1747 à 1785* (Paris: H. Laurens, 1912), 138, cites works by Mariette, Watelet, the Abbé Leblanc, Lieudé de Sepmanville, St. Yves Estève, Baillet de Saint-Julien, and the Marquis d'Argens as espousing positions in support of the supremacy of history painting.
32. Crow (*PPL,* 91) cites a lively letter to M. de Poiresson from 1741, describing a semiriotous scene in a crowd disbarred from the Salon as mixing up "humor, politics, and style" all together, in a species of antirococo skirmish.
33. Crow points out that far from being devotees of rococo, Tournehem and his family were "driven to rebuild the Academy's capacity to generate publicly oriented narrative pictures that were stylistically and morally disciplined by the classicism of the past century" (*PPL,* 111).
34. Thus argues Crow, *PPL,* 10.
35. R. G. Saisselin, "Neo-Classicism: Images of Public Virtue and Realities of Private Luxury," *Art History* 4 (March 1981): 14–36, locates the origin of neoclassicism in court circles, whereas Crow sees it as the creature of the bourgois and the parlementaires. Crow, *PPL* 112–113.
36. Crow, *PPL,* 119. Joan Landes has chosen to root her analysis of women's altered status in the

Revolution in Rousseau's representations of them, while conceding that "there are some interesting parallels to the works of earlier aristocratic reformers in that Rousseau favors many of the same sexualized metaphors of despotism and also yearns for a domestic republic" (67). I seek here to place this struggle at the center of a wider and longer struggle of taste and value and its use of misogyny as an arm of polemics.

37. "*Noblesse de robe,*" Albert Mathiez, *The French Revolution,* tr. Alison Phillips (New York: Grosset Dunlap, 1964), 7. "Culmination," Crow, *PPL,* 125.
38. "Ambitious painting," Crow, *PPL,* 117. "Emphasis on history painting," Saisselin, 19.
39. In eighteenth-century parlance, *caillettes* are chatty little dolls or chicks. *Oeuvres complètes* (Paris: Club français du livre, 1970) 6:41.
40. See Posner, 76, on the swing as a theme.
41. Bryson, *Word and Image,* 95–96.
42. Here is Michel Florisoone's dismissal, for one: "History has attached all too much importance to the adventures of a profuse art for which all of France must do penance" (23).

1. INFANT EROS AND HUMAN INFANT

1. Lawrence Stone, *The Family, Sex, and Marriage in England, 1500–1800* (London: Wiedenfeld and Nicolson, 1977), 395.
2. D. G. Charlton, *New Images of the Natural in France: A Study in European Cultural History 1750–1800* (Cambridge: Cambridge University Press, 1984), 139.
3. Paul Hazard, for one, in his *La Pensée européenne au XVIIIe siècle—de Montesquieu à Lessing* (Paris: Boivin, 1964).
4. See Michel Vovelle, "Le Tournant des mentalités en France, 1750–1789: la 'sensibilité' prérévolutionnaire," tr. John Hoyles, *Social History* 5 (1977): 621.
5. Vovelle, "Tournant," 608. He cautions us, however, to reconcile ourselves to uncertainty as to whether or how much such trends affected the ideas and feelings of ordinary people.
6. Vovelle, "Tournant," 609 and 611.
7. Acidalius, summoned before justice at Leipzig, himself disclaimed this work, saying it was the work of a Pole, a mere "theological joke," according to Pierre Darmon, *La Mythologie de la femme dans l'ancienne France* (Paris: Seuil, 1982), 22. "Emergence of monsters" Darmon, 22.
8. See Felix Gaiffe, *Envers du grand siècle* (Paris: A. Michel, 1924), passim, and Felix Roquain, *L'Esprit révolutionnaire avant la Révolution 1713–1789* (Paris: Plon, 1878; rpt. Geneva: Slatkine, 1971), 313 and 108.
9. John Crawford, as cited by Robert Mauzi in *L'Idee du bonheur au XVIIIe siècle* (Paris: A. Colin, 1960), 29. We find Rousseau in *La Nouvelle Héloïse* partially confirming this while noting the harshness of the men of Paris and the relative generosity of its women: "Paris being the business center of the greatest people in Europe, those who transact it are also the hardest of men. Therefore people turn to the women when they need favors; it is to them that the unfortunate turn; the women listen to them, console them, help them" (letter 21).
10. D. A. Coward, "Eighteenth-Century Attitudes to Prostitution," *Studies on Voltaire and the Eighteenth Century* 189 (1980): 364.
11. See Peter Brooks, *The Novel of Worldliness in Eighteenth-Century France* (Princeton: Princeton University Press, 1969), for an exploration of its elaborations in the novel.
12. Diane Alstad, *The Ideology of the Family in Eighteenth-Century France* (Ann Arbor: University Microfilms International, 1971), 52. I want to acknowledge my indebtedness to this fine Yale doctoral dissertation for its thoroughness and insight.
13. In 1700 there were 21 million French, in 1750 25 million, and in 1800 29 million, according to Lionel Gossman, *French Society and Culture: Background for Eighteenth-Century Culture,* (Englewood Cliffs, N.J.: Prentice Hall, 1972), 54.
14. Edward Shorter, *The Making of the Modern Family* (New York: Basic Books, 1975), 4.
15. Robert de Luppé affirms this in his *Les Jeunes Filles à la fin du XVIIIe siècle* (Paris: Champion, 1925), 16.
16. We think of one of Molière's demented fathers standing misguidedly in the way of the reasonable inclinations of his children.
17. Shorter, *MMF,* 4.

18. Elisabeth Badinter devotes her book *L'Amour en plus* (Paris: Poche Flammarion, 1980) to precisely this question.
19. Shorter, *MMF,* 74. See Natalie Zemon Davis's essential and influential "Women on Top," in her *Society and Culture in Early Modern France* (Stanford: Stanford University Press, 1975), which finds sixteenth-century precedents for the ritual of turning the tables.
20. Shorter, *MMF,* 75. Compare Pierre Bourdieu's more nuanced description of enduring twentieth-century peasant male affectivity: "Everything that falls in the domain of intimacy is banished from conversation. If he consents to express or listen to a freer mode of discourse, the peasant remains discreet regarding his own sexual life and even more so with respect to his emotions." "Célibat et condition paysanne," *Etudes rurales* 5–6 (1962): 103.
21. For marriage of daughters, Yvonne Knibiehler and Catherine Fouquet, *L'Histoire des mères, du moyen âge à nos jours* (Paris: Montalba, 1980), 118. For statistics from the Artois, Jean-Louis Flandrin, *Les Amours paysannes, XVIe au XIXe siècles* (Paris: Gallimard, 1975), 59.
22. "Female beauty," Flandrin, *AP,* 245. "Big boys," *Le Paysan perverti,* chapter 3, as quoted by Flandrin, *AP,* 145.
23. "Girl in the streets," Flandrin, *AP,* 60, 135. "Hope of emancipation," Bourdieu, 32–135, 103.
24. Arthur Young reports in 1787, "Women gathering grass and weeds by hand in the woods for their cows is a sign of poverty." Also, "Poverty and poor crops to Amiens; women are now ploughing with a pair of horses to sow barley. The difference of the customs of the two nations is in nothing more striking than in the labors of the sex; in England, it is very little that they will do except to glean and make hay; the first is a party of pilfering, and the second of pleasure: in France they plough and fill the dung cart." In speaking of pretty young girls, he observes that "hard labor destroys both person and complexion." *Travels in France During the Years 1787, 1788, 1789* (London: 1889), 7–8, 62. For the *tireuse,* Alain Decaux, *Histoire des Françaises* (Paris: Perrin, 1972), 1:427.
25. For the life of the *servante,* Olwen Hufton, "Women and the Family Economy in Eighteenth-Century France," *French Historical Studies* (Spring 1975): 4, 6. Pregnancy declarations had been required by law since the reign of Henri II in the sixteenth century. Vulnerability of serving women, Hufton, "Women and the Family Economy," 8.
26. Sara Maza, *Servants and Masters in Eighteenth Century France: The Uses of Loyalty* (Princeton: Princeton University Press, 1983), 132. Maza here draws upon Jacques Depauw, "Illicit Sexual Activity in Eighteenth-Century Nantes," in *Family and Society,* ed. Robert Forster and Orest Ranum, and Cissie Fairchilds, "Female Sexual Attitudes and the Rise of Illegitimacy: A Case Study," *Journal of Interdisciplinary History* 8:63–64; rpt. in *Marriage and Fertility: Studies in Interdisciplinary History,* ed. Robert I. Rotberg and Theodore K. Rabb (Princeton: Princeton University Press, 1980).
27. See Hufton, "Women and the Family Economy," 11, on living conditions, and for "sheer determination" (20–22).
28. Cited by Decaux, 429. Compare with Coward's figure of thirty thousand (364).
29. Vovelle, "Tournant," 615.
30. Cited by Shorter, *MMF,* 50.
31. Charles-Elie de Ferrières, *La Femme dans l'ordre social et dans l'ordre de la nature* (London: 1787), cited by André Maindron, "Fondements Physiologiques et Transposition littéraire dans les romans français du 19e siècle" thesis for Doctorat d'Etat, (University of Nantes, 1985), 114.
32. See Claude Delasselle, "Abandons d'enfants à Paris au XVIIIe siècle," *Annales: Economies, Sociétés, Civilisations* 30 (January–February 1975): 188.
33. Nicolas-Edmé Restif de la Bretonne, *La Vie de mon père,* chapters 7 and 8, as quoted by Flandrin, *AP,* 51–52. Flandrin claims we may doubt the authenticity of this scene, since it falls so fulsomely into readerly expectations. But the point is that these *were* the readerly expectations, even when transgressed.
34. Edward Shorter, "Illegitimacy, Sexual Revolution, and Social Change," in Rotberg and Rabb, 85. Cissie Fairchilds claims that these illegitimacies "can be adequately explained as a product of the persistence of sexual attitudes in the changing economic context of urbanization and modernization" (164). She sees little direct evidence of what women's attitudes, about which Shorter speculates so abundantly, were in fact. Hers is a skepticism I share.
35. For prostitution, see Coward, 363, 378, 379.
36. *Représentations à monsieur le lieutenant général de police de Paris sur les courtisanes à la mode et les demoiselles de bon ton* (Paris: 1760), 145, quoted by Coward, 391.

37. Paul-Henri, Baron d'Holbach, *La Morale universelle* (Amsterdam: 1766), 1:229, as quoted by Alstad, 61; "sense of crisis," Vovelle, "Tournant," 607.

38. Carol Pateman, *The Sexual Contract* (Stanford: Stanford University Press, 1988), 207.

39. Although I point here to certain specific discourses on gender as exemplifying trends that seem central to me, I agree with Dorinda Outram's insistence that we find "a plurality of discourses on competing regimens and images of the body" in this era. *The Body and the French Revolution: Sex, Class, and Political Culture* (New Haven: Yale University Press, 1989), 19.

40. Diderot's own introduction to *Le Fils naturel* (*The Illegitimate Son*). *Oeuvres complètes,* 15 vols. (Paris: Club français de livre, 1970), 3:24. Subsequent references in the text to this and other Diderot writings are to this edition, unless otherwise noted.

41. "No, . . . love and friendship in no way press equal duties upon me, especially this senseless love they know nothing about and which must be snuffed out" (3:42).

42. Listen to his Silvia, in act 2, scene 1 of *La Double Inconstance* (*Double Infidelity*) (1723), engaged to Arlequin, but visiting the court of the prince for the first time:

    > There's really something dreadful about this country! Never have I seen women so courteous or men so honorable. Their manners are so gentle, they make so many bows and compliments to you, show so many signs of friendship! You'd think they were the best people in the world, full of conscience and heart. But they're not at all! Out of the whole lot, there isn't a single one who hasn't come up to me to say in a confidential tone: 'Mademoiselle, believe me, I advise you to abandon Arlequin and marry the prince'; but they advise this absolutely naturally, without shame, just as if they were advising me to do something good. 'But,' I tell them, 'I've made a promise to Arlequin; where is faithfulness, integrity, good faith?' They hear nothing of all that. . . . It's as if I were speaking Greek to them. They laugh right in my face, tell me I'm being a child, that a grown girl like me must be reasonable! Isn't that lovely? To be worthless, to deceive your fellow being, fail in your pledge to him, to be two-faced and lying; that's what duty means to the high and mighty people of the accursed place. What are these people? Where to they come from? What are they made of?

    Nevertheless, both Silvia and Arlequin are made by the verbal and psychological play of the work not merely to change their minds and love objects, but to love that change.

43. Compare this view with that of Dr. Theophile Bordeu in his *Recherches anatomiques sur les glandes* (1751), reiterated by the physician Jacques-Louis Moreau de la Sarthe in his *Histoire naturelle de la femme* (1803), who held that women's temperament was by nature morbid and unruly, since they were thought to be governed by frequent changes in their internal organs, above all the uterus. From Paul Hoffman, *La Femme dans le pensée des lumières* (Paris: Ophrys, 1977), 168.

44. Dorval's and Clairville's relationship is another example of the male bond merely triangulated by the woman that Eve Kosofsky Sedgwick has so tellingly explored in her *Between Men* (New York: Columbia University Press, 1985).

45. This play concentrates on the alienation of the woman's will by moral torture as much as does Marivaux's *Double Inconstance.* Arlequin's and Silvia's manipulation by the more artful characters into a change of object is conveyed in a seriocomic register. Here Dorval's change of mind is rational and free: only Rosalie's is wrested from her outright, hence melodramatized.

46. Unless his remark is meant ironically, it underscores the gap between representation and society. Women "out there" have always been far more varied and unpredictable than the forms into which they have been pressed by art.

47. In Peter Nagy, *Libertinage et révolution,* tr. Christiane Grémillon (Paris: Gallimard, 1975) 22; Grimod's *Réflexions philosophiques sur le plaisir* (Neufchâtel: 1783), in Nagy, 34.

48. "Mme de Gancé," as quoted by Patrick Wald Lasowski, *Libertines* (Paris: Gallimard: 1980), 71.

49. "Libertine imagination," Lasowski, 71.

50. Delasselle (213) cites this passage from book 7 of Rousseau's *Confessions.* Commentary from Montlinot's *Observations sur les Enfants-trouvés dans les Municipalités de Soissons* as cited by Delasselle, 213. Delasselle notes the following occupations given for parents of children abandoned at the Hôtel-Dieu there in 1778. The mothers were mainly domestic servants or textile workers. The fathers' occupational range was more extensive: Parisian bourgeois came first, with 33.1 percent; then followed master-artisans and merchants (24.5 percent), salaried workers (13.5 percent) and jobbers and bearers (12.3 percent). Five to 10 percent were

servants. Also represented in small numbers were members of liberal professions (29), employees (23), soldiers (22), a handful of noblemen (4), and civic administrators (12). Of course upper-class men were able to buy their way out of having such inconvenient fatherhood attributed to them. Delasselle reckons that the Parisian bourgeoisie furnished half of such paternities that year (201–203). This social tableau of reproductive life, along with Montlinot's reflection, suggests that the structural paradigm advanced by Dorinda Outram (6) of a "struggle between the 'closed body' of the bourgeoisie and the 'carnivalesque' [Bakhtinian] body of the lower orders" in the Revolutionary era is an explicator somewhat remote from the ground of bodily history, in its too ready assumption of lower-class sexual "freedoms" and bourgeois repressions.

51. Jean-Louis Flandrin, "L'Attitude à l'égard du petit enfant et les conduites sexuelles dans la civilisation occidentale: structures et évolution," *Annales de démographie historique,* 1973:163. This view is confirmed by Jehanne Charpentier: "According to advanced views, prejudice against illegitimate birth . . . has lost none of its virulence in either high society or among the unenlightened *peuple*. The unmarried mother and her child are both still stigmatized." *Le Droit de l'enfance abandonnée* (Paris: PUF, 1967), 107.

52. "General Mortange's letters to his wife between 1760 and 1780 enable us to gauge the progress made by a concept of the family which had become identical with that of the nineteenth and twentieth centuries": Philippe Ariès, *Centuries of Childhood: A Social History of Family Life,* tr. Robert Baldick (New York: Vintage, 1962), 400. John McManners, *Death and the Enlightenment* (Oxford: Clarendon Press, 1981), 67, 66.

53. See Flandrin, "L'Attitude," 145–146. *Enfants-trouvés,* Delasselle, 188, 193. Louis-Sébastien Mercier, *Tableau de Paris* III, cclxxi, 234, quoted by Delasselle, 193.

54. Desbois de Rochefort's article "Enfant-trouvé" in the *Encyclopédie méthodique,* as cited by Delasselle, 193. Feeding and statistics, Delasselle, 195. Desbois de Rochefort on *le petit peuple,* Delasselle, 207. Legitimate abandoned children, Delasselle, 208–209.

55. As quoted by Delasselle, 210.

56. Mercier, in Delasselle, 213; McManners, 11.

57. Charpentier, 106.

58. Vovelle, "Tournant," cites as evidence of the decline men's decreased participation in *de mortuis* rites and funeral processions, as well as their lessened recourse to religious *confréries* (617–619). E. Leroi Ladurie, "Démographie et 'funestes secrets:' le Languedoc (fin XVIIIe début XIXe siécle)," *Annales d'histoire de la Révolution française* (1965): 973.

59. George D. Sussman, *Selling Mother's Milk: The Wet-Nursing Business in France 1715–1914* (Urbana: University of Illinois Press, 1982), 19.

60. Charles-Pierre Le Noir, *Détail sur quelques éstablissements de la ville de Paris, demandé par sa majesté impériale la reine de hongrie* (Paris: 1970), 63, in Sussman, 20. Conflicts between nursing and earning, Sussman, 24.

61. *Crise de conscience,* Sussman, 27. "Before eighth birthday," Sussman, 66–67.

62. Letter of Dr. Jousset, quoted in *De la mortalité des nourissons en France* (Paris: 1866), 51–52, in Shorter, *MMF,* 179.

63. Badinter, *L'Amour,* 179, 182.

64. I posited a related thesis earlier, in the section entitled "The Rise of Social Woman and the Reaction to It" (258–269) in my article "Lacos and 'le sexe:' The Rack of Ambivalence," *Studies on Voltaire and the Eighteenth Century* 189 (1980), 247–294. Joan B. Landis asserts a similar thesis in her *Women and the Public Sphere* (20–21).

65. For Mme de Moysan, Decaux, 433. Man as "not-woman" is the thesis of Jean Bethke Elshtain's *Public Man, Private Woman* (Princeton: Princeton University Press, 1981).

66. Pierre Roussel, *Système physique et moral de la femme* . . . (Paris: 1775), 103–104; L. Racine, *La Religion,* chant 2, in *Oeuvres* II, iii, 28, as quoted by Roger Mercier, *L'Enfant dans le société française du XVIIIe siècle* (Dakar: Université de Dakar, 1961), 32; "mere machines, " R. Mercier, 35.

67. *Dissertation sur l'éducation physique des enfants* (Haarlem: 1763), 175, quoted by Etienne and Francine van de Walle, "Allaitement, stérilité, et contraception: les opinions jusqu'au XIXe siècle," *Population* 27 (1972): 691; Boudier and Restif, Van der Walle, 693.

68. *Eloge historique de Michel de l'Hospital* (Paris: 1778), 126, and H. E. Estienne, *Introduction au traité de la conformité des merveilles anciennes et modernes* (sur les Hasles: 1607), 273, both cited in van de Walle, 698; Moheau, in *Recherches et considérations sur la population de la*

France, 2:99–100, in Jean-Louis Flandrin, *Familles, parenté, maison, sexualité dans l'ancienne société* (Paris: Seuil, 1984), 214.

69. Philip Stewart, "The Child Comes of Age," *Yale French Studies* 40 (1968): 136. Stewart finds this thesis set forth by Philippe Ariès and by Jean Calvet, in his *L'Enfant dans la litterature francaise* (Paris: F. Lanore, 1931); "prestige of real being," 137–138. For "child," see also Henri Peyre, *Saturday Review,* Dec. 2, 1967, 32. Stewart correctly points out that Rousseau fails in his own novel, and despite its sentimentality over children, to convincingly depict a child (140).

70. Marie-France Morel, "Théories et pratiques de l'allaitement en France au XVIIe siécle," *Annales de démographie historique* 1977:394.

71. *Traité de l'éducation corporelle des enfants en bas âge ou Réflexions pratiques sur les moyens de procurer une meilleure constitution aux citoyens* (Paris: 1760). Further references to this work will be cited in the text.

72. Léchevin, in Morel cites the feeding of goat's milk by spoon to infants at Aix in 1777 (423–424). Note the tide of apprehension about depopulation unfounded in fact.

73. Darmon, 41.

74. Jean Polman, *Le Chancre ou le couvre-sein* (Douai: 1635), 15, quoted by Darmon, 142.

75. "Concert of society," Darmon, 44; "instruments of generation," Darmon, 22.

76. See Morel's article for a full account of the wider debate by other commentators.

77. Of course this was never true: Rousseau has been tirelessly attacked by opinion for his hypocrisy about his fatherhood.

78. I refer to the Garnier edition of the *Emile* (Paris: 1964), putting page references in the text.

79. This desire for transparency is explored in Jean Starobinski's *Jean-Jacques Rousseau: La Transparence ou l'obstacle* (Paris: Gallimard, 1971). Even the nursing of animals may miscarry. Rousseau never dreams that any problem might arise in the nursing relationship.

80. We see confirmation of this in Rousseau's "naturalization" of incest in his *Essai sur l'origine des langues* (*Essay on the Origins of Language*).

81. I refer to the 1960 Garnier edition. For the *Confessions,* the edition is New York: French and European Publications, 1968, 2 vols.

82. The Valaisans are the Swiss peopling the region of Lake Geneva.

83. "He disputes whether man be so gregarious an animal, though the long and helpless state of infancy seems to point him out as particularly impelled to pair, the first step toward herding." *A Vindication of the Rights of Women* (1792) (New York: Norton, 1967), 42.

84. In the *Emile* Rousseau in fact puts patronizing strictures on the wet nurse's teaching of the infant: "I don't disapprove of the wet nurse's amusing the child with songs and gay and varied tones of voice; but I do disapprove of her confusing him with a multitude of useless words about which he can comprehend nothing but the tone in which they're spoken. I would like the first sounds he hears to be rare, distinct, frequently repeated, and for the words they express to connect with concrete objects that can be shown to the child" (53). Giddy nonsense is to be forbidden, can have no pedagogic function.

85. Discussed throughout this volume is a debate among modern scholars surrounding Rousseau's views on women as well as the character and extent of his influence upon them. Ruth Graham sees that the women of the Revolutionary generation used Rousseau's language of women's moral ascendancy to defend their various pleas: "Rousseau's Sexism Revolutionized," in *Women in the Eighteenth Century and Other Essays,* ed. Paul Fritz and Richard Morton (Toronto: Hakkert, 1976). Gita May, "Rousseau's Antifeminism Reconsidered," in *French Women and the Age of Enlightenment,* ed. Samia I. Spencer (Bloomington: Indiana University Press, 1984), tries to moderate hasty modern feminist judgments of his views, seeing the profound impact Rousseau exerted upon Germaine de Staël, Manon Roland, and George Sand. "Curiously enough, these exceptionally intelligent women obediently and unquestioningly subscribed to those views of Rousseau that no modern feminist in her right mind would endorse." These women refused to confront any discrepancy between his views and their aspirations (312). Both Graham's and May's articles rightly correct the record of Rousseau's influence upon women. The questions remain: Why were so many so taken with himself and his opinions of them? And how did their acceptance of his terms (which were not his only, but the most potent expression of an apparent consensus) affect their ability to think about their own aspirations? I hope this present work will contribute to this argument.

86. After Mlle de Saint-Yves reluctantly has sex with a powerful official to set her beloved free,

Voltaire's narrator tells us. "Her adventure was more instructive than four years in a covent." *L'Ingénu,* in *Romans et contes de Voltaire* (Paris: Garnier, 1960), 269. Rousseau relates, for example, his sexual exhibitionism, the "innocent" purchase of a child for sexual use, and a serial use of a woman along with Grimm and Klupffel, in his *Confessions.*

87. *Supplément au Voyage de Bougainville; ou Dialogue entre A et B sur l'inconvénient d'attacher des idées morales à certaines actions physiques que n'en comportent pas.* (Supplement to Bougainville's voyage; or dialogue between A and B about the bothersomeness of attaching moral ideas to certain physical acts that involve none) *Oeuvres complètes,* vol. 10. Further references in the text are to this volume.

88. See *L'Ingénu,* 239, and Zvi Lévy, "*L'Ingénu* ou l'anti-Candide," *Studies on Voltaire and the Eighteenth Century* 183 (1980): 45–67.

89. The finesse and subtely of Janet Whatley's reading in "*The Supplement to Bougainville's Voyage,* Un retour secret vers la forêt: The Problem of Privacy and Order in Diderot's Tahiti," *Kentucky Romance Quarterly* 24, no. 2 (1977): 199–208, much inflects my own. "No mystery," Whatley, 201.

90. "Set into stone," Whatley, 203.

91. For Greuze and Diderot, see Whatley, 204. She points out that Diderot had just married off his only and much beloved daughter, Angélique, as he wrote this *Supplement.* His advice to her in his letter of September 13, 1772, was to make herself entirely subordinate to her husband, to "have for your husband all the gracious compliance imaginable," to "conform to his reasonable tastes," to "try to think only what you can say to him: let him be unceasingly deep in your soul. Do nothing he could not witness. Be in all things and at all times as if under his eye. . . . You cannot show too much regard for your husband: it's a sure means of keeping immoral men away from you" (*Oeuvres complètes* 10:956). His entirely patriarchal protectiveness of his own daughter's chastity is ludicrously remote from the Tahitian's free offering of his daughter: but the sense of male prerogative is just as strong in both texts.

92. Whatley, 205.

93. For we find it too in Diderot's *D'Alembert's Dream.* See A. E. Pilkington's essay, "Nature as Ethical Norm," in *Languages of Nature,* ed. L. Jordanova (New Brunswick: Rutgers University Press, 1986), 12–13.

94. Mauzi, 269, 273, 280.

95. See Carol Duncan's "Fallen Fathers: Images of Authority in Pre-Revolutionary French Art," *Art History* 4:2 (June 1981): 186–202, for her superb survey of the ambivalences in the paintings of the period around the figures of the father. My discussion of Diderot's play owes much to her insights. The long quotation is from 186–187; "figures of pathos," 189; "old-fashioned patriarchy," 190.

96. Janet Whatley refers to this work as "a museum piece" (204). I would argue that it represents Oedipal struggle at least as much as does *Bougainville* and that, like *The Illegitimate Son,* it conveys a species of bourgeois anguish in sorting out its ideals of family and intimacy.

97. *Sophie:* Sergi [Saint-Albin] is your son!
    The Father: He loves and respects you, but his passion would end in your ruin and his, if you were to foster it. (304)

98. Denis Diderot, *Salons,* ed. Jean Seznec (Oxford: Clarendon Press, 1957–67), 2:122.

3. BETWEEN NATURE AND CULTURE

1. Richard Wilbur's translation, "*Tartuffe*" and "*The Misanthrope,*" act 5, scene 3 (New York: Harcourt Brace Jovanovich, 1965), 149–150.

2. "Euphoria of conversational interchange" is Erving Goffman's term, used by Elizabeth Goldsmith to describe Mlle de Scudéry's précieux salon exchanges (46). See 44–45 for background on the salon.

3. Ian MacLean, *The Renaissance Notion of Woman* (Cambridge: Cambridge University Press, 1980), 64.

4. Though there were women among the members of the Academy, they were fewer than a handful. The struggle over their admission is related, passim, by Vivian Cameron, *Women as Image and Image-Makers in Paris during the French Revolution* (Ann Arbor: University Micro-

films, 1984). Cameron's dissertation provides valuable illumination with regard to women in representation and as shapers of images in this era.

5. In *The Second Sex,* tr. H. M. Parshley (New York: Bantam, 1961), xxvii, 57 and *passim.*

6. From *A Journey from St. Petersburg to Moscow,* ed. Roderick Page Thaler, tr. Leo Wiener (Cambridge, Mass.: Harvard University Press, 1958), as quoted by Carolyn Hope Wilburger, "The View from Russia," in *French Women and the Age of Enlightenment* ed. Samia I. Spencer (Bloomington: Indiana University Press, 1984), 386.

7. From David Hume, *The Philosophical Works,* ed. T. H. Green and T. H. Crose, 4 vols. (Darmstadt: Scientia Verlag Aalen, 1964), 4:296, 301, as quoted by Katherine M. Rogers in "The View from England," in Spencer, 357–368.

8. G. P. Gooch, *Louis XV: The Monarchy in Decline* (London: Longmans Green, 1956), 95–99.

9. We recall the erotic message of the mule, from chapter 1.

10. For material on Pompadour and the Deerpark, see Gooch, 156–157.

11. I employ Michel Delon's image from his "Un monde d'eunuques," *Europe* 55 (1977): 79.

12. As cited by Olivier Bernier, *The Eighteenth-Century Woman* (Garden City, N.Y.: Doubleday & Co., 1981), 41.

13. For "*parvenue,*" see Karl Toth, *Woman and Rococo in France, Seen through the works of a Contemporary, Charles Pinot Duclos* (Philadelphia: Lippincott, 1931) 172–173; for Voltaire's remark, see Bernier, 41. My own version of Voltaire's verse.

14. Toth, 298.

15. Toth, 300.

16. I use the Garnier edition, ed. P. Vernière (Paris: 1960). References in the text are to letter rather than to a page, to facilitate access in other editions.

17. Notice the rapprochement with Crawford's observation in Chapter 1 about the "decent freedom" of French mores in this period. Again, we seem to have something more of a myth of pre-Revolutionary degeneracy than may have been warranted.

18. Arthur Young (85) notes having attended in the late 1780s, even in the French countryside, a dinner with two ladies and "five and six and twenty gentlemen; such a thing could not happen in England." Despite his surprise, we note how small a minority of such a company these women in fact were.

19. For a recent summary of women's legal status, see Adrienne Rogers, "Women and the Law," in Spencer; for a more extensive treatment of women's status under French law, see Léon Abensour's classical study *La Femme et le féminisme avant la révolution* (Paris: Ernest Leroux, 1923). Badinter, *L'Amour en plus,* 33; Terry Eagleton, *The Rape of Clarissa* (Bloomington: Indiana University Press, 1982), 95; Roger Picard, *Les Salons littéraires et le société française 1610–1789* (New York: Brentano's, 1943); Josephine A. J. d'Abrantès, *Histoire des salons de Paris* (Brussels: 1837), 3:316.

20. Dena Goodman, "Enlightenment Salons: The Convergence of Female and Philosophic Ambitions," *Eighteenth-Century Studies* 22, no. 3 (Spring 1989): 343. I recommend Goodman's able sifting out of the elements contributing to salon culture and her evaluation of its political place. Jean LeRond d'Alembert, *Eloge de Saint-Aulaire* in *Oeuvres de d'Alembert* (Paris: 1821–22), 3:295, as quoted by Craveri, 59.

21. Marguerite Glotz and Madeleine Maire, *Les Salons du XVIIIe siècle* (Paris: Nouvelles Editions Latines, 1949), 19.

22. The "paradox" lay in the actor's control in expressing emotions not actually felt, but amazingly simulated by him or her. The "portrait" of Mme de Boufflers (Mme de Luxembourg) is in *Horace Walpole's Correspondence,* 6:83–84.

23. Philippe Perrot provides an account of the secret marriage of Mme de Montesson and the Duke d'Orleans in 1773, where as the Marquis of Valançay presented the duke with the nuptial shirt, that groom "offered the spectacle of a complete depilation, down to the waist, in accordance with the rules of the most brilliant gallantry of the day. The princes and grandees neither consummated marriages nor received the first favors of a mistress before having this operation performed on their persons." From J. L. Soulavie, *Mémoires historiques et politiques du règne de Louis XVI* (Paris: 1801), 2:99, in Perrot, 227, note 92.

24. "To the point that all that remains of sexual dimorphism are broad anatomical and vestimentary differences." Perrot, 56.

25. "The Enlightenment Debate on Women," *History Workshop* 6 (1984): 106.

26. Delon, "Un monde d'eunuques," 79.

27. Sigmund Freud, "The most prevalent Form of Degradation in Erotic Life," 203–217, *Collected Papers,* tr. Joan Riviere (New York: Basic Books, 1959), 4:213.

28. In his study "A Special Type of Object of Choice Made by Men," *Collected Papers,* 5:192–202.

29. "Happiness," Mauzi, 111. *Anomie,* Delon, "Un monde d'eunuques," passim.

30. Bernard Le Bovier de Fontenelle (1657–1757), author and member of the Academy of Sciences, was a prominent salon figure whose presence straddled two centuries. I acknowledge my debt here to Benedetta Craveri's superb reconstruction of *Mme du Deffand et son monde,* from which I have extracted much of my documentation in the discussion that follows. Formont's portrait, 71–72.

31. One might then think that M. Formont is an antithesis to Romantic man: but not at all. Romantic man, à la René and Adolphe, will *also* fail to will, or love; it is merely that he will perceive this lack as a deep narcissistic wound. For more illumination on this score, Margaret Waller, "*Cherchez la femme:* Male Malady and Narrative Politics in the French Romantic Novel," *PMLA* 104, no. 2, (March 1989): 141–151.

32. In *Amours paysannes.* For Freud, see *Collected Papers,* 5:208. We recall the elaborate stratagems of women in society, depicted in novels like Crébillon's *Egarements* or Laclos's *Liaisons* as well as many others, to maintain their facade not of mere modesty, but of a prudery calculated to protect them from public ridicule as sexual beings.

33. Delon, "Un monde d'eunuques," 82.

34. Louis XV was said to have sobbed uncontrollably at the loss to death of the Pompadour, one of the few persons whom he trusted.

35. Craveri, 11–12. From letter to Grimm, June 1756, in Friedrich-Melchior Grimm, *Correspondance littéraire et critique, adressé à un souverain d'Allemagne depuis 1753 jusqu'en 1769,* 2:45–47. Compare Zillia's novelistic letter on the convent: "The Virgins who live in this place are in an ignorance so profound they cannot satisfy my least curiosity. Their worship of the Divinity of this land demands that they renounce all his gifts, give up all the mind's knowledge, the heart's feelings, I believe even reason; at least their speech makes one think this to be true." Françoise de Graffigny, *Lettres d'une Péruvienne,* ed. Gianni Nicoletti (Bari: Adriatica Editrice, 1967), 223.

36. Craveri, 360, note 29.

37. *Vie privée du maréchal de Richelieu* (Paris: 1791), 3:244–245, in Craveri, 16.

38. Charles Pinot Duclos, *Considérations sur les moeurs de ce siècle* (1751) in *Oeuvres complètes* (Paris: 1820–21), 1:135.

39. Picard, 303.

40. For "the reek of cadaverous flesh," see the *Mémoires* of the Baron de Besenval as cited by Collé, *La Vérité dans le vin, ou les Désagréments de la galanterie, comédie* (Paris: 1846), 4:48, in Craveri, 75. See also the *Vie privée du maréchal Richelieu,* 2:312, in Craveri, 76. For Rousseau on Mme de Luxembourg, *Confessions,* (New York: French and European Publications, 1968), 2:279.

41. *Horace Walpole's Correspondence* 6:83–84.

42. "Portrait de Mme du Deffand par M. de Forcalquier," *Walpole Correspondence* 6:51–52.

43. M. du Chatel to Mme du Deffand, 1742. *Correspondance complète de la marquise de Deffand avec ses amis* (Paris: 1865; rpt. Repr. 2 vols. Geneva: Slatkine, 1971), 1:81, in Craveri, 86.

44. This is Jean Bethke Elshtain's formulation of Jurgen Habermas's position (311).

45. For "naturalness," Craveri, 88; Nicolas Chamfort, *Maximes et pensées,* in *Oeuvres complètes* (Paris: 1801), 2:41, in Craveri, 88.

46. The other great drama was her passionate attachment to Horace Walpole, which does not impinge on our story here.

47. "Portrait de M. d'Alembert par Mme du Deffand," *Walpole Correspondence,* 6:94, in Craveri, 92.

48. See Craveri, chapter 8.

49. See Charles-Augustin de Sainte-Beuve, "Mémoires de Mme de Staal-Delaunay," *Oeuvres* (Paris: Pléiade, 1950–51), 2:897; Jean Le Rond d'Alembert, "Portrait de Mlle de Lespinasse," in *Lettres de Mlle de Lespinasse,* ed. Eugène Asse (Paris: n.d.), 346.

50. "Children of love," d'Alembert to Voltaire, May 26, 1760, in Craveri, 160–161. "Get a good laugh," *Mémoires de Marmontel* (Paris: 1891), 2:378, in Craveri, 155. "Worsening storm," M.-P. de Ségur, "Julie de Lespinasse: Le Couvent de St.-Joseph," *Revue des deux mondes* (April 1905): 892, in Craveri, 161.

51. Goodman, 339.

52. We recall Julie de Lespinasse's obsessive, self-destructive love for Mora. See Dena Goodman's

"Julie de Lespinasse: A Mirror for the Enlightenment," in *Eighteenth-Century Women and the Arts,* ed. Frederick Keener and Susan E. Lorsch (New York: Greenwood, 1988), 3–10.

53. *Salons,* 2:51.
54. *Salons,* 2:86.
55. Robert Muchembled, *Popular Culture and Elite Culture in France 1400–1750,* tr. Lydia Cochrane (Baton Rouge: Louisiana State University Press, 1985), 73–74; for *veillées,* 69.
56. Muchembled, 189, 191.
57. Muchembled, 165. This view is confirmed by Eugen Weber's reading of late nineteenth and early twentieth century notes in chapter 4, "Affections and Disaffections," of his *France—Fin de Siècle* (Cambridge, Mass.: Belknap–Harvard University Press, 1986).
58. One random example: Nearly 15 percent of the crimes committed in Arras between 1528 and 1529 were attributed to women: 20 percent of robberies, 10 percent of physical blows or injuries, and 18 percent of cases of resistance to authority. Of morals offense cases, 24 percent were charged to women. Muchembled, 192. "When they rose in revolt during periods of famine, when women looted the granaries of rich citizens, merchants and abbeys, such actions were considered serious and put down harshly." Muchembled, 122. See also 217.
59. Muchembled, 166.
60. See 298–299.
61. Arlette Farge, *Le Miroir des femmes* (Paris: Montalba, 1982), 13; for "a real monkey," 32.
62. Mireille Laget, "Petites écoles en Languedoc au XVIIIe siècle," *Annales: Economies, Sociétés, Civilisations* (1971): 1409.
63. Luc Thoré, "Langage et sexualité," in *Sexualité humaine* (Centre d'etudes Laënnec) (Paris: Aubier-Montaigne, 1970), 68. Bourdieu, 56.
64. Bourdieu, 104.
65. *Mari et femme dans la société paysanne,* exposition catalogue (Paris: Flammarion, 1980), 57.
66. Segalen, *Mari . . . paysanne,* 65.
67. "The man makes a woman, he socializes her in the true sense of the word, he makes her exist as a social and cultural being" (Segalen, *Mari . . . paysanne* 136). Wash-house, Segalen, *Mari . . . paysanne* 151. Assembled women, Farge, 61. Proverbs, Segalen, *Mari . . . paysanne* 167.
68. Segalen, *Mari . . . paysanne* 171.
69. Segalen, *Mari . . . paysanne* 182–183.
70. The verbal malaise in Bourdieu's modern study was relaxed in the sole case of courting, and only after authorization was obtained. "Camaraderie between boys and girls does not exist in the countryside" (102).
71. Jean-Jacques Rutlidge, *Essai sur le caractère et les moeurs des Français comparées [sic] à celles des Anglais* (London: 1776).
72. Among the population at large, "in social life, many were prepared to blame women for—or at least associate them with—the apparent disorder. . . . Luxury in particular and conspicuous consumption in general are taken to be specifically female failings." Elizabeth Fox-Genovese, "Women at Work," in Spencer, 114. The very variegation of approaches of the Encyclopedists is itself revealing. Note Susan Procious Malueg's summation in her "Women and the *Encyclopédie,*" in Spencer, 265: "While the Encyclopedists in their treatment of women are often guilty of common forms of bias—invisibility, stereotyping, imbalance and selectivity, unreality, fragmentation—the *Encyclopédie* nonetheless presents the other side of the coin as well. The good and the bad, the profound and the superficial, the complimentary and the uncomplimentary coexist." As examples of this range she cites Jaucourt's view favoring the equality of women and men within marriage; Desmahis's assessment of women as vain and deceitful; Barthez's that a woman, though perhaps an *homme manqué* or defective man, might yet be capable of improvement through education; and Boucher d'Argis's description of women's present legal disabilities as contrasted with their potential, as demonstrated by the learned women of Italy. Such an array of views, all of them lacking inner coherence and none by a major figure except for d'Alembert's powerful but parenthetical discussion of women's capacities in the article "Geneva," perfectly reflects the state of flux which thinking about women had entered.
73. David Williams, "The Politics of Feminism in the French Revolution," in *The Varied Pattern: Studies in the Eighteenth Century,* ed. P. Hughes and D. Williams (Toronto: A. M. Hakkert, 1971), 337. See also A. Rogers and Abensour.
74. See Frédéric Deloffre's discussion of the feminist tendencies of the "new preciosity" of Mme Lambert's circle, in *Une Préciosité nouvelle: Marivaux et le marivaudage* (Paris: A. Colin, 1967),

18–25 and passim. I also refer readers to the pioneering study by Georges Ascoli, "Histoire des idées féministes en France," *Revue de synthèse historique* 13 (1906): 25–57, 161–84.

75. "Women and the Reform of the Nation," in *Women in Society in Eighteenth-Century France,* ed. Eva Jacobs et al. (London: Athlone Press, 1979), 3–18.

76. Tomaselli (109) provides an example from the Scottish physician William Alexander's 1779 *History of Women from the Earliest Antiquity to the Present Time:* "In every age, and in every country, while the men have been partial to the persons of the fair sex, they have left their minds altogether without culture, or biased them with a culture of a spurious nature; suspicious, perhaps, that a more rational one would have opened their eyes, shown them their real condition, and prompted them to assert the rights of nature; rights of which men have perpetually, more or less, deprived them." On women and nature, see particularly Charlton and the distinguished work of Ludmilla Jordanova, "Natural Facts: A Historical Perspective on Science and Sexuality," and M. Bloch and J. H. Bloch, "Women and the Dialectics of Nature in Eighteenth-Century Thought," both in C. McCormack and M. Strathern, eds., *Nature, Culture, and Gender* (Cambridge: Cambridge University Press, 1980).

77. Tomaselli, 106, 107; Rutlidge, 154.

78. Tomaselli (105) argues they were a factor only for social history. The dichotomies are Ludmilla Jordanova's list from her "Naturalizing the Family: Literature and the bio-Medical Sciences," in *Languages of Nature,* ed. L. Jordanova (New Brunswick: Rutgers University Press, 1986), 91–92.

79. Denis Diderot, *Des Femmes, Oeuvres complètes* 10:44; Antoine-Léonard Thomas, *Essai sur le caractère, les moeurs, et l'esprit des femmes dans les différents siècles* (Paris: 1772), 3.

80. Emilie du Chatelet, *Discours sur le bonheur,* ed. Robert Mauzi (Paris: Les Belles Lettres, 1961), 21.

81. Laurent Versini, *Laclos et la tradition* (Paris: Klincksieck, 1968), 140, 135.

82. Quoted in Versini, 136.

83. "I should strongly approve of a law," jokes the narrator, "that would condemn the man who had seduced and abandoned a good woman to the love of courtesans: the commonplace man to the commonplace woman." Diderot, *Jacques, O.C.,* 12:189.

84. Godard d'Ancour, *Lettre du chevalier D'Auteuil et de Mlle de Thélis* (1742), in Versini, 140–141; Villaret, in Roland Mortier, "Libertinage littéraire et tension sociale dans la littérature de l'Ancien régime," *Revue de littérature comparée* 46 (1972): 44; Goncourt, *La Femme,* 6–7, 332. See also Toth.

    "A good deal of the French nobility's physical degeneracy in Rococo may be related to the criminal prejudice that conjugal obligations had to be discharged like an irksome burden . . . ; not less, however, to the increasing unnaturalness of motherhood itself. Each childbed in this tight-laced and bepatched generation becomes a life-and-death affair. Fear of a ruined bosom-line scares these women from the sweet sacrifice of suckling their children, and thus severs at the root the spiritual bond between mother and child. As for attending to their children's education! It has to be a question of impressing a third party before these women bring themselves even to the mere gesture of anxious motherhood" (332).

85. See Ruth Plaut Weinreb's edition, *Lettres à mon fils: Essais sur l'éducation et morceaux choisis* (Concord, Mass.: Wayside, 1989).

86. *Oeuvres de Mme d'Epinay, Mes Moments heureux* (Paris: 1869), 2:8, as quoted by Elisabeth Badinter, *Emilie, Emilie: L'Ambition féminine au XVIIIe siècle* (Paris: Flammarion, 1983), 369.

87. *Pseudo-Memoires de Mme d'Epinay, Historie de Mme de Montbrillant,* ed. Georges Roth, 3 vols., (Paris: Gallimard, 1951), Badinter, 370.

88. See Badinter, *Emilie, Emilie,* for a consideration of just this phenomenon, as well as a fuller account of Mme d'Epinay's career. Louis d'Epinay would become a gambler whose mother ended up putting him in jail to prevent him from squandering the family's fortune. Her daughter she married off at fourteen to a brain-damaged marquis living deep in the countryside.

89. We recall Rousseau's sexual fascination from childhood on with the whippings administered to him by Mlle Lambercier and Mlle Goton, as related in book 1 of the *Confessions.* For Rousseau, see *Les Confessions,* 2 vols. (New York: French and European Publications, 1968); further page references are within the text.

90. Note the resemblance here to Diderot's description of Mme de la Pommeraye's white-hot anger.

91. Rousseau claims he assumed she was pregnant and that he was being invited along to be used as her dupe.

92. *Lettre à M. d'Alembert sur son Article "Genève" dans le septième volume de l'Encyclopédie, et particulièrement sur le projet d'établir un théâtre de comédie en cette ville,* in *Du contrat social* (Paris: Garnier, 1962). References in text are to this edition. We recall that d'Alembert had included an eloquent plea for women's potentialities in his own argument.

93. My emphasis. Here is the preferred spectacle he proffers to that of theatrical entertainments.

94. He reports a desire so overwhelming it overcame him on his way to their rendezvous. "While walking I dreamed of the one I was to meet and of the caressing greeting she would give me, of the kiss awaiting me. . . . This sole kiss, this fatal kiss seeped into my blood even before I received it, to such a degree that I lost my head and was blinded with vertigo; my trembling knees could hold me up no longer; I was forced to stop and sit down; my entire being was in disorder: I was ready to fall into a faint. . . . I would arrive at Eaubonne weak, exhausted, wrung out, scarcely able to stand. The moment I saw her all was repaired; I felt by her side only the importunity of an inexhaustible potency, forever futile" (*Confessions,* 2:196).

95. Rousseau affirms, for example, that divorce was little resorted to in Greece and Rome, and that the Roman law allowing it lay inert on the books for five hundred years before anyone thought of using it. Neither assertion is accurate. Sarah B. Pomeroy asserts that divorce was easily attainable in Greek society with no stigma attached to it, and that in Rome it could be obtained without difficulty, in both cultures principally by men, of course. *Goddesses, Whores, Wives, and Slaves: Women in Classical Antiquity* (New York: Schocken Books, 1975), 64, 158.

96. Compare Germaine de Staël: "Finally [Rousseau] believes in love; he is forgiven; what does it matter to women that his reason fights against their power, when his heart is submissive to them? What does it even matter to women whom nature has made tender of soul that the false honor of governing the one they love is to be taken away from them?" *Lettres sur le caractère et les écrits de Jean-Jacques Rousseau,* in *Oeuvres de Madame de Staël-Hostein,* 3 vols. (Paris: 1838), 1:8.

97. Judith Shklar, "Rousseau's Two Models: Sparta and the Age of Gold," *Political Science Quarterly* 81 (1966): 43. It is in this sense that Rousseau's misogynous rejection of memory recapitulates classical misogyny, which reads women's being as representing men's mortality.

98. Sarah Kofman, *Le Respect des femmes* (Paris: Slatkine, 1982), 68.

99. We recall Diderot's discomposure with the image of the prostitute mixing with the senator.

100. There is of course an inherent paradox here for the author of the *Confessions,* which reveal so many of his own perplexities. But Rousseau's memoirs constitute an apologia for a specific individual life. Unlike the *Confessions,* a Racine play is generalizable to its public in its imaginary representations of persons in the thick of their dilemmas. Drama leaves our reading of such dilemmas to us, its spectators: Rousseau prearranges our reading of his.

His anger at the bracketing by theater of virtuous men in conflict is nowhere more evident, of course, than in his treatment of Molière's Alceste. In his letter he roundly scolds Molière for pandering to his stylish public by deliberately mocking him whom one ought not mock: "This tough, harsh aspect, which gives him at times so much spleen and bitterness also distances him . . . from any childish pique without reasonable foundation and from any excess of self-interest" (*Lett.* 153). The forthright stripper of illusion and lover of virtue cannot be funny, have an absurd dimension, for Rousseau. Molière ought to have made Philinte, the *homme de société,* the more ridiculous figure. It is significant to note here that Fabre d'Eglantine, the Jacobin, picks up on Rousseau's suggestion that the moderate Philinte is the figure on whom to concentrate attack, as he writes *Philinte, ou la suite du Misanthrope* (1790).

The name of Célimène never appears in Rousseau's extensive discussion of Molière's *Misanthrope, Lett.,* 150–158.

101. As he had formerly, in his *Discours sur les sciences et les arts* (1750).

4. THE WAR OF THE SEXES

1. Anita Brookner, *Jacques-Louis David* (New York: Harper and Row, 1980), 44.

2. "Le malheur de nos armées ne tira pas plus . . . Louis XV de son inertie que ne l'en avait tiré la détresse de ses peuples" (The misfortunes of our armies no more drew Louis XV out of his inertia than had the distress of his people). Félix Rocquain, *L'Esprit Révolutionnaire avant la Révolution 1715–1789* (Paris: 1878) 108. Helvetius, as cited by Rocquain, 310, from the

Mémoires de [Louis Petit de] *Bachaumont* (January 1774), 7:120–121. The scolding, Roc-quain, 312, from Siméon-Prosper Hardy, *'Mes loisirs,' par S. P. Hardy, journal d'evenements tels qu'ils parviennent à ma connaissance,* ed. M. Tourneux and M. Vitrac (Paris: Picard, 1912.)

3. "The prestige of royalty disappeared. It would never be reborn" (Rocquain, 313). Observe the terms of comparison between the two royal mistresses attributed to Choderlos de Laclos. The Pompadour is "that cheerful woman who gave mistresses to the king, ministers to his council, generals to his armies, priests to his Church, dungeons to those who allowed themselves any impudent whispers; contemptible woman, whom a few mercenary poets have hidden from disgrace, but whose name will not escape it." Whereas he writes of Jeanne Bécu, la Du Barry, "Elmire was thrown, almost despite herself, into the midst of conspirators and was carried along by the whirlwind of intrigue. . . . But remorse troubled her soul, even in a country where it passes for weakness. . . . Elmire will not fear posterity's judgment . . . ; it will forgive the delirium of the senses of a woman who has made her lover neither cruel nor unjust." *Galeries des dames françaises,* in Laclos, *Oeuvres complètes,* ed. Larent Versini (Paris: Pléiade, 1979), 752–754.

4. See Reinhard Koselleck's assessment of Turgot's administration in *Le Règne de la critique,* tr. Hans Hildenbrandt (Paris: Editions de minuit, 1959).

5. On the impact of libelles upon the queen, see Chantal Thomas, "L'héroïne du crime—Marie-Antoinette dans les pamphlets," in *La Carmagnole des Muses,* ed. Jean-Claude Bonnet (Paris: Armand Colin, 1988), and Elizabeth Colwill, "Just Another *Citoyenne?* Marie-Antoinette on Trial, 1790–1793," *History Workshop* 28 (Autumn 1989): 63–87. For the verse, see Robert Darnton, *The Literary Underground of the Old Regime* (Cambridge, Mass.: Harvard University Press, 1982), 201; Darnton's translation, slightly retouched by me.

6. Darnton refers here to Pierre Goubert's *L'Ancien régime* (Paris: Gallimard 1969), 1:152. See Darnton, 205, 155.

7. C. Thomas, 255.

8. See George May, *Le Dilemme du roman au XVIIIe siècle* (Paris: PUF, 1963), on the relationship of women as readers and writers to the "subversions" of the novel.

9. Nina Rattner Gelbart, "*Le Journal des dames* and its Female Editors: Censorship and Feminism in the Old Regime Press," in *Press and Politics in Eighteenth-Century France,* ed. Jack R. Censer and Jeremy Popkin (Berkeley: University of California Press, 1987). I am highly indebted to Gelbart's study in this section. Joan Landes also integrates Gelbart's findings into her own rich work, 57–61. See also Gelbart's *Feminine and Opposition Journalism in France* (Berkeley: University of California Press, 1989), published too late to be considered here.

10. From Marie-Anne Roumier Robert's *Voyage de Mylord Ceton dans les sept planètes ou le Nouveau Mentor* (The Hague: 1765–66), in Gelbart, 27–28.

11. Gelbart, 30, 32–33.

12. *Journal des dames* (Nov. 1761): 103–105, in Gelbart, 35. I cannot pursue here as Gelbart does the fascinating details of Mme Beaumer's ties with freemasonry, her troubles with the censor Malesherbes, her universalism, or her advocacy of every kind of work for women, as "painters, shopowners, sculptors, rugmakers, clockmakers, lensgrinders, collectors, taxider-mists, weavers, chemists and singers."

13. *JD* (Oct. 1761): 62–63, in Gelbart, 35. Feminist resistance to Rousseau, as we see here, began immediately in the wake of the publication of his works: it did not await the innumerable late twentieth-century deconstructions of Shulamith Firestone, Zillah Eisenstein, or Sarah Kofman, to name only a few.

14. *JD* 39: 63, in Gelbart, 44. Although, Gelbart writes, Mme de Maisonneuve "treated piquant issues, she stayed always within fashionable limits, striking the perfect balance of spice with respectability. There was none of her predecessor's belligerent rhetoric" (49).

15. For Mme de Montanclos, see Gelbart, 59, 64, 65.

16. I refer readers to Vivian Cameron's commentary on the popularity and nature of treatments of Cornelia (126–153). Cameron cites the painter Carmontelle's republican critique of Cor-nelia's stance before "the Campanian Woman" as "too craven" (130) toward wealth and posi-tion. Cameron sees Carmontelle's resentment of Hallé's art here as springing, like the Grub Streeters', from jealousy of an artist crowned with every privilege available to an academician in the court's favor.

17. Mme de Montanclos was followed as editor by Louis-Sébastien Mercier. For the rise of cafés, salons, etc, see François Furet, *Penser la Révolution française* (Paris: Gallimard, 1978), 59.

Furet uses the expression "democratic sociability" to allude to the "world of political sociability" based on opinion (59). He terms it democratic in its openness, even though it failed to extend to the peuple. See also Gabriel Sénac de Meilhan, *Du Gouvernment, des moeurs, et des conditions en France avant la Révolution* (Paris: 1795), 132.

18. Louis-Sébastien Mercier, *Tableau de Paris* (Amsterdam: 1782–88), 1:183.
19. Sénac, 37.
20. For L.-S. Mercier, see *TP*, 1:232. Suzanne Necker's huge contribution to the capital was the gift of a hospital, l'Hôpital Necker, whose operations she oversaw for a period of ten years. For Mme Necker's adulation of her husband, see Suzanne Curchod Necker, *Mélanges extraits des manuscrits de Mme Necker* (Paris: 1798), passim. An example displaying how this tendency remained at the core of Staël's own life project: "Any just man who examines M. Necker's public conduct will always find it in the principle of virtue." From Mme de Staël's posthumous *Considérations sur les principaux événements de la Révolution française*, 3 vols. (Paris: 1818), 1:64.
21. See my "Mme de Staël, Rousseau, and the Woman Question," *PMLA* 86, no. 1 (Jan. 1971): 100–109.
22. Coward, 376. C.-N. Ledoux, *L'Architecture considérée sous le rapport de l'art, des moeurs, et de la législation* (Paris: 1804), in Coward, 393.
23. Coward, 395.
24. Perrot, 99, 65, 68.
25. From Bressy's *Recherches sur les vapeurs* (London: 1789), 136, in Perrot, 80, 81.
26. The painting *Marie-Antoinette Wearing a "Gaulle"* by Vigée-Lebrun was so severely censured that it had to be removed from the 1784 Salon. Its offense lay in exposing "august persons . . . to the public wearing clothes reserved for the privacy of their palace. The queen was also accused of trying to ruin the Lyons silk industry by wearing English linens." Stella Blum, catalogue of exhibition, *Eighteenth-Century Women* (New York: Metropolitan Museum of Art, 1981), 138.
27. Heels had been so high that women "were forced to throw their bodies backward to stay in equilibrium while struggling against their natural bent, which carried them forward." Count de Verblanc, *Souvenirs* (Paris: 1838), 1:262, in Perrot, 232, note 66.
28. Note L.-S. Mercier: "Only in Paris do women of sixty still dress as they did at twenty, and offer us made-up faces with mouches and even a beribboned head." *TP*, 1:234. For discussion of hairstyle, see S. Blum, 13.
29. L.-S. Mercier, *TP*, 1:232.
30. J. Bloch, 8.
31. Riballier, (avec la collaboration de Mlle Cosson), *De l'éducation physique et morale des femmes avec une notice alphabétique de celles qui se sont distinguées* (Bruxelles: 1779), 17.
32. Riballier, 67.
33. Riballier, vii.
34. Riballier, 23–24.
35. Versini, 239.
36. J. Bloch, 15, Miremont, *Traité de l'éducation des femmes*, 2:503, 505, in Versini, 545.
37. L.-S. Mercier, *TP*, 2:224–225. All subsequent references here are to this volume.
38. The French word *charmes* refers also to physical seductiveness and has a more extended meaning than the English *charms*.
39. Hufton, "Women and the Family Economy," 20–21, 22.
40. J.-J. Bachelier, *Mémoire sur l'Education des filles, présenté aux Etats-Généraux* (Paris: 1789), rpt. in *Les Femmes dans la Révolution Française* (Paris: Edhis, 1982), vol. 1, doc. 4, p. 8.
41. "Pleurez sur ce jeune imprudent . . ." (Weep for this heedless young man) (10).
42. Nagy, 30.
43. See my "Laclos and 'le Sexe'" for a global view of Laclos's oeuvre about women.
44. Jordanova, "Naturalizing the Family" in *Languages of Nature*, 90–92.
45. I think of Joan Landes's and Dorinda Outram's searching studies of Rousseau's novel.
46. André Gide's preface to Ernest Dowson's 1940 translation *Les Liaisons dangereuses* (*Dangerous Acquaintances*) (London: Nonesuch Press) argues (viii) that the work was not a fully willed one, and Glauco Natoli saw it as expressing otherwise repressed matter in his "Figure e problemi della cultura francese," *Biblioteca di cultura contemporanea* (Messina-Florence) 19 (1956): 220.

47. Versini, 135, 139.
48. Nancy Miller, *The Heroine's Text: Readings in the French and English Novel 1722–1782* (New York: Columbia University Press, 1980), 117.
49. The edition of Laclos's work referred to in the text will be Laurent Versini's edition of the *Oeuvres complètes* (Paris: Pléiade, 1979). References to the *Liaisons dangereuses,* however, will be to letter numbers to facilitate access in other editions.
50. Crow, *PPL,* 221.
51. See Jean-Noël Vuarnet's "Massacre des femmes," *Nrf* (1977): 90, which characterizes Laclos as "the most feminist author" in French literature.
52. A phrase I use in my Laclos article, 275.
53. Versini (in Laclos, *Oeuvres,* 1364, note 1) observes that Valmont seeks to subdue Cécile's senses, Merteuil's brain, and Tourvel's heart, ambitions Merteuil notes in letter 84.
54. Versini reminds us that the Paris public thought it recognized in Merteuil Stéphanie de Genlis, the severely moralistic royal governess and author whom Laclos attacked in his *Galeries des dames* for having taken up the pen (in Laclos, *Oeuvres,* 750).
55. In Laclos, *Oeuvres,* 1377, note 5.
56. I owe to Nancy Miller's skillful juxtaposition of the Merteuil and Tourvel texts (142–143) my own reading of them. See also Paul Hoffmann, "Aspects de la condition féminine dans *les Liaisons dangereuses,*" *L'Information littéraire* (March–April 1963), 48, and Miller, 135.
57. Aram Vartanian, "The Marquise de Merteuil: A Case of Mistaken Identity," *Esprit Créateur* (Winter 1963): 176.
58. Versini compares this manipulative gallantry with Valmont's letters 31, 36, 58, and 83 of the *Liaisons. Oeuvres,* 1589, note 1 on p. 760.
59. This ferment, I suggest, may in fact have spurred Laclos to his astonishing first *Essay on Women* (the first of three), in which he invites them to revolt, as the only appropriate path to redressing the wrongs done them. See my "Laclos and 'le Sexe,'" 281.
60. In Dominique Aury's amazing summation of this backlash: "Never, perhaps, in any period except the two or three decades that preceded the French Revolution, in any milieu, if not in this closed milieu, half-aristocratic, half-bourgeois, of what was then called society, were [women] so cruelly pressured and entrapped with techniques usually employed in the hunt, with horn blasts and cries." "La Révolte de Mme de Merteuil," *Les Cahiers de la Pléiade* (1951): 101.
61. The word used, translated as "efficacity," is *énergie,* but Versini, supported by the *Dictionnaires de Trevoux* and *de l'Académie,* substitutes *efficacity* for it. Laclos's intent is obscure here. *O.c.,* 1592, note 2 to p. 762.
62. Aury, 93.
63. Norbert Elias, *The History of Manners: The Civilizing Process* (New York: Urizen, 1978), 184.
64. "Originally a gay and lightly carried off scene full of vitality, the theme becomes an allegory, more calculated, colder perhaps." Jean-Paul Bouillon, Antoinette Ehrard, and Michel Melot, eds., *Aimer en France 1780–1800,* exposition (City of Clermont-Ferrand: 1977), 12.
65. Pierre Roussel, *Système physique et moral de la femme . . .* (Paris: 1775), 216.
66. Cited by Nagy, 70.
67. Again we recall Grimod de la Reynière's remark: "People celebrate libertinism as much as they do lack of faith, and we would blush as much at appearing virtuous as we've long blushed at showing our faith." Cited note 42 from his *Réflexions philosophiques sur le plaisir* (Paris: 1783), 3–4. See Nagy, 26, 30.
68. *Les Gynographes, ou idées de deux honnêtes-femmes sur un Projet de Règlement proposé à toute l'Europe, pour mettre les femmes à leur place, et opérer le bonheur des deux sexes—avec des notes historiques et justificatives, suivies des noms de femmes célèbres,* 2 vols. (The Hague: 1777). References are to this edition.
69. N.-E. Restif de la Bretonne, *Le Pornographe,* ed. Beatrice Didier (Paris: Régine Desforges, 1976), 45, 43.
70. Restif, *Le Pornographe,* 46.
71. L.-S. Mercier, *TP,* 4:24; Restif, *Les Gynographes,* 2:42.
72. Roussel, 2–3.
73. From this weakness, of course, flow many of women's inferiorities: women's learning, therefore, is "a vain phantom" (152).
74. In slight mitigation of the harshness of this statement, Roussel adds here that women may apply themselves to self-cultivation, but only of the ornamental arts. 152.

75. As Elisabeth Badinter puts it: "At the end of the eighteenth century, it will be necessary to call upon [woman's] sense of duty, to spur her sense of guilt and even to threaten to return her to nurturant and maternal functions, spoken of as natural and spontaneous." *L'Amour en plus*, 182.

76. Badinter provides several examples of fathers deeply concerned for the welfare of their daughters; Jacob-Nicolas Moreau, writing in 1776, and General Mortange, in his correspondence (1756–82), the former grieving over his daughter's death, the latter over his child's illness. *L'Amour en plus*, 255. Her book provides cogent demonstrations of the crisis I allude to here. Badinter speaks of "complicity between fathers and mothers in parental neglect." *L'Amour en plus*, 182.

77. One small chink of evidence for this in this period lies in the terms of Rousseau's objection to Locke's contention that the conjugal tie was a natural one, to ensure the survival of the couple's young. In nature, Rousseau replies, "once appetite is satisfied, man has no more need of a given woman, nor a woman of a given man. The former has not the slightest concern, nor even the least idea of the consequences of his act." *Discours sur l'origine de l'inégalité*, in *Le Contrat social*, 116.

78. It is to this idea of universal man that Rousseau of course appeals: "O homme, de quelque contrée que tu sois" (Oh Man, whatever your nation), in his description of his "original" state, *De l'origine de l'inégalité*, 40. Rousseau believes it was in observing others' ways of conducting themselves that men concluded that their mode of thinking was "entirely in conformity" with their own. *De l'origine de l'inégalité*, 68. Rousseau is the spokesperson for all men in his own eyes.

79. *De l'origine de l'inégalité*, 42.

80. *Le Contrat social*, 236.

81. Roussel, 371. For the return to paternal sentiment, see Badinter, *L'Amour en plus*, 124.

82. L.-S. Mercier, *TP*, 2:194, 195.

83. L.-S. Mercier, *TP*, 10:201 and 8:195.

84. Dennis Fletcher, "Restif de la Bretonne and Woman's Estate," in Jacobs et al., 99, quotes from the *Philosophie de Monsieur Nicolas* (Paris: 1796), 179.

85. Restif, *PMN*, 254, in Fletcher, 99. It must be recalled that Restif's ideas were conditioned by the spermaticist biological theory that shaped beliefs concerning conception until the role of the ovum was finally confirmed in 1827, when Karl Ernst von Baer provided his demonstration of the existence of the until then invisible mammalian egg. See Thomas Laqueur, "Orgasm, Generation, and the Politics of Reproductive Biology," in *The Making of the Modern Body: Sexuality and Society in the Nineteenth Century*, ed. Catherine Gallagher and Thomas Laqueur (Berkeley: University of California Press, 1987), 25. Laqueur's article raises an issue closely related to the mental alterations I am attempting to adduce here: that is, the "dramatic revaluation of the female orgasm that occurred in the late eighteenth century and the even more dramatic reinterpretation of the female body in relation to that of the male." What Laqueur perceives is borne out by this study: "A new model of incommensurability triumphed over the old hierarchical model in the wake of new political agendas" (18). However, I am arguing that this model precedes and conditions the political agenda, as we may judge from the heat of Restif's sexual separatism.

86. Andrea Dworkin, *Pornography: Men Possessing Women* (New York: Putnam-Perigee, 1981), 128.

87. Fletcher emphasizes the link between these beliefs and "Restif's priapic fantasies," which impelled him to claim paternity of huge numbers of children. "Man is a candle, who lights up a hundred, a thousand others." *PMN*, 258, in Fletcher, 99. Again we see how spermaticist biology buttressed, and reflected, ancient suppositions concerning the male's primacy in conception and in the child's genetic makeup.

88. Ferrières, 119. Jean-Jacques Rutlidge had commented on "the frequent indifference of men for what they have so little reason to believe is their posterity" (153).

89. *PMN*, 529–530, in Fletcher, 100. For Mercier on beatings, *TP*, 10:173, and John Lough, "Women in Mercier's 'Tableau de Paris,'" in Jacobs et al. For "absolute dissymetry," see Roussel, who sees the "difference in function between man and woman in the work of generation as sufficing to set aside any idea of similarity" in organs. Since, for him, she is made to receive, he to give, there is simply no evidence in her of "an active, powerful sexuality" (134–135).

90. Lough, 120. L.-S. Mercier, *TP*, 9:173.

91. Fletcher, 104. As Fletcher notes concerning the M. and Mme Nicolas of Restif's novel, this ideal of gender is a backward-looking utopian myth of a *Vieille France*, buttressed by precedents even more antique.

92. Roussel, 372.
93. *Le Paysan perverti,* 346–347, in Fletcher, 107.
94. Michel Delon, "La Mère coupable ou la fête impossible," in *Fêtes de la Révolution Colloque de Clermont-Ferrand (1974),* ed. J. Ehrard and P. Viallaneix (Paris: Société des études robespier-ristes, 1977), 377.
95. For a "spermatic style," see letter to Mme de Godeville, *Lettres à Madame de Godeville 1777–1779,* ed. Maxime Formont, (Paris: 1928), 175, in Undank, 852. Jack Undank's re-markable study, "Beaumarchais' Transformations," *Modern Language Notes* 4 (Sept. 1985), has been a fruitful point of departure for my discussion, and I am much obliged to him for the use of it here. The censors who first reviewed the play in 1781 were ready to allow its performance, but after the king had himself read it, he forbad its production, claiming it would bring down the Bastille. Meanwhile the scandal of its censure was such that Catherine II demanded that it be previewed in Russia. It was finally premiered on April 27, 1784. Beaumarchais had waited six years to see it produced. Beaumarchais refers to Suzanne as Figaro's property in his preface. See Classiques Larousse edition, *La Mariage de Figaro,* 2 vols. (Paris: 1971), 1:40.
96. It has been frequently pointed out that the *jus primae noctis* (right to the first night) that the Count Almaviva is presumed in the play to be attempting to preempt from Figaro was not a right invoked literally by feudal lords over vassals. Here it is rather a metaphor for the "unfair" force of nobility and money in their effortless coercion of lower-class women's collaboration with sexual desire.
97. See Undank, 843, 847.
98. Preface to *Mariage,* 1:41.
99. Undank (857) would look upon it as one of Beaumarchais's healing "anironic countervisions of a grace and peace that quite literally pass all understanding."
100. It must be remembered that male lampoons of women's complaints were not infrequent at this time. See chapter 5 for the problem of ventriloquism in reading women's *cahiers de doléance.*
101. Undank, 863, 868.
102. Knibiehler and Fouquet, 150. Roussel, 354. Bordeu, in his *Recherches sur les glandes,* (1759) wrote that the mother attaches herself all the more to her nursling in that he rewards her by exciting a sensation that evokes tenderness in her, and in his *Analyse médicinale du sang* (*O.c.* 953), he stated that the "exchange of sensibility between nursing mother and child is evi-dently well established"; see Hoffmann, notes 41 and 42, 131–132. Shorter, *MMF,* 182.
103. George Gromont, *Le Hameau de Trianon* (Paris: Vincent, Frail, 1928), 63.
104. M.-F. Morel, 407, quoting from A. Franklin, *La Vie privée d'autrefois* (Paris: 1896), 46.
105. Sussman, 22.
106. "Degeneration," Morel, 413, quoting J. Raulin, *De la conservation des enfants ou les moyens de les fortifier, de les préserver, et de les guérir des maladies,* 3 vols. (Paris: 1768–69), 2:191. "Guilty" midwives, Morel, 408, citing an article in the *Journal de Paris,* October 15, 1784.
107. L.-S. Mercier, *TP,* 4:144. Mme de Genlis, Knibiehler and Fouquet, 147. Prost de Royer, *Mé-moire sur la conservations des enfants* (Lyon: 1778), 12, in Morel, 410. Rise in percentage of in-fants nursed by mothers, Sussman, 110–112. Persistence of wet-nursing, Sussman, chapter 5.
108. *Essais historiques sur la vie de Marie-Antoinette, reine de France, pour servir à l'histoire de cette princesse* (1789), 35, in C. Thomas, 253.
109. See, for amplification of this phenomenon, H. R. Hays, *The Dangerous Sex* (New York: P. G. Putnam, 1964), Wolfgang Lederer, *The Fear of Women* (New York: Harcourt Brace Jovanovich, 1968), Andrea Dworkin, *Woman Hating* (New York: E. P. Dutton, 1974), and Karen Horney (cited herein).
110. *Le Cadran des plaisirs de la Cour ou les Aventures du petit page Chérubin, pour servir de suite à la vie de Marie-Antoinette, ci-devant reine de France* (*The Calendar of court pleasures or the adven-tures of the little page Cherubin, to serve as sequel to the life of Marie-Antoinette, former queen of France*) (1789), 38. Note that she was still queen at this date.
111. C. Thomas, 256.
112. *Lettres écrites de Lausanne,* in Isabelle de Charrière, *Romans* (Paris: Le Chemin vert, 1982), 22. Further page references are in the text.
113. It is of no little interest that Charrière, never a biological mother, though buying into the arguments for maternity as women's highest estate, was sufficiently detached from the emo-

tions surrounding the maternal biological imperative to be a more effective thinker regarding women's education by women than many of those who were.

114. With the notable exceptions of her *Réflexions sur le procès de la reine* (see chapter 7), and her play *La Sunamite*. References to Staël's texts are in *Oeuvres de Madame de Staël-Holstein,* 3 vols (Paris: 1838), vol. 1. Page numbers are in the text.

115. This wise course was not one Charrière adopted herself, of course: she wrote.

116. His sheer dispiritedness continues the vein of the antihero (of the "eunuch") that had persisted in French literature since the time of Jean-Baptiste Gresset's *Sidney* (1745) at the least.

117. I discussed the implications of this ending in the light of the evolution of Staël's fictional types in my *Madame de Staël, Novelist* (Urbana: University of Illinois Press, 1978), 70–72.

118. My own thinking about Mme Roland has been much informed by Gita May's fine study, *Madame de Roland and the Age of Revolution* (New York: Columbia University Press, 1970), and by Mary Trouille's probing dissertation, *Eighteenth-Century Women Writers Respond to Rousseau: Sexual Politics and the Cult of Sensibility,* Northwestern University, 1980 (Ann Arbor: Dissertation Abstracts, 1988). I strongly recommend Dorinda Outram's excellent reading of the problematics of Manon Roland's self-conception, 129–152.

119. *Mémoires de Madame Roland* (Paris: Mercure de France, 1986), 212. Further references to Roland's memoirs are in the text. Much as i agree with Outram (137) that novelistic structures had a profound influence on Manon Roland, I concur with Gita May's and Harold Parker's estimate, also buttressed by Trouille's reading, that Plutarch and her society laid their imprint upon her just as much as did the novel. See Harold Parker, *The Cult of Antiquity and the French Revolution* (Chicago: University of Chicago Press, 1937).

120. Germaine de Staël experienced a parallel dissatisfaction with her mother's want of warmth; See my *Madame de Staël,* 31–35. Reflections such as this one of Manon Roland's made the Goncourt brothers conclude in their study of eighteenth-century women that "the maternity of that time knows nothing of the intimate family habits that endow children with a confident gentleness." *La Femme,* 6.

121. See Outram, 133–137. Examine Roland's pages on her nascent need to please, *Mémoires,* 251–255.

122. Letter to Sophie Cannet, December 10, 1776, in *Lettres de Madame Roland—Nouvelle Série, 1767–1780,* ed. Claude Perroud and Marthe Conor, 4 vols. (Paris: Imprimerie nationale, 1913), as quoted by Mary Trouille, "Revolution in the Boudoir: Mme Roland's Subversion of Rousseau's Ideals," *Eighteenth-Century Life* 13, no. 2 (May 1989): 84, note 11. "I am quite bored," *Lettres,* 274–275, cited by Mary Trouille, *Eighteenth-Century Women Writers,* 26.

123. By Jacques van den Heuvel, in his introduction to Bernardin's *Paul et Virginie* (Paris: Poche, 1974), 14. Jean Fabre yoked Paul et Virginie with the *Liaisons dangereuses* as novelistic antagonists in "*Paul et Virginie,* pastorale," in *Lumière et romantisme: Energie et nostalgie,* ed. Jean Fabre (Paris: Klincksieck, 1963), 234.

124. Marcel Hénaff, *Sade, l'Invention de corps libertin* (Paris: PUF-Croisier, 1978), 291.

125. Hénaff, 304. The woman as erotic adventuress has a far older pedigree than Hénaff acknowledges: we have only to think of Fernando de Rojas's *La Celestina* (1492). Max Horkeimer and Theodor Adorno in their chapter on Sade in *Dialectic of Enlightenment* (New York: Herder and Herder, 1972), as well as Henaff, stress the capitalist vein of Sade's outlook, as does Joan de Jean in her *Literary Fortifications* (Princeton: Princeton University Press, 1984), 294–302. Hénaff (295) places Sade's structuring of women's relationship to men in the context of Lévi-Strauss's characterization of women as objects of exchange.

126. Van den Heuvel cites these examples from Bernadin's *Etudes de la nature* in his preface to *Paul et Virginie,* 8. See Horkeimer and Adorno, 89–90.

127. This is true despite the classical and other origins adduced by Fabre for Bernardin's work, which remain, I believe, quite external to it. Sade, *Justine ou les malheurs de la vertu* (Paris: Soleil Noir, 1950), 55. Subsequent page references are in the text.

128. In Bernardin's tale, Europe's links with money and the past reveal it as an evil entity that submerges the divine little colony. For Hénaff, see 309.

129. Karen Horney, "The Dread of Women: Observations on a Specific Difference in the Dread Felt by Men and by Women Respectively for the Opposite Sex," *International Journal of Psychoanalysis* 13 (1932): 355.

130. Horney, 358.

131. Among reports concerning the kingdom of Butua is one by Sarmiento; a father "makes no

distinction among his daughters, his sons, his slaves, or his wives: all serve his licentious debauches undifferentiatedly." Sade's *Aline et Valcour,* in *Oeuvres complétes,* 16 vols. (Paris: Cercle du livre précieux, 1966–67), 3:219. Jean Gilibert observes, "We may try to deduce from the Sadean novelistic world of terror a family novel that would profoundly implicate a rivalrous dialectic between a criminal nature (maternal) and a man (child), her rival in crime. Who will kill more, who will kill better?" "L'Emprise sadienne," in *Sade, écrire la crise* (Colloque de Cerisy), (Paris: Pierre Belfond, 1983), 277.

132. Pateman, 186. Sade, *Aline et Valcour, Oeuvres,* vol. 3–4, 213.
133. An important treatment of Virginie's modesty and death is Clifton Cherpack's "Paul et Virginie and the Myth of Death," *PMLA,* 90, no. 1 (1975): 2–255. See also Philip Robinson, "Virginie's Modesty, Thoughts on Bernardin de St. Pierre and Rousseau," *British Journal for Eighteenth-Century Studies* 5, (1982): 35–48.
134. "Elegant adornments:" Such notes of the persistence of rococo are not lacking either in Sade, whose characters refer to the penis as "Venus's rod" and speak constantly, if sarcastically, of "graces."
135. See Ruth Thomas, "The Death of an Ideal: Female Suicides in the Eighteenth-Century French Novel," in Spencer, 326.
136. I treat related material in "1788—Civil Rights and the Wrongs of Women," in *A Harvard History of French Literature* (Cambridge, Mass.: Harvard University Press, 1989), ed. Denis Hollier, 558–566. On Condorcet, see Barbara Brookes, "The Feminism of Condorcet and Sophie de Grouchy," *Studies on Voltaire and the Eighteenth Century* 189 (1980): 291–361.
137. The duke of Saint-Simon mentions in his *Mémoires* that it was Louis XIV who made the decision about when a grandson was of age to dispense with the frock.
138. I am unfortunately in no position to assess the popularity or influence of Condorcet's views. This is an area that calls out for further research.
139. Antoine Nicolas Caritat, Marquis de Condorcet, *Lettres d'un bourgeois de New-Haven,* in Filippo Mazzei, *Recherches historiques et politiques sur les Etats-Unis de l'Amérique septentrionale, par un citoyen de Virginie* (Paris: 1788). Further references in text.
140. For example, Thomas Crow, "The Oath of the Horatii in 1785: Painting and Prerevolutionary Radicalism in France," *Art History* 1, no. 4 (1978): 424–471; Robert Rosenblum, *Transformations in Late Eighteenth-Century Art* (Princeton: Princeton University Press: 1967); and Brookner, 83.
141. D. L. Dowd, "Art and Theater during the French Revolution: The Role of Louis David," *Art Quarterly* 23 (Spring 1960): 5.
142. L. D. Ettinger points out that La Font de Saint-Yenne had, long before, proposed to artists the subject of Brutus's private martyrdom to public imperatives, and that the subject set by the Academy in 1785 was "Brutus causing his own children to be punished by death." In "Jacques-Louis David and Roman Virtue," *Journal of the Royal Society of Arts* 115 (Jan. 1967): 117. Such a concentration as we witness here on a public display of "heroic stoicism" is explored by Outram, chapter 5. Rosenblum discusses this neoclassical posture extensively, 50ff.
143. See "Oath," 462. Crow ties the moralism of the work to the aura of gossip surrounding the Kornmann affair, the lip-smacking, sexually polarizing scandal of that year, in which people chose sides for or against husband or wife. Kornmann had accused his wife's lover of abducting her, and aroused sympathy in public opinion for himself and his children, against his wife. The profound schism of David's Brutus strikes me as the emanation of a more generalized gender malaise, of which the reaction to the Kornmann case might be seen as a symptom.
144. For Voltaire's *Brutus,* see Ettinger, 118; for David's conception, see J.-L. David, *Gazette des beaux-Arts* (1875), 414ff, as quoted by Ettinger, 117.
145. However, as Crow points out, the work was criticized for its patent infidelity to Roman burial customs. *PPL,* 253. This is a Frenchman's visualization of the state versus the family from within the senator's house.
146. Norman Bryson, in *Word and Image,* notes that Brutus here "seems to be in communion with the primitive statue of Roma, which should face the room, but instead faces Brutus alone: beneath the statue we see a frieze of the wolf suckling Romulus and Remus, indicating the origin of Rome in the abrogation of the natural family—a motif which will be taken up in *The Intervention of the Sabine Women,* where it will have a very clear semantic function of placing negatively the dedication of the Roman male to the state over nature" (25).
147. Jean Clay, *Romanticism* (Secaucas: Chartwell, 1981), 54: Crow, "Oath," 462.

148. Robert A. Schumann, "Virility and Grace: Neo-Classicism, Jacques-Louis David, and the Culture of Pre-Revolutionary France," unpublished, p. 2.
149. Outram, 84–85. "He sits alone in his 'psychic autonomy'" (86).
150. Pateman, 96. See Yvon Belaval, "La Crise de la géométrisation de l'univers dans la philosophie des lumières," *Revue internationale de philosophie* 21 (1952): 337–345.
151. *PPL,* 251.
152. Ronald Paulson, *Representations of Revolution, 1789–1820* (New Haven: Yale University Press, 1983), 31.
153. Paulson views this Brutus richly as psychomachia, a depiction of divided loyalties "deriving from the conflicting emotions of the father and the mother, which materializes the mixed emotions of the father himself. The painting is about Brutus. In the larger terms of what is happening in France and what will happen, it deals with the situation of duty carried out despite human feelings" (33).
157. G.-T.-F. Raynal, *Histoire des deux Indes* (Paris: 1770, 1780), 700.

5. WOMEN'S EARLY REVOLUTION

1. The characterization is Dominique Godineau's. She goes on to say that generally "women are presented apart from or to the side of the Revolution, . . . not included in the revolutionary processes, which are envisaged without reference to their participation." She offers the corrective that when one takes women as the center, as she does in her remarkable volume *Citoyennes tricoteuses* (Aix-en-Provence: Alinea, 1988), it is the Revolution that instead appears as only a backdrop (12).
2. Elisabeth Guibert-Sledziewski, "Les Femmes, Sujet de Révolution," in *Mouvements populaires et conscience sociale* (Paris: CNRS-Maloine, 1985), 504.
3. Michel Vovelle, *La Mentalité révolutionnaire* (Paris: Messidor, Editions sociales, 1985), 41, 24.
4. See Fred Weinstein and Gerald M. Platt, *The Wish to Be Free: Society, Psyche, and Value Change* (Berkeley: University of California Press, 1986), 117, on repression of affective attachments. Lynn Hunt, *Politics, Culture, and Class in the French Revolution* (Berkeley: University of California Press, 1984), 12–13.
5. Carol Blum, *Rousseau and the Republic of Virtue: The Language of Politics in the French Revolution* (Ithaca: Cornell University Press, 1986), 132. This work courageously rereads and unveils aspects of Rousseau's thought otherwise obfuscated.
6. Carol Blum (135) recalls that in 1781 a collection of tunes called "Les Consolations des misères de la vie de Jean-Jacques Rousseau" was published, the proceeds to be donated to the foundling home. Among its patrons were Marie-Antoinette, the Princess de Lamballe, the Duchess de Choiseul, Melchior Grimm, and Benjamin Franklin.

I am quite aware of the unending debate about whether or not the Revolutionaries were or were not "Rousseauists." What concerns me here is an amorphous and publicly affirmed climate of attachment to the persona and any or all of the master's ideas, not to commitment to any specific tenet of his social, educational, or political philosophies.
7. Joseph-Alexandre de Ségur, *Les Femmes: Leur condition et leur influence chez différents peuples anciens et modernes* (Paris: 1803), 7–8.
8. I offer this rationale in elaboration of Ruth Graham's well-taken thesis that, acting in a mode contrary to our present assessments of the value of his view of them, the Revolution's educated women espoused Rousseau's *Weltanschauung.* I have tried to demonstrate how little this was a question of choice for them. But even within the Rousseauist canon, we see that the aspects of it they chose to embrace are his *Nouvelle Héloïse's* still courtly emphasis on the excellence and centrality to human destiny of the beloved woman, and his powerfully appealing stress on the importance of maternal love and breast-feeding. See my "Woman as Mediatrix, from Rousseau to Mme de Staël," in *Woman as Mediatrix,* ed. Avriel H. Goldberger (New York: Greenwood Press, 1987), on Staël's attraction to Rousseau's Julie as model, and how she yet refashions it to make it tolerable to herself.
9. This present view is an enlargement for me over my previous conception, in "Woman as Mediatrix," where I still saw Staël's positions as adopted essentially as personal choices, rather than as I do here, as part of a wider ideological gender struggle.

10. Letter 1 of the *Lettres sur les écrits et le caractère de Jean-Jacques Rousseau,* in *Oeuvres,* vol. 1.
11. Elshtain, 158.
12. Anon., *Avis aux dames* (Paris: 1788).
13. This despite the fact that France is thought to have practiced contraception in advance of and more widely than other European countries. See Jean-Louis Flandrin, "Contraception, Mariage, et relations amoureuses dans l'Occident chrétien," *Annales E.S.C.* 24 (1969): 1370–1390; and Antoinette Chamoux and Cecile Dauphin, "La Contraception avant la Révolution française," *Annales Economies Societes Civilisations* 24 (1969): 622–684.
14. For legal code, see François Bluche, *La Vie quotidienne au temps de Louis XVI* (Paris: Hachette, 1980), 330; for the Salpêtrière, Decaux, 1:430–431.
15. Guibert-Sledziewski, 586.
16. *Les Femmes dans la Revolution Française,* 2 vols. (Paris: Edhis, 1982), vol. 1, doc. 1, pp. 2, 4. Referred to below as *FRF-Edhis.*
17. Women still indulge in such verbal and vocal strategies of indirection and appeasement, as research on women's language in the United States of the twentieth century attests.
18. *Griefs et plaintes des femmes malmariées* (1789?), in *FRF-Edhis,* vol. 1, doc. 20, p. 4.
19. Crane Brinton wrote that the French Old Regime was in fact not notably cruel to natural children, who could own property, marry, transmit property, make wills, and demand sustenance of either or both parents. Excluded from office, they could still become mayors and judges with the consent of the prince. Peuchet, Mme Grandval, and Léonard Robin were advocates of the antibastardy legislation, but the Jacobins were not moved to act on this issue until 1793. *French Revolutionary Legislation on Illegitimacy 1789–1804* (Cambridge: Harvard University Press, 1936), 24–26.
20. *Lettres d'une citoyenne à son amie . . . , 1789* in *FRF-Edhis,* vol. 1, doc. 6, pp. 5–6, 14. For readers of English, I strongly recommend the annotated anthology of documents by Darline Gay Levy, Harriet B. Applewhite, and Mary D. Johnson, *Women in Revolutionary Paris* (Urbana: University of Illinois Press, 1979).
21. *Griefs* (see note 18), pp. 18, 19.
22. See Roderick G. Phillips, "Women's Emancipation, the Family, and Social Change in Eighteenth-Century France," *Journal of Social History* 12, no. 4 (1979): 553–567. I discuss this further.
23. Eliane Brault, *La Franc-Maçonnerie et l'émancipation des femmes* (Paris: Dervy, 1967), 43. See Bluche, 330, on lodges.
24. Observe the Rousseauist ploy in the fourth sentence. *Remontrances, plaintes, et doléances des dames françaises à l'occasion de l'assemblée des Etats-Generaux* (Paris: 1789), in *FRF-Edhis,* vol. 1, doc. 5, pp. 4, 12.
25. Betty Rizzo, "Women's Class Mobility: Potentialities and Limits," paper presented to American Society for Eighteenth-Century Studies, 1990 (Minneapolis). She is discussing English society, but I believe the structural story she relates applies largely to France as well, with some important nuances of difference in women's perceived status.
26. Camille Bloch, "Les Femmes d'Orléans pendant la Révolution," *La Révolution française* 43 (1902): 50.
27. Alphonse Aulard, "Le Féminisme pendant la Révolution," *Revue bleue,* 19 March 1889: 364.
28. Louis Devance, following Aulard's suggestion, attempts quite fruitfully to make such a distinction in his article, "Le Féminisme pendant la Révolution française," *Annales historiques de la Révolution française* 49 (1977): 341–376. Even he points out that "it is not possible to separate feminist actions and feminine actions during the Revolution. Feminism—the profound justification, formulated or not—of women's political action, finds both its sustenance and its best rationale in such action" (342).
29. *Motion adressée à l'Assemblée nationale en faveur du sexe* (Paris: 1789), in *FRF-Edhis,* vol. 1, doc. 10, pp. 5, 10.
30. *Motion de la pauvre Javotte, députée des pauvres femmes, lesquelles composent le second order du Royaume depuis l'abolition du Clergé et de la Noblesse* (Paris: 1790), in *FRF-Edhis,* vol. 1, doc. 23, pp. 10–13, passim.
31. *Griefs* (see note 18), p. 5. "Feigning passion," *Motion de Javotte* (see preceding note), 2. As Ruth Graham observes, "Reading the women's pamphlets of 1789 and 1790, we sense their marriages were not happy" (129).
32. For example, even the gutsy Mlle Jodin writes that "nowhere else have women whose first duty it is to be circumspect and reserved provoked so boldly the only sex meant to attack."

Vues législatives pour les femmes, adressés à l'Assemblée nationale par Mlle Jodin, fille d'un citoyen de Genève, in *FRF-Edhis,* vol. 1, doc. 24, p. 11.

33. See Jodin (preceding note), 17–18. Aulard ("feminisme") summarizes two early reviews of the women's cahiers in 1863, by Chassin (*Génie de la Révolution*) and Amédée le Faure (*Le Socialisme pendant la Révolution*) and concludes, "These were not radical analyses: not to be slaves, to be educated, that they not be left out of inheritances, that's what women wanted above all in 1789. However, masculine privilege was de facto attacked in principle" (362).

34. Condorcet, "Sur l'Admission des femmes au droit de cité," head article in *Journal de la Sociéte de 1789,* 5 (3 July 1790), in *FRF-Edhis,* vol. 2, doc. 25. For quotations in this paragraph, see pp. 3, 11.

35. Condorcet ("Sur l'Admission," 6–7) was far more probing in this regard than Sigmund Freud, who simply reiterated this oft-repeated prejudicial view.

36. Condorcet, "Sur l'Admission," 12. Condorcet noted the retrogression involved in having allowed women to select members of the First Estate, and now withdrawing that right altogether.

37. Bachelier, 8. *FRF-Edhis,* vol. 1, doc. 4.

38. Pierre Guyomar, *Le Partisan de l'égalité politique entre les individus, ou problème important de l'égalité en droits et de l'inégalité en fait* (Convention, April 29, 1793), in *FRF-Edhis,* vol. 2, doc. 45, pp. 10, 12, 13.

39. Guyomar, 20. See Judith Schlanger's discussion of the intensity of the relationship of the Revolutionaries to antiquity, chapter 4 of her *L'Enjeu et le débat—l'invention intellectuelle* (Paris: Denoël/Gonthier, 1979).

40. Edmond and Jules de Goncourt, *Paris pendant la Révolution* (Paris: 1854), 378.

41. C. Bloch, 51.

42. Louis-Sébastien Mercier, *Paris pendant la Révolution ou le nouveau Paris 1789–1798* (Paris: Le Livre Club du Libraire, 1962), 83.

43. Victorine de Chastenay, *Mémoires,* 2 vols. (Paris: 1896), 1:89.

44. Simon Schama, *Citizens: A Chronicle of the French Revolution* (New York: Knopf, 1989), 210. There are still those who believe the queen was not entirely uninvolved in this affair.

45. John Moore, M.D., *A Journal During a Residence in France from the Beginning of August to the Middle of December, 1792* 2 vols. (London: 1794), 1:64.

46. The full flavor of the word *Autrichienne,* the last syllable of which forms the word *bitch* in French, cannot be recreated in English. See C. Thomas, (251). Quotations are from C. Thomas and *Le Cadran des plaisirs de la cour ou les aventures du petit page Chérubin, pour servir de suite à la vie de Marie-Antoinette, ci-devant reine de France* (1789), 13, 38, in C. Thomas, 253–254; also from *Le Bordel royal, suivi d'un entretien entre la reine et le cardinal de Rohan après son entrée aux Etats-Généraux* (1789), 6, in C. Thomas, 253.

47. C. Thomas, 251; see also 256.

48. Pierre Bessand-Massenet, *Les Femmes sous la Révolution* (Paris: Plon, 1962), 31–32.

49. Neil Hertz, "Medusa's Head: Male Hysteria under Political Pressure," *Representations* 4 (1983): 27–54.

50. Edmund Burke, *Reflections on the Revolution in France* (Chicago: H. Regnery, 1968), 111, 113.

51. Bernard Beugnot, *Mémoires de Beugnot,* 3 vols, (Paris: 1866), 1:108.

52. Cited by Hector Fleischmann, *Les Filles publiques sous la terreur* (Paris: Albert Méricaut, 1908), 209. La Harpe was a politician and litterateur of Swiss origin.

53. The popular Necker's order into exile by the king on July 11 was the act that precipitated the fall of the Bastille on July 14.

54. Daniel Hamiche, *Le Théâtre et la Révolution: La Lutte des classes au théâtre en 1789 et 1793* (Paris: U.G.E., 1973), 49.

55. Naturally, I have no intention of reopening the question of the degree of Catherine de Medici's responsibility for the Saint Bartholomew's Massacre. She certainly colluded in it, at the least. It is a separate issue. What interests me here is the conflation of the two women.

56. Moore, 124. For *tapes-dur,* Hamiche, 158; "almost incendiary," Chastenay, 1:397, *Révolutions de Paris,* Hamiche, 63.

57. Hufton, 94; Godineau, 41. Jules Michelet, *Les Femmes de la Révolution,* ed. Pierre Labracherie and Jean Dumont (Paris: Hachette, n.d.), 52.

58. N.-E. Restif de la Bretonne, *Les Nuits de Paris ou le spectateur nocturne* (Paris: Livre Club du Libraire, 1960), 173.

59. Jane Kromm, "'Marianne' and the Madwoman," *Art Journal* 46, no. 4 (Winter 1987): 302.

60. E. Lairtullier, *Les Femmes célèbres de 1789 à 1795 et leur influence dans la Révolution* (Paris: 1840), 202.

61. As quoted by Annette Rosa, *Citoyennes: Les Femmes et la Révolution française* (Paris: Messidor, 1987), 77.

62. Deposition 343, June 18, 1790, from *Procédure criminelle instruite au Châtelet de Paris* (Paris: 1790), in Levy, Applewhite, and Johnson, 50. Their translation.

63. Chastenay, 1:131.

64. Decaux, 1:477, 475.

65. L.-S. Mercier, *Paris pendant la Révolution*, 90.

66. "Figures de prove" (585) is Guibert-Sledziewski's term. An "aberration of nature," in Mary Durham Johnson, "Old Wine in New Bottles: The Institutional Changes for Women of the People during the French Revolution," in *Women, War, and Revolution*, ed. Carol R. Berkin and Clara M. Lovett (New York: Homes and Meier, 1980), 117. Poissardes song in Cornwell B. Rogers, *The Spirit of Revolution in 1789* (Princeton: Princeton University Press, 1949), 183, note 24; Rogers's translation, slightly amended. Quote from *Les Entrennes*, in Evelyne Sullerot, *Histoire de la presse feminine en France, des origines à 1848* (Paris: Armand Colin, 1966), 48–49.

67. Introduction by Paul Roux to Mme Roland's *Mémoires*, 21. On her salon comportment, see Gita May: "Manon's was a decidedly political salon with a spartan flavor. She officiated with tact and, what was more appreciated, in silence" (184).

68. A sample of the marquis's prose, which expresses the vicissitudes of paternity and would probably have delighted Voltaire, is this reply to Olympe's attempt to claim her relationship to him: "I can believe without difficulty, and most unfortunately for me, that you are not a stranger to me; but you have no right to demand of me the title of father. You were born legitimate, and under the troth of marriage. If it remains true that Nature speaking within you and the imprudent caresses I gave you in childhood as well as your mother's confession assure you I am your father, imitate me and sigh over the fate of those who gave you life. God will not abandon you if you pray sincerely." In Olympe de Gouges, Oeuvres, ed. Benoîte Groult (Paris: Mercure de France, 1986), 17.

69. Fleury, for example, was inspired by her example to write, "All women who are authors by profession are in a false position, whatever talent we may imagine them to possess." In Gouges, 24.

70. Gouges, 26–27. Biographical details are from those supplied by the editor, Benoîte Groult, 25–26.

71. Gouges, 28. We observe the lèse-Rousseauism of this use of Ninon as reasoner: Rousseau, in book 5 of the *Emile*, had made her the model of all that was unwomanly in those women who claimed membership in men's society.

72. Gouges, 159.

73. We find some flavor of Hippel's systematic yet impassioned treatise in his exclamation, "Truly, the laws of the state as they apply to women are almost more contradictory than a frivolous love affair." Theodor Gottfried von Hippel, *On Improving the Status of Women*, tr. and ed. Timothy F. Sellner (Detroit: Wayne State University Press, 1979), 80–81.

74. Page references within the text are to the *Oeuvres*.

75. Commentary by Groult, in Gouges, 43.

76. Graham, 136. Graham reads the end of the *Declaration* as Rousseauist. I cannot altogether agree. While Olympe accepts his view that women must be moral regenerators, as Graham sees, her view of marriage could not have been more opposed than it was to Rousseau's traditional, nay retro, view of it.

77. I do not necessarily mean to imply that she did not agree with any of these characterizations of women; simply, they are so anchored in the prevailing rhetoric as to be mandatory verbal flourishes. Like static, they shroud her utterance.

78. Lairtullier, 125.

6. GODDESSES AND ALLEGORIES

1. A report of March 1794 by Le Breton on the activities of prostitutes near the rue Favart, telling how the rain scattered them from their posts, states that "several goddesses com-

plained" of being disturbed. Charles-Aime Dauban, *La Démagogie à Paris en 1794* (Paris: 1868), 207. Mercier provides a most striking instance of such usage in a passage Genet might have written. He is in an elegant brothel. "At a given signal the ceiling half opens and from the skies chariots . . . driven by Venus descend; sometimes it's Aurora, sometimes Diana come to seek her dear Endymion. All are dressed as goddesses. The customers choose, and the divinities, not of Olympus but of the ceiling, mix with the mortals." *PPR,* 116.

2. Marie-Hélène Huet, *Rehearsing the Revolution: The Staging of Marat's Death, 1793-1797,* tr. Robert Hurley (Berkeley: University of California Press, 1982); Hunt, *PCC,* 27-28.

3. Angus Fletcher, *Allegory: The Theory of a Symbolic Mode* (Ithaca: Cornell University Press, 1964), 16 note 29, 17, 23. Paul de Man, "Pascal's Allegory of Persuasion," in *Allegory and Representation: Selected Papers from the English Institute, 1978* (Baltimore: Johns Hopkins University Press, 1981), 80. E. H. Gombrich, "The Use of Art for the Study of Symbol," *American Psychologist* 20 (Jan. 1965): 45. E. H. Gombrich, "The Dream of Reason: Symbolism of the French Enlightenment," *British Journal for Eighteenth-Century Studies* 2 (1979): 195. See also chapter 6, "Le peuple au front gravé," of Schlanger's *L'Enjeu et le débat.*

4. de Beauvoir, 131, 133.

5. Some of this material recurs in my paper "The Rights and Wrongs of Woman: The Defeat of Feminist Rhetoric by Revolutionary Allegory," presented at the Dartmouth College Conference on Representation and Revolution, July 1989, published by the University Press of New England in *The Revolutionary Moment* (1992).

6. A. Fletcher, 283; Fenichel's *The Psychoanalytic Theory of the Neuroses* is quoted by A. Fletcher, 288.

7. Marina Warner, *Of Monuments and Maidens: The Allegory of the Female Form* (New York: Atheneum, 1985), 39; Hunt, "The Political Psychology of Revolutionary Caricatures," in *French Caricature and the French Revolution 1789-1799* (Los Angeles: Grunwald Center for the Graphic Arts, 1988), 39.

8. Warner, 37.

9. I will have more to say of such figures in the sections on "Maenads" and "Breasts," chapters 8 and 9.

10. Mona Ozouf, "De Thermidor à brumaire: Le discours de la Révolution sur elle-même," *Revue historique* 243 (1970): 43.

11. Hunt, PCC, 93. Hunt cites the Abbé Grégoire's view following Condillac's theory of cognition, that a legislator must control the production of signs so as to mold the people's understanding (92). See also James Leith's essential *The Idea of Art as Propaganda in France, 1789-1799* (Toronto: University of Toronto Press, 1965).

12. See Hunt, PCC, 96-97; she credits Darline Gay Levy with the essential insight that these dates were related (104).

13. Hunt, PCC, 104.

14. Mercier, *PPR, Nouveau Paris,* 4:115, "Chaumette," J.B.B., March 20, 1794, in Dauban, 271.

15. Rosa, 186. For Hébert's links with women, see Albert Soboul, "Sentiment religieux et cultes populaires," *Annales historiques de la Révolution française* 29 (July-Sept. 1957): 211. Alphonse Aulard, *Le Culte de l'Etre Suprême 1793-1794* (Aalen: Scientia Verlag, 1975), 99.

16. Quoted in Aulard, *Culte,* 287.

17. The architect Lequeu's design for the Arch of the People of 1794 contains a similarly huge construction of a Hercules seated atop the arch, with a lion's skin hung from his shoulder and holding a tiny effigy of the goddess of Liberty. See James Leith, "Deradicalization and Militarization: Some Architectural Projects under the Directory," *Consortium on Revolutionary Europe Proceedings 1985* (Athens, Ga: 1986), fig. 1.

18. I refer, for example, to the theoretical works of Dorothy Dinnerstein (1977) and Nancy Chodorow (1978), based on the psychoanalytic formulations, drawn from clinical observations, of Melanie Klein.

19. Furet, 42; Ozouf, 54. See also Hunt, *PCC* 118, on the huge, silent 1798 image of a Liberty, who "simply sits and waits."

20. Though remnants of course remain. In an exchange of views in the volume *Les Fêtes de la Révolution,* Edouard Guitton refers to historian Mona Ozouf as "la Déesse Raison de notre colloque" (the Goddess Reason of our conference," whose voice "surprises and enchants" him and fills him with admiration. For him, she is "an enchanting siren" (634).

7. LIMITS TO ACTION AS EMPOWERMENT

1. Again, I refer readers to Louis Devance's attempt to disentangle, at least in part, the feminist from the purely patriotic stands (341).
2. Quoted in Godineau, 112.
3. See Gary Kates, *The Cercle Social, the Girondins, and the French Revolution* (Princeton: Princeton University Press, 1985). These were the circles most hospitable to women. Cobb confirms the preponderant separatist tendencies of political life. "In most clubs one side of the hall was reserved for women, and often only married couples were allowed to sit together. Women were excluded from some clubs altogether, and the efforts of politically-minded citizenesses to form clubs of their own were eyed with disfavor: the *Société républicaine des deux sexes,* known derisively by the Paris Sans-Culottes as the *Société hermaphrodite,* was suppressed. A ruthless war was waged on prostitutes, who were held to be counter-revolutionary: the revolutionary authorities particularly attempted to drive them from the garrison towns." "The Revolutionary Mentality in France," *History* 17 (Oct. 1957): 189.
4. *Révolutions de Paris* 79 (226–235), 122 (355–357), and 126 (492–500). Page references are in the text.
5. My emphasis: an apparent allusion to the rejection of the chivalric code by the revolutionaries.
6. L.-S. Mercier, *TP* 1:82. For February 25–26, see M. D. Johnson, 123; Godineau, 111.
7. See Darline Gay Levy and Harriet B. Applewhite, "Women, Democracy, and Revolution in Paris, 1789–94," in Spencer. Godineau, 113.
8. Godineau, 118.
9. Godineau, 126.
10. See Nancy Huston's discussion of the male cultural equation of war as childbirth. "The Matrix of War: Mothers and Heroes," in *The Female Body in Western Culture: Contemporary Perspectives,* ed. Susan R. Suleiman (Cambridge, Mass.: Harvard University Press, 1986), 127–131.
11. One-third were from 25 to 40 years of age, but fully another third were from 60 to 70. It is noteworthy that these latter were women who came to maturity between 1745 and 1755, at the acme of women's influence in eighteenth-century France, before the reaction.
12. Théroigne de Méricourt, *Aux 48 Sections* (Paris: 1792), in *FRF-Edhis,* vol. 2, doc. 44.
13. Godineau, 146.
14. Godineau, 161.
15. *Archives de la préfecture de Police,* in Godineau, 161. Mercier, *TP,* 1:102–103.
16. Godineau, 153.
17. *La Gazette française* no. 533, in Godineau, 164.
18. Godineau, 164, 166.
19. Godineau, 165.
20. Godineau, 167.
21. Duhet, 145.
22. A similar note is struck with popular mockery of women who cut their hair short, *à la jacobine,* thereby appearing too dangerously androgynous to the dominant mentality. We note Citizen Rolin's report that when a group of these women tried to get the minister of the interior to pay attention to their needs as dependents of men at the front, he told them that "although they could not doubt his love for the female sex, the republican costume they chose to wear was not the one most pleasing to him." (Dauban, 258). Godineau, 170. Naomi Schor, *Reading in Detail: Aesthetics and the Feminine* (New York: Methuen, 1987), 45.
23. Godineau, 172.
24. See Jacqueline Dauxois, *Charlotte Corday* (Paris: Albin-Michel, 1982), 262, and Roland, 212.
25. *Le Moniteur universel. Réimpression de l'ancien Moniteur . . .* (mai 1789–novembre 1799), 32 vols. (Paris: 1840–1845), vol. 18 (1793), 127.
26. Thomas Waters Griffith, *My Scrap Book of the French Revolution,* ed. Elizabeth Wormley Latimer (Chicago: 1898), 42.
27. A more extended analysis of Staël's text is to be found in my article, "Nature, Cruauté, et femmes immolées: *Les Réflexions sur le procès de la reine,*" in *Le Groupe de Coppet et la Révolution française,* ed. Etienne Hofmann and Anne-Lise Delacrétaz (Lausanne: Institut Benjamin Constant, 1988), 123–140. Staël, *Oeuvres,* 1:55, 61.
28. It is not that such views were not aired before: simply that they had not received official sanction. See the citations from the *Révolutions de Paris,* note 4.

29. *Réimpression de l'Ancien Moniteur,* Oct. 30 (9 brumaire), vol. 18 (1793), 300.
30. *AM,* 300.
31. "Let's have an end to that simplistic and far from unbiased image of women solely as victims of male misogyny and power" (Godineau, 174). This author views the attack on women as an attack on the *peuple:* but she also believes the women were simply becoming too clamorous to be ignored (176). This explanation evades dealing with the issue of why women were dealt with thus *as a sex.*
32. Carol Blum comments, "All four were guillotined, and their execution lent weight to the condemnations of female claims that were taking place" (213).
33. M. D. Johnson, 128.
34. Richard Cobb notes the numerous mentions he has uncovered of the popular despair after the defeat of Prairial: "The police speak of the rising tide of suicides, among whom are counted many among the young women, who throw themselves into the Seine with their children." Suicides, especially among mothers of families, are also recorded in Amiens, Sotteville, and Versailles. *Terreur et Subsistances 1793–95* (Paris: Librarie Clavreuil, 1965), 315.

8. SEX, POLITICS, AND MURDEROUSNESS

1. Euripides, *The Bacchae,* tr. and ed. Michael Cacoyannis (New York: Mentor, 1982), 166–169).
2. We think again of the insightful account of comparable turnabout compensatory rituals in early modern France given by Natalie Davis in her "Women on Top."
3. Eva C. Keuls, *The Reign of the Phallus: Sexual Politics in Ancient Athens* (New York: Harper and Row, 1985), 367, reports that Pausanias (10, 4) tells of second-century A.D. Athenian women going "to Delphi doing Maenadic dances all along the way . . . there [being] joined [by] their sisters for rituals on Mt. Parnassus."
4. A sample: "Cease profaning that touching and sacred name of *le peuple* by tying it to the idea of corruption." Maximilien de Robespierre, *Oeuvres* (rpt. New York: Burt Franklin, 1970), 2:167.
5. According to Cobb, during the Revolution "it was both immoral and unlawful for a man to dress as a woman or a woman as a man." Mentalité," 189.
6. Vovelle, *Mentalité,* 214.
7. Vovelle, *"Mentalité,"* 215; Hunt, *PCC,* 39–45. I particularly recommend Hunt's discussion there of the French people's suspicion of organized politics and the resultant faith in a rhetoric of the emotions.
8. L.-S. Mercier, *TP* 2:102–103. Pourvoyeur, Report of 26 pluviôse, Year III, in Hufton, "Women in Revolution," 101, note 34.
9. I think of allusions like Villon's to women's "bon bec de Paris." It can only be that tastes were changing from a less frankly folkloric to a more sedate and bourgeois model of female comportment. Soboul, "Femmes," 17. Cobb, *Terreur.* 8. 60.
10. "Volcanic joy," Cobb, *The Police and the People* (Oxford: Clarendon, 1970), 51; L.-S. Mercier writes, "this brutal, depraved language which has conquered almost all the classes is a terrible scandal for our times" (*PPR,* 118).
11. Men's language, Cobb, *Police,* 87. Women's language, Hufton, "Women in Revolution," 101.
12. Mercier, *TP* 1:38.
13. *Arch. Nat.* W191, Report of 26 Pluviôse, Year III, in Hufton, "Women in Revolution," 101.
14. Weber in Gustave Lenôtre, *Les Massacres de Septembre* (Paris: Perrin, 1907), 53–54. Belzunce, in Rosa, 75. Restif, in *Nuits,* VI, 172. Angélique Voyer in Louis Mortimer-Ternaux, *Histoire de la Terreur 1792–1794,* 8 vols. (Paris: 1864), 4, 631.
15. For the Place de la Révolution, see Pierre Bessand-Massenet, *De Robespierre à Bonaparte* (Paris: Fayard, 1970), 206–207. L.-S. Mercier, *TP* 1:108.
16. L.-S. Mercier, *TP* 1:55.
17. Cobb, *Terreur,* 22. Lady MacBeth, in Hufton, "Women in Revolution," 101; femme Colon from *Tableau des crimes du comité révolutionnaire de Moulins,* in Cobb, *Police,* 385.
18. Docteur Augustin Cabanès and L. Nass, *La Névrose révolutionnaire,* 2 vols. (Paris: Albin Michel, 1924), 1:138. See the chapter on public whippings, 136–153.

19. Cabanès and Nass, 1:141, citing L. Scioult, *Histoire de la Constitution civile du clergé,* vol. 3.
20. *La Loi et la Religion vengées des violences commises aux portes des églises catholiques de Lyon,* by Simon (Jordan) in Cabanès and Nass, 1:149. Even accounting for the anti-Jacobin bias of such accounts, they convey an entirely believable mood of sexual animus.
21. Cobb, *Police,* 326.
22. Schama, 631.
23. Schama, 635.
24. Restif, *Nuits,* 10:230. For Petit-Mamin, Mortimer-Ternaux, 633.
25. Cabanès and Nass, 1:114.
26. Mortimer-Ternaux, 319, 317. A curious aspect of all the massacres is in fact the deep silence that attended them. A letter attributed to M. de la Vigne Dampierre reports that "the most unbelievable thing is that in all of Paris, except for the prison areas, the greatest tranquility reigned during the Massacres. Faces looked absolutely unmoved; you would have suspected nothing." From P. de Vaissière, *Lettres d'aristocrates: La Révolution racontée par des correspondances privées 1789–1794* (Paris: Perrin, 1907), 124, in Pierre Caron, *Les Massacres de Septembre* (Paris: Maison du livre français, 1935), 144. See also Caron, 59.
27. Caron's own determined reticence concerning the events at the Salpêtrière smacks of such a coverup mentality. The *Moniteur* simply remained silent about the massacres until September 10 before giving its official version. Schama (631), following Bluche, has underscored how historical scholarship has recapitulated or even heightened these first hypocrisies in the treatment of the Massacres.
28. As the *Révolutions de Paris* (182) observed, "the atrocious spectacle of these 45 women [Caron claims there were only 35] struck down in cold blood . . . was the more revolting in that these unfortunate victims were unacquainted with the plots woven against the Revolution" (Caron, 148). For Mme Roland, *Lettres,* ed. Pernoux, 2:436, in Caron, 63.
29. Restif, *Nuits,* 10:231–232, 235.
30. Restif, *Nuits,* 10:235, 236, 237.
31. Cobb, *Terreur,* 50.
32. Michel Delon, *L'Idée d'énergie au tournant des lumières (1770–1820)* (Paris: PUF, 1988), 521.
33. Mortimer-Ternaux, 414–415.
34. Quoted in Mortimer-Ternaux, 419, 417, 418.
35. P.-J.-B. Buchez and P. C. Roux, *Histoire parlementaire de la Révolution française,* vol. 24, (April 1793): 61.
36. See Gustave Lenôtre, *Les Massacres de Septembre* (Paris: Perrin, 1907) 307, 318.
37. Restif, *Nuits,* 7:166. Godineau cites the report of Perrière, who claimed that some women fainted at the sight of the guillotine or the death-carts (230).
38. For rape in the military, Susan Brownmiller, *Against Our Will: Men, Women, and Rape* (New York: Simon and Schuster, 1975), chapters 1–5. Cobb cites Restif's *Monsieur Nicolas,* (2, 702) where he states that nothing is "more deplorable than the fate of a prostitute whose protector is a soldier in the Gardes-Françaises. Not only will she be at the disposal of the whole regiment, she will be subjected to the brutality of a corps notorious for its cruelty and violence." *Police,* 238, note 3. Pierre Klossowski, "Préface à *la Philosophie dans le boudoir,*" *Oeuvres complètes du Marquis de Sade,* 3:254; Delon, *L'Idée d'energie,* 307; Cobb, *Police,* 131.
39. The heads of De Launay, the governor of the Bastille, and of Flesselles, trophies of the taking of the Bastille, and Berthier's and Foulon's heads, taken some days later, were all paraded before enthusiastic crowds.
40. *Les Républicains avignonnais . . . au peuple français* (Valence: 24 Floréal, An V), in Cobb, *Police,* 351.
41. Mercier, *TP,* 1:41.
42. Colette Caubisens-Lafargue, "Les Salons de peinture de la Révolution française," *L'Information d'histoire de l'art* 5 (May-June 1960), 69.
43. Godineau cites Arlette Farge's *La Vie fragile: violence, pouvoirs et solidarités à Paris au XVIIIe siècle* (Paris: Hachette, 1986), 218–223, and Devance's article for their discussions of this phenomenon.
44. E. Lairtullier, *Les Femmes célèbres de 1789 à 1795 et leur influence dans a Révolution* (Paris: 1840), 200–201.
45. Godineau, 232; see D. Arasse, *La Guillotine et l'imaginaire de la Terreur* (Paris: Flammarion, 1987).

46. *Le Moniteur universel. Réimpression de l'ancien Moniteur* ... (mai 1789–novembre 1799), 32 vols. (Paris: 1840–1845), vol. 18 (1793), 450.

47. Restif, *Nuits*, 3:160–161. Freud's remark is suggestive, if understated, here. "Wild beasts are as a rule employed by the dream-work to represent passionate impulses of which the dreamer is afraid. ... It might be said that the wild beasts are used to represent the libido, a force dreaded by the ego and combatted by means of repression." *The Unconscious—Standard Edition*, 14:183–184, cited by Klaus Theweleit, *Male Fantasies, 1: Women, Floods, Bodies, History*, tr. Stephen Conway (Minneapolis: University of Minnesota Press, 1989), 194.

48. A "new Venus," in Rosa, 78. "Let us arm," in *FRF-Edhis*, vol. 2, doc. 3, p. 3. For Sisina,

> Avez-vous vu Théroigne, amante du carnage,
> Excitant à l'assaut un peuple sans souliers,
> La joue et l'oeil en feu, jouant son personnage,
> Et montant, sabre au poing, les royaux escaliers?
> *Les Fleurs du mal* 59

49. Schama, 874–875. *Les origines de féminisme contemporain. Trois femmes de la Révolution: Olympe de Gouges, Théroigne de Méricourt, Rose Lacombe* (Paris: Plon, 1900).

50. Schama seems to have swallowed whole Paul Garnier's evaluation, cited by Lacour (390), that Théroigne belonged to that army of the unstable who enter the lists in times of trouble and was an "exaltée." We note Dr. Guillois's amazingly general conclusion that "numerous women, especially those playing an active role in the Revolution and played a sanguinary role in it, were unstable types." *Etude médico-psychologique sur Olympe de Gouges, considérations générales sur la mentalité des femmes pendant la Révolution* (Lyons: A. Rey, 1904), 88.

51. As Colwill puts it: "Revolutionary antagonism toward the political prerogatives of queenship had evolved into a general proscription of female action" (80). Hébert's *Père Duchesne* is cited by Colwill, 79; see 78 for her own remarks.

52. In Jean Epois, *L'Affaire Corday-Marat, prélude à la Terreur* (Paris: Cercle d'or, 1980), 47.

53. Epois, 207.

54. *La Démagogie en 1793 à Paris ou Histoire jour par jour de l'année 1793, accompagnée de documents contemporains* ... (Paris: Plon, 1868), 277. Erostrates was a martyr to his country.

55. *L'Ancien Moniteur* 18, 450.

56. Duhet, in *Les Femmes et la Révolution française* (Paris: Juillard, 1971) 220–221, characterizes racism as "the valorization ... of differences, real or imaginary, that profit the accuser to the detriment of his victim, so as to justify his privilege and his aggression." "Was Corday a member," Duhet, 145. "Monsters without number," in *Peuple, Réveille-toi, il est temps*, Godineau, 405, note 17.

57. I again refer readers to Neil Hertz's remarkable "Medusa's Head: Male Hysteria under Political Pressure," *Representations* 4 (1983): 27–54.

58. Horney, 349, 356, 359. Wedekind's neo-Romantic fantasies are heightened versions of the flood of such images at the end of the nineteenth century and the beginning of the twentieth, disinterred by both Bram Dijkstra and Klaus Theweleit.

59. Ozouf, 45.

60. Weinstein and Platt theorize that "if the pressures stemming from conflict prove to be too great, behavior regressive in content and reflecting continued attachments to the mandates of the traditional structure" can be expected to follow (37).

61. Cobb, *Police*, 327.

62. Rapport de Prévost, 8 Brumaire, An II, in Godineau, 266.

63. E. & J. de Goncourt, *Histoire de la société française pendant la Révolution* (Paris: 1854), 12.

64. Michelet, 271.

65. Thomas Carlyle, *The French Revolution* (New York: Modern Library, n.d.), 201. Of course Dickens's conception of that unforgettable tricoteuse Mme Defarge springs partially from Carlyle's heated prose.

66. Konrad Engelbert Oelsner, "Letter from Paris," August 14, 1792, as quoted by Suzanne Zantop in her paper, "Crossing the Boundaries: The French Revolution and the German Literary Imagination," presented at the Dartmouth College conference "The French Revolution and Representation," July 1989, which she graciously has shared with me. Published in *The Revolutionary Moment*, James Jeffernan, ed. (Hanover: University Press of New England, 1992).

9. IMAGERIES OF THE BREAST

1. Buffie Johnson, *Lady of the Beasts: Ancient Images of the Goddess and Her Sacred Animals* (San Francisco: Harper and Row, 1987), 44.

2. Margaret Miles, *Images as Insight: Visual Understanding in Western Civilization and Secular Culture* (Boston: Beacon Press, 1985), 78.

3. Warner writes: "A link does exist between [Mary's] nourishing the child Jesus at her breast like any mortal mother and the exalted nakedness of allegorical figures like Liberty; . . . they are stating that nature is good. Mary affirms . . . fruitfulness and our animal condition at the same time, and she transforms the erotic dangerousness of the breast in Christian imagery to a symbol of comfort, of candor, of good" (245).

4. Jacques-René Hébert, *Père Duchesne*, 280. In French:

> De ces effrayantes femelles
> Les intarissables mamelles
> Comme de publiques gamelles,
> Offrent à boire à tout passant;
> Et la liqueur qui coule,
> Et dont' l'abominable foule
> Avec aridité se saoule,
> Ce n'est pas du lait, mais du sang.

5. B. Johnson, 270.

6. "Her nourishment, the passport to kingship, provides the sustenance that protects him on his journey to the next world, where she alone presides. Her maternal care confers eternal divinity on the kings. The bull's tail that hung from the belts of the pharoahs was a reminder of their debt to Hathor and remained part of the pharaonic ceremonial garb for three millennia." B. Johnson, 276.

7. See Theweleit, 337–339.

8. Raynal, 4:23.

9. Marie-Joseph Chénier, and C. Dusausoir, et al., *Office des Décades, ou hymnes et prières en usage dans les temples de la Raison* (Paris: 1793), 10. Further page references in text.

10. *FRF-Edhis,* vol. 1: *Lettres d'une citoyenne,* doc. 6, pp. 8–9; *Discours des citoyennes d'Avallon,* doc. 34, p. 3; Marie Martin, *Le patriotisme des dames citoyennes,* doc. 27, p. 7.

11. We see this in Condorcet's concessions that women must breast-feed their infants and watch over their early years. He does not stop there, and calls for women to vote and engage in public service. In general, however, the emotional undertow of the maternalists' demands capsizes reflection.

12. Claire Lacombe, *FRF-Edhis,* vol. 2, doc. 43, *Discours prononcé à la barre de l'assemblée* (25 Juillet 1792), p. 2. Etta Palm, *FRF-Edhis,* vol. 2, doc. 33, *Appel aux Françoises sur la régénération des moeurs,* p. 26.

13. "Instead of compensating us through education and laws in our favor, it seems you form us solely for your pleasure." *FRF-Edhis,* vol. 2, doc. 32, *Discours de Mme Palm d'Aelders,* p. 3.

14. Palm, *Appel,* 43, 44 (see note 12).

15. *FRF-Edhis,* doc. 68, poster: Départment de Paris, le 30 juin 1793. Imprimerie Ballard.

16. Dauban comments, "O virtuous men! Your tender hearts, faced with the sight of alarmed innocence and modesty unveiled, remained deaf to the voice of nature!" *Démagogie,* (274).

17. Paul Ginisty, *Mémoires d'une danseuse de corde* (Paris: Flammarion, 1943), in Judith Chazin-Benahum, *Dance in the Shadow of the Guillotine* (Carbondale: Southern Illinois University Press, 1988), 194.

18. Gombrich noted a precedent in Raphael's fresco on the ceiling of the Stanza della Segnatura on two accessory figures. "Dream of Reason," 195.

19. Lewis Spence, *The Religion of Ancient Mexico* (London: Thinker's Library, 1945), 116, in Erich Neumann, *The Great Mother—An Analysis of the Archetype* (Princeton: Princeton University Press, 1963), 126.

20. Neumann, 276–277, 288.

21. I am indebted to Prof. Mary Sturgeon of the Art History Department of the University of North Carolina for her assistance in identifying the Piranesi as a source for me.

22. Gravelot and Cochin, 107. See Ann Hope, "Cesare Ripa's Iconology and the Neoclassical Movement," *Apollo* 86, Supplement 1-4. Medicine in Gravelot and Cochin is an old woman holding a multibreasted Nature, "the continual object of her observation" (55).
23. Rousseau, *Discours sur l'origine de l'inégalité* (*Discourse on the Origin of Inequality*), in *Contrat Social,* 99. Darwin's *The Descent of Man,* 41, as quoted by Bram Dijkstra, *Idols of Perversity: Fantasies of Feminine Evil in Fin-de-siècle Culture* (New York: Oxford Universtiy Press, 1986), 238. For Flaubert, see Dijkstra's rapprochment of text and image, and his translation, 239, and see Flaubert's own *Tentation* (Paris: Garnier, 1954), 184.
24. Dauban, *Démagogie,* 322.
25. To borrow Outram's terminology of desacralization, the female body's nurturant capacity has been trivialized by fetishization, expressive of the mood of concern for, and yet ambivalence toward, it.
26. We notice Tolstoy's kindred formulation, as quoted by Dijkstra (216): "Every woman, however she may call herself and however refined she may be, who refrains from childbirth without refraining from sexual relations, is a whore."
27. François de Neufchâteau's "Hymn to Liberty" begins, "Enfants d'une mère commune . . . *Children of one mother,* men are equal in their rights," and ends, "Let France offer them . . . a Family united by nature and by love."

POSTLUDE

1. *Archives parlementaires,* December 20, 1793, 22.
2. Alstad, 252.
3. Marcel Garaud, *La Révolution française et la famille* (Paris: PUF, 1978), 172.
4. Garaud, 172–173, from Fenet, *Recueil complet des travaux préparatoires du Code civil,* 15 vols. (Paris: 1827), 1:156.
5. Portalis, *Présentation du Projet de Code Civil IX,* 177–178, in Garaud, 173.
6. Roderick Phillips, "Women and Family Breakdown in Eighteen-Century France: 1780–1900," *Social History* 2 (May 1975): 203, 205. "The depositions of these miserable wives before the family and civil courts were veritable cahiers de doleances of married women. It is evident why divorce was beneficial to women and why women had greater resort to it" (216).
7. Despite the fiction that spouses "owed each other fidelity," a woman's adultery could be grounds for divorce under the Code, while a man would have to bring his concubine into the conjugal home to enable his wife to sue. Women also ran risks of imprisonment for adultery. Phillips, "Women and Family Breakdown," 216.
8. See Brinton, 22.
9. Brinton, 43, 66, 50–51.
10. Léon A. Lanzac de Laborie, *Paris sous Napoléon III, la cour et la ville, la vie et la mort* (Paris: Plon-Nourrit, 1906), 185, cites a figure for this area of one-third of all births in 1806, moving upwards to 42 out of 100 in 1812. For a "crowd of individuals," see *Bulletin de police* 14 août 1806, 184.
11. Brinton, 64.
12. Pateman, 123, 199, 225.
13. Brinton, 61. John Stuart Mill, "The Subjection of Women," in *Essays on Sex Equality,* ed. Alice S. Rossi (Chicago: University of Chicago Press, 1970), 141.
14. J. J. Virey, *De la femme sous ses rapports physiologique, moral, et littéraire* (1775) (Paris: 1823), 204, 240–241.
15. P.J.G. Cabanis, *Rapports du physique et du moral de l'homme* (Paris: An X [1802]), 1:322–323, 324, 348. My emphasis.
16. Cabanis, 1:351, 362.
17. C. Blum, 64. "Desire causes the current," Gilles Deleuze and Felix Guattari, *Anti-Oedipus: Capitalism and Schizophrenia* (Minneapolis: University of Minnesota Press, 1983), 6, in Theweleit, 260. "Streams of desire," Theweleit, 261.
18. Note C. Blum on Rousseau: "If sexuality was not innate, it was an aggressive intruder" (89). Also 81.

19. Lanzac de Laborie (2:225) observes in 1906 that in Napoleonic society "the most inconsequential occasion sufficed to provoke in these men [otherwise so free of neuroses and engrossed in military activity] attacks of lachrymose sensibility that only the greatest public or private catastrophes could occasion in our own time." André Maindron emphasizes the importance for this period of Senancour's formula that all of existence lay in the alternative *jouir ou souffrir* (know pleasure, or suffer). Maindron ironizes it thus: "the male who has pleasure causes suffering, and she who suffers brings pleasure" (214).

20. See my essay, "The Engulfed Beloved: Representations of Dead and Dying Women in the Revolutionary Era," in *Rebel Daughters: Women and the French Revolution,* ed. Sara Melzer and Leslie Rabine (New York: Oxford University Press, 1992).

21. Michelet, 38 and passim.

22. Theweleit, 283.

23. Bryson, *Tradition,* 929–993.

24. Maurice Agulhon, in *Marianne au combat: l'Imagerie et la symbole républicaines de 1789 a 1880* (Paris: Flammarion, 1979), will find elements of her recurrence in Delacroix's 1830 avatar. It is rather her being in motion, not any actual characteristic, that relates the two. For me, Rude's statue of La Marsellaise on the Arch of Triumph, in her own rush into action, combines elements of them both.

25. Anita Brookner particularly remarks on the seductiveness of the gesture of the pleading woman who embraces Tatius's leg (139).

26. Antoine Schnapper in *David* (Paris: Bibliothèque des arts, 1980), 193.

27. *Sur la condition des femmes dans les Républiques* (Paris: An VII [1799]). It must be emphasized, without space to elaborate here, that Theremin writes against the background of misogynist "jokes" like Sylvain Maréchal's 1801 *Proposal for a Law Forbidding Women to Learn to Read* (*Projet de loi portant défense aux femmes d'apprendre à lire*), retorted to spiritedly by *Les Femmes vengées de la sottise d'un philosophe du jour, ou réponse au projet de S.M.* (*Women Avenged for the Silliness of a Philosophe of Our Day, or Reply to S. M.'s Proposed Law*), by Mme Gacon-Dufour.

28. Theremin, 48, note 1; 51, 70.

29. Theremin, 72–73, 74, 76.

30. Duhet, 202.

31. Stéphane Michaud, *Muses et madones: Visages de la femme de la Révolution française aux apparitions de Lourdes* (Paris: Seuil, 1985), 25.

32. J. Van Baal, *Reciprocity and the Position of Women* (Atlantic Highlands, N.J.: Anthropological Papers, 1975), 114.

33. Van Baal, 115, 117.

34. See Alain Corbin, "La Prostituée," in *Misérable et glorieuse, la femme au XIXe siècle,* ed. Jean-Paul Aron (Paris: Fayard, 1980), 48. Jean Tulard also points out that the chief intellectual salons after 1800, those of Cambacérès, Talleyrand, and Renault de Saint-Jean-d'Angely, were all led by men; *La Vie quotidienne des Français sous Napoléon* (Paris: Hachette, 1978), 217. Bertie Greatheed, an English visitor to Paris in 1803, wrote of a party at Mme Bonaparte's that was "filled with men and a small portion of ladies." *An Englishman in Paris: 1803* (London: Geoffrey Bles, 1953), 83.

35. Claire-Élisabeth de Rémusat, *Essai sur l'éducation des femmes* (Paris: Hachette, 1902), See also Elisabeth Vigée-Lebrun, *Souvenirs,* tr. and ed. Morris F. Tyler (New York: 1880), 331–332, and Staël, *De la littérature,* in *Oeuvres,* 2:359–360.

36. Staël, *De la littérature,* in *Oeuvres,* 2:362.

WORKS CITED

Period Sources:

Abrantès, Joséphine Amet Junot d', *Histoire des salons de Paris,* 3 vols. (Brussels: 1837).

Alembert, Jean Le Rond d', "Portrait de Mlle de Lespinasse," in *Lettres de Mlle de Lespinasse,* ed. Eugène Asse (Paris: n.d.).
 Avis aux dames (Paris: 1788).

Beaumarchais, Pierre Augustin Caron de, *Le Mariage de Figaro,* 2 vols. (Paris: Classiques Larousse, 1971).

Bernardin de Saint-Pierre, Jacques-Henri, *Paul et Virginie,* ed. Jacques van den Heuvel (Paris: Poche, 1974).

Buchez, P.-J.-B., and P. C. Roux, *Histoire parlementaire de la Révolution française on Journal des assem-blées nationales depuis 1789 jusqu'en 1815,* 40 vols. (Paris: 1836).

Burke, Edmund, *Reflections on the Revolution in France* (Chicago: H. Regnery, 1968).

Cabanis, P. J. G., *Rapports du physique et du moral de l'homme,* 2 vols. (Paris: An X [1802]).

Charrière, Isabelle de, *Romans* (Paris: Le Chemin vert, 1982).

Chastenay, Victorine de, *Mémoires,* 2 vols. (Paris: 1896).

Chatelet, Emile du, *Discours sur le bonheur,* ed. R. Mauzi (Paris: Les Belles Lettres, 1961).

Chénier, Marie-Joseph, C. Dusausoir, et al. *Office des Décades, ou hymnes et prières en usage dans les temples de la Raison* (Paris: 1793).

Condorcet, Jean-Antoine-Nicolas de Caritat, "Sur l'Admission des femmes au droit de cité," head article in *Journal de la Société de 1789,* July 3, 1790, in *FRF-Edhis,* vol. 2, doc. 25.
 "Lettres d'un bourgeois de New-Haven," in Filippo Mazzei, *Recherches historiques et politiques sur les Etats-Unis de l'Amérique septentrionale, par un citoyen de Virginie* (Paris: 1788).

Des Essartz, Jean-Charles, *Traité de l'éducation corporelle des enfants en bas âge ou Réflexions pratiques sur les moyens de procurer une meilleure constitution aux citoyens* (Paris: 1760).

Diderot, Denis, *Jacques le fataliste et son maître,* in *Oeuvres,* ed. André Billy (Paris: Pléiade, 1951).
 Oeuvres complètes, 15 vols. (Paris: Club français de livre, 1970).
 Salons, ed. Jean Seznec, 2 vols. (Oxford: Clarendon Press, 1957–67).

Duclos, Charles Pinot, *Considérations sur les moeurs de ce siècle* (1751), in *Oeuvres complètes,* 9 vols. (Paris: 1820–21).

Epinay, Louise Florence d'Esclavelles d', *Lettres à mon fils: Essais sur l'éducation et morceaux choisis,* ed. Ruth P. Weinreb (Concord, Mass.: Wayside, 1989).

Ferrières, Charles-Elie de, *La Femme dans l'ordre social et dans l'ordre de la nature* (London: 1787).

Formont, Maxime, ed., *Lettres à Madame de Godeville 1777–1779* (Paris: 1928).

FRF-Edhis, *Les Femmes dans la Révolution française,* 2 vols. (Paris: Edhis, 1982).
 Bachelier, Jean-Jacques, *Mémoire sur l'éducation des filles, présenté aux Etats-Généraux* (Paris: 1789), vol. 1, doc. 4.
 Griefs et plaintes des femmes malmariées. n.p., n.d. (end of 1789?), vol. 1, doc. 20.
 Guyomar, Pierre, *Le Partisan de l'égalité politique entre les individus, ou problème important de l'égalité en droits et de l'inégalité en fait* (Convention, April 29, 1793), vol. 2, doc. 45.
 Lettres d'une citoyenne à son amie sur les avantages que procurerait à la Nation le patriotisme des Dames, (Grenoble-Paris: 1789), vol. 1, doc. 6.
 Motion adressée à l'Assemblée nationale en faveur du sexe (Paris: 1789), vol. 1, doc. 10.
 Motion de la pauvre Javotte, députée des pauvres femmes, lesquelles composent le second ordre du royaume depuis l'abolition du Clergé et de la Noblesse (Paris: 1790), vol. 1, doc. 23.
 Remontrances, plaintes et doléances des dames françaises, à l'occasion des Etats-Généraux (Paris: 1789), vol. 1, doc. 5.

Vues législatives pour les femmes adressées à l'Assemblée nationale par Mlle Jodin, fille d'un citoyen de Genêve (Angers: 1790), vol. 1, doc. 24.

Gouges, Olympe de, *Oeuvres*, ed. Benoîte Groult (Paris: Mercure de France, 1986).

Graffigny, Françoise de, *Lettres d'une Péruvienne*, ed. Gianni Nicoletti (Bari: Adriatica Editrice, 1967).

Gravelot, Hubert-François Bourguignon, and Nicolas Cochin, *Iconologie, on Traité de la science des allégories . . . en 350 figures*, 4 vols. (Paris, n.d.).

Greatheed, Bertie, *An Englishman in Paris: 1803* (London: Geoffrey Bles, 1953).

Hébert, Jacques-René, *Je suis le véritable père Duchesne, foutre!* 5 vols. (Paris: 1791–1794).

Hippel, Theodor Gottfried Von, *On Improving the Status of Women*, tr. and ed. Timothy F. Sellner (Detroit: Wayne State University Press, 1979).

La Font de Saint-Yenne, *Réflexions sur quelques causes de l'état présent de la Peinture en France* (The Hague: 1747).

Laclos, Pierre Choderlos de, *Oeuvres complètes*, ed. Laurent Versini (Paris: Pléiade, 1979).

Marivaux, Pierre Carlet, *Théâtre*, 2 vols. (Paris: Poche-Gallimard, 1966).

Mercier, Louis-Sébastien, *Paris pendant la Révolution ou le nouveau Paris 1789–1798* (Paris: Le Livre Club du Libraire, 1962).

Tableau de Paris, 12 vols. (Amsterdam: 1782–88).

Méricourt, Théroigne de, *Aux 48 Sections* (Paris: 1792), in *FRF-Edhis*, vol. 2, doc. 44.

Molière (Jean-Baptiste Coquelin), *"Tartuffe" and "The Misanthrope,"* tr. Richard Wilbur (New York: Harcourt Brace Jovanovich, 1965).

Le Moniteur universel. Réimpression de l'ancien Moniteur . . . (mai 1789–novembre 1799), 32 vols. (Paris: 1840–1845).

Mortimer-Ternaux, Louis, *Histoire de la Terreur 1792–1794 d'après des documents authentiques et inédits*, 8 vols. (Paris: 1864).

Moore, John, M.D., *A Journal during a Residence in France from the Beginning of August to the Middle of December 1792*, 2 vols. (London: 1794).

Necker, Suzanne Curchod, *Mélanges extraits des manuscrits de Mme Necker* (Paris: 1798).

Raynal, Guillaume-Thomas-François, Abbé de, *Histoire philosophique et politique des établissements du commerce des Européens dans les deux Indes*, 10 vols. (Geneva: 1780).

Reynière, Grimod de la, *Réflexions philosophiques sur le plaisir* (Paris: 1783).

Rémusat, Claire-Elisabeth Jeanne Gravier de Vergennes de, *Essai sur l'éducation des femmes* (Paris: Hachette, 1903).

Restif de la Bretonne, Nicolas-Edmé. *Les Gynographes, ou idées de deux honnêtes-femmes sur un Projet de Règlement proposé à toute l'Europe, pour mettre les femmes à leur place, et opérer le bonheur des deux sexes—avec des notes historiques et justificatives, suivies des noms de femmes célèbres* (The Hague: 1777).

Les Nuits de Paris ou le spectateur nocturne (Paris: Livre Club du Libraire, 1960).

Le Pornographe, ed. Beatrice Didier (Paris: Regine Desforges, 1976).

Riballier, (avec la collaboration de Mlle Cosson), *De l'éducation physique et morale des femmes avec une notice alphabétique de celles qui se sont distinguées* (Bruxelles: 1779).

Roland, Marie-Jeanne Phlipon, *Mémoires de Madame de Roland* (Paris: Mercure de France, 1986).

Rousseau, Jean-Jacques, *Les Confessions*, 2 vols. (New York: French and European Publications, 1968).

Discours sur l'origine de l'inégalité, in *Du Contrat social* (Paris: Garnier, 1962).

Du Contrat social (Paris: Garnier, 1962).

L'Emile (Paris: Garnier, 1964).

Lettre à M. d'Alembert sur son Article "Genève" dans le septième volume de l'Encyclopédie, et particulièrement sur le projet d'établir un théâtre de comédie en cette ville, in *Du Contrat social* (Paris: Garnier, 1962).

Julie, ou la Nouvelle Héloïse (Paris: Garnier, 1960).

Roussel, Pierre, *Système physique et moral de la femme . . .* (Paris: 1775).

Rutlidge, Jean-Jacques, *Essai sur le caractère et les moeurs des Français comparées [sic] à celles des Anglais* (London: 1776).

Sade, Donatien-Alphonse-François de, *Justine ou les malheurs de la vertu* (Paris: Soleil Noir, 1950). *Oeuvres complètes du Marquis de Sade*, 16 vols. (Paris: Cercle du livre précieux, 1966–67).

Ségur, Joseph-Alexandre de, *Les Femmes: Leur condition et leur influence chez différents peuples anciens et modernes* (Paris: 1803).

Sénac de Meilhan, Gabriel, *Du Gouvernement, des moeurs, et des conditions en France avant la Révolution* (Paris: 1795).

Shaftesbury, Earl of, *The Life, Unpublished Letters, and Philosophical Regimen of Anthony, Earl of Shaftesbury*, ed. Benjamin Rand (London: Swann Sonenschein, 1900).

Staël, Germaine de, *Considérations sur les principaux événements de la Révolution française*, 3 vols. (Paris: 1818).

   Oeuvres de Madame de Staël-Holstein, 3 vols. (Paris: 1838).

Theremin, Louis, *Sur la condition des femmes dans les Républiques* (Paris: An VII [1799]).

Thomas, Antoine-Léonard, *Essai sur le caractère, les moeurs, et l'esprit des femmes dans les différents siècles* (Paris: 1772).

Vigée-Lebrun, Elisabeth, *Souvenirs*, tr. and ed. Morris F. Tyler (New York: 1880).

Virey, J. J., *De la femme sous ses rapports physiologique, moral, et littéraire* (1775) (Paris: 1823).

Voltaire, Jean-Marie Arouet de, *L'Ingénu*, in *Romans et contes de Voltaire* (Paris: Garnier, 1960).

Walpole, Horace, *Horace Walpole's Correspondence with Mme du Deffand and Wiart*, ed. W. S. Lewis and Warren Huntington Smith, 39 vols. (New Haven: Yale University Press, 1937–1974).

Secondary Works:

Abensour, Léon, *La Femme et le féminisme avant la révolution* (Paris: Ernest Leroux, 1923).

Agulhon, Maurice, *Marianne au combat: l'Imagerie et la symbole républicaines de 1789 à 1880* (Paris: Flammarion, 1979).

Alstad, Diane, *The Ideology of the Family in Eighteenth-Century France* (Ann Arbor: University Microfilms International, 1971).

Arasse, D., *La Guillotine et l'imaginaire de la Terreur* (Paris: Flammarion, 1987).

Ariès, Philippe, *Centuries of Childhood: A Social History of Family Life,* tr. Robert Baldick (New York: Vintage, 1962).

Ascoli, Georges, "Histoire des idées féministes en France." *Revue de synthèse historique* 13 (1906): 25–27, 99–106, 167–184.

Aulard, Alphonse, *Le Culte de l'Etre Suprême 1793–1794,* rept. (Aalen: Scientia Verlag, 1975).

   "Le Féminisme pendant la Révolution," *Revue bleue,* March 19, 1889, 361–366.

Aury, Dominique, "La Révolte de Mme de Merteuil," *Les Cahiers de la Pléiade* (1951): 91–101.

Badinter, Elisabeth, *L'Amour en plus* (Paris: Poche-Flammarion, 1980).

   Emilie, Emilie: L'ambition féminine au XVIIIe siècle (Paris: Flammarion, 1983).

Beauvoir, Simone de, *The Second Sex,* tr. H. M. Parshley (New York: Bantam, 1961).

Belaval, Yvon, "La Crise de la géométrisation de l'univers dans la philosophie des lumières," *Revue internationale de philosophie* 21 (1952): 337–355.

Berger, John, *Selected Essays and Articles* (London: Penguin, 1972).

Bernier, Olivier, *The Eighteenth-Century Woman* (Garden City, N.Y.: Doubleday, 1981).

Bessand-Massenet, Pierre, *Les Femmes sous la Révolution* (Paris: Plon, 1962).

   De Robespierre à Bonaparte (Paris: Fayard, 1970).

Beugnot, Bernard, *Mémoires de Beugnot,* 3 vols. (Paris: 1866).

Bloch, Camille, "Les Femmes d'Orléans pendant la Révolution," *La Révolution française* 43 (1902): 49–67.

Bloch, Jean, "Women and the Reform of the Nation," in Jacobs et al. (London: Athlone Press, 1979).

Bluche, François, *La Vie quotidienne au temps de Louis XVI* (Paris: Hachette, 1980).

Blum, Carol, *Rousseau and the Republic of Virtue: The Language of Politics in the French Revolution* (Ithaca: Cornell University Press, 1986).

Blum, Stella, catalogue of exhibition, *Eighteenth-Century Women* (New York: Metropolitan Museum of Art, 1981).

Bouillon, Jean-Paul, Antoinette Ehrard, and Michel Melot, eds., *Aimer en France 1780–1800,* exposition (City of Clermont-Ferrand: 1977).

Boulant, Micheline, "La Famille en miettes: Sur un aspect de démographie du XVIIe siècle," *Annales* 27 (1972): 959–968.

Bourdieu, Pierre, "Célibat et condition paysanne," *Etudes rurales* 5–6 (1962): 32–135.

Brady, Patrick, *Rococo Style versus Enlightenment Novel* (Geneva: Slatkine, 1984).

Brault, Eliane, *La Franc-Maçonnerie et l'émancipation des femmes* (Paris: Dervy, 1967).

Brinton, Crane, *French Revolutionary Legislation on Illegitimacy 1789–1804* (Cambridge: Harvard University Press, 1936).

Brookes, Barbara, "The Feminism of Condorcet and Sophie de Grouchy," *Studies on Voltaire and the Eighteenth Century* 189 (1980): 297–361.

Brookner, Anita, *Jacques-Louis David* (New York: Harper and Row, 1980).

Brooks, Peter, *The Novel of Worldliness in Eighteenth-Century France* (Princeton: Princeton University Press, 1969).

Brownmiller, Susan, *Against Our Will: Men, Women, and Rape* (New York: Simon and Schuster, 1975).

Bryson, Norman, *Tradition and Desire: From David to Delacroix* (Cambridge: Cambridge University Press, 1984).

   Word and Image: French Painting of the Ancien Régime (Cambridge: Cambridge University Press, 1980).

Cabanès, Docteur Augustin, and L. Nass, *La Névrose révolutionnaire,* 2 vols. (Paris: Albin Michel, 1924).

Cameron, Vivian, *Women as Image and Image-Makers in Paris in the French Revolution* (Ann Arbor: University Microfilms, 1984).

Carlyle, Thomas, *The French Revolution* (New York: Modern Library, n.d.).

Caron, Pierre, *Les Massacres de Septembre* (Paris: Maison du livre français, 1935).

Caubisens-Lafargue, Colette, "Les Salons de peinture de la Révolution française," *L'Information d'histoire de l'art* 5 (May–June 1960): 67–73.

Chamoux, Antoinette, and Cecile Dauphin, "La Contraception avant la Revolution française," *Annales: Economies, Sociétés, Civilisations* 24 (1969): 662–684.

Charlton, D. G., *New Images of the Natural in France: A Study in European Cultural History 1750–1800* (Cambridge: Cambridge University Press, 1984).

Charpentier, Jehanne, *Le Droit de l'enfance abandonnée* (Paris: PUF, 1967).

Chazin-Benahum, Judith, *Dance in the Shadow of the Guillotine* (Carbondale: Southern Illinois University Press, 1988).

Clay, Jean, *Romanticism* (Secaucus: Chartwell, 1981).

Clements, Candace, "The Academy and the Other: *Les Graces* and *Le Genre Galant,*" paper presented at conference, "Women and the Rococo," University of Missouri, Columbia, October 1987.

Cobb, Richard, *The Police and the People* (Oxford: Clarendon, 1970).

   "The Revolutionary Mentality in France," *History* 17 (Oct. 1957): 181–196.

   Terreur et Subsistances 1793–95 (Paris: Libraire Clavreuil, 1965).

Colwill, Elizabeth, "Just Another *Citoyenne?* Marie-Antoinette on Trial, 1790–1793." *History Workshop* 28 (Autumn 1989): 63–87.

Corbin, Alain, "La Prostituée," in *Misérable et glorieuse, la femme au XIXe siècle* ed. Jean-Paul Aron (Paris: Fayard, 1980).

Coward, D. A., "Eighteenth-Century Attitudes to Prostitution," *Studies on Voltaire and the Eighteenth Century* 189 (1980): 363–399.

Craveri, Benedetta, *Madame du Deffand et son monde,* tr. Sibylle Zavriew (Paris: Seuil, 1978).

Crow, Thomas, "The Oath of the Horatii in 1785: Painting and Prerevolutionary Radicalism in France," *Art History* 1, no. 4 (1978): 424–471.

   Painters and Public Life in Eighteenth-Century Paris (New Haven: Yale University Press, 1985).

Darmon, Pierre, *La Mythologie de la femme dans l'ancienne France* (Paris: Seuil, 1982).

Darnton, Robert, *The Literary Underground of the Old Regime* (Cambridge, Mass.: Harvard University Press, 1982).

Dauban, Charles-Aimé, *La Démagogie en 1793 à Paris ou Histoire jour par jour ... accompagnée de documents contemporains* (Paris: 1868).

Dauxois, Jacqueline, *Charlotte Corday* (Paris: Albin Michel, 1982).

Davis, Natalie Zemon, "Women on Top," in *Society and Culture in Early Modern France* (Stanford: Stanford University Press, 1975).

Decaux, Alain, *Histoire des Françaises,* 2 vols. (Paris: Perrin, 1972).

Delasselle, Claude, "Abandons d'enfants à Paris au XVIIIe siècle," *Annales: Economies, Sociétés, Civilisations* 30 (Jan.–Feb. 1975): 187–218.

Deloffre, Frédéric, *Une Préciosité nouvelle: Marivaux et le marivaudage* (Paris: A. Colin, 1967).

Delon, Michel, *L'Idée d'énergie au tournant des lumières (1770–1820)* (Paris: PUF, 1988).

   "La Mère coupable ou la fête impossible," in *Fêtes de la Révolution, Colloque de Clermont-Ferrand (1974),* ed. J. Ehrard and P. Viallaneix (Paris: Société des études robespierristes, 1977).

   "Un monde d'eunuques," *Europe* 55 (1977): 79–88.

Devance, Louis, "Le Féminisme pendant la Révolution française," *Annales historiques de la Révolution française* 49 (1977): 341–376.

Dijkstra, Bram, *Idols of Perversity: Fantasies of Feminine Evil in Fin-de-siècle Culture* (New York: Oxford University Press, 1986).

Dowd, D. L., "Art and Theater during the French Revolution: The Role of Louis David," *Art Quarterly* 23 (Spring 1960): 2–22.

Duhet, Paule-Marie, *Les Femmes et la Révolution française* (Paris: Juillard, 1971).

Duncan, Carol, "Fallen Fathers: Images of Authority in Pre-Revolutionary French Art," *Art History* 4:2 (June 1981): 186–202.

——— "Happy Mothers and Other New Ideas in French Art," *Art Bulletin* 55 (1973): 570–583.

Dworkin, Andrea, *Pornography: Men Possessing Women* (New York: Putnam-Perigee, 1981).

——— *Woman Hating* (New York: E. P. Dutton, 1974).

Eagleton, Terry, *The Rape of Clarissa* (Bloomington: Indiana University Press, 1982).

Elias, Norbert, *The History of Manners: The Civilizing Process* (New York: Urizen, 1978).

Elshtain, Jean Bethke, *Public Man, Private Woman* (Princeton: Princeton University Press, 1981).

Epois, Jean, *L'Affaire Corday-Marat, prélude à la Terreur* (Paris: Cercle d'or, 1980).

Ettinger, L. D., "Jacques-Louis David and Roman Virtue," *Journal of the Royal Society of Arts* 115 (Jan. 1967): 105–123.

Fabre, Jean, "Paul et Virginie, pastoral," in *Lumière et romantisme: Energie et nostalgie,* ed. Jean Fabre (Paris: Klincksieck, 1963).

Fairchilds, Cissie, "Female Sexual Attitudes and the Rise of Illegitimacy: A Case Study," *Journal of Interdisciplinary History* 8:63–642; rpt. in Rotberg and Rabb.

Farge, Arlette, *Le Miroir des femmes* (Paris: Montalba, 1982).

Flandrin, Jean-Louis, *Les Amours paysannes, XVIe au XIXe siècles* (Paris: Gallimard, 1975).

——— "L'Attitude à légard du petit enfant et les conduites sexuelles dans la civilisation occidentale: structures et évolution," *Annales de démographie historique,* 1973: 143–210.

——— "Contraception, Mariage, et relations amoureuses dans l'Occident chretien," *Annales Economies, Sociétés, Civilisations* 24 (1969): 1370–1390.

——— *Familles, parenté, maison, sexualité dans l'ancienne société* (Paris: Seuil, 1984).

Fleischmann, Hector, *Les Filles publiques sous la terreur* (Paris: Albert Méricaut, 1908).

Fletcher, Angus, *Allegory: The Theory of a Symbolic Mode* (Ithaca: Cornell University Press, 1964).

Fletcher, Dennis, "Restif de la Bretonne and Woman's Estate," in Jacobs et al.

Florisoone, Michel, *La Peinture française: le dix-huitième siècle* (Paris: Pierre Tisné, 1948).

Fox-Genovese, Elizabeth, Introduction to *French Women and the Age of Enlightenment,* in Spencer.

Freud, Sigmund, *Collected Papers,* 5 vols., tr. Joan Riviere (New York: Basic Books, 1959).

Fritz, Paul, and Richard Morton, eds., *Women in the Eighteenth Century and Other Essays* (Toronto: Hakkert, 1976).

Furet, François, *Penser la Révolution française* (Paris: Gallimard, 1978).

Gadamer, Hans-Georg, *Truth and Method* (New York: Crown, 1985).

Gaiffe, Felix, *Envers du grand siècle* (Paris: A. Michel, 1924).

Garaud, Marcel, *La Révolution française et la famille* (Paris: PUF, 1978).

Gelbart, Nina Rattner, "*Le Journal des dames* and its Female Editors: Censorship and Feminism in the Old Regime Press," in *Press and Politics in Eighteenth-Century France,* ed. Jack R. Censer and Jeremy Popkin (Berkeley: University of California Press, 1987).

Gilibert, Jean, "L'Emprise sadienne," in *Sade, écrire la crise* (Colloque de Cérisy), (Paris: Pierre Belfond, 1983).

Glotz, Marguerite, and Madeleine Maire, *Les Salons du XVIIIe siècle* (Paris: Nouvelles Editions Latines, 1949).

Godechot, Jacques, "Compte-rendu de Paule-Marie Duhet, *Les Femmes et la Révolution 1794,*" in *Annales historiques de la Révolution française* (1971): 635–636.

Godineau, Dominique, *Citoyennes tricoteuses* (Aix-en-Provence: Alinea, 1988).

Goldsmith, Elizabeth, *Exclusive Conversations: The Art of Interaction in Seventeenth-Century France* (Philadelphia: University of Pennsylvania Press, 1988).

Gombrich, E. H., "The Dream of Reason: Symbolism of the French Enlightenment," *British Journal for Eighteenth-Century Studies* 2 (1979): 187–217.

——— "The Use of Art for the Study of Symbol," *American Psychologist* 20 (Jan. 1965): 34–50.

Goncourt, Edmond and Jules de, *La Femme au XVIIIe siècle* (Paris: 1862).

——— *Histoire de la société française pendant la Révolution* (Paris: 1854).

Gooch, G. P., *Louis XV: The Monarchy in Decline* (London: Longmans Green, 1956).

Goodman, Dena, "Enlightenment Salons: The Convergence of Female and Philosophic Ambitions," *Eighteenth-Century Studies* 22, no. 3 (Spring 1989): 329–367.

Gossman, Lionel, *French Society and Culture: Background for Eighteenth-Century Culture* (Englewood Cliffs, N.J.: Prentice-Hall, 1972).

Graham, Ruth, "Rousseau's Sexism Revolutionized," in Fritz and Morton.

Griffith, Thomas Waters, *My Scrap Book of the French Revolution,* ed. Elizabeth Wormley Latimer (Chicago: 1898).

Gromont, George, *Le Hameau de Trianon* (Paris: Vincent, Frail, 1928).

Guibert-Sledziewski, Elisabeth, "Les femmes, sujet de Revolution," in *Movements populaires et conscience sociale* (Paris: CNRS-Maloine, 1985), 583–590.

Gutwirth, Madelyn, "1788—Civil Rights and the Wrongs of Women," in *A Harvard History of French Literature,* ed. Denis Hollier (Cambridge, Mass.: Harvard University Press, 1989).

   "The Engulfed Beloved: Representations of Dead and Dying Women in the Revolutionary Era," in *Rebel Daughters, Women and the French Revolution,* ed. Leslie Rabine and Sara Melzer (New York: Oxford University Press, 1992).

   "Laclos and 'le Sexe:' The Rack of Ambivalence," *Studies on Voltaire and the Eighteenth Century* 189 (1980): 247–294.

   Madame de Staël, Novelist: The Emergence of the Artist as Woman (Urbana: University of Illinois Press, 1978).

   "Mme de Staël, Rousseau, and the Woman Question," *PMLA* 86, no. 1 (Jan. 1971): 100–109.
      "Nature, Cruauté, et femmes immolées: *Les Reflexions sur le procès de le reine,*" in *Le Groupe de Coppet et la Révolution française,* ed. Etienne Hofmann and Anne-Lise Delacrétaz (Lausanne: Institut Benjamin Constant, 1988).

   "The Rights and Wrongs of Woman: The Defeat of Feminist Rhetoric by Revolutionary Allegory," in *The Revolutionary Moment,* ed. James Heffernan (Hanover: University Press of New England, 1992).

   "Woman as Mediatrix, from Rousseau to Mme de Staël," in *Woman as Mediatrix,* ed. Avriel H. Goldberger (New York: Greenwood Press, 1987).

Hamiche, Daniel, *Le Théâtre et la Révolution: La Lutte des classes au théâtre en 1789 et 1793* (Paris: U.G.E., 1973).

Hays, H. R., *The Dangerous Sex* (New York: P. G. Putnam, 1964).

Hazard, Paul, *La Pensée européenne au XVIIIe siècle—de Montesquieu à Lessing* (Paris: Boivin, 1964).

Heffernan, James, ed., *The Revolutionary Moment* (Hanover: University Press of New England, 1992).

Hénaff, Marcel, *Sade, l'Invention de corps libertin* (Paris: PUF-Croisier, 1978).

Hertz, Neil, "Medusa's Head: Male Hysteria under Political Pressure," *Representations* 4 (1983): 27–54.

Hoffmann, Paul, "Aspects de la condition féminine dans *les Liaisons dangereuses,*" *L'Information littéraire* (March–April 1963): 47–53.

   La Femme dans le pensée des lumières (Paris: Ophrys, 1977).

Hope, Ann, "Cesare Ripa's Iconology and the Neoclassical Movement," *Apollo* 86, Supplement 1-4.

Horkeimer, Max, and Theodor Adorno, *Dialectic of Enlightenment,* tr. John Cumming (New York: Herder and Herder, 1972).

Horney, Karen, "The Dread of Women: Observations on a Specific Difference in the Dread Felt by Men and by Women Respectively For the Opposite Sex," *International Journal of Psychoanalysis* 13 (1932): 348–360.

Huet, Marie-Hélène, *Rehearsing the Revolution: The Staging of Marat's Death, 1793–1797,* tr. Robert Hurley (Berkeley: University of California Press, 1982).

Hufton, Olwen, "Women and the Family Economy in Eighteenth-Century France," *French Historical Studies* (Spring 1975): 1–22.

Hunt, Lynn, "Engraving the Republic: Prints and Propaganda in the French Revolution," *History Today* (Oct. 1980): 11–17.

   "The Political Psychology of Revolutionary Caricatures," in *French Caricature and the French Revolution 1789–1799* (Los Angeles: Grunwald Center for the Graphic Arts, 1988).

   Politics, Culture, and Class in the French Revolution (Berkeley: University of California Press, 1984).

Huston, Nancy, "The Matrix of War: Mothers and Heroes," in *The Female Body in Western Culture: Contemporary Perspectives,* ed. Susan R. Suleiman (Cambridge, Mass.: Harvard University Press, 1986).

Jacobs, Eva, et al., eds., *Woman and Society in Eighteenth-Century France: Essays in Honour of John Stephenson Spink* (London: Athlone, 1979).

Johnson, Buffie, *Lady of the Beasts: Ancient Images of the Goddess and Her Sacred Animals* (San Francisco: Harper and Row, 1987).

Johnson, Mary Durham, "Old Wine in New Bottles: The Institutional Changes for Women of the People during the French Revolution," in *Women, War, and Revolution*, ed. Carol R. Berkin and Clara M. Lovett (New York: Homes and Meier, 1980).

Jordanova, Ludmilla, "Natural Facts: A Historical Perspective on Science and Sexuality," in *Nature, Culture, and Gender*, ed. C. MacCormack and M. Strathern (Cambridge, Eng.: Cambridge University Press, 1980).

"Naturalizing the Family: Literature and the Bio-Medical Sciences," in *Languages of Nature*, ed. L. Jordanova (New Brunswick: Rutgers University Press, 1986).

Kates, Gary, *The Cercle Social, the Girondins, and the French Revolution* (Princeton: Princeton University Press, 1985).

Keuls, Eva C., *The Reign of the Phallus: Sexual Politics in Ancient Athens* (New York: Harper and Row, 1985).

Klossowski, Pierre, "Préface à *la Philosophie dans le boudoir*," in Sade, See *Oeuvres complètes*, vol. 3.

Knibiehler, Yvonne, and Catherine Fouquet, *L'Histoire des mères, du moyen âge à nos jours* (Paris: Montalba, 1980).

Kofman, Sarah, *Le Respect des femmes* (Paris: Slatkine, 1982).

Koselleck, Reinhard, *Le Règne de la critique*, tr. Hans Hildenbrandt (Paris: Editions de minuit, 1959).

Kromm, Jane, "'Marianne' and the Madwoman," *Art Journal* 46, no. 4 (Winter 1987): 209–304.

Lacour, Lópold, *Les origines du féminisme contemporain. Trois femmes de la Révolution: Olympe de Gouges, Théroigne de Méricourt, Rose Lacombe.* Paris: Plon, 1900.

Ladurie, E. Leroi, "Démographie et 'funestes secrets': le Languedoc (fin XVIIIe début XIXe siècle)", *Annales d'histoire de la Révolution française* (1965): 385–400.

Laget, Mireille, "Petites écoles en Languedoc au XVIIIe siècle," *Annales Economies, Sociétés, Civilisations* (1971): 1398–1418.

Lairtullier, E., *Les Femmes célèbres de 1789 à 1795 et leur influence dans la Révolution* (Paris: 1840).

Landes, Joan B., *Women and the Public Sphere in the French Revolution* (Ithaca: Cornell University Press, 1988).

Lanzac de Laborie, Léon A. de, *Paris sous Napoléon III, la cour et la ville, la vie et la mort,* (Paris: Plon-Nourrit, 1906).

Laplanche, Jean, and J. B. Pontalis, "Fantasy and the Origin of Sexuality," part 1, *Journal of Psychoanalysis* 49 (1968): 1–18.

Laqueur, Thomas, "Orgasm, Generation, and the Politics of Reproductive Biology," in *The Making of the Modern Body: Sexuality and Society in the Nineteenth Century*, ed. Catherine Gallagher and Thomas Laqueur (Berkeley: University of California Press, 1987).

Lasowski, Patrick Wald, *Libertines* (Paris: Gallimard, 1980).

Laufer, Roger, *Style rococo, style des "lumières"* (Paris: Corti, 1963).

Lederer, Wolfgang, *The Fear of Women* (New York: Harcourt Brace Jovanovich, 1968).

Leith, James, "Deradicalization and Militarization: Some Architectural Projects under the Directory," *Consortium on Revolutionary Europe Proceedings 1985* (Athens, Ga.: 1986): 29–44.

The Idea of Art as Propaganda in France, 1789–1799 (Toronto: University of Toronto Press, 1965).

Lenôtre, Gustave, *Les Massacres de septembre* (Paris: Perrin, 1907).

Levey, Michael, *From Rococo to Revolution* (New York: Frederick W. Praeger, 1966).

Levy, Darline Gay, and Applewhite, Harriet B., "Women, Democracy, and Revolution in Paris, 1789–94," in Spencer.

Levy, Darline Gay, Harriet B. Applewhite, and Mary D. Johnson, eds., *Women in Revolutionary Paris* (Urbana: University of Illinois Press, 1979).

Lévy, Zvi, "*L'Ingénu* ou l'Anti-Candide," *Studies on Voltaire and the Eighteenth Century* 183 (1980): 45–67.

Locquin, Jean, *La Peinture d'histoire en France de 1747 à 1785* (Paris, H. Laurens, 1912).

Lough, John, "Women in Mercier's 'Tableau de Paris,'" in Jacobs-Spink et al.

Luppé, Robert de, *Les Jeunes Filles à la fin du XVIIIe siècle* (Paris: Champion, 1925).

MacLean, Ian, *The Renaissance Notion of Woman* (Cambridge: Cambridge University Press, 1980).

McManners, John, *Death and the Enlightenment* (Oxford: Clarendon Press, 1981).

Maindron, André, "Fondements Physiologiques et Transposition littéraire dans les romans français du 19e siècle," thesis for Doctorat d'Etat, University of Nantes, 1985.

Malueg, Susan Procious, "Women and the *Encyclopédie*," in Spencer.

Man, Paul de, "Pascal's Allegory of Persuasion," in *Allegory and Representation: Selected Papers from the English Institute, 1978* (Baltimore: Johns Hopkins University Press, 1981).

Mathiez, Albert, *The French Revolution,* tr. Alison Phillips (New York: Grosset Dunlap, 1964).

Mauzi, Robert, *L'Idee du bonheur au XVIIIe siècle* (Paris: A. Colin, 1960).

May, George, *Le Dilemme du roman au XVIIe siècle* (Paris: PUF, 1963).

May, Gita, *Madame de Roland and the Age of Revolution* (New York: Columbia University Press, 1970). "Rousseau's Antifeminism Reconsidered," in Spencer.

Maza, Sara, *Servants and Masters in Eighteenth-Century France: The Uses of Loyalty* (Princeton: Princeton University Press, 1983).

Melzer, Sara, and Leslie Rabine, eds. *Rebel Daughters: Women and the French Revolution* (New York: Oxford University Press, 1992).

Mercier, Roger, *L'Enfant dans la société française du XVIIIe siècle* (Dakar: Université de Dakar, 1961).

Michaud, Stéphane, *Muses et madones: Visages de la femme de la Révolution française aux apparitions de Lourdes* (Paris: Seuil, 1985).

Michelet, Jules, *Les Femmes de la Révolution,* ed. Pierre Labracherie and Jean Dumont (Paris: Hachette, n.d.).

Miles, Margaret, *Images as Insight: Visual Understanding in Western Civilization and Secular Culture* (Boston: Beacon Press, 1985).

Mill, John Stuart, "The Subjection of Women," in *Essays on Sex Equality,* ed. Alice S. Rossi (Chicago: University of Chicago Press, 1970).

Miller, Nancy, *The Heroine's Text: Readings in the French and English Novel 1722–1782* (New York: Columbia University Press, 1980).

Mitchell, Jeri, "'Le Commerce des femmes': Sexuality and Sociability in Eighteenth-Century French Representation," paper presented at conference, "Women and the Rococo," University of Missouri, Columbia, October 1987.

Montesquieu, *Les Lettres persanes,* ed. P. Vernière, (Paris: Garnier, 1960).

Morel, Marie-France, "Théories et pratiques de l'allaitement en France au XVIIe siécle," *Annales de démographie historique* (The Hague: Mouton, 1977): 393–427.

Mortier, Roland, "Libertinage littéraire et tension sociale dans la littérature de l'Ancien régime," *Revue de littérature comparée* 46 (1972): 35–45.

Mortimer-Ternaux, Louis, *Histoire de la Terreur 1792–1794* (Paris: 1864).

Muchembled, Robert, *Popular Culture and Elite Culture in France 1400–1750,* tr. Lydia Cochrane (Baton Rouge: Louisiana State University Press, 1985).

Nagy, Peter, *Libertinage et révolution,* tr. Christiane Grémillon (Paris: Gallimard, 1975).

Neumann, Erich, *The Great Mother—An Analysis of the Archetype* (Princeton: Princeton University Press, 1963).

Outram, Dorinda, *The Body and the French Revolution: Sex, Class, and Political Culture* (New Haven: Yale University Press, 1989).

Ozouf, Mona, "De Thermidor à brumaire: Le discours de la Révolution sur elle-même," *Revue historique* 243 (1970): 31–66.

Parker, Harold, *The Cult of Antiquity and the French Revolution* (Chicago: University of Chicago Press, 1937).

Pateman, Carol, *The Sexual Contract* (Stanford: Stanford University Press, 1988).

Paulson, Ronald, *Representations of Revolution, 1789–1820* (New Haven: Yale University Press, 1983).

Perrot, Philippe, *Le Travail des apparences ou les transformations du corps féminin, XVIIIe–XIXe siècle* (Paris: Seuil, 1984).

Phillips, Roderick G., "Women's Emancipation, the Family, and Social Change in Eighteenth-Century France," *Journal of Social History* 12, no. 4 (1979): 553–567. "Women and Family Breakdown in Eighteenth-Century France: 1780–1900," *Social History* 2 (May 1975): 197–217.

Picard, Roger, *Les Salons littéraires et la société française 1610–1789* (New York: Brentano's, 1943).

Pilkington, A. E., "Nature as Ethical Norm," in *Languages of Nature,* ed. L. Jordanova (New Brunswick: Rutgers University Press, 1986).

Pomeroy, Sarah, *Goddesses, Whores, Wives, and Slaves: Women in Classical Antiquity* (New York: Schocken Books, 1975).

Posner, Donald, "The Singing Women of Watteau and Fragonard," *Art Bulletin* 69 (March 1982): 75–88.

Rizzo, Betty, "Women's Class Mobility: Potentialities and Limits," paper presented to American Society for Eighteenth-Century Studies, 1990 (Minneapolis).

Rocquain, Félix, *L'Esprit Révolutionnaire avant la Révolution 1715–1789* (Paris: 1878).

Rogers, Adrienne, "Women and the Law" in Spencer.

Rogers, Cornwell B., *The Spirit of Revolution in 1789* (Princeton: Princeton University Press, 1949).

Rogers, Katherine M., "The View from England," in Spencer.

Rosa, Annette, *Citoyennes: Les Femmes et la Révolution française* (Paris: Messidor, 1987).

Rosenblum, Robert, *Transformations in Late Eighteenth-Century Art* (Princeton: Princeton University Press: 1967).

Rotberg, Robert I., and Theodore K. Rabb, eds., *Marriage and Fertility: Studies in Interdisciplinary History* (Princeton: Princeton University Press, 1980).

Sahlins, Marshall, *Islands of History* (Chicago: University of Chicago Press, 1987).

Sainte-Beuve, Charles-Augustin de, "Mémoires de Mme de Staal-Delaunay," *Oeuvres* (Paris: Pléiade, 1950–51).

Saisselin, Rémy, "Neoclassicism: Images of Public Virtue and Realities of Private Luxury," *Art History* 4 (March 1981): 14–36.

Schama, Simon, *Citizens: A Chronicle of the French Revolution* (New York: Knopf, 1989).

Schlanger, Judith, *L'Enjeu et le débat—l'invention intellectuelle* (Paris: Denoël/Gonthier, 1979).

Schnapper, Antoine, *David* (Paris: Bibliothèque des arts, 1980).

Schor, Naomi, *Reading in Detail: Aesthetics and the Feminine* (New York: Methuen, 1987).

Schumann, Robert A., "Virility and Grace: Neo-Classicism, Jacques-Louis David, and the Culture of Pre-Revolutionary France," unpublished.

Sedgwick, Eve Kosofsky, *Between Men* (New York: Columbia University Press, 1985).

Segalen, Martine, *Mari et femme dans la France rurale traditionnelle* (Paris: Flammarion, 1980).
   Mari et femme dans la société paysanne, exposition catalogue (Paris: Flammarion, 1980).

Sheriff, Mary, "The Erotics of Decoration," paper presented at conference, "Women and the Rococo," University of Missouri, Columbia, October, 1987.

Shklar, Judith, "Rousseau's Two Models: Sparta and the Age of Gold," *Political Science Quarterly* 81 (1966): 25–51.

Shorter, Edward, "Illegitimacy, Sexual Revolution, and Social Change," in Rotberg and Rabb.
   The Making of the Modern Family (New York: Basic Books, 1975).

Soboul, Albert, "Sentiment religieux et cultes populaires," *Annales historiques de la Révolution française* 29 (July–Sept. 1957): 193–213.
   "Sur l'activité militante des femmes dans les sections parisiennes en l'an II," *Bulletin d'Histoire économique et sociale de la Révolution française* (1979): 15–27.

Spence, Lewis, *The Religion of Ancient Mexico* (London: Thinker's Library, 1945).

Spencer, Samia I, ed., *French Women and the Age of Enlightenment* (Bloomington: Indiana University Press, 1984).

Starobinski, Jean, *Jean-Jacques Rousseau: La Transparence ou l'obstacle* (Paris: Gallimard, 1971).
   L'Invention de la liberté (Geneva: Skira, 1964).

Stewart, Philip, "The Child Comes of Age," *Yale French Studies* 40 (1968): 134–141.
   "Representations of Love: The French Eighteenth Century," *Studies in Iconography* 4 (1978): 125–148.

Stone, Lawrence, *The Family, Sex, and Marriage in England, 1500–1800* (London: Wiedenfeld and Nicolson, 1977).

Sullerot, Evelyne, *Histoire de la presse féminine en France, des origines à 1848* (Paris: Armand Colin, 1966).

Sussman, George D., *Selling Mother's Milk: The Wet-Nursing Business in France 1715–1914* (Urbana: University of Illinois Press, 1982).

Theweleit, Klaus, *Male Fantasies, 1: Women, Floods, Bodies, History,* tr. Stephen Conway (Minneapolis: University of Minnesota Press, 1989).

Thomas, Chantal, "L'héroïne du crime—Marie-Antoinette dans les pamphlets," in *La Carmagnole des Muses,* ed. Jean-Claude Bonnet (Paris: Armand Colin, 1988).

Thomas, Ruth, "The Death of an Ideal: Female Suicides in the Eighteenth-Century Novel," in Spencer.

Thoré, Luc, "Langage et sexualité," in *Sexualité humaine* (Centre d'études Laënnec) (Paris: Aubier-Montaigne, 1970).

Tomaselli, Silvana, "The Enlightenment Debate on Women," *History Workshop* 6 (1984): 101–124.

Toth, Karl, *Woman and Rococo in France, Seen through the Life and Works of a Contemporary, Charles-Pinot Duclos* (London: Harrap, 1931).

Trouille, Mary, *Eighteenth-Century Women Writers Respond to Rousseau: Sexual Politics and the Cult of Sensibility.* Northwestern University, 1980 (Ann Arbor: Dissertation Abstracts, 1988).

    "Revolution in the Boudoir: Mme Roland's Subversion of Rousseau's Feminine Ideals," *Eighteenth-Century Life* 13, no. 2 (May 1989): 65–86.

Tulard, Jean, *La Vie quotidienne des Français sous Napoléon* (Paris: Hachette, 1978).

Undank, Jack, "Beaumarchais' Transformations," *Modern Language Notes* 4 (Sept. 1985): 831–870.

Van Baal, J., *Reciprocity and the Position of Women* (Atlantic Highlands, N.J.: Anthropological Papers, 1975).

van de Walle, Etienne and Francine, "Allaitement, stérilité, et contraception: les opinions jusqu'au XIXe siècle," *Population* 27 (1972): 685–701.

Vartanian, Aram, "The Marquise de Merteuil: A Case of Mistaken Identity," *Esprit Créateur* (Winter 1963): 172–180.

Versini, Laurent, *Laclos et la tradition* (Paris: Klincksieck, 1968).

Vovelle, Michel, *La Mentalité révolutionnaire* (Paris: Messidor, Editions sociales, 1985).

    "Le Tournant des mentalités en France 1750–1789: la 'sensibilité' pré-révolutionnaire," tr. John Hoyles, *Social History* 5 (1977): 605–629.

Vuarnet, Jean-Noël, "Massacre des femmes," *Nrf* (1977), 85–91.

Warner, Marina, *Of Monuments and Maidens: The Allegory of the Female Form* (New York: Atheneum, 1985).

Weinstein, Fred, and Gerald M. Platt, *The Wish to Be Free: Society, Psyche, and Value Change* (Berkeley: University of California Press, 1986).

Whatley, Janet, "*The Supplement to Bougainville's Voyage,* Un retour secret vers la forêt: The Problem of Privacy and Order in Diderot's Tahiti," *Kentucky Romance Quarterly* 24, no. 2 (1977): 199–208.

Wilburger, Carolyn Hope, "The View from Russia," in Spencer.

Williams, David, "The Politics of Feminism in the French Revolution," in *The Varied Pattern: Studies in the Eighteenth Century,* ed. P. Hughes and D. Williams (Toronto: A. M. Hakkert, 1971).

Wollstonecraft, Mary, *A Vindication of the Rights of Women* (1792) (New York: Norton, 1967).

Young, Arthur, *Travels in France During the Years 1787, 1788, 1789* (London: 1889).

Zantop, Suzanne, "Crossing the Boundaries: The French Revolution and the German Literary Imagination," presented at the Dartmouth College conference "The French Revolution and Representation," July 1989, and in *The Revolutionary Moment,* ed. James Heffernan (Hanover: University Press of New England, 1992).

Index

Numerals in italics represent pages on which illustrations appear.

women (*continued*)
"reign" of, 4–5; representations of in crowds, *241, 243, 240,* 323; requests to bear arms by, 289, 302, 338; in the Revolution's global history, 213; rhetorical timidity of, 218–219, 220, 222, 223; rights of association banned, 275; and the queen, 242–243; and the rococo, 3–22; as servantes, 28; status of, 13, 89–90, 109–112; unmarried, unnatural, 152–153; violence of speech, 309–310; vote for Estates-General, 222. *See also* salon; salon women; sexuality; violence

women of letters, Mme Roland's view of, 194–195

Yeats, William Butler, 94

Zantop, Suzanne, 339